Handbook of Information Security

Handbook of Information Security

Edited by **Audrey Coon**

WILLFORD PRESS
New York

Published by Willford Press,
118-35 Queens Blvd., Suite 400,
Forest Hills, NY 11375, USA
www.willfordpress.com

Handbook of Information Security
Edited by Audrey Coon

International Standard Book Number: 978-1-68285-302-3 (Hardback)

The publisher's policy is to use permanent paper from mills that operate a sustainable forestry policy. Furthermore, the publisher ensures that the text paper and cover boards used have met acceptable environmental accreditation standards.

Trademark Notice: Registered trademark of products or corporate names are used only for explanation and identification without intent to infringe.

Printed in the United States of America.

Contents

Preface

Information security is a set of processes that defends information from unauthorized accesses, modification or disruption. Information security programs are significant in maintaining the confidentiality of valuable data. The chapters included in this book are a compilation of updated information on topics such as cryptography, biometrics, cloud privacy, etc. It also glances at signal processing and encryption, network security and hardware security. This text is an assimilation of case studies and researches by renowned experts from around the world. As this field is emerging at a rapid pace, the contents of this book will help the readers understand the modern concepts and applications of the subject.

After months of intensive research and writing, this book is the end result of all who devoted their time and efforts in the initiation and progress of this book. It will surely be a source of reference in enhancing the required knowledge of the new developments in the area. During the course of developing this book, certain measures such as accuracy, authenticity and research focused analytical studies were given preference in order to produce a comprehensive book in the area of study.

This book would not have been possible without the efforts of the authors and the publisher. I extend my sincere thanks to them. Secondly, I express my gratitude to my family and well-wishers. And most importantly, I thank my students for constantly expressing their willingness and curiosity in enhancing their knowledge in the field, which encourages me to take up further research projects for the advancement of the area.

Editor

Assessing JPEG2000 encryption with key-dependent wavelet packets

Dominik Engel[1,2], Thomas Stütz[1,2]* and Andreas Uhl[2]

Abstract

We analyze and discuss encryption schemes for JPEG2000 based on the wavelet packet transform with a key-dependent subband structure. These schemes have been assumed to reduce the runtime complexity of encryption and compression. In addition to this "lightweight" nature, other advantages like encrypted domain signal processing have been reported. We systematically analyze encryption approaches based on key-dependent subband structures in terms of their impact on compression performance, their computational complexity and the level of security they provide as compared to more classical techniques. Furthermore, we analyze the prerequisites and settings in which the previously reported advantages actually hold and in which settings no advantages can be observed. As a final outcome it has to be stated that the compression integrated encryption approach based on the idea of secret wavelet packets can not be recommended.

1. Introduction

For securing multimedia data–like any other type of data–full encryption with a state-of-the-art cipher, is the most secure option. However, in the area of multimedia many applications do not require the level of security this option provides, and seek a trade-off in security to enable other requirements, including low processing demands, retaining bitstream compliance and scalability, and the support for increased functionality, such as, transparent encryption [1] and region of interest (ROI) encryption, or signal processing in the encrypted domain (adaptation, searching, watermarking, ...).

JPEG2000 is the most recent and comprehensive suite of standards for scalable coding of visual data [2,3]. JPEG2000 filled areas of application that JPEG could not provide for, especially where applications require a scalable representation of the visual data. Recently JPEG2000 has evolved into the format of choice for many specialized and high end applications. For example, the Digital Cinema Initiative (DCI), an entity created by seven major motion picture studios, has adopted JPEG2000 as the compression standard in their specification for a unified Digital Cinema System [4]. As a second example, in 2002, the Digital Imaging and Communications in Medicine (DICOM) committee approved the final text of DICOM

Supplement 61, marking the inclusion of Part 1 of JPEG2000 in DICOM (ISO 12052). Furthermore, in the ISO/IEC 19794 standard on Biometric Data Interchange Formats JPEG2000 is included for lossy compression, in the most recently published version (ISO/IEC FDIS 19794-6 as of August 2010) as the only format for iris image data.

Security techniques specifically tailored to the needs of scalable representation in general and JPEG2000 in particular have been proposed recently, e.g., [5-10]. An overview and discussion of the proposed approaches in the context of JPEG2000 can be found in [11]. JPEG2000 security is discussed in JPEG2000 Part 8 [12,13]. This part has the title "Secure JPEG 2000" and is referred to as JPSEC. It "intends to provide tools and solutions in terms of specifications that allow applications to generate, consume, and exchange Secure JPEG 2000 codestreams" (p. vi). JPSEC extends the codestream syntax to allow parts which are created by security tools, e.g., cipher or authentication tools. Encryption is implemented with conventional ciphers, e.g., AES.

The approaches discussed in this article perform encryption by constructing a secret transform domain. The principal idea of such schemes is that without the key the transform coefficients cannot be interpreted or decoded and therefore no access to the source material is possible (or only at a very low quality). Other than with bitstream-oriented methods, which operate on a final

* Correspondence: tstuetz@cosy.sbg.ac.at
[1]University of Applied Sciences, Urstein Sued 1, 5412 Puch/Salzburg Austria
Full list of author information is available at the end of the article

coded media bitstream, these methods apply encryption integrated with compression. In terms of applicability they are therefore restricted to scenarios where the final media bitstream is not yet available (video conferencing, live streaming, photo storage, transmission, and storage of surveillance data etc.).

Transparent encryption was introduced in the context of TV broadcasting [1,14] and denotes encryption schemes for which public access is granted for a preview image, i.e., anyone can decode an image of reduced quality from the encrypted stream, even without the key data. The difference to other media encryption schemes that guarantee a certain degree of distortion is that the preview image has to be of a (specified) minimum quality, i.e., apart from the *security requirement*, there is also a *quality requirement* [10,15]. Broadcasting applications, for example, can benefit from transparent encryption, as they, rather than preventing unauthorized viewers from receiving and watching their content completely, aim at promoting a contract with non-paying watchers, for whom the availability of a preview version (in lower quality) may serve as an incentive to pay for the full quality version. The reason for considering transparent encryption as target application scenario is that it has been shown [16], that the lowest resolution contained in a JPEG2000 file encrypted using the techniques discussed in this article can always be decoded by an attacker. This makes the approaches suitable for transparent encryption only, but prevents usage in applications requiring a higher degree of confidentiality.

In [17] the authors suggest to use secret Fourier-based transforms for the encryption of visual data. Other proposals in the area of lightweight encryption [18] propose the encryption of the filter choice used for a wavelet decomposition. However, this suggestion remains vague and is not supported by any experiments, while [19,20] propose encrypting the orthogonal filterbanks used for an non-stationary multi-resolution analysis (NSMRA) decomposition. The use of concealed biorthogonal parametrized wavelet filters for lightweight encryption is proposed by [21]. The use of key-dependent wavelet packet decompositions is proposed first by [22,23]. The latter study [23] evaluates encryption based on key-dependent subband structures in a zerotree-based wavelet codec. Parametrized wavelet filters have been employed for JPEG2000 lightweight encryption by [24,25], however, this approach was shown to be insecure in later study [26]. The scrambling of discrete cosine transform (DCT) and discrete wavelet transform (DWT) coefficients is proposed in [27]. Recently secret DCT-based transforms have been proposed for image and video encryption [28].

In the context of JPEG2000, the degrees of freedom in the wavelet transform are a prime candidate for constructing a secret transform domain. JPEG2000, Part 2, allows the definition of custom wavelet filters and user-defined isotropic and anisotropic wavelet packet subband structures [29]. Exemplary wavelet packets are shown in Figure 1.

Key-dependent wavelet packets in JPEG2000 have been proposed for a lightweight encryption scheme in earlier studies [16,30,31]. This approach is in the focus of interest in this study. The suggested scheme can be seen as a form of header encryption, as only the information pertaining to the transform domain needs to be encrypted, the rest of the data remains in plaintext. This approach has the advantage that only the parameters of the secret transform domain need to be kept secret. Therefore the demands for the encryption stage are minimal as compared to a more traditional, bitstream-oriented encryption approach [16]. Due to the shift in complexity from actual encryption to the compression pipeline, the scheme has been termed "lightweight". An overview of the two different systems KDWP encryption and conventional encryption is shown in Figure 2.

In this article, we evaluate, analyze, and discuss earlier proposed JPEG2000 encryption techniques that use key-dependent wavelet packets (KDWP) to establish a secret transform domain. Wavelet packets (WP) are introduced in Section 2.. We assess KDWP encryption with respect to the following three main properties of an image encryption scheme:

- *Compression impact*: KDWP encryption reduces compression performance, the actual decrease is evaluated in Section 3..
- *Computational demand*: The main argument for introducing the general concept of secret transform domains in encryption has always been an improved runtime performance, as the *conventional encryption* step is not needed. This assumption is in-depth evaluated and analyzed in Section 4..
- *Security*: The security of KDWP is in-depth analyzed in Section 5.. Special care has been taken to employ the suitable notion of security for multimedia encryption.

In Section 6. we combine the individual assessments of the previous sections and in-depth discuss other potential advantages of KDWP. Another potential advantage of KDWP encryption is the capability of performing signal processing operations on the protected data ("encrypted domain processing"), which are compared to the operations possible on a conventionally encrypted JPEG2000 bitstream. Final conclusion are drawn in Section 7..

2. Wavelet packets

The wavelet packet (WP) transform [32] generalizes the pyramidal wavelet transform. In the WP transform, apart from the approximation subband also the detail

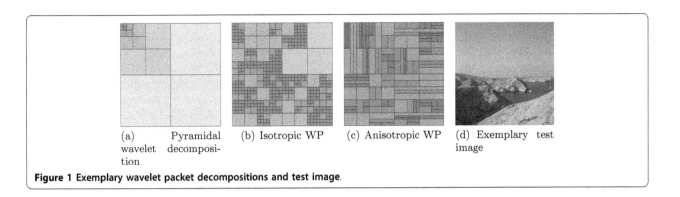

(a) Pyramidal wavelet decomposition   (b) Isotropic WP   (c) Anisotropic WP   (d) Exemplary test image

Figure 1 Exemplary wavelet packet decompositions and test image.

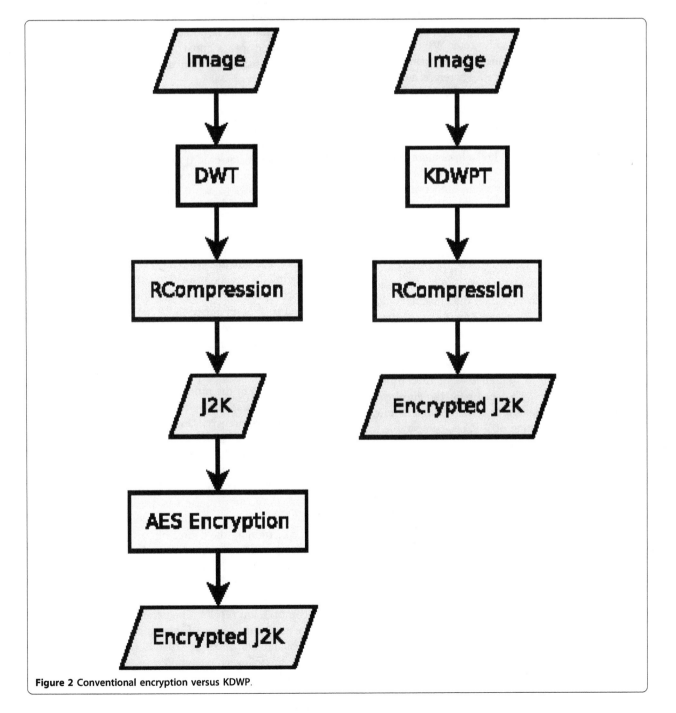

Figure 2 Conventional encryption versus KDWP.

subband can be decomposed; an example is shown in Figure 1. The WP can be adapted to take the properties of the image to be transformed into account, for example by using the best basis algorithm [32-36]. In this article we refer to each such a WP basis by the terms "WP subband structure", "decomposition structure" or briefly "WP".

The anisotropic WP transform is a generalization of the isotropic case: whereas in the latter, horizontal and vertical wavelet decomposition are always applied in pairs for each subband to be decomposed, this restriction is lifted for the anisotropic WP transform (for an example see Figure 1c).

Note that for the isotropic WP transform a single decomposition refers to both horizontal and vertical filtering and downsampling. For the anisotropic WP transform, a decompositions refers to filtering and downsampling in one direction (horizontal or vertical). Therefore, a decomposition depth of 2 g in the anisotropic case is comparable to a decomposition depth of g in the isotropic case.

2.1 WP in JPEG2000
Part 2 of the JPEG2000 standard [29] allows more decomposition structures than Part 1. Every subband resulting from a highpass filtering can be decomposed at most two more times (either horizontally, vertically or in both directions).

In order to maximize keyspace size for the proposed encryption scheme, we have implemented full support for arbitrary isotropic and anisotropic wavelet decomposition structures in JPEG2000, based on the JJ2000 reference implementation.[a] The source code for the implementation underlying all results in this paper can be downloaded from http://www.wavelab.at/sources.

2.2 Randomized generation of isotropic WPs
A WP can be derived by a sequence of random binary decomposition decisions. The seed s for the employed secure random number generator is the main parameter for the randomized generation of WP, i.e., comparable to the key in a symmetric crpyto system.

2.2.1 Uniform distribution
A uniformly distributed selection is achieved with the following randomized algorithm. For each subband (starting at the root subband, i.e., the entire image) it is randomly decided whether the subband is further decomposed. The probability of a decomposition of a subband depends on the number of sub-transforms within the subband, which is equivalent to Q_{g-l} where g is the maximum decomposition depth and l is the level of the subband.

$$p_u(l) = 1 - \frac{1}{Q_{g-l}}, \quad Q_j = Q_{j-1}^4 + 1, \quad Q_0 = 1$$

Subsequently, this distribution is referred to *isouni*.

2.2.2 Compression-oriented distribution
The compression-friendly randomized algorithm for WP selection enforces the decomposition of the approximation subbands, for all other subbands a possible decomposition is determined by a layer-dependent probability, $p_c(l)$, which depends on two input parameters, the base value b and the change factor c, which serves as multiplier for the level l:

$$p_c(l) = 1 - \frac{b + cl}{2}$$

Only the parameters, b, c and the seed of the random number generator need to be encrypted. Subsequently, these distributions are denoted/abbreviated by *iso* and further classified into a constrained (the LL is always further decomposed) and an unconstrained case.

2.3 Randomized generation of anisotropic WPs
The main motivation to introduce anisotropic WPs in the context of lightweight encryption is a significant increase in keyspace size [30,31]. This increase is due to the fact that the anisotropic transform has substantially more WP for a comparable maximum decomposition depth. The number anisotropic WP is given by the following recursion:

$$R_j = 1 + 2R_{j-1}^2 - R_{j-2}^4, \quad R_{-2} = R_{-1} = 0$$

Even more than in the case of isotropic WPs, there are anisotropic WP decompositions that are ill-suited for energy compaction. The compression-oriented selection method tries to eliminate these subband structures.

2.3.1 Uniform distribution
We use the case distinction introduced by [37] to construct a uniform distribution for the selection of a random subband structure: the probability for any case to be chosen is the ratio of the number of subband structures contained in the case to the total number of subband structures. Subsequently, this distribution is often denoted/abbreviated by *anisouni*.

2.3.2 Compression-oriented distribution
The basic algorithm for the compression-oriented generation of randomized anisotropic WPs is similar to the isotropic case, only the direction of the decomposition (vertical or horizontal) is additionally chosen at random. However, constraining the degree of anisotropy is necessary in order to prevent subbands from being decomposed excessively in a single direction, as, especially in the case of the approximation subband, this would lead to inferior energy compaction in the transform domain and thus to inferior compression results. The parameter q is used to restrict the maximum degree of anisotropy for the approximation subband. For the degree of anisotropy Υ of a subband we use the following definition:

$$\Upsilon(h, v) = v - h \qquad (1)$$

where h and v are the decomposition depths in horizontal and vertical direction, respectively. If at any node during the randomized generation of an anisotropic WP subband structure, decomposition of the subband at this node in the randomly chosen direction would result in the degree of anisotropy exceeding the maximum degree of anisotropy, the direction of the decomposition is changed. The degree of anisotropy for the approximation and detail subbands influence both, compression performance and keyspace size.

The other parameters are used in the same way as in the isotropic case: The base value b sets the basic probability of decomposition, the change factor c alters this base probability depending on the current decomposition level l.

3. Evaluation of compression performance

In previous study [16,30] parameter settings for the compression-oriented distribution have been determined for a small number of test images. For the isotropic wavelet packet transform it is proposed to force a maximum decomposition depth for the approximation subband. For the anisotropic wavelet packet transform, in addition to forcing a maximum decomposition depth, the maximum degree of anisotropy for the approximation subband needs to be restricted to preserve compression performance.

The parameters proposed by [16,30] were obtained empirically by a number of experiments. A large number of different parameter settings were used, but only on three test images. The parameters that were obtained for these three test images are a base value b of 0.25 and a change factor c of 0.1. For the isotropic case the global decomposition depth g has been set to 5. For the anisotropic case g has been set to 10 and the maximal degree of anisotropy of the approximation subband q has been set to 1. Recall that we follow the convention to give the decomposition depth of the isotropic wavelet packet transform in pairs of (horizontal and vertical) decompositions, whereas in the anisotropic case each (horizontal or vertical) decomposition step is counted separately.

We use these parameters in our experiments and evaluate their performance for a larger set of test images. We verify the compression performance of the compression-oriented selection method by an empirical study based on an extended set of images. For this purpose we use a set of 100 gray-scale images of 512×512 pixels (taken with four different camera models).

We use five different bitrates: 0.125, 0.25, 0.5, 1, and 2 bpp. For each of the test images we performed the following JPEG2000 compression tests at each of these bitrates:

- Pyramidal (1 subband structure, level 5),
- Isouni: random isotropic wavelet packets drawn according to the uniform distribution with $g = 5$ (100 randomly selected subband structures),
- Iso (constrained): random isotropic wavelet packets drawn according to the compression-oriented distribution with $g = 5$, $b = 0.25$, and $c = 0.1$ (100 randomly selected subband structures),
- Anisouni: random anisotropic wavelet packets drawn according to the uniform distribution with $g = 10$ (100 randomly selected subband structures), and
- Aniso (constrained): random isotropic wavelet packets drawn according to the compression-oriented distribution with $g = 10$, $b = 0.25$, $c = 0.1$, and $q = 1$ (100 randomly selected subband structures).

To ensure comparability the same seeds (and therefore the same decomposition structures) were chosen for each image at each of the five different rates. The standard CDF 9/7 biorthogonal wavelet was used for transformation in all experiments. The results of our empirical study are summarized for the five categories and all bitrates in Figure 3.

For the compression-oriented setup, the loss in compression performance is smaller for the anisotropic randomized decomposition method (below 1dB). Due to the fact that randomized anisotropic wavelet packets require fewer decompositions for the same keyspace size, the compression performance achieved in the anisotropic setup is superior to the isotropic setup. For the set of natural test images the pyramidal decomposition remains the setup with the best compression performance. In part this is due to the overhead in header data that is introduced in the JPEG2000 bitstream by increasing the number of subbands (as is usually the case in KDWP). Table 1 shows the average ratio of header data to packet data for all test images at different bitrates. As the header size is less affected by bitrate it can be seen that the ratio increases when the bitrate decreases and can make up a substantial part of the bitstream.

As regards the difference between uniform and compression-oriented selection, it can be seen that the compression performance of the latter is above the compression performance of the former. The difference is more evident for the anisotropic case, for which a predominant decomposition of the approximation subband in a single direction, which leads to inferior energy compaction for natural images, is possible. Restricting the

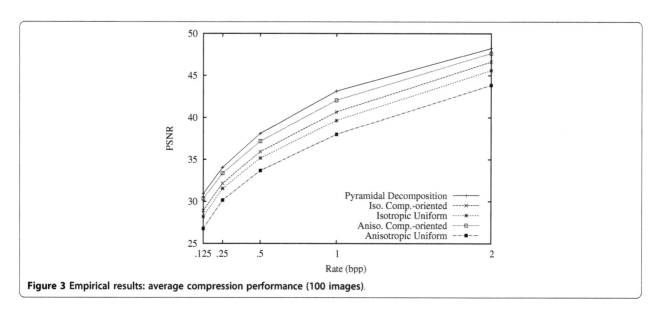

Figure 3 Empirical results: average compression performance (100 images).

maximum degree of anisotropy for the approximation subband in the compression-oriented selection leads to a compression performance that is closer to the pyramidal decomposition.

From an compression performance point of view, the compression-oriented distributions are favorable, although, even these distributions considerably decrease compression efficiency.

4. Computational complexity

In order to compare the computational complexity of KDWP encryption compared to conventional compression and encryption it is sufficient to determine the difference. The main difference between KDWP encryption and conventional compression and encryption is the transform stage, a random WP is chosen for KDWP encryption, while in a conventional encryption approach the pyramidal decomposition is employed. In the commonly applied PCRDO coding approach (post-compression-rate-distortion optimization) the complexity of the remaining compression (labeled "RCompression" in Figure 2) is almost completely independent of the bitrate and thus the difference in complexity is almost completely due to the difference in the transform stage. In the conventional approach there is an additional encryption

process after compression, which is linearly bit-rate-dependent. First we present experimental performance results in Section 4..1 and complement the findings with a theoretical performance analysis in Section 4..2.

4.1 Experimental performance evaluation

The experimental results have been obtained using our JJ2000-based implementation. The test set consisted of 100 grey-scale images with a resolution of 512 × 512. Both the implementation and the test set will be publicly available at http://www.wavelab.at/sources/. The tests were conducted on an Intel Core 2 CPU 6700 @2.66 GHz. Table 2 summarizes the results for the pyramidal decomposition and the different selection schemes, the uniform distribution ("isouni") and the compression-oriented distribution ("isouni"). The results are averages of hundred trials. Additionally we need to determine the complexity of AES encryption, which is given in Table 3 [11]. These results enable us to determine the complexity in dependence of a varying bit-rate, which is shown in Figure 4. The bit-rate in bpp (bit per pixel) is plotted against the complexity given in average processing time for in image in seconds. Clearly the additional complexity of AES encryption is negligible, compared to the complexity introduced by the KDWP. Furthermore the anisotropic

Table 1 Ratio of header data to packet data for different compression rates (16 quality layers)

Rate	pyramidal	iso	aniso
0.125	15.9%	32.8%	20.8%
0.25	10.0%	20.8%	15.1%
0.5	6.1%	13.6%	9.6%
1	3.7%	9.2%	5.9%
2	2.5%	6.4%	3.9%

Table 2 Average compression complexity with our implementation

structure	avg. t	avg. fps
pyramidal	0.643 s	1.55 fps
iso	1.005 s	1 fps
isouni	1.147 s	0.87 fps
aniso	0.726 s	1.34 fps
anisouni	1.891 s	0.53 fps

Table 3 Runtime performance of encryption routines

AES encryption			
Method	throughput	codestreams	with 2bpp
AES OFB	42.71 MB/s	0.0015 s	683.36 fps

uniform distribution performs worst by far, which is to some extend implementation-specific. Very anisotropic subbands are obviously not very efficiently dealt with our implementation.

However, one might argue that our Java based implementation does not reflect the state-of-the-art. One of the fastest implementations, the Kakadu implementation[b], even achieves 39.88 fps compared to 1.55 fps with our implementation (compression with the pyramidal decomposition, 2 bpp, 5 level wavelet decomposition and no quality layers), and thus is about 25 times faster. Therefore we also show results for an hypothetical optimized implementation that even outperforms Kakadu by a factor of 2, i.e., is 50 times faster than our implementation (see Figure 5). Nonetheless the basic assessment stays the same, no performance benefits with KDWP can be gained even with an optimized implementation.

The final question is whether it is at all possible to gain any performance benefits with KDWP (even with the most optimized implementation) compared to AES encryption. This question can only be answered with a theoretical analysis.

4.2 Theoretical performance analysis
We determine the computational complexities on a random access machine with an instruction set of basic operations, such as $\wedge$, $\&$, $+$, $*$, and $\%$.

As we are only interested in the difference of the complexities it is sufficient to determine the complexity of the pyramidal wavelet transform, the average WP transform, and AES encryption.

The wavelet transform stage consists of iterated filter operations, the number of filter operations depends on the WP and the number of pixels. For every input pixel and decomposition level two filter operations are required for the isotropic case. A single filter operation with an n-length filter consists of n multiplications, n additions, n MemReads and a single MemWrite, which yields 25 operations for $n = 8$ (JPEG2000's 9/7 irreversible filter).

In order to determine the average/expected complexity of the KDWP, we determine the expected average decomposition depth of the WP drawn from one of the two proposed selection schemes. The complexity analysis based on the average decomposition depth allows us to analyze the complexity of the WT and the KDWP independent of the image resolutions, as for every pixel the computational complexity is given by the average decomposition depth times the number of necessary operations for filtering. For the pyramidal wavelet decomposition with decomposition depth g, the average decomposition depth D_g^p is given by:

$$D_g^p = \sum_{i=0}^{g} 1/4^i \overset{g \to \infty}{=} 4/3 \approx 1.33333$$

The expected average decomposition depth for the uniform distribution on isotropic WP with a maximum decomposition depth g, D_g can be derived recursively:

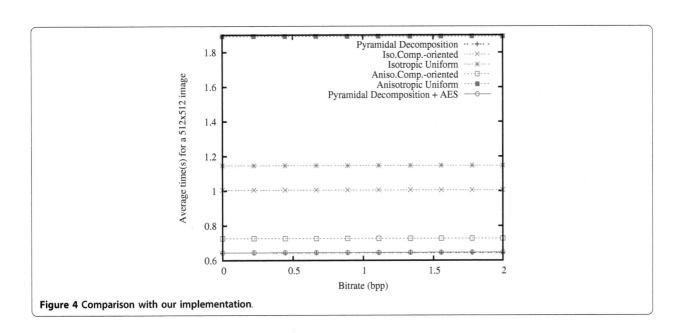

Figure 4 Comparison with our implementation.

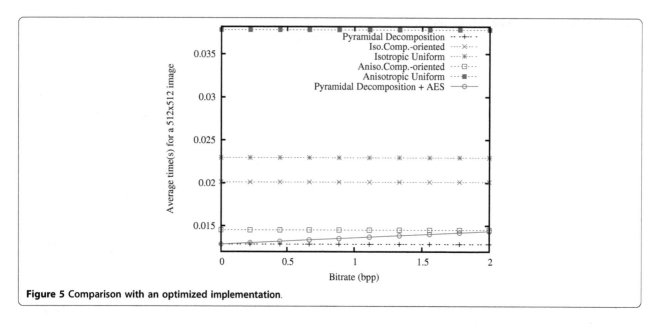

Figure 5 Comparison with an optimized implementation.

$$D_g = \frac{Q_g - 1}{Q_g}\left(D_{g-1} + 1\right), \quad D_0 = 0$$

$$g - 1 \leq D_g \leq g - 1/2, \quad D_{k+1} \approx k + 0.41174$$

The expected decomposition depth for the compression-oriented distribution without considering the forced decomposition of the approximation subbands is denoted D_g^c. For briefness we denote $p_c(l) = p_l$ and the probability of the converse event as $q_l = 1 - p_l$. $D_{l,g}^c$ gives the expected decomposition depth of a subband at level l with a maximum decomposition depth of g.

$$D_g^c = D_{0,g}^c, \quad D_{g,g}^c = 0, \quad D_{l,g}^c = \left(D_{l+1,g}^c + 1\right)p_l = \sum_{i=l}^{g-1}\prod_{k=l}^{i} p_k$$

If $c = 0$ and $1 - \frac{b}{2} < 1$, then:

$$D_g^c =^{g \to \infty} \frac{2}{b} - 1$$

If we take the enforced decomposition of approximation subbands into account (constrained case), we denote the expected average decomposition depth D_g^f.

$$D_g^f = \frac{g}{4^{g-1}} + \sum_{i=1}^{g-1}\frac{3}{4^i}\left(D_{i,g}^c + i\right)$$

If $c = 0$ and $0 < 1 - \frac{b}{2} < 1$, then:

$$D_g^f =^{g \to \infty} \frac{2}{b} + 1/3$$

Table 4 shows the average decomposition depths of D_g, D_g^c, and D_g^f for different maximum isotropic decomposition depths.

The expected decomposition depth for a uniform distribution on anisotropic WP is denoted D_g^a and can be determined by the following recursion:

$$\forall i \in \mathbb{N}: A_{-i} = 0, \quad A_g = 1 + 2A_{g-1}^2 - A_{g-2}^4$$

$$\forall i \in \mathbb{N}: D_{-i}^a = 0, \quad D_g^a = \frac{1}{A_g}\left(2A_{g-1}^2\left(D_{g-1}^a + 1\right) - A_{g-2}^4\left(D_{g-2}^a + 2\right)\right)$$

$$D_g^a \approx g - 1 + 0.5301$$

The expected decomposition depth for the compression-oriented distribution is denoted D_g^{ac}. $D_{l,g}^{ac}$ gives the expected decomposition depth of a subband at level l with a maximum decomposition depth of g.

$$D_g^{ac} = D_{0,g}^{ac}, \quad D_{g,g}^{ac} = 0, \quad D_{l,g}^{ac} = \left(D_{l+1,g}^{ac} + 1\right)p_l = \sum_{i=l}^{g-1}\prod_{k=l}^{i} p_k$$

If $c = 0$ and $0 < 1 - \frac{b}{2} < 1$, then:

$$D_g^{ac} =^{g \to \infty} \frac{2}{b} - 1$$

Table 5 shows the average decomposition depths of D_g^a, and D_g^{ac} for different maximum anisotropic decomposition depths.

Table 4 The expected average decomposition depth for isotropic WP distributions ($b = 1/4$, $c = 0$)

Iso. g	D_g	D_g^c	D_g^f
1	0.5	0.857	1
2	1.41176	1.6406	1.90625
3	2.41174	2.3105	2.70703
4	3.41174	2.89673	3.40967
5	4.41174	3.40946	4.02496

Table 5 The expected average decomposition depth for anisotropic WP distributions ($b = 1/4$, $c = 0$)

Aniso. g	D_g^a	D_g^{ac}
2	1.55556	1.64063
4	3.53125	2.89673
6	5.53020	3.85843
8	7.53014	4.59474
10	9.53014	5.15847

According to [38] and backed-up by our own analysis 352.625 operations are necessary for the encryption of a single byte with AES with a 128-bit key in CTR-mode.

The overall results are shown in Figure 6, the bitrate in bpp is plotted against the computational complexity in unit cost for the different approaches. Also the theoretical analysis backups the basic claim that no performance improvements can be gained from isotropic KDWP for the relevant bitrate ranges. Anisotropic uniform KDWP performs worst (similar to our experimental results). However, the difference to the other approaches is much smaller, clearly indicating that the JJ2000 implementation does not cope well with very anisotropic subbands. Only the anisotropic compression-oriented KDWP can theoretically perform slightly better for bit-rates in excess of 1.4 bpp. Note that even in the most optimized implementations this will not be achievable as AES has much more faster local data access, compared to the KDWP. Faster local data access is not reflected in our computational model.

5. Security evaluation

In order to assess the security of a multimedia encryption approach, we first need to define "security" of a multimedia cryptosystem more precisely. Conventional notions of security for cryptosystems require that the ciphertext does not leak any information (information-theoretic approach [39]) or any efficiently computable information (the approach of modern cryptography [40]) of the plaintext. This kind of security notions are also referred to as MP-security (message privacy) [41]. However this type of security is rarely met nor targeted by multimedia encryption schemes. Thus multimedia encryption is often analyzed with respect to a full message recovery, i.e., how hard is it for an attacker to reconstruct the (image) data. This type of security notion is referred to as MR-security (message recovery) [41]. However, a reconstruction of a multimedia datum (on the basis of the ciphertext) may have excellent quality and even be perceived as identical by a human observer, while the perfect recovery of the entire message remains impossible.

Thus in the context of multimedia encryption it is required to take the quality of a reconstruction (by an adversary on the basis of the ciphertext) into account. An adversary, who tries to break a multimedia encryption system, is successful if she can efficiently compute a "high quality" reconstruction of the original multimedia datum. Which quality constitutes a security threat highly depends on the targeted application scenario [11]. In [42] this multimedia-specific security notion is termed MQ-security (message quality), similar concepts can be found in the multimedia encryption literature [43,44].

5.1 Usual security analysis: key space

Commonly a multimedia encryption security analysis consists of counting the key space. The common conclusion is that if the key space is large enough the proposed approach is believed to be secure. The number of

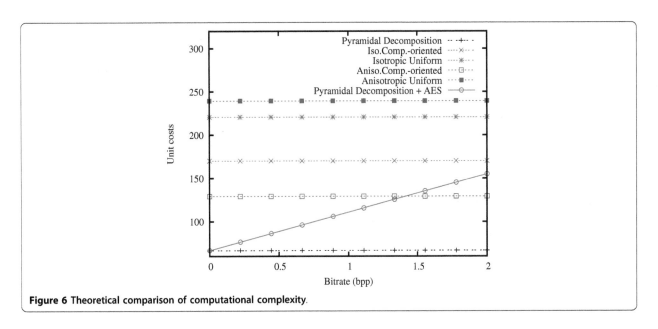

Figure 6 Theoretical comparison of computational complexity.

possible WP is huge even for moderate maximum decomposition depths (e.g., $2^{261.6}$ for isotropic $g = 5$, and $2^{1321.9}$ for an anisotropic depth of 10). Thus the common conclusion would be to consider the scheme secure. Additionally the quality of a reconstruction with a wrong key is often analyzed in literature. However, if we try to decode a JPEG2000 codestream with a wrong WP the decoder will not be able to decode an image, as the WP is required for the decoding. Information, such as the subband/codeblock size and the number of code-blocks in a subband, which is required to make sense of the coded data, is missing. Thus a naive attacker would need to test half of the possible WP before the correct is identified (on average). A futile approach given the number of WP!

5.2 Improved security analysis: entropy

We have presented two basic KDWP selection schemes, namely uniform and compression-oriented. So far the compression-oriented scheme shows advantages, both in terms of compression efficiency and runtime perfor-mance. However, the key space counting approach only reflects a security analysis if the WP are drawn according to a uniform distribution. How can we properly assess the security of the compression-oriented distribution? The appropriate measure is the entropy $H(X)$ of the com-pression-oriented distribution. An attacker needs to test $2^{H(X)-1}$ keys (WP) on average to find the correct key. The entropy $H(X)$ for the compression oriented distribution is a bit tricky to compute (see Appendix 1). Table 6 sum-marizes the results for previously proposed parameters and for the isotropic case.

Still the numbers are sufficiently large such that we have to conclude that KDWP in JPEG2000 are secure. Since entropy values in excess of state-of-the-art ciphers key set sizes (128 bit) can be considered secure, security is sufficient for $g > 5$ in the compression oriented case and for $g > 4$ in the case of uniform WP distribution.

Since the number of anisotropic WP is by far greater than the number of isotropic WP (for comparable maxi-mum decomposition depths, remember an isotropic decomposition depth g corresponds to an anisotropic decomposition depth of $2\,g$), the anisotropic case has to be considered secure as well.

Table 6 Entropy of the isotropic compression-oriented distribution ($b = 1/4$, $c = 0$) and the uniform distribution

g	Entropy (iso)	Entropy (isouni)
2	2.4	4.1
3	9.1	16.3
4	32.4	65.4
5	114.0	261.6
6	399.5	1046.4

Note that this analysis holds for every scheme that strongly requires the WP for decoding. However, the key question now is whether this requirement is strong for JPEG2000 or whether it can be weakened by exploit-ing specifically tailored attacks.

In the following we will argue that such specifically-tailored attacks can be designed for KDWP with JPEG2000 and that they will be even more effective if only the permissible WP of JPEG2000 Part 2 are employed.

5.3 Specific attacks against KDWP in JPEG2000

Due to JPEG2000 coding the LL subband can be recon-structed by an attacker with a special-purpose decoder. The LL subband can be decoded, because the coded LL subband data is located at the start of JPEG2000 file. Thus an attacker can decode a low-resolution image, a fact that has already been highlighted in previous study [16]. The previous conclusion has been that KDWP in JPEG2000 are only suitable for the application scenario of transparent encryption.

In this study we pose a new question: can an attacker go further and decode subsequent resolutions, i.e., images with an higher quality than targeted? In fact resolution only loosely corresponds to perceived quality, but as every subsequent improvement an attacker can achieve (by image enhancement operations) starts from a pre-viously deciphered lower resolution it makes sense to use resolution as sole quality indicator within the scope of this work. The quality of an attacked image is determined as the fraction of original resolution divided by the obtained resolution (given in the number of pixels).

Thus the attacker's problem is: given access to a low-resolution image how hard is it to obtain/decode the next resolution? Figure 7 illustrates the problem for iso-tropic and anisotropic decompositions.

Therefore, we first need to answer whether the next resolution can be decoded from the codestream (indepen-dently of the higher resolutions). This is the case in the coding framework of JPEG2000. A resolution can be decoded independently from the remaining higher resolu-tions (definitely for resolution progression and at least at the lowest quality for layer progression and always if SOP and EPH markers are employed which signal packet borders).

The next question is whether it is decidable that the employed subband decomposition structure is the cor-rect one. It is also highly likely that it can be decided whether the correct decomposition structure has been employed in the decoding of a resolution: Firstly, the wavelet resolutions are not independent, i.e., statistical cross-resolution dependencies are highly likely to iden-tify the correct decomposition. Secondly, the codestream syntax and semantics must also be met while decoding

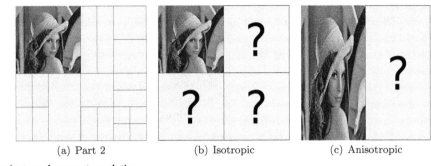

| (a) Part 2 | (b) Isotropic | (c) Anisotropic |

Figure 7 Attack against a subsequent resolution.

with a subband decomposition structure, i.e., decoding errors clearly indicate an incorrect decomposition structure.

Thus the decomposition structure of a resolution can be determined independently of the higher resolutions in JPEG2000.

Now, how hard is it for an adversary to decode a certain resolution? We first discuss the standardized case of JPEG2000 Part 2.

5.3.1 JPEG2000 Part 2

In JPEG2000 Part 2 a high frequency subband may only be decomposed two more times (either isotropic or anisotropic). In the case of isotropic WP, every next resolution may only be secured by $Q_2^3 = 17^3 = 4913$ possibilities. In the case of anisotropic WP, a subband has only $R_2 = 18$ possibilities to be further decomposed. Thus the restrictions of Part 2 and both distinct cases do not offer security for each subsequent resolution. An attacker would need only 4913/2 or 18/2 trials on average to decode each subsequent resolution.

However, JPEG2000 Part 2 allows to specify either horizontal, vertical or horizontal and vertical decomposition for a subband, i.e., there are four different subband structures for a single subband (no decomposition, vertical, horizontal, or both) in one step. The low resolution subband can have three high frequency subbands (HL, LH, HH) or one high frequency subband (either horizontal or vertical). These high frequency subbands may be decomposed two more times, which yields $4^4 + 4^2 + 4^2 - 1 = 287$ different subband decomposition structures for such a subband. 4^4 is the number of possibilities after a decomposition in both directions and 4^2 is the number of possibilities after either a horizontal or a vertical decomposition, one WP is counted three times (thus -2) and no decomposition also has to be counted (+1). Figure 7a shows the case with three subbands. There are three cases:

- Three subbands (HL, LH, HH), which leads to $287^3 = 23639903$ possible WP.
- One vertical subband, which has 287 possible WP.

- One horizontal subband, which has 287 possible WP.

In summary there are about $2^{24.49}$ possible WP for a subsequent resolution in Part 2. Though less than 2^{24} checks are quite an effort, this number of checks is still computationally feasible.

Thus the application of a JPEG2000 Part 2 encoder and KDWP can not be considered secure (neither MR-secure nor MQ-secure) due to the restrictions in terms of admissible WP. For non-standard WP security is expected to be increased.

5.3.2 Non-standard WP

The complexity an adversary has to face is given by the entropy of the distribution on the WP on a certain resolution. Tables 7 and 8 summarize the results, while details on the computation are given in Appendix 2). An attacker has to try $2^{H(X)-1}$ WP on average to decode a certain resolution/quality.

In the isotropic case the compression oriented distribution all obtained entropy values are below state-of-the-art cipher key-length (AES has at least 128 bit). The uniform distribution also results in entropy values below AES minimum key length, except for the highest resolution. The anisotropic case with uniform distribution shows higher entropy values, but at a quality of 1/16 security drops far below AES minimum key length. The anisotropic case with the compression oriented

Table 7 Entropy for the distribution on resolutions of the isotropic compression-oriented distribution ($g = 5$, $b = 1/4$, $c = 0$) and the uniform distribution

Res. at level	Quality	Entropy (iso)	Entropy (isouni)
0	1	114.0	261.6
1	1/4	28.7	65.4
2	1/16	7.5	16.3
3	1/64	2.2	4.1
4	1/256	0.8	1.0
5	1/1024	0.0	0.0

Table 8 Entropy for the distribution of decomposition structures of a resolution as induced by the anisotropic uniform distribution ($g = 10$, $b = 1/4$, $c = 0$)

Res. at level	Quality	Entropy (anisouni)
0	1	1321.9
1	1/2	660.5
2	1/4	329.7
3	1/8	164.4
4	1/16	81.7
5	1/32	40.3
6	1/64	19.7
7	1/128	9.3
8	1/256	4.2
9	1/512	1.5
10	1/1024	0.0

distribution is expected to be far below the security levels of the uniform distribution. In general an attacker can compute lower resolutions, while only the higher resolutions remain well-protected.

6. Discussion

Media encryption schemes relying on secret transform domains have been proposed mainly motivated by the significant reduction of the computational demand for encryption as compared to traditional transparent encryption methods and by potential capabilities in encrypted domain signal processing. A thorough analysis of the properties of the KDWP approach has revealed that significant disadvantages as compared to conventional compression and encryption schemes exist.

- *Compression impact*: The KDWP approach obviously reduces compression performance. If all possible subband structures are equally likely, the approach is not be suitable for application due to the high variance of obtained compression results. The approach of pruning the set of all subband structures (compression oriented distribution) improves the compression performance, however, still with this technique, a significant loss exists. On the other hand, conventional encryption of course does not at all influence compression performance.

- *Computational demand*: Although the additional complexity of encryption with KDWP in a compression framework, such as JPEG2000, seems to be negligible at a first glance, our careful analysis and our evaluation results clearly show that runtime advantages can not be achieved compared to state-of-the-art cryptographic ciphers (AES). In general we advise to carefully reconsider statements about an improved runtime performance of transform based image and video encryption schemes.

- *Security*: From a security point of view, state-of-the-art cryptographic ciphers are superior to KDWP. The KDWP schemes cannot prevent access to lower resolutions and are thus less secure in terms MQ-security. Within the standardized framework of JPEG2000 Part 2, the KDWP approach is completely insecure, i.e., an attacker is able to reconstruct the entire image.

From the proposed KDWP schemes, the anisotropic compression oriented scheme is best performing. However, even this approach is overall outperformed by conventional compression and encryption, which shows no decrease in compression performance, better runtime performance and cryptographic security.

Apart from an improved runtime performance, image encryption schemes can offer an improved functionality. On the one hand improved functionality could be suitability for specific applications, such as transparent encryption. However, transparent encryption can also be implemented in the conventional approach [10], the small resolution portion of the JPEG2000 file is simply left in plaintext. A standardized tool, namely JPSEC, can be employed to signal all the meta-data (keys, plaintext parts). Even completely JPEG2000-compliant implementations are possible [10], which do not require special software for decoding, a great advantage for real-world deployment of transparent encryption. Transparent encryption with KDWP requires a special decoder, i.e., an attacker's decoder, that can cope with wrong or missing WP structure information, while JPSEC-based approaches require a JPSEC-capable decoder. Thus, the support of transparent encryption by KDWP is not an advantage compared to other approaches, which are more flexible. The conventional approach offers full confidentiality/cryptographic security (MP-security).

Image encryption schemes may also allow special encrypted domain processing, which may justify their application although there are disadvantages in compression, computational demand and security. A good example is encrypted content that can still be robustly watermarked; this feature would outweigh many disadvantages.

6..1 Encrypted domain processing

In fact for KDWP in JPEG2000, the encrypted domain is a scrambled JPEG2000 bitstream and only signal processing operations that can be conducted in this domain are possible. In fact the only possible processing is the truncation of the scrambled bitstream, which results in an almost rate-distortion optimal rate adaptation (in case the underlying bitstream is in quality progression order). However, truncation of an encrypted bitstream is also possible with conventional block ciphers if the are used in the proper mode, e.g., counter mode.

Signal processing operations which rely on transform coefficient data cannot be applied to KDWP protected data as these data can not be decoded. Given the results of our evaluation and analysis (decreased compression performance, increased computational complexity, decreased security, no other advantages) it has to be stated that hardly any sensible realistic application scenarios can be identified for KDWP-based encryption at the present time.

7. Conclusion

A primary argument for proposing KDWP-based encryption has always been its "lightweight" nature, introduced by shifting complexity from encryption into the compression pipeline. When comparing JPEG2000 encryption with key-dependent wavelet packets (KDWP) to the conventional approach (AES encryption), we have assessed an overall increase in computational complexity through additional complexity introduced in the compression step.

Signal processing in the encrypted domain, often used as a second argument favoring transform-based image encryption schemes, does not offer advantages compared to the appropriate application of conventional ciphers. The security of JPEG2000 encryption with KDWP has been analyzed in depth and has been found to be less secure than conventional encryption, as smaller resolution images remain accessible. Security can not be achieved at all if only permissible subband structures of JPEG2000 Part 2 are employed.

All these facts taken together with a slight decrease in compression efficiency as compared to classical (pyramidal) JPEG2000 make KDWP-based encryption approaches not suitable for most application scenarios.

The presented assessment should serve as guideline in the future development of image and video encryption schemes. The following general conclusions may be drawn: Computational complexity will need to be carefully (re)considered for transform-based image and video encryption schemes. Security has to be analyzed with respect to a multimedia specific security notion (MQ-security). Image and video encryption schemes have to provide conclusive evidence for improved functionality, such as encrypted domain signal processing.

Appendix 1: Details on the entropy computation of WP distributions

A WP (wavelet packet subband structure) is derived by the following randomized algorithm (see Section 2..2.2): every subband at depth l is further decomposed with a certain probability p_b, which may only depend on the depth l.

Game tree

This randomized algorithm can be illustrated with the corresponding *game tree*. A game tree $\mathcal{G}_g$ is the tuple (V, E, l, p):

$$V \ldots \text{set of vertices}, \quad E \subset V \times V \ldots \text{set of edges}, \quad l : E \to \{0, 1\}^*, \quad p : E \to \mathbb{R}^+$$

The vertices of a game tree correspond to a certain WP. The edge label (l) in a game tree indicates decomposition decisions and is associated with the probability p that this decomposition decisions are selected in the randomized algorithm. In Figure 8a game tree is illustrated, showing the edge labels and the vertices. The first decision is whether the entire image gets decomposed (split into four subbands), there are two outcomes, an edge labeled with a "0" indicates no decomposition, an edge labeled with a "1" indicates a decomposition into four distinct subbands. A "0" in the label of a edge is replaced by "0000" in the label of a next edge, in order to obtain same length labels at a certain depth of the tree. A "1" in the label of a edge is replaced by one of the strings "0000",... ,"1111" in the label of the next edge, which indicates the further decompositions of the 4 subbands. I.e., the string "0000" indicates that no subband is decomposed, the string "0001" indicates that the last subband (HH) is decomposed, ..., and the string "1111" indicates that all subbands are decomposed. A label uniquely identifies a further decomposition. Note that 0^{16} denotes the string 0000000000000000 and analogous is the meaning of 1^{16}. A unique code for a node is derived by a separated concatenation of the edge labels from a path from the root to the node. We use "," as a separator. Each node corresponds to a certain WP. Figure 8b shows how the edges and edge labels are determined by the predecessor edge. The function pre: $E \to E$ gives the predecessor edge of an edge, e.g., in Figure 8b the predecessor of the edge labeled y, $l(e) = y$, is the edge labeled x, i.e., $l(\text{pre}(e)) = x$. $S(x, r_1, ..., r_n)$ denotes the string obtained by applying the substitution rules r_1 to r_n to string x. If there is a complex rule, which allow choices, i. e., the right side of one rule is a set of strings, $S(x, r_1,...,r_n)$ denotes the set of all possible substitutions. In Figure 8b new edges are added to the vertex (s, x) depending on the edge label x: the label of the first edge is obtained by substituting every "0" in x by "0000" and every "1" by "0000". The labels of all outgoing edges of (s, x) are obtained by all possible substitutions of a "1" in x. The last edge (see Figure 8b) is obtained by substituting all "1"s by "1111". A predecessor label determines the edges and edge labels in the following way:

$$l(e) = y, \quad l(\text{pre}(e)) = x, \quad x \in \{0, 1\}^n, \quad x = (x_1, ..., x_n), \quad x_i \in \{0, 1\}$$
$$y \in S(x, 0 \to 0000, 1 \to \{0000, ..., 1111\}) \subset \{0, 1\}^{4n}$$

The function p assigns each edge a probability (the probabilities of the outgoing edges of a node sum up to 1). The probability of an edge can be determined by its label y and the label of its predecessor x, by simply considering the number of actual decomposition decisions (Σy_i) and the number of maximally possible decomposition decisions ($4\Sigma x_i$):

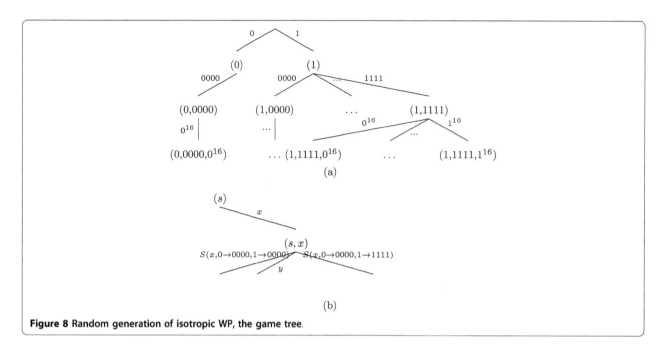

Figure 8 Random generation of isotropic WP, the game tree.

$$l(e) = \gamma, \quad l(\mathrm{pre}(e)) = x, \quad p(\gamma) = p_l^{\Sigma \gamma_i}(1-p_l)^{4\Sigma x_i - \Sigma \gamma i}$$

Every leaf of a game tree with depth g corresponds to exactly one WP ψ with maximum decomposition depth g, the probability of a WP ψ is derived by the product of the edge weights p of the path from the root to the leaf.

$$\psi \in V : p(\psi) = \Pi_{e \in \mathrm{Path}(\mathrm{root}, \psi)} p(e)$$

We denote the entropy of corresponding distribution for a game tree $\mathcal{G}_g$ by:

$$H(\mathcal{G}_g) = \sum_{\psi \in \mathrm{Leaves}(\mathcal{G}_g)} -p(\psi) 1 \mathrm{d} p(\psi)$$

However, as the number of leaves at depth g is $Q(g)$ the computation of the entropy of the distribution on WPs on the basis of this formula is soon infeasible with growing g.

Cumulative game tree
A simpler representation of a game tree $\mathcal{G}_g$ is its corresponding *cumulative game tree* (CuGa-Tree), $\mathcal{C}_g$. A CuGa-Tree $\mathcal{C}_g$ is the tuple (V, E, l, p, n):

$$l : E \to \mathbb{N}, \quad p : E \to \mathbb{R}^+, \quad n : E \to \mathbb{N}$$

A CuGa-Tree summarizes the edges of a node with the with the same probability p, i.e., with the same number of decomposition decisions, i.e., with the same number of "1"s in the edge label of the game tree. Thus the edge label of a CuGa-Tree indicates the number of decomposition decisions, i.e., the number of subbands which are further decomposed. We have to keep track

how many edges of the game tree are summarized by an edge of a CuGa-Tree, therefore we introduce a weight function $n : E \to \mathbb{N}$. A CuGa-Tree with depth 2 is shown in Figure 9.

The edges and edge labels are determined by the predecessor edge (see Figure 9b): the successors of an edge with label $l(e) = i$ (this number of subbands have been decomposed) can be in the range of 0 to $4i$, as every subband may have up to four children:

$$l(\mathrm{pre}(e)) = i, \quad l(e) \in \{0, ..., 4i\}$$

The probability for an edge is similar to game trees:

$$p(e) = p_l^{l(e)}(1-p_l)^{4l(\mathrm{pre}(e))-l(e)}$$

The number of edges in the game tree with the same probability is derived by counting the number of edges with the same number of "1"s, i.e., decomposition decisions in the edge label: There are $4l(\mathrm{pre}(e))$ possible positions for $l(e)$ "1"s and thus there are $\binom{4l(P\mathrm{pre}(e))}{l(e)}$ edges with the same probability in the game tree:

$$n(e) = \binom{4l(P\mathrm{pre}(e))}{l(e)}$$

The probability p and weight n are defined for vertices $\psi \in V$ in the following way:

$$p(\psi) = \Pi_{e \in \mathrm{Path}(\mathrm{root}, \psi)} p(e)$$
$$n(\psi) = \Pi_{e \in \mathrm{Path}(\mathrm{root}, \psi)} n(e)$$

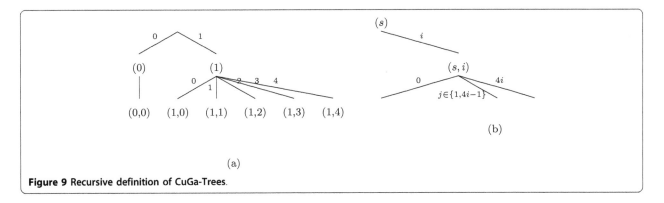

Figure 9 Recursive definition of CuGa-Trees.

The entropy of the corresponding distribution of a CuGa-Tree $\mathcal{C}_g$ can be computed by:

$$H\left(\mathcal{C}_g\right) = \sum_{\psi \in \text{Leaves}(\mathcal{C}_g)} -n(\psi)p(\psi)1\mathrm{d}p(\psi)$$

The nodes can be uniquely identified by the path from the root, i.e., by tuple of edge labels. A node at depth g is a g-tuple of edge labels $(x_1,..., x_g)$. The set of all nodes at depth g is given by $\{(x_1,...,x_g)|x_1 \in \{0,1\}, x_{i+1} \leq 4x_i\}$.

Appendix 2: Details on the entropy computation of distributions of decomposition structures on resolutions

In order to assess the MQ-security of KDWP we need to compute the entropy of the resulting distribution of the decomposition structures on a resolution, i.e., on the subband is the result of always decomposing the low pass band further (no high pass filtering, i.e., either the LL, LX or XL subband). Thus only the case of a low pass band decomposition is of interest up to the depth d of the targeted resolution (see Figure 10). The entropy of the decomposition structures of a resolution corresponds to the entropy of the tree of Figure 10, the depth of the resolution has to be considered for the split-probability in sub-tree $\mathcal{C}_{g-d}$, which is indicated by the notation $\mathcal{C}_{g-d}(p_d)$. Thus entropy computation is straight-forward, namely the entropy of the

$$q = 1 - \Pi_{l=0}^{d-1}p_l \overbrace{\qquad\qquad\qquad} p = \Pi_{l=0}^{d-1}p_l$$

$$\mathcal{C}_{g-d}(p_d)$$

(a) $\mathcal{R}_{g,d}$

Figure 10 The entropy of distributions of decomposition structures on resolutions.

decomposition structures for a resolution d can be computed by:

$$q = 1 - \Pi_{l=0}^{d-1}p_l, \quad p = \Pi_{l=0}^{d-1}p_l$$
$$H\left(\mathcal{R}_{g,d}\right) = q1\mathrm{d}l/q + p1\mathrm{d}l/p + pH\left(\mathcal{C}_{g-d}\left(p_d\right)\right)$$

Endnotes
[a]http://jj2000.epfl.ch/. [b]Linux binaries in version 6.3.1 from http://www.kakadusoftware.com.

Acknowledgements
This work was funded by the Austrian Science Fund under Project 19159. The authors thank Stefan Huber and Rade Kutil, and Roland Kwitt for the valuable discussions and contributions.

Author details
[1]University of Applied Sciences, Urstein Sued 1, 5412 Puch/Salzburg Austria
[2]Dept. of Computer Sciences, University of Salzburg, Jakob Haringer Str. 2, 5020 Salzburg, Austria

Competing interests
The authors declare that they have no competing interests.

References
1. BM Macq, JJ Quisquater, Cryptology for digital TV broadcasting. Proc IEEE. 83(6):944–957 (1995)
2. ISO/IEC 15444-1, Information technology–JPEG2000 image coding system. Part 1: Core coding system. (2000)
3. D Taubman, M Marcellin, *JPEG2000–Image Compression Fundamentals, Standards and Practice.* (Kluwer Academic Publishers, Boston, 2002)
4. Digital Cinema Initiatives, LLC (DCI), Digital cinema system specification v1.1, online presentation. (2007)
5. R Grosbois, P Gerbelot, T Ebrahimi, Authentication and access control in the JPEG2000 compressed domain. in *Applications of Digital Image Processing XXIV, ser Proceedings of SPIE*, vol. 4472, ed. by Tescher A (San Diego, CA, USA, 2001), pp. 95–104
6. H Kiya, D Imaizumi, O Watanabe, Partial-scrambling of image encoded using JPEG2000 without generating marker codes. in Proceedings of the IEEE International Conference on Image Processing (ICIP'03), vol. III. (Barcelona, Spain, 2003), pp. 205–208
7. T Stütz, A Uhl, On format-compliant iterative encryption of JPEG2000. *Proceedings of the Eighth IEEE International Symposium on Multimedia (ISM'06).* (IEEE Computer Society, San Diego, CA, USA, 2006), pp. 985–990
8. M Grangetto, E Magli, G Olmo, Multimedia selective encryption by means of randomized arithmetic coding. IEEE Trans Multimedia. 8(5):905–917 (2006)

9.   Y Yang, BB Zhu, Y Yang, S Li, N Yu, Efficient and syntax-compliant JPEG2000 encryption preserving original fine granularity of scalability. EURASIP J Inf Security (2007). 2007:056365

10.   T Stütz, A Uhl, On efficient transparent JPEG2000 encryption. *Proceedings of ACM Multimedia and Security Workshop, MM-SEC '07.* (New York, NY, USA, ACM, 2007), pp. 97–108

11.   D Engel, T Stütz, A Uhl, A survey on JPEG2000 encryption. Multimedia Syst. **15**(4):243–270 (2009)

12.   ISO/IEC 15444-8, Information technology–JPEG2000 image coding system. Part 8: Secure JPEG2000. (2007)

13.   ITU-T T.807, Information technology–JPEG2000 image coding system. Part 8: Secure JPEG2000. (2006)

14.   B Macq, J Quisquater, Digital images multiresolution encryption. J Interactive Multimedia Association Intellectual Property Project. **1**(1):179–206 (1994)

15.   T Stütz, V Pankajakshan, F Autrusseau, A Uhl, H Hofbauer, Subjective and objective quality assessment of transparently encrypted JPEG2000 images. *Proceedings of the ACM Multimedia and Security Workshop (MMSEC'10).* (ACM, Rome, Italy, 2010), pp. 247–252

16.   D Engel, A Uhl, Secret wavelet packet decompositions for JPEG2000 lightweight encryption. in Proceedings of 31st International Conference on Acoustics, Speech, and Signal Processing, ICASSP'06, vol. V. (Toulouse, France, 2006), pp. 465–468

17.   G Unnikrishnan, K Singh, Double random fractional fourier-domain encoding for optical security. Opt Eng. **39**(11):2853–2859 (2000)

18.   L Vorwerk, T Engel, C Meinel, A proposal for a combination of compression and encryption. in ser Proceedings of SPIE, vol. 4067. (Perth, Australia, 2000), pp. 694–702

19.   A Pommer, A Uhl, Wavelet packet methods for multimedia compression and encryption. *Proceedings of the 2001 IEEE Pacific Rim Conference on Communications, Computers and Signal Processing.* (Victoria, Canada: IEEE Signal Processing Society, 2001), pp. 1–4

20.   A Pommer, A Uhl, Lightweight protection of visual data using high-dimensional wavelet parametriza-tion. in *Image Analysis and Processing - ICIAP 2005, ser. Lecture Notes on Computer Science,* vol. 3617, ed. by Roli F, Vitulano S (Cagliari, Italy, 2005), pp. 645–652

21.   A Uhl, A Pommer, Are parameterised biorthogonal wavelet filters suited (better) for selective encryption? in *Multimedia and Security Workshop 2004,* ed. by Dittmann J, Fridrich J (Magdeburg, Germany, 2004), pp. 100–106

22.   A Pommer, A Uhl, Selective encryption of wavelet packet subband structures for secure transmission of visual data. in *Multimedia and Security Workshop, ACM Multimedia,* ed. by Dittmann J, Fridrich J, Wohlmacher P (Juan-les-Pins, France, 2002), pp. 67–70

23.   A Pommer, A Uhl, Selective encryption of wavelet-packet encoded image data–efficiency and security. ACM Multimedia Syst (Special issue on Multimedia Security). **9**(3):279–287 (2003)

24.   T Köckerbauer, M Kumar, A Uhl, Lightweight JPEG2000 confidentiality for mobile environments. in Proceedings of the IEEE International Conference on Multimedia and Expo, ICME'04, vol. 2. (Taipei, Taiwan, 2004), pp. 1495–1498

25.   D Engel, A Uhl, Parameterized biorthogonal wavelet lifting for lightweight JPEG2000 transparent encryption. *Proceedings of ACM Multimedia and Security Workshop, MM-SEC'05.* (New York, NY, USA, 2005), pp. 63–70

26.   D Engel, R Kutil, A Uhl, A symbolic transform attack on lightweight encryption based on wavelet filter parameterization. *Proceedings of ACM Multimedia and Security Workshop, MM-SEC'06.* (Geneva, Switzerland, 2006), pp. 202–207

27.   W Zeng, S Lei, Efficient frequency domain selective scrambling of digital video. **5**(1):118–129 (2003)

28.   S-KA Yeung, S Zhu, B Zeng, Partial video encryption based on alternating transforms. IEEE Signal Process Lett. **16**(10):893–896 (2009)

29.   ISO/IEC 15444-2, Information technology–JPEG2000 image coding system. Part 2: Extensions. (2004)

30.   D Engel, A Uhl, Lightweight JPEG2000 encryption with anisotropic wavelet packets. *Proceedings of International Conference on Multimedia & Expo, ICME'06.* (Toronto, Canada, 2006), pp. 2177–2180

31.   D Engel, A Uhl, An evaluation of lightweight JPEG2000 encryption with anisotropic wavelet packets. in *Security, Steganography, and Watermarking of Multimedia Contents IX, ser Proceedings of SPIE,* ed. by Delp EJ, Wong PW (SPIE, San Jose, CA, USA, 2007), pp. 65 051S1–65 051S10

32.   M Wickerhauser, *Adapted Wavelet Analysis from Theory to Software.* (A.K. Peters, Wellesley, Mass, 1994)

33.   K Ramchandran, M Vetterli, Best wavelet packet bases in a rate-distortion sense. IEEE Trans Image Process. **2**(2):160–175 (1993)

34.   T Stütz, B Mühlbacher, A Uhl, Best wavelet packet bases in a JPEG2000 rate-distortion sense: the impact of header data. *Proceedings of the IEEE International Conference on Multimedia & Expo, ICME'10.* (Singapore, 2010), pp. 19–24

35.   T Stütz, A Uhl, Efficient wavelet packet basis selection in JPEG2000. *Proceedings of the IEEE International Conference on Image Processing, ICIP'11.* (Brussels, Belgium, 2011), pp. 317–320

36.   T Stütz, A Uhl, Efficient and rate-distortion optimal wavelet packet basis selection in JPEG2000. IEEE Trans Multimedia. (in press)

37.   R Kutil, D Engel, Methods for the anisotropic wavelet packet transform. Appl Comput Harmonic Anal. **25**(3):295–314 (2008)

38.   A Pommer, A Uhl, Selective encryption of wavelet packet subband structures for obscured transmission of visual data. *Proceedings of the 3rd IEEE Benelux Signal Processing Symposium (SPS 2002).* (IEEE Benelux Signal Processing Chapter, Leuven, Belgium, 2002), pp. 25–28

39.   CE Shannon, Communication theory of secrecy systems. Bell Syst Tech J. **28**, 656–715 (1949)

40.   O Goldreich, *The Foundations of Cryptography.* (Cambridge University Press, Cambridge, 2001)

41.   M Bellare, T Ristenpart, P Rogaway, T Stegers, Format-preserving encryption. in Proceedings of Selected Areas in Cryptography, SAC'09, vol. 5867. (Calgary, Canada, 2009), pp. 295–312

42.   T Stütz, A Uhl, Efficient format-compliant encryption of regular languages: block-based cycle-walking. in *Proceedings of the 11th Joint IFIP TC6 and TC11 Conference on Communications and Multimedia Security, CMS'10, ser. IFIP Advances in Information and Communication Technology,* vol. 6109, ed. by Decker BD, Schaum?ü?ller-Bichl I (Springer, Linz, Austria, 2010), pp. 81–92

43.   A Said, Measuring the strength of partial encryption schemes. Proceedings of the IEEE International Conference on Image Processing (ICIP'05). **2**, 1126–1129 (2005)

44.   Y Mao, M Wu, A joint signal processing and cryptographic approach to multimedia encryption. IEEE Trans Image Process. **15**(7):2061–2075 (2006)

2

Do private and portable web browsers leave incriminating evidence?: a forensic analysis of residual artifacts from private and portable web browsing sessions

Donny J Ohana[*] and Narasimha Shashidhar

Abstract

The Internet is an essential tool for everyday tasks. Aside from common use, the option to browse the Internet privately is a desirable attribute. However, this can create a problem when private Internet sessions become hidden from computer forensic investigators in need of evidence. Our primary focus in this research is to discover residual artifacts from private and portable web browsing sessions. In addition, the artifacts must contain more than just file fragments and enough to establish an affirmative link between user and session. Certain aspects of this topic have triggered many questions, but there have never been enough authoritative answers to follow. As a result, we propose a new methodology for analyzing private and portable web browsing artifacts. Our research will serve to be a significant resource for law enforcement, computer forensic investigators, and the digital forensics research community.

Keywords: Private browsing; Portable web browsers; Internet forensics; Portable browsing; Web browser artifacts; RAM analysis

1. Introduction

In the last 20 years, the Internet has become drastically essential for everyday tasks associated with stationary and mobile computer devices. Aside from common Internet usage, people desire the option to browse the Internet while keeping their user information private. As a result, new web browsing features were slowly developed for all major web browsers, asserting the option of 'private browsing.' This method works by either removing information at the end of a private session or by not writing the data at all. Other private browser features may include concealing additional information such as cookie discoverability from websites.

According to one study [1] there are two private browsing objectives. The first objective is to allow users to browse the Internet without leaving any trace. The second is to allow users to browse the Internet while limiting identity discoverability to websites. While both of these goals are

* Correspondence: djo007@shsu.edu
Department of Computer Science, Sam Houston State University, Huntsville, TX 77340, USA

important, our research will focus on discovering information from local storage devices since the majority of computer investigations involve search and seizure of local machines. One alternative to using private browsing modes is to surf the Internet using a portable web browser, such as one stored on a Universal Serial Bus (USB) flash drive. Therefore, web browsing sessions are more likely to be stored on the portable storage device itself instead of the computer or host machine.

Private and portable web browsing artifacts, such as usernames, electronic communication, browsing history, images, and videos, may contain significant evidence to an examiner. Prior research in this area is very limited. Referring back to one of the main studies on private browsing modes [1], this research lacks an in-depth analysis of deleted and volatile information pertaining to private browsing sessions. In another study focused on portable web browsers [2], many statements were made without the basis of true experimental findings. Furthermore, there are virtually no published studies on residual artifacts from current portable web browsers existing on host machines.

In the past, similar studies have been conducted on the SanDisk U3 flash drive and its portable applications. Since U3-USB devices had a pre-installed read-only partition, it was challenging for forensic investigators to discover electronic evidence. In the latter year of 2009, SanDisk began phasing out support for U3 Technology and it has been discontinued because of many irresolvable issues [3].

Private and portable web browsing artifacts can be extremely valuable. Prior research either lacks significant findings or does not provide sufficient answers. We plan to overcome these shortcomings by analyzing both allocated and unallocated space on entire disks while measuring our results against multiple web browsers. Furthermore, we plan to analyze volatile data that may be available in an incident response.

This paper is organized as follows: Section 2 provides a list of background terms. Section 3 describes prior and related work in private browsing modes and portable web browsers. Section 4 discusses the four major browsers and their privacy capabilities. Section 5 discusses several different portable web browsers. Section 6 details the implementation and experiments. Sections 7 and 8 conclude the paper with some open questions, future work, and discussion.

2. Background definitions

In this section, we provide a list of background terms and definitions (Table 1) to assist readers with some of the terminology used in this research.

3. Related work
3.1. Private browsing

In the study [1] on private browsing modes in modern browsers, researchers presented a list of inconsistencies between private browsing goals and browser implementations. They also defined private browsing modes to have two primary goals: privacy against the web and privacy against local machines. Meaning, the user's identity should not be identified over the Internet (web), and the user's activity should not be recorded on the machine (local). One example is that Mozilla Firefox and Google Chrome both take steps to remain private against websites during private mode. Apple Safari on the other hand takes measures to only protect against local machines, but through our research, we will exploit some of the vulnerability to that method.

The researchers found that all the web browsers (tested) failed in one way or another when analyzing policies. This is mainly because of complications introduced by browser plug-ins and extensions. It was also shown that extensions can weaken private browsing modes and therefore activities can still be recorded. One example is that Google Chrome disables all extensions during private browsing mode and Firefox does not. With regard to inconsistencies within a single browser, the researchers found that cookies set in public mode in Firefox 3.6 are not available to the web when browsing privately, however SSL certificates and passwords are.

Ultimately, this study establishes a good foundation for private browsing analysis but lacks significant findings. The areas primarily studied were policy inconsistencies,

Table 1 Terms and definitions

Terminology	Definition
Residual artifacts	Remaining data such as files, images, documents, and web content
Affirmative link	Judicially devised standard to aid Courts in determining sufficiency of evidence between subject and offense
ISO image	A computer file that is an exact copy of an existing file, CD, DVD, etc.
Virtual machine	Simulation of a real machine
Prefetch files (Windows)	Each time an application is run on a Windows machine, a Prefetch file referencing the loaded application is created to speed boot time
$I30/$MFT	New Technology File System (NTFS) Index Attribute/Master File Table
Browser cache	Temporary Internet files (storage) for increasing speed
RAM	Working memory that is volatile
Pagefile (paging)	Virtual memory designated on disk
Memdump	Action of dumping volatile memory into a file to view contents
Drive free space	Referencing the unallocated space on disk
Slack space/file slack	Unused space in a disk cluster (area between end of file and end of disk cluster)
System volume information	Volume shadow copy (snapshots) for system restore/backup
FTK orphan directory	Contains files that no longer have a parent, and the parent folder is overwritten (using $MFT as a reference)
Data carving	There are many different types of data carving techniques (block-based, statistical, semantic, etc.) but essentially, most data carvers extract content by looking for file headers/footers and then 'carving' data blocks in between

browser extension weaknesses, private browsing usage, website user discoverability, and Firefox vulnerabilities. Various files and folders which were privately modified and accessed are pointed out by the researchers, but they do retrieve specific data that is deleted after a private session is terminated. Also, volatile memory artifacts were ignored because they wanted to show discoverability after the memory was cleared. When a small experiment was conducted running a memory leaking program, certain artifacts from private browsing sessions were discovered in the memory. The reason for this was explained that operating systems often cache DNS resolutions, and therefore by analyzing the cache and TTL values, an investigator can learn if and when the user visited a particular site. In addition, the Operating System can swap memory pages leaving further traces of user activity.

In contrast to this research, we plan to examine all four major web browsers utilizing a different acquisition method. Our goal is to extract as much data as possible, including deleted and volatile data, to obtain sufficient information within the artifacts retrieved. One research article [4] argues that browser vendors deliver exactly what they claim but consumers have limited knowledge as to what private browsing modes can actually do. Comparing this article to the first study [1] proves otherwise. There are clearly private policy inconsistencies within the four major browsers according to the data.

3.2. Portable web browsing

One study on portable web browsers [2] explained that portable web browsing artifacts are primarily stored where the installation folder is located (removable disk). Residual artifacts, such as USB identifiers and portable programs, can be discovered by analyzing the Windows Registry and Windows Prefetch files. Furthermore, they state that if the removable disk is not accessible to the investigator, it is *impossible* to trace any further information. In regard to portable software discoverability, the researchers stated that it was difficult to determine portable web browser usage on a host machine. The majority of these statements were made without the basis of any true experimental findings. Therefore, every one of these statements will be fully tested in our research to determine authoritative answers. We plan to recover significant residual artifacts located on host machines testing several different portable web browsers. Even though USB identifiers are important to obtain, it is even more important to establish an affirmative link between user and session.

3.3. Flash drive

In comparison to current portable software, Sandisk and Microsoft worked together many years ago on a project called U3 Technology [5]. Essentially, the idea was to allow consumers to carry a portable disk containing personalized files and web browsers. U3 flash drives were pre-installed with a U3 Launchpad, similar to an OS start menu with various programs installed. There are two partitions to the U3 flash drive structure: one is a mass storage device and the other is a virtual CD-ROM. The virtual partition was actually an ISO image, which was why information was read but not written to the disk. According to one study [6], U3 devices created a folder on host machines and recorded user activity. Once the disk was ejected, a cleanup program was executed and automatically removed all user activity from that system. By analyzing the Windows Prefetch files, researchers were able to identify which programs were run from the U3 device.

In another study on battling U3 anti-forensics [7], U3 identifiers were discovered as well by analyzing the Windows Registry and Prefetch directory. The majority of traces were located within slack space and free space of the hard drive. For this reason, our research experiments will be conducted using separate physical hard drives to incorporate the possibility of discovering data within these areas. Even though sufficient evidence was obtained to support which U3 programs were launched, it was still extremely difficult for researchers to identify other significant artifacts. We will probably face the same barriers in our research. Overall, the U3 portable disk provided a sense of privacy and personalization to users. Over time, there had been numerous complaints about U3 devices such as potential incompatibility and malware-like behavior. SanDisk began phasing out support for U3 Technology in late 2009 [3] and the U3 disk has been discontinued.

4. Major browsers and private browsing

In this section, we discuss four major web browsers and their private browsing implementations.

4.1. Microsoft Internet Explorer

Microsoft Internet Explorer (IE) is one of the most commonly used web browsers on Windows machines. A list of areas where most IE web browsing artifacts are located is as follows:

- Cookies (Index.dat)
- History (Index.dat)
- Registry (typed URLs, search queries, auto-complete, protected storage)
- NTUSER.dat
- Temporary Internet Files and Index.dat Entries
- Downloads.

IE also offers users a private browsing feature called InPrivate Browsing. According to Microsoft [8], InPrivate Browsing enables users to surf the Internet without leaving a trace on their computer. However, while using InPrivate Browsing, some information such as cookies and temporary files are temporarily stored so that web pages will work correctly. Once the browsing session is ended, all of that data is discarded. Table 2 shows a list of areas affected by InPrivate Browsing and is available to the public on Microsoft's webpage. In regard to web browser extensions, IE disables all toolbars and extensions during InPrivate Browsing sessions to ensure better privacy. IE also does not clear toolbars and extensions after a private session is ended.

4.2. Google chrome

Google Chrome is another very popular web browser that can be found on both Windows and Mac operating systems. A list of common areas where Chrome web browsing artifacts can be located is as follows:

- JSON (JavaScript Object Notation) structure - text based open standard design for human readable data
- Downloads
- Bookmarks
- Web data
- Keyword search terms
- Keywords
- URL database
- History index (YYY-MM)
- Current and last sessions
- Top sites database
- Media cache.

Chrome also offers something called Incognito mode for users to browse the Internet in a private setting. According to Google [9], Incognito mode does not record any browsing or download histories, and all created cookies will be removed when exiting a session completely. Additionally, Google states that if users are

working in Chrome OS, surfing the Internet under guest browsing essentially does the same thing. Once the guest session is closed, all browsing information is completely erased.

4.3. Mozilla Firefox

Mozilla Firefox is another popular web browser that can be found on multiple platforms. Web browsers such as Chrome and Firefox can also be found on mobile devices such as Androids, iPads, etc. A list of common areas where Firefox web browsing artifacts can be located is as follows:

- Sqlite database structure
- Prefs.js (user preferences)
- Signons.txt (encrypted data for website authentication)
- Formhistory.sqlite
- Cookies.sqlite
- Firefox cache
- Places.sqlite (bookmarks and history)
- Downloads.sqlite.

Just like all other major web browsers, Firefox offers a discreet browsing mode called Private Browsing. According to Mozilla [10], Private Browsing mode allows users to surf the Internet without saving any information about visited sites or pages. Table 3 shows a list of areas affected by Private Browsing and is available to the public on Mozilla's webpage. Mozilla makes it clear that private browsing modes do not make users anonymous from web sites, ISP's, and networks. In other words, Private Browsing is merely affected in the Application Layer recognized in the OS. Aside from other privacy features, there is an option to enable the Do-Not-Track feature in Firefox which requests that websites do not track user browsing behavior. This request is honored voluntarily and Apple Safari offers the same. In the experimental phase of our

Table 2 Microsoft IE InPrivate browsing features

Data	How InPrivate browsing affects data
Cookies	Contained in working memory but cleared after session
Temporary internet files	Stored on disk but deleted after session
Webpage history	Not stored
Form data and passwords	Not stored
Anti-phishing cache	Temporary information is encrypted and stored
Address bar and auto-complete	Not stored
Automatic cache restore	Restore is successful only if tab crashes and not entire session
Document object model storage	Discarded after session

Table 3 Mozilla private browsing features

Data	How private browsing affects data
Visited pages	Will not be added in History menu, Library history, or other bar list
Form and search bar entries	Nothing entered will be saved for Form Auto-complete
Passwords	No new passwords will be saved
Download list entries	No downloaded files will be listed under Downloads
Cookies	Does not save
Cached web content	Not saved
Flash cookies	Latest version of Flash must be used to prevent saving
Offline web content and user data	Not saved

Figure 1 PortableApps launchpad.

Figure 2 Hard drive setup with labels.

research, these types of features will be optimized for full privacy.

4.4. Apple safari

The Apple Safari web browser is primarily used on Mac/iOS operating systems but is also available for Windows. A list of common areas where Safari web browsing artifacts can be located is as follows:

- .plist (Propert List) structure
- Cookies.plist
- Bookmarks.plist
- History.plist
- WebpageIcons.db
- Keychains.plist
- Downloads.plist

Apple's latest version of the Safari web browser for Windows is Safari 5.1.7 [11]. When Safari launched 6.0, they did not update the Windows versions. Most people have assumed that Apple is moving away from Windows compatibility. According to Apple, Private Browsing mode ensures that web pages are not added to the history list, cookie changes are discarded, searches are not added to

the search fields, and websites cannot modify information stored on the computer.

5. Portable software

In this section, we discuss several major web browsers that are made available in portable formats and were used for this research.

5.1. Portable application and web browsers

To allow for certain portable browsers to work, a free program called PortableApps [12] was used for this research. PortableApps is similar to the previously mentioned U3 Launchpad in that it allows you to take portable applications with you as you go. It is based on an open source platform and will work with almost any portable storage device. Figure 1 shows how the launchpad is structured. In our study, the application was installed on a USB flash drive. Three portable web browsers were selected through PortableApps: Mozilla Firefox Portable 18.0.1 [13], Google Chrome Portable 24.0.1312.52 [14], and Opera Portable 12.12 [15]. The reason Apple Safari Portable was not selected because it was not in fact portable. The most updated version located was not a standalone executable program and it had to be installed onto the machine. According

Figure 3 DaemonFS monitoring example.

to Mozilla, the Portable Edition leaves no personal information behind on the machine it runs on [13]. All the portable browsers were essentially designed for users to carry customized browsers without leaving traces on machines. That is why artifacts, such as web browsing history, passwords, and auto-fill forms, are stored where the portable browser installation folder is located. Privacy modes can also be enabled to help block flash cookies and other artifacts from storing within the installation folder.

6. Implementations and experiments
In this section, we provide a brief overview of private and portable web browsing sessions that will be analyzed using computer forensics.

6.1. Tools and setup
The following tools were used for the assessments, acquisitions, examinations, and analysis:

Hardware

- 1- Desktop (PC - forensic workstation - 4-GB RAM)
- 1- Laptop (PC - forensic workstation - 6-GB RAM)
- 8–160 GB SATA Hard Drives (one dedicated drive for lab)
- 1- USB Flash Drive (8 GB)
- 1- USB External Drive (1 TB WD Passport)
- 1- SATA to USB Adapter
- 1- Tableau USB Write Blocker (IDE/SATA)
- Antistatic Bags and Antistatic Wrist Strap

Software

- Microsoft Windows 7 Professional (64)
- Internet Explorer, Firefox, Safari, Chrome
- VMware - virtualization software
- DaemonFS - file integrity monitoring program
- Disk Wipe - to replace data on disk with zeros
- Nirsoft Internet Tools - history, cache, and cookie viewers

Table 4 Browser analysis during normal browsing sessions

Browser	Primary changes
Internet explorer 8.0	Temp File Directory files (Content.IE, History.IE5, Cookies, Recovery, Custom Destinations, Index.dat) are created, modified, and deleted
Google chrome 23.0.1271.95	Directory Chrome\User Data (Safe Browsing Whitelist, Default\ Cache, Current Session, Default\History, Default\Session Storage) files are created, modified, and deleted
Firefox 17.0.1	Directory Firefox\Profiles (Cache, jumpListCache, etc.) and Win CustomDestinations, files are created, modified, and deleted
Safari 5.1.7	Directory AppleComputer\Safari (Cache, History, Webpage Previews, Cookies, WebpageIcons.db) files are created, modified, and deleted

Table 5 Browser analysis during private browsing sessions

Private browser	Noticeable change
IE InPrivate Browsing	Everything gets deleted when exiting the browser and the entire session is terminated
Google Chrome Incognito Mode	Safe Browsing databases, Cookies, and History are modified, no changes during session but the chrome_shutdown_ms.txt is replaced with a new timestamp when session ends
Firefox Private Browsing	Safe Browsing database gets modified, nothing appears to be written while surfing, but when session ends, some Firefox\Profile files are modified
Safari Private Browsing	Only NTuser.dat appears to be modified

- Live View - Java based tool to convert .dd to .vmdk
- PortableApps - portable application Launchpad
- Firefox Portable, Chrome Portable, Opera Portable
- FTK Imager - used to create forensic images
- FTK Imager Lite - portable version
- AccessData FTK version 3.2 (Licensed) - used to analyze forensic images and organize information

The key to our research was for us to conduct a standardized test across multiple controlled environments. Therefore, all the experiments were handled in a forensically sound manner as if we were handling real evidence. Photographs were taken, forensic images were created, procedures were properly documented, and evidence was safely preserved.

We began by taking every hard drive and removing residual data using Disk Wipe [16]. Each disk was connected to a secondary forensic workstation (laptop) through a SATA to USB Adapter. The Disk Wipe tool provides several different wiping options and writes over data with zeros. The first disk was tested by examining it forensically after wiping it with only one pass. Since there was some residual data that was found, a DoD Algorithm was selected next to wipe the disk using three passes; this method proved to be more efficient. After every disk was successfully wiped, each one was installed with Windows 7 Professional - 64 bits. The 64-bit version was used so that more random-access memory (RAM) could later be tested.

Next, each disk was installed with only one specific Internet browser pre-loaded from an external hard drive, except for the portable applications. The web browsers installed were Microsoft Internet Explorer, Mozilla Firefox, Apple Safari, and Google Chrome. Each browser was configured to launch automatically into private browsing mode except for Safari, which had to be done manually. It is important to note, since prior research [1] showed browser plug-ins and extensions to cause weakness to private browsing sessions, none were installed. It is also important to note that everything was pre-configured before connecting to the Internet. Figure 2 shows the hard drives being configured and labeled.

6.2. Preliminary analysis
While the disks were being properly developed, a baseline was established using a laptop with VMware and a file integrity monitoring program called DaemonFS [17]. This assisted with having a general idea for which areas were modified and accessed during normal, private, and portable web browsing sessions. Once DaemonFS was launched, it was set to monitor all activity within the local hard drive (root). After the logical parameter was set, each web browser was individually launched and tested using a series of standardized steps. Figure 3 shows how the log is generated during activity. These steps included article searches, image searches, video searches, email account logins, bank account logins, and online purchase attempts. See Tables 4, 5, and 6 for results.

6.3. Private ate browsing experiments
Author[1] has a background in law enforcement and has experience analyzing digital media for a vast array of crimes. The Internet activities used for these experiments were adapted from an abundance of information to include past experience and knowledge. It is important to note that these principles can still be applied to all aspects of Internet forensics regardless of whether or not the scope relates to a crime. These types of browsing sessions can very well be conducted without any criminal intent. The overall purpose of digital forensics is to help establish and

Table 6 Browser analysis using portable web browsers

Portable browser	Host machine activity
Opera portable	Temp files appear to be created on disk and then are deleted when session ends
Firefox portable	Mozilla\Roaming directory was modified, and a few temp files under Local AppData were created/deleted
Google chrome portable	Folder called GoogleChromePortable had files created, modified, and deleted, including Sys32\Winevt\Logs, and Portable Chrome Cache
Safari portable	Setup files are portable but must be installed on system (not standalone.exe) therefore will not be used for testing

articulate an affirmative link between A (artifact) and B (person, place, or thing). By collecting and analyzing enough data, evidentiary content can be produced.

To begin the main experiments, each disk was separately utilized as a single primary drive. Every step was manually recorded with timestamps for future reference points. For the first four disks, only private browsing sessions were tested using the installed web browsers. For the purpose of these experiments, a 'browsing session' will refer to all activity conducted on one specific web browser. Once a private browsing session was launched, the same series of steps were performed for each browser. Table 7 shows the details of these standardized sessions.

After each browsing session was complete, the web browser process tree was terminated (verified) and the RAM was dumped into a file using FTK Imager Lite (installed on USB). Not only was the memory dumped but Registry files were obtained, the pagefile.sys was extracted, and an .ad1 image file of the RAM was created as well. The location of the RAM dump was stored on the target machine's Desktop due to reasons that will later be explained. This would probably not be preferred in a real setting unless it was absolutely necessary. In any event, it is always important to document the footprints left behind on a live environment. Initially, the data was extracted to an external hard drive. The machine was then unplugged from the back and the disk was carefully removed. As noted, a few extra things were done to preserve sound results. The working memory was dumped before and after every disk session, to ensure that residual data was not left over in the RAM from the session before. In addition, several Internet tools from Nirsoft [18], such as cache viewer, history viewer, and cookie viewer, were executed after each browsing session was terminated and yielded negative results. Meaning, nothing could be discovered using these tools after private browsing sessions were used.

6.4. Portable browsing experiment

The next three disks were used in conjunction with portable web browsers running from a USB flash drive. The flash drive was installed with a program called PortableApps. Essentially, PortableApps allows you to run different programs from a flash drive similar to an OS Start menu. After setting up the Launchpad, three portable web browsers were installed on the flash drive: Mozilla Firefox Portable, Google Chrome Portable, and Opera Portable. Again, each hard disk was separately used as a primary hard drive but this time without any other web browsers installed. Each portable web browser was individually launched while performing the same series of standardized steps as the first four disks (Table 7). Whenever a disk was complete, it was carefully placed into an antistatic bag and into a cool dry place for storage. In addition, an antistatic wrist band was used while handling all internal electronic components.

6.5. Forensic acquisition and analysis

The last hard disk was developed with Windows 7 and FTK 3.2 to make it a dedicated computer forensic workstation. AccessData's Forensic Toolkit (FTK) [19] is a court accepted program used for examining computers and mobile devices at the forensic level. Each disk was individually connected to the Desktop using a hardware-based write blocker (Tableau), to protect any data from being altered by the computer. Digital evidence preservation is the most important factor next to chain of custody, when it comes to forensic integrity. Using FTK Imager, a bit stream image of each evidence disk was created as a compressed E01 image file and was verified by several different hashes. Each image took anywhere from 3 to 5 h to complete. Next, individual images were forensically examined, analyzed, and classified by FTK 3.2. One disk image took up to 72 h to process and the disks with the installed browsers took the longest.

Table 7 Internet sessions used for experiments

Website	Standardized steps
Google	Search for various images, sites, and forums targeted for criminal activity; click on top five links; save/download different files and images
Yahoo!	Search for various sites and forums targeted for criminal activity; click on top five links; save/download available files
YouTube	Search for how-to videos on different types hacking (social media, bank accounts, and WiFi connections); click on links to open
Gmail	Send email with attachments
Hotmail	Send email with attachments
Yahoo! Mail	Send email with attachments
SHSU Mail	Send email with attachments
Online Banking	Log into several accounts (stores cookies and certificates)
Ammunition-to-Go	Attempt to purchase large amounts (2,000+) of ammunition (various high powered rounds) by searching and adding to cart
Online Firearms Store	Search for high capacity magazines and various weapons
Craigslist	Search for different types of items for sale that might be flagged as stolen

Table 8 Private web browsing artifacts

	Artifacts	Discovered	Target locations
Microsoft internet explorer 8.0 (InPrivate browsing)	Private browsing indicator	Y	Memdump; Free/Slack Space ('Start InPrivate Browsing' - prior to URL history); $I30 (...\Content.IE5- 'inprivate [1]'- prior to list of *.jpeg's); Pagefile
	Browsing history	Y	Memdump; Free space; File slack (Temporary Internet Folder, Roaming\...\Custom Destinations); SysVol Info; $LogFile; $J; AppData\...\IE\Recovery\Active
	Usernames/email accounts	Y	Memdump; Freespace; Temporary Internet Folder; User\AppData...\IE\Recovery \Active
	Images	Y	Memdump (partial photos); Free space (full content); File slack (full content)
	Videos	N	N/A
Google chrome 23.0.1271.95 (Incognito)	Incognito indicators	Y	Memdump; Chrome\...\Installer\chrome.7z & chrome.dll (timestamp matches); $I30 (safebrowsing timestamp) AppData\Local\Google\Chrome\User Data\chrome_shutdown_ms.txt (always updates with timestamp); AppData\Local\Google\Chrome\User Data\Default\Extension State*.log (declarative_rules.incognito.declaritiveWeb Request- timestamp matches session start); ~\SysVol Information (new incognito window with timestamps); AppData\Roaming\Microsoft\Windows\Recent\Custom Destinations (new incognito window with timestamps); Chrome\UserData\Safebrowsingcookies.db (modified timestamp)
	Browsing history	Y	Memdump; SysVol Info (matching timestamps); Pagefile.sys (downloaded file)
	Usernames/email accounts	N	N/A
	Images	Y	Carved from Memdump (Mostly partial images)
	Videos	N	N/A
Mozilla Firefox 17.0.1 (Private browsing)	Private browsing indicators	Y	Memdump (browsing mode); SysVolume Information (Enter Private Browsing and Window's User listed below- file timestamp accurate)
	Browsing history	Y	Memdump; Free space- AppData\...\Temp; Win\Prefetch (.rtf temp file download discovered); AppData\...\Firefox\Profiles (blacklist.xml- matching timestamps); Firefox\Profiles\ (file timestamps update)
	Usernames/email accounts	N	N/A
	Images	Y	Carved from Memdump (Mostly partial images)
	Videos	N	N/A
Apple Safari 5.1.7 (Private browsing)	Private browsing indicators	Y	Memdump; ~\SysVol Information (com.apple.Safari.PrivateBrowsing timestamp)
	Browsing history	Y	Memdump; Free/Slack Space (URL History); AppData\Local\AppleComp\Safari\Webpageicons.db> > tables; AppData\Local\AppleComp\Safari\ (databases timestamp updates); AppData\...\AppleComp\Safari & Preferences\(several *.plist timestamp updates) Pagefile (URL's and modified timestamps update)
	Usernames/email accounts	N	N/A
	Images	Y	Carved from Memdump (Mostly partial images)
	Videos	N	N/A

Aside from the default processing options in FTK, additional refinements were selected to carve different types of data and parse complex information. Once FTK finished processing the evidence files, numerous hours were spent sifting through the data. We found that it was also beneficial to use a program called Live View [20] to have a better understanding of the artifacts found. Live View is an open source program that can convert a raw image to a virtual disk. The disk must be booted into safe mode for the virtual machine to work correctly without having to activate Windows. By using two screens simultaneously, one with a live virtual

environment and the other with the forensic image in FTK, it allowed us to fully grasp and understand the connections. See Tables 8 and 9 for complete results.

6.6. Results analysis

Private browsing modes and portable web browsers do in fact leave incriminating evidence, but it depends on the browser. Some web browsers left enough information to establish an affirmative link and some did not. Out of the four major web browsers, Internet Explorer provided the most residual artifacts but not where common artifacts are typically sought. This was fairly consistent

Table 9 Portable web browsing artifacts

	Artifacts	Discovered	Target Locations
Google chrome portable - 24.0.1312.52	Browser indicators	Y	NTFS Allocated and Unallocated Space; Prefetch; Pagefile; Memdump; $Logfile; Users\AppData\Roaming\Microsoft\Windows\Recent\CustomDestinations; ~\System Volume Information; AppData\Local\Temp; AppData\LocLow\Mic\CryptnetUrlCache; Win\AppCompat\Prog\RecentFileCache; Win\Mic.NET\Framework\log (fileslack); Win\Sys32\LogFiles\WUDF\ (fileslack)
	Browsing history	Y	NTFS Allocated and Unallocated Space; Memdump; Orphan Directory; Pagefile; Users\AppData\Roaming\Microsoft\Windows\Recent\CustomDestinations (Carved .lnk)
	Usernames/email accounts	Y	[Orphan] directory and NTFS Unallocated Free/Slack Space
	Images	Y	Carved (NTFS Unallocated Space and Orphan Directory)
	Videos	N	N/A
Opera portable - 12.12	Browser indicators	Y	NTFS Allocated and Unallocated Space; Pagefile; Memdump; $LogFile; ~\System Volume Information; NTUSER.DAT; AppData\Local\Mic\Win\UsrClass.dat; Users\AppData\Roaming\Microsoft\Windows\Recent\CustomDestinations (Carved .lnk); Win\Prefetch; Win\Sys32\LogFiles\SQM\SQMLogger
	Browsing history	Y	Memdump; AppData\Roaming\Mic\Win\Rec\CustomDestinations (Carved .lnk files with Last Access Times)
	Usernames/email accounts	N	N/A
	Images	Y	Carved from Memdump (Mostly partial images and difficult to view full content)
	Videos	N	N/A
Mozilla fireFox portable - 18.0.1	Browser indicators	Y	Memdump; SysVol Information file timestamp (Firefox Portable appinfo)
	Browsing history	Y	Memdump; SysVol Information (Email only)
	Usernames/email accounts	Y	Memdump; SysVol Information (Email Account History)
	Images	Y	Carved from Memdump (Mostly partial images and difficult to view full content)
	Videos	N	N/A

with all the browsers. For example, the Index.dat (history) and Registry > TypedURLs were empty, but we were still able to recover virtually all cached images, URL history, and usernames with their associated accounts. Everything was recoverable except for playable videos. Even though most of the data was recovered from RAM, free space, and slack space areas, there were sufficient findings within allocated space as well. Figure 4 shows an '[InPrivate]' indicator within RAM prior to an online search for hacking. In regard to indicators, there were a few areas where 'InPrivate' and 'Start InPrivate Browsing' were noted prior to a URL history log. Figure 5 shows one of these indicators within allocated space. It was also noted that the Microsoft 'PrivacIE' directory was found empty.

The three remaining browsers were a little more difficult to recover residual artifacts from. It appeared that the overall best way to recover residual data was to obtain the evidence from RAM or working memory, but that is not always possible for investigators. For Google Chrome Incognito artifacts, there were many browsing indicators and changes in timestamps to show Chrome usage. However, it was difficult to establish an affirmative link between the user and session because none of the usernames and other historical information was accessible; the same resulted for Mozilla Firefox. In both of these cases, any documents that were temporarily opened from the Internet were recoverable. This information is important because browsing indicators along with timestamps may be able to explain why something like as URL history is not there. For example, if a live search using regular expressions was used to locate one of these hidden artifacts in an unfamiliar location, an investigator can now understand why they were not found in other common areas.

Apple Safari seemed to fall in the middle by keeping most things private while still leaving traces on the machine. The easiest way to view the browsing history

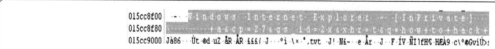

Figure 4 [InPrivate] search for 'how + to + hack + ...' within RAM (Hex view).

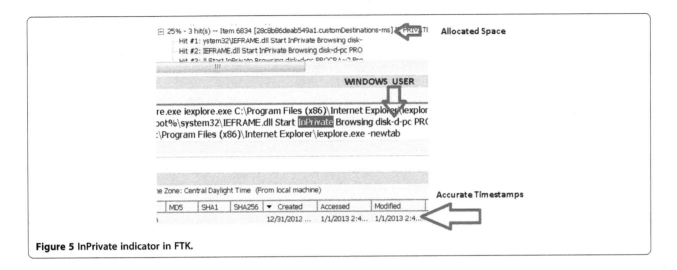

Figure 5 InPrivate indicator in FTK.

for Safari private browsing sessions was to locate the 'WebpageIcons' database under Safari artifacts. This database provided a good log of every visited URL along with other pertinent information. Figure 6 shows some of the database artifacts using FTK. It is important to realize that this can be used to explain to courts as to why URL history would be located here and nowhere else under Safari data. It is not always about what is present, but what is absent is also of value.

With regard to residual portable browsing artifacts, it appeared that everything was just as easily obtained from the memory dumps as it was with the installed browsers. However, not everything was located on the target hard drives. Out of the three portable web browsers tested, Google Chrome Portable left the most residual artifacts on the host machine. The recovery seemed as if Chrome was installed on the machine itself. Almost all artifacts to include images, browsing history, browsing method, and usernames with associated accounts, were located on the disk. Also note, these recovered artifacts were obtained without the flash drive. The importance for an investigator to distinguish that these artifacts came from Google Chrome Portable is for two reasons: (a) to be able to explain why Chrome artifacts were not located under common areas and (b) to alert the investigator that further evidence may be found on a flash

drive that the investigator did not originally consider. Figure 7 provides a comparison of all the browsers tested and the strength of evidence which can be found.

Opera Portable, on the other hand, did not leave as much information as Chrome. There were many portable browsing indicators but most history artifacts were limited; none of the usernames or accounts could be recovered. Firefox Portable resulted in similar findings; however, some user activity was found to be recoverable. All of the usernames associated with their respected email accounts were recovered along with Firefox browsing indicators.

In reference to carved images from RAM, most of them were distorted but a few of the images could be seen as a whole. One solution was to try and match a distorted image from RAM with a whole image on the hard drive using FTK's fuzzy hash option. This would be a great way to link carved contraband to working memory artifacts and therefore strengthening evidence against the user. The program attempts to match files by determining a fundamental level of similarity between hashes. This method did not always work as hoped. Some of the thumbnails stored in RAM were successfully matched with ones on the disk but none specific to user activity. Perhaps on a machine with a much higher capacity of RAM, this would be more useful.

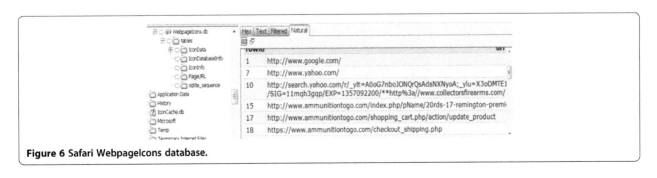

Figure 6 Safari WebpageIcons database.

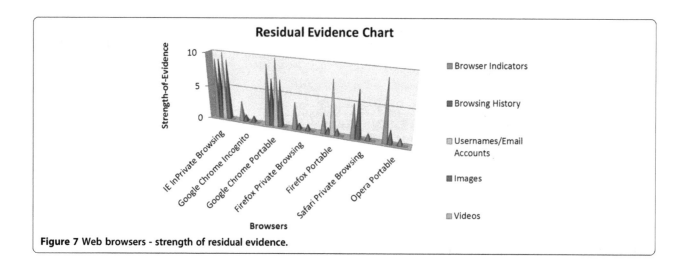

Figure 7 Web browsers - strength of residual evidence.

6.7. Additional forensic results

Aside from discovering hidden web browsing artifacts, there is another finding worth mentioning due to its significant linking of users and machines. Every time the external hard drive (WD Passport) was connected to one of the machines via USB, not only did it leave unique identifiers but also a log of every folder located on the Passport. This information was transferred directly to the Windows machine while remaining on the hard drive and RAM. For this reason, a flash drive was later used to dump the memory on the Desktop to preserve data integrity without further contamination. The Passport files were discovered within several different locations on the hard drive. One was within a log file called the Circular Kernal Context Logger (BootCKCL.etl), and the other was within Trace*.fx files. Most probably the reason for the Trace*.fx files was due to the activity of a USB device configured for ReadyBoost (virtual memory).

This finding raises a number of questions and concerns. An investigator can easily document certain footprints such as plugging in devices and checking running processes. It is the unknown footprints which can cause a problem. This could violate certain policy and procedures that were once considered forensically sound. On the other hand, it could provide an investigator with enough information to understand that the file paths may be pointing to an external device. So not only will information from the Registry provide unique identifiers but this could also be used to know what type of contraband may be on the 'missing evidence.' This information would be extremely helpful when trying to establish an affirmative link between user and target machine.

7. Future work

Future work may include further RAM experiments, and more efficient methods to extract information

over an extended period of time instead of one controlled browsing session. In addition, forensic tools or carving options may be developed to provide investigators with whether or not these browsing artifacts exist (0/1 = False/Positive), and parse these artifacts accordingly.

8. Conclusion

The majority of recovered artifacts were discovered in RAM, slack/free space, and FTK [Orphan] directories. That being said, information was still obtained within allocated space. Another commonality between the browsers was information contained within the System Volume Information directory. The bottom line is that our research clearly establishes authoritative answers to which were never there before. In addition, some of our authoritative results contradict prior research statements. For example, one study [2] made the statement that it would be *impossible* to trace residual information, other than USB identifiers, if a portable storage device was not accessible to the investigator. Our research clearly shows that further data can still be recovered on host machines without the portable storage device being present. Overall, our research is a valuable resource pertaining to private and portable web browsing artifacts. Not every web browser will leave incriminating evidence but some will, depending on the situation. These residual artifacts may or may not be important to a case, but on the other hand it may be the only way to explain certain results. Computer forensic investigators must treat digital environments like a real crime scene. It is not only important to document what is found but to also note what is not there and ask why. Our research now provides an alternative way to perceive these types of findings and explain the results. We conclude that just because something is not there does not mean it never happened.

Competing interests

The authors declare that they have no competing interests.

References

1. G Aggarwal, E Bursztein, C Jackson, D Boneh, An analysis of private browsing modes in modern browsers, in *Proc. Of 19th Usenix Security Symposium* (, Washington, DC, 2010), pp. 11–13
2. JH Choi, KG Lee, J Park, C Lee, S Lee, *Analysis framework to detect artifacts of portable web browser* (Center for Information Security Technologies, Seoul, 2012)
3. SanDisk, *U3 Launchpad End of Life Notice*, 2010. Available: http://kb.sandisk.com/app/answers/detail/a_id/5358/~/u3-launchpad-end-of-life-notice. Accessed 28 July 2012
4. C Soghoian, *Why private browsing modes do not deliver real privacy* (Center for Applied Cyber security Research, Bloomington, 2011)
5. Wikipedia, *U3*, 2013. Available: http://en.wikipedia.org/wiki/U3. Accessed 22 July 2012
6. R Tank, PAH Williams, *The impact of U3 devices on forensic analysis* (Australian Digital Forensics Conference, Perth, 2008)
7. T Bosschert, Battling anti-forensics: beating the U3 stick. J Digit Forensic Pract **1**(4), 265–273 (2007)
8. Microsoft, *InPrivate Browsing*, 2012. Available: http://windows.microsoft.com/en-US/internet-explorer/products/ie-9/features/in-private. Accessed 03 September 2012
9. Google, *Incognito mode*, 2012. Available: https://www.google.com/intl/en/chrome/browser/features.html#privacy. Accessed 03 September 2012
10. Mozilla, *Private Browsing*, 2012. Available: http://support.mozilla.org/en-US/kb/private-browsing-browse-web-without-saving-info. Accessed 03 September 2012
11. Apple, *Safari 5.1: Browse Privately*, 2012. Available: http://support.apple.com/kb/PH5000. Accessed 03 September 2012
12. PortableApps, , 2013. Available: http://portableapps.com/ Accessed 27 July 2012
13. PortableApps, *Mozilla Firefox, Portable Edition*, 2013. Available: http:// portableapps.com/apps/internet/firefox_portable. Accessed 27 July 2012
14. PortableApps, *Google Chrome Portable*, 2013. Available: http://portableapps.com/apps/internet/google_chrome_portable. Accessed 27 July 2012
15. PortableApps, *Opera, Portable Edition*, 2013. Available: http://portableapps.com/apps/internet/opera_portable. Accessed 27 July 2012
16. Disk Wipe, *Disk Wipe*, 2009. Available: http://www.diskwipe.org/. Accessed 12 December 2012
17. DaemonFS, *Sourceforge: DaemonFS*, 2010. Available: http://sourceforge.net/projects/daemonfs/. Accessed 27 July 2012
18. Nir Sofer, *NirSoft Freeware Utilities*, 2013. Available: http://nirsoft.net. Accessed 12 December 2012
19. AccessData, *FTK*, 2013. Available: http://www.accessdata.com/products/digital-forensics/ftk. Accessed 18 December 2012
20. Carnegie Mellon, *Live View*, 2006. Available: http://liveview.sourceforge.net. Accessed 18 December 2012

3

An enhanced audio ownership protection scheme based on visual cryptography

Rimba Whidiana Ciptasari[1,2]*, Kyung-Hyune Rhee[3] and Kouichi Sakurai[2]

Abstract

Recently, several ownership protection schemes which combine encryption and secret sharing technology have been proposed. To reveal the original message, however, they exploited XOR operation which is similar to a one-time pad. It is fairly losing the reconstruction simplicity due to the human visual system (HVS). It should be noted that it is completely different from the original concept of visual cryptography proposed by Naor and Shamir. To decrypt the secret message, Naor and Shamir's concept stacked k transparencies together. The operation solely does a visual OR of the shares rather than XOR, the way HVS does. In this paper, we, consequently, adopt Naor and Shamir's concept to apply correct theory of visual cryptography. Furthermore, audio copyright protection schemes which exploit chaotic modulation or watermark integration into frequency components have been widely proposed. Nevertheless, security issue against intentional distortions has not been addressed yet. In this paper, we aim to construct a resilient audio ownership protection scheme to enhance the security by integrating the discrete wavelet transform and discrete cosine transform, visual cryptography, and digital timestamps. In the proposed scheme, the watermark does not require to be embedded within the original audio but is used to generate a secret image and a public image. The watermark is then acquired by performing OR between the secret and public image. We can alleviate the trade-off expenses between the capacity of data payload and two other important properties such as imperceptibility and robustness without modifying the original audio signals. The experiments against a variety of audio signals processing provided by StirMark confirm superior robustness of the proposed scheme. We also demonstrate the intentional distortion by modifying the original content via experiments, it reveals comparable reliability. The proposed scheme can be widely applied to the area of audio ownership protection.

Keywords: Digital watermarking; Audio ownership protection; Visual cryptography; Transform domain; Timestamp

1 Introduction

1.1 Background

Protection of an intellectual property has become a major problem in the digital age. It is possible to duplicate digital information a million-fold and distribute it over the entire world in seconds through the Internet. There are various techniques for preventing and/or minimizing the risk of copying, making copying easier to detect, and assisting in proving infringement. One of the technical measures is to embed a 'digital watermark' in the host data. The watermark is regarded as a code, which is impossible or very difficult to detect and/or remove, and it can be used to identify the source of the copied data [1]. This aids users in proving copyright infringement.

Among the development of digital watermarkings in a various multimedia, digital audio watermarking provides a special challenge because the human auditory system (HAS) is extremely more sensitive than a human visual system (HVS) [2]. Most audio watermark algorithms insert the information as a plain-bit or adjusted digital signal using a key-based embedding algorithm. The embedded information is hidden and linked inseparably with the source data structure. For the optimal watermarking application trade-offs among competing criteria such as robustness, non-perceptibility, capacity, non-detectability, and security have to be considered. However, there is always trade-off between capacity and other two important properties, non-perceptibility and robustness. A higher capacity is always obtained at the expense of

*Correspondence: rmb@ittelkom.ac.id
[1] Department of Informatics, Telkom University, Bandung 40257, Indonesia
[2] Graduate School of Information Science and Electrical Engineering, Kyushu University, 744 Motooka, Nishi-ku, Fukuoka 819-0395, Japan
Full list of author information is available at the end of the article

either robustness or non-perceptibility (or both) [3]. Further, some audio quality degradations inevitably occur due to the embedding process.

1.2 Related work

In order to eliminate the trade-offs among competing criteria aforementioned, several audio ownership protection schemes [4-6], which are different from the traditional watermarking, have been proposed. These schemes are referred to as *zero-watermarking*. In the paper [4], three-level discrete wavelet decomposition (DWT) is applied to get the low-frequency subband of the host audio, which is the perceptually significant region of it. To make the scheme resist lossy compression operation such as MP3 compression, discrete cosine transform (DCT) is performed on the obtained low-frequency wavelet coefficients. And by considering the Gaussian signal suppression property of higher-order cumulant, the fourth-order cumulants of the obtained DWT-DCT coefficients are calculated to ensure the robustness of the scheme against various noise addition operations. Finally, the essential features extracted based on DWT, DCT, and higher-order cumulant are used for generating binary pattern. In addition, the scheme introduced the presence of the authentication center to keep the copyright information such as the secret keys, original host audio, and the corresponding digital timestamp used in copyright demonstration.

Wang and Hu [5] proposed the scheme created by selecting some maximum absolute value of low frequency wavelet coefficients of original audio. The construction of the watermark is random by chaotic sequence. After generating the watermark, chaotic inverse search is adopted to get the initial value of another watermark sequence that is identical to the original one. In verification phase, instead of using an original audio, they exploited chaotic modulation to generate the original watermark sequence. In order to reduce the processing time, they cut the watermark into fifty sections. According to our experiment, despite long hours of executing the initial value searching process, we could not achieve the convergence condition. The initialization of its initial value is a somewhat trial-and-error process. The time complexity of each section is $O(NM)$ where N indicates the watermark's size, and M refers to the number of iterations. In this case, we cannot predict the M value. We, therefore, argue that their algorithm is not efficient. Moreover, their scheme indeed requires the length of its original watermark sequence to generate original watermark W in extraction stage. This value was not kept either in secret key K or initial vector H. In other words, their scheme cannot be regarded as a blind watermarking.

The authors also proposed a modification of Chen and Zhu's scheme for generating secret keys in their earlier work [6]. Compared to that of Chen and Zhu's, the key's size is relatively the same as its watermark. The scheme, however, is claimed to have good degree of robustness, imperceptibility, and payload capacity.

Furthermore, some ownership protection schemes which combine encryption and secret sharing technology [7-12] have also been proposed, and they achieved good results. Several works in visual cryptography [7,9,11] were performed in a distinctive way. In order to retrieve the secret image, they exploit XOR operation among shares instead of stacking them. This mechanism is considered as an appropriate way to be employed in ownership protection area. Lou et al. [11] proposed the scheme that extracts the feature from the protected image by utilizing the secret key and the relation between the low and middle sub-band wavelet coefficients. Then, the feature and watermark are used to generate a secret image by the codebook of visual cryptography technique. To provide further protection, the secret image, with the exception of the secret key and codebook, is registered to certification authority (CA). In the verification procedure, public image is first generated from the suspected image. The extracted watermark is obtained by performing XOR operation between secret and public image. However, such an impressive combination has not yet been proposed for audio.

Lee and Chen [10] introduced cryptographic tools into the watermarking process to provide security against malicious attacks. As a first step, a gray-level original image was decomposed by exploiting wavelet transform. Vector quantization was then exploited to generate indices set I that would be signed by the owner with digital signature technique. Lastly, the owner sent signed indices set S to a trusted CA. CA digitally added time and date when it received them. This scheme can protect the indices set from alteration, and everyone can use it to verify the copyright logo corresponding to the test image.

Chen and Horng [12] improved their earlier work [10]. In order to resist against geometric distortions, the watermark was first permutated based on two-dimension pseudorandom permutation generated by seed s. Then, the polarity table T was constructed to be used in computing the verification key K. They included digital signature and timestamp to avoid either counterfeit or copy attacks and to make public verification possible. The advantage of their scheme was that it is resistant to blind pattern matching attack.

1.3 Challenge issues

Based on related work, we summarize the following challenge issues:

1. Consider the watermarking scheme proposed by Chen and Zhu [4]. The embedding process takes host

audio A and watermark w as input and generates three secret keys. These keys imply the information of selected frames, extracted feature points, and its watermark, where respectively this information is denoted by K_1, K_2, and K_3. Consider the case when an adversary intends to produce a watermarked file using the same procedure in the paper [4]. The adversary simply extracts the information of selected frames and then applies exclusive-or operation for adversary's watermark like binary image to obtain the K_3. In an extreme case, it is sufficient for the adversary to modify K_3. Thus, K_3 contains the information of watermark. As a result, an adversary can easily produce the information K_1, K_2, and K_3 from an audio file and can claim that the file contains his/her watermark. This situation shows that Chen and Zhu's scheme suffers from security weakness. Referring to the concept which is described in [3,13], the security of watermark algorithms depends on the secret keys used for embedding and recovery process. In contrast to this concept, Chen and Zhu's secret keys are somewhat public knowledge rather than confidential information. The first challenge issue is on how to improve the scheme in order to fulfill an appropriate watermarking concept.

2. As previously mentioned, some image ownership protection schemes [7-12], which combine encryption and secret sharing technology have also been proposed. Regarding original visual cryptography (VC) proposed by Naor and Shamir [14], the ciphertext is supposed to be revealed directly by a HVS. In that case, HVS does a visual OR rather than XOR operation. Unfortunately, most aforementioned existing schemes exploited XOR operation. Hence, the second challenge issue is on how to employ VC correctly in a digital watermarking area.

3. In terms of audio intellectual property protection, both Chen and Zhu [4] and Wang and Hu [5] do not provide any experimental results dealing with security aspects of their scheme against intentional distortions. Although Chen and Zhu [4] registers their secret keys, host original image, and timestamp to CA for copyright demonstration, it reflects that the timestamp is not digitally added by CA. They do not provide a detailed explanation on this issue as well. We argue whether this situation leads to owner's deception. Furthermore, most watermarking algorithms cannot resist against malicious manipulations of the content. Such manipulations may distort audio data as well as readily destroy or even remove the watermark. The last challenge issue is on how to enhance security against intentional distortions.

1.4   Contribution

This paper proposes a novel audio watermarking based on visual cryptography that can be exploited in ownership protection area. Akin to our previous work [6], we extract the feature by performing H-level wavelet decomposition to obtain low-frequency subband of segmented host audio. To make the proposed scheme resistant to lossy compression operation, discrete cosine transform is performed to the obtained low-frequency wavelet coefficients. We use the whole DWT-DCT coefficients rather than a certain part of coefficients to adjust matrix dimension.

In the proposed scheme, the watermark does not require to be embedded into the original audio but is used to generate secret and public share images by using the visual cryptography technique. In a nutshell, feature extraction is first accomplished to obtain digital audio's features by frequency-domain functions. The sharing matrices referred to as *codebook* are then generated in such ways that have two properties: contrast and secrecy. Instead of data embedding, audio's features and binary-valued watermark are integrated to construct secret shares based on generated codebook. In other words, the image shares contain watermark information. In contrast to existing schemes [7-12] that exploit XOR operation, we employ a visual OR of the shares to reveal the original watermark as its original concept stated in [14].

Further, product registration to a trusted authority is a well-established way of protecting intellectual property rights as well as offering indisputable proof of original ownership and legal rights [15]. In order to prevent any intentional distortion, digital timestamping is incorporated in a proposed scheme. Referring to timestamping's mechanism [16], we simplify the protocol by using CA as a trusted party which is responsible for the issuing and verification of timestamps as well as issuing a digital certificate that contains a name of the holder, a serial number, expiration date, and a holder's public key. Therefore, the steps of generating a timestamp are as follows. At first, the owner signs his protected data using his private key and generates a fingerprint by using a digital signature function. Then, the fingerprint is sent to CA. The CA generates a timestamp based on the owner's fingerprint and the date and time obtained from an accurate time source. The timestamp is sent back to the owner. The CA keeps a record of the timestamp for future verification.

The rest of the paper is organized as follows. Section 2 describes the development of an ownership protection scheme. In Section 3, the proposed scheme is investigated against incidental and intentional distortions. Finally, the conclusion is provided in Section 4.

2   Proposed scheme

The proposed scheme comprises two stages: *share image generation stage* and *watermark verification stage*. Host audio is first segmented into several frames, and each frame contains N samples. Next, the sample features are extracted by performing wavelet decomposition to obtain the low-frequency coefficients. Then, DCT is exploited only to the obtained low-frequency wavelet coefficients. Afterward, features of DCT coefficients are calculated. Finally, encoding utilizes these features and binary-valued watermark to generate secret share images according to the concept of Naor and Shamir's scheme [14]. One of the secret share image is then registered to CA for further protection and will be used for watermark verification purpose.

To retrieve the watermark, the received audio is segmented into several frames that contain N samples each. Then, the samples' features are extracted by performing wavelet decomposition to obtain the low-frequency coefficients. Next, DCT is exploited to the obtained low-frequency wavelet coefficients, and the DCT coefficients are calculated. The decoding exploits these features and registered share image to generate a public share image. The watermark is recovered by performing OR operation between secret and public share images and then used to verify the ownership. The following subsections provide more detailed description on each stage.

2.1 Main process in the proposed scheme

2.1.1 Feature extraction

To accomplish feature extraction, the host audio is first segmented into several frames in which each frame contains N samples and T-level wavelet decomposition is performed on each frame. Then, approximated coefficients in the LL_T subband are transformed to DCT coefficients. Let $A^{TC} = DCT(A^T) = \{a^{TC}(n)|n = 1,\ldots,\frac{N}{2^T}\}$ be the obtained DCT coefficients. The output array of DCT coefficients contains real numbers, and they have a range from -1 to 1. The feature type t is then obtained by the following conditions:

$$t = \begin{cases} 1 & -1 \leq a^{HC}(n) \leq 0 \\ 2 & 0 < a^{HC}(n) \leq 1. \end{cases} \quad (1)$$

2.1.2 Encoding and decoding

In principle, encoding is the process of generating secret shares by integrating binary value of the watermark and digital audio's features, while decoding refers to process of revealing the original watermark message by stacking those secret shares.

Formally, the basic model of visual secret sharing is denoted as k out of n problem. Given a secret message, we would like to generate n transparencies so that the original message is visible if any k of them are stacked together; otherwise, the message is totally invisible. We exploit original encryption problem proposed by Naor and Shamir

[14], that is a 2 out of 2 or (2,2)-secret sharing problem. The watermark is visible if two shares are stacked together; otherwise, it does not provide any information.

In this paper, the watermark consists of a collection of black and white pixels. Each original pixel appears in n shares, one for each transparency. Each share consists of m black and white sub-pixels. The resulting sharing matrices can be represented as two collections of $n \times m$ Boolean matrices $\mathbf{S}=\{S_0, S_1\}$. To share either a white or black pixel, one randomly chooses one of the matrices in either S_0 or S_1, respectively. When transparencies $i_1, i_2, \ldots, i_k$ are stacked together, the black subpixels appearing on a combined share are represented by OR operation of rows $i_1, i_2, \ldots, i_k$ in sharing matrices $\mathbf{S}$. The gray level of this combined share is proportional to the Hamming weight $H(V)$ where V is the m-vector of the resulting OR operation [14].

The sharing matrices should satisfy two properties, namely *contrast* and *secrecy*.

1. In case of contrast, the gray level G is deemed valid if the following condition is satisfied.

$$G = \begin{cases} \text{black} & \text{if } \mathbf{H(V)} \geq d \\ \text{white} & \text{otherwise} \end{cases} \quad (2)$$

for a threshold $1 \leq d \leq m$. In order to comply with a condition (2), the codebook shown in (3) and (4) is arranged in such a way that H(V) is 2 or 3 in S_0, while it is 4 in S_1.

2. In terms of secrecy, the number of 1's in $\mathbf{S}$ should have same probability distribution, i.e., codebook shown in (3) and (4) has probability $\text{Prob}(S_i =' 1'/0) = \text{Prob}(S_i =' 1'/1) = 0.5$. Let $S = [s_{ij}]$ be a Boolean matrix with a row for each share and a column for each subpixels. For each pixel, the share matrix must be chosen at random and must be known only by the sender (owner) and receiver (CA), while the codebook is publicly known.

The examples of share matrix representations used in our proposed scheme are described as follows.

$$S_0 = \left\{ \begin{pmatrix} 1 & 0 & 0 & 1 \\ 1 & 0 & 0 & 1 \end{pmatrix} \begin{pmatrix} 1 & 1 & 0 & 0 \\ 0 & 1 & 1 & 0 \end{pmatrix} \begin{pmatrix} 0 & 1 & 0 & 1 \\ 0 & 0 & 1 & 1 \end{pmatrix} \begin{pmatrix} 0 & 1 & 1 & 0 \\ 0 & 1 & 0 & 1 \end{pmatrix} \right\} \quad (3)$$

$$S_1 = \left\{ \begin{pmatrix} 0 & 1 & 1 & 0 \\ 1 & 0 & 0 & 1 \end{pmatrix} \begin{pmatrix} 1 & 0 & 0 & 1 \\ 0 & 1 & 1 & 0 \end{pmatrix} \begin{pmatrix} 1 & 1 & 0 & 0 \\ 0 & 0 & 1 & 1 \end{pmatrix} \begin{pmatrix} 1 & 0 & 1 & 0 \\ 0 & 1 & 0 & 1 \end{pmatrix} \right\} \quad (4)$$

2.1.3 Watermark reduction

Since it is accomplished by applying four subpixels per pixel, it affects the aspect ratio of original image. In order to compute bit error rate (BER), it is required to have extracted watermark in the same size as its original. Let $W(M \times N)$ be the original watermark image. Note that the extracted watermark W' will be equal to $M \times 4N$. In order to yield the same watermark size as its original one, it is necessary to accomplish the reduction process of extracted watermark. Assume that black pixel is assigned as 1 and white pixel value is 0, the reduction process is performed based on the following conditions:

$$\text{Reduction result} = \begin{cases} 1 & \text{if the number of black pixel } > 3 \\ 0 & \text{otherwise.} \end{cases}$$

$$(5)$$

2.2 Share image generation and verification procedure
2.2.1 Share image generation procedure
Figure 1 illustrates the secret share image generation, and the procedure is described as follows.

Input: host original audio $A = \{a(i)|i = 1, \ldots, L_{\text{sample}}\}$, binary image watermark $W(N \times N) = \{w(i,j)|w(i,j) \in \{0,1\}\}$, and codebook C.

Output: secret share images $S_A(N \times mN)$ and $S_B(N \times mN)$ where m is the number of subpixels per pixel.

Step 1. Firstly, A is segmented into F frames, denoted as $Fr = \{fr_i|i = 1, \ldots, F\}$, and each frame contains N samples. Next, T-level wavelet decomposition is performed on each frame fr_i to yield its coarse signal A^T and detail signal $D^T, D^{T-1}, \ldots, D^1$. Then, to take advantage of low-frequency coefficient, which is robust against signal processing manipulations, DCT is only performed on A^T

and obtained DCT coefficients are denoted as

$$A_k^{TC} = \text{DCT}(A_k^T) = \left\{ a_k^{HC}(n) \mid n = 1, \cdots, \frac{N}{2^T} \right\}. \quad (6)$$

Step 2. Construct a new sequence $B_n^{TC} = \{b_n^{TC}(n)|n = 1, \ldots, N/2^T\}$ by taking the first n frames of A_k^{TC}.

Step 3. Let x be 1.

    a. Obtain the feature type t from B_n^{TC} based on Equation (1).
    b. Construct a secret share block $S(x)$ by utilizing a codebook C as described in (3) and (4), feature type t, and a corresponding watermark pixel value $w(i,j)$.
    c. Add x to one. If $x \leq N \times N$ then go to **a**.

Step 4. The secret share images $S_A(N \times mN)$ and $S_B(N \times mN)$ are generated. Note that the security of our scheme is based on the $S_A(N \times mN)$.

Step 5. The next step is timestamping for the protected data. The owner signs the security parameter by using digital signature scheme:

$$f = DS_{OPK}(S_A, C) \quad (7)$$

where $DS_{OPK}(.)$ is a digital signature function by using the owner's private key OPK, and f stands for owner's fingerprint. Afterward, owner sends f, S, and C to the CA. CA creates a timestamp TS with the owner's fingerprint f, and the time t and date d obtained from an accurate time source as

$$TS = TS_{CAPK}(f, t, d) \quad (8)$$

where $TS_{CAPK}(.)$ is a timestamp function by using CA's private key $CAPK$. After creating the timestamp TS, it is

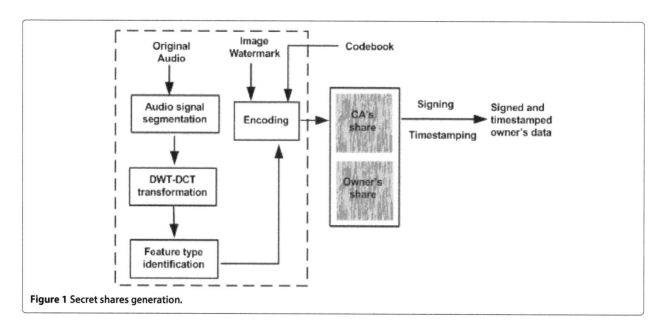

Figure 1 Secret shares generation.

sent back to the owner and kept as an archive by CA as well. Subsequently, f, TS, S_A, and C are used by CA in verification purpose when the dispute arises. Note that timestamping mechanism is completed by CA so that detail discussion of digital signature is beyond the scope of this paper.

2.2.2 Watermark verification and extraction procedure

The presence of original audio is not required in verification and extraction phase. In order to verify the copyright of an audio, anyone can use CA's public key to validate the timestamp TS and owner's public key to validate the signature f. When a dispute arises or multiple claims occur, the earlier registered data will be regarded as the original one. In the meantime, S_A and C are used to verify copyright watermark's logo corresponding to the received audio.

As depicted in Figure 2, the extraction procedure is similar to share image generation procedure and is illustrated as follows:

Input: a received audio $\{A' = a(s) | s = 1, \ldots, L_{sample}\}$, a secret share image $S(N \times N)$, and a codebook C.

Output: an extracted watermark logo $EW(N \times N)$

Step 1. A' is segmented into F frames, denoted as $Fr = \{fr_i | i = 1, \ldots, F\}$, and each frame contains N samples. Next, T-level wavelet decomposition is performed on each frame fr_i to yield its coarse signal A^T and detail signal $D^T, D^{T-1}, \ldots, D^1$. Then, DCT is on A^T and obtained DCT coefficients are denoted as $A_k^{TC} = \mathrm{DCT}(A_k^T) = \{a_k^{HC}(n) | n = 1, \cdots, N/2^T\}$.

Step 2. Construct a new sequence $B_n^{TC} = \{b_n^{TC}(n) | n = 1, \ldots, N/2^T\}$ by taking the first n frames of A_k^{TC}.

Step 3. Let x be 1.

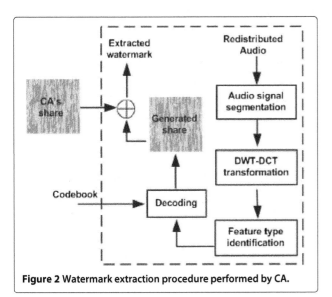

Figure 2 Watermark extraction procedure performed by CA.

a. Obtain the feature type t from B_n^{TC} based on Equation (1).
b. Construct a public share block $S_B x$ by utilizing a codebook C as described in (3) and (4) and feature type t.
c. Add x to one. If $x \leq N \times N$ then go to **a**.

Step 4. A public share image $S_B N \times mN$ is yielded. An extracted watermark $W'(N \times mN)$ is obtained by

$$W' = S_A \mathrm{OR} S_B. \tag{9}$$

Step 5. Afterward, watermark reduction process is performed according to Equation 5 to obtain the recovered watermark $EW(N \times N)$.

3 Experimental results

To demonstrate the feasibility of the proposed scheme in terms of ownership protection requirements, some experiments are conducted. Bit error rate is employed to measure robustness of the zero-watermarking system,

$$\mathrm{BER} = \frac{B}{MN} 100\% \tag{10}$$

where B is the number of erroneously extracted bits. Signal-to-noise ratio (SNR) is the ratio of quality sound to noise. The higher the decibel (dB) value, the better is the quality of the sound. For instance, a signal-to-noise ratio of 90 or 100 decibels is considered high fidelity. In this paper, SNR

$$\mathrm{SNR} = 10\log_{10}\left(\frac{\sum_{i=0}^{N-1} f^2(n)}{\sum_{i=0}^{N-1} (g(n) - f(n))^2}\right) \tag{11}$$

is applied to evaluate the quality comparison between the attacked audio and original audio. Where $f(n)$ is an original audio sample, and $g(n)$ is an attacked audio sample. SNR value is getting larger, thus leading to better audio quality.

Pearson's correlation, denoted as $\rho(x,y)$,

$$\rho(x,y) = \frac{K\sum_{i=1}^{K} X_i Y_i - (\sum_{i=1}^{K} X_i)(\sum_{i=1}^{K} Y_i)}{\sqrt{[K\sum_{i=1}^{K} X_i^2 - (\sum_{i=1}^{K} X_i)^2][K\sum_{i=1}^{K} Y_i^2 - (\sum_{i=1}^{K} Y_i)^2]}} \tag{12}$$

is employed to represent correlation between two images where $\rho(x,y)$ is a correlation coefficient (CC) between x and y, X is an image 1, Y is an image 2, and K is the number of image bits.

All the audio signals used in this test are audio with 16 bits/sample, 44.1 KHz sample rate, and 15 s long. We take various audio data files with the most commonly related to copyright protection issue. Therefore, three types of audio, including classical (violin and bass), jazz (singer and band), and instrumental (solo piano, solo guitar), are used in the experiments. The watermark to be embedded is a

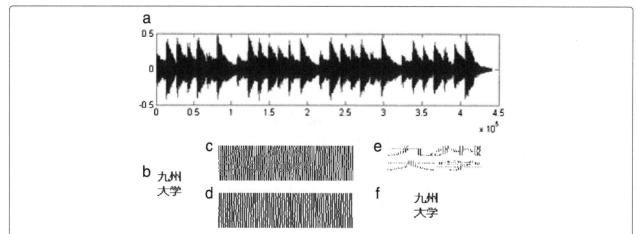

Figure 3 Watermark extraction result without being attacked. (a) Original audio signal, **(b)** original watermark, **(c)** secret share, **(d)** public share, **(e)** extracted watermark, and **(f)** reduced watermark.

visually recognizable binary image of size 64 × 64. Three-level wavelet decomposition is performed, and the frame length is 512 samples.

3.1 Watermark extraction

We first investigate our proposed scheme in recovering the watermark without being attacked. According to the experimental results described in Figure 3, BER and correlation coefficient values of all types of audio files are respectively 0% and 1. It demonstrates that each bit of watermark data is completely extracted and identical to the original one.

On the other hand, an erroneous condition is discovered in embedding phase of Chen and Zhu's scheme [4]. Consider the binary image watermark $W = \{w_{i,j} | w_{i,j} \in \{0, 1\}, i = 0, \ldots, M-1; j = 0, \ldots, N-1\}$.

Table 1 BER and correlation coefficient of extracted watermark attacked by StirMark

Attacks	Instrumental		Jazz		Classical		CC in [4]
	BER	CC	BER	CC	BER	CC	
a. AddBrumm	1.90%	0.92	0.85%	0.96	2.24%	0.91	0.98
b. AddDynNoise	5.57%	0.80	2.25%	0.91	3.17%	0.87	-
c. AddNoise	5.25%	0.81	1.81%	0.92	3.66%	0.86	0.99
d. *AddSinus*	*0.098%*	*0.99*	*0.44%*	*0.98*	*1.17%*	*0.95*	*0.92*
e. Amplify	0%	1	0%	1	0%	1	1
f. BassBoost	2.39%	0.90	7.67%	0.75	2.05%	0.91	-
g. BitChanger	0%	1	0%	1	0%	1	-
h. *Compressor*	*0%*	*1*	*0.68%*	*0.97*	*0%*	*1*	*0.99*
i. Echo	26.44%	0.47	18.70%	0.55	23.34%	0.50	1
j. ExtraStereo	5.91%	0.80	1.54%	0.93	4.27%	0.84	-
k. FlippSample (2000)	33.86%	0.4	17.11%	0.57	27.61%	0.45	-
FlippSample (100)	10.84%	0.68	3.34%	0.87	8.54%	0.72	-
l. LSBZero	0%	1	0%	1	0%	1	-
m. NoiseMax	4.79%	0.82	1.61%	0.93	3.91%	0.85	-
n. RCHighPass	3.49%	0.86	8.94%	0.72	3.10%	0.87	-
o. RCLowPass	1.22%	0.95	0.51%	0.98	1.001%	0.96	1
p. ReplaceSamples	13.14%	0.64	5.03%	0.81	15.73%	0.59	-
q. Smooth	4.37%	0.83	0.81%	0.96	2.37%	0.90	0.99
r. Smooth2	3.10%	0.87	0.71%	0.97	2.51%	0.90	-
s. Stat1	4.76%	0.82	2.29%	0.90	4.42%	0.83	0.94
t. Stat2	1.68%	0.93	0.29%	0.99	1.05%	0.95	1
u. ZeroCross	3.78%	0.85	1.34%	0.94	3.83%	0.86	0.97
v. Resampling	0%	1	0%	1	0%	1	1

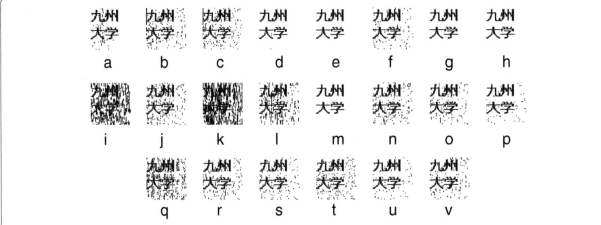

Figure 4 Examples of extracted watermark from attacked audio by StirMark. The music type of Instrumental is taken as an example. **(a to v)** The extracted watermark from StirMark attacks.

To generate watermark key, they first constructed binary pattern matrix $B = \{b_{t,p}|b_{t,p}\epsilon\{0,1\}, t = 0, \ldots, T - 1; p = 0, \ldots, P - 1\}$ where T is the number of selected frame and P is the number of selected coefficient cumulants on all selected frame. Then, the watermark key K_3 was generated by performing XOR operation between binary pattern matrix B and image watermark W. Notice that matrix dimension of K_3 will be equal to B. It is reflected by the provided formula in [4] on how to find each pixel position in W that corresponds to B. In the extraction phase, the extracted watermark W' is revealed by conducting XOR operation between K_3 and B. The dimension between W' and W is different, thus causing the extracted watermark to be unrecognizable and unusable for verification purpose. To improve the problem, we simply utilize the entire of the obtained DWT-DCT coefficients rather than employ certai coefficients.

3.2 Robustness against incidental distortions

Incidental distortion refers to the distortions introduced from real applications which do not change the content of the multimedia data [17]. To evaluate the robustness to such distortions, the scheme is tested by performing various attacks of audio signal processing provided by StirMark for Audio (SMFA) version 1.03 [18] as well as exploiting their default values. The aim of SMFA is to delete, remove, or destroy the digital watermark by modifying the signal of the audio file. According to the Table 1, the minimum acceptable value of BER and CC are located on FlippSample attack, which are approximately 26.19% and 0.47, respectively, and the extracted watermark is still visually recognizable. This attack flips 2,000 samples every 10,000 with sample 6,000 ahead. However, when the attack only flips 100 samples, the average of BER and CC have both improved to approximately 7.57% and 0.76, respectively. Thus, it leads to assertion that in general the proposed scheme has a satisfactory performance against StirMark attacks, especially BitChanger, Compressor, and LSBZero as depicted in Figure 4.

Table 2 Performance over various durations

Attacks	00:01:38		00:02:20		00:04:08	
	BER	CC	BER	CC	BER	CC
a. AddBrumm	2.44%	0.90	0.90%	0.96	3.88%	0.85
b. AddDynNoise	3.15%	0.87	3.22%	0.87	4.49%	0.83
c. AddNoise	6.61%	0.77	2.73%	0.89	7.91%	0.74
d. AddSinus	0.46%	0.98	0.31%	0.99	1.83%	0.92
e. Amplify	0%	1	0%	1	0.02%	0.99
f. BassBoost	5.81%	0.79	10.08%	0.69	13.75%	0.63
g. BitChanger	0%	1	0%	1	0%	1
h. Compressor	0%	1	0.6836%	0.9687	0%	1
i. Echo	18.43%	0.56	21.48%	0.52	24.80%	0.48
j. ExtraStereo	15.67%	0.60	17.26%	0.57	10.52%	0.68
k. FlippSample (2000)	21.34%	0.52	11.35%	0.67	30.44%	0.43
FlippSample (100)	5.98%	0.79	3.10%	0.87	8.30%	0.73
l. LSBZero	0%	1	0.02%	0.99	0.02%	0.99
m. NoiseMax	6.60%	0.77	1.78%	0.92	6.23%	0.78
n. RCHighPass	9.59%	0.70	17.79%	0.57	19.09%	0.55
o. RCLowPass	0.42%	0.98	0.27%	0.99	0.66%	0.97
p. ReplaceSamples	16.77%	0.58	6.13%	0.78	0%	1
q. Smooth	0.49%	0.98	0.32%	0.99	0.68%	0.97
r. Smooth2	0.85%	0.96	0.44%	0.98	1.05%	0.95
s. Stat1	1.83%	0.92	1.10%	0.95	2.10%	0.91
t. Stat2	0.37%	0.98	0.12%	0.99	0.29%	0.99
u. ZeroCross	8.74%	0.72	1.78%	0.92	8.50%	0.73

The next attack conducted is downsampling generated by Cool Edit Pro 2.1. The sample of audio rate is adjusted from 44,100 to 22,050 Hz, and then, its sample rate is readjusted to 44,100 Hz. This process might cause an alteration in some parts of audio data. Consequently, the watermark data cannot be completely extracted. However, the BER and correlation coefficient value as shown in Table 1, which are 0% and 1, respectively, indicate that the proposed scheme resists to such attack.

To evaluate the robustness of proposed scheme, we draw a comparison to earlier method [4] subjected to StirMark attacks as well as short duration. In more detail, all the audio signals used in [4] were audio with 16 bits/sample, 44.1 KHz sample rate, and 28.73 s long. The music styles used throughout their experiment were not explicitly reported. In order to properly compare the schemes, we deliberately exploit various music styles. We expect the music styles used in [4] to be any of ours. BER and correlation coefficient values are reported in Table 1, and the extracted watermark against those attacks is illustrated in Figure 4. The results indicate that our proposed scheme outperforms Chen's scheme [4] on AddSinus and Compressor attacks. In case of other attacks, we still achieve considerable results compared to Chen's scheme.

Furthermore, to verify the efficacy of the proposed scheme, evaluation over various durations is conducted as well. The duration is ranging from 1 to 4 min. However, we did not perform comparative experiments because the duration either in [4] or [5] is approximately below 60 s. The experimental results against SMFA are reported in Table 2. In general, the findings show that longer duration provides fairly the same performance as short duration. For example, BitChanger attack indicates exactly the same results, while amplify and LSBZero attacks demonstrate

that the number of error bit is only one. To confirm the findings, the resulting extracted watermarks are provided in Figure 5.

3.3 Robustness against intentional distortions

Intentional distortion refers to distortions conducted by deliberately modifying the host content [17]. It can be performed by overwriting or removing the watermark. In the following subsection, we address two types of intentional distortions: *counterfeit attack* and *multiple claims situation*.

3.3.1 Counterfeit attack

In some cases, the adversary tries to confuse ownership by creating a faked original or faked watermarked audio. In this case, an adversary performs a distortion by modification of a set of features of received audio A' so-called faked original audio A^f. By doing so, it is expected that the original watermark will be destroyed. One simple way to alter the features is to modify the sample data in such a way that the SNR is still acceptable. Figure 6 demonstrates spectrogram of original audio signal and its faked version due to sample data alteration. The vertical axis represents frequencies up to 20,000 Hz, the horizontal axis shows positive time toward the right, and the colors represent the most important acoustic peaks for a given time frame, with red representing the highest energies, then in decreasing order of importance, orange, yellow, green, cyan, blue, and magenta.

Once the faked signal is constructed, the adversary may embed his watermark onto it and produce another watermarked audio. In the verification phase, the adversary's audio signal is verified by using registered secret share image. As shown in Table 3, the number of error bits is approximately in ranges 49 to 118 bits from 4,096 bits, and the owner's watermark is completely extracted. It indicates that the proposed scheme performs well in

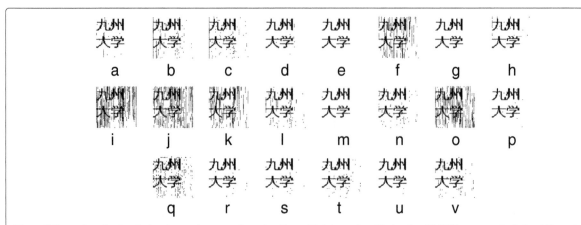

Figure 5 Examples of extracted watermark over various durations. We take audio with duration 00:02:20 as a sample. **(a to v)** The extracted watermark from StirMark attacks reported in Table 2.

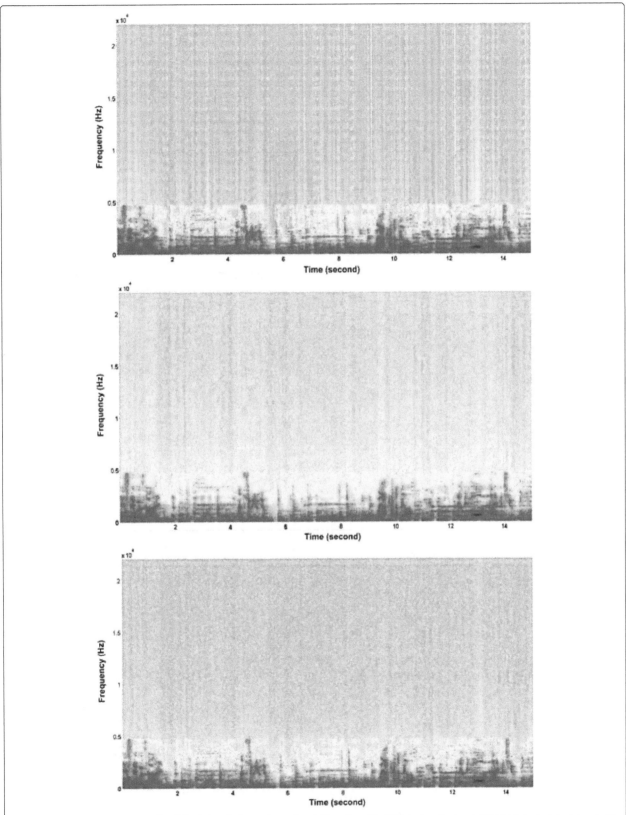

Figure 6 Spectrogram of Jazz and its faked signals due to intentional distortion. (Top) Original audio signal. (Middle) Faked original signal with SNR = 20.9949 dB. (Bottom) Faked original signal with SNR = 27.0155 dB. The figure is intended for color reproduction on the Web and in print.

Table 3 Watermark extraction performance against intentional distortion

Adversary's watermark	Extracted watermark	SNR	BER	CC
 九州 大学	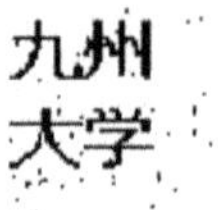	26.2626 dB	1.1963%	0.9467
ARTSPACE	 九州 大学	20.242 dB	2.8809%	0.8824

watermark verification phase and possesses an unambiguous property.

3.3.2 Multiple claims

In this situation, the adversary attempts to provoke a dispute by embedding his/her own message. The following is the model of the proposed scheme. In such a scheme, let $\mathbf{x} = (x(1) \ldots x(N_f))^T$ be a feature vector extracted from the audio content with length-N_f. The message to be hidden is a binary matrix W of size $N \times N$. The scheme exploits (2,2)-secret sharing. The codebook C comprises two $2 \times n$ boolean matrices (C_i^0, C_i^1) with:

- $i = (1 \ldots f)$, f is the number of feature type.
- C_i^0 and C_i^1 are the base matrices for black and white pixel, respectively.

The scheme is defined as the four-tuple $(W, \mathcal{E}, \mathcal{D}, C)$, where:

- $\mathcal{E}: \mathbf{x} \times W \times C \rightarrow \mathcal{S}$ is the encoder mapping a sequence $\mathbf{x}$, a hidden message W using codebook C to a secret share image $\mathcal{S}$.
- $\mathcal{D}: \mathbf{x} \times C \rightarrow \mathcal{P}$ is the decoder mapping a sequence $\mathbf{x}$ using codebook C to a public share image $\mathcal{P}$.

According to our scheme, $\mathcal{S}$ is kept by CA while $\mathcal{P}$ as well as codebook are publicly known. Suppose the adversary intends to rewrite the content with his hidden message. We would like to show that all his efforts are fairly unworthy.

Suppose $\mathbf{x}^*$, C^*, and W^* are the feature vector extracted from the retrieved audio content, adversary's codebook, and adversary's hidden message, respectively. Based on aforementioned statement, we might convey that $C^* \equiv C$ such that

- $\mathcal{E}: \mathbf{x}^* \times W^* \times C^* \rightarrow \{\mathcal{S}^*, \mathcal{P}^*\}$ where $\mathcal{S}^*$ is the adversary's secret share. Note that $\mathcal{S}^*$ is not required since the original $\mathcal{S}$ have been registered by the owner in advance.

九州
大学

Figure 7 The example of extracted watermark of multiple claims condition.

- $\mathcal{D}: \mathbf{x}^* \times C^* \rightarrow \mathcal{P}^*$ where $\mathcal{P}^*$ is the adversary's public share. Due to the property of our scheme, it is obvious that $\mathbf{x}^* \equiv \mathbf{x}$ which implies that $\mathcal{P}^* \equiv \mathcal{P}$. Thus the adversary's hidden message will never be extracted. □

To evoke multiple claims situation, the adversary embeds his watermark, which is depicted in Table 3, onto the $\mathbf{x}^*$. Figure 7 shows that original's watermark remains extracted.

4 Conclusions

This paper investigates the problem of constructing an audio ownership protection scheme in order to resist against both intentional and incidental distortions. To achieve these goals, we have integrated wavelet transform, visual cryptography, and digital timestamp into an ownership protection scheme. The trade-off between data payload and two other properties, imperceptibility and/or robustness, can be reduced, while preserving its audio signal quality. According to experimental results, the proposed scheme fulfills several properties of ownership protection including perceptual transparency, blindness, robustness, security, and unambiguousness. In terms of security, it is achieved by means of visual cryptography method. Without possessing both shares, it is infeasible for anyone to retrieve the secret image from each share. The integrity of codebook and its secret share image is guaranteed by certification authority through timestamp mechanism. It indicates that audio ownership protection can take advantage from the combination of visual cryptography and watermarking and proposed scheme can be widely applied to the area of audio ownership protection.

Competing interests
The authors declare that they have no competing interests.

Acknowledgements
The authors wish to thank the anonymous reviewers for their very constructive and helpful comments. Research support for the first author was provided by the Directorate General of Higher Education, Ministry of National Education, Indonesia. The second author acknowledges support provided by Grant NRF-2011-013-D00121 from the National Research Foundation of Korea. This is an expanded version of a paper [6] presented at the Seventh International Conference on Intelligent Information Hiding and Multimedia Signal Processing (IIHMSP 2011) with further analysis and some new simulation experiments.

Author details
[1] Department of Informatics, Telkom University, Bandung 40257, Indonesia.
[2] Graduate School of Information Science and Electrical Engineering, Kyushu University, 744 Motooka, Nishi-ku, Fukuoka 819-0395, Japan. [3] Department of IT

Convergence and Application Engineering, Pukyong National University,
599-1, Daeyeon 3-Dong, Nam-Gu, Busan 608-737, Korea.

References
1. S Stokes, *Digital Copyright: Law and Practice*, 2nd edn. (Hart Publishing, New York, 2005), p. 120
2. X-Y Wang, Y-R Cui, H-Y Yang, H Zhao, A new content-based digital audio watermarking algorithm for copyright protection, in *Proceedings of the 3rd International Conference on Information Security (SEC)*, vol. 85 (ACM, New York, 2004), pp. 62–68
3. M Barni, F Bartolini, *Watermarking systems engineering: enabling digital assets security and other applications*, (Marcel Decker, New York, USA, 2004), pp. 6–11
4. N Chen, J Zhu, A robust zero-watermarking algorithm for audio. EURASIP J. Adv. Signal Process. **2008**, 453580 (2008)
5. R Wang, W Hu, Robust audio zero-watermark based on LWT and chaotic modulation, in *Proceeding International Workshop Digital Watermarking (IWDW)*, (Springer, Heidelberg, 2007), pp. 373–381
6. RW Ciptasari, A Fajar, FA Yulianto, K Sakurai, An efficient key generation method in zero-watermarking for audio, in *Proceeding of 7th IEEE International Conference on Intelligent Information Hiding and Multimedia Signal Processing (IIHMSP)*, (IEEE, Washington DC, 2011), pp. 336–339
7. Z Wang, CC Chang, HN Tu, MC Li, Sharing a secret image in binary images with verifcation. J. Inform. Hiding Multimedia Signal Process. **2**(1) (2011)
8. CC Chang, JC Chuang, An image intellectual property protection scheme for gray-level images using visual secret sharing strategy. Pattern Recognit. Lett. **23**, 931–941 (2001)
9. SL Hsieh, LY Hsu, IJ Tsai, A copyright protection scheme for color images using secret sharing and wavelet transform, in *Proceedings of World Academy of Science, Engineering And Technology*, (World Academy of Science, Engineering and Technology, Egypt, 2005), pp. 17–23
10. WB Lee, TH Chen, A public verifiable copy protection technique for still images. J Syst. Software, 195–204 (2002)
11. DC Lou, HK Tso, JL Liu, A copyright protection scheme for digital images using visual cryptography technique. J. Comput. Stand. Interfaces **29**, 125–131 (2006)
12. TH Chen, GB Horng, WB Lee, A publicly verifiable copyright-proving scheme resistant to malicious attacks. IEEE Trans. Ind. Electron. **52** (1), (2005)
13. IJ Cox, ML Miller, JA Bloom, *Digital Watermarking* (Morgan Kauffman Publisher, San Francisco, 2002), pp. 45–47
14. N Naor, A Shamir, Visual cryptography. Advances in Cryptology: Eurocrypt. **94**, 1–12 (1995)
15. G Voyatzis, I Pitas, Protecting digital image copyrights: a framework. IEEE Comput. Graph. Appl. **19**(1), 18–24 (1999)
16. Electronic Time-stamping. https://www.digistamp.com/technical/how-a-digital-time-stamp-works/. Accessed 25 Oct 2011.
17. D He, Q Sun, Multimedia authentication, in *Multimedia Security Technologies for Digital Rights Management*, ed. by W Zeng, H Yu, and CY Lin (Academic Press, London, 2006), pp. 111-138
18. A Lang, StirMark benchmark for audio, http://sourceforge.net/projects/stirmark/files/. Accessed 17 November 2011

4

Taxonomy of social network data types

Christian Richthammer[*†], Michael Netter[†], Moritz Riesner[†], Johannes Sänger[†] and Günther Pernul[†]

Abstract

Online social networks (OSNs) have become an integral part of social interaction and communication between people. Reasons include the ubiquity of OSNs that is offered through mobile devices and the possibility to bridge spatial and temporal communication boundaries. However, several researchers have raised privacy concerns due to the large amount of user data shared on OSNs. Yet, despite the large body of research addressing OSN privacy issues, little differentiation of data types on social network sites is made and a generally accepted classification and terminology for such data is missing. The lack of a terminology impedes comparability of related work and discussions among researchers, especially in the case of privacy implications of different data types. To overcome these shortcomings, this paper develops a well-founded terminology based on a thorough literature analysis and a conceptualization of typical OSN user activities. The terminology is organized hierarchically resulting in a taxonomy of data types. The paper furthermore discusses and develops a metric to assess the privacy relevance of different data types. Finally, the taxonomy is applied to the five major OSNs to evaluate its generalizability.

Keywords: Taxonomy; Privacy; Data types; Online social networks; Social identity management; Classification; Privacy relevance metric

1 Introduction

Online social networks (OSNs) have reached major importance due to their increased usage and ubiquity, rising membership, and presence in the media. Allowing their users to create custom profile sites, express relationships with other users, and explore the resulting social graph [1], they combine previously available communication and self-representation functions, such as personal blogs, forums, and instant messaging with novel social functions. Also, they allow reaching new contacts. The user base of OSNs is no longer restricted to private end users and college communities [2] but extends to professionals while serving as collaboration tools [3].

1.1 Privacy threats and the need for different data types

With the increased usage frequency and ubiquitous usage of OSNs, the quantity and sensitivity of user data that is stored on OSNs has grown tremendously as well. This is fostered by the availability of social networking services on mobile devices that provide location-based features and camera functions, for instance, allowing users to publish their current activity and location. For service providers, it is possible to derive rich profiles of their users [4], leading to *social footprints* [5].

Further privacy issues occur not only due to the service provider's data usage but also because other OSN users have access to user data. Similar to the physical world, OSNs need to offer means to create different images of the self, such as facets to cover the professional aspects of OSN-facilitated communication and further facets for family and friend-related representations of one's personality. Historically, creating and managing multiple facets of one's identity is not a OSN-specific phenomenon but part of everyday life. In historical records of ancient Greece, for instance, Plato refers to social interaction as the 'great stage of human life' (in Burns [6]). Sociologist Erving Goffman labels people's desire to control their appearances for different audiences as impression management [7]. Privacy is violated if information intended for a particular audience (such as one's family) unintentionally becomes available to another audience (such as one's employer). This understanding of privacy as respecting social norms of intended contexts is also referred to as contextual integrity [8].

On OSNs, on the one hand, the disembodied environment of these sites emphasizes the communication part

*Correspondence: christian.richthammer@wiwi.uni-regensburg.de
†Equal contributors
Department of Information Systems, University of Regensburg, Regensburg 93053, Germany

of social interaction. On the other hand, most communication is conducted in an asynchronous manner, i.e., OSNs *need to provide a variety of different data types* to adequately map social interaction onto the World Wide Web and to cover all aspects of social communication. This need for targeted and selective disclosure of personal information to create several facets of the self - representing different areas of the physical world - and keep them separated is also referred to as *Social Identity Management* (SIdM) [9].

1.2 Existing privacy-related research

Prompted by these developments, privacy concerns have been voiced by researchers. Numerous studies have been conducted on privacy issues on OSNs in general [10,11] as well as on people's awareness in this context [12,13] and on potential hazards [14,15]. Proposals for improving the user's understanding of disclosed information [16], enhanced access control models [17], and improved privacy protection on OSNs [18] have been made.

Observing the literature on privacy and user control in OSNs shows that there is little work describing data elements that are associated with the users, albeit surveying the application programming interface (API) of the popular site Facebook that reveals a large number of distinct data elements that can be associated with a user [19]. Related work in assessing the access control models in OSNs (e.g., [20,21]) does not differentiate between different attributes of the user identity, while others only focus on singular aspects such as the owner and creator of items [22]. Still, it is seldom or only briefly [23] considered that attributes on OSNs vary widely in implementation, semantics, applicable policies [24], and privacy controls [25] and thus carry far-reaching implications for the user.

This paper aims at tackling the lack of a generally accepted terminology for describing and differentiating data types on OSNs by developing and proposing a detailed taxonomy.[a] It is intended to benefit discussions among researchers, alleviate difficulties when comparing data elements within and across OSNs, and provide guidance for end users when assessing the privacy implications in dealing with particular OSN data types. To further ease the assessment of privacy threats, the paper introduces steps toward a metric to quantitatively assess the privacy relevance of particular data types.

The remainder of the paper is organized as follows. Work related to classifying OSN data types and privacy metrics is discussed and compared to our contribution in Section 2. The scope and methodology of the research are defined in Section 3. The proposed taxonomy is introduced in Section 4 accompanied by an analysis of related

literature and a conceptualization of fundamental OSN user activities involving user data. Based on the data types identified in the taxonomy, a privacy relevance metric is developed in Section 5. The taxonomy is evaluated in Section 6 by applying it to five major OSNs before concluding the paper in Section 7.

2 Related work

This section provides an overview of important related work with respect to our work. We outline research regarding the study of user activities on OSNs, the conceptualization of data types, and the development of privacy metrics for OSNs. Furthermore, we point out how our paper distinguishes from related publications.

2.1 User activities on OSNs

Surma and Furmanek [26] and Zhang et al. [27] describe fundamental user activities on OSNs. The former work [26] focuses on user activities accustomed to a small community of OSNs, which is why it does not allow to draw generic conclusions. The latter work [27] is conducted on a high level of abstraction containing only three different entities and is used as a basis for the explanation of the variables of a heterogeneous network. Despite the unsuitable degree of abstraction and the completely different purposes, the study of user activities conducted in this paper in order to derive originating data types has been inspired by the user-centric approaches introduced above.

2.2 Data types on OSNs

Ho et al. [10] mention two different approaches for categorizing data. The first one is based on a survey in which users of OSNs were asked which data they would place on their profile. Consequently, the resulting classification only considers the items that were mentioned by the participants of the survey. In the second approach presented by Ho et al. [10], user data is divided by focusing on the data's impact on privacy. While reasonable for categorizing privacy settings, it is unsuitable for developing a general-purpose taxonomy as many other dimensions would be omitted. Similarly, Park et al. [4] also focus on certain aspects of data on OSNs. Data is categorized on the basis of its visibility (i.e., private or public) and its creator (i.e., the user himself or others). As a consequence, unlike this work, the categorization proposed by Park et al. [4] lacks a discussion of activity-related data types and solely focuses on the two dimensions mentioned before.

Beye et al. [28] follow a different approach that builds upon the definition of OSN by Boyd [sic] and Ellison [1] from which three data types are deduced. Additional six data types are derived by focusing on the goals of different OSNs. Compared to the approaches discussed so far,

Beye et al.'s work [28] contains a well-founded explanation on the origin of the data types. However, their definition (e.g., the definition of the data type *Messages*) can be considered too coarse-grained. No distinction is made concerning the item's visibility, its creator, and the domain in which it is created. These aspects are of major importance when analyzing the user's capabilities on modern OSNs.

Unlike other approaches which developed their classifications only as a basis for further examinations, Schneier [23] focuses solely on the task of establishing a taxonomy. However, his brief discussion lacks a structured methodology and does not mention any explanation on how he deduced the data types. Moreover, his taxonomy does not cover all important aspects of OSNs. For example, there are no data types in which the user's relationships or his connection-related attributes (e.g., Internet Protocol (IP) address) can be arranged. Årnes et al. [29] pick up the ideas proposed by Schneier [23]. Although being a meaningful extension to the work presented by Schneier [23], this approach also does not go into detail about the particular data types and is limited to a short definition and a list of examples for each category.

A major distinction between all previously discussed approaches and this paper is the level of granularity. Rather than aiming at a high-level classification, this work proposes a fine-grained taxonomy. In addition, the individual data types are arranged hierarchically, which is a common feature of taxonomies.

2.3 Privacy scoring for OSNs

Besides data types in OSNs and their classification, current research lacks an analysis of the privacy risks which single data types of the proposed taxonomies are accompanied with. A first step toward this direction has been made by Liu and Terzi [30] who proposed a framework for computing the privacy scores of users on OSNs. They developed mathematical models to assess the sensitivity and visibility of disclosed information. Their privacy score as an aggregation of combined sensitivity and visibility values provides a measure for the privacy risk a user faces. As the data basis for this score only involves the user's current privacy settings and the user's position in the social network, the authors assume that the user alone is responsible for the dissemination of his privacy-relevant data. However, as we will point out during the development of our taxonomy, privacy is significantly impacted by the creator and the publisher of data as well as the domain information is published in. The fact that privacy relevant data can be disclosed outside the user's domain bears additional potential risks. Further approaches to measure privacy risks include the work of Cutillo et al. [31] and Becker et al. [32]. The former

assesses the achievable privacy degree in an OSN based on graph topology measures, such as degree distribution, clustering coefficient, and mixing time. Becker et al. [32], in contrast, measure the privacy risks attributed to direct social contacts. Similar to the work published by Liu and Terzi [30], these approaches do not make a differentiation between different data types but provide an aggregated value to measure the comprehensive privacy risks a user faces.

3 Research scope and approach
3.1 Problem scope

This work aims at developing a taxonomy for describing and classifying data types on OSNs, thereby benefiting three areas. The first goal is to improve comparability of user data within and across OSNs. Further, it intends to provide a clear terminology for discussions among researchers. Lastly, it aims at improving the understanding of attribute characteristics on OSNs and their implications by end users.

The goal of this paper is not to provide an exhaustive list of all attributes and data elements that are available or disclosed on current OSNs. Rather, it intends to develop a taxonomy to describe important characteristics of data types on OSNs and understand their differences, especially with regards to characteristics specific to OSNs and SIdM.

Note that this work focuses on centralized OSNs and only covers data types related to user actions that occur directly on them. External aspects like social plugins (e.g., Facebook's Like button) create extensive privacy issues. However, they have to be discussed separately and are out of the scope of this paper. Also, note that the subsequent discussions are solely based on facts and that no assumptions regarding the actions of OSN service providers are made.

3.2 Research approach

Aiming at delivering a taxonomy consisting of *constructs* for describing data types on OSNs that are used for abstracting from particular data types, a design-oriented research approach [33,34] is applicable to the problem scope. For conducting design-oriented research, a process model consisting of six steps - problem identification, elicitation of solution objectives, solution design, demonstration, evaluation, and communication - has been proposed [34].

The research approach employed in this work adapts the process proposed by Peffers et al. [34]. The first step has been performed in the previous two sections by identifying the problem and motivating the need for a taxonomy for data types on OSNs. Also, the corresponding research gap has been identified. Subsequently, the objectives of developing the taxonomy have been identified previously in this section, thus constituting the second step of the design research process.

The research model depicted in Figure 1 shows the core steps performed in this paper. As a preparation for developing the taxonomy, the body of the related literature is analyzed with regards to possible elements of an OSN attribute taxonomy (Section 4). A conceptualization of fundamental user activities between the user, the OSN, and possibly the user's contacts that affect user data complements this analysis (step 1 in Figure 1). Based on these foundations, the proposed taxonomy is discussed thoroughly, which corresponds to the third step of the design research process model [34].

Evaluation is deemed as a *central and essential activity* [35] and a *key element* [36] in design-oriented research. Correspondingly, the design research process [34] contains both a demonstration and a dedicated evaluation step. The taxonomy is demonstrated (step 2 in Figure 1) by applying it to five major OSNs and identifying actually implemented data types for each element of the taxonomy (Section 6). Besides demonstration, the taxonomy is evaluated by identifying all data types of the OSN Facebook and iterating over all these data types and mapping them into the taxonomy (step 3 in Figure 1).

The presentation of results in this paper concludes one iteration of the design science process and corresponds to the communication step.

4 Proposed taxonomy

To arrive at a taxonomy for OSN data types, this section follows the previously outlined research model. In an initial step and based on Section 2, a thorough literature analysis reveals in essence the following three related approaches: Schneier [23], its refinement by Årnes et al. [29], and the classification by Beye et al. [28]. Figure 2 correlates the data elements of these approaches and the taxonomy proposed in this work, while the subsequent

discussion of this section highlights conceptual similarities and deviations.

The analysis of Figure 2 leads to several observations: Firstly, it reveals that to some extent terminology is not consistently used, such as the different understanding of behavioral data [23,29] and behavioral information [28]. Secondly, a general lack of granularity can be attributed to some existing data type definitions, as observable in Beye et al.'s generic conceptualization of profiles [28]. Consequently, it is difficult to precisely specify data elements as needed in scientific discussions. Lastly, some related work either does not cover all available data types, such as the missing specification of data related to the connection with other users in Schneier's proposal [23], or focuses on data elements whose existence is difficult to verify (e.g., the probability-based derived data in Schneier's [23] and in Årnes et al.'s [29] work that stems from the combination of several other data types).

Based on the analysis of existing literature, this work follows a user-centric approach by studying data that is created during possible user activities on OSNs. Figure 3 illustrates OSN entities and possible activities. As can be seen, most activities are either initiated by the user or one of his contacts. The subsequent elicitation of data types will refer to the numbered steps in Figure 3 to clarify the origin of a particular data element.

As a taxonomy is commonly regarded a hierarchical classification, this paper takes a top-down approach stepwise subdividing the set of data types into non-redundant partitions. The process is repeated until all data types are classified. At the first level, a distinction is made based on the stakeholder for whom a particular data type is of use. From a privacy point of view, two stakeholders are distinguishable [37]: *service providers* and *OSN users*. The former group offers OSN platforms and related services whereas personal data commonly provides the basis of their business model. For OSN users as the second

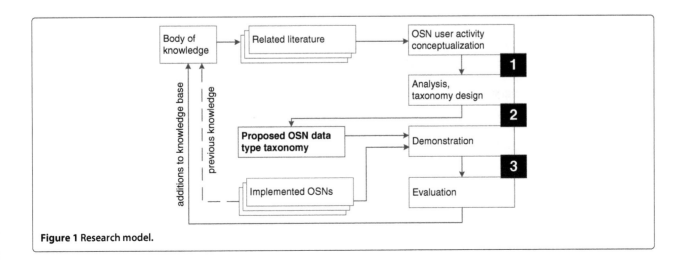

Figure 1 Research model.

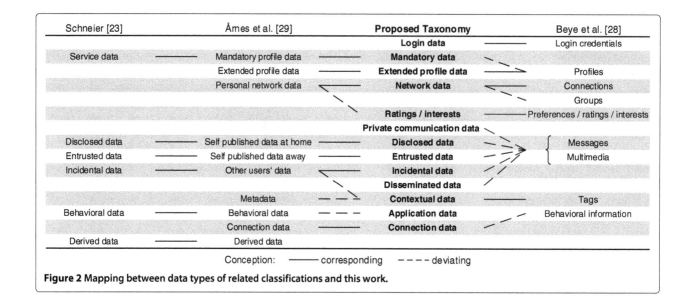

Figure 2 Mapping between data types of related classifications and this work.

stakeholder, personal data is used for the purpose of SIdM. In the following, accruing data types for each stakeholder are discussed in detail.

4.1 Service provider-related data types

Note that while service providers of centralized OSNs typically have access to personal data that is generated in user-related activities, this section discusses only data that originates from the service usage. Drawing on user activities identified in Figure 3, several service provider-related activities can be identified. In the following, data emerging

from these activities is classified into three separate data types. To assess the privacy impact of service provider-related data types in general, it is valuable to recall that privacy is a social concept. In more detail, privacy is breached if other people that have a relationship with the user gain access to this data. For service providers, in contrast, such a relationship does commonly not exist. Moreover, data is typically processed by machines and algorithms without human interaction. Nevertheless, in the longer run, the data types which are subsequently discussed may lead to social privacy implications. For

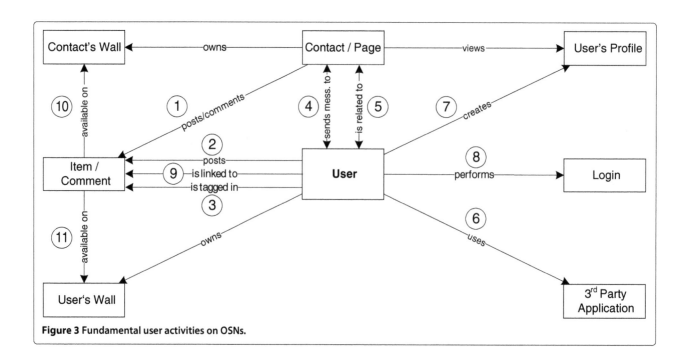

Figure 3 Fundamental user activities on OSNs.

instance, if such data becomes publicly available (e.g., through data breaches), people that do have a relation with the user can use this data to gain more knowledge and thereby invade his privacy. Consequently, protection is necessary and therefore discussed for each of the service provider-related data types.

4.1.1 Login data

OSN service usage requires prior user authentication to prevent identity theft, which is represented by activity 8 in Figure 3 and is consistent with Beye et al.'s respective data type [28] (cf. Figure 2). Consequently, login data is considered a data type that is required by the OSN service provider to provide evidence of a claimed identity. Common instances of this data type are identifiers such as username and email address as well as passwords used to verify an identity. From a privacy perspective, identifiers such as the user's email address may facilitate the linkability of different partial identities and may lead to the compilation of a more comprehensive profile. In addition, inadequate protection of login data may allow other users to access a user's profile and gain access to personal information that was not intended for them. This may cause a violation of privacy in the sense of contextual integrity (cf. Section 1).

4.1.2 Connection data

While not OSN-specific, requesting - i. e., connecting to and using - Internet-based services (activity 8 in Figure 3) leads to a variety of digital traces created by protocols on several layers of the OSI model. Figure 2 shows that the definition is consistent with the work presented by Årnes et al. [29], while a broader conceptualization is used by Beye et al. [28]. Instances include the user's IP address, the type of communication unit (such as mobile devices), information related to the browser and the operating system, and location (derived from the IP address or using GPS). Especially browser-related information and location are deemed sensitive and entail privacy implications when being available to OSN service providers, such as for acquiring detailed user information through cookies and browsing history or for creating a movement profile based on location data. Attacks, such as browser fingerprinting, have been successfully demonstrated, allowing users to be identified solely based on their HTTP headers even if they update their browser version [38]. In this case, it is not the actual data that is contained in this data type which is of privacy importance but rather the potential to use this data to de-anonymize users, link previously unrelated personal information, and thereby invade privacy.

4.1.3 Application data

Besides OSN platform usage, data originating from the use of third party services (activity 6 in Figure 3) running within the boundaries of the OSN platform or having

API access can be differentiated. None of the related work explicitly focuses on this type of data. Common examples are player statistics of OSN games, application usage statistics, or in-app purchase data such as credit card information. This data type may entail both privacy and security risks. On the one hand, data security largely depends on the trustworthiness and protection mechanisms of the service provider and third party services. Breaches may lead to serious consequences such as credit card fraud. On the other hand, privacy may be threatened if third party usage statistics become available. For instance, an employer may notice that one of his employees is playing OSN games during working hours.

4.2 User-related data types

To model the diversity of a user's personality and his ways of social interaction, an OSN account offers a variety of means to express oneself and communicate with other users. Fundamentally, two classes of data can be distinguished: *semantically specified* and *semantically unspecified* data. The first category refers to data instances that have a clearly defined meaning and whose content is clearly understood. Examples include predefined attribute types of an OSN profile such as name, birthdate, and hometown. Yet, OSN service providers have acknowledged that it is difficult to force all aspects of a user's personality into well-specified conceptual boxes. Hence, semantically unspecified data types are provided to freely express some facets of one's personality, such as status posts whose content is not semantically predefined. Note that for some data types, a selective classification is difficult as parts of the data type are semantically specified while others remain unspecified. For this taxonomy, we focus on the data type's value for classification. For example, while the concept of a shared photograph is semantically defined, its value is difficult to interpret and consequently the data type is semantically unspecified. As another example, for friend lists, not only the concept itself but also its value (a set of contacts (which is also a clearly specified concept)) is semantically defined.

4.2.1 Semantically specified

Data elements available for self-description and expression of one's personality can be further subdivided into mandatory and optional data types.

4.2.1.1 Mandatory data Similar to the physical world, a minimal set of data is required to initiate social interaction. Consequently, this class covers data that is needed for an OSN service to be useful and to enable basic functionalities such as user discovery and verification purposes. Mandatory data refers to personal information that needs to be provided by the user during the registration or profile creation process (activity 7 in Figure 3), which -

except from the terminology used - corresponds with the works presented by Schneier [23] and Årnes et al. [29] (*cf.* Figure 2). A common example is the user's name serving as an identifier for other users to create a social graph. Due to age verification processes because of possibly inappropriate content and in order to preclude immature users, the user's birthday is also a frequently required attribute. Privacy implications for mandatory data depend on the concrete implementation by a OSN service provider. It needs to be examined whether mandatory data becomes part of the OSN user's profile and if privacy settings are available to restrict its visibility.

4.2.1.2 Optionally provided data Besides the mandatory data, several data types with clearly specified semantics exist on OSNs that are subsequently discussed.

Extended profile data: OSNs offer a variety of predefined attribute types that may be used to further describe particular aspects of one's personality. Note that extended profile data solely refers to the user's profile while other parts of an OSN account are covered by further data types. Consequently, properties of extended profile data are the following: profile-centricity, optionality, predefined attribute types with clear semantics, and in some cases predefined attribute values. Typically, the process of providing extended profile data (activity 7 in Figure 3) is guided by a form that contains input fields for attribute types, like address, education, favorite music, favorite films, hobbies, and interests. The profile picture, which is a common feature of OSNs, is also arranged in this category. According to Figure 2, this is in line with the conceptualizations presented by Schneier [23] and Årnes et al. [29], while the profiles' category presented by Beye et al. [28] is considered too coarse-grained. From the optionality of this data type, it follows that privacy risks are manageable as it is down to the user to decide whether to disclose a particular personal attribute. On closer examination, available privacy settings are to be considered as these define the granularity of the potential audience that may access an attribute.

Ratings/Interests: Besides the extended profile data that allows for a rich description, the study of user activities (activities 5 and 9 in Figure 3) reveals that binary or predefined multi-value attributes related to existing entities such as pages and shared items which are used to refine how one is seen by others (e.g., by liking favorite bands). Corresponding with the data type proposed by Beye et al. [28] in Figure 2, this class of data covers expressed interests such as Facebook's Like and Google's +1 and the rating of photos shared by other users. With regards to privacy, two aspects need to be discussed. On the one hand, privacy implications and privacy control depend on default or available visibility settings. On the other hand and in contrast to the structured listing of

mandatory and extended profile data, ratings and interests are typically bound to items shared by others and hence are widely distributed across the OSN. Thus, awareness of previously expressed ratings and interests becomes increasingly important as it may allow others to draw inferences from all instances of this data type about the user's personality.

Network data: As social interaction is an inherent property of OSNs, users are encouraged to express their relationship with other users (activity 5 in Figure 3). The collection of all connections of a particular user is often referred to as his social graph [28] and describes data concerning the network the user has built around himself on the OSN, which conforms to the definition of Årnes et al. [29] as presented in Figure 2. From the viewpoint of a particular user, a single instance of network data has a binary value, i.e., a connection either exists or not. Network data may be uni- or bidirectional and differ in the strength of a connection. Common examples include the notions of friend, friend-of-friend, follower, and someone you are following. Depending on its concrete implementation, network data may be visible by default or access to it can be controlled by the user. Access to network data can be considered to have a significant impact on privacy. On the one hand, knowledge of a user's social graph allows to draw inferences about his identity and enables sybil attacks on other OSNs by forging the user's identity and connected identities [39]. On the other hand, it has been demonstrated that (partial) knowledge of a user's social graph (such as knowledge of groups he is member of) is sufficient to reveal his identity [40].

Contextual data: While some data shared on OSNs contains an atomic piece of information (such as the user's birthdate), other items such as pictures enclose a multitude of information. This class of data refers to a property of an existing item that is made explicit and provided with semantics, hence forming a new data type. Common examples include the tagging feature, allowing to make peoples' names (and eventually their identity) in an existing picture explicitly available to other OSN users (activity 3 in Figure 3). Further instances are the location of a picture and the relation of a shared item to an activity or an event. The comparison of existing taxonomies in Figure 2 shows that while corresponding with Beye et al.'s taxonomy [28], this type of data is only partly covered by Schneier [23] and Årnes et al. [29]. Two aspects of contextual data are particularly of importance when assessing the privacy risk. Firstly, contextual data is often a byproduct of its primary data type and as such is sometimes not explicitly visible to the user. As an example, a shared picture may contain a variety of information including the camera model, camera owner and location. Secondly, contextual data is often machine-processable (while its host data type can be semantically unspecified). Consequently, it allows service providers to extrapolite from contextual data to the content of the host data type.

4.2.2 Semantically unspecified

Semantically unspecified data refers to data elements provided by the OSN where the data format is predefined but whose content is left to the user and cannot trivially be interpreted by machines. For instance, a photo album feature predefines the format (digital photos) but leaves the picture's content to the user (yet it is notable that OSN service providers are increasingly making progress on face recognition technologies). As a consequence, on the one hand, it is difficult to make generalizations on privacy risks associated with semantically unspecified data types where risks largely depend on the content. On the other hand, the lack of semantic specification impedes OSN service providers from automatically processing this data. To further refine the classification, a distinction can be made between data used in 1:1 and 1:n communication.

4.2.2.1 Private communication data
This class covers data elements that originate from private communication (i.e., 1:1 communication) between two OSN users (activity 4 in Figure 3), which is only partly covered in Beye et al. [28] as illustrated in Figure 2. While private communication may comprise text messages as well as other media formats, their content is not semantically specified. Examples include private messages with or without attachments, private video chats as well as smaller interactions such as poking other users. Private communication data is not accompanied with privacy risks as long as the communication partner can be trusted, the OSN security mechanisms prevent third parties from gaining access, and the OSN service provider does not inspect the messages to an extent greater than roughly scanning them for illegal content.

4.2.2.2 1 : n communication
Besides private communication between two users, data with semantically unspecified content can be shared with an audience of n other users where n defines the degree of publicness. Each of the subsequently discussed data types is concerned with semantically unstructured data such as photos, status messages, and comments, yet a differentiation is made between creator, publisher, and the domain in which the element is published (see Table 1). As can be seen from Figure 2, the first three data types subsequently discussed are based on the work presented by Schneier [23] and Årnes et al. [29].

Disclosed data: A frequent user activity on OSNs is to post information on one's wall (activities 2 and 11 in Figure 3). In conceptual terms, the data is generated and published by a user in his own domain. Privacy of disclosed data largely depends on the availability of visibility

Table 1 Differences between disclosed data, entrusted data, incidental data, and shared data

	Creator	Publisher	Domain
Disclosed data	User	User	User
Entrusted data	User	User	Contact
Incidental data	Contact	Contact	User
Disseminated data	User	Contact	Contact

settings and the concrete implementation of the OSN service provider. Apart from this, privacy is not affected as the user is both the creator and publisher of the item (i.e., he intentionally wants the data instance to be visible to others), and it is shared within the domain of the user (no other users are affected with the shared item).

Entrusted data: In contrast, entrusted data refers to information that is both user-generated and user-published but in the domain of a contact (activities 2 and 10 in Figure 3), i.e., the former is able to shape the latter's representation on the OSN. Consequently, once the data is shared, control passes over to the domain owner that is from then on able to define its visibility. Whether this ability is only extended or shifts completely depends on the concrete OSN. Examples include posts and comments made on another user's wall or a similar space. Privacy implications mainly arise from the loss of control once the data element is published.

Incidental data: Incidental data originates from a contact sharing a data element on the user's wall (activities 1 and 11 in Figure 3), i.e., the contact is both the creator and publisher, however, the information is shared in the user's domain. In this scenario, a contact is able to shape the presentation of the user on the OSN. As a consequence, the user gains control over the item, whereas the extent depends on the concrete implementation.

Disseminated data: In the last case of Table 1, user-generated data elements that are considered are further disseminated by a contact within his own domain (activities 1 and 10 in Figure 3). This may include data elements that the user has initially shared with the contact or provided to him using other communication channels. In the first case, which is also discussed by Hu et al. [22], the OSN may prevent the contact from publishing the item with a larger than the user's intended audience and grant additional permissions to the user. However, in the second case, the contact remains the only person to control the visibility of the data element, raising serious privacy implications.

4.3 Summary

Figure 4 provides an overview of the proposed taxonomy based on the previous discussion. It comprises 13 data types that are integrated in a hierarchical structure. The

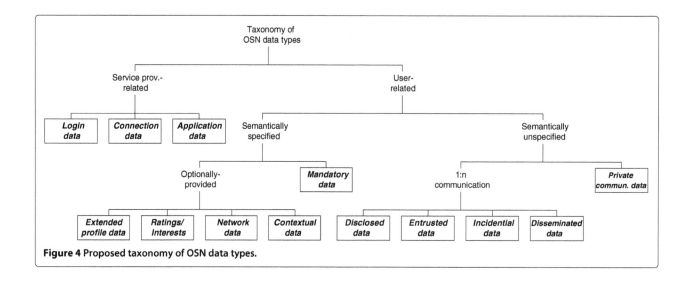

Figure 4 Proposed taxonomy of OSN data types.

analysis of privacy implications of data types revealed that privacy mainly depends on the interplay of a data element's content, the extent and granularity of user control, and its concrete implementation. The content may be easily accessible to service providers for data types with clear semantics, while semantically unspecified data requires human cognition for interpretation. Besides, each service provider decides whether the collection and visibility of a particular data type is user-controllable. If user control exists, its granularity largely depends on the concrete OSN implementation.

5   Toward a metric for assessing privacy relevance

Taking a bird's-eye view on our taxonomy, it becomes clear that the data types classified differ in the privacy risks they are accompanied with. Private communication data, for instance, is obviously not privacy critical as long as the communication partner is known and trusted. Disclosed data, in contrast, can be critical since one may easily lose track of who is able to read the content. Furthermore, permissions or social graph structures could change over time. As a result, a user could suddenly see messages that were originally not visible to him. In order to make the privacy relevance quantitatively measurable, a privacy relevance metric (PRM) is needed.

OSN data is always created within a specific context, which can be described through various attributes. The range comprises general factors such as audience size or audience composition as well as content-specific attributes like the topic of a message. These attributes form a finite context set $C = \{c_1, c_2, \ldots, c_n\}$. Based on this context set which serves as an input, our metric should calculate the privacy relevance of a data type. For this purpose, we compare the input context set (subsequently denoted as b) to a reference context set (subsequently

denoted as a) which describes a scenario having no privacy issues. The outcome of the comparison should be a value within the range [0,1] with 0 denoting no privacy relevance (reference value) and 1 denoting maximum privacy relevance.

To this end, we first provide a generic PRM that can easily be adapted to a set of preselected context attributes. Secondly, we show how this generic PRM can be implemented for the three context attributes *audience size*, *domain*, and *creator and publisher*. In the evaluation section, we finally demonstrate our PRM by measuring the privacy relevance of the data types classified in our taxonomy for a fictive profile on Facebook.

To further ease the understanding, we will use the following worked example during the development of our metric: OSN user Jane posts a photograph within her domain (e.g., on her wall) and sets the visibility to all of her 150 friends (i.e., audience size = 150). Using the taxonomy, this is classified as *disclosed data*. For Jane, the size of the audience and who is creator and publisher is twice as important as the domain in which the photograph is posted.

5.1   Metric space and distance function

Context attributes can be modeled as a dimension in a vector space. Therefore, we define an n-dimensional metric space M, where each dimension is derived from one context attribute of the context set $C(|C| = n)$. We furthermore introduce n mapping functions $f_i(c)$ to range the context attributes to a predefined interval (either continuous or discrete). To measure the distance of points in the metric space M, various distance functions can be used. A function

$$d : M \times M \to \mathbb{R}$$

is called distance function if it satisfies the following conditions for all $a, b \in M$:

1. $d(a,b) \geq 0$
2. $d(a,b) = 0$ if and only $a = b$
3. $d(a,b) = d(b,a)$
4. $d(a,c) \leq d(a,b) + d(b,c)$

Exemplary distance measures are the Manhattan distance or the Euclidean distance which are two types of the generic Minowski distance. The decision which distance measure to use depends on the application area. In this work, we chose the Manhattan distance which is more robust to outliers.

To implement an exemplary PRM, we selected the three context attributes *audience size*, *domain*, and *creator and publisher*. These attributes form our context set $C = \{c_1, c_2, c_3\}$, where c_1 takes values of the discrete interval $C_1 = \{0, 1, 2, \ldots\}$, while c_2 and c_3 take values of the nominal sets $C_2 = \{$user, contact$\}$ and $C_3 = \{$ (user, user), (user, contact), (contact, contact)$\}$.

The space M^{prae} is defined as follows:

$$M^{\mathrm{prae}} : = C_1 \times C_2 \times C_3$$

In M^{prae}, the single attributes are not comparable in their values. This might lead to a bias in the final context value. The *audience size*, for instance, is not necessarily bounded from above allowing very high distances between its members. The distances between members of the nominal sets *domain* and *creator and publisher* must be transformed before they can be measured. Hence, we define three mapping functions $f_i(c)$ to range the values within an interval of $[0, \gamma_i]$. γ_i is the weight factor that allows to weight single context attributes based on their importance. For $\gamma_1 = \gamma_2 = \gamma_3$, each dimension has the same impact on the global PRM. Thus, we define the final metric space M as

$$M : = [0, \gamma_1] \times [0, \gamma_2] \times [0, \gamma_3]$$

To make the privacy relevance measurable, we define the distance function $\tilde{d}$ in our metric space M as follows:

$$\tilde{d} : M \times M \to \left[0, \sum_{i=1}^{3} \gamma_i \right], \quad (a, b) \mapsto \sum_{i=1}^{3} (b_i - a_i)$$

A reasonable and intuitively understandable value range for the distance as a relevance measure is [0,1] with 1 denoting a maximum privacy relevance and 0 denoting no privacy relevance (absolute congruence to reference set). Therefore, $\tilde{d}$ is scaled by the inverse of $\tilde{d}_{\max} = \sum_{i=1}^{3} \gamma_i$

which quantifies the length of the diagonal in the metric space. That leads to the final distance function d:

$$d : M \times M \to [0, 1]$$

$$d(a, b) := \frac{\tilde{d}(a, b)}{\tilde{d}_{\max}} = \frac{\sum_{i=1}^{3} (b_i - a_i)}{\sum_{i=1}^{3} (\gamma_i)}$$

5.2 Context dimensions

The context dimensions depict the single attributes of the context set C. Since the context attributes consist of both structured and unstructured data of random values, modeling the mapping functions $f_i(c)$ can turn out to be difficult. However, this is an important step because parameters that vary greatly in size may have a much bigger impact on the distance than parameters that differ only slightly, even though slight distinctions could have an equal impact on the changes in context. In the following paragraphs, we define the mapping functions $f_i(c)$ for the three context attributes *audience size*, *domain*, and *creator and publisher*. In more detail, for each of the three attributes of input context set b, a mapping function $f_i(c)$ is defined. The same mapping functions are used for each of the three attributes of reference context set a.

5.2.1 Audience size

As stated above, the audience size is critical for privacy issues since an increased audience leads to a higher privacy risk. However, privacy relevance is not static and exactly the same for similar classes in different profiles. It depends on a user's number of friends. To capture this, we propose the following function:

$$f_1(c_1) = \gamma_1 * \left(1 - e^{\frac{c_1 * \ln(0.5)}{n_f}} \right)$$

with c_1 depicting the audience size and n_f quantifying a user's number of friends. The outcome of this function ranges in the interval of $[0, \gamma_1)$. Content that is only visible to the creator (audience size = 0) results in a value of 0, whereas content visible to the user's friends is reflected in a value of $0.5\gamma_1$. The value converges to γ_1 for content being visible to all friends-of-friends or all users. The logic modeled in this metric states that the growth of perceived privacy risk decreases with an increasing audience size. This coherence can be easily understood thinking of a user who shares a secret with one person. Having told two persons instead, the perceived privacy risk would have been notably higher. Now think of 1,000 persons. The difference of perceived privacy risk compared to sharing the private information with 1,001 persons instead would have been marginal.

Continuing the worked example introduced previously and assuming a weight factor of 2, the privacy relevance of Jane's audience size of 150 friends is calculated as follows:

$$f_1(c_1) = 2 * \left(1 - e^{\frac{150*\ln(0.5)}{150}}\right) = 1$$

5.2.2 Domain

Data can either be published in the user's or in a contact's domain. If shared in the own domain, the user is the data owner and can regulate the visibility and availability. Published in a contact's domain, in contrast, one passes these privileges. That may lead to increased privacy risk. We therefore model the domain function as follows:

$$f_2(c_2) = \begin{cases} 0, & \text{if } c_2 = \text{user} \\ \gamma_2, & \text{if } c_2 = \text{contact} \end{cases}$$

In the worked example, a weight factor for the domain of 1 was assumed. Hence, the privacy relevance of the domain attribute is calculated as follows:

$$f_2(c_2) = 1 * 0 = 0$$

5.2.3 Creator and publisher

Serious privacy concerns are raised if the user creates content that is further disseminated by a contact within his own domain. The user thereby loses control of his own content. The third function is designed to cover this case:

$$f_3(c_3) = \begin{cases} \gamma_3, & \text{if } c_3 = \{\text{user, contact}\} \\ 0, & \text{else} \end{cases}$$

A weight factor of 2 for the creator and publisher attribute in our worked example leads to the following calculation:

$$f_3(c_3) = 2 * 0 = 0$$

Based on these results, the overall privacy relevance for Jane in the worked example can be calculated. As previously defined, the privacy relevance for each attribute of the reference context set a is 0. Hence the overall privacy relevance is

$$d(a,b) = \frac{(1-0) + (0-0) + (0-0)}{2+1+2} = \frac{1}{5} = 0.2$$

6 Evaluation

Two approaches are used to evaluate the proposed taxonomy, namely, demonstration (which is described as a light-weight evaluation by Venable et al. [35]) of its efficiency to solve a certain problem [34] and evaluation of its suitability to map all data types of a given OSN. In

the first part of the evaluation, five major OSNs - Facebook, Google+, Twitter, LinkedIn, and Instagram - are analyzed under the aspect of using the proposed taxonomy. Note that the intention of the analysis is to show the feasibility of the taxonomy in general and to present the most common and most important examples for each data type. With the help of these examples, the main differences between the inspected OSNs can be shown in a descriptive way that is comprehensible for casual OSN users as well. The differences are highlighted by referring to the availability and importance of the data types on the particular OSN but also by pointing out existing privacy implications and user control mechanisms. The second part of the evaluation takes the opposite direction, setting the starting point to the OSN (i.e., Facebook) with all its data types. These data types are mapped into the taxonomy in order to show that it is able to cover all of them. Finally, we demonstrate our privacy relevance metric and discuss its benefits and shortcomings.

6.1 Application of the taxonomy to OSNs

Table 2 gives an overview on the data types of the inspected OSNs as available on 4 March 2014.

6.1.1 Service provider-related data types

Login data can be found on all OSNs. Facebook, Google+, Twitter, and LinkedIn all provide a login via email and password. On Facebook, the phone number can replace the email. On Twitter, a login is alternatively possible via username and password. As opposed to the other four OSNs, Instagram does not provide a login via email but only via username.

Connection data is collected by all OSNs. In order to inspect the items arranged in this category, the privacy policies of the five OSNs have been analyzed. It is important to state that these policies do not list every single data item collected through the use of the platform. For example, Google tries to arrange the collected data into categories (e.g., device information, log information, location information) and then mentions the most important examples with the help of expressions like 'such as' and 'may include.' However, splitting up connection data in the three data types mentioned above does not lead to better results regarding the taxonomy because the analyzed providers do not define them in the same way. Moreover, the five inspected OSNs differ in the examples they list and their level of detail. Nevertheless, all OSNs collect similar data items that can be arranged in the categories used by Google, which is why we also employ them in Table 2.

Application data is available on all five inspected OSNs because for all of them, there are connectors for external websites or unofficial smartphone apps. On Facebook and Google+, the number of third party applications

Table 2 Demonstration of the taxonomy on Facebook, Google+, Twitter, LinkedIn, and Instagram

Data types	Facebook	Google+	Twitter	LinkedIn	Instagram
Login data	Email, phone, password	Email, password	Email, username, password	Email, password	Username, password
Connection data	Device, log, and location information, cookies	Device, log, and location information, cookies	Device, log, and location information, cookies	Device, log, and location information, cookies	Device, log, and location information, cookies
Application data	Usage statistics, credit card data	Usage statistics, credit card data	Usage statistics	Usage statistics	Usage statistics
Mandatory data	Name, email, birthday, gender	Name, email, birthday, gender	Name, email	Name, email, job status, country, postal code	Name, email
Extended profile data	General-purpose input fields	General-purpose input fields	Bio, location, website	Professionally related input fields	Phone, gender, bio, website
Ratings/Interests	Page, status/photo/video	Page, status/photo/video	Verified account, Tweet	Organization, status	Photo/video
Network data	Unidirectional, bidirectional	Unidirectional	Unidirectional	Bidirectional	Unidirectional
Contextual data	Tag in status/comment, on photo, at location	Tag in status/comment, on photo, at location	Mention in Tweet	Tag in status/comment	Tag on photo
Private commun. data	Private message, video chat, poke	Private message, video chat	Private message	Private message, InMail	N/A
Disclosed data	Text post, photo (album), video, check-in	Text post, photo (album), video, check-in	Text post, single photo	Text post, single photo, file attachments	Single photo, video
Entrusted data	See disclosed data	Restricted to comments	N/A	Restricted to comments	Restricted to comments
Incidental data	See disclosed data	Restricted to comments	N/A	Restricted to comments	Restricted to comments
Disseminated data	See disclosed data	See disclosed data	See disclosed data	See disclosed data	See disclosed data

is bigger by far as there are a lot of providers for games. As mentioned in Section 4, games may process credit card information because of in-app purchases, whereas website connectors and smartphone apps do not collect additional data (i.e., in addition to the data already available without using the application) except for the usage statistics. An important characteristic of application data is its optionality, i.e., the user decides about the use of third party applications. In the majority of cases, confirmation for requested permissions is required before being able to use an application. Consequently, user control is implemented on a binary decision basis.

6.1.2   User-related data types

As all OSNs include profiles, mandatory data and extended profile data always exist. Basic items of *mandatory data* are name, email, birthday, and gender. The first two items are mandatory on all inspected OSNs; the latter two items are only required on Facebook and Google+. There is a peculiarity regarding email being mandatory on Google+. Users do not have to provide an email account in the first place but Google will automatically create one for them, which is why we treat email also as mandatory here. LinkedIn forces a new user to indicate his country and postal code for networking purposes. Moreover, his job status is mandatory as well, which is motivated by the way LinkedIn describes itself - as a network for professionals. Note that email, birthday, and gender can usually be hidden from other users, giving the user the ability to alleviate certain threats (e.g., social engineering attacks with the help of personalized emails). If mandatory attributes are hidden, they are only used for internal purposes, such as using the user's gender in order to address him with the correct pronouns.

Which *extended profile data* is ultimately present in addition to the profile photo and the cover photo - each inspected OSN uses at least the concept of the profile photo - depends on whether the OSN is a platform for general purposes (e.g., Facebook, Google+) or for rather specialized ones (e.g., LinkedIn). Facebook and Google+ offer the user the ability to provide a variety of attributes such as basic info, contact info, work, education, and living. Similarly, LinkedIn offers additional data elements to refine one's profile but with a professional focus (such as experience, skills, publications, and awards). In contrast to the three OSNs mentioned before, Twitter does not focus on this detailed self-presentation in one's profile and only offers three single input fields for extended profile data. Instagram also only offers the input fields of Twitter and adds the phone number as a fourth data item. Although the provision of extended profile data is optional on all OSNs, only Facebook and Google+ offer a selective disclosure of attribute values. On Twitter, LinkedIn, and

Instagram, they are either publicly visible or only available to oneself.

Ratings/Interests is a category that possesses differing importance on OSNs but can be observed on all of them. On Facebook and Google+, it is possible to express one's preference for all kinds of pages (e.g., persons, products, sports). On Twitter and LinkedIn, the pages mainly resemble verified accounts of well-known persons and organizations, respectively. Moreover, the focus lies more on staying informed about these pages rather than publicly demonstrating certain interests. Instagram is quite similar to Twitter with regards to following pages of well-known persons in order to stay up-to-date on them. However, there are currently no indicators that officially verify a celebrity page. Besides the pages mentioned above, the inspected OSNs all provide mechanisms to express one's favor for the items that are available as disclosed data. When focusing on the user's control over the visibility of his preferences, pages and disclosed data have to be discussed separately. For disclosed data, the visibility of one's favor always depends on the visibility of the corresponding item, whereas for pages, the visibility options are different on the inspected platforms. As following pages on Twitter and Instagram is done by establishing a unidirectional connection to them, the visibility properties are them same as for network data (see below), which means that the pages users follow are publicly visible. Users of Facebook and Google+ have the option to hide their preferences.

As the term *Online Social Network* already indicates, OSNs always include *network data*. The main difference between OSNs is whether the connections are bidirectional (e.g., Facebook, LinkedIn) or unidirectional (e.g., Google+, Twitter, Instagram). As shown in Table 2, Facebook is the only OSN that supports both types of connections at the same time. However, the unidirectional connections have to be enabled by the user before others are able to follow him without befriending him. Another important difference can be observed when analyzing the user's ability to hide his social graph from other users. Facebook, Google+, and LinkedIn implement this feature, whereas Twitter and Instagram always reveal your followers and the users you are following.

Further differences between the inspected OSNs can be observed when analyzing the presence of *contextual data*. On Facebook and Google+, the user has the ability to tag his contacts in text posts/comments, on photos, and at locations. Although being limited to text posts, Twitter's tagging feature creates more extensive privacy issues than the ones provided by Facebook and Google+ because Twitter's users lack the ability to remove these tags on their own. LinkedIn also limits the tagging feature to referencing contacts in text posts/comments but here, these references can be easily removed. Instagram supports tags on photos.

Private communication data can be found on all inspected OSNs except Instagram. Facebook and Google+ offer this feature via instant messaging and without any limitations concerning availability and text length. On Twitter, private messages are provided via *Direct Messages*, which resemble a private *Tweet* and therefore are limited to 140 characters. Apart from messages to contacts, LinkedIn provides a feature called *InMail*, which is advertised as a professional and credible way to reach anyone on LinkedIn without prior introduction but which is only available to premium users. In addition to text messages, Facebook and Google+ offer video chats as another type of private communication data. Facebook also has the poking feature mentioned in Section 4. The only way of privately contacting another user on Instagram is to use Instagram Direct, a feature that was introduced in December 2013, and disclose a photo or video item only for that particular person. Thus, the two users are able to chat via the comments under the item.

Significant discrepancies concerning the availability of the data types have been identified when posting items. Firstly, there are differences in the complexity of the items and secondly, the ability to post them may be restricted to the user's own domain. Facebook and Google+ enable their users to post text, photos, photo albums, videos, their current location, and other objects (e.g., questions, events). LinkedIn users are also able to post text and single photos but cannot create entire albums. However, they can enrich their status updates with other documents, such as MS Office files or PDF files. In contrast, Twitter limits its *Tweets* to text and single photos. Note that users have the possibility to enrich their text posts with their current location or a link to an uploaded video but not to disclose these elements outside of a Tweet. Posting on Instagram is - because of its specialized character - limited to single photos and videos, which can also be enriched with a location. Regardless of the complexity of the items, the user is always able to post them in his own domain (*disclosed data*) as well as to share the ones originally published by his contacts (*disseminated data*). On the contrary, posting in foreign domains without any content-wise limitations is only possible on Facebook (*entrusted data* and vice versa *incidental data*). However, Facebook's users can turn off this feature in their privacy settings and are able to control the visibility of incidental data on a fine-grained level. On Google+, LinkedIn, and Instagram, posting in foreign domains is limited to commenting on items disclosed by the domain's owner. These comments inherit the visibility of their corresponding items, giving the domain's owner full control over them. To be precise, LinkedIn users are able to post on organizations' pages. But what we understand by foreign domains are the domains of other human contacts. Publicly addressing contacts on Twitter is done by making a response (e.g., @johndoe), which does not appear in the contact's domain and therefore is not treated as entrusted data. With Instagram Direct, users are able to directly share photos and videos with 1 to up to 15 contacts. But similar to Twitter, media shared in this way stay in the user's domain and do not represent entrusted data. Moreover, Instagram Direct has to be seen as some kind of access control mechanism rather than posting in foreign domains. As incidental data is just the opposite of entrusted data, it is limitedly present on Google+, LinkedIn, and Instagram, and cannot be found on Twitter.

Summarizing the application of the taxonomy, most of its elements can be found on all of the five inspected OSNs demonstrating the suitability to describe the most important characteristics of OSNs. Furthermore, it demonstrated the taxonomy's capability of capturing different instantiations of a particular data type on different OSNs and the number of items contained in it. This is especially true for extended profile data where Twitter and Instagram provide only a few additional input fields because self-presentation is achieved by posting items and not by entering static profile information here, and where LinkedIn focuses more on work and science affiliated attributes because of the orientation toward professional networks. Another important observation is that Facebook has most features, especially concerning the distinctive data types, i.e., entrusted/incidental data and contextual data. Hence, there are more potential hazards for casual OSN users and more aspects that might be interesting for researchers in this area.

6.2 Mapping of Facebook data types into the taxonomy

In the previous section, we successfully applied the taxonomy to compare different OSNs, demonstrating its usefulness in one of its major usage scenarios. Subsequently, we evaluate its ability to cover all data types existing on OSNs by iterating overall OSN data types and mapping them into the taxonomy. Hereunto, Facebook as the currently largest and most popular OSN is used.

Facebook's Graph API reference [19] is employed in order to capture all data types. In particular, the focus is on the root node */user* including all of its edges and fields except for */user/home* and */user/notifications*, which are only used internally by Facebook for notification purposes related to other data types. Besides the */user* node, few other nodes contain data types related to the user. They are marked by an asterisk (*) in Figure 5, which provides an overview of the mapping of the aforementioned data types into our taxonomy. Note that the denomination of the root node */user* is omitted to improve readability. A prefixed slash (/) is used to distinguish edges from fields. In order to cover all user-related data types on Facebook, we

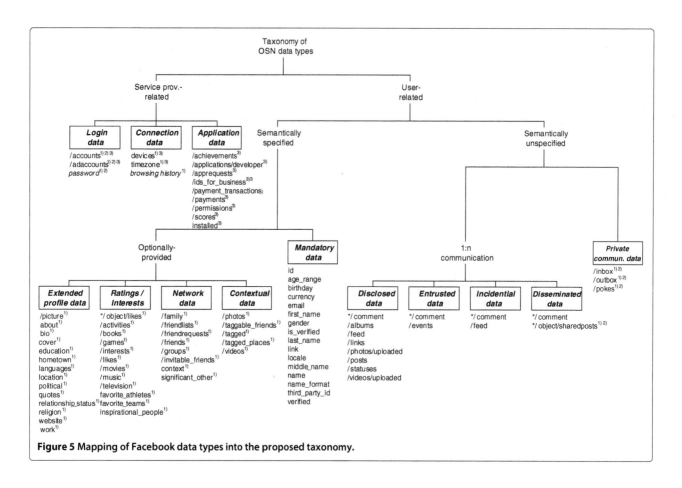

Figure 5 Mapping of Facebook data types into the proposed taxonomy.

further include additional data types (such as connection data and login data, e.g., the user's password and browsing history) into our analysis in addition to Facebook's Graph API reference.

Sections 2 and 4 already contain some exemplary remarks concerning the shortcomings of the previously published taxonomies. In order to illustrate their limitations in detail, in Figure 5, we show their inability to map some of Facebook's data types (i.e., no suitable data type exists in their taxonomies). Data types that cannot be mapped into the taxonomy introduced by Schneier [23] are marked with [1], while those that cannot be mapped into the taxonomies introduced by Årnes et al.[29] and Beye et al. [28] are marked with [2] and [3], respectively. For instance, Schneier's taxonomy [23] can be criticized for not being able to cover login data, connection data, extended profile data, ratings/interests, network data, contextual data, disseminated data, and private communication data. The work presented by Årnes et al. [29] improves on this but still does not feature any equivalents for login data, disseminated data, and private communication data. The taxonomy of Beye et al. [28] has shortcomings related to its insufficient definitions of login credentials as well as behavioral information and, additionally, is missing an equivalent for application data.

Although it is possible to map the data types related to $1:n$ communication and private communication into the categories proposed by Beye et al. [28], a lot of privacy-relevant information is lost when treating all of them simply under the general term *Messages*.

6.3 Evaluation of the privacy relevance metric

As pointed out, privacy relevance depends on multiple factors and varies for different OSNs and user profiles. To demonstrate our metric, we created a fictive user profile on Facebook that has 150 friends ($n_f = 150$). We mainly used Facebook's default privacy settings. However, we changed the visibility of extended profile data to 'friends' in order to demonstrate the differences. For login data, connection data, and application data, a value of 0 was defined since the service provider is assumed to be trusted. As weighting parameter we chose $\gamma_1 = 2$, $\gamma_2 = 1$, and $\gamma_3 = 2$. The reference context set is defined to entail no privacy risk ($c_1 = 0$, $c_2 =$ user, $c_3 = $ {user,user}). For the friends of our fictive user, we assumed the same privacy settings, leading to the following values as depicted in Table 3.

The privacy relevance metric introduced could clarify that the different data types of OSN data classified in our taxonomy greatly vary in the privacy risks they carry.

Table 3 Proposed PRM for classes of the taxonomy by the example of a Facebook profile

Data types	PRM-value
Login data	0
Connection data	0
Application data	0
Mandatory data	0.4
Extended profile data	0.2
Ratings/ interests	0.6
Network data	0.4
Contextual data	0.6
Private commun. data	≈ 0
Disclosed data	0.2
Entrusted data	0.6
Incidental data	0.2
Disseminated data	0.8

These findings can help end users to increase their privacy awareness when dealing with OSN data, on the one hand. Particularly, the fact that the loss of control over own data carries high risk is an essential and valuable insight gained. The service providers, on the other hand, can benefit as well, since this metric may suggest which concepts should be revised in order to foster user privacy and improve the quality of their services with regard to privacy.

This quite generic approach also brings some limitations that need to be discussed. Currently, the metric does not consider different expectations of the end users toward privacy. To cover this issue, the context dimensions could be extended by user sensitivity. In this paper, however, our aim is to emphasize the difference of privacy risks attributed to distinct data types. Thus, we left varying end user perceptions out of consideration for the moment. The weight parameters were furthermore only exemplary chosen to demonstrate the functioning. To create a more realistic setting, empirical tests to find appropriate values should be conducted in the future.

7 Conclusions

Despite the growing body of research addressing OSN privacy issues, currently, *data* as one of the fundamental building blocks of OSN is not well understood. The lack of a generally accepted terminology and classification for existing data elements as well as the small number of publications considering implications of differing semantics of data types for social identity management further substantiates the argument.

Yet, data is at the core of any discussion of privacy issues on OSNs. Without a precise terminology and classification of all types of data on OSNs, it is difficult to unambiguously specify privacy-related problems which ultimately impedes the development of appropriate solutions.

To address these shortcomings, a taxonomy for OSN data types was developed in this paper. Based on a design-oriented methodology, first, the body of literature was analyzed to identify possible data elements and terminological inconsistencies. Subsequently, a hierarchically structured taxonomy was derived by studying fundamental user activities on OSNs and step-wise classifying the identified data types into non-redundant partitions. The discussion of data types revealed that privacy mainly depends on the interplay of a data element's content, the extent and granularity of user control, and its concrete implementation. Based on the understanding of privacy implications of different data types, a privacy relevance metric was proposed which allows to quantitatively assess privacy threats for a given context. The subsequent evaluation of applying the taxonomy to five major OSNs demonstrates its applicability to existing OSNs and reveals implementation-specific differences in privacy settings of various data types. A detailed evaluation using all of Facebook's data types further shows that it is possible to map all these data types into the taxonomy.

Endnote

[a]Note that this article is an extended version of the paper by Richthammer et al. presented at the 2013 ARES conference [41].

Competing interests

The authors declare that they have no competing interests.

Acknowledgements

The authors would like to thank the anonymous reviewers for their helpful comments. This research is partly funded by the European Union within the PADGETS project (no. 248920), the European Regional Development Funds (ERDF) within the SECBIT project (http://www.secbit.de/) and by the 'Bavarian State Ministry of Education, Science and the Arts' as part of the FORSEC research association (http://www.bayforsec.de/).

References

1. D Boyd, N Ellison, Social network sites – definition, history, and scholarship. J. Comput.-Mediated Commun. **13**, 210–230 (2007)
2. MM Skeels, J Grudin, When social networks cross boundaries: a case study of workplace use of Facebook and LinkedIn, in *Proceedings of the International SIGGROUP Conference on Supporting Group Work* (ACM New York, 2009)
3. K Riemer, A Richter, Tweet inside: microblogging in a corporate context, in *Proceedings of the 23rd Bled eConference eTrust: Implications for the Individual, Enterprises and Society*, (2010)
4. J Park, S Kim, C Kamhoua, K Kwiat, Optimal state management of data sharing in online social network (OSN) services, in *Proceedings of the 11th IEEE International Conference on Trust, Security and Privacy in Computing and Communications (TrustCom)* (IEEE Computer Society Washington, DC, 2012)
5. D Irani, S Webb, K Li, C Pu, Large online social footprints – an emerging threat, in *Proceedings of the 12th IEEE International Conference on*

Computational Science and Engineering (CSE) (IEEE Computer Society Washington, 2009)

6. T Burns, *Erving Goffman*. (Taylor & Francis, New York, 1991)

7. E Goffman, *The Presentation of Self in Everyday Life*. (Anchor, New York, 1959)

8. H Nissenbaum, *Privacy in Context - Technology, Policy, and the Integrity of Social Life*. (Stanford University Press, Stanford, 2010)

9. M Netter, M Riesner, G Pernul, Assisted social identity management, in *Proceedings of the 10th International Conference on Wirtschaftsinformatik* (AIS Electronic Library Zurich, 2011)

10. A Ho, A Maiga, E Aimeur, Privacy protection issues in social networking sites, in *Proceedings of the 2009 ACS/IEEE International Conference on Computer Systems and Applications (AICCSA)* (IEEE Computer Society Los Alamitos, 2009)

11. M Madejski, M Johnson, S Bellovin, The failure of online social network privacy settings. Technical report, (Columbia University 2011). http://academiccommons.columbia.edu/download/fedora_content/download/ac:135407/CONTENT/cucs-010-11.pdf. Accessed 19 July 2014

12. C Ngeno, P Zavarsky, D Lindskog, R Ruhl, User's perspective: privacy and security of information on social networks, in *Proceedings of the 2nd IEEE International Conference on Social Computing (SocialCom)* (IEEE Computer Society Washington, DC, 2010)

13. M Netter, M Riesner, M Weber, G Pernul, Privacy settings in online social networks – preferences, perception, and reality, in *Proceedings of the 46th Hawaii International Conference on Systems Science* (IEEE Computer Society Washington, DC, 2013)

14. D Rosenblum, What anyone can know: the privacy risks of social networking sites. IEEE Secur. & Privacy. **5**, 40–49 (2007)

15. D Michalopoulos, I Mavridis, Surveying privacy leaks through online social networks, in *Proceedings of the 14th Panhellenic Conference on Informatics (PCI)* (IEEE Computer Society Washington, DC, 2010)

16. H Lipford, A Besmer, J Watson, Understanding privacy settings in Facebook with an audience view, in *Proceedings of the 1st Conference on Usability, Psychology, and Security (UPSEC)* (USENIX Association Berkeley, 2008)

17. B Carminati, E Ferrari, R Heatherly, M Kantarcioglu, B Thuraisingham, Semantic web-based social network access control. Comput. & Secur. **30**(2–3), 108–115 (2011)

18. W Luo, Q Xie, U Hengartner, FaceCloak: an architecture for user privacy on social networking sites, in *Proceedings of the 12th IEEE International Conference on Computational Science and Engineering (CSE)* (IEEE Computer Society Washington, DC, 2009)

19. Facebook Graph API Reference. https://developers.facebook.com/docs/graph-api. Accessed 4 July 2014

20. P Fong, M Anwar, Z Zhao, A privacy preservation model for Facebook-style social network systems, in *Proceedings of the 14th European Conference on Research in Computer Security (ESORICS)* (Springer Berlin, Heidelberg, 2009)

21. J Park, R Sandhu, Y Cheng, ACON: activity-centric access control for social computing, in *Proceedings of the 6th International Conference on Availability, Reliability and Security (ARES)* (IEEE Computer Society Washington, DC, 2011)

22. H Hu, G-J Ahn, J Jorgensen, Detecting and resolving privacy conflicts for collaborative data sharing in online social networks, in *Proceedings of the 27th Annual Computer Security Applications Conference (ACSAC)* (ACM New York, 2011)

23. B Schneier, A taxonomy of social networking data. IEEE Security & Privacy. **8**, 88–88 (2010)

24. M Riesner, G Pernul, Maintaining a consistent representation of self across multiple social networking sites – a data-centric perspective, in *Proceedings of the 2012 ASE/IEEE International Conference on Social Computing and 2012 ASE/IEEE International Conference on Privacy, Security, Risk and Trust* (IEEE Computer Society Washington, DC, 2012)

25. M Riesner, M Netter, G Pernul, An analysis of implemented and desirable settings for identity management on social networking sites, in *Proceedings of the 7th International Conference on Availability, Reliability and Security (ARES)* (IEEE Computer Society Washington, DC, 2012)

26. J Surma, A Furmanek, Improving marketing response by data mining in social network, in *Proceedings of the 2010 International Conference on Advances in Social Networks Analysis and Mining (ASONAM)* (IEEE Computer Society Los Alamitos, 2010)

27. J Zhang, J Tang, B Liang, Z Yang, S Wang, J Zuo, J Li, Recommendation over a heterogeneous social network, in *Proceedings of the 9th International Conference on Web-Age Information Management (WAIM)* (IEEE Computer Society Washington, DC, 2008)

28. M Beye, A Jeckmans, Z Erkin, P Hartel, R Lagendijk, Q Tang, Privacy in online social networks, in *Computational Social Networks: Security and Privacy* (Springer London, 2012)

29. A Årnes, J Skorstad, L Michelsen, Social network services and privacy. Technical report, Datatilsynet (2011). http://www.datatilsynet.no/global/english/11_00643_5_parti_rapport_facebook_2011.pdf. Accessed 19 July 2014

30. K Liu, E Terzi, A framework for computing the privacy scores of users in online social networks. ACM Trans. Knowl. Discov. Data. **5**(1), 1–30 (2010)

31. LA Cutillo, R Molva, M Önen, Analysis of privacy in online social networks from the graph theory perspective, in *Proceedings of the 2011 IEEE Global Telecommunications Conference (GLOBECOM)*, (2011), pp. 1–5

32. J Becker, H Chen, Measuring privacy risk in online social networks, in *Proceedings of W2SP 2009: Web 2.0 Security and Privacy*, (2009). http://w2spconf.com/2009/papers/s2p2.pdf. Accessed 19 July 2014

33. A Hevner, S March, J Park, S Ram, Design science in information systems research. MIS Q. **28**, 75–105 (2004)

34. K Peffers, T Tuunanen, M Rothenberger, S Chatterjee, A design science research methodology for information systems research. J. Manag. Inform. Syst. **24**, 45–77 (2007)

35. J Venable, J Pries-Heje, R Baskerville, A comprehensive framework for evaluation in design science research, in *Proceedings of the 7th International Conference on Design Science Research in Information Systems: Advances in Theory and Practice* (Springer Berlin, Heidelberg, 2012)

36. A Hevner, S Chatterjee, *Design Research in Information Systems: Theory and Practice*. (Springer, New York, 2010)

37. M Ziegele, O Quiring, Privacy Online. Perspectives on Privacy and Self-Disclosure in the Social Web (Springer Heidelberg, 2011)

38. P Eckersley, How unique is your web browser?, in *Proceedings of the 10th International Conference on Privacy Enhancing Technologies* PETS'10 (Springer Berlin, Heidelberg, 2010), pp. 1–18

39. B Carminati, E Ferrari, M Viviani, Security and Trust in Online Social Networks. Synthesis Lectures on Information Security, Privacy, and Trust. **4**(3), 1–120 (2013)

40. G Wondracek, T Holz, E Kirda, C Kruegel, A practical attack to de-anonymize social network users, in *Proceedings of the 2010 IEEE Symposium on Security and Privacy. S & P 2010* (IEEE Computer Society Washington, DC, 2010), pp. 223–238

41. C Richthammer, M Netter, M Riesner, G Pernul, Taxonomy for social network data types from the viewpoint of privacy and user control, in *Proceedings of the 8th International Conference on Availability, Reliability and Security (ARES)* (IEEE Computer Society Washington, DC, 2013), pp. 141–150

5

Cross-country analysis of spambots

Vaibhav Garg[1*], Thomas Koster[2] and Linda Jean Camp[2]

Abstract

Spam is a vector for cybercrime and commonly legally prohibited. Why do certain national jurisdictions produce a higher percentage of spam than others despite its prohibition? Why do some countries have a higher percentage of systems acting as spambots compared to other countries? We begin to answer there questions by conducting a cross-country empirical analysis of economic factors that correlate with the prevalence of spam and associated botnets. The economic factors under consideration are grounded in traditional theories of crime offline, as well as prior research in security economics. We found that more than 50% of spam can be attributed to having originated from merely seven countries, indicating that deterrence through policy is both feasible and economically rational. As expected, higher Internet adoption is correlated with higher percentage of spam from a country. Counterintuitively, Internet adoption is also positively correlated with the percentage of infected machines.

Keywords: Economics; Spam; Botnets; Security; Cybercrime

Introduction

The problem of junk email or spam was recognized as early as 1975 [1,2]. In 2010, Symantec reported that 89% of email messages were spam [3], while 88% of spam activity was attributed to spambots [4]. The existence of spambots is attributed to the existence of insecure software on the production side and lack of patching or adoption of security software, e.g., anti-virus software, by end-users (or consumers). This, however, does not (completely) explain why the percentage of spambots is different across countries. Some countries, such as India, always have a high proportion of spambots, and others, e.g., Sweden, do not. Unlike other bot activities, spambots need to be online for a shorter period of time. Thus, all bots are equally valued for sending spam [3]; bots with poor Internet connectivity, such as those in India, are as valuable as those in Sweden, which are likely to have more persistent connections.

The success of cybercrime is contingent on availability of such (spam) botnets. However, individuals whose systems are being exploited as bots do not typically agree to facilitate criminal enterprise. For example, Anonymous (a hacktivist group) tweaked its 'voluntary' botnet software, Low Orbit Ion Canon (LOIC), to trick unsuspecting bystanders into launching a distributed denial-of-service

(DDoS) attack on the US Justice Department [5]. Similarly, end-users, who are not technically savvy, may unsuspectingly participate as spambots. Deterrence-based approaches when applied to such unsuspecting naive end-users would be undesirable [6]. It would be unrealistic to expect such users to be responsible for their systems or hold them accountable for illicit activities, i.e., sending spam.

Spam, however, is not merely an annoyance but in fact has a significant financial impact. Spam campaigns are integral to the success of online scams, e.g., phishing, pharmaceutical spam [7]. The annual loss due to phishing, and possible gain to phishers, has been claimed to be as much as $178.1 million dollars a year [8]. Pharmaceutical spam revenues have been approximated to $3.5 million dollars [9], with transactions worth $170 million conducted over several years [10].

To alleviate the incentives for cyber-criminals to engage in illegal enterprise online, defenders endeavor to make attacks more expensive [11]. Simultaneously, criminals can be deterred through legal and regulatory solutions, i.e., prosecution [12] or takedowns by law enforcement [13]. While legal deterrence is promising [14], its impact may be limited [15]. For example, even when cyber-criminals are prosecuted, in the long term, they can move to another jurisdiction that is more forgiving of undesirable behavior. Note that for countries with non-extant legitimate information communication technology

*Correspondence: me@vaibhavgarg.net
[1]Department of Computer Science, Drexel University, Philadelphia, PA 19104, USA
Full list of author information is available at the end of the article

(ICT) market, it may be economically rational to allow cybercrime to persist [16]. For example, in a country like Nigeria, 419 scams result in an increased inflow of capital which corresponds with improved (local) social welfare [17].

Current regulatory solutions have been prosecution based. Laws such as the graduated response or the three strikes law [18] have tried to hold individuals accountable for their systems security [19]. Simultaneously, regulators have targeted the prosecution of cybercriminals and other punitive approaches such as takedowns. These punitive regulations are limited in their scope [16], can lead to collateral damage [20], and may be more expensive than the damages due to criminal activity [21].

A third ancillary approach examines the economic indicators of macro behaviors (e.g., participation in botnets) rather than address the micro incentives to protect/attack individual systems [22]. (In fact, there are limited if any incentives for end-users from protect individual systems. From a rational economics perspective, it is better for an individual to free ride since the security of their system depends on the security investment of others [23]. Simultaneously, investment in security is a certain loss, while the loss associated with a security breach is uncertain. Behavioral economics argues that individuals will choose probable rather than certain losses, even when the expected value of the loss is equal [24].) Thus, we need to examine why the percentage of spambots and associated spam differs on a macro level, i.e., across national jurisdictions.

Eeten et al. [25], for example, found that the number of infected machines is driven primarily by the size of an internet service provider's (ISP's) user base. Our research is distinct is three ways. First, the unit of analysis is country rather than ISPs. Second, Eeten et al. exclusively examined countries that were members of Organization for Economic Co-operation and Development (OECD). Our focus is global rather than strictly European. Third, the data for independent variable used here is compiled from the World Bank database, which is free and publicly available. Simultaneously, it is not a one-time measure. Thus, it allows for future research to use the same factors, where the findings would not be an artifact of the measurement strategies for a specific variable. To the extent that measurement impinges the findings, their impact would be consistent across different studies.

We offer preliminary answers to two research questions. First, we investigated why certain countries send a higher total volume of spam than others. Second, we examined why some countries have a higher percentage of infected machines, i.e., spambots, to support spam. Answering these questions required that this work be theoretically grounded in traditional criminology as well as emergent literature on cybercrime economics. With this grounded,

we were able to explore the underlying country-level factors that appear to encourage spam and associated botnet infrastructure.

The practical applications for this research are in the guidance of infrastructure investment, and policy formulation. The cross-country analysis of economic variables that correlate with spam/spambots informs not only previously unexplored avenues for policy but also can illuminate the risks of some policies under consideration. (For example, a promising anti-cybercrime effort has been the German Anti-Botnet initiative [26], which provides end-user technical support. However, it is possible that economic constraints prevent the end-user from implementing the recommendations provided, for example, the purchase of anti-virus software. Then, the success of German Anti-Botnet efforts would be contingent on software subsidies for low income markets in some jurisdictions.) This research can serve as a foundation to determine the potential for more widespread patch availability, i.e., a reduction in the number of systems acting as spambots and consequently overall reduction in spam.

Background

Spam requires users to spend a significant amount of time identifying legitimate emails from unsolicited ones. If the web is an attention span economy, then spam is mass theft [27,28]. In addition to costs for the individual end-user, spam also impinges costs on the society as it is often a vector for cybercrime.

Spam has no easy fixes [29]. On the technical side, the effort has been to automate the process of separating spam from legitimate email. This has essentially become an escalating arms race between spammers and security professionals. Anti-spam technologies range from IP address-based techniques [30] to machine learning approaches [31,32]. However, anti-spam efforts are often overcome by strategic innovations by spammers. For example, botnets have emerged as a response to IP blacklisting. Moore et al. [33] investigated temporal correlation between phishing websites and spam campaigns. They found that fast flux attacks pose the greatest threat. While fast flux-based websites comprise only 3% of the hosts, they account 68% of the spam sent.

Spam, like other cybercrime activities, is profit driven [3,34]. Thus, it is only (economically) rational to send spam when the cost of spamming is lower than the respective profits [35]. Moore et al. [34] argue that unlike crime offline, cybercrime is committed by well-educated individuals who do not have comparable financial opportunities in local markets. They recommend public/private partnerships to share information, for example, regarding phishing websites, to facilitate faster take down. They also suggest that ISPs should be made liable for certain activities if due diligence is not observed. Kanich et al. note that for stand alone retail spam to be profitable, the cost of sending spam should be 20 times cheaper than it currently is [9]. Alternatively, for spam to be profitable, it is must be vertically integrated with the associated scam architecture, i.e., the same individuals running the scam campaigns are also responsible for the associated spam. Economically efficient strategies for takedown are contingent on the analysis of these larger criminal networks as a whole [36].

Given the low marginal revenue, spam is economically sensitive and susceptible to new defenses [37]. Recognizing this, researchers have investigated economic solutions to spam seeking, for example, to raise the cost of sending bulk unsolicited email [38]. For example, CAPTCHAs are used to make the sender prove that they are human. CAPTCHAs, however, can be overcome by using crowdsourced labor markets such as Amazon's Mechanical Turk [39] and its more notorious counterpart Freelancer [40]. Some other techniques to increase the cost of bulk email include proof of work [41] and greylisting [42].

Current economic solutions to both spam in particular and cybercrime in general imagine the attackers to be *homo economicus*, are grounded in microeconomic investigations of individual stakeholder motivation and are thus informed by deterrence theory of crime. Complementary economic insights on a national level, both theoretical [16] as well as empirical [43], have been limited.

Garg et al. [16] proposed an economic model of cybercrime building on the model of smuggling [44]. They assumed certain legitimate networked services to be the smuggled analogue to botnets, in that they both provide bandwidth and computation cycles. Thus, botnets were modeled as an instantiation of eSmuggling. They found that existing illegal markets can act as a prohibitive tariff suppressing the development of legal services. Surprisingly, they found that cybercrime can be welfare increasing in local jurisdictions skewing the incentives for local law enforcement to crack down on such activities, creating a local maximum that can perversely suppress the development of a legitimate market.

Osorio [43] examined the economic factors that drove software copyright infringement. He concluded that copyright violations are a function of access and affordability, being explained by GDP per capita and availability of post sales software support in local markets. A deterrence-based solution to piracy then, such as Stop Online Piracy Act (SOPA) [45], is potentially less effective than Netflix, which allows individuals to participate legitimately [46].

Osorio considered a three-dimensional model [43]: (1) accessibility, (2) affordability, and (3) legal framework. Accessibility was operationalized as the ability of the software to fit local needs, presence of after sales support and corporate presence. Affordability was operationalized as gross domestic product (GDP) per capita. Legal

framework was operationalized using the work of Easterly et al. [47]. GDP refers to the market value of all goods and services produced in a country. Osorio's paper empirically examined the theoretical assertions of prior research [48-50].

Osorio's model presumes voluntary participation in illicit activity. However, while this applies to illegal copies of software, this assumption is unlikely to hold for botnets. Facilitators of cybercrime are frequently naive end-users, whose systems have been hijacked, often to support activities of which they do not approve [5]. While these cybercrime activities such as spam and phishing campaigns are short lived, the same is not true for the infrastructure, such as botnets, that supports these activities. What factors facilitate the presence of spambots and associated spam in a country? In this paper, we begin to answer this question by a cross-country examination of the underlying economic variables. We discuss data and methodology in the section immediately following.

Methodology

In this paper, we conduct a cross-country empirical analysis of the economic factors that correlate with and appear to encourage the percentage of spam and associated bots. We implement an ordinary least squared (OLS)-based linear regression analysis, using independent variables that are grounded in traditional theories of crime offline [51] as well as prior research in economics of cybercrime [43]. We consider two dependent variables. First, we investigate the total amount of spam originating from a country as a percentage of total amount of spam received. Second, we examine the number of infected systems in a country as a percentage of total number of spambots.

Independent variables

The independent variables under consideration are grounded in traditional theories of crime offline, specifically: (1) routine activity theory, (2) economic deprivation theory, and (3) social support/altruism theory. These variables have all been operationalized using the publicly available data from the World Bank. The World Bank database provides a consistent measure of country-level economic variables. To the extent that there are measurement errors, the mistakes should be unbiased, evenly distributed, and thus not effect final results (i.e., noise). This database is widely used in economic research [52]. Table 1 lists all the independent variables along with the corresponding year.

Routine activity theory of crime considers crime to be a function of motivated offenders[a], available targets, and absence of guardianship [53]. For spambots, available targets are the vulnerable systems which could be exploited as spambots. A larger population of Internet users creates more potentially vulnerable machines. Thus,

Table 1 Five-dimensional regression model

Model variables	Description	Year
Availability (AVA)	Fixed broadband subscribers	2010
	Fixed broadband subscribers (per100 people)	2010
	Internet users (per 100 people)	2010
Security of ICT infrastructure (SEC)	Secure internet servers	2010
	Secure internet servers (per one million people)	2010
Economic resources or affordability (ECO)	GDP per capita	2010
	GDP per capita by PPP	2010
Governance or legal framework (LEG)	Government effectiveness	2010
	Regulatory quality	2010
	Rule of law	2010
	Control of corruption	2010
Security skills or education (EDU)	Computer, comm., and other services (% imports)	2010
	Computer, comm., and other services (% exports)	2010

we consider the number of Internet users and the number of fixed broadband subscribers. (We use both Internet users and fixed Internet broadband subscribers to account for the difference in resources. For example, broadband subscribers are likely to have higher bandwidth than those that use dial up modem. Simultaneously, broadband subscribers would likely be online more often.) To account for the differences in the proportion of population online, we also included measures of the number of fixed Internet broadband subscribers and Internet users per 100 people in the analysis.

Further, we consider the security of the existing ICT infrastructure, as a variable that measures guardianship. This is operationalized as the number of secure Internet servers (SIS) and SIS per million people. Secure Internet servers is defined by the World Bank as 'servers using encryption technology in Internet transactions[b].'

The resilience of the associated infrastructure has been shown to impinge the volume of spam and the percentage of infected systems [54]. (To account for the difference in population, we also consider the number of secure Internet servers per one million people.) Admittedly, this term is vaguely defined. However, it does allow a uniform, consistently available measure that is likely to be repeated over time by the World Bank. This will allow other researchers to reproduce our work and conduct broader empirical examinations of Internet readiness, cybercrime, etc. A more perfect one-time measurement is almost certainly possible, but it would prevent this

work from being subject to replication or later repetition and as such be less of a contribution to the science of cybersecurity.

Economic deprivation theory of crime argues that individual participation in crime may be driven by absolute [55] or relative economic deprivation [56]. The lack of economic resources limits the ability of the individual to participate legally in the market. For example, individuals with limited resources may not be able to pay for licensed copies of software, thereby (often) blocking their access to timely security updates and software patches. Alternatively, limited resources would impinge the end-users' ability to purchase protection services such as anti-virus, making them more vulnerable. Thus, we consider GDP per capita and GDP per capita by purchasing power parity (PPP). Given that GDP is used as a measure of economic resources available to a nation, GDP per capita corresponds to the absolute deprivation of the individual in the country while GDP per capita by PPP indicates the relative deprivation with respect to other countries. Economic deprivation is similar to affordability under Osorio's [43] framework.

The impact of resource deprivation can be alleviated by *social support and altruism* [57]. *Social support* is provided by the government by conditions conducive to adoption of security technologies, for example, through direct and indirect subsidies. An example of a indirect security subsidy is the German Anti-Botnet initiative [26], where offending system owners are informed of malware on their systems as well as advised on how to address the infection. A direct subsidy can be in the form of NSA secure linux in the USA, whereby individuals have a clear signal in the market for secure software as well as free access to it.

Then, better governance should lead to more mature local ICT markets, providing better and cheaper access to ICT technologies and creating an indirect subsidy for the end-user. We operationalize social support using a subset of World Governance Indicators (WGI) [58]: (1) government effectiveness, (2) regulatory quality, (3) rule of law, and (4) control of corruption, i.e., perception of corruption within a country. Government effectiveness measures the perceived quality of public services, quality of civil service, and the degree to which it is independent from political manipulation, the quality of policy formulation and implementation, and the perceived credibility of the government to commit to said policies. Regulatory quality quantifies the perceived ability of the government toward sound policy and the degree to which regulations formulation and implementation encourage private sector development. Rule of law indicates the degree to which the legal framework is implemented. The legal framework can also be thwarted by corruption or perceptions thereof. Control of corruption measures perceptions of corruption, where corruption is defined as misuse of public power for private gain. Governance is similar to legal framework under Osorio's [43] framework.

In addition to social support through public bodies, we also consider *altruism* through private bodies. A developed ICT market should be more invested in protecting its resources. For example, it may be cheaper for the ISPs to proactively protect their networks than provide customer support related to security issues [59]. It would then be rational for ISPs to invest in detection of malware on their networks and actively engage users to clean their machines.

Simultaneously, a bigger ICT market, for example, would result in a larger number of staff personnel who have been trained in basic security practices to address the information security needs of that organization. This information would be relevant when the end-user is using their home machines as well as those at work. Some companies in fact provide access to anti-virus software for home computers as employees often take work home. Thus, we consider the size of the ICT market as a proxy for private altruism. This is operationalized by considering the percentage export and import of computer, communications, and other services. Thus, this variable is used as a proxy to the technical security skills available to the market as a whole[c].

Datasets

Recall we had two research questions. Why do certain national jurisdictions produce a higher percentage of spam than other? Why do some countries have a higher percentage of systems acting as spambots than others? Consequently, we examine two dependent variables and two datasets.

The first dependent variable corresponds to the number of spam emails that appear to originate from a specific geographic location. The data for this variable was procured from an academic source, i.e., computer science servers of Indiana University, Bloomington (in the USA). These servers are primarily used by faculty and staff in computer science. The strategy behind the data collection has been detailed in the Appendix along with the assumptions.

The second dependent variable corresponds to the percentage of infected systems acting as spambots in individual countries. The data corresponding to this variable was obtained from Microsoft's Security Intelligence Report 2011 (Volume 11) [60]. The spambot data is generated by Microsoft's Forefront Online Protection for Exchange (FOPE), which uses a two-stage filter. The first uses a reputation-based filtering at the network edge. The second uses content-based rules and detects issues such as malicious email attachments. The report provides data for

the first and the second quarters of 2011. The list is limited to the top 80 countries that host at least 0.1% of the IP addresses used by spambots.

Clearly, we cannot assert if spambot data does or does not represent botnet owners and controllers. However, our research only examines why spambots occur more frequently in certain countries than others. We do not address if command and control centers for such botnets are also endemic to national jurisdictions with specific economic properties. As the focus here is upon the involuntary participation, the issue of botnet control is orthogonal.

Data analysis

We examine two regression Equations 1 and 2, which correspond to the two research questions. For Equation 1, N1 refers to the amount of spam in different countries as a percentage of the total spam volume. The data for dependent variable in this equation is that from Indiana University (Bloomington). For Equation 2, N2 refers to the percentage of infected machines that act as spambots in distinct national jurisdictions. The data for N2 is that from Microsoft. Both Equations 1 and 2 were evaluated using OLS regression, and thus were examined for the underlying assumptions of (the absence) of multicollinearity and heteroskedasticity.

$$N1 = \epsilon_1 + \beta_{11} * \text{AVA} + \beta_{12} * \text{SEC} + \beta_{13} * \text{ECO} + \beta_{14} * \text{LEG} + \beta_{15} * \text{EDU} \tag{1}$$

$$N2 = \epsilon_2 + \beta_{21} * \text{AVA} + \beta_{22} * \text{SEC} + \beta_{23} * \text{ECO} + \beta_{24} * \text{LEG} + \beta_{25} * \text{EDU} \tag{2}$$

We began by calculating the variance inflation factor (VIF) to discover and address the presence of multicollinearity in the regression model[d]. The four aspects of WGI were significantly collinear, i.e., VIF>5. Thus, we combined the four governance factors into one by adding all four and called it WGI. Similarly, GDP per capita as well as GDP per capita by PPP were also significantly collinear, i.e., VIF>5. We excluded GDP per capita, while GDP per capita by PPP was retained as an indicator of relative deprivation. Number of fixed broadband Internet subscribers was significantly collinear with the number of Internet users, i.e., VIF>5. Since number of fixed broadband Internet subscribers had less number of missing values, we retained it variable in the model instead of the number of Internet users. For the remaining model VIF values did not indicate strong multicollinearity, i.e., VIF<5.

We also examined the model for heteroskedasticity[e]. We plotted the residuals for the model as a histogram. We also computed the Shapiro test to examine whether the residuals were normally distributed. For Equation 1, the *p* value for the test was much less than 0.001, i.e., the evidence indicates heteroskedasticity. For Equation 2, the p value was 0.715, i.e., the null hypothesis cannot be rejected or there is not enough evidence for heteroskedasticity. For the first model, we then used the White-Huber method to generate heteroskedasticity-corrected covariance matrices.

To facilitate the regression analyses, we transformed both the dependent and the independent variables. Some independent variables, e.g., GDP per capita by PPP, had a wide range and thus the regression will be dominated by the size effect. For such variables, we log transformed the data. Appropriate variables were identified by noticing the presence of outliers in the box plots. Independent variables log transformed were GDP per capita by PPP, number of fixed broadband Internet subscribers, secure Internet servers, and secure Internet servers (per million people).

Given that OLS regression is a parametric test, it makes additional assumptions regarding the dependent variable; specifically, OLS assumes that the dependent variable is continuous and normally distributed. Recall we had two dependent variables: (1) volume of spam and (2) percentage of spambots. The counts for spam volume were converted to percentages, i.e., we divided the amount of spam from a country by the total volume of spam (from all countries in this dataset). The corresponding histogram as well as the Shapiro test did not indicate that the data was normally distributed; p value for the Shapiro test was ≈ 0. Simultaneously, the box plot indicated several outliers. Thus, this dependent variable was also log transformed.

The second dependent variable was the percentage of spambots within a country for different countries. The normality assumption was not satisfied, either by eyeballing the histogram, or by the Shapiro test; p value for the Shapiro test was $<<0.001$. The box plot again indicated several outliers. Thus, this dependent variable was log transformed.

Results

Tables 2 and 3 presents the summary statistics for all the dependent and independent variables. The spam dataset from Indiana University (Bloomington) was highly correlated with the spambot dataset from Microsoft; cor = 0.87, p value $<<0.001$, $n = 79$ (where n is the number of countries compared). The correlations between the dependent variables and independent variables is given in Table 4[f]. OLS was applied to Equations 1 and 2[g]. The results are given in Tables 5 and 6; the effective sample sizes were 117 and 69, respectively.

Discussion

The relative volume of spam is highly skewed in its distribution. The top seven countries accounted for 51.53% of the total volume of spam received by Indiana University

(Bloomington), indicating that most of the offending bots are concentrated jurisdictionally; these seven countries were India, Russian Federation, USA, Vietnam, Indonesia, Brazil, and China, respectively, with India accounting for the largest volume of spam. Previous research noted this

Table 2 Summary statistics: without transformation

	Mean	Standard deviation
Dependent variable		
Indiana University*	38,510.0	106,352.2
Microsoft*	2.453	3.83
Independent variable		
GDP per capita by PPP*	14,017.2	15,117.01
Fixed broadband Internet subscribers (FBIS)*	2,859,683	11,877,249
Fixed broadband Internet subscribers (per 100 people)	9.96	12.14
Internet users (per 100 people)	35.47	28.00
Secure Internet servers*	5,560.237	34,338.54
Secure Internet servers (per one million people)*	367.6445	1,151.99
Computer, comm., and other services (% exports)	29.08	19.49
Computer, comm., and other services (% imports)	30.81	16.18
World governance indicators (WGI)	305.7658	158.0306

Asterisk (*) indicates that these variables have *not* been transformed.

Table 3 Summary statistics

	Mean	Standard deviation
Dependent Variable		
Indiana University*	-3.29	2.76
Microsoft*	2.45	3.83
Independent Variable		
GDP per capita by PPP*	8.90	1.25
Fixed broadband Internet subscribers (FBIS)*	11.45	3.14
Fixed broadband Internet subscribers (per 100 people)	9.96	12.14
Internet users (per 100 people)	35.47	28.00
Secure Internet servers*	4.62	2.84
Secure Internet servers (per one million people)*	3.09	2.90
Computer, comm., and other services (% exports)	29.08	19.49
Computer, comm., and other services (% imports)	30.81	16.18
World governance indicators (WGI)	205.06	111.38

Asterisk (*) indicates that these variables have been transformed as described in the text.

Table 4 Correlations between spam/spambots and economic factors

Economic variable	Indiana University (n)	Microsoft (n)
GDP per capita by PPP	0.46*** (145)	0.15 (75)
Fixed broadband Internet subscribers (FBIS)	0.84*** (164)	0.68*** (77)
Fixed broadband Internet subscribers (per 100 people)	0.39*** (164)	0.17 (77)
Internet users (per 100 people)	0.43*** (156)	0.12 (77)
Secure Internet servers	0.74*** (172)	0.46*** (78)
Secure Internet servers (per one million people)	0.23** (172)	0.08 (78)
Computer, comm, and other services (% exports)	0.29*** (141)	0.29* (73)
Computer, comm, and other services (% imports)	0.28*** (141)	0.27* (73)
World governance indicators (WGI)	0.29*** (168)	0.08 (79)

Significant codes: '***' <0.001, '**' <0.01, '*' <0.05.

Table 6 OLS regression model: Microsoft [Spambots]

Linear regression	Estimate	Standard error	Pr(> |t|)
(Intercept)	-4.057	2.592	0.123
GDP per capita by PPP	-0.133	0.392	0.736
Fixed broadband Internet subscribers	0.255	0.125	0.046 *
Fixed broadband Internet subscribers (per 100 people)	-0.019	0.025	0.469
Internet users (per 100 people)	-0.016	0.013	0.210
Secure Internet servers	0.388	0.146	0.010 *
Secure Internet servers (per one million people)	-0.011	0.198	0.954
Computer, comm., and other services (% exports)	0.002	0.008	0.742
Computer, comm., and other services (% imports)	0.018	0.010	0.062
World governance indicators (WGI)	-0.002	0.002	0.295

Significant codes: '***' <0.001, '**' < 0.01, '*' <0.05; residual standard error, 0.8288 on 60 degrees of freedom; multiple R-squared, 0.6057; adjusted R-squared, 0.5466; F-statistic, 10.24 on 9 and 60 DF; p value, 2.284e-09.

concentration even for ISPs, i.e., most of the spambots are concentrated to the handful of ISPs. Simultaneously, such ISPs were popular, well established, and thus potentially susceptible to regulatory pressure. Given that most spam is concentrated in a handful of countries, regulatory solutions to spam then appears to be a tangible and tractable option; only a small subset of countries would need to agree to regulate an admittedly larger but still a relatively malleable set of ISPs.

Table 5 OLS regression model: Indiana University [Spam]

Linear regression	Estimate	Standard error	Pr (> |t|)
(Intercept)	-11.657	2.622	≈0***
GDP per capita by PPP	0.059	0.403	0.883
Fixed broadband Internet subscribers	0.705	0.172	≈0***
Fixed broadband Internet subscribers (per 100 people)	-0.051	0.033	0.123
Internet users (per 100 people)	0.002	0.016	0.918
Secure Internet servers	0.242	0.212	0.257
Secure Internet servers (per one million people)	0.208	0.161	0.201
Computer, comm., and other services (% exports)	-0.002	0.010	0.835
Computer, comm., and other services (% imports)	-0.006	0.014	0.658
World governance indicators (WGI)	-0.007	0.003	0.0137 *

Significant codes: '***' <0.001, '**' <0.01, '*' <0.05; residual standard error, 1.327 on 108 degrees of freedom; multiple R-squared, 0.7649; adjusted R-squared, 0.7453; F-statistic, 39.03 on 9 and 108 DF; p value, <2.2e-16.

Overall the evidence in the paper indicates that the prevalence of both spam and spambots is best explained by routine activity theory of crime [53], which considers crime as a function of motivated offenders, available targets, and lack of guardianship. We tested two of these variables, i.e., available targets and guardianship, both of which were important in predicting the volume of spam; the third variable, motivated offenders, is not relevant online as all targets can be considered proximal and thus appropriate for infection[h]. Unlike crime offline, spam and spambots appear to increase with the availability of guardianship. Therefore, previous policy prescriptions grounded in routine activity theory may not be directly applicable online. However, the exploration and translation of such prescriptions from offline to online does suggest a first step in providing potential solutions that can complement regulatory efforts grounded in deterrence.

Availability

We find that all measures of availability, number of users connecting to the Internet, were directly and statistically significantly correlated with the total volume of spam (Table 4). Intuitively, as the number of users increases, so would the number of individual systems and email accounts that can then be used to send out spam. Relative volume of spam is driven by the number of fixed broadband Internet subscribers from a country, as it is the only measure of availability that is statistically significant in the regression analysis (Table 5). In previous research, Eeten et al. [25] similarly noted that the total volume of spam from an ISP was driven by the size of its user base.

The percentage of systems acting as spambots in a country is, however, not statistically correlated with all measures of availability. In fact, only the total number of fixed broadband Internet subscribers (FBIS) was statistically correlated with the percentage of spambots (Table 4). FBIS was also the only statistically significant measure of availability in the regression model (Table 6). This indicates that higher adoption may lead to higher percentage of spambots. This is contrary to previous work by Eeten et al. [25], who found that while bigger ISPs might do worse in total volume of spam, they perform marginally better in terms of percentages. ISPs and national economies may then differ in this respect. Alternatively, the difference might be an artifact of the countries under analysis; Eeten et al. [25] concentrated on OECD countries.

There are several potential explanations for why Internet adoption may increase the percentage of spambots. The foremost and simplest explanation is that increased Internet adoption may simply mean more number of people clicking on links and navigating to different websites, increasing their risk exposure. Then, higher Internet adoption would not just indicate more spambots and spam, but also more malware infections and bots in general. This explanation can be tested by examining the correlations between measures of availability and malware-infected machines and zombies in future studies using other datasets. In concurrent work, we find evidence that suggests that this hypothesis may not be accurate, as number of malware infected machines was negatively correlated with FBIS [61].

A second explanation is that early adopters are typically those who are interested in new technologies, are more technically literate, and have higher education and income. They would be more aware of security risks and more capable of risk mitigation. However, as Internet adoption progresses, systems would be available less informed and economically constrained individuals who would then be limited in their incentives and ability to protect their systems. This explanation is contingent on two variables: education and income (which is highly correlated with education [62]). Education can be examined by using country-level measures of individual literacy rates as well as community-based measures, such as public spending on education. Correspondingly, there would be distinct policy implications[i].

A third potential but tenuous hypothesis may be that when Internet adoption is low, those that adopt technologies are more homogenous. To the extent that security awareness and corresponding mitigation strategies are contingent on stories exchanged in communities [63], the exposure of a homogenous community would be lower. While it is difficult to test this relationship on a country level, it may be possible by looking at indicators of income inequality, e.g., GINI index.

A fourth possibility is the higher penetration allows faster spread of infections as epidemiological models are driven by concentrations [54]. However, there is limited evidence for this. None of the measures for concentration, e.g., Internet users per 100 people, were correlated with the percentage of spambots in a country. However, it is difficult to access the epidemiological impact of malware spread as this is a static model with static independent variables. It may be better to consider the rate of change in the number of Internet users for individual countries. The optimal solution would be to conduct a time series analysis on historical spam data. Such data is, however, not currently available to the researchers.

Guardianship

Security (or guardianship), i.e., secure Internet server (SIS), was directly correlated with both the relative volume of spam from a country as well as the percentage of spambots in individual countries (Table 4). These correlations were statistically significant. However, SIS was not significant in the regression model for the relative volume for spam (Table 5). It may be that the relationship between SIS and relative volumes of spam is not linear as Spearman's coefficient indicates both linear and non-linear correlations. SIS was, however, significant in explaining the percentage of spambots in individual countries (Table 6).

A first explanation for this is that as the number of users in the local market increases, the number of SIS would consequently have to increase. Thus, more SIS is simply an indicator of Internet adoption. As noted earlier in this section, Internet adoption may lead to more infections. Thus, as the Internet grows not only does the volume of spam increases so does the percentage of spambots. It could be argued that SIS do not need to be jurisdictionally co-located with their target market. However, given that SIS is highly correlated with all measures of availability (p value $<<0.001$), this hypothesis has limited support.

A second explanation then could be that the security of the SIS itself is broken. Personnel in charge may simply be following 'best practices' to secure such servers, which is security often means 'common practices' rather than indicate a measure of quality. It may then be that due to inadequate security, these servers may themselves have become vector for spambot-related malware infections. From a rational choice perspective, trusted systems would attract more attacks as the return on investment would be higher. Problems with SSL implementations are well documented [64]; this could easily extend to other encryption implementations on such servers. However, concurrent research indicates that more SIS do not lead to higher rate of malware infections in general [61]. Thus, this hypothesis currently does not have support.

Economic deprivation

The sole indicator of economic resources, i.e., GDP per capita by PPP, was directly and significantly correlated with the relative volume of spam. However, the correlation with percentage of spambots was not significant. GDP per capita by PPP was also not significant in either of the regression models. Overall, there seems to be limited evidence for the influence of economic resources on prevalence or spam or associated botnets. The evidence that is available indicates a positive relationship; both the correlations are positive and so are the signs for the estimates in both regression models. This is counterintuitive based on previous research. To the extent that economic resources constrain individual ability to purchase legal copies of software [43], higher rates of software piracy should be positively correlated with spam [25]. Similarly, if limited expendable income impinges, the individual ability to purchase security technologies, e.g., anti-virus software, higher GDP per capita by PPP should also lower spam and spambots.

There are two possible explanations for this counterintuitive observation. The simplest explanation is that to the extent that economic resources impact Internet adoption, GDP per capita by PPP also indicates the individual ability to participate in the market as an Internet user. As noted earlier in this section, adoption may lead to higher volume of spam and percentage of spambots. A second, more tenuous, behavioral explanation is that as GDP per capita by PPP increases, adoption of legal software as well as anti-malware technologies is proportionally impinged. However, individuals compensate for risk mitigating technologies by demonstrating higher risk behavior. There is evidence for such static risk budgets offline. For example, the introduction of ABS did not reduce overall risk as drivers compensated by driving closer to other vehicles [65]. Both these hypotheses can be tested by replacing GDP per capita by PPP with more direct measures of economic resources such rates of software copyright infringement and market penetration of anti-virus software. While statistics for copyright infringement are readily available from Business Software Alliance, similar data for market penetration of security technologies is admittedly harder to acquire.

Social support/altruism

Indicator of legal framework and overall governance, i.e., World Governance Indicator (WGI), was significantly and positively correlated with the volume of spam (though not with the percentage of spambots) (Table 4). On the ISP level, better specific governance initiatives have been found to be correlated with lower levels of botnet activity [25]; however, the specific independent variables under consideration were different. WGI was also significant in the regression model for the relative percentage of spam

from individual countries (Table 5). To the extent that better governance creates a subsidy for individual end-user consumption of ICT technologies by facilitating the evolution of local ICT markets, this subsidy may not extend to individual investment in security. This is not unexpected, as from a macro-behavioral perspective the security market suffers from clear signals and is thus a market of lemons [66].

Both proxies for technical skills were positively and significantly correlated with both the relative volume of spam as well as the percentage of spambots. These measures do not directly measure either individual literacy rates or technical education in general; instead, they indicate the amount of technical skills that are available to the economy as a whole. Technical skills then indicate a weak relationship with lowering the incidence of spam or spambot, as they were not significant in either of the regression models. The statistical significance of their correlations with the volume of spam and percentage of spambots can be explained as a function of Internet adoption. The relationship between (export and imports of) computer, communications, and other services and Internet adoption is obvious; more exports and imports of ICT services should indicate higher Internet adoption in the local market.

Conclusions

Spam is concentrated, both jurisdictionally and on the network. Merely seven countries appear to generate more than 50% of spam. Similarly, most spam is concentrated to a handful of ISPs. We argue that this allows the possibility of deterrence through regulation. Appropriate legal incentives in less than ten countries would address more than half the spam in the world. Simultaneously, the enforcement of such legislation would be relatively cheap, as only a handful of actors (roughly 50 ISPs) would need to be monitored. Absent the influence of economic deprivation on the prevalence of spam/spambots, there is no argument for software subsidies in low-income markets as a solution to botnets. In fact, the problem of spam seems to be a macro level lack of governance; simultaneously, spambots are impinged by broader infrastructure management issues as those with secure Internet servers. Governance efforts such as the German Botnet Initiative have been promising. Simultaneously, minimum security can be mandated for network providers such as secure Internet servers. While specific policy prescriptions are beyond the scope of this paper, in concurrent research, we argue for ex-ante regulations for addressing spambots [20]. Future research should address the relative costs of policy prescriptions as public or private interventions vs. a common-pool regime.

Of the different theories of criminology tested in this paper, routine activity theory was the most significant driver of spam and associated botnets. As expected as

Internet adoption increases, the total volume of spam goes up. Counterintuitively, Internet adoption also increases the percentage of offending machines. The likely explanation is that investments in Internet adoption are not proportionally matched by those in education. Lack of education impinge individuals in two ways. First, they are limited in their awareness of security risks. Second, even when they are aware, they may not have enough information to adequately assess the risk and construct an appropriate response.

Unlike in traditional routine activity theory, where crime is driven by lack of guardianship, spam and associated bots are instead correlated with the presence of secure Internet servers. This difference does not allow us to directly transfer policy insights offline to countering spam. However, it does provide an alternative perspective to the problem and allow us to develop a framework for systematic inquiry toward engendering long-term public policy and technical solutions.

In this paper, we addressed two research questions. First, what economic factors explain the variance in the relative volume of spam seen from different countries. Second, what economic factors explain the variance the percentage of systems acting as spambots across different nations. We find that large volumes of spam and/or spambots are correlated with higher rates of Internet adoption and presence of secure Internet servers. Our research is theoretically grounded in previous investigations of security economics online as well as criminology offline. While some of our results reify previous microeconomic investigations, others are contradictory. Thus, research investigating individual markets may not be generalizable national economies.

Future work includes repeating this analysis over time to evaluate if changes in the population of spambots are correlated with economic changes; this would be helpful in establishing a causal link rather than just a correlational one. Further, our hope is to collaborate with additional institutions who might share their data. In particular, institutional data sets from corporations and non-US institutions are ideal tests of this model.

Endnotes

[a] In our analysis we do not consider the presence of motivated offenders. Offline motivated offenders is given by proximity to the target. Online, however, all attackers are proximal. It may be that attackers prefer to attack systems that are fewer hops away; however, we do not know of any evidence that indicates support for this hypothesis online. Arguably, it is possible to compute a distance metric for the average distance between two systems in two different countries. However, given that we do not have information on the command and control center for the spambots in out data set, even if such distance metric was available, it could not possibly be applied to this data.

[b] See http://data.worldbank.org/indicator/IT.NET.SECR.P6.

[c] Eeten et al. [25] used education as a proxy variable for technical skills. Unfortunately, the World Bank data for education was sparsely populated. Then, using education as a proxy variable would have left out several countries from our analyses. Thus, we decided on a different proxy variable. Note that the size of the ICT market does not encapsulate individual security education, but instead provides a measurement for security skills available to the market as a whole.

[d] Multicollinearity is observed when two or more independent variables are highly correlated, i.e., at least one of the independent variables can be computed as a linear combination of the rest to a statistically significant degree. If the independent variables are multicollinear, then the results for the ordinary least squared regression may be computed incorrectly.

[e] Heteroskedasticity is observed when the residuals for a model are not normally distributed. This happens when the variance of a variable does not increase or decrease proportionally with respect to a second variable.

[f] Since we use Spearman's rank correlation coefficient (which is sensitive to outliers), the variables were transformed as described above before computing the specific values. Note that we do not use Pearson's coefficient as many of the independent variables are not normally distributed. Furthermore, since log transformation is order preserving, it does not impact Spearman. However, log transformation allows us to have a data set without outliers.

[g] Note that while the independent variables are not normally distributed, OLS is still applicable as the sample size is large [67].

[h] For example, previous research has noted that most botnets include bots that are spread over 30 to a 100 countries [68]. Simultaneously, for spam, the associated bots do not require extra bandwidth or longer uptime, it is unlikely that bots in one country would be preferred over another [3].

[i] Eeten et al. [25] note that higher education levels did in fact indicate lower rates of spam. However, as noted by other findings in this paper, results from ISPs may not directly apply to national economies or those from OECD to countries globally.

Appendix
Indiana University (Bloomington) data collection strategy

The spam data spans between 25 July 2010 and 27 March 2011 ($\approx$ 8 months). There were 9.7 million messages. Of these, 6.0 million were classified as spam and 3.7 million were deemed legitimate. From this data set, we have ≈ 62% spam which is below the upper bound given by Symantec.

All email messages are subjected to two spam filters. The primary filter is an IP address based blacklist. This filter provides a binary output as either an 'OK', which results in the message being exposed to the second filter or a 'REJECT' at which time it is discarded and deemed spam. Additionally, the output of the first filter also provides a time and date stamp as well as an IP address. The second filter subjects the email to several spam classifiers. The email is accepted if the message is internal, has less than a 60% probability of being spam, and is on a whitelist or department supported mailing list, or a virus is successfully removed. Spam messages are accepted but considered to be spam if there is a greater than 60%, but less than 99%, probability of being spam. Messages may be accepted with a warning notification regarding suspicious attachments. Messages are rejected if they have a virus, an illegal attachment type, a greater than 99% probability of being spam or other instantiation of a virus. For our analysis, we combined messages that were accepted spam, rejected spam, as well as messages regarding viruses in one spam category.

We make three assumptions. First, we assume that spam and only spam are caught by the two filter systems, i.e., no spam gets let through accidentally and legitimate messages do get tossed away accidentally. Second, we assume that IP addresses and hostnames correspond to spambots and are not spoofed. Third, we assume that all the spam was sent by spambots.

Additionally, there were messages aborted during reception due to a dropped connection or invalid recipient addresses. It is unknown if these were blanket spam attacks that put in incorrect addresses, people accidentally mistyping emails, or people/organizations that had not updated their email lists and were emailing people no longer at Indiana University (Bloomington) and whose email addresses were no longer valid. Thus, these messages have not been included in the current analysis.

There is also a 'none' status in the second filter, which was used twice in the 8 months, but it is unknown what this status meant. These messages were thrown out, as 2 messages out of 9.7 million are insignificant.

Each line of the spam data from the second filter contained a unique identifier, stating whether a message is local, (from) Indiana (University), or external, a time and date stamp, anonymized 'from' and 'to' tags, the result of the analysis of the email, filters, the percent chance that it is spam (if it does not hit one of the automatic exceptions, e.g., the whitelist), and the relay hostname or IP address. We used an IP lookup database with a 95% accuracy rate to determine the spam 'messages' country of origin. For the secondary messages without IP addresses, we looked at country-level domains (.br, .ua, .gov, etc.) to determine the originating country of spam messages. For all top-level domains (.com, .net, .org), we had to throw these spam messages into an unknown origins category for a lack of accuracy with respect to the originating location. These methods are reflected in other spam studies [9,69].

Microsoft data

There were a total of 80 countries in the data set. India had the higher percentage of spambots with 10.9% of the machines acting as spambots in the first quarter of 2011 and 11.0 % in the second. Jordan had the lowest percentage with 0.06% of machines acting as spambots in the first quarter of 2011 and 0.10 % in the second. Table 7 provides summary statistics for the data.

Table 7 Summary statistics for Microsoft spambot data

Statistics	1Q11	2Q11
Minimum	0.06	0.10
First quarter	0.21	0.19
Median	0.45	0.45
Mean	1.14	1.31
Third quarter	1.30	1.00
Maximum	10.90	11.00

Competing interests
The authors declare that they do not have any competing interests.

Acknowledgements
We would like to thank Prof. Angela Sasse and Nathaniel Husted for their insights and comments. We are also thankful to the Stat/Math Center at Indiana University, specifically Thomas Jackson, for their help with the statistical analysis. Last but not the least, we are indebted to the anonymous reviewers whose feedback was critical to improving this research. Any mistakes in the paper are the authors' own.

Author details
[1] Department of Computer Science, Drexel University, Philadelphia, PA 19104, USA. [2] School of Informatics and Computing, Indiana University, Bloomington, IN 47408, USA.

References
1. J Postel, On the junk mail problem. Request for comments. Netw Working Group (1975)
2. P Denning, Electronic Junk. Commun. ACM **25**(3), 163–165 (1982)
3. B Stone-Gross, T Holz, G Stringhini, G Vigna, in *Proceedings of the 4th USENIX conference on Large-scale exploits and emergent threats*, LEET'11. The underground economy of spam: a botmaster's perspective of coordinating large-scale spam campaigns (USENIX Association Berkeley, CA, 2011), p. 4. http://dl.acm.org/citation.cfm?id=1972441.1972447. Accessed 29 October 2013
4. MessageLabs, MessageLabs Intelligence; 2010 Annual Security Report. Tech. rep., MessageLabs (2010)

5. Q Norton, Anonymous Tricks Bystanders Into Attacking Justice Department. Tech. rep., Wired (2012), http://www.wired.com/threatlevel/2012/01/anons-rickroll-botnet/. Accessed 29 October 2013

6. P Yu, The graduated response. Fla. Law Rev. **62**, 1373–1430 (2010)

7. C Grier, K Thomas, V Paxson, M Zhang, in *Proceedings of the 17th ACM conference on Computer and communications security*, CCS '10. @spam: the underground on 140 characters or less (ACM, New York, NY, 2010), pp. 27–37. http://doi.acm.org/10.1145/1866307.1866311. Accessed 29 October 2013

8. T Moore, R Clayton, in *Workshop on the Economics of Information Security*. An empirical analysis of the current state of phishing attack and defence. http://weis07.infosecon.net/papers/51.pdf. Accessed 29 October 2013

9. C Kanich, C Kreibich, K Levchenko, B Enright, GM Voelker, V Paxson, S Savage, in *Proceedings of the 15th ACM Conference on Computer and Communications security*, CCS '08. Spamalytics: an empirical analysis of spam marketing conversion (ACM, New York, 2008), pp. 3–14. http://doi.acm.org/10.1145/1455770.1455774. Accessed 29 October 2013

10. D McCoy, A Pitsillidis, G Jordan, N Weaver, C Kreibich, B Krebs, GM Voelker, S Savage, K Levchenko, in *Proceedings of the 21st USENIX conference on Security symposium*, Security'12. PharmaLeaks: understanding the business of online pharmaceutical affiliate programs (USENIX Association, Berkeley, 2012), p. 1. http://dl.acm.org/citation.cfm?id=2362793.2362794. Accessed 29 October 2013

11. Z Li, Q Liao, in *Managing Information Risk and the Economics of Security*. A Striegel, Botnet Economics: Uncertainty Matters (Springer US, 2009), pp. 245–267. http://dx.doi.org/10.1007/978-0-387-09762-6_12. Accessed 29 October 2013

12. T Holz, M Engelberth, F Freiling, in *Proceedings of the 14th European conference on Research in computer security*, ESORICS'09. Learning more about the underground economy: a case-study of keyloggers and dropzones (Springer-Verlag, Berlin, Heidelberg, 2009), pp. 1–18. http://dl.acm.org/citation.cfm?id=1813084.1813086. Accessed 29 October 2013

13. D Bleaken, Botwars: the fight against criminal cyber networks. Comput. Fraud Secur. **2010**(5), 17–19 (2010)

14. G Higgins, A Wilson, B Fell, An application of deterrence theory to software piracy. J. Crim. Justice Pop. Cult. **12**(3), 166–184 (2005)

15. I Png, C Wang, Q Wang, The deterrent and displacement effects of information security enforcement: international evidence. J. Manag. Inf. Syst. **25**(2), 125–144 (2008)

16. V Garg, N Husted, N Camp, in *eCrime Researcher's Summit*. Smuggling Theory Approach to Organized Digital Crime (IEEE, San Diego, 2011), pp. 1–7. http://ieeexplore.ieee.org/xpl/abstractAuthors.jsp?arnumber=6151980. Accessed 29 October 2013

17. J Buchanan, AJ Grant, Investigating and prosecuting Nigerian fraud. U. S. Attorneys' Bull. **49**(6), 39–47 (2001)

18. PK Yu, The graduated response. Fla. Law Rev. **62**, 1373 (2010)

19. P Sayer, French court levies first fine under three-strikes law on illegal downloads under Hadopi. Tech. rep., Computer World (2012)

20. V Garg, J Camp, in *The Research Conference on Communication, Information, and Internet Policy*. Ex Ante vs. Ex Post: Economically Efficient Sanctioning Regimes for Online Risks (Arlington, VA, 27–29, September 2013)

21. R Anderson, C Barton, R Böhme, R Clayton, M van Eeten, M Levi, T Moore, S Savage, in *Workshop on the Economics of Information Security*. Measuring the Cost of Cybercrime (Berlin, 25–26 June 2012)

22. TC Schelling, *Micromotives and macrobehavior*. (WW Norton & Company, New York, 2006)

23. H Varian, *System Reliability and Free Riding* (Kluwer Academic Publishers, Norwell, 2004), pp. 1–15

24. B Schneier, in *Proceedings of the Cryptology in Africa 1st International Conference on Progress in Cryptology*, AFRICACRYPTŠ08. The psychology of security (Springer-Verlag Berlin, Heidelberg, 2008), pp. 50–79. http://dl.acm.org/citation.cfm?id=1788634.1788642. Accessed 29 October 2013

25. M van Eeten, JM Bauer, H Asghari, S Tabatabaie, The Role of Internet Service Providers in Botnet Mitigation: An Empirical Analysis Based on Spam Data. OECD Science, Technology and Industry Working Papers 2010/5, OECD Publishing (2010). http://dx.doi.org/10.1787/5km4k7m9n3vj-en. Accessed 29 October 2013

26. S Karge, The role of Internet intermediaries in advancing public policy objectives. Tech. rep., OECD (2009)

27. T Lewis, Something for nothing [electronic commerce]. Comput. **32**(5), 120–118 (1999)

28. R Kannan, An empirical study of long-run impact of Internet advertising on consumer response behavior. *PhD thesis*, Massachusetts Institute of Technology, 2006

29. L Cranor, B LaMacchia, Spam! Commun. ACM **41**(8), 74–83 (1998)

30. H Esquivel, A Akella, T Mori, in *Proceedings of the 2nd International Conference on COMmunication Systems and NETworks*, COMSNETS'10. On the effectiveness of IP reputation for spam filtering (IEEE Press, Piscataway, 2010), pp. 40–49. http://dl.acm.org/citation.cfm?id=1831448. Accessed 29 October 2013

31. I Androutsopoulos, J Koutsias, KV Chandrinos, CD Spyropoulos, in *Proceedings of the 23rd Annual International ACM SIGIR Conference on Research and Development in Information Retrieval*. An experimental comparison of naive Bayesian and keyword-based anti-spam filtering with personal e-mail messages (ACM, New York, 2000). pp. 160–167

32. A Bratko, B Filipič, G Cormack, T Lynam, B Zupan, Spam filtering using statistical data compression models. J. Mach. Learn. Res. **7**, 2673–2698 (2006)

33. T Moore, R Clayton, H Stern, in *Proceedings of the 2nd USENIX Conference on Large-scale Exploits and Emergent Threats: Botnets, Spyware, Worms, and more*, LEET'09. Temporal correlations between spam and phishing websites (USENIX Association, Berkeley, 2009), p. 5. http://dl.acm.org/citation.cfm?id=1855676.1855681. Accessed 29 October 2013

34. T Moore, R Clayton, R Anderson, The economics of online crime. J. Econ. Perspect. **23**(3), 3–20 (2009)

35. E Allman, The economics of spam. Queue **1**(9), 80 (2003)

36. Y Nadji, M Antonakakis, R Perdisci, W Lee, in *International Symposium on Research in Attacks, Intrusions, and Defenses*. Connected Colors: Unveiling the Structure of Criminal Networks (Rodney Bay, 23–25 October 2013)

37. H Liu, K Levchenko, M Félegyházi, C Kreibich, G Maier, GM Voelker, S Savage, in *Proceedings of the 4th USENIX conference on Large-scale Exploits and Emergent Threats*, LEET'11. On the effects of registrar-level intervention (USENIX Association, Berkeley, 2011), p. 5. http://dl.acm.org/citation.cfm?id=1972441.1972448. Accessed 29 October 2013

38. J Goodman, G Cormack, D Heckerman, Spam and the ongoing battle for the inbox. Commun. ACM **50**(2), 24–33 (2007)

39. E Bursztein, S Bethard, C Fabry, JC Mitchell, D Jurafsky, in *Proceedings of the 2010 IEEE Symposium on Security and Privacy*, SP '10. How Good Are Humans at Solving CAPTCHAs? A Large Scale Evaluation (IEEE Computer Society, Washington, 2010), pp. 399–413. http://dx.doi.org/10.1109/SP.2010.31. Accessed 29 October 2013

40. M Motoyama, K Levchenko, C Kanich, McD Coy, GM Voelker, S Savage, in *Proceedings of the 19th USENIX conference on Security*, USENIX Security'10. Re: CAPTCHAs: understanding CAPTCHA-solving services in an economic context (USENIX Association, Berkeley, 2010), p. 28. http://dl.acm.org/citation.cfm?id=1929820.1929858. Accessed 29 October 2013

41. D Liu, LJ Camp, in *Workshop on the Economics of Information Security*. Proof of Work can Work. Cambridge, 26–28 June 2006

42. D Twining, MM Williamson, M Mowbray, M Rahmouni, in *USENIX Annual Technical Conference, General Track*. Email Prioritization: Reducing Delays on Legitimate Mail Caused by Junk Mail (Boston, MA, 27 June–02 July 2004), pp. 45–58

43. C Osorio, in *Program on Internet and Telecoms Convergence*. A contribution to the understanding of illegal copying of software: empirical and analytical evidence against conventional wisdom (MIT, 2002). http://hdl.handle.net/1721.1/1479. Accessed 29 October 2013

44. J Bhagwati, B Hansen, A theoretical analysis of smuggling. Q. J. Econ. **87**(2), 172–187 (1973)

45. B Barrett, What is SOPA? Tech. rep., Gizmodo (2012)

46. J Sanchez, SOPA Internet Regulation And the Economics of Piracy. Tech. rep., CATO Institute (2012)

47. W Easterly, M Sewadeh, *Global Development Network Growth Database*. (World Bank Group, Washington, 2001). http://go.worldbank.org/ZSQKYFU6J0. Accessed 29 October 2013

48. I Al-Jabri, A Abdul-Gader, Software copyright infringements: an exploratory study of the effects of individual and peer beliefs. Omega **25**(3), 335–344 (1997)

49. M Katz, C Shapiro, Technology adoption in the presence of network externalities. J. Pol. Econ. **94**(4), 822–841 (1986)

50. H Varian, *Economics of Information Technology*. (University of California, Berkeley, 2001)

51. T Pratt, F Cullen, Assessing macro-level predictors and theories of crime: a meta-analysis. Crime Justice **32**, 373–450 (2005)
52. C Kilby, Supervision and performance: the case of World Bank projects. J. Dev. Econ. **62**, 233–259 (2000)
53. M Felson, L Cohen, Human ecology and crime: a routine activity approach. Hum. Ecol. **8**(4), 389–406 (1980)
54. T Kelley, L Camp, in *11th Annual Workshop on the Economics of Information Security*. Online promiscuity: prophylactic patching and the spread of computer transmitted infections (WEIS, Berlin, 2012). http://weis2012. econinfosec.org/papers/Kelley_WEIS2012.pdf. Accessed 29 October 2013
55. W Bonger, *Race and Crime* (Patterson Smith, Montclair, 1969)
56. J Blau, P Blau, The cost of inequality: Metropolitan structure and violent crime. Am. Sociol. Rev. **47**, 114–129 (1982)
57. F Cullen, Social support as an organizing concept for criminology: presidential address to the academy of criminal justice sciences. Justice Q. **11**(4), 527–559 (1994)
58. D Kaufmann, A Kraay, M Mastruzzi, The worldwide governance indicators: methodology and analytical issues. SSRN eLibrary (2010). http://papers. ssrn.com/sol3/papers.cfm?abstract_id=1682130. Accessed 29 October 2013
59. MJ van Eeten, JM Bauer, Economics of Malware: Security Decisions, Incentives and Externalities. OECD Science, Technology and Industry Working Papers 2008/1, OECD Publishing (2008). http://ideas.repec.org/ p/oec/stiaaa/2008-1-en.html. Accessed 29 October 2013
60. Microsoft, Microsoft Security Intelligence Report (Volume 11). Tech. rep., Microsoft (2011). http://www.microsoft.com/security/sir/default.aspx. Accessed 29 October 2013
61. V Garg, LJ Camp, in *Network and Distributed System Security Symposium Extended Abstracts*. Macroeconomic Analysis of Malware (San Diego, CA, 24–27 February 2013)
62. S Baum, J Ma, Education pays for individuals and society. High. Educ. **57**(4), 1–48 (2007)
63. E Rader, R Wash, B Brooks, in *Proceedings of the Eighth Symposium on Usable Privacy and Security, SOUPS '12*. Stories as informal lessons about security (ACM, New York, 2012), pp. 6:1–6:17. http://doi.acm.org/10.1145/2335356.2335364. Accessed 29 October 2013
64. M Marlinspike, in *BlackHat DC*. New tricks for defeating SSL in practice (Arlington, VA, 16–19 February 2009)
65. B Jonah, R Thiessen, E Au-Yeung, Sensation seeking, risky driving and behavioral adaptation. Accid. Anal. Prev. **33**(5), 679–684 (2001)
66. R Anderson, in *Proceedings of the 17th Annual Computer Security Applications Conference*, ACSAC '01. Why Information Security is Hard-An Economic Perspective (IEEE Computer Society, Washington, 2001), p. 358. http://dl.acm.org/citation.cfm?id=872016.872155. Accessed 29 October 2013
67. P Diehr, T Lumley, The importance of the normality assumption in large public health data sets. Annu. Rev. Publ. Health **23**, 151–169 (2002)
68. L Zhuang, J Dunagan, DR Simon, HJ Wang, JD Tygar, in *Proceedings of the 1st Usenix Workshop on Large-Scale Exploits and Emergent Threats*, LEET'08. Characterizing botnets from email spam records (USENIX Association, Berkeley, 2008), pp. 2:1–2:9. http://dl.acm.org/citation.cfm?id=1387711. Accessed 29 October 2013
69. A Ramachandran, N Feamster, in *Proceedings of the 2006 Conference on Applications, Technologies, Architectures, and Protocols for Computer Communications*, SIGCOMM '06. Understanding the network-level behavior of spammers (ACM, New York, 2006), pp. 291–302. http://doi.acm.org/10.1145/1159913.1159947. Accessed 29 October 2013

6

Edge-based image steganography

Saiful Islam[*], Mangat R Modi and Phalguni Gupta

Abstract

This paper proposes a novel steganography technique, where edges in the cover image have been used to embed messages. Amount of data to be embedded plays an important role on the selection of edges, i.e., the more the amount of data to be embedded, larger the use of weaker edges for embedding. Experimental results have shown that the proposed technique performs better or at least at par with the state-of-the-art steganography techniques but provides higher embedding capacity.

Keywords: Steganography; Steganalysis; Information hiding; Edge detection

1 Introduction

Steganography is an art of secure transmission of messages from a sender to a receiver. It should ensure that no one can reliably conclude on the secret communication between the sender and the receiver. To achieve such a secrecy, the message is hidden in some cover media which may not raise any suspicion on the possibility of carrying the secret message to the third party. Embedding introduces distortion in the cover medium. The embedding distortion in visual and statistical properties of the cover medium may lead steganographic detectability. The objective of any steganographic technique is to preserve these properties while embedding the message in the cover media.

Images are preferred medium for the current steganography techniques. Content adaptability, visual resilience, and smaller size of images make them good carrier to transmit secret messages over the internet. There exists a large number of image steganography techniques which are accompanied by various attacks on the steganography systems. Security of any steganography technique depends on the selection of pixels for embedding. Pixels in noisy and textured area are better choice for embedding because they are difficult to model. Pixels in edges can be seen as noisy pixels because their intensities are either higher or lower than their neighboring pixels due to sudden change in the coefficient gradient. Due to these sharp changes in the visual and statistical properties, edges are difficult to model in comparison to pixels in

smoother area. Therefore, edges make a better option to hide secret data than any other region of an image where a small distortion is much more noticeable. Figure 1a is an image with 20% of pixels modified to produce distortion. The image has some smooth parts such as sky and some parts with high concentration of edges, such as trees and buildings. Some areas from both smoother part and high texture part are cropped and zoomed as shown in Figure 1b,c. It can be seen that the modified pixels in the smoother parts are clearly noticeable, whereas it is hard to detect these distortions in the high texture parts. In this paper, we have proposed a steganography technique which can hide the secret message only in the edges of the cover image. The proposed steganography technique is found to have excellent security against steganalysis attacks. The performance of the technique is analyzed by testing on 'break our steganography system' (BOSSbase) ver. 1.01 [1] and 'break our watermarking system' (BOWS2)[a] databases, each having 10,000 grey scale images.

The paper is organized as follows. Section 2 discusses some well-known steganographic techniques. Various observations which are used to propose the steganographic technique are discussed in Section 3. An efficient edge-based steganography technique has been presented in Section 4. Experimental results have been analyzed in Section 5. Conclusions are given in the last section.

2 Literature review

There exist several steganographic techniques to embed data securely in a carrier medium and tools to detect reliably the presence of any secret message in a steganogram.

*Correspondence: sislam@cse.iitk.ac.in
Department of Computer Science and Engineering, Indian Institute of Technology Kanpur, Kanpur 208016, India

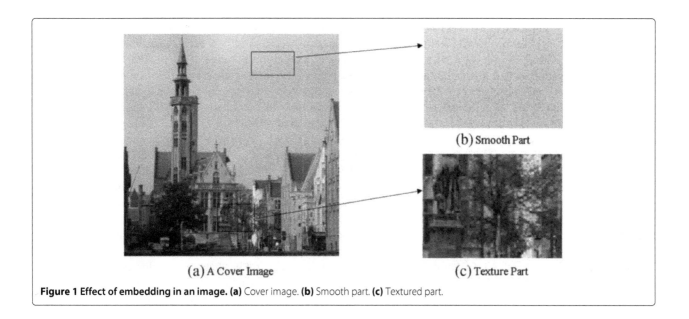

(a) A Cover Image

(b) Smooth Part

(c) Texture Part

Figure 1 Effect of embedding in an image. (a) Cover image. **(b)** Smooth part. **(c)** Textured part.

Steganographic technique consists of embedding and extracting mechanism. Image-based steganographic techniques can be classified into two categories: spatial domain and frequency (transform) domain.

A secret message is generally considered as an encrypted data, where bits of encrypted message are embedded in pixels of the cover image. The trivial steganography technique is based on the least significant bit (LSB) substitution in which the LSB of the pixels is modified to embed the secret message. In the spatial domain, this type of techniques can be broadly classified into two categories: LSB replacement and LSB matching. In case of LSB replacement [2,3], the least significant bit of each pixel of the cover image is replaced by the next bit of the secret message to be embedded. In LSB matching [4], if there is a mismatch between least significant bit of a byte in the cover image and next bit of the secret message to be embedded, then embedding, in general, is done by increasing or decreasing randomly the content of the byte of the cover image by 1, except at the boundary values. In some techniques, the decision to increase or decrease the content of a byte is governed by the score of the distortion function [5]. Embedding in two least significant bits is an extension of LSB replacement. There are multiple ways to embed data by flipping the least and the second least bits of a cover image [6].

In case of transform domain, the LSB-based embedding is done by modifying the LSB of non-zero DCT coefficients of a cover image. There exist several ways to embed data in transform domain such as modification of quantization table, heuristic based, utilizing non-shared selection, and side information at sender side [7].

Steganalysis tools track the distortion caused during the data embedding to detect the presence of the secret message in an image. These tools are classified as visual, structural, and non-structural [8,9]. Visual steganalysis attacks analyze images for some distortions which are visible to human vision system. The distortions could be visible in stego image or in LSB plane extracted from the stego image. Structural attacks analyze structural properties of an image to find any anomaly which are introduced by steganography. Structural detectors such as histogram attack [10], sample pair analysis (SPA) [11], RS method [12], and weighted stego [13] can reliably detect presence of stego data and even estimate message length. Non-structural detectors use feature extractors to model cover image and to compute distortion between the cover and the stego image to detect embedding. A classifier is trained by the feature set from large number of stego and cover images. During training, the classifier learns the differences in features, and this learning is used to classify a fresh image into stego or clean image. Non-structural detectors such as subtractive pixel adjacency matrix (SPAM) [14] and spatial-rich model (SRM) [15] claim better probability of detection of embedding in a stego image. Features based on steganalysis techniques use support vector machine (SVM) or ensemble classifiers [16] for supervised learning. SVM is not suitable for any high-dimension feature vector, while this is not the case with ensemble classifier but its performance is comparable to SVM.

Most of the current steganography techniques are based on model-preserving principles. These techniques are designed by finding a model for cover images, and embedding modifications are done in such a way that this model is preserved. Highly undetectable stego (HUGO) [5], ASO [17], universal wavelet relative distortion (UNIWARD) [18], and maximum mean discrepancy (MMD) [19] are designed on this principle. HUGO preserves features used by SPAM for steganalysis, thus preserving features space model. Similarly, UNIWARD preserves a wavelet-based model, while MMD preserves parametric-based model. Generally, these techniques embed message by minimizing a defined embedding distortion function heuristically. But, in [20], a non-heuristic distortion function is used to preserve the Kullback Leibler distance.

In [21], an embedding technique, known as pixel value difference technique (PVD) has been proposed. In this technique, the image is divided into non-overlapping blocks of adjacent pixels which are randomly selected, and data is embedded into each of its pixels. The amount of data embedded, i.e., the number of last significant bits used, is directly proportional to the differences in the intensities of adjacent pixels. This uneven embedding in PVD leads to unusual steps in the histogram of pixel difference in the stego image. An improved technique (IPVD), proposed in [22], has exploited this vulnerability. Adaptive edge LSB technique (AE-LSB) [23] has also removed this uneven pixel difference by introducing a readjusting phase and has provided better capacity. All these techniques are edge adaptive in a way that they can embed more data where pixel difference is high but they have one fundamental limitation. These techniques consider pixel pair at random, rather than selecting on the basis of higher differences. So, they may end up by embedding data at random places in the image and by distorting the texture in LSB plane of the image. Performance of these techniques are found to be poor [24].

In hiding behind corners (HBC) [25][b] technique, corner pixels are used to contain hidden data. Data is embedded by using simple LSB substitution. Such embedding leads to many structural asymmetries and could easily be detected by structural steganalysis tools like chi-square [10], sample pair analysis (SP) [26], and weighted stego (WS) [27]. Thus, the HBC technique which maintains texture in LSB plane, offers poor security.

Edge adaptive image steganography (EALMR) [24] technique is based on LSB matching revisited (LSBMR) [3] technique which alleviates some of the above said limitations. EALMR calculates the difference between two adjacent pixels. If this difference is greater than a predefined threshold, then both pixels are marked as edge pixels, and one bit of data is hidden in each of them using LSBMR. This technique has some limitations. Difference of intensities of adjacent pixels may not be an edge point; any such technique may embed data in smoother parts even though there are some unused prominent edges. So, any well-known edge detection algorithm can be used to find edge pixels and to hide data in the detected edges. Further, since EALMR compares a pixel with its adjacent pixel, it can find edges only in one direction. To

overcome this limitation, an image can be divided into some non-overlapping but equal size blocks, and each block is rotated in the range of set {0°, 90°, 180°, 270°} to see edge pixels in more than one direction inside a given block. But, poor edge selection results in detection by steganalysis tools like targeted attack [28] and blind attacks SPAM [14] and SRM [15].

In [5], HUGO steganographic technique is presented. Its design is derived from the image model obtained from the feature set of SPAM steganalyzer. It is based on the minimum-embedding impact principle, where embedding is done in such a way that the distortion in a stego image is minimum. It preserves a model utilized by SPAM steganalyzer to derive steganalytic features in such a way that it does not over-fit to a SPAM feature set. Dimensionality of the feature set has been tremendously enhanced so that the technique is not detectable by minor modification in SPAM steganalyzer. Instead of using Markov transition matrix to compute SPAM features, co-occurrence matrix is used to derive those features. But, it may have minor degradation in performance. Detectable parts of the model are identified by Fisher linear discriminant (FLD criteria) [29]. It rates individual features' importance for embedding changes. The parts of the model not vulnerable to embedding changes are identified using criteria optimized in FLD. In [30], it is shown that HUGO is vulnerable against steganalysis that uses other models drawn from different domains.

In [31], embedding distortion cost is computed through directional residual obtained using Daubechies wavelet filter bank [32]. The objective is to limit the embedding changes to those parts of the cover image that are difficult to model in multiple directions. Embedding is done in textures or noisy parts and avoiding smooth regions and clean edges of empirical cover images. Distortion function, called as UNIWARD [31], is used to compute delectability map. Syndrome trellis code (STC) [33] and detectability map are used to embed payload while minimizing the embedding distortion. The same distortion design technique can be used for spatial and transform domains.

3   Some observations

This section discusses some observations that are used to design an edge-based steganography technique. The edges are difficult to model, and the pixels belonging to each selected edge are considered as noisy pixels for embedding. In Figure 2, it is seen that embedding in edge pixels leads to changes in edges of the stego image. Consider the cover image shown in Figure 2a. The edges in the cover image for maximum possible embedding capacity are shown in Figure 2b, and corresponding edges in the stego image are depicted in Figure 2c. Finally, Figure 2d shows the locations where edges in stego and cover image

Figure 2 Change in the number of edge pixels due to embedding. (a) Cover image. **(b)** Edge pixels in a cover image. **(c)** Edge pixels in a stego image. **(d)** Edge pixel mismatch.

do not match. As a result, it makes it impossible to retrieve the embedded message from the stego image. But, the secret message must be extracted from the stego image. Therefore, just by using any edge detection algorithm to detect edges and embedding in those locations may not be sufficient for designing an edge-based steganography technique.

3.1 Masking cover image

In order to keep no changes in edges before and after embedding, the LSBs of the cover image are masked, and edge detectors are applied on the masked cover images. Since LSB replacement does not modify any bit other than LSB, a pixel of a cover image, the edges in cover and stego images remain identical as shown in Figure 3. It has been observed that the number of pixels belonging to edges does not change much by masking LSB or the least two significant bits (2LSB).

Table 1 lists the difference in the number of pixels belonging to edges between cover image and its modified images by masking 2LSB for BOSSbase database ver. 1.01 of 10,000 natural images. It can be seen that the average difference for different edge detectors and masking 2LSB is limited to less than 2%. However, there is a outlier case, shown in Figure 4, where the difference is 61%. It can be noted that for both databases, the number of pixels belonging to edges are increased after masking 2LSB. Hence, masking at least two significant bits does not effect the edges in the cover image for most of the cases.

3.2 Embedding in LSB or 2LSB

Most of the steganographic techniques embed data in LSB of pixels in the cover image pixel. Embedding is done by either LSB replacement or LSB matching. LSB replacement is detected by most of the structural detectors, but

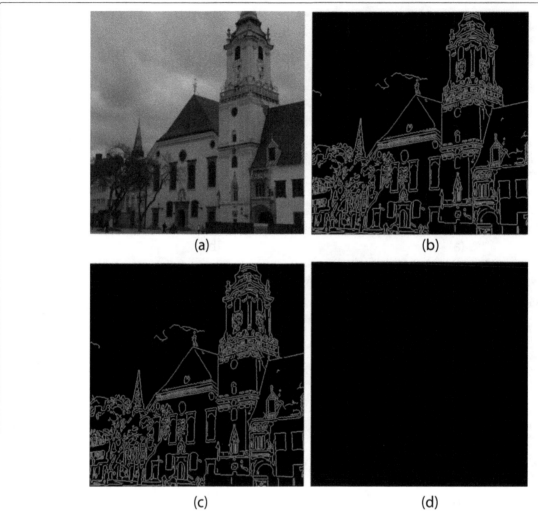

Figure 3 Change in the number of edge pixels due to embedding. (a) Cover image. **(b)** Edge pixels in a cover (masked). **(c)** Edge pixels in a stego (masked). **(d)** No edge pixels mismatch.

LSB matching is reliably detected through non-structural detector SPAM and SRM. Hence, if one embeds in the LSB plane, then there is a high probability of detection of presence of the message. To overcome these structural and non-structural detectors, embedding is done in 2LSB plane of the cover image. Embedding in 2LSB plane violates the basic assumption of structural detectors, and it has been observed that even SPAM and SRM are less

accurate in detecting the presence of the message for less amount of data embedding in comparison to LSB replacement. It is shown in [6,34] that embedding in 2LSB plane is preferable to embed in LSB plane.

4 Proposed technique

This section proposes a new steganography technique which hides secret messages in the edges of the carrier

Table 1 Average difference in number of edge pixels between image and its (2LSB) masked image

Algorithm	Total pixels	Edge pixels (average)	Edge pixels (%)	Edge pixels (masked)	Difference (average)	Difference (%)
Canny	262,144	23,818	9.1	24,201	383	1.61
Sobel	262,144	8,451	3.2	8,458	7	0.09
Prewitt	262,144	8,407	3.2	8,415	8	0.10
LOG	262,144	18,220	6.9	18,357	137	0.80

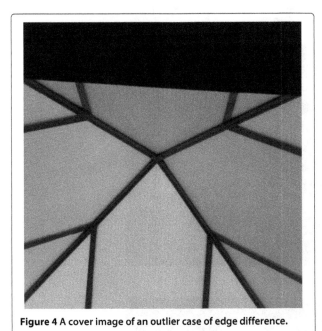

Figure 4 A cover image of an outlier case of edge difference.

image. It is an extension of edge embedding in color image [35]. To get true edges, Canny edge detection technique [36] has been used. The selection of edges for embedding is dependent on the length of payload and the image. As the payload size increases, a weak threshold for the selection of edges is used so that more edges can be selected to accommodate the increased amount of data. For a given payload, the sharpest possible edges are selected to embed the message. The flow graph shown in Figure 5 shows the proposed steganography technique which consists of two primary tasks: threshold selection and embedding. Threshold selection is to find Canny high threshold t_h so that sufficient number of edges are selected to embed the given payload in a cover image, while embedding is done by computing edge-map based on threshold. Payload is

embedded in a cover image in a random order based on the stego key and the edge map.

4.1 Threshold selection

Canny edge detection algorithm returns [36] edges in a image on the basis of three parameters, namely, high threshold (t_h), lower threshold (t_l), and width of Gaussian kernel. Threshold t_h is used to identify strong edges, where t_l helps to identify weaker edges. The t_h value is dynamically adjusted on the basis of message size in such a way that enough number of edges in the cover image are selected to embed the secret message. Experimentally, the t_l value is set to $0.4 \times t_h$. The effect of change in the threshold value for edge detection is shown in Figure 6. The sharper edge means sharp change in visual and statistical properties in the image which make the detection of hidden data tougher. Canny edge detector's sensitivity to noise is controlled by width of the kernel. Increase of the kernel width decreases detector's noise sensitivity and vice versa. Initially, the width of the kernel is taken as constant to obtain the threshold value. Initial guess of the threshold is obtained through Algorithm 1. Later, fine tuning of the threshold and width of the Gaussian kernel are done to improve the embedding algorithm. Figure 7 shows the effect of width of kernel w on thresholds t_h and t_l and number of pixels selected for embedding.

It is to be noted from Table 2 that for each image, different sets of thresholds are obtained to fix the width of the kernel. There is no way to obtain the best value of width of the kernel, but it has been observed that high value of t_h and low value of w are better options for embedding. For experimental purpose, fine tuning is done by increasing the threshold value and decreasing width of the Gaussian kernel. The results are evaluated for fixed values of w and embedding rates. Sets of stego images are evaluated for security, and the best result among all cases is reported. Threshold selection tries to avoid clean edges by fixing $t_l = 0.4 \times t_h$ and by reducing the width of Gaussian kernel.

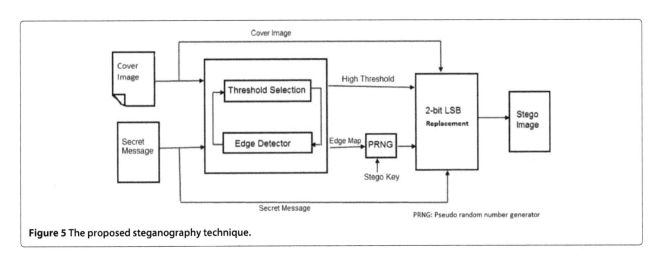

Figure 5 The proposed steganography technique.

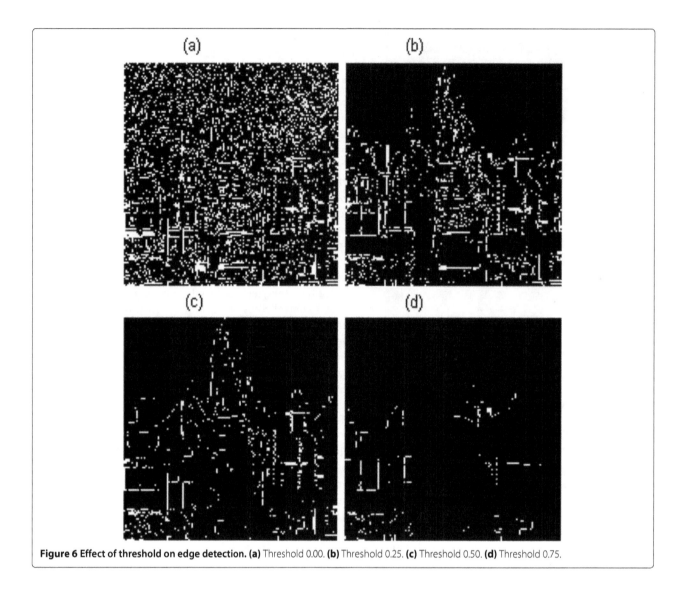

Figure 6 Effect of threshold on edge detection. (a) Threshold 0.00. **(b)** Threshold 0.25. **(c)** Threshold 0.50. **(d)** Threshold 0.75.

To facilitate the extraction of message at the receiver end, the length of the secret message is pre-fixed to the message to form an augmented message. The structure of the augmented message is shown in Figure 8. The message size field of the augmented message is of fixed length (C bits). The augmented message is a binary string with the assumption that C bits are sufficient to store the message size information.

The threshold value is computed at the time of embedding, and it has to be sent to the receiver separately. The threshold value and width of the kernel are stored in IEEE 754 floating point half precision format. They require only 16 bits and are embedded in non-edge pixels of the cover image.

Algorithm 1 finds the suitable high threshold value for the Canny edge detector. Initially t_{min} is set to 0 and t_{max} equal to 1. The high threshold value t_h lies between these two values. Let the number of pixels in edges returned by Canny edge detector for the given threshold which is median between t_{min} and t_{max} be n_e. Binary search is used to find the threshold value. It is quite possible that number of pixels n_e belonging to edges may not be exactly same as length of the secret message N. If this condition occurs, binary search cannot return the threshold value. To alleviate this problem, the terminating condition of the search is modified so that it returns the number of pixels greater than or equal to N, and *limit* is used to set upper bound on n_e. It has been found that *limit* of 1% is sufficient for BOSSbase ver. 1.01 and BOW2 database. If n_e is less than the required number of edge pixels N, then t_h has to be greater than the median threshold, t_{min} is set to the median threshold, and the process is repeated. Similarly, if n_e is greater than ($N + 0.01N$), the median threshold is set to t_{max}, and the process is repeated until the difference between the number of edge pixels, n_e and N, is less than the *limit*.

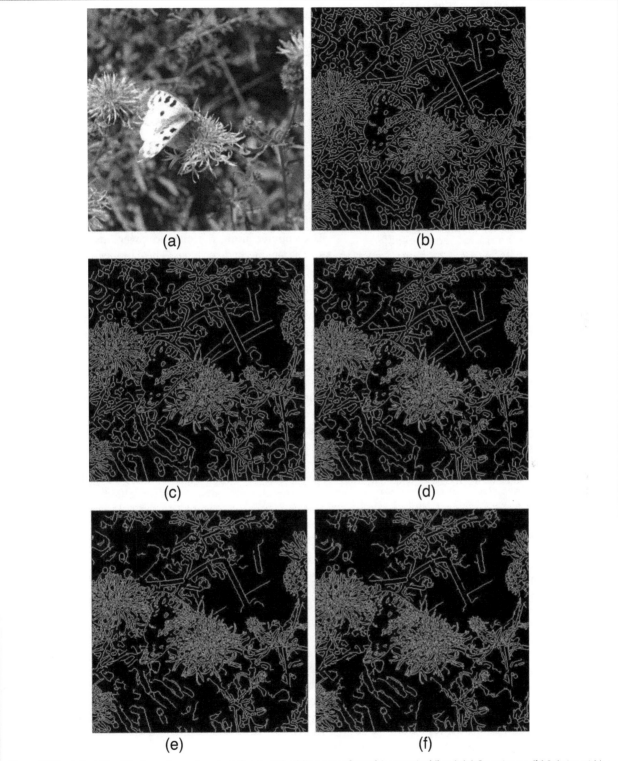

Figure 7 Effect of width of the kernel on edge pixels for an embedding rate of 0.10 bits per pixel (bpp). **(a)** Cover image. **(b)** Relative width = 1.0. **(c)** Relative width = 0.8. **(d)** Relative width = 0.6. **(e)** Relative width = 0.4. **(f)** Relative width = 0.2.

4.2 The embedding

Embedding in the cover image is done by least two-significant-bit substitutions (2LSB). It means that each of the least two significant bits in the pixel intensity holds one bit of message. Bits of a pixel are flipped whenever they are not equal to the message bits. Only six most

Table 2 Effect of width of kernel on edge pixels

High threshold (t_h)	Low threshold (t_l)	Width (w)	Pixels required (range in bits)	Embedding capacity (bits)
0.070	0.0280	1.0	26,234 to 28,835	28,801
0.105	0.0420	0.8	26,234 to 28,835	28,598
0.105	0.0420	0.6	26,234 to 28,835	28,506
0.095	0.0380	0.4	26,234 to 28,835	28,798
0.095	0.0380	0.2	26,234 to 28,835	28,422

Algorithm 1: getThreshold(I, N, w)

Data: I: Image, N: Length of augmented message to be embedded, w: width of the Gaussian Kernel

Result: threshold: t_h for Canny to get N pixels

```
// limit is set to 1% of the message
   length
// no. of edge pixels, n_e ≤ N + 0.01 × N
   and n_e ≥ N
// n_e = number of edge pixels in I, when
   Canny edge detector is used on I with
   high threshold t_h and low threshold
   t_l = 0.4 * t_h and width w
```

$limit \longleftarrow 0.01 \times N$;
$t_{max} \longleftarrow 1$;
$t_{min} \longleftarrow 0$;
$set \longleftarrow false$;
repeat
> $t_h \longleftarrow \lfloor (t_{max} + t_{min})/2 \rfloor$;
> $n_e \longleftarrow$ getEdgePixelCount(Canny(I, t_h, t_l, w));
> ```
> // it returns the number of pixels in
>    the edges obtained through Canny
>    edge detector
> ```
> $diff \longleftarrow n_e - N$;
> **if** $diff > limit$ **then**
> > $t_{min} \longleftarrow t_h$;
>
> **end**
> **else if** $diff < 0$ **then**
> > $t_{max} \longleftarrow t_h$;
>
> **end**
> **else**
> > $set \longleftarrow false$;
>
> **end**

until $set = true$;
return t_h

---

significant bits participate in edge detection to form an edge map of the gray scale cover image.

In Algorithm 2, two least significant bits of the cover image are masked to form an edge map (e). Threshold is computed using the masked cover image and length of the augmented message. The number of edge pixels used to embed the augmented message is half of the augmented message bits because each edge pixel carries two bits of the augmented message. The edge map e obtained through the Canny edge detector is randomly arranged using stego key P by calling *randomPermute(e,P)*. It ensures that only the intended users can extract data from the stego image. The secret message M is embedded in the randomly permuted S using edge map e by modifying the least two bits of pixel $S_{x,y}$ to the corresponding two consecutive message bits $M_{index+1}$ and M_{index} . The threshold and width are embedded in non-edge pixels of the stego image. Non-edge pixel map e' is obtained by taking complement of e for minimum values of t_h and w. The threshold and width are embedded in the first 32 bits of S corresponding to e'. Image S is reshuffled to get the stego image.

4.3 Extraction

It is the process to retrieve the augmented message from the given stego image. The threshold value and width are extracted from the non-edge pixels of the stego image. Stego key has been used as the seed to permute the set of edge pixels. Extraction is similar to the embedding process. The least two significants bits of the stego image S is masked, and edge map e is computed. It is permuted using stego key P to retrieve the message in the same order as it has been embedded. The value corresponding to the least

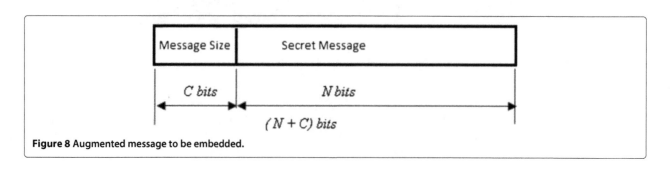

Figure 8 Augmented message to be embedded.

Algorithm 2: embed(*I, M, P, w*)

Data: *I*: Image, *M*: Augmented message in binary, *P*: Stego key, *w*: width of the Gaussian kernel

Result: *S*: Stego image

$S \longleftarrow I$;
// Mask 2LSB and find edges
$I \longleftarrow$ bitand(I,252);
$L \longleftarrow |M|$;
// Length of the augmented message
// Compute Threshold
$t_h \longleftarrow$ getThreshold(I, L, w);
// Obtain e: e is edge map obtained by calling Canny edge detector algorithm with high threshold t_h and low threshold $t_l = 0.4 * t_h$ and width w
$e \longleftarrow$ Canny(I, t_h, t_l, w);
// Shuffle e and **S** using Stego key *P*
$e \longleftarrow$ randomPermute(e,P);
$S \longleftarrow$ randomPermute(S,P);
// e is the set of edge pixels
$index \longleftarrow 0$;
for *each edge pixel i in* **e do**
    $S_{x,y} =$ bitand($S_{x,y}$,252); // x,y are co-ordinates of pixel *i*
    $S_{x,y} = S_{x,y} + 2*M_{index+1} + M_{index}$;
    $index \longleftarrow index + 2$;
end
// Embed threshold and width in non-edge pixels of *S*
$e \longleftarrow$ Canny($I, 0, 0, 0.1$); // Pixels in e are maximum number of edge pixels for a given image
$e' \longleftarrow$ complement(e); // Pixels in e' are non-edge pixels
for *i = 1: 16 in e'* **do**
    $S_{x,y} =$ bitand($S_{x,y}$,254); // x,y are co-ordinates of pixel *i*
    $S_{x,y} = S_{x,y} + t_{h(i)}$;
    // t_h is represented in 16 bits IEEE 754 floating point half precision
end
for *i = 17: 32 in e'* **do**
    $S_{x,y} =$ bitand($S_{x,y}$,254); // x,y are co-ordinates of pixel *i*
    $S_{x,y} = S_{x,y} + w_{(i-16)}$;
    // w is represented in 16 bits IEEE 754 floating point half precision
end
$S \longleftarrow$ randomPermute(S,P); // Reshuffle *S* to get Stego Image: *S*
return *S*;

Algorithm 3: decode: retrieve secret message

Data: *I*: stego image, *T*: Threshold, *P*: stego key, *w*: Kernel width

Result: *M*: Secret message

$S \longleftarrow I$;
// Mask least 2 bits and find edges
$S' \longleftarrow$ bitand(S,252);
// Obtain e: e is edge map obtained by calling Canny edge detector algorithm with high threshold t_h and low threshold $t_l = 0.4 * t_h$ and width w
$t_h \longleftarrow T$;
$t_l \longleftarrow 0.4 * t_h$;
$e \longleftarrow$ Canny(S', t_h, t_l, w);
$e \longleftarrow$ randomPermute(e,P);
// Shuffle *S* to get order of embedding
$S \longleftarrow$ randomPermute(S, P);
$index \longleftarrow 0$;
for *each edge pixel i in e* **do**
    $val \longleftarrow$ bitand($S_{x,y}$,3); // x,y are co-ordinates of pixel *i*
    $M_{index+1} \longleftarrow val$ mod 2;
    $val \longleftarrow val/2$;
    $M_{index} = val$;
    $index \longleftarrow index + 2$;
end
// extract first C bits to get message size
$msg\_size \longleftarrow M[1:C]$;
$M \longleftarrow M[C + 1 : msg\_size]$;
return (M);

---

two significant bits of each edge pixel is extracted to *val*. Two consecutive bits $M_{index+1}$ and M_{index} of payload are retrieved from *val* for each edge pixel belonging to *e*. This retrieved payload consists of message size, actual message, and few extra bits. Message size *msg_size* is extracted from the first *C* bits of the payload which is used to retrieve the actual message $M[C+1:msg\_size]$. Extra bits beyond *msg_size* are discarded, and the secret message *M* is returned. Algorithm 3 delineates the extraction module.

5 Experimental results

The proposed technique has been tested on BOSSbase database ver. 1.01 and BOWS2 database. Each database contains 10,000 8-bit gray scale images with size of 512×512. Images of BOSSbase taken from eight different cameras, resized and uncompressed. Secret message is randomly generated by a pseudo random number generator (PRNG) to simulate encryption of the secret message. For experimental purpose, payload is taken to be 10% bits per pixel (bpp) of the cover image to show the effectiveness of the proposed technique. In both databases, the total number of pixels belonging to edges is found to be less than 10%. Further, the technique is also analyzed for variable payload and for the best threshold and width of the Gaussian filter. It is compared with LSBM, existing edge adaptive techniques HBC and EALMR, and minimizing distortion-based techniques HUGO and S-UNIWARD. The steganographic security is evaluated against visual, structural, and blind steganalysis attacks.

5.1 Visual attacks

All well-known techniques do not create any visible mark on the stego image. However, when the LSB plane is filtered to remove the significant part of the cover image, the difference becomes obvious. The technique like LSBM embeds data, irrespective to the nature and structure of image damaged texture in the LSB plane. One of the reasons to use edge-based steganography is to preserve the texture in the LSB plane. Texture in LSB plane can be seen in Figure 9b which has some white and black patches; these are the clusters of pixels having same LSB value. This property is more prominent in smoother areas of the image like bright sky or dark shadow. So, any change in the smoother part of the image may change LSB value of the pixels in these clusters. This is visible in Figure 9c, which is a stego image generated by LSBM, corresponding to the area marked in Figure 9b. Here, LSBM writes some message bits, causing some black pixels to appear. On inspection, these black pixels on the white patch may raise suspicion. On the other hand, all other edge-based techniques in Figure 9 have not caused any noticeable change. It can be concluded that the edge-based steganography resists visual attacks.

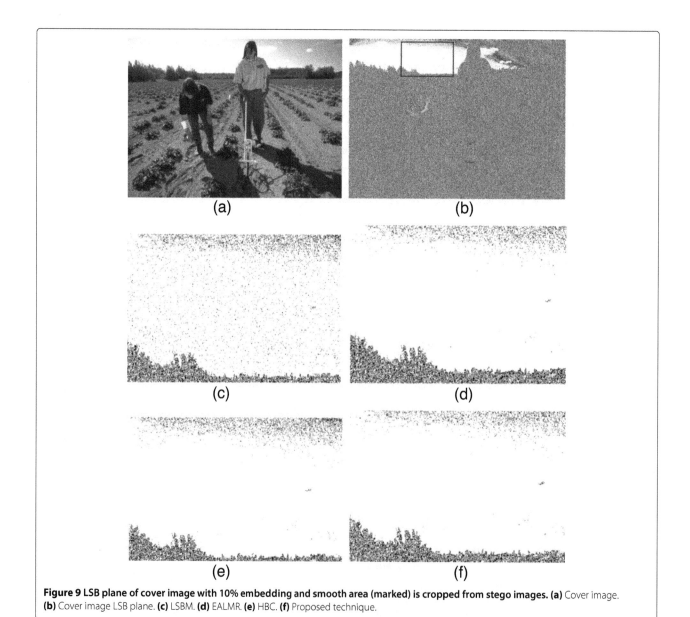

Figure 9 LSB plane of cover image with 10% embedding and smooth area (marked) is cropped from stego images. **(a)** Cover image. **(b)** Cover image LSB plane. **(c)** LSBM. **(d)** EALMR. **(e)** HBC. **(f)** Proposed technique.

5.2 Structural attacks

Embedding data in an image leads to statistical modification in the structure of cover image. Any such modification in a cover image can be observed by first- and second-order statistics. SP [26] analysis and WS [27] are two popular structural attacks. Both SP and WS estimate the length of the embedded message by giving the percentage of pixels which may hold data.

Table 3 lists the result of SP and WS for various steganography techniques. It can be noted that the relative message length for HBC lies close to 10%, but that for LSBM, EALMR, and the proposed technique is 0.2%, 0.06%, and 2.6%, respectively. For better understanding, SP and WS are executed on the original databases to get the mean value of relative message length. LSBM, EALMR, and the proposed technique are found to be close to the mean value of the natural images. One possible reason for these results could be the use of LSB matching and 2LSB-based embedding which do not lead to asymmetry in pixels intensity. Therefore, the relative message length for any edged-based technique does not raise any suspicion.

5.3 Blind steganalysis using feature extraction

Edge-based steganographic techniques, minimizing embedding distortion-based techniques, and the proposed technique are analyzed using SPAM and SRM.

5.3.1 Steganalysis by Subtractive Pixel Adjacency Matrix (SPAM)

Analysis of these techniques is performed by taking feature sets from their respective stego images and natural images. These features are used to train SVM to learn the difference in features caused by steganography [37]. Testing is done in fivefold cross-validation. For each technique, cover and corresponding stego sets of images are divided into five parts. SVM is trained for four sets of randomly selected sample images, and the results have been validated for the remaining set. This process is repeated five times, and the average of all the tests is reported as the final result. The results from SVM may vary greatly with the values of two parameters: penalization cost (C) and gamma (γ). However, there are few rules to determine optimal values of these parameters. High or low values of

both false positive (F_p) and false negative (F_n) indicate that the classifier is biased towards one class. For a good classifier, average value of F_p and F_n should be low. So, the values of C and γ are adjusted to achieve minimum average value of F_p and F_n. In [38], fivefold cross-validation is used with the multiplicative grid

$$C \in \{0.001, 0.01, \ldots 10000\}$$
$$\gamma \in \left\{ 2^i \mid i \in \{-d-3, \ldots, -d+3\} \right\},$$

where $d = \log_2(x)$, x is the number of features in the subset. But, the range of γ has been extended as it has been observed that the accuracy of SPAM increases for the larger value of γ. Hence, for experimental purpose, the following multiplicative grid is used:

$$C \in \{0.001, 0.01, \ldots 10000\}$$
$$\gamma \in \{0, 0.01, 0.1, 1, 2, 4, 8, 16\}.$$

Table 4 shows that LSBM is detected with an accuracy of 93.0%. HBC and EALMR both do not use any well-known edge detection algorithm; therefore, they are easily detected by SPAM and have accuracy rate of 89.6% and 70.8%, respectively. The maximum detection accuracy achieved by the proposed technique is 51.1%, and it can be attributed to the selection of noisy pixels through true edge detection [36]. It can be noted that accuracy of 50% is like a random guess about cover and stego images. This means that features extracted by SPAM have failed to produce any considerable difference between stego and natural images for the proposed technique.

5.3.2 Steganalysis by spatial-rich model

SRM consists of 39 symmetrized sub-models quantized with three different quantization factors with a total dimension of 34671. Due to its large dimensionality, it is implemented using machine learning tool, ensemble classifier [16] which consists of many base learners such as FLD [29]. Each of them is trained on a set of a cover and stego images. The accuracy of the model is evaluated using the ensemble's unbiased estimate of the testing error known as the 'out-of-bag' error, E_{OOB}. It is an accurate estimate of the testing error.

This subsection presents the results of the tests conducted for relative payloads 0.05, 0.10, and 0.20 bpp. It has been observed in Table 1 that for BOSSbase database,

Table 3 SP and WS relative message length for various steganography techniques (estimation results)

Database	Attacks	LSBM	HBC	EALMR	Cover image	Proposed
BOWS2	SP	0.20	15.6	0.06	2.40	2.60
	WS	0.12	8.34	0.01	0.84	1.30
BOSSbase ver. 1.01	SP	0.32	9.60	0.09	0.01	0.07
	WS	0.10	7.20	0.06	0.00	0.05

Table 4 SPAM accuracy against edge embedding algorithms

Algorithm	Accuracy
LSBM	93.0%
HBA	89.6%
EALMR	70.8%
Proposed	51.1%

the number of pixels belonging to edges is less than 10%. The number of pixels belonging to edge can be increased by decreasing threshold and kernel width. This increase in the number of pixels is, on average, limited to 34.6% of cover images of the database. Relative payloads of 0.30, 0.40, and 0.50 bpp are not considered in the database because it is not possible to embed payload of 0.30 bpp in large number of images by the proposed technique. The number of cases for which the payload is more than the number of pixels belonging to edges increases considerably for embedding rate greater than 0.30 bpp. The simulation results of the proposed technique is compared with those of HUGO and S-UNIWARD [18]. The results are obtained through fine tuning of threshold and width of the Gaussian kernel and embedding using LSBMR. LSBMR is used, instead of 2LSB, because HUGO and S-UNIWARD embed at most 1 bit per pixel. The HUGO simulator with default settings is used to create the stego images. Similarly, the sets of stego images are obtained from the S-UNIWARD simulator. Figure 10 presents E_{OOB} errors of the proposed technique, HUGO and S-UNIWARD. It is seen that the proposed technique outperforms HUGO and performs equivalent to the S-UNIWARD for embedding rate up to 20%. Embedding rate beyond 20% cannot correctly be evaluated because there are large number of outlier cases as shown in Table 5. For relative payload of 30%, there are 1,331 cover images having less than 30% of total pixels belonging to edge. Therefore, embedding is not possible for the given payload in these images.

6   Conclusions

In this paper, a new technique for steganography in gray scale images has been proposed. Data is hidden at the edges of the cover image, and the edges are dynamically selected based on the length of the message. The proposed technique can resist visual, structural, and non-structural

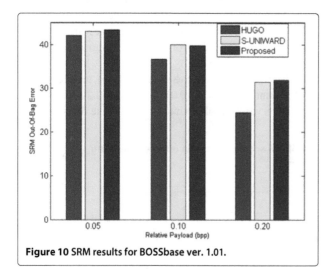

Figure 10 SRM results for BOSSbase ver. 1.01.

Table 5 Number of outlier cases for the proposed technique

Bits per pixel	Outliers
0.05	2
0.10	2
0.20	25
0.30	1,331

attacks better than the existing edge-based techniques. HBC is detected by structural detectors due to anomalies created by LSB substitution. These anomalies are well resisted by LSBM, but it does not discriminate between smooth areas and the edges in an image causing some distortion in LSB plane of stego image. EALMR is resistant to structural attacks because it uses LSBMR for embedding. It fails to discriminate between prominent edges and smothered area for a given threshold. Hence, there is a possibility of embedding in smoother parts of image. The proposed technique uses two-bit LSB substitution for embedding, and as a result, it decreases the number of pixels to be distorted. Modification of two bits of the selected pixels leads to significant change in pixel intensity, but this change does not lead to detectability due to sharp difference in intensity of edge and non-edge pixels. Hence, embedding in edges does not produce any visual distortion in stego images. The performance of the proposed technique is also found to be better than that of HUGO for embedding rate less than 10% bpp and slightly better than that of S-UNIWARD for embedding rate of 5%. An embedding rate greater than 10% bpp leads to embedding payload in weak edges. It tries to avoid clean edges by fixing $t_l = 0.4 \times t_h$ and reducing width of Gaussian kernel, but there is no rule of thumb to accurately discriminate between clean and non-clean edges in an image. Further, reduction of width of the Gaussian kernel improves the performance of the proposed technique as some finer details are also selected as edges. The performance of the proposed technique is expected to be improved if one uses syndrome coding to reduce the amount of distortion that occurred due to embedding.

Endnotes
[a]BOWS-2 in http://bows2.ec-lille.fr/ (2013)
[b]Digital invisible ink toolkit in http://diit.sourceforge. net/files/HidingBehindCorners.pdf (2014)

Competing interests
The authors declare that they have no competing interests.

Acknowledgements
The authors would like to thank antonymous reviewers for their valuable comments and sharing their knowledge in improving this article.

References

1. P Bas, T Filler, T Pevný, ed. by T Filler, T Pevný, S Craver, and A Ker, "Break our steganographic system": The ins and outs of organizing BOSS, in *Lecture Notes in Computer Science: Information Hiding*, vol. 6958 (Springer Berlin, 2011), pp. 59–70
2. C-K Chan, L-M Cheng, Hiding data in images by simple LSB substitution. Pattern Recognit. **37**(3), 469–474 (2004)
3. A Ker, ed. by J Fridrich, Improved detection of LSB steganography in grayscale images, in *Lecture Notes in Computer Science: 6th International Workshop on Information Hiding, Toronto, Canada*, vol. 3200 (Springer Berlin, 2004), pp. 97–115
4. AD Ker, Steganalysis of LSB matching in grayscale images. IEEE Signal Process. Lett. **12**(6), 441–444 (2005)
5. T Pevný, T Filler, P Bas, ed. by R Böhme, PWL Fong, and Safavi-Naini R, Using high-dimensional image models to perform highly undetectable steganography, in *Lecture Notes in Computer Science: 12th International Conference on Information Hiding, Calgary, AB, Canada* (Springer Berlin, 2010), pp. 161–177
6. AD Ker, Steganalysis of embedding in two least-significant bits. IEEE Trans. Inf. Forensics Security **2**(1), 46–54 (2007)
7. JJ Fridrich, T Pevný, J Kodovský, Statistically undetectable jpeg steganography: dead end challenges, and opportunities. Paper presented at the 9th workshop on multimedia & security (MM&Sec), Dallas, TX, USA, 20–21 Sep 2007, pp. 3–14
8. AD Ker, ed. by M Barni, J Herrera-Joancomartí, S Katzenbeisser, and F Pérez-González, A general framework for the structural steganalysis of LSB replacement, in *Lecture Notes in Computer Science: 7th International Workshop on Information Hiding, Barcelona*, vol. 3727 (Springer Berlin, 2005), pp. 296–311
9. N Provos, P Honeyman, Hide and seek: an introduction to steganography. IEEE Secur. Privacy **1**(3), 32–44 (2003)
10. A Westfeld, A Pfitzmann, ed. by A Pfitzmann, Attacks on steganographic systems - breaking the steganographic utilities EzStego, Jsteg, Steganos, and S-Tools - and some lessons learned, in *Lecture Notes in Computer Science: 3rd International Workshop on Information Hiding, Dresden, Germany*, vol. 1768 (Springer Berlin, 1999), pp. 61–76
11. S Dumitrescu, X Wu, Z Wang, ed. by FAP Petitcolas, Detection of LSB steganography via sample pair analysis, in *Lecture Notes in Computer Science: 5th International Workshop on Information Hiding, Noordwijkerhout, The Netherlands*, vol. 2578 (Springer Berlin, 2002), pp. 355–372
12. JJ Fridrich, M Goljan, D Hogea, D Soukal, Quantitative steganalysis of digital images: estimating the secret message length. Multimedia Syst. **9**(3), 288–302 (2003)
13. JJ Fridrich, M Goljan, On estimation of secret message length in LSB steganography in spatial domain. Paper presented at the SPIE security, steganography, and watermarking of multimedia contents VI, San Jose, CA, USA, 18–22 Jan 2004, vol. 5306, pp. 23–34
14. T Pevný, P Bas, JJ Fridrich, Steganalysis by subtractive pixel adjacency matrix. IEEE Trans. Inf. Forensics Security **5**(2), 215–224 (2010)
15. JJ Fridrich, J Kodovský, Rich models for steganalysis of digital images. IEEE Trans. Inf. Forensics Security **7**(3), 868–882 (2012)
16. J Kodovský, JJ Fridrich, V Holub, Ensemble classifiers for steganalysis of digital media. IEEE Trans. Inf. Forensics Security **7**(2), 432–444 (2012)
17. S Kouider, M Chaumont, W Puech, Adaptive steganography by oracle (ASO). Paper presented at the IEEE international conference on multimedia and expo (ICME), San Jose, CA, USA, 15–19 July 2013, pp. 1–6
18. V Holub, J Fridrich, T Denemark, Universal distortion function for steganography in an arbitrary domain. EURASIP J. Inform. Secur. **2014**(1) (2014). doi:10.1186/1687-417X-2014-1
19. T Filler, JJ Fridrich, Design of adaptive steganographic schemes for digital images. Paper presented at the media watermarking, security, and forensics XIII, part of IS&T SPIE electronic imaging symposium, San Francisco, CA, USA, 24 Jan 2011, vol. 7880, pp. 1–14
20. JJ Fridrich, J Kodovský, Multivariate Gaussian model for designing additive distortion for steganography. Paper presented at the IEEE international conference on acoustics, speech and signal processing (ICASSP), Vancouver, BC, Canada, 26–31 May 2013, pp. 2949–2953
21. D-C Wu, W-H Tsai, A steganographic method for images by pixel-value differencing. Pattern Recogn. Lett. **24**(9-10), 1613–1626 (2003)
22. X Zhang, S Wang, Vulnerability of pixel-value differencing steganography to histogram analysis and modification for enhanced security. Pattern Recogn. Lett. **25**(3), 331–339 (2004)
23. C-H Yang, C-Y Weng, S-J Wang, H-M Sun, Adaptive data hiding in edge areas of images with spatial LSB domain systems. IEEE Trans. Inf. Forensics Security **3**(3), 488–497 (2008)
24. W Luo, F Huang, J Huang, Edge adaptive image steganography based on LSB matching revisited. IEEE Trans. Inf. Forensics Security **5**(2), 201–214 (2010)
25. K Hempstalk, Hiding behind corners: using edges in images for better steganography. Paper presented at the second computing women congress (CWC), Hamilton, New Zealand, 11–19 Feb 2006, pp. 1–4
26. S Dumitrescu, X Wu, N Memon, On steganalysis of random LSB embedding in continuous-tone images. Paper presented at the international conference on image processing, Rochester, NY, USA, 22–25 Sept 2002, vol. 3, pp. 641–644
27. AD Ker, R Böhme, Revisiting weighted stego-image steganalysis. Paper presented at the SPIE electronic imaging, security, forensics, steganography, and watermarking of multimedia xontents X, Orlando, FL, USA, 27–31 Jan 2008, vol. 6819, pp. 5–1517
28. S Tan, B Li, Targeted steganalysis of edge adaptive image steganography based on LSB matching revisited using b-spline fitting. IEEE Signal Process. Lett. **19**(6), 336–339 (2012)
29. RO Duda, PE Hart, DG Stork, *Pattern Classification*, 2nd edn. (Wiley, New York, NY, 2001)
30. G Gul, F Kurugollu, ed. by T Filler, T Pevný, S Craver, and A Ker, A new methodology in steganalysis: breaking highly undetectable steganography (HUGO), in *Lecture Notes in Computer Science: 13th International Conference on Information Hiding, Prague, Czech Republic*, vol. 6958 (Springer Berlin, 2011), pp. 71–84
31. V Holub, J Fridrich, Digital image steganography using universal distortion. Paper presented at the first ACM workshop on information hiding and multimedia security, Montpellier, France, 17–19 June 2013, pp. 59–68
32. V Holub, J Fridrich, Designing steganographic distortion using directional filters. Paper presented at the IEEE international workshop on information forensics and security (WIFS), Tenerife, Spain, 2–5 Dec 2012, pp. 234–239
33. T Filler, J Judas, J Fridrich, Minimizing additive distortion in steganography using syndrome-trellis codes. IEEE Trans. Inf. Forensics Security **6**(3), 920–935 (2011)
34. S Islam, P Gupta, Revisiting least two significant bits steganography. Paper presented a the 8th international conference on intelligent information processing (ICIIP), Seoul, Republic of Korea, 1–3 April 2013, pp. 90–93
35. MR Modi, S Islam, P Gupta, ed. by D-S Huang, V Bevilacqua, JC Figueroa, and P Premaratne, Edge based steganography on colored images, in *Lecture Notes in Computer Science: 9th International Conference on Intelligent Computing (ICIC)*, vol. 7995 (Springer Berlin, 2013), pp. 593–600
36. J Canny, A computational approach to edge detection. IEEE Trans. Pattern Anal. Mach. Intell. **8**(6), 679–698 (1986)
37. C Cortes, V Vapnik, Support-vector networks. Mach. Learn. **20**(3), 273–297 (1995)
38. T Pevný, JJ Fridrich, AD Ker, From blind to quantitative steganalysis. IEEE Trans. Inf. Forensics Security **7**(2), 445–454 (2012)

7

Enhancing the security of LTE networks against jamming attacks

Roger Piqueras Jover[1*], Joshua Lackey[1] and Arvind Raghavan[2]

Abstract

The long-term evolution (LTE) is the newly adopted technology to offer enhanced capacity and coverage for current mobility networks, which experience a constant traffic increase and skyrocketing bandwidth demands. This new cellular communication system, built upon a redesigned physical layer and based on an orthogonal frequency division multiple access (OFDMA) modulation, features robust performance in challenging multipath environments and substantially improves the performance of the wireless channel in terms of bits per second per Hertz (bps/Hz). Nevertheless, as all wireless systems, LTE is vulnerable to radio jamming attacks. Such threats have security implications especially in the case of next-generation emergency response communication systems based on LTE technologies. This proof of concept paper overviews a series of new effective attacks (smart jamming) that extend the range and effectiveness of basic radio jamming. Based on these new threats, a series of new potential security research directions are introduced, aiming to enhance the resiliency of LTE networks against such attacks. A spread-spectrum modulation of the main downlink broadcast channels is combined with a scrambling of the radio resource allocation of the uplink control channels and an advanced system information message encryption scheme. Despite the challenging implementation on commercial networks, which would require inclusion of these solutions in future releases of the LTE standard, the security solutions could strongly enhance the security of LTE-based national emergency response communication systems.

Keywords: LTE; Jamming; Security; OFDMA

1 Introduction

As mobile phones steadily become more powerful and bandwidth demands skyrocket, cellular operators are rapidly deploying broadband data services and infrastructure to enhance capacity. The long-term evolution (LTE) is the recently deployed standard technology for communication networks, offering higher data speeds and improved bandwidth. This new cellular communication system is the natural evolution of 3rd Generation Partnership Project (3GPP)-based access networks, enhancing the Universal Mobile Telecommunications System (UMTS).

LTE provides capacity to user equipments (UEs) by means of a centralized assignment of radio resources. A newly enhanced physical (PHY) layer is implemented based on orthogonal frequency division multiple access (OFDMA) and substantially improves the performance of the former wideband code division multiple access (W-CDMA) [1]. The new modulation scheme provides a large capacity and throughput, potentially reaching a raw bit rate of 300 Mbps in the downlink with advanced multiple input multiple output (MIMO) configurations [1].

Due to its spectrum efficiency and great capacity, LTE is planned to be adopted as the basis for the next-generation emergency response communication system, the Nationwide Interoperable Public Safety Broadband Network [2]. In this context, the characteristics of such LTE-based public safety networks are already under consideration in the industry [3]. Note that, specially in the case of this application, the security requirements of LTE communication networks are of paramount importance.

Despite the tremendous capacity and system enhancements implemented by LTE, cellular networks are known to be, as any kind of wireless network, vulnerable to radio jamming. Although it is a simple and well-known attack, radio jamming is the most common way to launch

*Correspondence: roger.jover@att.com
[1] AT&T Security Research Center, New York, NY 10007, USA
Full list of author information is available at the end of the article

a localized denial of service (DoS) attack against a cellular network [4]. The impact of such attacks is very local and mainly constrained by the transmitted power of the jamming device. The attacker is only able to deny the service locally to UEs located in its vicinity. However, more sophisticated attacks have been discovered as a potentially more effective way to jam LTE networks [5,6]. These smart jamming attacks aim to saturate specifically the main downlink broadcast channel of LTE networks in order to launch a local DoS attack that requires less power, making it stealthier. Further complex attacks, such as low-power smart jamming, identify the actual physical resource blocks (PRBs) assigned to essential uplink control channels by capturing the unprotected broadcast messages sent from the base station (eNodeB). The interception of such unencrypted network configuration data allows the attacker to selectively saturate uplink control channels in order to extend the range of the attack to an entire cell or sector. Note that network configuration contained in the broadcast channel can also be leveraged to deploy an effective rogue base station and other kinds of attacks.

Although radio jamming attacks have a rather local range, they become highly relevant in the current cybersecurity scenario. Reports of very targeted and extremely sophisticated attacks have emerged over the last 2 years [7]. These attacks, popularly known as advanced persistent threats (APTs), span over months or even years and target large corporations and government institutions with the goal of stealing intellectual property or other valuable digital assets [8]. The advent of APTs has substantially changed the set of assumptions in the current threat scenario. When it comes to very well-planned and funded cyber attacks, the scale of the threat is not important anymore. Instead, achieving a very specific and localized goal for economic benefit or military advantage is the key element. In this context, scenarios such as a local DoS attack against the cell service around, for example, a large corporation's headquarters or the New York Stock Exchange becomes very relevant. DoS is also often a tool used to knock a phone off a secure network and force it down to an insecure radio access network (RAN) to pursue further attacks and data exfiltrations [9].

The goal of this proof of concept paper is to raise awareness on the traditionally overlooked threat of radio jamming and to propose a combination of potential research directions and LTE RAN enhancements against sophisticated jamming attacks. This theoretical enhanced security architecture relies on a boost of the jamming resiliency of the main downlink broadcast channels and the encryption of the data broadcasted in it. The potential results would be twofold. On one hand, an attacker would not be able to easily jam the downlink broadcast channels and, therefore, deny the service to UEs in its vicinity. On the other hand, no network configuration information could be intercepted and decoded, preventing an attacker to gain knowledge on each cell's specific configuration, which could be leveraged in security attacks. Finally, a proactive smart jamming multi-antenna cancelation technique is presented.

Some of the proposed security solutions involve substantial changes at the PHY layer of LTE networks which could be very challenging to implement on a commercial network and would require collaboration within the industry. Nevertheless, such security architecture could substantially increase the reliability and resiliency against security attacks of the Nationwide Interoperable Public Safety Broadband Network [2]. Anti-jamming enhancements could be included to the list of requirements for LTE-based public safety networks that are not in the scope of current releases of the LTE standard, such as direct communication and group communication [3].

The remainder of the paper is organized as follows. Section 2 briefly overviews the cell selection procedure in LTE networks, the main downlink broadcast channels, and the feasibility of eavesdropping unprotected broadcasted network configuration messages. Three attacks against LTE networks are described in Section 3. The proposed research directions and theoretical architecture to mitigate radio jamming attacks is introduced in Section 4. Finally, related work is reviewed in Section 5, and the concluding remarks are presented in Section 6.

2 Initial access to LTE networks

This section overviews the basic procedures necessary for a phone to synchronize with and connect to an LTE network. Any UE willing to access the network must first perform a cell selection procedure. After this procedure, the UE decodes the physical broadcast channel (PBCH) to extract the basic system information that allows the other channels in the cell to be configured and operated. The messages carried on this channels are unencrypted and can be eavesdropped by a passive radio sniffer. Once at this point, the UE can initiate an actual connection with the network by means of a random access procedure and establish a radio access bearer (RAB) in order to send and receive user traffic. The whole process is portrayed in Figure 1.

2.1 Cell search procedure

The cell search procedure consists of a series of synchronization steps that allow the UE to determine time and frequency parameters required to detect and demodulate downlink signals as well as to transmit uplink signals with the right timing. The three major steps in this procedure are symbol timing acquisition, carrier frequency synchronization, and sampling clock synchronization. To achieve full synchronization, the UE detects and decodes the

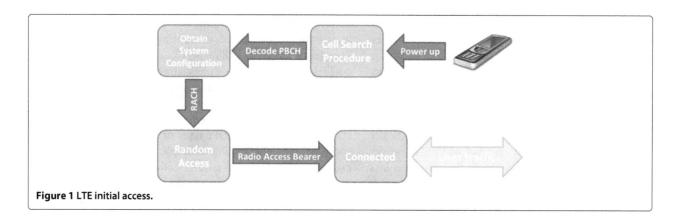

Figure 1 LTE initial access.

primary synchronization signal (PSS) and the secondary synchronization signal (SSS), which are fully described in [10]. The mapping of the PSS and SSS in the central subcarriers of the LTE frame as well as the main functions of these synchronization signals is shown in Figure 2.

The PSS enables the UE to acquire the time slot boundary independently from the cyclic prefix configuration of the cell, which at this point is unknown to the UE. Based on the downlink frame structure, the PSS is transmitted twice per radio frame. This enables the UE to get time synchronized on a 5-ms basis, which simplifies the required inter-frequency and inter-RAT measurements. The PSS is transmitted occupying the six central PRBs of the LTE frequency configuration [11]. With 12 subcarriers per PRB, this results in 1.08 MHz of bandwidth (BW). This way, independently of the BW configuration of the cell, the UE is able to decode it.

The next step is to obtain the radio frame timing and the group identity of the cell, which is found in the SSS. In the time domain, the SSS is transmitted in the preceding symbol to the PSS. The SSS also has a 5-ms periodicity and occupies 62 of the 72 central subcarriers so it can be decoded without knowledge of the system BW configuration.

Decoding this signal, the device determines the unique identity of the cell. At this point, the terminal can get fully synchronized with the eNodeB because the reference signals are transmitted in well-defined resource elements and the current synchronization allows locating them. A reference symbol from the generated reference signal pattern is transmitted on every sixth subcarrier. In the time domain, every fourth OFDM symbol holds a reference symbol. This results on four reference symbols per PRB.

2.2 LTE physical broadcast channel

The LTE PBCH is crucial for the successful operation of the LTE radio interface. Therefore, its transmission has to be optimized so it can be reliably decoded by cell edge users with low latency and low impact on battery life.

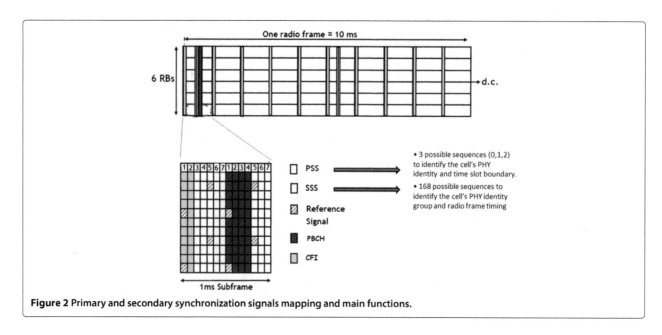

Figure 2 Primary and secondary synchronization signals mapping and main functions.

This is achieved by means of low system overhead (the effective data rate is of just 350 bps) and transmission with the lowest modulation and coding scheme (MCS) in order to minimize the bit error rate (BER) for a given signal-to-noise ratio (SNR) [1].

The main LTE system information is transmitted over the PBCH within the master information block (MIB). This message contains the most frequently transmitted parameters, essential for an initial access to the cell, such as the system BW, the physical hybrid ARQ indicator channel (PHICH) structure and the most significant eight bits of the system frame number (SFN).

The remainder of the system configuration is encoded in the system information blocks (SIBs), which are modulated on the physical downlink shared channel (PDSCH). These messages can be mapped on the PDSCH based on their broadcast id, the system information RAN temporary identifier (SI-RNTI), which is fixed in the specifications and therefore known *a priori* to all UEs and potential attackers. The SIB-1 message contains transport parameters necessary to connect to the cell as well as scheduling information, and the SIB-2 message contains information on all common and shared channels. Subsequent SIB messages define multiple parameters, such as the power thresholds for cell re-selection and the list of neighboring cells.

2.3 MIB and SIB message eavesdropping

The MIB and SIB messages are broadcasted on PRBs known *a priori* and transmitted with no encryption. Therefore, a passive sniffer is able to decode them. This simplifies the initial access procedure for the UEs but could be potentially leveraged by an attacker to craft sophisticated jamming attacks, optimize the configuration of a rogue base station or tune other types of sophisticated attacks. Figure 3a,b presents our lab system configuration eavesdropped with a commercial of-the-shelf LTE wireless traffic sniffer. Note that details such as the system BW, the cell identity, and the MCC and the mobile network code (MNC) of the eNodeB are broadcasted in the clear. These values have been faded out on purpose in the figures.

Similarly, using the same commercial traffic sniffer, the subsequent SIB messages can be intercepted. For example, the SIB-2 messages contains the PRB mapping of other control channels, such as the uplink (UL) resources reserved for the UE random access procedure on the random access channel (RACH).

Note that a commercial traffic sniffer is not necessary to obtain this information. A skilled programmer could design a PBCH traffic sniffer implemented on a cheap software-defined radio (SDR) platform such as the universal software radio peripheral (USRP) [12], which is commonly used as radio transceiver in GSM (Global

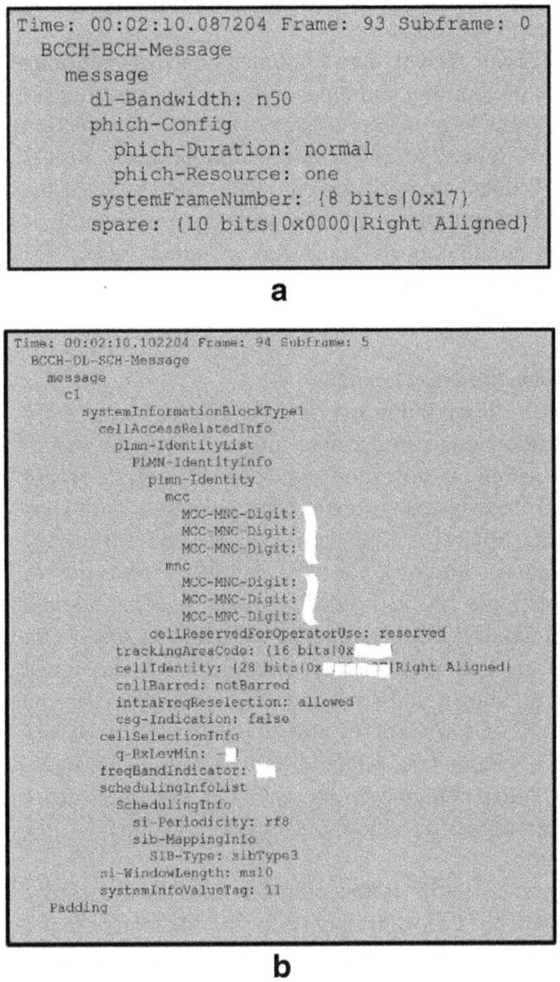

```
Time: 00:02:10.087204 Frame: 93 Subframe: 0
 BCCH-BCH-Message
   message
     dl-Bandwidth: n50
     phich-Config
       phich-Duration: normal
       phich-Resource: one
     systemFrameNumber: {8 bits|0x17}
     spare: {10 bits|0x0000|Right Aligned}
```

a

```
Time: 00:02:10.102204 Frame: 94 Subframe: 5
 BCCH-DL-SCH-Message
   message
     c1
       systemInformationBlockType1
         cellAccessRelatedInfo
           plmn-IdentityList
             PLMN-IdentityInfo
               plmn-Identity
                 mcc
                   MCC-MNC-Digit:
                   MCC-MNC-Digit:
                   MCC-MNC-Digit:
                 mnc
                   MCC-MNC-Digit:
                   MCC-MNC-Digit:
                   MCC-MNC-Digit:
             cellReservedForOperatorUse: reserved
           trackingAreaCode: {16 bits|0x
           cellIdentity: {28 bits|0x       |Right Aligned}
           cellBarred: notBarred
           intraFreqReselection: allowed
           csg-Indication: false
         cellSelectionInfo
           q-RxLevMin:
           freqBandIndicator:
         schedulingInfoList
           SchedulingInfo
             si-Periodicity: rf8
             sib-MappingInfo
               SIB-Type: sibType3
         si-WindowLength: ms10
         systemInfoValueTag: 11
 Padding
```

b

Figure 3 MIB (a) and SIB-1 (b) LTE messages eavesdropped with a commercial traffic sniffer.

System of Mobile Communications) open source projects [13].

3 Attacks against cellular networks

Radio jamming is the deliberate transmission of radio signals to disrupt communications by decreasing the SNR of the received signal. This attack essentially consists of blasting a high-power constant signal over the entire target band of the system under attack [4,14].

This attack is broadly known as a simple and common way to attack a wireless network and has been widely studied in the literature in the context of wireless local area networks (WLAN) [4], sensor networks [15], and cellular networks [14]. Despite the attack's simplicity, often, the only solution is to locate and neutralize the attacker, specially in the situation where the entire band of the system is being jammed. The very large amount of transmitted power, though, results in a reduced stealthiness so more elaborated schemes to jam cellular networks are being proposed in the literature.

It has been shown that a standard barrage jamming attack is the optimal jamming strategy when the attacker has no knowledge of the target signal [16]. This section overviews specific derivations of radio jamming attacks against cellular networks based on the knowledge of the target LTE signal that an attacker can obtain from publicly available documents and standards. A popular new threat vector that can be exploited as a result of such attacks is also described.

3.1 Downlink smart jamming

Downlink smart jamming consists of generating malicious radio signals in order to interfere with the reception of essential downlink control channels. A recent report introduces the potential theoretical results of jamming the PBCH of LTE networks [5]. The authors of the original study expanded the details of this study in a recent paper [6]. This attack, which could be applied to both 2G and 3G networks as well, targets this channel because, as described in Section 2.1, its assigned PRBs are known *a priori* and always mapped to the central 72 subcarriers of the OFDMA signal. Given that this channel is required to configure and operate the other channels in the cell, this jamming attack is characterized by a low duty cycle and a fairly low bandwidth.

The range of the jammer in this case is still rather small, with a very localized impact. The transmission and modulation characteristics of the PBCH still require a fairly high-power interfering signal to deny the service to noncell edge users. Note that, in order to outpower the legitimate signal, the attacker is bounded by the large transmitted power at the eNodeB and the potentially low transmitted power of the jamming device.

More sophisticated versions of this attack have been proposed, targeting the downlink pilot signals used by the UE to estimate the channel for signal equalization [17]. However, Release 10 of the LTE standard covers the concepts of heterogeneous networks (HetNets), with strong enhancements in the pilot signals to avoid strong interference between the pilots sent by different overlaying cells (macrocells and pico/femto/metrocells) [18]. As a consequence of the inter-cell interference coordination (ICIC) efforts of Release 10, the downlink (DL) pilot signals might experience an enhancement in their resiliency against jamming.

3.2 Uplink (low-power) smart jamming

Low-power smart jamming takes a step further by targeting essential uplink control channels. Note that, as depicted in Figure 4, the range of an uplink smart jamming attack is less local and covers the entire cell or sector. This is because the attacker jams UL control channels, preventing the eNodeB from receiving essential UL signaling messages required for the correct operation of the cell. By overwhelming reception at the eNodeB by means of a jamming signal, the attacker is effectively preventing the base station to communicate with every UE in the cell, thus extending the range of the attack to the entire cell.

Moreover, the attacker is not bounded by the high power of downlink signals transmitted by the eNodeB (often in the range of 48 dBm), but by the maximum power, a legitimate UE can transmit, which is fixed at 23 dBm in the case of LTE [19]. In this case, an attacker sitting in the vicinity of the eNodeB transmitting at the same power level as any legitimate smartphone could potentially jam the uplink control messages of all the UEs within a given cell or sector. Furthermore, the attacker could use a very directive antenna pointed towards the eNodeB and substantially enhance the effectiveness of the attack.

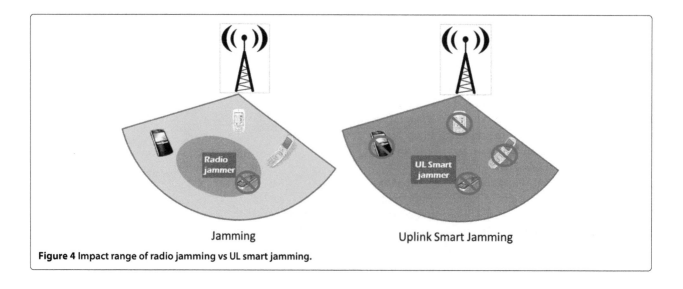

Jamming   Uplink Smart Jamming

Figure 4 Impact range of radio jamming vs UL smart jamming.

This type of attack has been previously demonstrated in the context of GSM networks targeting the uplink RACH [20].

The first message exchange on this channel allows the UE to synchronize in the uplink and, after the initial access procedure, radio resources can be allocated to the UE.

In order to target a specific LTE uplink control channel, the attacker would need to know the actual PRBs assigned to it at the PHY layer. This PRB assignment can be obtained from publicly available documentation. Nevertheless, as it will be presented in Subsection 4.4, if the actual location of this signals in the time-frequency LTE frame was randomized or scrambled, such radio resource assignment information could still be obtained from the SIB unprotected messages carried by the PBCH and PDSCH.

In the context of a sophisticated and highly targeted attack, one should note that the MCC and MNC of an eNodeB are also encoded in the SIB-1 message. Eavesdropping of this information would allow an attacker, for example, to selectively target a jamming charge against base stations from a specific cellular network operator.

Note that uplink smart jamming, while being much more effective than basic jamming or downlink smart jamming, is a more complex attack. In order to selectively jam the PRBs assigned to, for example, the RACH channel, an attacker should be perfectly synchronized in time and frequency with the LTE signal. Moreover, the attacker should be able to capture and decode the MIB and SIB messages in order to extract the actual RACH PRB allocation information. Therefore, a skilled attacker and moderate development work on, for example, software-defined radio would be required.

3.2.1 LTE link budget

To illustrate the gain in transmitted power and, therefore, range of uplink smart jamming, we compute the link budget for a typical 10 MHz LTE system in both the uplink and downlink. The main parameters of this LTE configuration are described in Table 1. Such calculations can be done with multiple open access tools available online such as [21].

Given an eNodeB transmitting at the standard power (48 dBm), the received power at a UE located at the edge of a cell is of −100.80 dBm for the largest possible cell with radius 0.4 Km (i.e., −100.80 dBm is the receiver sensitivity in the DL). Although the maximum size of the cell is limited by the UL link, for the sake of comparison, we compute the received power at the eNodeB from a UE located at the cell edge, 0.4 km away from the UL receiver. This link budget results in −132.26 dBm received at the eNodeB. This difference of 31.46 dB between the received power in the UL and DL indicates that the power the eNodeB receives from a UE at the cell edge is 1,000 times

Table 1 LTE link budget parameters from a standard 10 MHz deployment

System parameters	Values
System BW	10 MHz
Subchannel reuse	One-three
Carrier frequency	2.5 GHz
#TX antennas	2
#RX antennas	2
Path loss model	Cost 231
BS antenna height	30 m
UE antenna height	1.5 m
MCS	QPSK 1/2
SNR_{min} for MCS	8.5 dB [22]
Thermal noise density	-174 dBm/Hz
Log-normal fading margin	6 dB
Downlink	
eNodeB max power	43 dBm
Multi-antenna gain	3 dB
TX antenna gain	17 dBi
Noise figure	4 dB
Uplink	
UE max power	23 dBm
Multi-antenna gain	0 dBm
TX antenna gain	-1 dBm
Noise figure	9 dB

lower than the power that the same UE at the cell edge receives from the eNodeB in the downlink. This gives a clear indication on the much lower jamming signal power requirements for an UL smart jamming strategy.

3.2.2 Attack complexity

Based on the characteristics of UL smart jamming, the attacker would require full synchronization in time and frequency with the LTE signal to be able to, for example, selectively jam the RACH. This raises the complexity of the attack as compared to DL smart jamming. Nevertheless, there are numerous of-the-shelf and open access tools that could be leveraged in this context.

The USRP is commonly used for GSM-related projects, but there are certain ongoing open source projects that could be used to write software radio applications that synchronize with an LTE signal. One example is the openLTE project [23]. Leveraging these tools, a skilled attacker could potentially implement an advanced jammer at a very low cost. Moreover, there are other off-the-shelf applications and tools that allow a user to synchronize with an LTE signal such as specialized LTE sniffing hardware and commercial software-based LTE base stations.

3.3 Rogue base station attacks

Rogue base station attacks have been proposed in the literature as a means to, for example, steal credentials or invade the privacy of mobile users [9,24]. These attacks are based on the deployment of a GSM rogue base station combined with jamming the UMTS and/or LTE network in order to force as many UEs as possible to camp on the fake GSM cell. Many security features of GSM have been defeated over the last few years [25]. Given that the authentication algorithm is not symmetric, the network is not required to authenticate, so the UE believes it is connected to a real base station.

An efficient technique to maximize the potential number of devices camping on the fake cell is by advertising the id of the rogue base station based on the list of neighboring cells broadcasted by legitimate base stations. Note that such information can be extracted from the unprotected downlink broadcast MIB and SIB messages. From the data sniffed from such broadcast messages, one can efficiently tune the transmitted power of the rogue cell as well such that the UEs will handoff to the rogue base station.

Note that both techniques leveraged to optimize a rogue base station attack (jamming of the LTE network and obtaining information from the unencrypted MIB and SIB messages) leverage the vulnerabilities introduced in Section 2.

4   LTE security solutions against jamming attacks

One of the goals of this proof of concept paper is to propose research directions to enhance the resilience of LTE against smart jamming threats. We introduce a set of security research directions at the PHY layer of LTE networks, aiming to enhance the resiliency of data communications against jamming. The envisioned security system would protect communication systems by mitigating the radio jamming attacks discussed in Section 3. These solutions would also minimize the system configuration information that an attacker can easily eavesdrop in order to leverage a jamming charge or the deployment of a rogue base station.

The proposed theoretical security system is based on an enhancement of the resiliency against radio jamming of the PBCH by means of a spread spectrum transmission. This can be combined with scrambling of the PRB allocation of UL control channels and a distributed encryption scheme for downlink control broadcast messages. On one hand, the system protects its most vulnerable resources, downlink control channels, which are the target of DoS attacks [6]. On the other hand, MIB and SIB messages are protected so an attacker cannot learn any information on the PRB allocation for the other control channels, which are now randomly allocated in time and frequency. Only with the information encoded and encrypted in the MIB and SIB messages an attacker would be able to aim to the UL control channels with a jamming charge. Full application of such security solutions render a jamming attack to be only as effective as basic barrage jamming. Note that in jamming mitigation studies, the goal is precisely to force any sophisticated jamming attack to be just as efficient as standard jamming [17].

Note that the full implementation of the proposed techniques would not be trivial, as it will be discussed throughout this section. For example, the scrambling of the PRB allocation of UL control channels will challenge the SC-FDMA scheduling in the uplink because it could potentially break up the continuity of user allocations. The successful implementation of some of these solutions would be very challenging in commercial networks. Nevertheless, such modifications at the PHY layer could be aimed for the development on the Nationwide Interoperable Public Safety Broadband Network, with a PHY layer based on LTE [2,3]. Such next-generation communication systems for emergency response present strict security requirements and should be protected against potential jamming attacks.

4.1   Spread-spectrum jamming resiliency

By means of jamming the central 1.08 MHz of any LTE signal, an attacker would deny the service to all UEs in its vicinity. Therefore, it is important to enhance the protection of the main broadcast channels at the PHY layer. The goal is to counteract the advantage in bandwidth and transmitted power the jammer has due to this LTE vulnerability [6].

Newly deployed LTE networks implement a completely redesigned modulation scheme that substantially maximizes the performance of the wireless channel in terms of bits per second per Hertz (bps/Hz). However, the implementation of an OFDMA-based PHY layer lacks of the inherent interference resilience features of code division multiple access (CDMA)-based networks. While OFDMA is often the choice because of its robust performance in challenging multipath environments, it is not optimal for scenarios where adversarial entities intentionally attempt to jam communications, such as in tactical scenarios [17].

The strong interference resiliency of CDMA-based networks is well known [26,27]. The application of a scrambling signal with a high chip rate to the transmitted signal spreads the spectrum to levels that, in some cases, can be masked by the thermal noise at the receiver. Upon reception of the signal, application of the same code, orthogonal with the code used in other base stations or UEs, allows to recover the original signal. Due to the nature of the transmitted signal in UMTS, based on W-CDMA, an interfering signal needs to be transmitted at a very high power in order to jam the communication. This is due to the fact that the process of despreading the signal spectrum at the receiver causes, assuming an interfering signal uncorrelated with the scrambling signal, an inherent reduction of the interference power by $\log_{10}(G)$ decibels (dBs), being G the spreading factor or processing gain of the W-CDMA signal [26].

Considering the characteristics of broadcast channels, one could envision an alternative transmission scheme where the main downlink broadcast channels are protected by a spread spectrum-based method. Although downgrading from OFDMA could potentially decrease the available throughput for broadcast messages, such control channels are known for having very low overhead and a low throughput of, in the case of the PBCH, just 350 bps [1].

4.1.1 System description

The proposed security solution applies a spread spectrum-based modulation to the downlink control channels in order to extend their spectrum over the available BW. This could be done by just expanding the BW of the downlink broadcast signals or by applying an actual CDMA-based modulation on this portion of the LTE signal.

This solution by itself would prevent a downlink jamming attack to be launched with a simple radio transmitter or jammer, which substantially increases the attack complexity and cost. To perform such attack, full synchronization in time and frequency would be required in order to apply the same CDMA spreading code to the jamming signal. In the case that an attacker does incur this cost, a further enhancement to this solution is described in Subsection 4.3.

Assuming a scrambling or spreading sequence with a rate of $R_b \cdot G$, with R_b being the rate of the PBCH messages, a jammer would theoretically require an extra $\log_{10}(G)$ dBs of transmitted power in order to achieve the same result. With the transmitted power kept constant, the BW of the jamming signal would be reduced by a factor of up to G times. With both power and BW kept constant, the range of the attack would be reduced.

4.1.2 Limitations and potential implementation

The main limitation of the solution is that the UE requires a finer synchronization with the DL signal. In addition to that, the effectiveness of the defense is directly proportional to the spreading factor of the broadcast signal. Therefore, either extra BW should be allocated for the PBCH or its PRB allocation should be modified and spread over the available 1.08 MHz. Nevertheless, with an effective throughput of just 350 bps, there is potentially room for improvement.

In order to be implemented in commercial cellular, this technique would require changes in the LTE standards. Moreover, it would not be backwards compatible with current LTE terminals unless the PBCH and broadcasting messages were transmitted both within the central subcarriers and with the spread spectrum enhancement. Nevertheless, this solution is feasible and could be implemented in the context of an anti-jamming security-enhanced LTE-based military or tactical network, which would use custom wireless devices and eNodeBs.

4.2 LTE, MIB, and SIB message encryption

As introduced in Subsection 2.2, the MIB and SIB messages broadcasted by an eNodeB contain essential network configuration parameters that aid the UE to synchronize and establish a connection with the network. Nevertheless, all these messages are transmitted in the clear with obvious security implications.

Assuming a hypothetical scenario with control broadcast messages encrypted but no specific protection for the PSS and SSS, an attacker could not obtain any configuration information by means of a commercial traffic sniffer. A skilled attacker could still synchronize with the network by means of a SDR platform. Extraction of network configuration information, though, would be impossible, assuming a strong encryption scheme. Therefore, the only way an attacker could obtain the network configuration details would be by using a legitimate wireless device and hijacking it to extract data from the baseband chip, which is unreachable from the user space.

4.2.1 Initial limitations

A simple encryption scheme cannot be applied to the system information messages. If the information in the PBCH was encrypted with a secret key, the mobile terminal must know that key *a priori*. Assuming the case of a mobile terminal being turned on or roaming to a new network, the device must still be able to decode the PBCH to establish a connection. In parallel, key exchange algorithms cannot be executed with the network at this stage because the device is not connected and authenticated yet. Therefore, the key that encodes the MIB and SIBs must be hard-coded in the UE.

Relying on one common key for all users and cells is not possible either. If this key was compromised by any means, the whole system would be useless. Therefore, the system must be able to operate with a large number of different keys or able to generate a large number of keys.

4.2.2 Assumptions

The main assumption for this security architecture is a global collaboration of all mobile operators. Subscriber identity module (SIM)-based authentication schemes allow to provide cellular services to a mobile terminal independently of the network being roamed (assuming, of course, that the user has roaming activated and the phone and network are compatible). Encryption of the MIB and SIB messages would require a similar collaboration among carriers.

It is important to note that, in the case of such encryption scheme being applied exclusively to a national LTE-based emergency response broadband network, such as the Nationwide Interoperable Public Safety Broadband Network, this limitation does not apply.

The proposed solution assumes that the UE is equipped with a trusted hardware (HW) platform which is secure and able to both securely store data and perform cryptographic operations. Note that all UEs are already provisioned with such element, the SIM card. Basing the encryption scheme on the SIM, though, could potentially allow an attacker to capture LTE wireless traffic and decode it afterwards with a legitimate SIM on a standard card reader connected to a personal computer. Therefore, such encryption scheme would only be effective if it was implemented on a protected trusted platform module (TPM) that can be only operated by, for example, the baseband of a cell phone. Note that there are initial plans in the industry to equip UEs with a TPM [28]. In the context of a national emergency response network, equipping mobile devices with a secure TPM is feasible. Finally, a strong private key encryption scheme is assumed.

4.2.3 System description

The proposed solution is depicted in Figure 5. On the network side, either each base station or a node in the EPC stores a set of N secret keys in a secure location. In the case of storing the keys in a centralized way, this secure storage could be the home subscriber server (HSS) or any other newly implemented network node. On the other hand, the TPM (or SIM card) in each mobile phone stores securely the same set of N keys. The value of N can be arbitrarily large.

Note that, in practice, only one secret key K would be required. Based on this initial secret key, each sub-key K_j $j = 1,...,N$ would be generated as $K_j = H(K|j)$, being H a hash function and '|' the concatenation operation.

Assuming a robust hash function, eventual leakage of a sub-key K_j would not provide an attacker any information on the actual secret key K. However, leakage of the main secret key K would relent this method useless.

The operation of the system is described as follows. The eNodeB selects a key K_j with id j. The broadcast MIB and SIB messages are encrypted with the key K_j and transmitted over the air. Along with the encryption of the broadcast message, for example $enc_{K_j}(MIB)$, the system transmits the id j in plain text. This way, any UE knows what key to use to decrypt the messages. Note that an attacker would learn the id j but would not be able to know the key K_j that is being used to encrypt the broadcast messages.

If at any point a key was compromised, the network would be able to switch to a different key K_i and continue operating normally. A broadcast message would be sent to the mobile devices to alert them of this change. Incoming connections, either via handovers from other cells or new devices being turned on, would just receive the updated broadcast messages $[i|enc_{K_i}(MIB)]$ and continue operating normally.

Note that the network could choose to use a different key at each cell/sector. This way, if an attacker managed to compromise a key, a potential attack during the time it would take the network to change to a new key would be localized and only impact one cell or sector.

In this section, the MIB message is used as example, but the same scheme could be applied to SIB messages as well.

4.2.4 Limitations and potential implementation

The main limitations for this security enhancement of LTE networks is the requirement for a global partnership of both cellular operators, device manufacturers (in the case of the deployment of a TPM), and SIM card providers. Moreover, a substantial editing of the standards would be necessary. Therefore, such a security solution, when

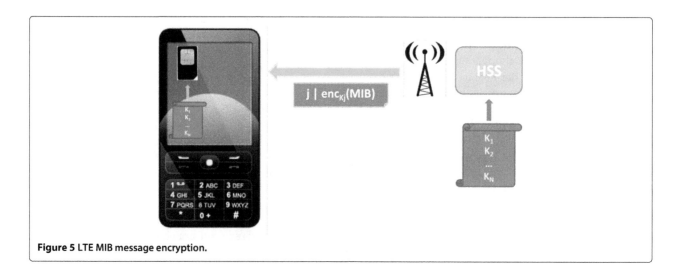

Figure 5 LTE MIB message encryption.

framed in the context of commercial wireless networks, would be more appropriate for the upcoming fifth generation of mobile networks, the standards of which are just being started.

In the context of high security demanding LTE-based communications, such as military networks or first responders, the encryption of broadcast messages is more feasible. Based on custom hardware equipped with state-of-the-art TPM and encryption schemes, such a system could be deployed.

It is important to note that, by itself, the encryption of the broadcast messages would not prevent an attack from jamming the LTE central subcarriers (downlink smart jamming) and block users from detecting and decoding the PSS and SSS and, therefore, connect to the cell.

4.3 Spread-spectrum and encryption combination

As introduced in Subsection 4.1, if an attacker obtained the sequence used to protect the central subcarriers of the LTE signal, the spread spectrum anti-jamming solution would be useless against a skilled attacker using a fully synchronized jamming device. In this section, we introduce an enhancement of the spread spectrum protection based on the encryption scheme described in Subsection 4.2.

4.3.1 Assumptions

In order to prevent an attacker from encoding the jamming signal with the right sequence and, therefore, bypass the protection, this spreading sequence must be only known by the UEs and the eNodeB. In parallel, the entire system cannot depend on a single spreading sequence because, if it was compromised, the protection would be bypassed. Therefore, the spreading sequence selection can be implemented as follows.

4.3.2 System description

The proposed enhanced security architecture is depicted on Figure 6. On the network side, either each eNodeB or the HSS stores a set of M secret spreading sequences. The value of M can be arbitrarily large. The eNodeB selects a sequence S_i with id i and scrambles the PBCH signal with it prior to broadcasting it. Along with the scrambled signal $PBCH(t) \cdot S_i(t)$, the eNodeB broadcasts the id i, either on the same channel or on a separate resource. This allows the UE to despread the PBCH with the right sequence. An attacker would just learn the id i but would not be able to extract the sequence C_i used to protect the DL signal.

Note that, when enhancing the resiliency against jamming of the MIB messages following this scheme, the sequence $S_i(t)$ used to scramble the signal can be seen as the equivalent of the key k_i used to encrypt the MIB.

4.3.3 Limitations and potential implementation

With the combination of the MIB and SIB message encryption and the spread spectrum protection against jamming, an attacker cannot leverage the knowledge of the id i, broadcasted in the clear, to optimize the attack. However, if the attacker was able to jam the actual broadcast transmission of the id i, the wireless system would be inoperative as no legitimate user would be able to determine what spreading code is being used in a given cell.

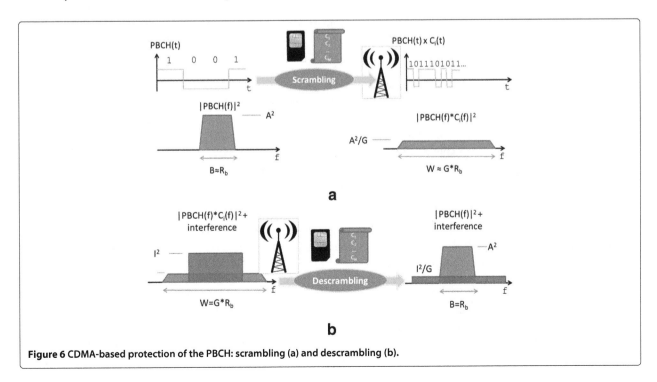

Figure 6 CDMA-based protection of the PBCH: scrambling (a) and descrambling (b).

This could be prevented in different ways. In the case of LTE-based systems with a specific application, such as military ad-hoc networks or first responder wireless systems, the id i could be distributed through an out of band secondary channel or known a priori before deploying the ad-hoc network. Alternatively, the id i could be broadcasted in a more complex yet secure manner, such as the primary scrambling code detection in UMTS networks [26]. In this case, a receiver detects which one of the 512 possible primary scramble codes is being used within a cell by applying a correlation receiver. The necessary signals for the primary scrambling code detection are often transmitted in a way that they can be received and decoded at a low SNR regime. A similar procedure could be implemented to, for example, broadcast which one of 512 possible sequences C_i with $i = \{1, 2, ..., 511\}$ is being used.

Finally, the sequence id could be broadcasted repeatedly in a frequency hopping scheme over the entire system bandwidth. Although this would require substantial changes to the LTE standards, it would force an attacker to jam the entire band to jam the id broadcasting operation. Therefore, the goal of counteracting the advantage a jammer has in LTE networks would be achieved as the only feasible option would be barrage jamming.

4.4 LTE UL control channel PRB scrambling

The PRB allocation of the Physical Uplink Control Channel (PUCCH) is known a priori as defined by the standards. The UL control signaling on this channel is transmitted in a frequency region on the edges of the system BW. In parallel, the PRB allocation of other essential UL control channels, such as the RACH, can be extracted from the SIB messages.

4.4.1 *System description*

The proposed security architecture scrambles the PRB allocation of UL control channels so they cannot be the target of an uplink smart jamming attack. Based on the encryption scheme described in Section 4.2, a legitimate UE would be able to decode the system configuration and normally operate on the UL control channels. An attacker, though, would not be able to locate any UL control channel and its best UL jamming strategy would be equivalent to a basic barrage jamming.

4.4.2 *Limitations and potential implementation*

Periodically modifying the PRB allocation of certain UL control channels, such as the RACH, would not be challenging given the multiple possible configurations of the RACH in current LTE networks. However, the allocation of the PUCCH away from the edges of the spectrum would generate new limitations. The frequency diversity achieved through frequency hoping would not be

maximized anymore. In parallel, the maximum achievable PUSCH data rate would decrease due to the fact that uplink allocations must be contiguous in frequency to maintain the single-carrier nature of the uplink LTE signal [1]. Random allocation of the UL control channels could potentially pose a challenge to SC-FDMA scheduling because it could break up the continuity of user allocations.

In this case, the implementation of this security solution would require changes in the LTE standards. However, a potential application for security-demanding military and first responder LTE-based networks could be implemented using nonstandard hardware on both transmitting and receiving sides.

4.5 Selective uplink smart jamming interference cancelation

In order to enhance their coverage range and apply diversity techniques, cell towers are equipped with multiple antennas. The number of antennas at the cell tower is commonly three but some network operators are pushing this number to five in LTE networks to expand further the system's capacity [29]. The cell range in the DL is often bounded by the base station's transmitted power, which is significantly higher than that of a UE. Therefore, the multiple antennas implement spatial diversity in the UL to extend the cell's range limited by the UE.

The proposed security architecture includes a further application that exploits the availability of multiple antennas to suppress the interfering signal of the smart UL jammer, defined in Subsection 3.2. Similar methods have been proposed in the literature aiming to mitigate the effects of a jamming signal in a wireless system by means of jointly mechanically adjusting an array with two antennas and applying an interference cancelation algorithm [30].

4.5.1 *System description*

The proposed security scheme implements beam-forming techniques at the eNodeB that leverage the availability of up to five antennas in reception. By means of a configurable signal feed, with variable delays and gains, the radiation pattern of an antenna array can be molded to achieve either enhanced directivity or strongly attenuate the signal coming from a specific direction [31]. Assuming the location of the jammer was known, a null in the antenna radiation pattern of the eNodeB could be generated to selectively block the interference. Figure 7 depicts an example of such application.

The attenuation of the interfering signal will depend on the null of the radiation pattern. In order to locate the source of the interference, a narrow directive radiation pattern can be shifted while monitoring SNR and traffic congestion metrics on the UL control channels, scanning

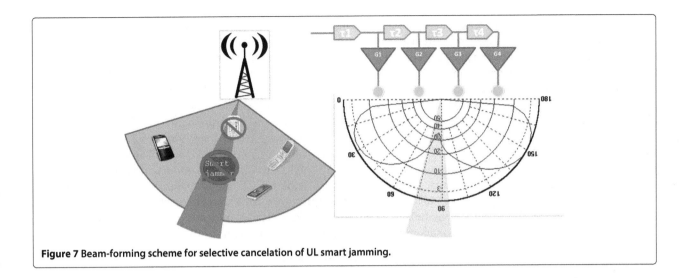

Figure 7 Beam-forming scheme for selective cancelation of UL smart jamming.

this way the entire cell or sector. This would allow to determine the angle of arrival of an incoming UL jamming signal.

4.5.2 Limitations and potential implementation

Note that the proposed architecture requires the multiple antennas of the eNodeB to perform both spatial diversity and beam-forming. The spatial separation between antennas required to optimize the diversity receiver substantially increase the phase or delay between each antenna element. In terms of the beam-forming, this could result in a suboptimal radiation pattern with considerable side lobes and a wider null in the radiation pattern. A trade-off should be found between the performance of the array in terms of diversity/MIMO and the ability to generate a narrow beam.

In parallel, all the UEs located in line with and in the close vicinity of the jammer would not be able to access the networks. Nevertheless, the range of the jammer would be significantly reduced, efficiently mitigating any uplink smart jamming attack.

It is important to note that this particular security enhancement is completely independent and both the hardware (multiple antennas at each eNodeB) and the technology (beamforming) already exist. A potential implementation could be framed within the concept of self-organizing networks (SON), as a an automatic smart jamming attack detection plus self-healing security function. Upon detection of an anomaly in a given eNodeB, in the shape of a strong decrease in the load or anomalous decrease in the SNR, the cell would go into detection mode. A narrow reception beam would scan the cell or sector. In the case of an ongoing uplink smart jamming attack, the cell would then go into a defense state, creating a null in reception and blocking the malicious interfering signal.

5 Related work

Jamming attacks are the main basic type of threat that wireless communication networks face given the fact that the threat vector exploited is inherent to the actual technology. There is no way to prevent an attacker from broadcasting high-power signals on the frequency band allocated to a commercial mobility network. The goal of this attack is often to prevent users to access communication networks, which catalogues this threat as a DoS attack. Several attacks proposed in the literature use radio jamming as a first step in order to force UEs to an insecure access network [24].

Jamming attacks have been in the scope of network and security research for several years already [16]. As new network standards arise, jamming attacks spread their threat over new technologies such as wireless sensor networks (WSNs) [15] and WLANs [4]. Mobility networks, the main commercial wireless networks, have also been considered in radio jamming studies [14].

In parallel, the potential of this kind of attack has lead to improvements and refinements, resulting in more sophisticated jamming techniques. Over the years, authors have proposed ways to launch DoS attacks against mobility networks by overloading the system at the paging channel [32] or with a spike in core network signaling messages [33]. Some other sophisticated jamming techniques have been proposed for UMTS networks [34].

The author of [20] was the first to implement an actual smart jamming attack against an UL control channel in a GSM network, opening a new simple but very effective attack vector to be leveraged in a radio jamming attack. The same idea has recently been proposed as a potential way to jam LTE networks [6].

Despite the prevalence and effectiveness of jamming in the context of wireless networks, there is a clear lack of security strategies to mitigate the impact of such attacks, specially in current mobility networks and upcoming LTE-based emergency response broadband systems. Current standardization bodies do not consider any jamming resiliency requirements for the next planned release of the LTE advanced standard. Nevertheless, some work has been done in addressing jamming attacks in WLANs [35] and WSNs [15].

6 Conclusions

Jamming attacks are one of the main types of security attack that mobility networks face. This threat is inherent to the actual wireless technology employed in this type of network, and in its most basic implementation (barrage jamming), there is no means to prevent an attacker from broadcasting a high power interfering signal on a commercial frequency band.

Despite that jamming attacks are well known and have been widely studied in the literature, no actual security and mitigation strategies have been proposed to enhance the resiliency against jamming attacks in mobility networks. This has resulted on a constantly growing list of new proposals for sophisticated DoS attacks against cellular networks based on jamming principles. However, standardization bodies do not include any anti-jamming guidelines or requirements for the upcoming new releases of LTE advanced. Nevertheless, the forecasted application of LTE-based technologies to implement national emergency response networks make the reliability and security requirements of LTE of paramount importance.

In this proof of concept paper, we overview a series of simple but effective jamming attacks that extend the range of basic jamming while requiring less power. Based on these new threats, classified as smart jamming, we propose a series of potential security research directions that could protect LTE cellular networks, forcing a potential attacker to rely on just basic jamming to attempt a DoS charge. The goal is to raise awareness on this traditionally overlooked threat and spark security research work in this area. We are, in parallel, implementing smart jamming in the lab as well as some of the proposed security solutions.

A potential enhancement of the anti-jamming properties of the main DL broadcast channels, importing concepts from spread spectrum modulations, protects the wireless interface from a smart jamming attack aimed to such control channels. In parallel, a randomization of the PRB allocation of UL control channels plus a sophisticated encryption method for DL system configuration messages, backed up by the deployment of a TPM in the UE, prevent an attacker from launching a smart jamming attack against these essential UL channels. Finally, a method that leverages the current availability of antennas at the eNodeB is proposed to filter out an UL smart jamming signal in order to block an UL smart jamming attack.

The limitations for all these solutions have been discussed as well.

Such enhancements, or similar proposals, should be considered in the scope and requirements of the upcoming releases for wireless cellular networks, specially for the Nationwide Interoperable Public Safety Broadband Network. Mobility networks, providing mobility services to billions of customers over the world, were never designed with a security perspective. The evolution from GSM to UMTS and finally LTE has addressed encryption and authentication issues, aiming to enhance the overall system security. The same kind of proactive approach should be taken in order to mitigate potential DoS jamming attacks against mobility networks.

Competing interests
The authors declare that they have no competing interests.

Authors' information
Dr. Raghavan participated in this work while being a member of the AT&T Radio Access and Devices team.

Author details
[1] AT&T Security Research Center, New York, NY 10007, USA. [2] Blue Clover Devices, San Bruno, CA 94066, USA.

References

1. S Sesia, M Baker, I Toufik, *LTE, The UMTS Long Term Evolution: From Theory to Practice.* (Wiley, New York, 2009)
2. Nationwide Public Safety Broadband Network. US Department of Homeland Security: Office of Emergency Communications (2012). http://goo.gl/AoF41. Accessed Feb 2014
3. T Doumi, M Dolan, S Tatesh, A Casati, G Tsirtsis, K Anchan, D Flore, LTE for public safety networks. IEEE Comm. Mag. **51**(2), 106–112 (2013)
4. W Xu, Y Zhang, T Wood, The feasibility of launching and detecting jamming attacks in wireless networks, in *ACM MOBIHOC; Urbana-Champaign* (ACM New York, 2005), pp. 46–57
5. D Talbot, *One simple trick could disable a city 4G phone network.* (MIT Technology Review, 2012). http://goo.gl/jROMe2.
6. M Lichtman, JH Reed, TC Clancy, M Norton, Vulnerability of LTE to hostile interference, in *Proceedings of the IEEE Global Conference on Signal and Information Processing,* GlobalSIP '13, Austin, TX (IEEE New York, 2013), pp. 285–288
7. When advanced persistent threats go mainstream. Emc corporation: security for business innovation council (2011). http://www.emc.com/collateral/industry-overview/sbic-rpt.pdf.
8. D Alperovitch, Revealed: operation shady RAT. Threat research, mcafee (2011). http://www.mcafee.com/us/resources/white-papers/wp-operation-shady-rat.pdf.
9. D Perez, J Pico, A practical attack against GPRS/EDGE/UMTS/HSPA mobile data communications, in *In BlackHat DC,* (2011). http://goo.gl/KGN3j.
10. A Rossler, Cell search and cell selection in UMTS LTE. White paper, Rhode & Schwarz (2009). http://goo.gl/ntWJPA.
11. 3rd Generation Partnership Project; Technical Specification Group Radio Access Network, LTE; Evolved Universal Terrestrial Radio Access (E-UTRA); Physical channels and modulation. 3GPP TS 36.211 vol. v9.1.0 (2010)
12. Ettus Research. USRP. http://www.ettus.com/. Accessed Mar 2014
13. Kestrel Signal Processing, Inc. The OpenBTS Project. http://openbts.sourceforge.net/.
14. M Stahlberg, Radio jamming attacks against two popular mobile networks, in *Helsinki University of Technology. Seminar on Network Security. Mobile Security,* (2000). Accessed Apr 2014
15. W Xu, K Ma, W Trappe, Y Zhang, Jamming sensor networks: attack and defense strategies. IEEE Netw. **20**(3), 41–47 (2006)

16. T Basar, The Gaussian test channel with an intelligent jammer. IEEE Trans. Inform. Theor. **29**, 152–157 (1983)

17. T Clancy, Efficient OFDM denial: pilot jamming and pilot nulling, in *Communications (ICC), 2011 IEEE International Conference on* (IEEE New York, 2011), pp. 1–5

18. P Bhat, S Nagata, L Campoy, I Berberana, T Derham, G Liu, X Shen, P Zong, J Yang, LTE-advanced: an operator perspective. IEEE Comm. Mag. **50**(2), 104–114 (2012)

19. 3rd Generation Partnership Project; Technical Specification Group Radio Access Network, LTE; Evolved Universal Terrestrial Radio Access (E-UTRA); User Equipment (UE) radio transmission and reception. 3GPP TS 36.101 vol. fv10.3.0 (2011)

20. D Spaar, A practical DoS attack to the GSM network, in *In DeepSec*, (2009). http://tinyurl.com/7vtdoj5.

21. LTE/WiMAX link budget calculator (2010). http://goo.gl/phn2we. Accessed Mar 2014

22. K Ramadas, R Jain, WiMAX system evaluation methodology, in *Wimax Forum, Jan*, (2007). http://goo.gl/sNlj70.

23. B Wojtowicz, OpenLTE. An open source 3GPP LTE implementation. http://sourceforge.net/projects/openlte/. Accessed Apr 2014

24. K Nohl, S Munaut, Wideband GSM sniffing. In 27th Chaos Communication Congress (2010). http://goo.gl/wT5tz.

25. E Gadaix, GSM and 3G security, in *In BlackHat Asia*, (2001). http://tinyurl.com/85plhlv.

26. J Pérez-Romero, O Sallent, Agustí R, MA Diaz-Guerra, *Radio Resource Management Strategies in UMTS*. (John Wiley & Sons, New York, 2005). http://books.google.com/books?id=581gFV8abl4C.

27. AJ Viterbi, *CDMA: Principles of Spread Spectrum Communication, Volume 129*. (Addison-Wesley Boston, MA, 1995)

28. P Vig, Trusted platform module. Microsoft secret weapon in the mobile arena. Zunited (2012). http://goo.gl/lqldu.

29. S Marek, AT&T's Rinne: using SON helps improve throughput and reduce dropped calls. FierceBroadband Wireless (2012). http://goo.gl/xV70k.

30. TD Vo-Huu, EO Blass, G Noubir, Counter-jamming Using mixed mechanical and software interference cancellation, in *Proceedings of the Sixth ACM Conference on Security and Privacy in Wireless and Mobile Networks*, WiSec '13 (ACM New York, 2013), pp. 31–42

31. C Balanis, *Antenna Theory: Analysis and Design*. (Wiley, New York, 1982)

32. J Serror J, Impact of paging channel overloads or attacks on a cellular network, in *Proceedings of the ACM Workshop on Wireless Security (WiSe)* (IEEE New York, 2006), pp. 1289–1297

33. P Lee, T Bu, T Woo, On the detection of signaling DoS attacks on 3G wireless networks, in *INFOCOM 2007. 26th IEEE International Conference on Computer Communications. IEEE*, (2007)

34. G Kambourakis, C Kolias, S Gritzalis, J Park, DoS attacks exploiting signaling in UMTS and IMS. Comput. Commun. **34**(3), 226–235 (2011)

35. S Khattab, D Mosse, R Melhem, Jamming mitigation in multi-radio wireless networks: reactive or proactive?, in *Proceedings of the 4th International Conference on Security and Privacy In Communication Netowrks, SecureComm '08* (ACM New York, 2008), pp. 27:1–27:10

8

Privacy-preserving distributed clustering

Zekeriya Erkin[1][*], Thijs Veugen[1,2], Tomas Toft[3] and Reginald L Lagendijk[1]

Abstract

Clustering is a very important tool in data mining and is widely used in on-line services for medical, financial and social environments. The main goal in clustering is to create sets of similar objects in a data set. The data set to be used for clustering can be owned by a single entity, or in some cases, information from different databases is pooled to enrich the data so that the merged database can improve the clustering effort. However, in either case, the content of the database may be privacy sensitive and/or commercially valuable such that the owners may not want to share their data with any other entity, including the service provider. Such privacy concerns lead to trust issues between entities, which clearly damages the functioning of the service and even blocks cooperation between entities with similar data sets. To enable joint efforts with private data, we propose a protocol for distributed clustering that limits information leakage to the untrusted service provider that performs the clustering. To achieve this goal, we rely on cryptographic techniques, in particular homomorphic encryption, and further improve the state of the art of processing encrypted data in terms of efficiency by taking the distributed structure of the system into account and improving the efficiency in terms of computation and communication by data packing. While our construction can be easily adjusted to a centralized or a distributed computing model, we rely on a set of particular users that help the service provider with computations. Experimental results clearly indicate that the work we present is an efficient way of deploying a privacy-preserving clustering algorithm in a distributed manner.

1 Introduction

As a powerful tool in data mining, clustering is widely used in several domains, including finance, medicine and social networks, to group similar objects based on a similarity metric. In many cases, the entity that performs the clustering operation has access to the whole database, while in some other cases, databases from different resources are merged to improve the performance of the clustering algorithms. A number of examples can be given as follows:

- *Social networks.* Users are clustered by the service provider based on their profile data. The clustering result can be used for creating self-help groups or generating recommendations. Obviously, in many cases, users would not like to share their profile data with anyone else but with the people that are in the same group.
- *Banking.* Several banks might want to merge their customer databases for credit card fraud detection or to classify their users based on past transactions to identify profitable customers.
- *Medical domain.* Different holders of medical databases might be willing to pool their data for medical research, either for scientific, economic or marketing reasons [1]. Another case can be the Centre for Disease Control that would like to identify trends based on data from different insurance companies [2].

However, regardless of the application setting with one or more data resources, in many cases, data are privacy sensitive or commercially valuable: the data owners might not want to reveal their sensitive data to the service provider, for instance in social networks, as the data can be processed for other purposes, transferred to other third parties without user consent or stolen by outsiders. In the case of multiple data resources from different entities as in banking, the data owners might not want to take risks in sharing their customer data with other competitors. Clearly, such privacy-related concerns might result in several drawbacks: people not joining social networks

*Correspondence: z.erkin@tudelft.nl
[1] Department of Intelligent Systems, Delft University of Technology, Delft, 2628 CD, The Netherlands
Full list of author information is available at the end of the article

or database owners preferring to process data on their own.

In this paper, we focus on a setting with a central entity that provides services based on clustering of multiple users, each one having a private preference vector. Our goal is to prevent the service provider from learning the privacy-sensitive data of the users, without substantially degrading the performance of the clustering algorithm. Thus, we focus on the following:

- *Privacy.* To protect the privacy of users, we encrypt the preference vectors and provide only these encrypted vectors to the service provider, who does not have the decryption key. However, it is still possible for the service provider to cluster people using our cryptographic protocol. Throughout the protocol, the preferences, intermediate cluster assignments and the final results of the clustering algorithm are all encrypted and thus unknown to the service provider or any other person in the network. This approach, which has proved itself useful in the field of privacy-enhanced technologies [3], guarantees privacy protection to the users of the social network without disrupting the service.
- *Performance.* While processing encrypted data as explained above provides privacy protection, it also comes with a price: expensive operations on the encrypted data, in terms of computational and communication costs. To improve the efficiency, we approach this challenge in two directions: (1) custom-tailored cryptographic protocols that use data packing and (2) a setting in which the service provider creates user sets and assigns additional responsibilities to one of the users in each set to be able to use less expensive cryptographic sub-protocols for the computations, avoiding expensive computations such as the ones in [4]. Moreover, having such a construction, centralized or distributed clustering scenarios can be realized, as discussed further below.

The service provider is defined as the entity that wants to cluster users based on their private preference vectors. Each user also participates in the clustering computations, and a set of users, named helper users, are chosen randomly to perform additional tasks. As the number of user sets increases, it becomes easier to parallelize operations and thus achieve better performance. However, this setting with one set of users and a single helper user can also be considered to realize clustering algorithms for the scenarios with multiple entities, each having a private database: users belong to different entities, and the helper user becomes a privacy service provider [4]. Thus,

our construction can easily be reshaped according to the application.

In this paper, we choose the K-means clustering algorithm for finding the group of similar people based on their similarities. We choose the K-means algorithm since it is known to be a very efficient data mining tool that is widely used in practice as its implementation is simple and the algorithm converges quickly [5]. Our goal is to provide an efficient, privacy-preserving version of the clustering algorithm. Even though the idea of processing encrypted data for clustering has been addressed before in the literature, its realization in an efficient way has been a challenge. To improve the state of the art, we contribute in the following aspects:

- We propose a flexible setting, which can be interpreted as a centralized or a distributed environment with several servers. This enables a wide variety of business models.
- We build our system based on the semi-honest security model, in which we assume that involved parties are following the protocol steps. For the application settings, where the central entity is expected to go beyond the bounds of the protocol, our protocol can be tweaked to work in the malicious model with a cost of increased computation and communication [6]. However, we provide an alternative that is in between: we distribute trust among a number of helper users instead of relying on a single party. Especially in a setting with distributed databases, this substantially limits the power of a malicious central party.
- We exploit the construction with helper users to avoid more expensive cryptographic protocols such as secure comparisons [4], achieving significant performance gain compared to related work in the field.
- We employ custom-tailored cryptographic protocols with data packing [4,7,8] to reduce the communication and computation costs of using homomorphic encryption.

We emphasize that our proposal is an improvement of the ideas from [9] and [10] in terms of efficiency and requires reasonable security and business assumptions. Our main contribution is to show that realizing privacy-preserving K-means clustering with existing tools is feasible to deploy. To prove our claim of achieving high efficiency, we also give the test results of our proposal on a synthetic data set of 100,000 users.

The rest of the paper is organized as follows: Section 2 gives an overview on the state of the art. Section 3 introduces K-means clustering algorithm and homomorphic encryption briefly and presents our security assumptions and the notation used throughout the paper. Section 4 describes the privacy-preserving version of the K-means clustering algorithm in detail. Section 5 discusses the security aspects of our proposal, and Section 6 presents the complexity analysis and the numerical test results. Section 7 gives a discussion on the practicality of deploying our protocol in real life. Finally, Section 8 concludes this paper.

2   Related work

The idea of privacy-preserving data mining was introduced by Agarwal and Srikant [11] and Lindell and Pinkas [1]. In their work, the aim is to extract information from users' private data without having to reveal individual data items. Since then, a number of privacy protection mechanisms for finding similar items or people have been proposed in [2,12-16], which address the widely applied K-means clustering algorithm. The proposed methods apply either cryptographic tools [2,12-14] or randomization techniques from signal processing [15,16] to protect the private data, which are either horizontally or vertically partitioned.

In general, the cryptographic proposals are based on secure multiparty computation techniques [6], which make any two-party privacy-preserving data mining problem solvable, for instance by using Yao's secure circuit evaluation method [17]. Even though Yao's method can be used to implement any function in a privacy-preserving manner, heavy computation or communication costs in such circuits make the solutions feasible only for small circuit sizes. However, algorithms like clustering require large circuit sizes for realization. In [2,12,14], the authors attempt to solve the clustering problem in a two-party setting which is suitable for deploying techniques based on secret sharing. Apart from the difference in settings, [2] suffers from a problem during the centroid update procedure where an integer division is misinterpreted as multiplication by the inverse, which is not correct, as explained with an example in [12]. On the other hand, [13] has a multiuser setting but requires three non-colluding entities for the clustering algorithm, and the authors overcome the problem of updating centroids by allowing users to perform the division algorithm locally. In order to do that, the users learn the intermediate cluster assignments, meaning more information leakage.

As a different approach from using secure multiparty computation techniques, Oliviera and Zaiane [15,16] suggested using techniques from signal processing based on randomization and geometric transformation of data to hide private data of individuals. In these works, the privacy of the users is achieved by perturbing their data in a predefined way. Then, the data is made publicly available for processing. This approach is fast since the operations can be handled by each user simultaneously. However, data perturbation leads to unavoidable data leakage [18,19].

In [9], Erkin et al. proposed a method based on encryption and secure multiparty computation techniques for clustering users in a centralized system. In that work, Erkin et al. kept the preference vector of each user in the system hidden from all other users and the service provider and reveal the centroid locations to the service provider for achieving better performance in terms of run-time and bandwidth. The proposed method requires the participation of all users, and the average communication and computation cost is high due to homomorphic encryption. In [10], Beye et al. proposed an improved version of K-means clustering by proposing a three-party setting. In that work, users' private data are stored by one party and the decryption key by the other. A third party helps with the computations. Due to this three-party setting, Beye et al. proposed a highly efficient algorithm based on garbled circuits [20] that does not require oblivious transfer protocols [6]. While the overall system is highly efficient, the authors rely on trusting three separate parties that may not collude.

3   Preliminaries

In this section, we briefly introduce the K-means clustering algorithm, present our security assumptions, describe homomorphic encryption and introduce the notation used throughout the paper.

3.1 K-means clustering

Data clustering is a common technique for statistical data analysis where data is partitioned into smaller subgroups with their members sharing a common property [5]. As a widely used technique, K-means clusters data into K groups using an iterative algorithm. Particularly, each user i is represented as a point in an R-dimensional space, denoted with $P_i = (p_{(i,1)}, \ldots, p_{(i,R)})$, and assigned to the closest cluster among K clusters, $\{C_1, \ldots, C_K\}$. The algorithm starts with choosing the constant value K, which is the number of clusters in the data set. Each cluster k is represented by its centre (also named centroid), $C_k = (c_{(k,1)}, \ldots, c_{(k,R)})$, which is initially a random point. In every iteration, the distances $D_{(i,k)}$ between the ith user P_i and cluster centre C_k for $k \in \{1, \ldots, K\}$ are calculated and each user is assigned to the closest cluster. Once every user is associated with a cluster, centroid locations are recalculated by taking the arithmetic mean of the users' locations within that cluster. For the next iteration, the distances are recalculated and users are assigned to the closest cluster. This procedure, given in Algorithm 1, is repeated until either a certain number of iterations is reached or centroid locations converge.

Algorithm 1 The K-means clustering algorithm.

Input: K (randomly) chosen locations as cluster centroid.
Output: Cluster indices for each user.

1: For each user P_i, compute the distances to each cluster centroid C_k for $k \in \{1, \dots, K\}$.
2: Assign each user to the closest cluster.
3: Recalculate the centroid locations by taking the arithmetic mean of the users' locations within that cluster.
4: Repeat steps 1, 2 and 3 until one of the termination conditions is reached: (a) a certain number of iterations or (b) centroid locations converge.
5: Output the cluster indices for each user.

3.2 Security assumptions

We consider the semi-honest security model, which assumes that the involved parties are honest and follow the defined protocol steps but are also curious to obtain more information. Therefore, the parties can store previously exchanged messages to deduce more information than they are entitled to. This model does not consider any malicious activity by the parties such as manipulating the original data.

We assume that the service provider creates groups of people randomly to help in computations, in which a number of people takes more responsibility in computations. Our assumption is that these randomly chosen users do not collude with the service provider in revealing other users' personal data. The risk of information leakage by such parties is reduced, as explained later, by randomly choosing such helper users in each iteration of the algorithm. Note that as the number of helper users increases, the security of the system improves since the trust is divided among multiple entities, rather than one single entity.

Note that even though we assume that the service provider acts according to the protocol description, it is possible that the service provider can create dummy users and assign them as helper users. There are two approaches to cope with this problem. Firstly, each user participating in the computations can be asked to use certifications to prove their identity. Secondly, the helper users can be chosen truly random by deploying another sub-protocol. For this, the ideas from [21] can be used. Furthermore, in the case of malicious acts requiring input verification by the users, the techniques known from cryptography like commitment schemes and zero-knowledge proofs can be deployed at the cost of increased complexity.

Finally, we also assume that all underlying communication channels are secure: both integrity and authentication of all messages are obtained via standard means, e.g. IPSec or SSL/TLS [22].

3.3 Homomorphic encryption

The public-key cryptosystem Paillier [23] is *additively homomorphic*, meaning that multiplication of two cipher texts results in a new cipher text whose decryption equals the sum of the two plain texts. Given the plain texts m_1 and m_2, the additively homomorphic Paillier works as follows:

$$\mathcal{D}_{sk}\left(\mathcal{E}_{pk}(m_1) \cdot \mathcal{E}_{pk}(m_2)\right) = m_1 + m_2,$$

where pk and sk are the public and secret keys, respectively. As a consequence of the additive homomorphism, any cipher text $\mathcal{E}_{pk}(m)$ raised to the power c results in a new encryption of $m \cdot c$ as

$$\mathcal{D}_{pk}\left(\mathcal{E}_{pk}(m)^c\right) = m \cdot c.$$

The encryption of a message, $m \in \mathbb{Z}_n$, by using the Paillier scheme is defined as

$$\mathcal{E}_{pk}(m) = g^m \cdot r^n \bmod n^2,$$

where n is a product of two large prime numbers, g generates a sub-group of order n and r is a random number in $\mathbb{Z}_n^*$. Note that the message space is $\mathbb{Z}_n$ and the cipher text space is $\mathbb{Z}_{n^2}^*$. For decryption and further details, we refer readers to [23].

In addition to the homomorphic property, Paillier is semantically secure. Informally, this means that one cannot distinguish between encryptions of known messages and random messages. This is achieved by having multiple possible cipher texts for each plain text and choosing randomly between these. This property is required as the messages to be encrypted in this paper are from a very small range compared to the message space of the cryptosystem. Throughout this paper, we denote a Paillier encryption of a message m by $[\![m]\!]_{pk}$ for the sake of simplicity.

3.4 Notation

We use uppercase and lowercase letters to represent a vector and its elements, respectively: $A_i = (a_{(i,1)}, a_{(i,2)}, \dots, a_{(i,R)})$. We represent the packed version of a vector as $\tilde{A}_i = a_{(i,1)} || a_{(i,2)} || \dots || a_{(i,R)}$. We present the variables used throughout the paper in Table 1.

4 Privacy-preserving user clustering

In this section, we present a cryptographic protocol that clusters users in a social network setting using the K-means algorithm. Our aim is to hide the private data of the users from the service provider. We define the private data as the preference vectors P_i, distances between the P_i

Table 1 List of symbols

Symbol	Description
M	Number of groups created by the service provider
N_u	Total number of users in the social network
K	Number of clusters
P_i	Preference set of user i
$\widetilde{P}_{\Sigma_{(m,r)}}$	Packed sum of preferences of users in G_m
$p_{(i,r)}$	rth coordinate of P_i
$c_{(k,r)}$	rth coordinate of cluster k
$\widetilde{P}_i$	Packed preference of user i
$\widetilde{C}_r$	Packed centroid for dimension r
$\gamma_{(i,k)}$	Binary value for the kth cluster: 1 for the closest cluster, 0 otherwise
$\widetilde{\Gamma}_{\Sigma_m}$	Packed total number of users in each cluster for G_m
w	Bit length of $p_{(i,r)}$ and $c_{(j,r)}$
$\alpha, \beta, \phi, \psi, \rho$	Random values
$[\![\cdot]\!]_H$	Encryption of a plain text using the public key of H_m
$\widetilde{S}_{(i,r)}$	Packed partial input of user i for dimension r
N_g	Number of users in each group
R	Dimension of preferences
G_m	Group m
$\widetilde{P}_i$	Packed preferences of user i
$\widetilde{P}_{\Sigma_r}$	Packed sum of preferences of all users for dimension r
C_k	Cluster centroid k
$D_{(i,k)}$	Euclidean distance between P_i and C_k
$\widetilde{D}_{(i,k)}$	Packed Euclidean distance between P_i and C_j
Δ	Compartment size of $\widetilde{\Gamma}_i$ in bits
$\widetilde{\Gamma}_i$	Packed vector of γ's for user i
$\widetilde{\Gamma}_\Sigma$	Packed total number of users in each cluster
σ	Statistical security parameter
H_m	Helper user of group m
n	Paillier modulus
ℓ	Compartment size of $\widetilde{C}$ in bits

and the centroid C_k, and the result of the clustering algorithm, which is the final cluster assignment of each user. We define the following roles for our construction:

1. The *service provider* has a business interest in providing services to users in a social network.
2. A *user* participates in a social network and would like to find similar other users based on his/her preferences.
3. A *helper* is a user who helps the service provider with the computations.

We assume that each user has a public key pair with valid certificates. We anticipate that the service provider

determines K points to be the initial cluster centroids. To cluster all users, the following steps are performed:

1. The service provider creates M groups of users and, for each group, G_m for $m \in \{1, \ldots, M\}$, selects a random user H_m for each iteration as illustrated in Figure 1. We assume that there are N_g users in each group and the total number of users is $N_u = N_g \cdot M$.
2. The service provider informs every user in G_m about the public key to be used for encryption in that iteration, which is the public key of H_m.
3. The service provider sends the encrypted cluster centroids to the users. Each user computes K encrypted Euclidean distances, one for every cluster centroid, and sends them to the service provider.
4. The service provider interacts with H_m to obtain an encrypted vector for each user, whose elements indicate the closest cluster to that user. Then, the service provider sends this vector to the user.
5. Each user computes his/her partial input for updating the centroid locations using the encrypted vector and sends it to the service provider.
6. The service provider aggregates the partial inputs from all users in G_m and interacts with H_m to obtain the clustering result of G_m in plain text.
7. Finally, the service provider combines the clustering results from all groups and obtains the new centroids for that iteration.

Steps 1 to 7 are repeated either for a certain number of iterations or up to a point where the cluster centroids do not change significantly. After the final iteration, the service provider runs a protocol with H_m to send the index of the closest cluster to each user. Hereafter, we describe the above procedure in detail for a single group.

4.1 Steps 1 and 2: grouping and key distribution
The first step of the K-means clustering algorithm is for the service provider to choose K points in an R-dimensional space as the initial cluster centroids. Next, the service provider creates M groups consisting of N_g users each and picks a random user from every group who will help the service provider with the computations for the current iteration. Note that in order for the helper users to be clustered, the service provider treats them as an ordinary user in a different group. Later, the service provider disseminates the public key of the helper user to the other users.

4.2 Step 3: computing the encrypted distances
In principle, the service provider and the users in G_m compute the Euclidean distances from each user's preference

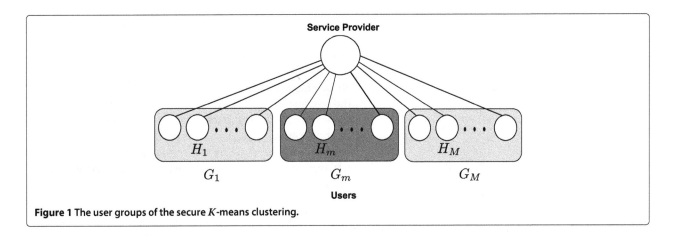

Figure 1 The user groups of the secure K-means clustering.

vector P_i to every cluster centroid C_k as given in Equation 1:

$$
D^2_{(i,k)} = ||\mathbf{P}_i - \mathbf{C}_k||^2 = \sum_{r=1}^{R} p^2_{(i,r)}
$$
$$
+ \sum_{r=1}^{R} (-2p_{(i,r)} c_{(k,r)}) + \sum_{r=1}^{R} c^2_{(k,r)}, \tag{1}
$$

where user i possesses P_i and the service provider holds cluster locations C_k, which are privacy sensitive and hence should be kept secret from the other party. To compute the Euclidean distance without revealing private data, the service provider and user i use the homomorphic property: given that encryption of C_k and sums $\sum_{r=1}^{R} c^2_{(k,r)}$ are provided by the service provider, the encrypted distance could be computed as follows [9]:

$$
\left[\!\left[D^2_{(i,k)}\right]\!\right]_H = \left[\!\left[\sum_{r=1}^{R} p^2_{(i,r)}\right]\!\right]_H \prod_{r=1}^{R} [\![c_{(k,r)}]\!]_H^{-2p_{(i,r)}} \cdot \left[\!\left[\sum_{r=1}^{R} c^2_{(k,r)}\right]\!\right]_H . \tag{2}
$$

The above approach to compute the encrypted distances in [9] uses the homomorphic property of the cryptosystem without any optimization and therefore introduces a considerable computational overhead for user i. More precisely, that computation requires $K(R+1)$ encryption by the service provider and one encryption, KR exponentiation and $K(R+1)$ multiplications by *each* user over mod n^2. Repeating these expensive operations for N_u users, the clustering algorithm becomes considerably expensive and thus impractical in real life.

To improve the efficiency in terms of communication and computation, we use data packing by following a similar approach as in [4,7,8]. Instead of computing separate Euclidean distances in the encrypted domain, users can compute a single *packed* value, which involves K distances, with the help of the service provider. For this

purpose, the service provider creates the following packed values:

$$
\widetilde{C}_1 = c_{(1,1)}||c_{(2,1)}|| \ldots ||c_{(K,1)}
$$
$$
\widetilde{C}_2 = c_{(1,2)}||c_{(2,2)}|| \ldots ||c_{(K,2)}
$$
$$
\vdots
$$
$$
\widetilde{C}_R = c_{(1,R)}||c_{(2,R)}|| \ldots ||c_{(K,R)}, \tag{3}
$$

where $||$ denotes concatenation. Formally, the above values are calculated as follows:

$$
\widetilde{C}_r = \sum_{k=1}^{K} c_{(k,r)} \cdot (2^\ell)^{k-1}, \text{ for } r \in \{1, \ldots, R\} . \tag{4}
$$

The bit length of each $\widetilde{C}_r$ is now $K \times \ell$ bits. We set the size of each compartment to $\ell = 2w + \lceil \log R \rceil$ bits, with w being the bit length of $c_{(k,r)}$, to accommodate the distances computed in the consequent steps, which are the sum of R positive numbers of size $2w$ bits.

In addition to the packed values above, the service provider prepares the following value:

$$
\widetilde{C}^2 = \sum_{r=1}^{R} c^2_{(1,r)}|| \sum_{r=1}^{R} c^2_{(2,r)}|| \ldots || \sum_{r=1}^{R} c^2_{(K,r)}, \tag{5}
$$

where the sums of squares are also packed in compartments of size ℓ-bits. Then, the service provider encrypts $\widetilde{C}^2$ and $\widetilde{C}_r$ for $r \in \{1 \ldots R\}$ with the public key of H_m and sends the encrypted values to the users. Next, each user i of G_m computes the packed distances as follows:

$$
\left[\!\left[\widetilde{D}^2_i\right]\!\right]_H = \left[\!\left[D^2_{(i,1)}||D^2_{(i,2)}|| \ldots ||D^2_{(i,K)}\right]\!\right]_H
$$
$$
= \left[\!\left[\widetilde{C}^2\right]\!\right]_H \cdot \prod_{r=1}^{R} \left[\!\left[\widetilde{C}_r\right]\!\right]_H^{-2p_{(i,r)}} \cdot \left[\!\left[\widetilde{P}^2\right]\!\right]_H , \tag{6}
$$

where

$$\widetilde{P}^2 = \underbrace{\sum_{r=1}^{R} p_{(i,r)}^2 || \cdots || \sum_{r=1}^{R} p_{(i,r)}^2 || \sum_{r=1}^{R} p_{(i,r)}^2}_{K \text{ times}} . \tag{7}$$

User i then sends $[\![\widetilde{D}_i^2]\!]_H$ to the service provider.

Remark 1. Each squared distance $D_{(i,k)}^2$ consists of at most ℓ-bits. We assume that $K \cdot \ell \ll n$, where n is the message space of the Paillier encryption scheme, meaning all of the K distances can be packed in one encryption. Note that $|p_{(i,r)} - c_{(k,r)}| \leq \max(p_{(i,r)}, c_{(k,r)})$, and thus, $D_{(i,k)}^2 \leq R \cdot 2^{2w}$.

Notice that due to the way we compute distances using data packing, there is a gain by a factor of K in the number of operations on the encrypted data compared to [9]. The computation of the packed encrypted distances only requires $R + 1$ encryption by the service provider and one encryption, R exponentiation and $R + 1$ multiplications by each user.

4.3 Step 4: finding the closest cluster
After having obtained $[\![\widetilde{D}_i^2]\!]_H$, the service provider interacts with H_m to find out the minimum distance, hence the closest cluster. To achieve this, the service provider sends the packed distances to H_m, who has the decryption key. H_m decrypts the cipher text and obtains the packed distances in clear. Note that H_m does not know the identity of the owner of the computed distances. After decryption, H_m unpacks the distances and creates a vector $(\gamma_{(i,1)}, \gamma_{(i,2)}, \ldots, \gamma_{(i,K)})$, where $\gamma_{(i,k)}$ is 1 if and only if $D_{(i,k)}^2$ is the minimum distance (so user i is in cluster number k), and 0 otherwise. Before sending these binary values to the service provider, H_m encrypts them using his/her public key.

Upon receiving the values $[\![\gamma_{(i,k)}]\!]_H$'s from H_m, the service provider packs them to reduce the bandwidth usage and to simplify the computations in the subsequent steps:

$$[\![\widetilde{\Gamma}_i]\!]_H = [\![\gamma_{(i,1)} || \gamma_{(i,2)} || \cdots || \gamma_{(i,K)}]\!]_H = \prod_{k=1}^{K} [\![\gamma_{(i,k)}]\!]_H^{2^{\Delta(k-1)}}$$

$$= \left[\!\!\left[\sum_{k=1}^{K} \gamma_{(i,k)} \cdot 2^{\Delta(k-1)}\right]\!\!\right]_H , \tag{8}$$

where $\Delta = w + \lceil \log N_u \rceil$, N_u being the number of total users in the system. This gives one packed $\widetilde{\Gamma}_i$ with a compartment size of $w + \lceil \log N_u \rceil$ bits. The service provider, then, sends $\widetilde{\Gamma}_i$ to the users.

Remark 2. Notice that in the above procedure, H_m will learn how many users in his/her group belong to each cluster. To hide this information from H_m, the service provider uses a different permutation, π_i, independently chosen for each user to shuffle the order of clusters during the creation of the $\widetilde{C}_r$ values. The order is corrected when the service provider applies the inverse permutation, π_i^{-1}, on the received $[\![\gamma_{(i,k)}]\!]$'s. As this permutation is necessary and can only be done by the service provider, H_m cannot apply data packing himself, which would simplify the computations otherwise.

Remark 3. We assumed in Equation 8 that packing K $\gamma_{(i,k)}$'s, each within a compartment size of $w + \lceil \log N_u \rceil$ bits, is possible. This is a valid assumption in practical cases since the Paillier modulus, even for a weak security, is 1,024 bits. Given that $K = 10$ and $w = 3$, N_u can be as large as 2^{99}.

4.4 Step 5: computing partial inputs
To update K cluster centroids, the service provider needs to take the average of user preferences in each cluster under encryption. To achieve this, upon receiving $[\![\widetilde{\Gamma}_i]\!]$, user i computes

$$[\![\widetilde{S}_{(i,r)}]\!]_H = [\![\widetilde{\Gamma}_i]\!]_H^{p_{(i,r)}} = [\![\gamma_{(i,1)} \cdot p_{(i,r)} || \cdots || \gamma_{(i,K)} \cdot p_{(i,r)}]\!]_H, \tag{9}$$

for $r \in \{1, \ldots, R\}$. The result of this operation is R encryptions, each of which contains K packed values. Each compartment of the encryptions contains the multiplication of $\gamma_{(i,k)}$ and $p_{(i,r)}$ for $k \in \{1, \ldots, K\}$. It is clear that $K - 1$ compartments consist of zeros and only one compartment that has the index of the closest cluster is exactly $p_{(i,r)}$. User i, finally, sends $[\![\widetilde{S}_{(i,r)}]\!]$ for $r \in \{1, \ldots, R\}$ to the service provider.

To update the cluster centroids, the service provider needs the number of users and the sum of preferences in each cluster. Since $[\![\widetilde{\Gamma}_i]\!]$'s are available to the service provider, it easily computes the number of users in each cluster for G_m under encryption:

$$[\![\widetilde{\Gamma}_{\Sigma_m}]\!]_H = \prod_{i \in G_m} [\![\widetilde{\Gamma}_i]\!]_H = \left[\!\!\left[\sum_{i \in G_m} \widetilde{\Gamma}_i\right]\!\!\right]_H$$

$$= \left[\!\!\left[\sum_{i \in G_m} \gamma_{(i,1)} || \sum_{i \in G_m} \gamma_{(i,2)} || \cdots || \sum_{i \in G_m} \gamma_{(i,K)}\right]\!\!\right]_H . \tag{10}$$

Similarly, the service provider computes $P_{\Sigma(m,r)}$, the sum of user preferences of G_m, for each cluster as follows:

$$[\![\widetilde{P}_{\Sigma(m,r)}]\!]_H = \prod_{i \in G_m} [\![\widetilde{S}_{(i,r)}]\!]_H = \left[\!\!\left[\sum_{i \in G_m} \widetilde{S}_{(i,r)}\right]\!\!\right]_H , \qquad (11)$$

for $r \in \{1, \ldots, R\}$. This results in R encryption, one for each dimension, and each of which has K packed sums of preferences of users in G_m.

4.5 Step 6: aggregating partial inputs

The next step for the service provider is to obtain the decryptions of $[\![\widetilde{\Gamma}_{\Sigma_m}]\!]_H$ and $[\![\widetilde{P}_{\Sigma(m,r)}]\!]_H$. For this reason, the service provider interacts with H_m. As these values are also privacy sensitive, the service provider prevents H_m from accessing the content of the cipher text by applying masking: it generates two sets of random numbers α_m and $\beta_{(m,r)}$ that are $K \cdot \Delta + \sigma$ bits long, where σ is a statistical security parameter in the range of 40 to 100 bits. After that, the server blinds $\widetilde{\Gamma}_{\Sigma_m}$ and $\widetilde{P}_{\Sigma(m,r)}$ by performing the following multiplications:

$$[\![\widetilde{\Gamma}_{\Sigma_m} + \alpha_m]\!]_H = [\![\widetilde{\Gamma}_{\Sigma_m}]\!]_H \cdot [\![\alpha_m]\!]_H ,$$
$$[\![\widetilde{P}_{\Sigma(m,r)} + \beta_{(m,r)}]\!]_H = [\![\widetilde{P}_{\Sigma(m,r)}]\!]_H \cdot [\![\beta_{(m,r)}]\!]_H , \qquad (12)$$

for $r \in \{1, \ldots, R\}$. Then, the service provider sends $[\![\widetilde{\Gamma}_{\Sigma_m} + \alpha_m]\!]_H$ and $[\![\widetilde{P}_{\Sigma(m,r)} + \beta_{(m,r)}]\!]_H$ to H_m. After decrypting them, H_m could send $\widetilde{\Gamma}_{\Sigma_m} + \alpha_m$ and $\widetilde{P}_{\Sigma(m,r)} + \beta_{(m,r)}$ to the service provider, who could remove the masking by subtracting the random values, but this would reveal sensitive information to the service provider about the distribution of users in each group. To avoid this information leakage, H_m also applies masking by adding random values, ϕ_m and $\psi_{(m,r)}$, which are computed as described below, and sends the resulting masked values to the service provider.

The random values ϕ_m and $\psi_{(m,r)}$ of size $K \cdot \Delta + \sigma$ bits are generated by a single helper user prior to the start of the iteration such that $\sum_{m=1}^M \phi_m = 0$ and $\sum_{m=1}^M \psi_{(m,r)} = 0$ for $r \in \{1, \ldots, R\}$. Each of these random values are then encrypted with the public key of the corresponding helper user and sent to the service provider, who passes them to the corresponding H_m. Finally, each helper user sends $\widetilde{\Gamma}_{\Sigma_m} + \alpha_m + \phi_m$ and $\widetilde{P}_{\Sigma(m,r)} + \beta_{(m,r)} + \psi_{(m,r)}$ to the service provider.

4.6 Step 7: obtaining the new cluster centroids

After receiving masked values from all of the M groups, the service provider obtains the masked packed sums of preferences and the number of users in each cluster, separately for each group. The service provider adds the plain texts from all H_m's and obtains

$$\sum_{m=1}^M (\widetilde{\Gamma}_{\Sigma_m} + \alpha_m + \phi_m) , \quad \sum_{m=1}^M (\widetilde{P}_{\Sigma(m,r)} + \beta_{(m,r)} + \psi_{(m,r)}) . \qquad (13)$$

Recall that $\sum_{m=1}^M \phi_m = 0$ and $\sum_{m=1}^M \psi_{(m,r)} = 0$. Since the service provider knows $\sum_{m=1}^M \alpha_m$ and $\sum_{m=1}^M \beta_{(m,r)}$, he subtracts them from the total and obtains $\widetilde{\Gamma}_\Sigma = \sum_{m=1}^M \widetilde{\Gamma}_{\Sigma_m}$ and $\widetilde{P}_{\Sigma_r} = \sum_{m=1}^M \widetilde{P}_{\Sigma(m,r)}$ for $r \in \{1, \ldots, R\}$. Notice that $\widetilde{P}_{\Sigma_r} = \sum_{i \in C_1} p_{(i,r)} || \ldots || \sum_{i \in C_K} p_{(i,r)}$ and $\widetilde{\Gamma}_\Sigma = \sum_{i \in C_1} \gamma_{(i,r)} || \ldots || \sum_{i \in C_K} \gamma_{(i,r)}$.

Finally, the service provider unpacks $\widetilde{\Gamma}_\Sigma$ and $\widetilde{P}_{\Sigma_r}$ and computes the new cluster centroids as follows:

$$c_{(k,r)} = \lceil \frac{\widetilde{P}_{\Sigma_r}(k)}{\Gamma_\Sigma(k)} \rceil , \qquad (14)$$

for $k \in \{1, \ldots, K\}$ and $r \in \{1, \ldots, R\}$, where $\Gamma_\Sigma(k)$ is the total number of users in cluster k and $P_{\Sigma_r}(k)$ is the rth coordinate of the sum of preferences in cluster k, obtained after unpacking. The result of this operation is then rounded to the nearest integer. The complete steps of the protocol for one iteration is given in Figure 2.

4.7 Termination control and obtaining the cluster index

The service provider checks whether the predetermined termination condition is reached at the end of each iteration. Since centroid locations and the number of iterations are known to the service provider in plain text, termination control is considered to be costless. Once the termination condition is reached, i.e. when a certain number of iterations is reached or when centroids do not move significantly, the cluster index of the user, which is the non-zero element in the encrypted vector $[\![\widetilde{\Gamma}_i]\!]_H$, should be delivered to the user in plain text. For this purpose, after the last iteration, the service provider sends $[\![\widetilde{\Gamma}_i]\!]_H$ to user i, who masks it with a random number ρ_i of size $\log(KR) + \sigma$ bits to get $[\![\widetilde{\Gamma}_i + \rho_i]\!]_H$, and sends it back to the service provider. The service provider sends the cipher text to H_m to be decrypted. After receiving the plain text, the service provider sends $\widetilde{\Gamma}_i + \rho_i$ to user i, who can easily obtain the cluster index by subtracting ρ_i from the decrypted value and checking the non-zero value in the compartments. Notice that all messages pass through the service provider instead of sending them directly to the helper user. This is unavoidable in our design as the users do not know the identity of the helper user. As an alternative approach, the encrypted random value ρ_i can also be sent directly to the service provider at the start of the protocol. Having this random number, the service provider can mask $\widetilde{\Gamma}_i$ and send it to the helper user to be decrypted. By this way, transmission of $\widetilde{\Gamma}_i$ to user i can be avoided.

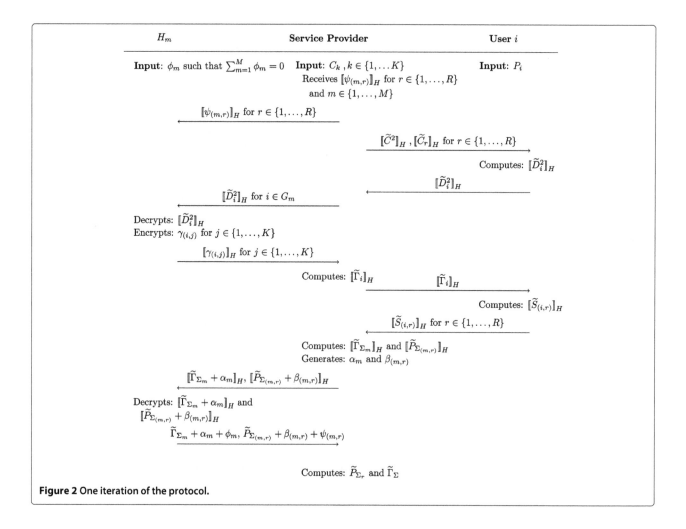

Figure 2 One iteration of the protocol.

5 Security discussion

In this section, we present arguments to show that our protocol is secure under the semi-honest security model. Recall that this model expects involved parties, namely the service provider, the helper users and all other users, to be honest in following the protocol steps. These parties are also assumed to be curious so they can keep previous messages to deduce more information than they are entitled to. This model does not consider corrupted parties. In this paper, we consider only one flavour of security threat: information leakage. In the following, we present an informal discussion on this issue.

Before discussing what information each party can derive from the received messages, we need to point out what information is allowed to be accessed. Remember that the number of clusters is public information. While the users to be clustered receive only the index of the cluster they are assigned to, the service provider does not obtain any information on the preferences of the users nor the final clustering results. However, a helper user obtains the distances between a user and the cluster centres. Even though the distances are permuted and the identity of the

user is unknown to the helper user, the helper user can still acquire information about the distances between clusters and the number of assignments for each cluster. Note that enabling helper users to access permuted distances seems to be a reasonable compromise to achieve better performance in computation. Although not formally proved, we believe that the privacy risks created here will be rather harmless to the users, particularly when the number of clusters grows. Considering that in each iteration a different user will be assigned as a helper user, the amount of information on the distances between centres diminishes.

Recall that every user, including the helper users, only interacts with the service provider using a secured channel. The public key of the helper user is also delivered to the users in that group by the service provider. On the basis of this information, we analyze what information can be inferred from exchanged messages.

5.1 Service provider

The service provider receives from the helper users encrypted packed distances of the users $[\![\widetilde{D}^2_{(i,k)}]\!]_H$ and the encrypted binary values $[\![\gamma_{(i,k)}]\!]_H$ that show the closest cluster for each user. As the Paillier cryptosystem is semantically secure, meaning that it is infeasible for a computationally bounded adversary to derive significant information about the plain text when its cipher text and the public key used are known, it is not feasible for the service provider from obtaining meaningful information from the cipher texts without the decryption key. However, the service provider also receives the sum of preferences and the number of users in each cluster within the group from the helper users in plain text. To prevent the service provider from accessing this information, the helper users mask their messages using random numbers, ϕ_m and $\psi_{(m,r)}$, in such a way that when these masked values are all added up, random values cancel each other out and the service provider gets the final result of the clustering for that iteration. The values received are statistically indistinguishable from random values with the same sum, but completely independent of the group sums. Therefore, the service provider does not have access to any information that might harm the users.

Notice that the way helper users perturb data prevents the service provider to obtain meaning information about each user group. This data perturbation technique will serve its purpose as long as the random numbers are generated accordingly, and helper users do not cooperate with the service provider. Within the semi-honest model, we assume that random number generation is performed properly. Selecting a number of helper users randomly for each iteration also reduces the risk of possible cooperation.

5.2 Helper user

In each group, all computations on the encrypted data are performed by using the public key of the helper user. As pointed out before, the helper user receives and sends data from and to the service provider only. To prevent the helper user from knowing the number of users in each cluster, the service provider applies a different permutation for each user during packing of the centroids. As a result of different permutations, the helper cannot observe the actual cluster with the minimum distance. Note that while the helper user learns the distances between users and K centroids, it is not possible to know the distance between a specific user and a certain cluster since both is kept hidden from the helper user. Furthermore, since in each iteration helper user changes, deducing meaningful information from computed distances becomes infeasible.

Hiding the sum of preferences in each group by applying permutation, on the other hand, is not possible. To hide this information, the service provider masks the values by adding random values, which guarantees that the helper user cannot infer meaningful information.

5.3 Users

Users receive encrypted messages from the service provider and without the decryption key, they cannot access the content. As a result, users cannot obtain information on the intermediate values of the clustering algorithm.

Although out of the scope of our semi-honest model, users are able to manipulate the clustering output by providing fake input data. As long as the size of the input is correct, such an attack would also not be prevented. However, since a user only obtains the index of his cluster, such an attack is not likely to lead to information leakage.

6 Performance

In this section, we present the complexity analysis of the privacy-preserving K-means clustering algorithm and experimental results on its performance.

6.1 Complexity analysis

The privacy-preserving version of the clustering algorithm presented in this paper has a number of disadvantages compared to the version in plain text. User preferences, which are usually small non-negative integers, grow to large numbers, e.g. 2,048 bits, after encryption. On top of that, addition and multiplication on the plain text become multiplication and exponentiation over mod n^2, which are computationally time-consuming. Moreover, transmission of the data from users to the service provider and vice versa requires more bandwidth than the plain version. Finally, realization of the algorithm involves interactive steps, requiring data exchange between the users and the service provider, which do not exist in the clustering algorithm with plain text data.

In Table 2, we present the complexity of our protocol in terms of expensive operations, namely encryption, decryption, multiplication and exponentiation, and communication cost for a single iteration and compare them with only [9]. Note that we assume the cost of operations on the plain text data is negligible compared to the ones on the encrypted data, and thus, we omit these operations.

As seen in Table 2, the privacy-preserving K-means clustering algorithm has linear complexity in the number of users similar to the original version on plain text. However, the cost of working in the encrypted domain has been significantly reduced compared to [9], which has a comparable complexity to [10]. The computational and communication gain come from the effective use of data packing, eliminating the need for an expensive secure comparison protocol in [9] and involving helper users in the computations.

The complexity analysis also shows that our proposal has lower complexity compared to the previous works in [2,12] and [14]. The communication complexity in [2] is $\mathcal{O}(N_u nKR)$ bits, and the computational complexity for the two-party setting is $\mathcal{O}(N_u KR)$ encryptions

Table 2 Communication and computational complexity for SP, H_m and user i for one iteration of the algorithm

	Our proposal			Algorithm in [9]	
	SP	H_m	User	SP	User
Encryption	$\mathcal{O}(N_uR)$	$\mathcal{O}(N_gK)$	$\mathcal{O}(1)$	$\mathcal{O}(N_uK(R+\ell))$	$\mathcal{O}(K(R+\ell))$
Decryption	-	$\mathcal{O}(N_gR)$	-	$\mathcal{O}(N_uK(R+\ell))$	-
Multiplication	$\mathcal{O}(N_uR)$	-	$\mathcal{O}(R)$	$\mathcal{O}(N_uKR)$	$\mathcal{O}(K(R+\ell^2))$
Exponentiation	$\mathcal{O}(N_uK)$	-	$\mathcal{O}(R)$	-	$\mathcal{O}(K(R+\ell^2))$
Communication	$\mathcal{O}(N_u(R+K))$	$\mathcal{O}(N_g(R+K))$	$\mathcal{O}(R)$	$\mathcal{O}(N_uK(R+\ell))$	$\mathcal{O}(K(R+\ell))$

In terms of Paillier encryptions. SP, service provider, H_m, helper user.

and multiplications for one party and $\mathcal{O}(N_uKR)$ exponentiations and multiplications for the other. [12] claims to have the same level of communication complexity with [2] but does not provide the computational complexity. [14], on the other hand, has a communication complexity of $\mathcal{O}(K^3nR)$. The computational complexity is $\mathcal{O}(K^3R)$ encryption and $\mathcal{O}(N_uK^3R)$ multiplications for one party and $\mathcal{O}(K^3R)$ exponentiation, $\mathcal{O}(K^2)$ encryption and $\mathcal{O}(N_uK^3R)$ multiplications for the other party.

6.2 Performance analysis

To test its performance, we implemented the cryptographic algorithm in C++ using GMP Library version 4.2.1 and tested our implementation on a single computer with 8 cores and 16 GB of RAM. Table 3 gives the list of parameters used in the tests. The values for K, n and k were taken from [9] for a fair comparison of the two protocols. In our test, we only assume that random numbers that are required for encryption and blinding are generated in advance as they are not dependent on the user data. This off-line computation consists of generating random numbers and raising them to the power of n for the fast encryption afterwards. For the values in Table 3, the total time for these computations was 97 min.

Table 3 Parameters

Symbol	Value
N_u	100,000
N_g	1,562
M	64
R	12
K	10
n	1,024 bits
ℓ	10
w	3 bits
σ	40 bits

However, note that these values for better on-line performance can be generated in the idle time of the service provider.

Figure 3 shows the run-times of our proposal and the protocol from [9], for ten iterations. To compare both protocols fairly, we took $M = 1$, meaning that there is only one helper user in the system. The run-time of the protocol in [9] for $N_u > 973$ users has been estimated. It is clear that the performance difference between the two protocols is drastic: the protocol in [9] takes approximately 110 h, while our proposal takes only 2.3 h for 100,000 users. This significant difference in performance is a result of employing data packing, which reduces the number of operations on the encrypted data, and avoiding the use of an expensive secure comparison protocol, thanks to using a helper user.

While our protocol outperforms the protocol from [9] even in the case of only two helper users, a drastic performance boost is achieved when there are multiple helper users in the system. Figure 4 shows the run-time of our protocol for different numbers of helper users and a varying number of users in each group. For every choice of M, the total number of users in the system is set to 100,000. While with two helpers, it takes approximately 80 min, with 64 helper users, it takes 26 min to cluster 100,000 users. Figure 4 shows that as the number of helper users increases, the total run-time decreases first sharply and later gradually. This means that for a fixed number of users in the system, increasing the number of helper users introduces a significant gain in performance. However, after a certain number of helper users, each having a negligible amount of work to accomplish, the performance of the overall system is determined by the tasks of the service provider. This fact is clearly seen in Figure 5, where for different numbers of helper users in the system, the work share between the helper users and the service provider is given by a percentage, omitting the users' participation, which is negligible compared to the helper users and the service provider. It is clear from the figure that the number of helper users should be chosen accordingly since the computational and

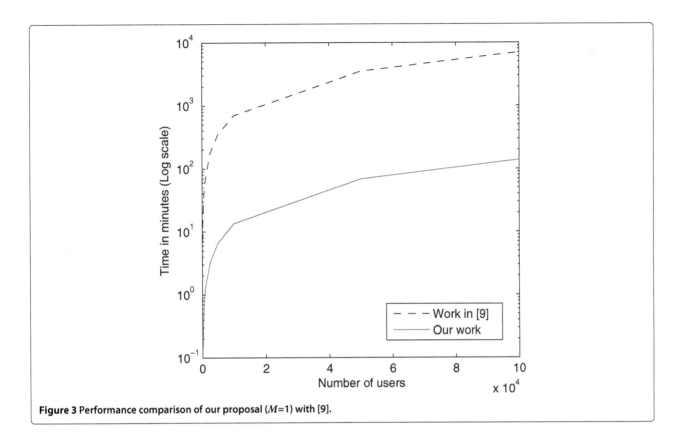

Figure 3 Performance comparison of our proposal (M=1) with [9].

communication loads become heavy with fewer helper users.

As for the bandwidth, we only consider the transmitted encrypted messages. For the parameters given in Table 3, the service provider sends and receives 1.215 GB of data, while the amount of data transmitted for a helper user is 9.4 kB. An ordinary user sends and receives only 6.8 kB of data. For the same set of parameters, the work in [9] requires the service provider and each user to transmit 7.8 GB and 82 kB of data, respectively. The significant difference in the amount of transmitted data is a result of data packing, as shown in the complexity analysis.

7 Discussion

Our proposal in this paper outperforms the most related protocol given in [9], which is also based on cryptographic tools within the semi-honest security model. Note that the privacy-preserving protocol in [10] that hides the cluster centroids from the service provider has a complexity comparable to [9]. Even though the numerical results on a data set of 100,000 show that our protocol is promising to be deployed in real life, we believe the performance of our proposal in a real implementation can be improved further for the following reasons. Firstly, an appropriate number of helper users can be determined by assessing the number of users in the system and the users' resources in terms of bandwidth and computation.

This leads to a number of groups, in which the helper user can process encrypted data without disrupting the user's other activities. Secondly, after choosing the optimum number of helper users based on the aforementioned criteria, the overall performance of the privacy-preserving clustering algorithm will be determined by the performance of the service provider. Note that all operations by the service provider can completely be performed in parallel. Since a multiple server model, or a cloud, is widely used in business, the overall runtime of the privacy-preserving clustering algorithm is expected to be within reasonable boundaries in real life.

With respect to bandwidth usage, our protocol employs data packing to the fullest extent. Note that using the Paillier cryptosystem, we face data expansion by a factor of 64, assuming that 32-bit numbers become 2,048-bit cipher text after encryption. We reduce this expansion considerably by deploying data packing.

A major aspect to be considered in deploying the privacy-preserving K-means clustering algorithm in real life is the security assumptions. Our model assumes the honest participation of all parties. While the semi-honest security model can be considered too simplistic, it is still good enough for real-world applications where the service provider and the users have incentives to act according to the protocol as seen in the sugar beet auction system

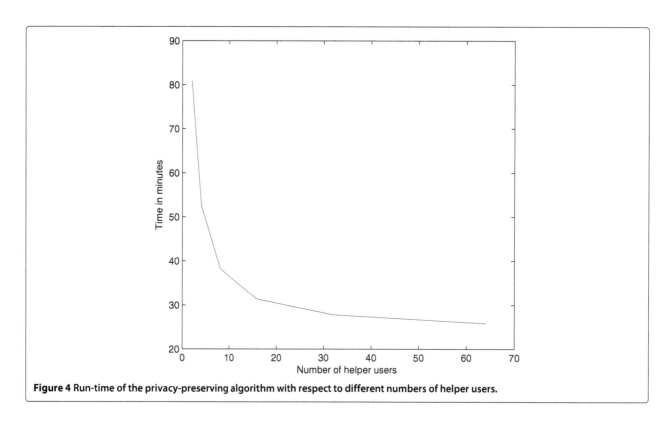

Figure 4 Run-time of the privacy-preserving algorithm with respect to different numbers of helper users.

[24]. Note that a protocol with 'proper measures against malicious parties' will be *much more expensive* computationally and hence impractical for large-scale deployment. A protocol with less strict but still realistic security guarantees is therefore preferred. To that end, we distribute the trust of the system between multiple parties, preventing a single malicious party to learn sensitive data. In a distributed model consisting of independent database owners, security risks are smaller because a collusion between the service provider and one of the helper users

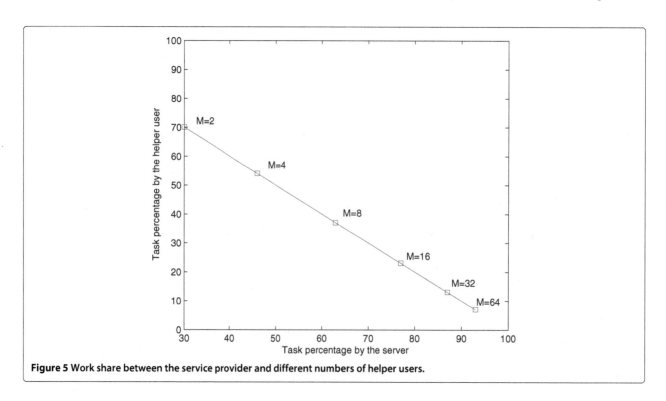

Figure 5 Work share between the service provider and different numbers of helper users.

will be less likely. A second aspect to consider is the active participation of all users in the system. It is our conclusion that without introducing (semi) trusted third parties, users' data cannot be processed without their participation. Fortunately, due to our construction, only the helper user needs to be on-line during the clustering procedure. Once the encrypted data are sent to the service provider, users can go off-line for the rest of the computation. If the same helper users are to be used, other users can stay off-line not only during that iteration but during the whole clustering; however, this would lead to minor changes in the protocol such as the encrypted distances should be computed by the service provider. Note that using the same helper users will lead to a similar setting to [10] with dedicated key holders. However, it is our motivation to distribute trust among multiple random helper users in each iteration for privacy protection, which requires helper users to be on-line during each iteration.

8 Conclusion

In this paper, we present an efficient, privacy-preserving K-means clustering algorithm in a social network setting. We present a mechanism where the private data of the users, sensitive intermediate values and the final clustering assignments are protected by means of encryption. The service provider, who does not have the decryption key, can still perform clustering without being able to access the content of private data. While the approach of processing encrypted data presents a concrete privacy protection for the users, it also introduces performance drawbacks compared to the version with plain text due to data expansion after encryption and expensive operations on the encrypted data. Previous work has shown different approaches to reduce the complexity of privacy-preserving K-means clustering such as using semi-trusted third parties. In this work, we build a mechanism on the common server-client model and reduce the costs by employing data packing. By this way, we reduce the number of encryption by a factor of K, thus introducing a considerable gain in terms of communication and computation. We also avoid interactive protocols such as secure comparison by exploiting the distributive setting. We also distribute trust among multiple random users for each iteration of the protocol, which introduces a computational gain proportional to the number of such users. The resulting cryptographic protocol is significantly more efficient compared to previous work in the semi-honest security model. We also analyze the effects of different choices of parameters on the performance of the cryptographic protocol. Experimental results support our claim on the feasibility of privacy-preserving K-means clustering such that it takes 26 min to cluster 100,000 users. This result, which can be improved further on a real

system, encourages the deployment of privacy-preserving K-means clustering algorithms based on homomorphic encryption.

Competing interests
The authors declare that they have no competing interests.

Acknowledgements
This work is supported by the Dutch COMMIT programme.

Author details
[1] Department of Intelligent Systems, Delft University of Technology, Delft, 2628 CD, The Netherlands. [2] TNO, P.O. Box 5050, Delft, 2600 GB, The Netherlands. [3] Computer Science Department, Aarhus University, IT-Parken, Åbogade 34, Aarhus N 8200, Denmark.

References
1. Y Lindell, B Pinkas, Privacy preserving data mining, in *CRYPTO '00: Proceedings of the 20th Annual International Cryptology Conference on Advances in Cryptology* (Springer, London, 2000), pp. 36–54
2. G Jagannathan, Wright R N, Privacy preserving distributed K-means clustering over arbitrarily partitioned data, in *KDD '05: Proceedings of the Eleventh ACM SIGKDD International Conference on Knowledge Discovery in Data Mining* (ACM, New York, 2005), pp. 593–599
3. R Lagendijk, Z Erkin, M Barni, Encrypted signal processing for privacy protection: encrypted signal processing for privacy protection. IEEE Signal Process. Mag. **30**(1), 82–105 (2013)
4. Z Erkin, T Veugen, T Toft, RL Lagendijk, Generating private recommendations efficiently using homomorphic encryption and data packing. IEEE Trans. Inf. Forensics Secur. **7**(3), 1053–1066 (2012)
5. K Fukunaga, *Introduction to Statistical Pattern Recognition* (Academic, San Diego, 1990)
6. O Goldreich, *Foundations of Cryptography II* (Cambridge University Press, Cambridge, 2004)
7. JR Troncoso-Pastoriza, S Katzenbeisser, MU Celik, AN Lemma, A secure multidimensional point inclusion protocol, in *ACM Workshop on Multimedia and Security* (ACM Dallas, 2007), pp. 109–120
8. T Bianchi, A Piva, M Barni, Composite signal representation for fast and storage-efficient processing of encrypted signals. IEEE Trans. Signal Process. **5**(1), 180–187 (2009)
9. Z Erkin, T Veugen, T Toft, R Lagendijk, Privacy-preserving user clustering in a social network, in *1st IEEE Workshop on Information Forensics and Security (WIFS09)* (IEEE, London, 2009), pp. 96–100
10. M Beye, Z Erkin, R Lagendijk, Efficient privacy preserving k-means clustering in a three-party setting, in *IEEE Workshop on Information Forensics and Security (WIFS '11)*. (Foz do Iguaçu, 29 Nov–2 Dec 2011)
11. R Agrawal, R Srikant, Privacy-preserving data mining, in *SIGMOD '00: Proceedings of the 2000 ACM SIGMOD International Conference on Management of Data, Volume 29(2)* (ACM, New York, 2000), pp. 439–450
12. P Bunn, R Ostrovsky, Secure two-party k-means clustering, in *Proceedings of the 14th ACM Conference on Computer and Communications Security* (ACM, New York, 2007), pp. 486–497
13. C Clifton, M Kantarcioglu, J Vaidya, Tools for privacy preserving distributed data mining. ACM SIGKDD Explorations **4**(2), 28–34 (2003)
14. G Jagannathan, K Pillaipakkamnatt, R Wright, A new privacy-preserving distributed k-clustering algorithm, in *Proceedings of the Sixth SIAM International Conference on Data Mining*. (Bethesda, 20–22 Apr 2006)
15. S Oliveira, O Zaiane, Privacy preserving clustering by data transformation, in *Proceedings of the 18th Brazilian Symposium on Databases*. (Manaus, 6–10 October 2003, pp. 304–318)
16. S Oliveira, O Zaiane, Achieving privacy preservation when sharing data for clustering, in *Secure Data Management*, ed. by W Jonker, M Petković. Proceedings of the VLDB 2004 Workshop, SDM 2004, Toronto, Canada, August 30, 2004. Lecture Notes in Computer Science, vol. 3178 (Springer, Berlin, 2004), pp. 67–82

17. ACC Yao, How to generate and exchange secrets (extended abstract), in *Proceedings of the 27th Annual IEEE Symposium on Foundations of Computer Science* (IEEE, Toronto, 1986), pp. 162–167

18. Z Huang, W Du, B Chen, Deriving private information from randomized data, in *SIGMOD '05: Proceedings of the 2005, ACM SIGMOD International Conference on Management of Data* (ACM, New York, 2005), pp. 37–48

19. H Kargupta, S Datta, Q Wang, K Sivakumar, On the privacy preserving properties of random data perturbation techniques, in *Proceedings of the ICDM 2003* (IEEE, Melbourne, 2003), pp. 99–106

20. V Kolesnikov, AR Sadeghi, T Schneider, Improved garbled circuit building blocks and applications to auctions and computing minima, in *Cryptology and Network Security,* ed. by JA Garay, A Miyaji, A Otsuka. Proceedings of the 8th International Conference, CANS 2009, Kanazawa, Japan, December 12–14, 2009. Lecture Notes in Computer Science, vol. 5888 (Springer, Berlin, 2009), pp. 1–20

21. D Kononchuk, Z Erkin, JCA van der Lubbe, RL Lagendijk, Privacy-preserving user data oriented services for groups with dynamic participation, in *Computer Security – ESORICS 2013,* ed. by J Crampton, S Jajodia, K Mayes. Proceedings of the 18th European Symposium on Research in Computer Security, Egham, UK, September 9–13, 2013. Lecture Notes in Computer Science, vol. 8134 (Springer, Berlin, 2013), pp. 418–442

22. N Doraswamy, D Harkins, *IPSec: The New Security Standard for the Internet, Intranets, and Virtual Private Networks* (Prentice-Hall, Upper Saddle River, 1999)

23. Paillier P, Public-key cryptosystems based on composite degree residuosity classes, in *Advances in Cryptology — EUROCRYPT '99,* ed. by J Stern. Proceedings of the International Conference on the Theory and Application of Cryptographic Techniques Prague, Czech Republic, May 2–6, 1999. Lecture Notes in Computer Science, vol. 1592 (Springer, Berlin, 1999), pp. 223–238

24. P Bogetoft, DL Christensen, I Damgård, M Geisler, TP Jakobsen, M Krøigaard, JD Nielsen, JB Nielsen, K Nielsen, J Pagter, MI Schwartzbach, T Toft, Multiparty computation goes live. IACR Cryptology ePrint Arch. **2008**, 68 (2008)

9

How can sliding HyperLogLog and EWMA detect port scan attacks in IP traffic?

Yousra Chabchoub[*], Raja Chiky and Betul Dogan

Abstract

IP networks are constantly targeted by new techniques of denial of service attacks (SYN flooding, port scan, UDP flooding, etc), causing service disruption and considerable financial damage. The on-line detection of DoS attacks in the current high-bit rate IP traffic is a big challenge. We propose in this paper an on-line algorithm for port scan detection. It is composed of two complementary parts: First, a probabilistic counting part, where the number of distinct destination ports is estimated by adapting a method called 'sliding HyperLogLog' to the context of port scan in IP traffic. Second, a decisional mechanism is performed on the estimated number of destination ports in order to detect in real time any behavior that could be related to a malicious traffic. This latter part is mainly based on the exponentially weighted moving average algorithm (EWMA) that we adapted to the context of on-line analysis by adding a learning step (supposed without attacks) and improving its update mechanism. The obtained port scan detecting method is tested against real IP traffic containing some attacks. It detects all the port scan attacks within a very short time response (of about 30 s) and without any false positive. The algorithm uses a very small total memory of less than 22 kb and has a very good accuracy on the estimation of the number of destination ports (a relative error of about 3.25%), which is in agreement with the theoretical bounds provided by the sliding HyperLogLog algorithm.

Introduction

Problem statement

Denial of service (DoS) attacks are one of the most important issues in network security. They aim to make a server resource unavailable by either damaging data or software or flooding the network with a huge amount of traffic. Thus, the server becomes unreachable by legitimate users, causing a significant financial loss in some cases. Port scan is a particular DoS attack that aims to discover available services on the targeted system [1]. It essentially consists of sending an IP packet to each port and analyzing the response to the connection attempts. Definitions found in the literature are enable to provide an absolute quantitative definition of port scan. The attack is rather defined by a comparison to the standard behavior. The attacker can discover not only available ports (or sevices) but also more relevant information about the victim such as its operating system, services owners, and the authentication method. Once the system vulnerabilities are identified, a future attack can be launched, engendering important damages. Various port scanning techniques have been developed and are very simple to install in order to launch serious port scan attacks. Nmap [2] is the most known port scan method. It was proposed by Fyodor in 2009. Zmap [3] is a faster scanning method developed by Durumeric et al. in 2013. It can scan the IPv4 address space in less than 45 min using a single machine.

Network operators are always looking for scalable solutions to detect on-line DoS attacks. Their objective is to stop the attack very quickly in order to avoid wasting network resources. So, the attack detection solution should ideally be deployed very close to the source of the attack, which is unrealistic as it means that it has to be implemented for each user. Moreover, the DoS attacks can be launched from several sources against a single victim, at the same time, and are called distributed attacks (DDoS) in this case. To detect such attacks, one has to consider the aggregated traffic issued from the several sources, because the contribution of each source can be considered as a normal traffic. Therefore, the attack detection solution has to be implemented in a core router network so as to analyze the traffic issued from several users. It has also to perform an on-line analysis and rise alarms in case of

*Correspondence: yousra.chabchoub@isep.fr
ISEP, 21 rue d'assas, Paris 75006, France

suspicious traffic. In the context of core network, the real-time processing is a big challenge. In fact, the analysis time of an IP packet has to be shorter packet inter-arrival time which is of only some nanoseconds in the current IP traffic carried by core networks (8 ns in an OC-768 link). Moreover, as attack detection is not the main role of the router, which can provide many other functions such as prioritization and quality of service, the amount of memory used for attack detection has to be very small.

Related work

The problem of DoS attack detection in IP traffic has been largely addressed by the network security community. Most of the proposed methods analyze the exhaustive traffic and maintain accurate statistics about the various flows (number of packets per communication (source-destination pair), number of SYN packets sent by each source address, etc.) (e.g., the threshold random walk method proposed in [4]). The memory size required by this kind of approach is proportional to the number of flows, which is clearly unscalable and not adapted to the current very high-bit traffic carried by very high speed links. To overcome this problem, it is necessary to dispense accurate statistics and to generate estimates which require less memory and are based on a faster processing. In this context, some recent probabilistic methods based on Bloom filters have been proposed (see [5,6], and [7]). A Bloom filter is an efficient data structure of a limited size that guarantees fast processing, thanks to the use of hash functions.

Attack detection algorithms must first generate on-line aggregate information and statistics on the observed traffic, and then identify, based on the obtained statistics, the suspicious traffic that could correspond to attacks. Probabilistic algorithms can be used to extract statistics and estimates quickly, but they must be complemented by a decision phase that identifies attacks.

Various methods can be used for the decision phase. In [8], a detailed study of the port scan detection approaches is provided by Monowar et al. The different methods are divided into five main classes (soft computing, algorithmic, rule-based, threshold-based, and visual approaches). The performance of these algorithms is compared (accuracy, response time, etc.,). The results show that methods combining the data mining and threshold-based analysis are the most efficient in terms of false positive rates, robustness, and scalability. A common weakness of the threshold-based methods is that their accuracy is closely related to traffic characteristics. As an example, the detection mechanism used in [5], and [9], is based on the well-known problem of finding the top k elements from a data stream. This means that at most, k simultaneous attacks can be detected. Therefore, the parameter k must be well chosen in order to minimize false alarms and

missed attacks. The aim of this paper is to use Bloom filters for the extraction of relevant information about the traffic and to automatically adapt a threshold-based algorithm to the on-line analysis context and the varying traffic conditions.

Organization of the paper

In this paper, we designed a new algorithm that detects on-line port scan attacks. The proposed method is mainly based on the sliding HyperLogLog algorithm [10] that we adapted to the context of port scan detection in IP traffic. Sliding HyperLogLog is an efficient algorithm that estimates the number of distinct elements over a sliding window. It is able to deal with a massive data stream and provides an accurate estimate using a very small memory. We used sliding HyperLogLog to analyze traffic and perform an on-line counting that we completed with a decisional mechanism that identifies port scan attacks.

The organization of this paper is as follows: The sliding HyperLogLog algorithm is presented in Section The sliding HyperLogLog algorithm. A detailed description of the proposed method for port scan detection is given in Section The proposed method for port scan detection. In this latter section, the counting method and the decisional mechanism are explained separately. The new detecting method is tested against experimental data collected from IP backbone network in Section Experimental results. It is also compared to other existing methods. Concluding remarks are presented in Section Conclusion.

The sliding HyperLogLog algorithm

The sliding HyperLogLog algorithm is mainly based on the HyperLogLog algorithm [11] designed by Flajolet et al. in 2007. The HyperLogLog algorithm is a very efficient probabilistic algorithm for cardinality estimation. It performs a single pass on data and gives an accurate estimation of the number of distinct elements, using a very small memory. The HyperLogLog algorithm is nowadays used in many fields such as databases and networks, where an exact counting is impractical because of memory consumption and high latency. An example of an application of HyperLogLog for the improvement of database queries in Google systems is provided in [12]. A new release of the well-known database management system, PostgreSQL, has been recently developed in 2013 to add HyperLogLog data structures as a native data type (see [13] for more details). The HyperLogLog algorithm is said to be probabilistic because it uses some randomness introduced by the hash function h. The objective is to estimate the cardinality of a given set S, where elements can be repeated (also called multiset). Each element v of S will be first hashed into a random value $h(v)$. The algorithm focuses on the following pattern '$0^\rho 1$' in the binary representation of $h(v)$ (ρ is the position of the leftmost 1). Let us denote by R the highest value of ρ among all the elements of the multiset S. The key idea of the algorithm is that with a larger cardinality, we are more likely to have a higher value of R. More precisely, 2^R is a good estimator of the multiset cardinality. To have a more robust estimation, a stochastic averaging process is introduced. It consists in splitting S into m subsets $S_1, \ldots S_m$, according the first b bits in the hashed value $h(v)$, where $m = 2^b$. $R[i]$ is computed and stored independently for each subset S_i. $R[1], \ldots, R[m]$ are initialized to $-\infty$ at the beginning.

$$R[i] = \max_{v \in S_i} \rho(v), \quad \rho \text{ is the position of the leftmost 1.}$$

The harmonic mean of $2^{R[i]}$, $i \in \{1, .., m\}$, is then computed using the following formula:

$$Z := \left(\sum_{j=1}^{m} 2^{-R[j]} \right)^{-1}.$$

The normalized harmonic mean is given by

$$E := \alpha_m m^2 Z \quad \text{where} \quad \alpha_m$$

$$:= \left(m \int_0^\infty \left(\log_2 \left(\frac{2+u}{1+u} \right) \right)^m du \right)^{-1}.$$

The full specification of the HyperLogLog algorithm is given by the following pseudo-code:

The HyperLogLog algorithm

Assume $m = 2^b, b \in N$
Initialize the m registers, $R[1], \ldots, R[m]$ to $-\infty$;

For $v \in S$ do

- set $x := h(A)$;
- set $i :=$ the subset identifier, given by the first b bits of x;
- set $x_{b+} := x$ stripped of its initial b bits;
- set $R[i] := max(R[i], \rho(x_{b+}))$, where $\rho(x_{b+})$ is the leftmost 1 position of x_{b+};

Compute the harmonic mean of $2^{R[i]}$, $Z := \left(\sum_{j=1}^{m} 2^{-R[j]} \right)^{-1}$
return the estimate $E := \alpha_m m^2 Z$, where $\alpha_m := \left(m \int_0^\infty \left(\log_2 \left(\frac{2+u}{1+u} \right) \right)^m du \right)^{-1}.$

The main advantage of the HyperLogLog algorithm is that it provides an excellent cardinality estimation, with a relative accuracy of about $1.04/\sqrt{m}$, using a very small memory equal to $m \log_2 \log_2(n/m)$ bits. m is the number of subsets, and n is the real cardinality of the multiset. In practice, using only 1.5 Kb, a cardinality of a one billion can be easily estimated with a typical standard error of about 2%.

The sliding window model is widely used in many applications requiring data stream management such as network monitoring, security, and financial applications. It consists of maintaining and updating some relevant statistics about the recent items of data stream. The sliding window can be logical or physical if it is, respectively, defined as the last N received items or the last time window T. Datar et al. [14] proposed a standard framework to adapt several applications (sums, averages, min, max, etc.) to the data stream context by adding a sliding window. They showed that their sliding window mechanism requires a memory overhead and adds a loss in the accuracy of the estimation. The additional error depends of course on the total used memory.

The sliding HyperLogLog algorithm proposed in [10] aims to adapt the original HyperLogLog algorithm to the context of data stream management. Its objective is to estimate the cardinality over a variable-bounded duration. In other words, one can answer at any time t the query about the number of distinct items seen over the last w units of time, where w is bounded by the window size W. For this purpose, it is compulsory to consider and store information about item arrival times (*timestamps*) to identify recent items at any time. Just like in Hyper-LogLog, each received item v will be hashed using the hash function h. Then, the corresponding subset will be identified with the first b bits of the hashed value. Finally, $\rho(v)$, defined as the position of the leftmost 1 in v stripped of its initial b bits, is computed. Thus, v will be associated to the pair $< t_v, \rho(v) >$, where t_v is the timestamp of the item v. The main idea of the sliding HyperLogLog algorithm is to maintain and update only relevant information, useful to answer at any time the query about the cardinality over the sliding window W. In particular, one must be able to compute, at any time, for each subset $i, i \in \{1, .., m\}$, the crucial parameter $R[i] = \max_{v \in S_i} \rho(v)$. For each subset i, a list called 'list of future possible maxima' (LFPM$_i$) will be stored. An element $< t_v, \rho(v) >$ remains in the LFPM$_i$ if and only if it is a possible maximum over a future window of time. In other words, $R[i]$ can be equal to $\rho(v)$ for a future possible query at a future time, t, concerning the last time window W. The LFPM$_i$ is updated as follows:

For each received item $< t_v, \rho(v) >$, associated to the subset i, do the following:

- Delete old items (items with a timestamp $t < t_v - W$) from all the lists $\text{LFPM}_i, i \in \{1, .., m\}$;
- Delete items v' with $\rho(v') \leq \rho(v)$ from the LFPM_i;
- Add$< t_v, \rho(v) >$ to the LFPM_i.

To answer at a given time t, the query about the number of distinct elements seen over the last w units of time, one has to follow the following steps:
For each $\text{LFPM}_i, i \in \{1, .., m\}$

- Extract items concerned by the query:
  $< t_v, \rho(v) >$, with $t_v < t - w$.
- Compute $R[i]$ over the extracted items.

Compute the harmonic mean and the cardinality estimation with the exactly the same manner as that in the HyperLogLog algorithm.

Two major results about accuracy and memory consumption of sliding HyperLogLog algorithm are detailed in [10]. First, unlike in [14], adding the sliding window does not modify the accuracy of the algorithm. So, the accuracy of the sliding HyperLogLog algorithm is exactly the same as that in the HyperLogLog algorithm (a standard error of $1.04/\sqrt{m}$). Second, an upper bound to the total used memory was established. The total size of the m lists LFPM is bounded is $\text{Id}_{size}mln(n/m)$ bytes, where Id_{size} is the size of the item identifier $< t_v, \rho(v) >$. In practice, the timestamp t_v is encoded on 4 bytes, and only 1 byte is sufficient for $\rho(v)$.

The proposed method for port scan detection

The aim of this paper is to propose a new method that detects on-line port scan attacks in the IP traffic. Such a solution is designed to be implemented on a core router of the backbone network of the operator. The router has to analyze on the fly the huge amount of data received at a very high bit rate in order to extract relevant statistics that will be used by the decisional mechanism to identify the suspicious traffic. The two different steps of the algorithm are illustrated in Figure 1. The on-line analysis is a real challenge because the router has very limited resources and many other functions to provide.

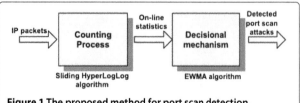

Figure 1 The proposed method for port scan detection.

Therefore, very efficient detecting methods are required to extract relevant statistics about the traffic and to make very quick decision about legitimacy of the traffic. In particular, the analysis of each packet has to be faster than the inter-arrival of the IP packets which is of only few nanoseconds.

Probabilistic counting method

We focus in this paper on a particular kind of port scan attack called vertical port scan [8]. It consists of scanning many ports for a given destination. The number of destination ports can theoretically reach $65,536$ as it is encoded on 2 bytes, but the commonly used destination ports are not very numerous. The used destination ports are mainly composed of the so-called, in [1], well-known ports (0-1023) and some registered ports (1024-49151). Therefore, the total number of distinct destination ports is a key observable to detect port scan attacks. In this context, the sliding HyperLogLog algorithm can be applied to count indefinitely, over a sliding window, the number of distinct destination ports. For each received packet (identified by the classical 5tuple composed of the source and destination addresses, the source and destination port numbers together with the protocol type), only the destination port will be considered and hashed into a random value. The sliding HyperLogLog algorithm will not perform an exact counting but will only provide an estimation. Therefore, a good choice of the parameters of the algorithm has to be done in order to ensure an acceptable error on the estimation. The number of buckets, m, is the crucial parameter of the counting method. With a high value of m, a smaller standard error can be achieved ($1.04/\sqrt{m}$), but a larger memory will be used ($\text{Id}_{size}mln(n/m)$ bytes). Moreover, m depends on the cardinality of the multiset: the number of distinct destination ports which can theoretically reach $65,536$. The number of distinct elements per bucket has to be high enough to perform significant statistics. With a total number of buckets of $1,024$ ($m = 1,024 = 2^{10}$), a standard error of only 3.25% can easily be achieved. Notice that this choice does not depend on the traffic trace and can be used for any port scan attack detection.

There is clearly a tradeoff in the choice of the size of the sliding time window W. With a larger time window, one can answer requests concerning larger durations, for example, the number of destination ports in the last 30 min. But to deal with a larger time window, more information has to be stored. More precisely, the upper bound of the used memory ($5mln(n/m)$ bytes) depends on n, the number of distinct destination ports, which is closely related to the size of the time window. Moreover, the standard duration of the attack must be considered in the choice of the size of the time window: W has to be large enough to notice the impact of the attack on the traffic.

The port scan attacks last about 20 min and should be detected from the first minute. Thus, $W = 60$ s is a good choice for the size of the time window. So, the total used memory will be less than 22 kB, which is very reasonable for a router.

Some slow attacks, also called progressive attacks, are more difficult to detect because the intensity of the attack is increasing slowly. The attack lasts more than the standard duration in this case. To detect this kind of attack, one has to aggregate more the traffic in time. For the sliding HyperLogLog algorithm, a larger time window $W' = 5$ min can be added. The algorithm is performed independently and in parallel for the two time scales: $W = 60$ s and $W' = 5$ min.

Decisional mechanism

Once relevant statistics related to port scan attacks are provided from the counting process, one has to filter and classify these information in two groups: 'standard behavior' and 'suspicious traffic'. This problem, also known as 'change-point detection' has been widely studied in the literature. Many methods have been developed by the community of statistics and data mining for several application fields.

In their [15] book entitled *Detection of Abrupt Changes: Theory and Application*, Basseville and Nikiforov provided the description and the performance analysis of a wide range of algorithms dealing with this problem of change detection. They classified these algorithms into three main categories: the elementary algorithms, the cumulative sum algorithm, and the Bayes-type algorithms.

The elementary algorithms use simple and intuitive concepts. They have many industrial applications, in particular, in the quality control field. One can cite the Shewart control charts algorithm that was first introduced by Walter Shewhart [16] in 1924. This technique has found many applications in improving the quality of manufacturing processes [17]. A more efficient method, called 'the geometric moving average control charts' algorithm, was proposed later by Roberts in 1965 [18]. This algorithm is also known as the 'exponentially weighted moving average' (EWMA) algorithm. Its key idea is to give different weights to the values of the observed process, to detect the change point: the recent values must be given more importance. Another solution presented in the 'finite moving average' (FMA) is to ignore very old observations by using a finite set of weights. The filtered derivative algorithm is another elementary algorithm introduced by Basseville and Gasnier [19] in 1981, based on the gradient techniques. It is widely used in the context of image edge detection.

The 'cumulative sum' (CUSUM) algorithm was designed by Page in 1954 [20]. It is based on the sum of the process past observations. The CUSUM algorithm is well adapted to the detection of systematic small variations of the process.

The Bayesian algorithms were first introduced by Girshick and Rubin in 1952 [21]. The main advantage of these methods is that they guarantee a robust performance with a formal proof of optimality, but they need an *a priori* knowledge about the observed process, more precisely, the distribution of the change time must be given in advance.

Roberts presents in [22] a comparative experimental study of all the different algorithms described above. The input parameters of all these algorithms are set to their optimal values, and the mean detection delays are compared. The main result is that the CUSUM algorithm outperforms the other algorithms when the observed process has small shifts.

Recall that in the context of on-line port scan detection, we focus on change-point detection in a high-speed data stream. Sequential data is provided on the fly from the counting process, and our purpose is to identify as quickly as possible the change point using a very small memory. According to Basseville and Nikiforov [15], all the approaches described above can be used in the context of on-line analysis. But, in our particular context of port-scan detection, no assumption about the distribution of the attack time can be made. So, the Bayesian algorithms are not adapted for such applications. Moreover, the total duration of an attack is about 20 min, so the detection delay must be small enough (less than 1 min) to stop the attack quickly. Therefore, the lack of reactivity of the CUSUM algorithm against abrupt change points may be a big weakness.

Sebastiao and Gama performed in [23] an experimental comparison between some particular algorithms well adapted for an on-line analysis. More precisely, they compared the efficiency of the four following algorithms: the statistical process control (SPC) [24], the adaptative windowing (ADWIN) [25], the fixed cumulative windows model (FCWM) [26], and the Page-Hinkley test (PHT) [20]. These methods are closely related to the the three kinds of algorithms presented above. The main result of this paper is that PHT and SPC are less time- and memory-consuming, but in some cases, they endanger a high rate of false alarms.

To achieve our objectives in terms of detection delay, on-line analysis (only one pass over the whole data) and without any *a priori* knowledge about IP traffic characteristics, we choose to focus in this paper on an elementary algorithm: EWMA [18] proposed by Roberts. The main idea of the EWMA algorithm is to define a threshold delimiting a 'standard behavior' and to handle and update periodically an average of the observed data stream. The change point is then declared as soon as the average exceeds the fixed threshold. This algorithm is very simple to implement. Unlike ADWIN, the past values of the observed data are not stored. It does not require any data structure. It also has a lower complexity because for each observed data, one has only to update a weighted average [27]. Compared to PHT and CUSUM, EWMA has the advantage to closely relate the importance of the observed data to its age which is more meaningful in the context of data stream. In PHT and CUSUM algorithms, all data history is equivalent and is considered in the same manner.

Our objective in this is to adapt the EWMA algorithm to the context of port scan detection and to experiment and evaluate the so obtained version. EWMA is an advanced control chart which calculates, over a sliding window, a weighted average of the data, taking into account the past observations. The older the observation, the less weight it has in the computation of the average. The sliding weighted average is updated as follows:

$$\begin{cases} \text{EWMA}(0) := \text{the average of all the observations} \\ \text{EWMA}(t) = \lambda * Y(t) + (1 - \lambda) * \text{EWMA}(t - 1), \text{ for } t > 0, \end{cases}$$

where $Y(t)$ is the observed value at time t. λ is a multiplicative factor ($0 < \lambda \leq 1$). It can be interpreted as a kind of correlation between $Y(t)$ and $\text{EWMA}(t)$. In practice, we want the moving average $\text{EWMA}(t)$ to follow carefully the variations of the observed process $Y(t)$. To give more importance to the past observations, than the current one, λ is very often taken smaller than 0.5. However, with very small value of λ, the algorithm becomes insensitive to some attacks having a small duration or a moderate intensity. That is why λ is usually between 0.2 and 0.5 in practice. $\text{EWMA}(0)$, also called the target, is the average of the whole data set.

In this control chart, an alarm is raised as soon as the moving average $\text{EWMA}(t)$ exceeds some thresholds called 'upper control limit' (UCL) and the 'lower control limit' (LCL), respectively, defined as

$$\text{UCL} = \text{EWMA}(0) + k * \sqrt{\lambda/(2 - \lambda)s_0^2}$$

$$\text{LCL} = \text{EWMA}(0) - k * \sqrt{\lambda/(2 - \lambda)s_0^2},$$

where the factor k is either set equal to 3 or chosen using the tables in Lucas et al. [28] in the enhanced version of EWMA proposed in 1990. s_0 is the standard deviation calculated on the whole data set.

It is clear that the so-described EWMA algorithm cannot be directly applied for the on-line data stream analysis because it clearly requires two passes over the whole data set. In fact, it needs first to compute $\text{EWMA}(0)$ and s_0 using the whole data to fix the threshold UCL. Then, all the data will be considered again to detect the change

points. To overcome this problem, we propose to add a learning step of some minutes at the beginning of the algorithm in order to initialize its parameters, namely, $\text{EWMA}(0)$ and s_0. No change-point detection will be performed during this learning step. So, we implicitly assume that this period corresponds to the 'standard behavior' and does not contain any anomaly.

Notice also that in the EWMA algorithm described above, the moving average $\text{EWMA}(t)$ is always updated even if it exceeds the detection threshold UCL. It turns out however that it is useless to update $\text{EWMA}(t)$ in this latter case as this can generate some false positives (false alarms) just after some intensive attacks. In fact, when $\text{EWMA}(t)$ gets very high, in case of an attack, it needs a long time (several slices of time windows) to reach its normal values (<UCL) when the attack is stopped. Thus, we propose the following update mechanism for $\text{EWMA}(t)$:

$$\begin{cases} \text{if } (\text{EWMA}(t) > \text{UCL}) \text{ then } \text{EWMA}(t) = \text{EWMA}(t - 1) \\ \text{else } \text{EWMA}(t) = \lambda * Y(t) + (1 - \lambda) * \text{EWMA}(t - 1). \end{cases}$$

Experimental results

Dataset

The so-obtained algorithm with the two complementary parts (the counting and the decisional mechanisms) is tested against real IP traffic containing some port scan attacks. The considered traffic trace was captured in December 2007, by Orange Labs, in the context of an ANR-RNRT project on network security called 'OSCAR'. The traffic capture was performed on a router belonging to the IP backbone network of Orange Labs. Some global characteristics of this traffic trace are given in Table 1.

The flow is defined as the set of those packets with the same source and destination addresses, the same source and destination port numbers, and the same protocol type.

Counting process

In this part, we focus on testing the counting process based on the sliding HyperLogLog algorithm. The number of distinct destination ports in the last time window W is estimated every 30 s. The time window is taken equal to 60 s, and the number of buckets m equals 1,024.

In Figure 2, the standard error on the estimated number of destination ports is plotted. One can notice that the standard error is most often within the theoretical

Table 1 Characteristics of the traffic trace used for attack detection

Duration	No. of IP packets	No. of flows
67 min	32.10^6	250.10^3

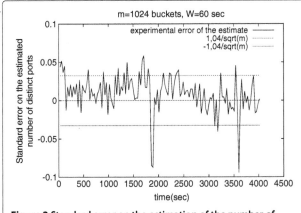

Figure 2 Standard error on the estimation of the number of distinct destination ports.

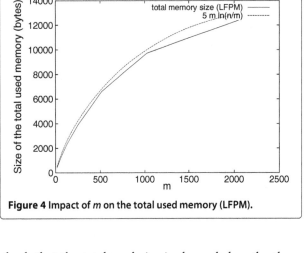

Figure 4 Impact of m on the total used memory (LFPM).

error σ of 3.25% ($\sigma = 1.04/\sqrt{m}$). It sometimes slightly exceeds this value, in fact σ is not an upper bound, but just an estimation of the standard error. As mentioned in [11], the estimate provided by HyperLogLog is expected to be within σ, 2σ, 3σ of the exact count in, respectively, 65%, 95%, and 99% of all the cases. Thus, the experiments confirm that adding the sliding window mechanism does not affect the accuracy of the original HyperLogLog algorithm.

In Figure 3, the size of the total used memory is plotted. It closely depends on n, the number of distinct destination ports. The results show that the total used memory (also called LFPM) is always below the theoretical bound of $5mln(n/m)$ bytes given in [10]. Recall that m is here constant (equal to $1,024$). This corresponds to a total used memory less than 22 kB.

Figure 4 shows the impact of m on the size of the total used memory. The mean size (calculated over the whole traffic trace) of the list LFPM is computed for different values of m, ($m = 16, 32, 64, \ldots 2,048$). One can easily

check that the total used size is always below the theoretical bound. In the sliding HyperLogLog algorithm, for each received packet, the LFPM is updated in order to erase very old elements. So, the number of elements in the LFPM impacts directly the complexity of the update operation. One can conclude that the value of the parameter m can be chosen according to a total memory usage constraint. Moreover, with a good choice of m, it is possible to control the complexity of the algorithm.

In the description of the counting method, an additional time window ($W' = 5$ min) is suggested to deal with slow or progressive attacks. Recall that the time window was fixed to 1 min in the previous experiments. So, one has to check that the total used memory remains reasonable for larger time windows. For this purpose, many time windows have been considered in Figure 5 (W between 1 and 5 min). m is constant, taken as equal to $1,024$. In a larger time window, more distinct destination ports can be seen. So, more information will be stored in the list of future possible maxima (LFPM); that is why a larger memory is

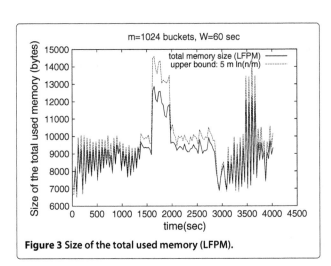

Figure 3 Size of the total used memory (LFPM).

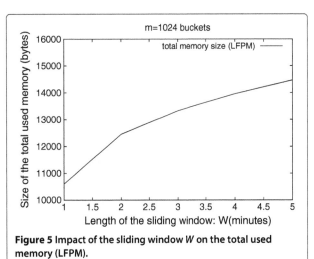

Figure 5 Impact of the sliding window W on the total used memory (LFPM).

required. But, the total used memory is still small as it is only multiplied by 1.5 when the time window grows from 1 to 5 min. This can be explained by the fact that the total number of distinct destination ports is bounded by $2^{16} = 65,536$. Moreover, many frequently used ports (well-known and registered ports) can be used over several 1-min time windows. This information is confirmed by Figure 6 which shows that the estimated number of distinct destination ports, with two time scales ($W = 1$ min and $W' = 5$ min).

Decisional mechanism using EWMA algorithm

The input of this decisional part is the estimated number of distinct destination ports provided by the counting process. This information is received every 30 s; it concerns the last 60-s time window. The input data is presented in Figure 6. One can easily see several peaks that are very likely to correspond to some port scan attacks. Our objective here is to automatically identify these peaks using the EWMA algorithm. The multiplicative update factor λ is taken equal to 0.3 and the detection parameter k equals to 3. All the implementations are performed with R.

In Figure 7, the original version of EWMA algorithm is tested. We considered first the whole data to compute the parameters of the algorithm: the target EWMA(0), the standard deviation S_0, and thus the upper bound UCL. A second pass on the data is performed to detect the port scan attacks. EWMA(t) is plotted; it is updated every 30 s. The detected port scan attacks are represented by squares: An alarm is raised each time EWMA(t) exceeds the upper bound UCL. We are not interested here in the lower bound LCL defined by the EWMA algorithm. Notice finally that the attacks are detected within a reasonable delay time of only 30 s.

Figure 8 concerns the first improvement added to the EWMA algorithm: To respect the on-line analysis constraint, only one pass on the data is performed. First

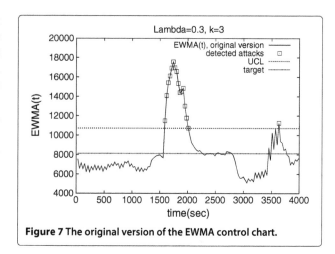

Figure 7 The original version of the EWMA control chart.

EWMA(0), S_0, and UCL are calculated in the introduced learning step taken equal to 10 min. Notice that the target EWMA(0) is lower than in the original version of EWMA. In fact, unlike in the original version, the attacks (where the observed data has high values) are not included in the computation of *EWMA*(0). So, with this proposed improvement, more attacks can be detected because UCL has also a lower value as it is closely related to EWMA(0).

In Figure 9, the second improvement is added: The weighted moving average EWMA(t) is not updated in case of attacks. It is constant, keeping its old value. The squares correspond to the calculated values of the weighted moving average, and as they exceed UCL, they are not affected by EWMA(t). So, in case of attack, EWMA(t) and thus the squares (calculated using EWMA(t)) have lower values than in the original version of the EWMA. This enables EWMA(t) to reach very quickly the normal behavior (<UCL) when the attack stops. That is why we have less alarms in this case (compared to Figure 8), in particular at the end of the attacks.

The same experiments as that in Figure 9 are performed with different values of λ in order to analyze

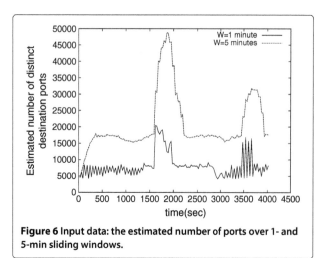

Figure 6 Input data: the estimated number of ports over 1- and 5-min sliding windows.

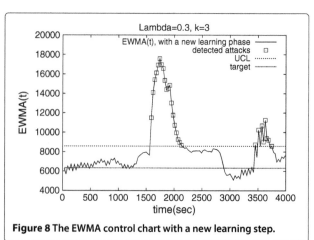

Figure 8 The EWMA control chart with a new learning step.

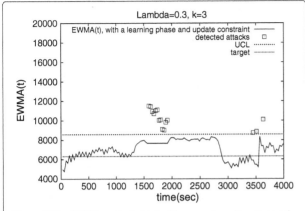

Figure 9 The EWMA control chart with a new learning step and an additional update constraint, $\lambda = 0.3$.

the impact of this parameter on the performance of the algorithm. Recall that λ is used to update the moving average $EWMA(t)$ and to compute the upper bound $UCL = EWMA(0) + k*\sqrt{\lambda/(2-\lambda)s_0^2}$. In Figure 9, λ is taken equal to 0.3. With a value of λ set to 0.5, roughly, the same results are obtained: the target $EWMA(0)$ is always equal to $6,333$ as it does not depend on λ. The upper bound, UCL, is higher ($9,297$ instead of $8,458$), but the same alarms are raised at the same moments. Figure 10 shows the obtained results for $\lambda = 0.1$. One can notice that in this case, UCL is very close to the target $EWMA(0)$; it is equal to $7,441$. In fact the difference $UCL - EWMA(0) = k*\sqrt{\lambda/(2-\lambda)s_0^2}$ is proportional to $\sqrt{\lambda/(2-\lambda)}$, which is an increasing function on $[0:1]$ with values in $[0:1]$. In this case, only small variations of $EWMA(t)$ are tolerated, and many false positives (false alarms) are generated by the algorithm. Thus, the results are consistent with the choice of λ (between 0.2 and 0.5) presented in the description of the EWMA algorithm.

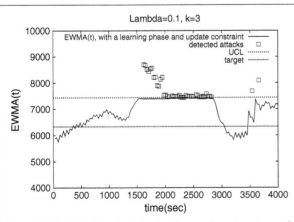

Figure 10 The EWMA control chart with a new learning step and an additional update constraint, $\lambda = 0.1$.

The use of the learning phase aims to adapt on-line the parameters of the algorithm to the initial characteristics of the traffic. $EWMA(0)$ and UCL only depend on the traffic of this training set. It is clearly assumed that this period (taken equal to 10 min in practice) corresponds to a standard data having no attacks. The performance of the algorithm is of course closely related to the effectiveness of this assumption. We propose the following solution to reduce the dependance on this assumption and improve the robustness of the algorithm: We define a lower bound LCL in the same manner as in the EWMA algorithm:

$$LCL = EWMA(0) - k*\sqrt{\lambda/(2-\lambda)s_0^2}$$

If, at any time t, $EWMA(t) < LCL$, then we restart the algorithm. The idea is that if we consider the worst case where the learning phase contains many port scan attacks, $EWMA(t)$ will have smaller values at the end of the attacks, which can be detected by comparing $EWMA(t)$ to the lower bound LCL defined in the learning phase. In other words, if there is no more correlation between the initial parameters calculated on the training set and the current values, the algorithm has to be restarted again. The learning phase is very useful as there is no absolute quantitative description of a port scan attack. The attack is simply defined as a significant deviation from a standard behavior that has to be learned online.

EWMA versus CUSUM algorithm

The CUSUM algorithm was first introduced by Page in 1954 [20]. It aims to detect small process shifts and is based on the cumulative sum C_t of the observed process $Y(i)$:

$$CUSUM(t) = \sum_{i=1}^{t}(Y(i) - \mu_0) = CUSUM(t-1) + (Y(t) - \mu_0),$$

where μ_0 is the target of the process given by its mean value. A process shift is declared if $CUSUM(t)$ exceeds the upper bound $k * \sigma$, σ being the standard deviation of the process $Y(i)$. Notice that in this original version of the CUSUM algorithm, σ and μ_0 are calculated on the whole process. Therefore, in our case, two passes on the dataset are required to detect the port scan attacks using the original version of CUSUM. This version is clearly not adapted to an online analysis. Figure 11 shows the result of the CUSUM algorithm on the dataset containing some port scan attacks. The CUSUM algorithm was implemented with R. According to the recommendations given in [27], the process $Y(i)$ was first normalized, and the CUSUM algorithm was applied on the $X(i)$ process defined by the following relation:

$$X(i) = \frac{Y(i) - \mu_0}{\sigma},$$

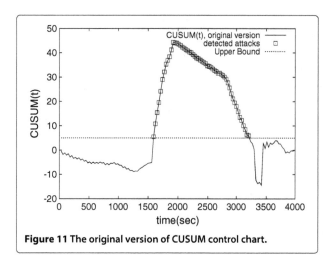

Figure 11 The original version of CUSUM control chart.

$X(i)$ has a mean of 0 and a standard deviation equal to 1. The upper bound k is taken equal to 5 to have good ARL properties as mentioned in [27]. Figure 11 shows that only the first attack is detected. The second attack that happens around the second 3,450 has a shorter duration and a smaller magnitude; that is why it has a limited impact on CUSUM(t) and can not be detected. Moreover, the duration of the first attack is largely overestimated. In fact CUSUM(t) is updated even in case of attacks, and unlike EWMA(t), in its original version, it takes a long time to reach normal values at the end of the attack. This can be explained by the fact that the CUSUM algorithm accumulates the effect of the attack over several sliding windows as it is based on a sum and gives the same weight to all the observed values.

Just like the EWMA algorithm, we introduced a learning step to adapt the CUSUM algorithm to the online analysis context. Thus, μ_0 and σ computation is only based on the first 10 min. Moreover, CUSUM(t) is not updated in case of attack. The results of the so-obtained version of CUSUM are given by Figure 12. The attack that

happens at the end of the traffic trace (around the second 3,450) is not detected. In addition, between the second 2,000 and 3,000, the mean of the input process is slightly higher, which is considered by the CUSUM algorithm as an attack. One can easily check that it is a false positive using Figure 6 which displays the aggregated input data over larger time window. In fact, the time aggregation has no additive impact on the observed data. As a conclusion, the EWMA algorithm is more adapted than the CUSUM algorithm to the context of port scan attack detection. It is more reactive to the attacks with a short duration and a relatively small magnitude, and it is less sensitive to the small shifts that are mainly related to the varying IP traffic conditions (activity depending on the time of the day, etc.)

Conclusion

In this paper, a new method identifying online port scan attacks in IP traffic is proposed. First, some relevant statistics are extracted from the data stream using the sliding HyperLogLog algorithm. A good choice of the parameters of the this algorithm has to be done in order to ensure an acceptable accuracy of the statistics. Second, a change point detection method based on the EWMA algorithm is used to identify suspicious traffic. It is mainly an adaption of the EWMA to the data stream context. For this purpose, a learning phase is added at the beginning of the algorithm in order to initialize its parameters. Then, a new constraint is added to the moving average EWMA(t) update to overcome the false-positive problem when this latter exceeds the UCL detection threshold. Finally, we run experiments on a real traffic trace captured in the IP backbone network of Orange Labs in December 2007 in the context of the ANR-RNRT OSCAR project. The obtained results confirm the efficiency of the adapted combination of the HyperLogLog and EWMA algorithms in terms of accuracy, memory usage, and time response.

Competing interests
The authors declare that they have no competing interests.

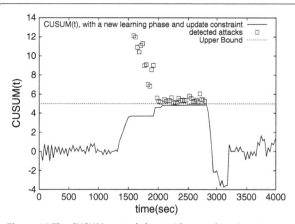

Figure 12 The CUSUM control chart with a new learning step and an additional update constraint.

References
1. M de Vivo, E Carrasco, G Isern, GO de Vivo, A review of port scanning techniques. SIGCOMM Comput. Commun. Review. **8**, 411–430 (1999)
2. S Staniford, JA Hoagland, Alerney McJM, *Nmap Network Scanning: The Official Nmap Project Guide to Network Discovery and Security Scanning*. (Insecure, 370 Altair Way Ste 113 Sunnyvale, California 94086-6161 US).
3. Z Durumeric, E Wustrow, Halderman JA, ZMap: Fast internet-wide scanning and its security applications. Paper presented at the 22nd USENIX security symposium. Washington, D.C., USA, 14–16 Aug 2013
4. J Jung, V Paxson, A Berger, Balakrishnan H, Fast portscan detection using sequential hypothesis testing. Paper presented at IEEE symposium on security and privacy. Claremont Resort Oakland, California, USA, 9–12 May 2004

5. J Mikians, P Barlet-Ros, J Sanjuas-Cuxart, J Sole-Pareta, A practical approach to portscan detection in very high-speed links. Lect. Notes Comput. Sc. **6579**, 112–121 (2011)

6. S Nam, H Kim, H Kim, Detector SherLOCK: enhancing TRW with Bloom filters under memory and performance constraints. Computer Networks. **52**, 1545–1566 (2008)

7. A Sridharan, T Ye, S Bhattacharyya, Connectionless port scan detection on the backbone. Paper presented at the 25th IEEE performance, computing, and communications conference (PCCC), Phoenix, AZ, USA, 0–12 April 2006

8. H Monowar, DK Bhattacharyya, JK Kalita, Surveying port scans and their detection methodologies. Comput. J. **54**(10), 1565–1581 (2011)

9. C Levy-Leduc, Detection of network anomalies using rank tests. Paper presented at the EUSIPCO, Laussane, Switzerland, 25–29 Aug 2008

10. Y Chabchoub, G Hebrail, Sliding HyperLogLog: estimating cardinality in a data stream over a sliding window. Paper presented at the ICDM workshop on large-scale analytics for complex instrumented systems (LACIS), Sydney, 13 Dec 2010

11. P Flajolet, E Fusy, O Gandouet, F Meunier, Hyperloglog: the analysis of a near-optimal cardinality estimation algorithm. Paper presented at the 13th conference on analysis of algorithm (AofA), Juan des Pins, 17–22 June 2007, 127–146

12. S Heule, M Nunkesser, A Hall, HyperLogLog in practice: algorithmic engineering of a state of the art cardinality estimation algorithm. Paper presented at the EDBT 2013 conference, Genoa, Italy, 18–22 March 2013

13. GitHub, PostgreSQL extension adding HyperLogLog data structures as a native data type. http://github.com/aggregateknowledge/postgresql-hll. Accessed 20 Dec 2013

14. M Datar, A Gionis, P Indyk, R Motwan, Maintaining stream statistics over sliding windows. SIAM J. Comput. **31**(6), 1794–1813 (2002)

15. M Basseville, I Nikiforov, *Detection of Abrupt Changes: Theory and Application*, (Prentice-Hall, Upper Saddle River, 1993)

16. W Shewhart, *Bell Telephone Laboratories series: Economic Control of Quality of Manufactured Product*. (D. Van Nostrand Company, Princeton, 1931)

17. GEP Box, G Jenkins, *Time Series Analysis, Forecasting and Control*. (Holden-Day, San Francisco, 1990)

18. SW Roberts, Control chart tests based on geometric moving averages. Technomearics. **1**, 239–250 (1959)

19. BE M Basseville, J Gasnier, Edge detection using sequential methods for change in level. Trans. Acoust. Speech Signal Processing. **29**, 24–31 (1981)

20. ES Page, Continuous inspection schemes. Biometrika. **41**, 100–115 (1954)

21. M Girshick, H Rubin, A Bayes approach to a quality control model. Ann. Math. Stat. **23**, 114–125 (1952)

22. S Roberts, A comparison of some control chart procedures. Technometrics. **8**(3), 411–430 (1966)

23. R Sebastiao, J Gama, A study on change detection methods. Paper presented at the 14th Portuguese conference on artificial intelligence (EPIA), Aveiro, Portugal, 12–15 Oct 2009

24. J Gama, P Medas, G Castillo, P Rodrigues, Learning with drift detection, in *Advances in Artificial Intelligence*, ed. by ALC Bazzan, S Labidi (Springer New York, 2004), pp. 286–295

25. A Bifet, R Gavalda, Learning from time-changing data with adaptive windowing. Paper presented at the 7th SIAM international conference on data mining, Minneapolis, MN, USA, 29 Sept–1 Oct 2007

26. R Sebastiao, J Gama, Monitoring incremental histogram distribution for change detection in data Streams, in *Lecture Notes in Computer Science: Knowledge Discovery from Sensor Data*, ed. by MM Gaber, RR Vatsavai, OA Omitaomu, J Gama, NV Chawla, and AR Ganguly (Springer New York, 2010), pp. 25–42

27. C Douglas, *Introduction to Statistical Quality Control*. (Wiley, New York, 2004)

28. JM Lucas, MS Saccucci, RVJ Baxley, WH Woodall, HD Maragh, FW Faltin, GJ Hahn, WT Tucker, JS Hunter, JF MacGregor, TJ Harris, Exponentially weighted moving average control schemes: properties and enhancements. Technometrics. **32**, 1–29 (1990). doi:10.1080/00401706.1990.10484583

Document authentication using graphical codes: reliable performance analysis and channel optimization

Anh Thu Phan Ho[1*], Bao An Mai Hoang[2], Wadih Sawaya[1] and Patrick Bas[3]

Abstract

This paper proposes to investigate the impact of the channel model for authentication systems based on codes that are corrupted by a physically unclonable noise such as the one emitted by a printing process. The core of such a system for the receiver is to perform a statistical test in order to recognize and accept an original code corrupted by noise and reject any illegal copy or a counterfeit. This study highlights the fact that the probability of type I and type II errors can be better approximated, by several orders of magnitude, when using the Cramér-Chernoff theorem instead of a Gaussian approximation. The practical computation of these error probabilities is also possible using Monte Carlo simulations combined with the importance sampling method. By deriving the optimal test within a Neyman-Pearson setup, a first theoretical analysis shows that a thresholding of the received code induces a loss of performance. A second analysis proposes to find the best parameters of the channels involved in the model in order to maximize the authentication performance. This is possible not only when the opponent's channel is identical to the legitimate channel but also when the opponent's channel is different, leading this time to a min-max game between the two players. Finally, we evaluate the impact of an uncertainty for the receiver on the opponent channel, and we show that the authentication is still possible whenever the receiver can observe forged codes and uses them to estimate the parameters of the model.

1 Introduction

The problem of authentication of physical products such as documents, goods, drugs, and jewels is a major concern in a world of global exchanges. The World Health Organization in 2005 claimed that nearly 25% of medicines in developing countries are forgeries [1], and according to the Organization for Economic Co-operation and Development (OECD), international trade in counterfeit and pirated goods reached more than US$250 billion in 2009 [2].

1.1 Addressed problem and related works

Authentication of physical products is generally done by using the stochastic structure of either the materials that composes the product or of a printed package associated to it. Authentication can be performed for example by recording the random patterns of the fiber of a paper [3], but such a system is practically heavy to deploy since each product needs to be linked to its high-definition capture stored in a database. Another solution is to rely on the degradation induced by the interaction between the product and a physical process such as printing, marking, embossing, carving, etc. Because of both the defaults of the physical process and the stochastic nature of the matter, this interaction can be considered as a physically unclonable function (PUF) [4] that cannot be reproduced by the forger and can consequently be used to perform authentication. In [5], the authors measure the degradation of the inks within printed color tiles and use discrepancy between the statistics of the authentic and print-and-scan tiles to perform authentication. Other marking techniques can also be used; in [6], the authors propose to characterize the random profiles of laser marks on materials such as metals (the technique is called LPUF for laser-written PUF) to use them as authentication features.

*Correspondence: phanho@telecom-lille.fr
[1] Institut-Telecom-LAGIS, Telecom-Lille, Rue Guglielmo Marconi, Villeneuve-d'Ascq 59650, France
Full list of author information is available at the end of the article

We study in this paper an authentication system which uses the fact that a printing process at very high resolution can be seen as a stochastic process due to the nature of different elements such as the paper fibers, the ink heterogeneity, or the dot addressability of the printer. Such an authentication system has been proposed by Picard et al. [7,8] and uses 2D pseudo-random binary codes that are printed at the native resolution of the printer (2,400 dpi on a standard offset printer or 812 dpi on a digital HP Indigo printer).

The principle of the studied system in this paper is depicted in Figure 1:

- The original code is secretly exchanged between the legitimate source and the receiver.

- Once printed on a package to be authenticated, the degraded code will be scanned then thresholded by an opponent (the forger). It is important to note that at this stage thresholding is necessary for the opponent because the industrial printers can only print dots, e.g., binary versions of the scanned code.

- The opponent then produces a printed copy of the original code to manufacture his forgery.

- The receiver performs a test on an observed scanned code, being either the scanned version of the original printed code or the scanned version of the fake code. Using his knowledge on the original code, he establishes a statistical test in order to perform authentication.

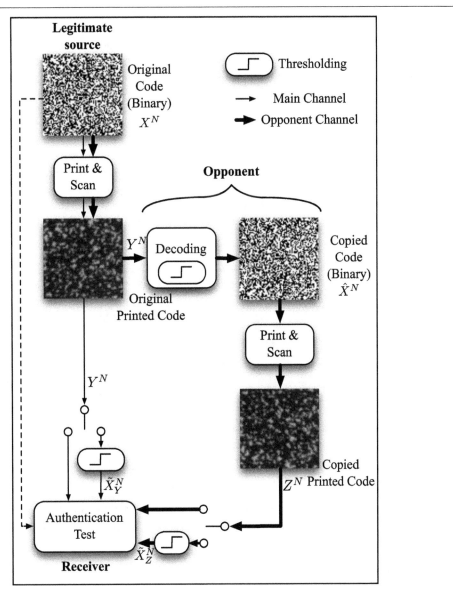

Figure 1 Principle of authentication using graphical codes.

One advantage of this system over previously cited ones is that it is easy to deploy since the authentication process needs only a scan of the graphical code under scrutiny and the seed used to generate the original one: no fingerprint database is required in this case.

The security of this system solely relies on the use of a PUF, i.e., the impossibility for the opponent to accurately estimate the original binary code. Different security analysis have already been performed with respect to (w.r.t.) this authentication system or to very similar ones. In [9], the authors have studied the impact of multiple printed observations of same graphical codes and have shown that the power of the noise due to the printing process can be reduced in this particular setup, but not completely removed due to deterministic printing artifacts. In [10], the authors use machine learning tools in order to try to infer the original code from an observation of the printed code; their study shows that the estimation accuracy can be increased without recovering perfectly the original code. In [11], the authors propose a print and scan model adapted to graphical code and derive attacks and adapted detection metrics to counter the attacks. In [12], the authors consider the security analysis in the rather similar setup of passive fingerprinting using binary fingerprints under informed attacks (the channel between the original code and the copied code is assumed to be a binary symmetric channel). They show that in this case the security increase with the code length, and they propose a practical threshold when type I error (originally detected as a forgery) and type II error (forgery detected as an original) are equal.

1.2 Notations

We denote sets by calligraphic font, e.g., $\mathcal{X}$, random variables (RV) ranging over these sets by the same italic capitals, e.g., X, and their outcomes in lowercase letters, e.g., x. $E_X[.]$ denotes the expectation over X. The cardinality of the set $\mathcal{X}$ is denoted by $|\mathcal{X}|$. The sequence of N variables $(X_1, X_2, ..., X_N)$ is denoted X^N.

1.3 Setup

The binary graphical code can be seen as an authentication sequence x^N chosen at random from the message set $\mathcal{X}^N$ and shared secretly with the legitimate receiver. In our authentication model, x^N is published as a noisy version y^N taking values in the set of points $\mathcal{V}^N$ (see Figure 1). An opponent may observe y^N and, naturally, tries to retrieve the original authentication sequence. He obtains an estimated sequence $\hat{x}^N$ and publish a forgery as a sequence z^N taking value in the same set of points $\mathcal{V}^N$, hoping that it will be accepted by the receiver as coming from the legitimate source. When observing a sequence o^N, which may be one of the two possible sequences y^N or z^N, the

destination has to decide whether this observed sequence comes from the legitimate source or not.

The authentication model involves two channels $\mathcal{X} \rightarrow (\mathcal{Y}, \mathcal{Z})$, and in the rest of the paper, we define the main channel as the channel between the legitimate source and the receiver, and the opponent channel as the channel between the legitimate source and the receiver but passing through the counterfeiter channel (see Figure 1). The two channels $\mathcal{X} \rightarrow (\mathcal{Y}, \mathcal{Z})$ are considered being discrete and memoryless with conditional probability distribution $P_{YZ|X}(y, z \mid x)$. The marginal channels $P_{Y|X}$ and $P_{Z|X}$ constitute the transition probability matrices of the main channel and the opponent channel, respectively.

As we shall see in the rest of the paper, authentication performances are directly impacted by the discrimination between the two channels and can be maximized by channel optimization.

Note that the authentication sequence x^N is generated using a secure pseudo-random number generator (PRNG) having a sufficiently large key space to prevent brute-force attacks. The seed of the PRNG can practically be transmitted using both a secure lossless communication channel and via a key distribution system so that the receiver can generate x^N from the seed. The security of such a system is beyond the scope of this paper.

1.4 Contributions of the paper

The goal of this paper is twofold:

- Firstly, it provides reliable performance measurements of the authentication system based on a Neyman-Pearson hypothesis test (i.e., to compute accurately the probability of rejecting an authentic code and the probability of non-detecting an illegal copy, denoted as type I and type II errors, respectively). An asymptotic expression which is more accurate than the Gaussian expression is first proposed to compute these probabilities of errors; then, the importance sampling simulation method is provided to practically estimate them. We evaluate the impact of the Gaussian approximation of the test with respect to its asymptotic expression.

- Secondly, the computation of type I and type II errors are used to derive the most favorable channels for authentication. We show first that it is in the receiver's interest to process directly the scanned grayscale code instead of a binary version. Then, the error probabilities are used to compute for a given channel model, the configuration which maximizes the authentication performance.

This paper is an extension of [13] in which we use the generalized Gaussian distribution family instead of the Gaussian distribution as in [13]. Moreover, the analytical formulation of these probabilities is practically confirmed by using an importance sampling method, a Monte Carlo strategy of numerical simulation that can be used to compute rare events. We also present how to design the channel in order to maximize the authentication performance for different cases of generalized Gaussian distributions and when the opponent is either passive (he undergoes the same channel as the receiver) or active (he can adapt his channel).

2 The authentication channel

2.1 Channel modeling

Let $T_{V|X}$ be the generic transition matrix modeling the whole physical processes used, more specifically the printing and scanning devices. The entries of this matrix are conditional probabilities $T_{V|X}(v \mid x)$ relating an input alphabet $\mathcal{X}$ and the output alphabet $\mathcal{V}$. In practical and realistic situations, $\mathcal{X}$ is a binary alphabet standing for black (0) and white (1) elements of a digital code, and the channel output set $\mathcal{V}$ stands for the set of gray-level values with cardinality K (for printed and scanned images, $K = 256$). Transition matrix $T_{V|X}$ may conceptually be any discrete distribution over the set $\mathcal{V}$, but we will focus in Section 4.4 on some common and realistic distributions when analyzing numerically the performance.

The marginal distribution of the main channel $P_{Y|X}$ is equivalent to one print and scan process, and consequently, we have $P_{Y|X} = T_{V|X}$. On the other hand, $P_{Z|X}$ depends on the opponent processing while he has to retrieve the original sequence before reprinting it. We aim here at expressing this marginal distribution considering that the opponent tries to restore the original sequence before publishing his fraudulent sequence z^N.

When performing a detection to obtain an estimated sequence $\hat{x}^N$ of the original code, the opponent undergoes errors. These errors are evaluated with probabilities $P_{e,W}$ when confusing an original white dot with a black and $P_{e,B}$ when confusing an original black dot with a white. This distinction is due to the fact that the distribution $T_{V|X}$ of the physical devices is arbitrary and not necessarily symmetric. Let $\mathcal{D}_W$ be the optimal decision region for decoding white dots obtained after using classical maximum likelihood decoding:

$$\mathcal{D}_W = \left\{ v \in \mathcal{V} : P_{Y|X}(v \mid X = 1) > P_{Y|X}(v \mid X = 0) \right\}. \tag{1}$$

Error probabilities $P_{e,W}$ and $P_{e,B}$ are then equal to

$$P_{e,B} = \sum_{v \in \mathcal{D}_W} P_{Y|X}(v \mid X = 0), \tag{2}$$

$$P_{e,W} = \sum_{v \in \mathcal{D}_W^c} P_{Y|X}(v \mid X = 1). \tag{3}$$

where $\mathcal{D}_W^c$ is the complementary region in the set $\mathcal{V}$. The channel $X \to \hat{X}$ can be modeled as a binary input binary output (BIBO) channel with transition probability matrix $P_{\hat{X}|X}$:

$$\begin{bmatrix} P_{\hat{X}|X}(\hat{x} = 0 \mid x = 0) & P_{\hat{X}|X}(\hat{x} = 1 \mid x = 0) \\ P_{\hat{X}|X}(\hat{x} = 0 \mid x = 1) & P_{\hat{X}|X}(\hat{x} = 1 \mid x = 1) \end{bmatrix}$$

$$= \begin{bmatrix} 1 - P_{e,B} & P_{e,B} \\ P_{e,W} & 1 - P_{e,W} \end{bmatrix} \tag{4}$$

As we can see in Figure 1, the opponent channel $\mathcal{X} \to Z$ is a physically degraded version of the main channel. Thus, $X \to \hat{X} \to Z$ forms a Markov chain with the relation $P_{\hat{X}Z|X}(\hat{x}, z \mid x) = P_{\hat{X}|X}(\hat{x} \mid x) T_{Z/\hat{X}}(z \mid \hat{x})$, where $T_{Z|\hat{X}}$ is the transition matrix of the counterfeiter physical device. Components of the marginal channel matrix $P_{Z|X}$ are

$$P_{Z|X}(v \mid x) = \sum_{\hat{x}=0,1} P_{\hat{X}Z|X}(\hat{x}, v \mid x)$$

$$= \sum_{\hat{x}=0,1} P_{\hat{X}|X}(\hat{x} \mid x) T_{Z|\hat{X}}(v \mid \hat{x}). \tag{5}$$

Finally, we have

$$P_{Z|X}(v \mid X = 0) = (1 - P_{e,B}) T_{Z|\hat{X}}(v \mid \hat{X} = 0) + P_{e,B} T_{Z|\hat{X}}(v \mid \hat{X} = 1), \tag{6}$$

$$P_{Z|X}(v \mid X = 1) = (1 - P_{e,W}) T_{Z|\hat{X}}(v \mid \hat{X} = 1) + P_{e,W} T_{Z|\hat{X}}(v \mid \hat{X} = 0). \tag{7}$$

2.2 Receiver's strategies: thresholding or not?

Two strategies are possible for the receiver.

2.2.1 Binary thresholding

As a first strategy, the legitimate receiver first decode the observed sequence o^N using a maximum likelihood criterion based on the main channel marginal distribution $P_{Y|X}$. He then restores a binary version $\tilde{x}^N$ of the original message x^N using the same decision region as defined by (1) and naturally undergoes errors.

- In the main channel, i.e., when $O^N = Y^N$, error probabilities are equivalent to (2) and (3).

- In the opponent channel, i.e., when $O^N = Z^N$, we make use of (6) and (7) to express the corresponding error probabilities:

$$\tilde{P}_{e,W} = \sum_{v \in \mathcal{D}_W^c} P_{Z|X}(v \mid X = 1), \tag{8}$$

$$\tilde{P}_{e,W} = (1 - P_{e,W}) \sum_{v \in \mathcal{D}_W^c} T_{Z|\hat{X}}(v \mid \hat{X} = 1)$$
$$+ P_{e,W} \sum_{v \in \mathcal{D}_W^c} T_{Z|\hat{X}}(v \mid \hat{X} = 0).$$

$$\tilde{P}_{e,W} = (1 - P_{e,W})P'_{e,W} + P_{e,W}(1 - P'_{e,B}) \tag{9}$$

where $P'_{e,W} = \sum_{v \in \mathcal{D}_W^c} T_{Z|\hat{X}}(v \mid \hat{X} = 1)$ and $P'_{e,B} = \sum_{v \in \mathcal{D}_W} T_{Z|\hat{X}}$ $(v \mid \hat{X} = 0)$. The same development yields

$$\tilde{P}_{e,B} = (1 - P_{e,B})P'_{e,B} + P_{e,B}(1 - P'_{e,W}). \tag{10}$$

For this first strategy, the opponent channel may be viewed as the cascade of two binary input/binary output channels:

$$\begin{bmatrix} 1 - \tilde{P}_{e,B} & \tilde{P}_{e,B} \\ \tilde{P}_{e,W} & 1 - \tilde{P}_{e,W} \end{bmatrix} = \begin{bmatrix} 1 - P_{e,B} & P_{e,B} \\ P_{e,W} & 1 - P_{e,W} \end{bmatrix}$$
$$\times \begin{bmatrix} 1 - P'_{e,B} & P'_{e,B} \\ P'_{e,W} & 1 - P'_{e,W} \end{bmatrix}. \tag{11}$$

As we will see in the next section, in this particular case, the test to decide whether the observed decoded sequence $\tilde{x}^N$ comes from the legitimate source or not is tantamount to counting the number of erroneous decoded dots.

2.2.2 Gray-level observations

In the second strategy, the receiver performs his test directly on the received sequence o^N without any given decoding. We will see in Section 3.3 that this strategy is better than the previous one (see Section 3.2).

3 Impacts of the receiver's strategies on hypothesis testing

We consider here testing whether, for a given fixed input $(x_1, \ldots, x_N)$, an observed independent and identically distributed (i.i.d.) sequence $(o_1, \ldots, o_N \mid x_1, \ldots, x_N)$ is generated from a given distribution $P_{Y|X}$ or if it comes from an alternative hypothesis associated to distribution $P_{Z|X}$, $(o_i \mid x_i)$ belonging to a discrete finite set $\mathcal{V}$. Practically, we are interested in performing authentication after observing a sequence of N samples $(o_i \mid x_i)$, attesting whereas this sequence comes from a legitimate source or from a counterfeiter. The receiver establishes then a decision based on a predefined statistical test and

assigns one of the two hypothesis H_0 or H_1 corresponding, respectively, to each of the former cases. According to this test, the space $\mathcal{V}^N$ will be partitioned into two regions $\mathcal{H}_0$ and $\mathcal{H}_1$. Accepting hypothesis H_0 while it is actually a fake (the observed N sample sequence belongs to $\mathcal{H}_0$ while H_1 is true) leads to an error of type II having probability β. Rejecting hypothesis H_0 while actually the observed sequence comes from the legitimate source (the observed N sample sequence belongs to $\mathcal{H}_1$ while H_0 is true) leads to an error of type I with probability α. It is desirable to find a test with a minimal probability β for a fixed or prescribed probability of type I. An optimal decision rule will be given by the Neyman-Pearson criterion. The eponymous theorem states that under the constraint $\alpha \leq \alpha^*$, β is minimized if only if the following log-likelihood test infers the choice of H_1:

$$\log \frac{P^N(o^N \mid x^N, H_1)}{P^N(o^N \mid x^N, H_0)} \geq \gamma, \tag{12}$$

where γ is a threshold verifying the constraint $\alpha \leq \alpha^*$.

3.1 Authentication via binary thresholding

In the first strategy, the final observed data is $\tilde{x}^N$ and the original sequence x^N is a side information containing two types of data ('0' and '1'). The conditional distribution of each random component $(\tilde{X}_i \mid x_i)$ of the sequence $(\tilde{X}^N \mid x^N)$ is the same for each given type. We compute now the probabilities that describe the two random i.i.d. sequences $(\tilde{X}^N \mid x^N)$, one per data type, and for each of the two possible hypothesis. We derive then the corresponding test from (12). Under hypothesis H_j, $j \in \{0, 1\}$, these probabilities are expressed conditionally to the known original code x^N. Let $\mathcal{N}_B = \{i : x_i = 0\}$ and $\mathcal{N}_W = \{i : x_i = 1\}$, with $N_B = |\mathcal{N}_B|$ and $N_W = |\mathcal{N}_W|$. Because of i.i.d. sequences, we have

$$P^N(\tilde{x}^N \mid x^N, H_j) = \prod_{i=1}^N P(\tilde{x}_i \mid x_i, H_j),$$

$$P^N(\tilde{x}^N \mid x^N, H_j) = \prod_{i \in \mathcal{N}_B} P(\tilde{x}_i \mid 0, H_j)$$
$$\times \prod_{i \in \mathcal{N}_W} P(\tilde{x}_i \mid 1, H_j).$$

Under hypothesis H_0 the channel $X \to \tilde{X}$ has distributions given by (2) and (3) and we have:

$$P^N\left(\tilde{x}^N \mid x^N, H_0\right) = (P_{e,B})^{n_{e,B}}(1 - P_{e,B})^{N_B - n_{e,B}}$$
$$\times (P_{e,W})^{n_{e,W}}(1 - P_{e,W})^{N_W - n_{e,W}},$$

where $n_{e,B}$ and $n_{e,W}$ are the number of errors $(\tilde{x}_i \neq x_i)$ when black is decoded into white and when white is decoded into black, respectively.

- Under hypothesis H_1, the channel $X \to \tilde{X}$ has distributions given by (9) and (10), and we have

$$P^N\left(\tilde{x}^N \mid x^N, H_1\right) = (\tilde{P}_{e,B})^{n_{e,B}}(1 - \tilde{P}_{e,B})^{N_B - n_{e,B}}$$
$$\times (\tilde{P}_{e,W})^{n_{e,W}}(1 - \tilde{P}_{e,W})^{N_W - n_{e,W}}.$$

Applying now the Neyman Pearson criterion (12), the test is expressed as

$$L_1 = \log \frac{P^N\left(\tilde{x}^N \mid x^N, H_1\right)}{P^N\left(\tilde{x}^N \mid x^N, H_0\right)} \underset{H0}{\overset{H1}{\gtrless}} \gamma, \tag{13}$$

$$L_1 = n_{e,B} \log\left(\frac{\tilde{P}_{e,B}(1 - P_{e,B})}{P_{e,B}(1 - \tilde{P}_{e,B})}\right)$$

$$+ n_{e,W} \log\left(\frac{\tilde{P}_{e,W}(1 - P_{e,W})}{P_{e,W}(1 - \tilde{P}_{e,W})}\right) \underset{H0}{\overset{H1}{\gtrless}} \lambda_1, \tag{14}$$

where $\lambda_1 = \gamma - N_B \log\left(\frac{1 - \tilde{P}_B}{1 - P_B}\right) - N_W \log\left(\frac{1 - \tilde{P}_W}{1 - P_W}\right)$. This expression has the practical advantage to only count the number of errors in order to perform the authentication task but at a cost of a loss of optimality.

3.2 Authentication via gray-level observations

In the second strategy, the observed data is o^N. Here again, the conditional distribution of each random component $(O_i \mid x_i)$ of the sequence $(O^N \mid x^N)$ is the same for each type of data of X. The Neyman Pearson test is expressed as

$$L_2 = \log \frac{P^N(o^N \mid x^N, H_1)}{P^N(o^N \mid x^N, H_0)} \underset{H0}{\overset{H1}{\gtrless}} \lambda_2, \tag{15}$$

which can be developed as

$$L_2 = \sum_{i \in \mathcal{N}_B} \log \frac{P_{Z|X}(o_i \mid 0)}{P_{Y|X}(o_i \mid 0)} \tag{16}$$

$$+ \sum_{i \in \mathcal{N}_W} \log \frac{P_{Z|X}(o_i \mid 1)}{P_{Y|X}(o_i \mid 1)} \underset{H0}{\overset{H1}{\gtrless}} \lambda_2,$$

$$L_2 = \sum_{i \in \mathcal{N}_B} \log\left((1 - P_{e,W})\frac{T_{Z|\hat{X}}(o_i \mid 0)}{T_{Y|X}(o_i \mid 0)} + P_{e,W}\frac{T_{Z|\hat{X}}(o_i \mid 1)}{T_{Y|X}(o_i \mid 0)}\right)$$

$$+ \sum_{i \in \mathcal{N}_W} \log\left((1 - P_{e,B})\frac{T_{Z|\hat{X}}(o_i \mid 1)}{T_{Y|X}(o_i \mid 1)} + P_{e,B}\frac{T_{Z|\hat{X}}(o_i \mid 0)}{T_{Y|X}(o_i \mid 1)}\right)$$

$$\underset{H0}{\overset{H1}{\gtrless}} \lambda_2. \tag{17}$$

Note that the expressions of the transition matrix modeling the physical processes $T_{Y|X}$ and $T_{Z|\hat{X}}$ are required in order to perform the optimal test.

3.3 Authentication with thresholding vs authentication without thresholding

In this setup and without loss of generality, we consider only the Gaussian model with variance σ^2 for the physical devices $T_{Y|X}$ and $T_{Z|\hat{X}}$. Figure 2 compares the receiver operating characteristic (ROC) curves associated with the two different strategies. Note that the error probabilities are computed using the results given in the next section (see Section 4.2). We can notice that the gap between the two strategies is important. This is not surprising since the binary thresholding removes information from the gray-level observation, yet this has a practical impact because one practitioner can be tempted to count the number of errors as given in (14) as an authentication score for its easy implementation. The information theoretical analysis presented in the Appendix confirms also that authentication is more accurate without thresholding, and this result is in line with *the remark of Blahut in [14] where in p108 he writes that 'information is increased if a measurement is made more precise [...] (i.e. with a refinement of the set of measurement outcomes).'*

Moreover, as we will see in Section 5, the plain scan of the graphical code can be used whenever the receiver needs to estimate the opponent's channel.

4 Toward reliable performance evaluation

In the previous section we have expressed the Neyman-Pearson test for the two proposed strategies resumed by (14) and (17). These tests may then be practically performed on the observed sequence in order to make a decision about its authenticity. We aim now at expressing the error probabilities of types I and II and comparing the two possible strategies described previously. Let $m = 1, 2$

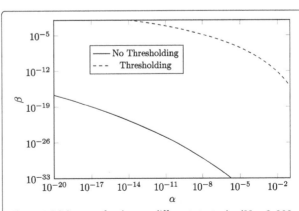

Figure 2 ROC curves for the two different strategies ($N = 2,000$, $\sigma = 52$). α is the probability of rejecting an authentic code and β the probability of non-detecting an illegal copy.

be the index denoting the strategy; a straightforward calculation gives

$$\alpha_m = \sum_{l > \lambda_m} P_{L_m}(l \mid H_0), \tag{18}$$

$$\beta_m = \sum_{l < \lambda_m} P_{L_m}(l \mid H_1). \tag{19}$$

where $P_{L_m}(l \mid H_j)$ is the distribution of the log-likelihood ratio L_m under hypothesis H_j.

4.1 Gaussian approximation

As the length N of the sequence is generally large, we use the central limit theorem to study the distributions P_{L_m}, $m = 1, 2$ (a similar strategy was proposed in [15]).

- For the binary thresholding strategy, $n_{e,W}$ and $n_{e,B}$ in (14) are binomial random variables depending on the origin of the observed sequence. Let N_x stand for the number of data of type x in the original code and $P_{e,x}$ the cross-over probabilities emerging from type x in the BIBO channels (4) or (11). When N is large enough, the binomial random variables can be approximated with a Gaussian distribution. We have

$$n_{e,x} \sim \mathcal{N}(N_x P_{e,x}, N_x P_{e,x}(1 - P_{e,x})). \tag{20}$$

From (14), L_1 is a weighted sum of Gaussian random variables and one can obviously deduce the parameters of the normal approximation describing the log-likelihood L_1.

- For the second strategy, i.e., when the receiver tests directly the observed gray-level sequence, the log-likelihood L_2 in Equation 17 may be expressed as two sums of i.i.d. and becomes

$$L_2 = \sum_{i \in \mathcal{N}_B} \ell(o_i, 0) + \sum_{i \in \mathcal{N}_W} \ell(o_i, 1) \underset{H0}{\overset{H1}{\gtrless}} \lambda_2, \tag{21}$$

where $\ell(v, x)$ is a function $\ell : \mathcal{X} \times \mathcal{V} \to \mathbb{R}$ having some distribution with mean and variance equal to

$$m_x = E[\ell(V, x) \mid H_j] = \sum_{v \in \mathcal{V}} \ell(v, x) P(v \mid x, H_j), \tag{22}$$

and

$$\text{var}[\ell(V, x) \mid H_j] = \sum_{v \in \mathcal{V}} (\ell(v, x) - m_x)^2 P(v \mid x, H_j), \tag{23}$$

with $P = P_{Y|X}$ (respectively $P = P_{Z|X}$) for $j = 0$ (respectively 1). The central limit theorem is then used again to approximate the distribution of L_2 and compute type I and type II error probabilities.

4.2 Asymptotic expression

In this section, we drop the subscribe m denoting the strategy as all the subsequent analysis is common for both of them. One important problem is the fact that the Gaussian approximation proposed previously provides inaccurate error probability values when the threshold λ in (18) and (19) is far from the mean of the log-likelihood random variable L. Chernoff bound and large deviation theory [16] are preferred in this context as very small error probabilities of types I and II may be desired [17]. Given a real number s, the Chernoff bound on type I and type II errors may be expressed as

$$\alpha = \Pr(L \geq \lambda \mid H_0) \leq e^{-s\lambda} g_L(s; H_0) \text{ for any } s > 0, \tag{24}$$

$$\beta = \Pr(L \leq \lambda \mid H_1) \leq e^{-s\lambda} g_L(s; H_1) \text{ for any } s < 0, \tag{25}$$

where the function $g_L(s; H_j)$, $j = 0, 1$ is the moment generating function of the random variable L defined as

$$g_L(s; H_j) = E_{P_L(L|H_j)} \left[e^{sL} \right]. \tag{26}$$

where expectation is performed with respect to distribution $P_L(L \mid H_j)$. Reminding that L is a sum of N independent random variables, asymptotic analysis in probability theory (when N is large enough) shows that bounds similar to (24) and (25) are much more appropriate for estimating α and β than the Gaussian approximation especially when λ is far from $E[L]$, namely when bounding the tails of a distribution [16,17]. The tightest bound is obtained by finding the value of s that provides the minimum of the right-hand side (RHS) of (24) and (25), i.e., the minimum of $e^{-s\lambda} g_L(s; H_j)$ for each $j = 0, 1$. Taking the derivative, the value s that provides the tightest bound under each hypothesis is such that [a]

$$\lambda = \left. \frac{\frac{dg_L(s; H_j)}{ds}}{g_L(s; H_j)} \right|_{s = \tilde{s}_j} = \left. \frac{d}{ds} \ln g_L(s; H_j) \right|_{s = \tilde{s}_j}. \tag{27}$$

We introduce the semi-invariant moment generating function after an acute observation of the identity (27). The semi-invariant moment generating function of L is

$$\mu_L(s; H_j) = \ln g_L(s; H_j). \tag{28}$$

This function has many interesting properties that ease the extraction of an asymptotic expression for (24) and (25) [17]. For instance, this function is additive for the sum of independent random variables, and we have

$$\mu_L(s; H_j) = \sum_{i \in \mathcal{N}_B} \mu_{i,0}(s; H_j) + \sum_{i \in \mathcal{N}_W} \mu_{i,1}(s; H_j), \tag{29}$$

where $\mu_{i,x}(s; H_j)$ is the semi-invariant moment generating function of the random component $\ell(O_i, x)$ when the observed sequence comes from the distribution associated to hypothesis H_j. In addition, relation (27) may be expressed as the sum of the derivatives at the value $\tilde{s}_j$ optimizing the bound:

$$\lambda = \sum_{i \in \mathcal{N}_B} \mu'_{i,0}(\tilde{s}_j ; H_j) + \sum_{i \in \mathcal{N}_W} \mu'_{i,1}(\tilde{s}_j ; H_j). \tag{30}$$

Chernoff bounds on type I and type II errors (24) and (25) may then be expressed as

$$\alpha = \Pr(L \geq \lambda \mid H_0)$$

$$\leq \exp\left[\sum_{i \in \mathcal{N}_B} \left(\mu_{i,0}(\tilde{s}_0 ; H_0) - \tilde{s}_0 \mu'_{i,0}(\tilde{s}_0 ; H_0) \right) \right. \tag{31}$$

$$\left. + \sum_{i \in \mathcal{N}_W} \left(\mu_{i,1}(\tilde{s}_0 ; H_0) - \tilde{s}_0 \mu'_{i,1}(\tilde{s}_0 ; H_0) \right) \right],$$

and

$$\beta = \Pr(L \leq \lambda \mid H_1)$$

$$\leq \exp\left[\sum_{i \in \mathcal{N}_B} \left(\mu_{i,0}(\tilde{s}_1 ; H_1) - \tilde{s}_1 \mu'_{i,0}(\tilde{s}_1 ; H_1) \right) \right. \tag{32}$$

$$\left. + \sum_{i \in \mathcal{N}_W} \left(\mu_{i,1}(\tilde{s}_1 ; H_1) - \tilde{s}_1 \mu'_{i,1}(\tilde{s}_1 ; H_1) \right) \right].$$

The distribution of each random component $(O_i \mid x_i)$ in the sequence $(O^N \mid x^N)$ is the same for each type of data X, and consequently, $\mu_{i,x}(s ; H_j) = \mu_x(s ; H_j)$, i.e., $\mu_{i,x}(s ; H_j)$ is independent from i for each type of data x. The RHS in (31) and (32) can be simplified as

$$\exp\left[N_B \left(\mu_0(\tilde{s}_j ; H_j) - \tilde{s}_j \mu'_0(\tilde{s}_j ; H_j) \right) + N_W \left(\mu_1(\tilde{s}_j ; H_j) \right. \right.$$
$$\left. \left. - \tilde{s}_j \mu'_1(\tilde{s}_j ; H_j) \right) \right]. \tag{33}$$

Roughly speaking, Cramér's theorem [16] states that for sufficiently large N, the upper bounds expressed for $j = 0, 1$ in (33) are also lower bounds for α and β, respectively. Thus, one can write for $N_B \approx N_W \approx N/2$:

$$\lim_{N \to \infty} \frac{2}{N} \ln \alpha = \left[\mu(\tilde{s}_0 ; H_0) - \tilde{s}_0 \mu'(\tilde{s}_0 ; H_0) \right], \tag{34}$$

$$\lim_{N \to \infty} \frac{2}{N} \ln \beta = \left[\mu(\tilde{s}_1 ; H_1) - \tilde{s}_1 \mu'(\tilde{s}_1 ; H_1) \right], \tag{35}$$

where $\tilde{s}_0 > 0$, $\tilde{s}_1 < 0$, $\mu(\tilde{s}_j ; H_j) = \mu_0(\tilde{s}_j ; H_j) + \mu_1(\tilde{s}_j ; H_j)$, $\mu'(\tilde{s}_j ; H_j) = \mu'_0(\tilde{s}_j ; H_j) + \mu'_1(\tilde{s}_j ; H_j)$. A modified asymptotic expression including a correction factor is evalu-

ated for the sum of an i.i.d random sequence (see [17], Appendix 5A), and for large N, we have

$$\alpha = \Pr(L \geq \lambda \mid H_0),$$
$$\underset{N \to \infty}{\to} \frac{1}{\tilde{s}_0 \sqrt{N \pi \mu''(\tilde{s}_0 ; H_0)}} \exp\left\{ \frac{N}{2} \left[\mu(\tilde{s}_0 ; H_0) - \tilde{s}_0 \mu'(\tilde{s}_0 ; H_0) \right] \right\}. \tag{36}$$

and

$$\beta = \Pr(L \leq \lambda \mid H_1),$$
$$\underset{N \to \infty}{\to} \frac{1}{|\tilde{s}_1| \sqrt{N \pi \mu''(\tilde{s}_1 ; H_1)}} \exp\left\{ \frac{N}{2} \left[\mu(\tilde{s}_1 ; H_1) - \tilde{s}_1 \mu'(\tilde{s}_1 ; H_1) \right] \right\}, \tag{37}$$

where $\mu''(\tilde{s}_j ; H_j) = \mu''_0(\tilde{s}_j ; H_j) + \mu''_1(\tilde{s}_j ; H_j)$ is the second derivative of the semi-invariant moment generating function of $\ell(V, x)$ defined by

$$\ell(v, 1) = \log\left((1 - P_{e,W}) \frac{T_{Z|\hat{X}}(v \mid 1)}{T_{Y|X}(v \mid 1)} + P_{e,W} \frac{T_{Z|\hat{X}}(v \mid 0)}{T_{Y|X}(v \mid 1)} \right), \tag{38}$$

$$\ell(v, 0) = \log\left((1 - P_{e,B}) \frac{T_{Z|\hat{X}}(v \mid 0)}{T_{Y|X}(v \mid 0)} + P_{e,B} \frac{T_{Z|\hat{X}}(v \mid 1)}{T_{Y|X}(v \mid 0)} \right). \tag{39}$$

4.3 Numerical computations of α and β via importance sampling

This section addresses the problem of estimating numerically type I and type II error probabilities, i.e., α and β. Monte Carlo simulation method [18] gives accurate solution since these probabilities can be expressed as expectations of a function of a random variable governed by a given probability distribution. We have

$$\alpha = \sum_{v^N \in \mathcal{H}_1} P^N(v^N \mid x^N, H_0), \tag{40}$$

$$= \sum_{v^N \in \mathcal{V}^N} P^N(v^N \mid x^N, H_0) \phi(v^N ; \mathcal{H}_1), \tag{41}$$

where $\phi(v^N ; \mathcal{H}_1) = 1$ whenever $v^N \in \mathcal{H}_1$ and zero if not. The probability of type I error is then expressed as the expectation of $\phi(v^N ; \mathcal{H}_1)$ under distribution $P^N(v^N \mid x^N, H_0)$. In the same way, type II error probability β is the expectation of $\phi(v^N ; \mathcal{H}_0)$ under distribution $P^N(v^N \mid x^N, H_1)$. In the sequel, we denote $P^N(v^N \mid x^N, H_0) = P^N_{Y|X}$ and $P^N(v^N \mid x^N, H_1) = P^N_{Z|X}$, and we have

$$\alpha = E_{P^N_{Y|X}} \left[\phi(V^N ; \mathcal{H}_1) \right], \tag{42}$$

$$\beta = E_{P^N_{Z|X}} \left[\phi(V^N ; \mathcal{H}_0) \right]. \tag{43}$$

Monte Carlo methods make use of the law of large numbers to infer an estimation for α and β by computing numerically an empirical mean for $\phi(v^N ; \mathcal{H}_1)$ and $\phi(v^N ; \mathcal{H}_0)$, respectively. Clearly, the computer runs N_{trials}, each one generating an i.i.d. vector v^N, where samples v_n are driven from distributions $P_{Y|X}$ and $P_{Z|X}$, respectively, which gives the following estimates:

$$\hat{\alpha} = \frac{1}{N_{\text{trials}}} \sum_{i=1}^{N_{\text{trials}}} \phi((v^N)^{(i)}; \mathcal{H}_1),$$

$(v_n)^{(i)}$ being generated from $P_{Y|X}$

$$\hat{\beta} = \frac{1}{N_{\text{trials}}} \sum_{i=1}^{N_{\text{trials}}} \phi((v^N)^{(i)}; \mathcal{H}_0),$$

$(v_n)^{(i)}$ being generated from $P_{Z|X}$.

The Monte Carlo estimator is unbiased ($\hat{\alpha} \to \alpha$ and $\hat{\beta} \to \beta$) almost surely, and the rate of convergence is $N_{\text{trials}}^{-1/2}$. Recalling that for a zero mean and unit variance Gaussian random variable U, $P(|U| \leq 1.96) = 0.95$, the confidence interval at 0.95 obtained from each estimation is

$$[\hat{\alpha} - \frac{1.96\sigma_\alpha}{\sqrt{N_{\text{trials}}}}, \hat{\alpha} + \frac{1.96\sigma_\alpha}{\sqrt{N_{\text{trials}}}}] \qquad (44)$$

$$[\hat{\beta} - \frac{1.96\sigma_\beta}{\sqrt{N_{\text{trials}}}}, \hat{\beta} + \frac{1.96\sigma_\beta}{\sqrt{N_{\text{trials}}}}], \qquad (45)$$

where σ_α (resp. σ_β) is the standard deviation of the random variable $\phi((V^N)^{(i)}; \mathcal{H}_1)$ (resp. $\phi((V^N)^{(i)}; \mathcal{H}_0)$). As $\phi((v^N)^{(i)}; \mathcal{H}_1)$ and $\phi((v^N)^{(i)}; \mathcal{H}_0)$ are Bernoulli random variables with parameter α and β, respectively, their variances are easily deduced, e.g., $\sigma_\alpha^2 = \alpha - \alpha^2 \approx \alpha$ and $\sigma_\beta^2 = \beta - \beta^2 \approx \beta$. When α and β are very small, accurate estimations are then difficult to achieve with realistic number of trials. Roughly speaking, the number of trials needed is $N_{\text{trials}} > \frac{10^3}{\alpha}$ (or $N_{\text{trials}} > \frac{10^3}{\beta}$) when the desired confidence interval at 0.95 is constrained to be about a tenth of the expected value of α or β. Actually, we need to evaluate numerically very small values of α and β to draw the curve $\beta(\alpha)$ evaluating the performance of a given test statistic. The required number of trials fails to be realistic. We propose then to use the importance sampling method [18] which enables us to generate rare events and thus reduce considerably the required number of trials. Let us consider distributions $Q_{Y|X}$ and $Q_{Z|X}$ over the set $\mathcal{V}$ such that $Q_{Y|X}$ and $Q_{Z|X} > 0$ and rewrite (42) and (43) as

$$E_{P_{Y|X}^N}\left[\phi(V^N; \mathcal{H}_1)\right] = E_{P_{Y|X}^N}\left[\phi(V^N; \mathcal{H}_1)\frac{Q_{Y|X}^N}{Q_{Y|X}^N}\right],$$

$$E_{P_{Z|X}^N}\left[\phi(V^N; \mathcal{H}_0)\right] = E_{P_{Z|X}^N}\left[\phi(V^N; \mathcal{H}_0)\frac{Q_{Z|X}^N}{Q_{Z|X}^N}\right].$$

One can then alternatively express type I and type II error probabilities by

$$\alpha = E_{Q_{Y|X}^N}\left[\phi(V^N; \mathcal{H}_1)\frac{P_{Y|X}^N}{Q_{Y|X}^N}\right], \qquad (46)$$

$$\beta = E_{Q_{Z|X}^N}\left[\phi(V^N; \mathcal{H}_0)\frac{P_{Z|X}^N}{Q_{Z|X}^N}\right]. \qquad (47)$$

Monte Carlo simulation with importance sampling method gives the following two estimates:

$$\hat{\alpha} = \frac{1}{N_{\text{trials}}} \sum_{i=1}^{N_{\text{trials}}} \phi\left((v^N)^{(i)}; \mathcal{H}_1\right) \times \left[\frac{P_{Y|X}^N((v^N)^{(i)} \mid x^N)}{Q_{Y|X}^N((v^N)^{(i)} \mid x^N)}\right],$$

$(v^N)^{(i)}$ being generated from $Q_{Y|X}^N$, $\qquad (48)$

$$\hat{\beta} = \frac{1}{N_{\text{trials}}} \sum_{i=1}^{N_{\text{trials}}} \phi\left((v^N)^{(i)}; \mathcal{H}_0\right) \times \left[\frac{P_{Z|X}^N((v^N)^{(i)} \mid x^N)}{Q_{Z|X}^N((v^N)^{(i)} \mid x^N)}\right],$$

$(v^N)^{(i)}$ being generated from $Q_{Z|X}^N$. $\qquad (49)$

The problem of importance sampling is to choose an adequate function $Q_{V|X}$ such that the variance of the estimated probabilities in (48) and (49) are very small. The number of trials will be considerably reduced and accurate estimations of very low values of α and β may be possible. Let

$$Q_{Y|X}(s, v \mid x) = \exp\left(-\mu_x(s; H_0) + s\ell(v, x)\right)P_{Y|X}(v \mid x)$$

and

$$Q_{Z|X}(s, v \mid x) = \exp\left(-\mu_x(s; H_1) + s\ell(v, x)\right)P_{Z|X}(v \mid x)$$

be tilted distributions over the set $\mathcal{V}$, and $\mu_x(s; H_j)$ the semi-invariant moment generating function of $\ell(v, x)$ distributed under hypothesis H_j.

Proposition 1. *The mean of the log-likelihood function $\ell(v, x)$ governed by the tilted distributions $Q_{Y|X}(s, v \mid x)$ is $\mu_x'(s; H_0)$.*

Proof. We have indeed

$$\sum_{v \in \mathcal{V}} \ell(v, x)Q_{Y|X}(s, v \mid x) = \sum_{v \in \mathcal{V}} \ell(v, x)\exp(-\mu_x(s; H_0) + s\ell(v, x))$$
$$\times P_{Y|X}(v \mid x),$$
$$= \frac{\sum_{v \in \mathcal{V}} \ell(v, x)\exp(s\ell(v, x))P_{Y|X}(v \mid x)}{\exp(\mu_x(s; H_0))};$$

since $\mu_x(s; H_0) = \log\big(g_x(s; H_0)\big)$, the denominator of the previous expression is simply $g_x(s; H_0)$:

$$\sum_{v\in\mathcal{V}}\ell(v,x)Q_{Y|X}(s,v\,|\,x) = \frac{\sum\limits_{v\in\mathcal{V}}\ell(v,x)\exp\big(s\ell(v,x)\big)P_{Y|X}(v\,|\,x)}{\sum\limits_{v\in\mathcal{V}}\exp\big(s\ell(v,x)\big)P_{Y|X}(v\,|\,x)},$$

$$= \frac{\frac{\mathrm{d}g_x(s;H_0)}{\mathrm{d}s}}{g_x(s;H_0)},$$

Finally, we have

$$\sum_{v\in\mathcal{V}}\ell(v,x)Q_{Y|X}(s,v\,|\,x) = \mu_x'(s; H_0). \tag{50}$$

The same development yields

$$\sum_{v\in\mathcal{V}}\ell(v,x)Q_{Z|X}(s,v\,|\,x) = \mu_x'(s; H_1). \tag{51}$$

When choosing $s = \tilde{s}_0$ for $Q_{Y|X}(s,v\,|\,x)$ and $s = \tilde{s}_1$ for $Q_{Z|X}(s,v\,|\,x)$, the mean of the log-likelihood function $\ell(v,x)$ governed by these tilted distributions will be equal to the threshold λ of the test 30. $\qquad\square$

Proposition 2. *The variances of the estimations in (48) and (49) go to zero as the number of dots is sufficiently large.*

Proof. To show this, let o^N be the observed samples coming from the main channel, e.g., driven from the tilted distribution $Q_{Y|X}^N(\tilde{s}_0, v^N\,|\,x^N)$. We have

$$Q_{Y|X}^N(\tilde{s}_0, o^N|x^N) = \exp\Bigg(-\sum_{i\in\mathcal{N}_B}\mu_{i,0}(\tilde{s}_0; H_0) - \sum_{i\in\mathcal{N}_W}\mu_{i,1}(\tilde{s}_0; H_0)$$

$$+ \tilde{s}_0\sum_{i\in\mathcal{N}_B}\ell(o_i,0) + \tilde{s}_0\sum_{i\in\mathcal{N}_W}\ell(o_i,1)\Bigg)$$

$$\times P_{Y|X}^N(o^N\,|\,x^N).$$

Recalling that $\mu(\tilde{s}_j; H_j) = \mu_0(\tilde{s}_j; H_j) + \mu_1(\tilde{s}_j; H_j)$, for $N_B \approx N_W \approx N/2$, we have

$$Q_{Y|X}^N(\tilde{s}_0, o^N\,|\,x^N) = \exp\Bigg(-\frac{N}{2}\mu(\tilde{s}_0; H_0) + \tilde{s}_0\Bigg(\sum_{i\in\mathcal{N}_B}\ell(o_i,0)$$

$$+ \sum_{i\in\mathcal{N}_W}\ell(o_i,1)\Bigg)\Bigg)P_{Y|X}^N(o^N\,|\,x^N).$$

By the law of large numbers, the sum of $N/2$ log-likelihood functions of the observed samples $(o_i\,|\,x)$ gov-

erned by the tilted distribution, converges in probability to its mean value as N is sufficiently large:

$$\sum_{i\in\mathcal{N}_B}\ell(o_i, 0) \xrightarrow{P} \frac{N}{2}\sum_{v\in\mathcal{V}}\ell(v, 0)Q_{Y|X}(\tilde{s}_0, v\,|\,0) = \frac{N}{2}\mu_0'(\tilde{s}_0; H_0),$$

$$\sum_{i\in\mathcal{N}_W}\ell(o_i, 1) \xrightarrow{P} \frac{N}{2}\sum_{v\in\mathcal{V}}\ell(v, 1)Q_{Y|X}(\tilde{s}_0, v\,|\,1) = \frac{N}{2}\mu_1'(\tilde{s}_0; H_0).$$

Recalling that $\mu'(\tilde{s}_j; H_j) = \mu_0'(\tilde{s}_j; H_j) + \mu_1'(\tilde{s}_j; H_j)$, and from proposition 1, we have

$$\Bigg(\sum_{i\in\mathcal{N}_B}\ell(o_i, 0) + \sum_{i\in\mathcal{N}_W}\ell(o_i, 1)\Bigg) \xrightarrow{P} \frac{N}{2}\mu'(\tilde{s}_0; H_0).$$

Equivalently, when observed samples come from the opponent channel, e.g., drawn from the tilted distribution $Q_{Z|X}^N(\tilde{s}_1, v^N\,|\,x^N)$, we have

$$\Bigg(\sum_{i\in\mathcal{N}_B}\ell(o_i, 0) + \sum_{i\in\mathcal{N}_W}\ell(o_i, 1)\Bigg) \xrightarrow{P} \frac{N}{2}\mu'(\tilde{s}_1; H_1).$$

Finally, we have

$$Q_{Y|X}^N(\tilde{s}_0, o^N\,|\,x^N) \xrightarrow{P} \exp\left(-\frac{N}{2}\big(\mu(\tilde{s}_0; H_0) - \tilde{s}_0\mu'(\tilde{s}_0; H_0)\big)\right)$$

$$\times P_{Y|X}^N(o^N\,|\,x^N) \tag{52}$$

and

$$Q_{Z|X}^N(\tilde{s}_1, o^N\,|\,x^N) \xrightarrow{P} \exp\left(-\frac{N}{2}\big(\mu(\tilde{s}_1; H_1) - \tilde{s}_1\mu'(\tilde{s}_1; H_1)\big)\right)$$

$$\times P_{Z|X}^N(o^N\,|\,x^N). \tag{53}$$

The variance of $\phi(V^N; \mathcal{H}_1)\frac{P_{Y|X}^N}{Q_{Y|X}^N}$ when V^N is governed by the tilted distribution $Q_{Y|X}^N(\tilde{s}_0, v^N\,|\,x^N)$ is then (the function $\phi(.)$ being 0 or 1)

$$\mathrm{var}_{Q_{Y|X}^N}\left[\phi(V^N; \mathcal{H}_1)\frac{P_{Y|X}^N}{Q_{Y|X}^N}\right]$$

$$= E_{Q_{Y|X}^N}\left[\phi^2(V^N; \mathcal{H}_1)\left(\frac{P_{Y|X}^N}{Q_{Y|X}^N}\right)^2\right] - \alpha^2,$$

$$= E_{P_{Y|X}^N}\left[\phi(V^N; \mathcal{H}_1)\left(\frac{P_{Y|X}^N}{Q_{Y|X}^N}\right)\right] - \alpha^2,$$

$$\xrightarrow{P} E_{P_{Y|X}^N}\left[\phi(V^N;\mathcal{H}_1)\left(\frac{1}{\exp\left(-\frac{N}{2}\big(\mu(\tilde{s}_0;H_0)-\tilde{s}_0\mu'(\tilde{s}_0;H_0)\big)\right)}\right)\right] - \alpha^2.$$

The denominator in the expectation, i.e., $\exp\left(-\frac{N}{2}\big(\mu(\tilde{s}_0; H_0) - \tilde{s}_0\mu'(\tilde{s}_0; H_0)\big)\right)$, is simply the inverse of the

Cramér-Chernoff bound proposed in (34). We then have

$$\text{var}_{Q^N_{Y|X}}\left[\phi(V^N;\mathcal{H}_1)\frac{P^N_{Y|X}}{Q^N_{Y|X}}\right] \xrightarrow{P} \alpha E_{P^N_{Y|X}}\left[\phi(V^N;\mathcal{H}_1)\right] - \alpha^2.$$

Finally, since $E_{P^N_{Y|X}}\left[\phi(V^N;\mathcal{H}_1)\right] = \alpha$ (42), the variance goes to zero as N is large enough:

$$\text{var}_{Q^N_{Y|X}}\left[\phi(V^N;\mathcal{H}_1)\frac{P^N_{Y|X}}{Q^N_{Y|X}}\right] \xrightarrow{P} 0.$$

The same development gives

$$\text{var}_{Q^N_{Z|X}}\left[\phi(V^N;\mathcal{H}_0)\frac{P^N_{Z|X}}{Q^N_{Z|X}}\right] \xrightarrow{P} 0.$$

$\square$

4.4 Practical performance analysis

Without loss of generality, we use in our analysis a generalized Gaussian distribution to model the physical device, i.e., the association of a printer with a scanner, used by the legitimate source $T_{Y|X}(v \mid x)$ and by the counterfeiter $T_{Z|\hat{X}}(v \mid \hat{x})$:

$$p(v \mid x) = \frac{b}{2a\Gamma(1/b)}e^{-(|v-m(x)|/a)^b}, \tag{54}$$

where $m(x)$ is the mean and the parameter a can be computed from the variance $\sigma^2 = \text{var}[V]$:

$$a = \sqrt{\sigma \Gamma(1/b)/\Gamma(3/b)}. \tag{55}$$

The parameter b is used to control the sparsity of the distribution, for example, when $b = 1$ the distribution is Laplacian, $b = 2$ the distribution is Gaussian, and $b \to +\infty$ the distribution is uniform. The resulting distribution is first discretized then truncated to provide values within $[0,\dots,255]$ to model a scanning process. Each channel is parametrized in this case by four parameters, two per each type of dots, $m_b = m(0)$ and σ_b for black dots and $m_w = m(1)$ and σ_w for white dots. Note that other print and scan models that take into account the gamma transfer function or additive noise with input dependent variance can be found in [19], but the general methodology of this paper is not dependent on the model and can still be applied.

Figure 3 illustrates the different effects of the generalized Gaussian distributions on the main and the opponent channels of same mean and variance and $b = 1$ (Laplacian distribution), $b = 2$ (Gaussian distribution), and $b = 6$, i.e., close to a uniform distribution.

In order to assess the accuracy of the computations of α and β using either the Gaussian approximation given by (18) and (19), the asymptotic expression given by (36) and (37), or the Monte Carlo simulations using importance sampling given by (48) and (49), we derive ROC curves for generalized Gaussian distributions and $b = \{1, 2, 6\}$.

Figure 4 illustrates the gap between the estimation of α and β using the Gaussian approximation and the asymptotic expression or the Monte Carlo simulations. The Monte Carlo simulations confirm the fact that the derived Cramér Chernoff bounds are tight, and the difference between the results obtained with the Gaussian approximation are very important especially for close to uniform channels. We can also notice that for the same channel power, the authentication performances are better for $b = 6$ then for $b = 2$ and $b = 1$.

5 Optimal configurations for authentication

The goal of this section is to derive configurations that are optimal regarding authentication, i.e., to derive configurations that for a given α minimize β.

5.1 Optimal configurations by modification of the printing channel

5.1.1 Problem setting

This authentication problem can be seen as a game where the main goal of the receiver, for a given false alarm probability α, is to find a channel that minimizes the probability of missed detection β. Practically, this means that the channel can be chosen by using a given quality of paper, a different ink, and/or by adopting an appropriate resolution. For example, if the legitimate source wants to decrease the noise variance, he can choose to use oversampling to replicate the dots; on the contrary, if the legitimate source wants to increase the noise variance, he can use a paper of lesser quality. It is important to recall that because the opponent will have to print a binary version of its observation, and because a printing device at this very high resolution can only print binary images, the opponent will in any case have to print with decoding errors after estimation $\hat{X}$.

We analyze two scenarios described below:

- The legitimate source and the opponent have identical printing devices; practically, this means that they use exactly the same printing setup. In this case, the legitimate source will try to look for the channel $\mathcal{C}$ such that for a given α, the legitimate party will have a probability of missed detection β^* such that

$$\beta^* = \min_{\mathcal{C}} \beta(\alpha). \tag{56}$$

In this case, the opponent is passive and has no strategy but duplicating the graphical code.

- The opponent can modify its printing channel $\mathcal{C}_o$ (here, we assume that he can change the variance of its noise), practically it means that he can modify one or several parameters of the printing setup without

Figure 3 Example of a 20 × 20 code which is printed and scanned by an opponent. Main and opponent channels are identical, $m_b = 50$, $m_w = 150$, $\sigma_b = 40$, and $\sigma_w = 40$.

being detected. The opponent then tries to maximize the probability of false detection by choosing the adequate printing channel, and the legitimate sources will adopt the printing channel $\mathcal{C}_l$ which will minimize the probability of false detection. We end up with what is called a min-max game in game theory, where the optimal β^* is the solution of

$$\beta^* = \min_{\mathcal{C}_l} \max_{\mathcal{C}_o} \beta(\alpha). \tag{57}$$

In this case, the opponent is active since he tries to adapt his strategy in order to degrade the authentication performance.

Because the expressions of $\beta(\alpha)$ is not simple and have to be computed using the asymptotic expressions (31) and (32), we cannot solve this problem analytically and we have to use numerical calculus instead.

We conduct this analysis for the generalized Gaussian model, where we assume that the parameters m_b and m_w are constant for the main and the opponent channels (which implies that the scanning process has the same calibration for the two types of images). We assume that the main channel and the opponent channel variances are respectively denoted σ_m^2 and σ_o^2 and are identical for black and white dots.

5.1.2 Passive opponent
Here, the opponent has to undergo a channel identical to the main channel; the only parameter of the optimiza-

tion problem (56) is consequently σ_m. Figure 5 presents the evolution of β w.r.t. σ_m for $\alpha = 10^{-6}$ and $m_b = 50$, $m_w = 150$. For each channel configuration, we can find an optimal configuration; this configuration offers a smaller probability of error for $b = 6$ than for $b = 2$ or $b = 1$. It is not surprising to notice that in each case, β is important whenever σ_m is very small (i.e., when the print and scan noise is very small, hence the estimation of the original code is easy) or very large (i.e., when the print and scan noise is so important that the original and forgery become equally noisy).

5.1.3 Active opponent
In this setup, the opponent can use a channel of different variance σ_o^2 than the main channel σ_m^2 and tries to solve the game defined in (57). Figure 6 shows the evolutions of β w.r.t. σ_o for different σ_m. We can see that in each case it is in the opponent interest to optimize his channel. Note that even if we assume that the opponent print and scan channel is perfect ($\hat{\mathbf{x}}^N = \mathbf{z}^N$), because the input of the printer has to be binary and because the opponent will make decoding errors by estimating the original code, the copied printed code will be necessarily different from the original printed code (see Figure 1), which implies a perfect discrimination between the two hypotheses.

Figure 7 shows the evolution of best opponent strategy $\max_{\sigma_o} \beta$ w.r.t. σ_m. By comparing it with Figure 5, we can see that the opponent's probability of non-detection can be multiplied by one or several orders of magnitude ($\times 10^7$ for $b = 1$, $\times 10^5$ for $b = 2$, and $\times 10$ for $b = 6$).

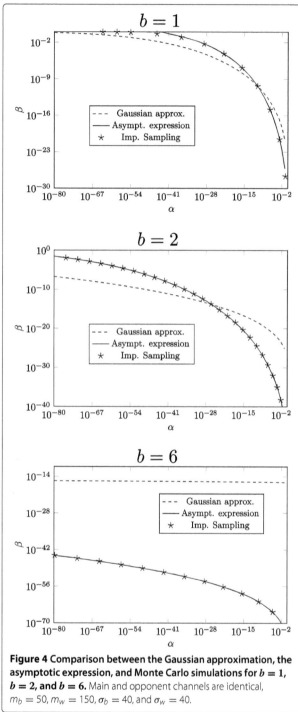

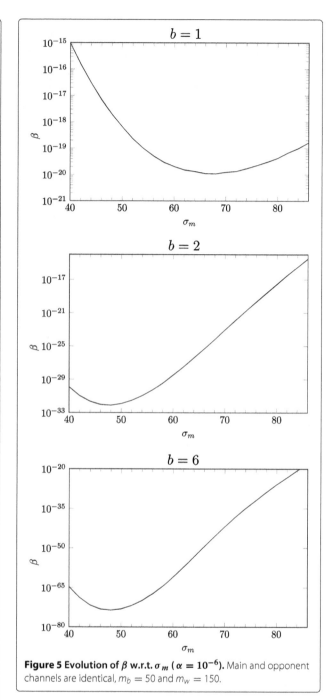

Figure 4 Comparison between the Gaussian approximation, the asymptotic expression, and Monte Carlo simulations for $b = 1$, $b = 2$, and $b = 6$. Main and opponent channels are identical, $m_b = 50$, $m_w = 150$, $\sigma_b = 40$, and $\sigma_w = 40$.

Figure 5 Evolution of β w.r.t. σ_m ($\alpha = 10^{-6}$). Main and opponent channels are identical, $m_b = 50$ and $m_w = 150$.

6   Impact of the estimation of the print and scan channel

The previous scenarios assume that the receiver has a full knowledge of the print and scan channel. Here, we assume that the receiver also has to estimate the opponent channel before performing authentication. From the estimated parameters, the receiver will compute a threshold and a log-likelihood test. Depending on the number of observations N_o, the estimated model and test will decrease the performance of the authentication system.

We consider that the opponent uses a different printing device unknown from the legitimate party. According to (6) and (7), the parameters to be estimated are $P_{e,W}$, $P_{e,B}$, m_b, m_w, and $\sigma = \sigma_b = \sigma_w$. We use the classical expectation maximization (EM) algorithm combined with Newton's method to solve the maximization step as these

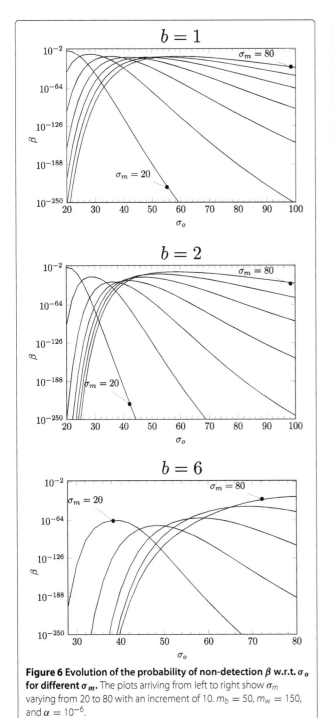

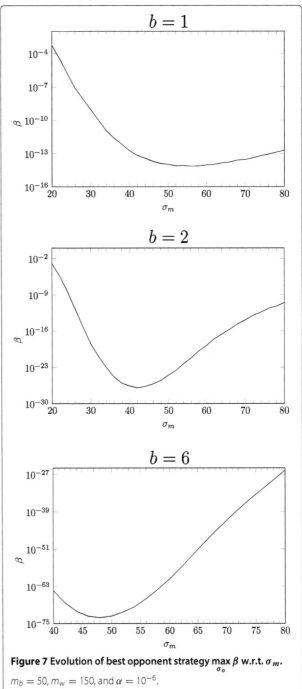

Figure 6 Evolution of the probability of non-detection β w.r.t. σ_o for different σ_m. The plots arriving from left to right show σ_m varying from 20 to 80 with an increment of 10. $m_b = 50$, $m_w = 150$, and $\alpha = 10^{-6}$.

Figure 7 Evolution of best opponent strategy $\max_{\sigma_o} \beta$ w.r.t. σ_m. $m_b = 50$, $m_w = 150$, and $\alpha = 10^{-6}$.

distributions are discrete and have the finite support of the gray-level range.

Figure 8 shows the authentication performances using an estimated Gaussian model ($b = 2$) from $N_o = 2,000$ observed symbols. We can notice that the performance is very close to an exact knowledge of the model. This analysis shows also that if the receiver has some assumptions of the opponent channel and enough observations,

he should perform model estimation instead of using the thresholding strategy. Figure 9 shows the importance of model estimation when comparing it to a blind authentication test when the receiver assumes that both the opponent channel and his channel are identical.

7 Conclusions

This paper brings numerous conclusions on the authentication using binary codes corrupted by a manufacturing stochastic noise:

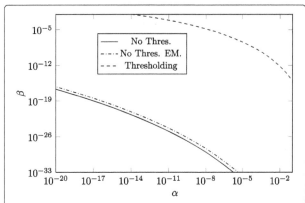

Figure 8 Authentication performance using model estimation with the EM algorithm ($N = 2,000$, $N_o = 2,000$, $\sigma = 52$, $m_b = 50$, and $m_w = 150$). The asymptotic expression is used to derive the error probabilities.

- The nature of the receiver's input is of upmost importance, and thresholding is a bad strategy with respect to getting an accurate version of the genuine or forged code, except if the system requires it, due for example to computational requirements.
- The Gaussian approximation used to compute the ROC of the authentication system are not valuable anymore for very low type I or type II errors. Cramér Chernoff bound or Monte Carlo simulations using importance sampling can be used instead to achieve accurate values of these probabilities. The proposed methodology is not impacted by the nature of the noise and can be applied for different memoryless channels that are more realistic for modeling the printing process.

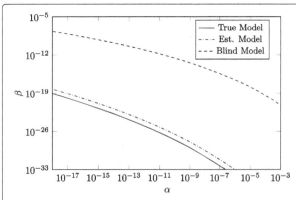

Figure 9 Importance of model estimation when compared to a blind authentication test. ROC curves comparing different degrees of knowledge about the opponent channel while the true opponent printing process model has parameters ($\sigma = 40$, $m_b = 40$, and $\mu_w = 160$). 'True model': the receiver knows exactly this model, 'Blind model': the receiver uses arbitrarily his printing process to model it, and 'Est. model': the receiver estimates the opponent channel using $N_o = 2,000$ observations.

- It is in the opponent's interest to adapt its channel in order to decrease the authentication performances of the system; this can be possible by solving a max-min game.
- If the opponent's print and scan channel remains unknown for the receiver, he can use estimation techniques such as the EM algorithm in order to estimate the channel.

Our future works will consist in evaluating the impact of the noise model on the authentication performance; this first analysis suggests that sparse distributions are less favorable for authentication than dense distributions, but this has to be confirmed by a deeper study.

Endnote

[a]One can show that $e^{-s\lambda} g_L(s ; H_j)$ is a convex function of s.

Appendix

Information theoretic comparison between hypothesis testing with and without thresholding

In this appendix, we aim at establishing an inequality between the average of the two log-likelihood tests (14) and (15). The greater is the discrimination between the two distributions involved in the log-likelihood test, the best is the authentication performance. The expected value of the log-likelihood test (12) with respect to any of the two distributions involved in the ratio is the Kullback-Leibler divergence or *discrimination* defined as

$$L(P_{Y|X}^N; P_{Z|X}^N) = \sum_{v^N \in \mathcal{V}^N} P_{Y|X}^N(v^N \mid x^N) \log \frac{P_{Y|X}^N(v^N \mid x^N)}{P_{Z|X}^N(v^N \mid x^N)},$$

(58)

the base of the logarithm being arbitrary. In the remainder of this paper, we settle on base 2.

In ([14], p. 114), the author provides an interesting inequality relating the discrimination to type I and type II errors in hypothesis testing. This relation is stated by the following lemma:

Lemma 1. *(see the former reference for the proof) For any partition ($\mathcal{H}_0$, $\mathcal{H}_1$) of the observation space $\mathcal{V}^N$, the probabilities of type I and II errors satisfy*

$$L(P_{Y|X}^N; P_{Z|X}^N) \geq \alpha \log \frac{\alpha}{1-\beta} + (1-\alpha) \log \frac{1-\alpha}{\beta}. \quad (59)$$

In our authentication model, the likelihood test is performed conditionally to an available side information involving two types of data x. One type for black points and the second one for white points in the original code. In accordance to this, we express now the discrimination quantity for the two proposed strategies in order to establish the desired inequality:

$$L(P^N(\tilde{X}^N \mid x^N, H_0) ; P^N(\tilde{X}^N \mid x^N, H_1))$$

$$= \sum_{\tilde{x}_1} \cdots \sum_{\tilde{x}_N} P^N\left(\tilde{x}^N \mid x^N, H_0\right) \log \frac{P^N\left(\tilde{x}^N \mid x^N, H_0\right)}{P^N\left(\tilde{x}^N \mid x^N, H_1\right)},$$

$$(60)$$

and

$$L(P^N(O^N \mid x^N, H_0) ; P^N(O^N \mid x^N, H_1))$$

$$= \sum_{v_1} \cdots \sum_{v_N} P^N_{Y|X}(v^N \mid x^N) \log \frac{P^N_{Y|X}(v^N \mid x^N)}{P^N_{Z|X}(v^N \mid x^N)}. \quad (61)$$

For the sake of simplicity, we develop proofs and details for the second strategy only and give results for the thresholding case for which all developments are likewise the former. Regarding the additivity theorem ([14], theorem 4.3.7) for independent sequences and reminding that the distribution of each component of the sequence $(O^N \mid x^N)$ is the same for each type of data x, the discrimination quantity becomes

$$L(P^N(O^N \mid x^N, H_0) ; P^N(O^N \mid x^N, H_1))$$

$$= N_W \times \sum_{v \in \mathcal{V}} P_{Y|X}(v \mid 1) \log \frac{P_{Y|X}(v \mid 1)}{P_{Z|X}(v \mid 1)} \quad (62)$$

$$+ N_B \times \sum_{v \in \mathcal{V}} P_{Y|X}(v \mid 0) \log \frac{P_{Y|X}(v \mid 0)}{P_{Z|X}(v \mid 0)}.$$

Given a composition (or relative frequency) for X $P_X = \{N_W/N , N_B/N\}$, we have

$$L(P^N(O^N \mid X^N, H_0) ; P^N(O^N \mid X^N, H_1))$$

$$= N \times L(P_{Y|X}; P_{Z|X} \mid P_X), \quad (63)$$

where $L(P_{Y/X}; P_{Z/X} \mid P_X)$ is the average discrimination. Similarly, we obtain for the first strategy the relation

$$L(P^N(\tilde{X}^N|X^N, H_0); P^N(\tilde{X}^N|X^N, H_1)) = N \times L(P_{e,x}; \tilde{P}_{e,x} \mid P_X).$$

$$(64)$$

Corollary 1. *Given an i.i.d outcome $X^N = x^N$ with composition, or type P_X, for any partition of the observation*

space $(\mathcal{H}_0, \mathcal{H}_1)$, *the probabilities of type I and II errors satisfy*

$$L(P_{Y|X}; P_{Z|X} \mid P_X) \geq \frac{1}{N} \left(\alpha \log \frac{\alpha}{1-\beta} + (1-\alpha) \log \frac{1-\alpha}{\beta}\right).$$

$$(65)$$

Proof. The proof is straightforward by combining (59) and (63). $\qquad\square$

Corollary 2. *Consider a partition of the observation space $(\mathcal{H}_0, \mathcal{H}_1)$ with probability of type I error α; then, the probability of type II error is lower bounded by*

$$\beta \geq 2^{-[NL(P_{Y|X}; P_{Z|X} \mid P_X) + h(\alpha)]/(1-\alpha)}. \quad (66)$$

Proof. From the previous corollary, we have

$$-(1-\alpha) \log \beta \leq NL(P_{Y|X}; P_{Z|X} \mid P_X) - \alpha \log \alpha$$

$$- (1-\alpha) \log(1-\alpha) + \alpha \log(1-\beta).$$

Setting $h(\alpha) = -\alpha \log \alpha - (1-\alpha) \log(1-\alpha)$, which is the binary entropy (≤ 1), and observing that $\alpha \log(1-\beta) \leq 0$, we can write the inequality

$$-(1-\alpha) \log \beta \leq NL(P_{Y|X}; P_{Z|X} \mid P_X) + h(\alpha). \quad (67)$$

$$\square$$

It is desired that this lower bound is very small which is obviously possible with large values of the quantity $L(P_{Y|X}; P_{Z|X} \mid P_X)$.

Theorem 1. *For the two strategies of the receiver, we have $L(P_{Y|X}; P_{Z|X} \mid P_X) \geq L(P_{e,x}; \tilde{P}_{e,x} \mid P_X)$*

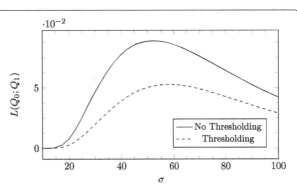

Figure 10 Comparison between the Kullback-Leibler divergences. Kullback-Leibler divergence function for the two different strategies w.r.t. the standard deviation of the Gaussian model of the physical devices.

Proof.

$$L(P_{Y|X}; P_{Z|X} \mid P_X)$$

$$= \sum_{x=0,1} P_X(x) \sum_{v \in \mathcal{V}} P_{Y|X}(v \mid x) \log \frac{P_{Y|X}(v \mid x)}{P_{Z|X}(v \mid x)},$$

$$\sum_{x=0,1} P_X(x) \sum_{v \in \mathcal{D}_{\mathcal{W}}} P_{Y|X}(v \mid x) \log \frac{P_{Y|X}(v \mid x)}{P_{Z|X}(v \mid x)},$$

$$+ \sum_{x=0,1} P_X(x) \sum_{v \in \mathcal{D}_{\mathcal{W}}^c} P_{Y|X}(v \mid x) \log \frac{P_{Y|X}(v \mid x)}{P_{Z|X}(v \mid x)},$$

$$\overset{(a)}{\geq} \sum_{x=0,1} P_X(x) \sum_{v \in \mathcal{D}_{\mathcal{W}}} P_{Y|X}(v \mid k) \log \frac{\sum_{v \in \mathcal{D}_{\mathcal{W}}} P_{Y|X}(v \mid x)}{\sum_{v \in \mathcal{D}_{\mathcal{W}}} P_{Z|X}(v \mid x)},$$

$$+ \sum_{x=0,1} P_X(x) \sum_{v \in \mathcal{D}_{\mathcal{W}}^c} P_{Y|X}(v \mid x) \log \frac{\sum_{v \in \mathcal{D}_{\mathcal{W}}^c} P_{Y|X}(v \mid x)}{\sum_{v \in \mathcal{D}_{\mathcal{W}}^c} P_{Z|X}(v \mid x)},$$

$$\overset{(b)}{=} \sum_{x=0,1} P_X(x) \left(P_{e,x} \log \frac{P_{e,x}}{\tilde{P}_{e,x}} + (1 - P_{e,x}) \log \frac{(1 - P_{e,x})}{(1 - \tilde{P}_{e,x})} \right),$$

$$= \sum_{x=0,1} P_X(x) L(P_{e,x}, \tilde{P}_{e,x} \mid x),$$

$$= L(P_{e,x}, \tilde{P}_{e,x} \mid P_X).$$

$\square$

(a) is obtained from the log-sum inequality: $\sum_{i=1}^{N} a_i$

$$\log \frac{a_i}{b_i} \geq \left(\sum_{i=1}^{N} a_i \right) \log \frac{\sum_{i=1}^{N} a_i}{\sum_{i=1}^{N} b_i}.$$

(b) since $P_{e,x} = \sum_{v \in \mathcal{D}_{\mathcal{W}}} P_{Y|X}(v \mid x)$, $\tilde{P}_{e,x} = \sum_{v \in \mathcal{D}_{\mathcal{W}}} P_{Z|X}(v \mid x)$,
$1 - P_{e,x} = \sum_{v \in \mathcal{D}_{\mathcal{W}}^c} P_{Y|X}(v \mid x)$, $1 - \tilde{P}_{e,x} = \sum_{v \in \mathcal{D}_{\mathcal{W}}^c} P_{Z|X}(v \mid x)$.

Figure 10 plots a comparison between the Kullback-Leibler divergences with and without thresholding w.r.t. the variance of Gaussian model of the physical devices, we can see that the divergence is smaller with thresholding than without.

Competing interests
The authors declare that they have no competing interests.

Acknowledgements
This work was partly supported by the National French project ANR-10-CORD-019 'Estampille'.

Author details
[1]Institut-Telecom-LAGIS, Telecom-Lille, Rue Guglielmo Marconi, Villeneuve-d'Ascq 59650, France. [2]LAGIS, Telecom-Lille, Rue Guglielmo Marconi, Villeneuve-d'Ascq 59650, France. [3]CNRS-LAGIS, Cite Scientifique, 59651, Villeneuve-d'Ascq 59650, France.

References
1. WCO, Global congress addresses international counterfeits threat immediate action required to combat threat to finance/health. http://www.wcoomd.org/en/media/newsroom/2005/november. Accessed 14 Nov 2005
2. WCO, Counterfeiting and piracy endangers global economic recovery, say global congress leaders. http://www.wipo.int/pressroom/en/articles/2009/article_0054.html. Accessed 3 Dec 2009
3. T Haist, HJ Tiziani, Optical detection of random features for high security applications. Optic. Comm. **147**(1–3), 173–179 (1998)
4. GE Suh, S Devadas, Physical unclonable functions for device authentication and secret key generation, in *Proceedings of the 44th Annual Design Automation Conference* (ACM, San Diego, 2007), pp. 9–14
5. MD Gaubatz, SJ Simske, S Gibson, Distortion metrics for predicting authentication functionality of printed security deterrents, in *16th IEEE International Conference on Image Processing (ICIP), 2009* (Cairo, IEEE, Piscataway, 2009), pp. 1489–1492
6. SS Shariati, FX Standaert, L Jacques, B Macq, MA Salhi, P Antoine, Random profiles of laser marks, in *Proceedings of the 31st WIC Symposium on Information Theory in the Benelux* (Rotterdam, 11–12 May 2010)
7. J Picard, J Zhao, Improved techniques for detecting, analyzing, and using visible authentication patterns. WO Patent WO/2005/067,586 (28 July 2005)
8. J Picard, C Vielhauer, N Thorwirth, Towards fraud-proof, ID documents using multiple data hiding technologies and biometrics, in *SPIE Proceedings–Electronic Imaging, Security and Watermarking of Multimedia Contents VI* (San Jose, 2004), pp. 123–234
9. C Baras, F Cayre, 2D bar-codes for authentication: a security approach, in *Proceedings of EUSIPCO 2012* (Bucarest, 27 Sept 2012)
10. M Diong, P Bas, C Pelle, W Sawaya, Document authentication using 2D codes: maximizing the decoding performance using statistical inference, in *Communications and Multimedia Security* (Springer, Kent, 2012), pp. 39–54
11. AE Dirik, B Haas, Copy detection pattern-based document protection for variable media. Image Process. IET. **6**(8), 1102–1113 (2012)
12. F Beekhof, S Voloshynovskiy, F Farhadzadeh, Content authentication and identification under informed attacks, in *2012 IEEE International Workshop on Information Forensics and Security (WIFS)* (IEEE, Tenerife, 2012), pp. 133–138
13. Ho A-T Phan, Mai B-A Hoang, W Sawaya, P Bas, Document authentication using graphical codes: impacts of the channel model, in *ACM Workshop on Information Hiding and Multimedia Security* (Montpellier, ACM, New York, 2013)
14. RE Blahut, *Principles and Practice of Information Theory*, vol. 1, ((Addison-Wesley, 1987)
15. J Picard, Digital authentication with copy-detection patterns. Electron. Imaging. **5310**, 176–183 (2004)
16. A Dembo, *Large Deviations Techniques and Applications*. Stochastic Modelling and Applied Probability, vol. 38. (Springer, 2010)
17. RG Gallager, *Information Theory and Reliable Communication*, vol. 15. (Wiley, 1968)
18. JM Hammersley, DC Handscomb, G Weiss, Monte Carlo methods. Phys. Today. **18**, 55 (1965)
19. C-Y Lin, S-F Chang, Distortion modeling and invariant extraction for digital image print-and-scan process, in *Proceedings of International Symposium on Multimedia Information Processing* (Taipei, Dec 1999)

Optimized combined-clustering methods for finding replicated criminal websites

Jake M Drew[*] and Tyler Moore

Abstract

To be successful, cybercriminals must figure out how to scale their scams. They duplicate content on new websites, often staying one step ahead of defenders that shut down past schemes. For some scams, such as phishing and counterfeit goods shops, the duplicated content remains nearly identical. In others, such as advanced-fee fraud and online Ponzi schemes, the criminal must alter content so that it appears different in order to evade detection by victims and law enforcement. Nevertheless, similarities often remain, in terms of the website structure or content, since making truly unique copies does not scale well. In this paper, we present a novel optimized combined clustering method that links together replicated scam websites, even when the criminal has taken steps to hide connections. We present automated methods to extract key website features, including rendered text, HTML structure, file structure, and screenshots. We describe a process to automatically identify the best combination of such attributes to most accurately cluster similar websites together. To demonstrate the method's applicability to cybercrime, we evaluate its performance against two collected datasets of scam websites: fake escrow services and high-yield investment programs (HYIPs). We show that our method more accurately groups similar websites together than those existing general-purpose consensus clustering methods.

Keywords: Clustering; Consensus clustering; Cybercrime; Escrow fraud; Hierarchical agglomerative clustering; HTML feature extraction; HYIP fraud; Ponzi schemes; High-yield investment programs; Unsupervised learning; Image similarity; Machine learning

1 Introduction

Cybercriminals have adopted two well-known strategies for defrauding consumers online: large-scale and targeted attacks. Many successful scams are designed for massive scale. Phishing scams impersonate banks and online service providers by the thousand, blasting out millions of spam emails to lure a very small fraction of users to fake websites under criminal control [1,2]. Miscreants peddle counterfeit goods and pharmaceuticals, succeeding despite very low conversion rates [3]. The criminals profit because they can easily replicate content across domains, despite efforts to quickly take down content hosted on compromised websites [1]. Defenders have responded by using machine learning techniques to automatically classify malicious websites [4] and to cluster website copies together [5-8].

Given the available countermeasures to untargeted large-scale attacks, some cybercriminals have instead focused on creating individualized attacks suited to their target. Such attacks are much more difficult to detect using automated methods, since the criminal typically crafts bespoke communications. One key advantage of such methods for criminals is that they are much harder to detect until after the attack has already succeeded.

Yet these two approaches represent extremes among available strategies to cybercriminals. In fact, many miscreants operate somewhere in between, carefully replicating the logic of scams without completely copying all material from prior iterations of the attack. For example, criminals engaged in advanced-fee frauds may create bank websites for non-existent banks, complete with online banking services where the victim can log in to inspect their 'deposits'. When one fake bank is shut down, the criminals create a new one that has been tweaked from the former website. Similarly, criminals establish fake escrow services as part of a larger advanced-fee fraud [9]. On the

*Correspondence: jdrew@smu.edu
Computer Science and Engineering Department, Southern Methodist University, 6425 Boaz Lane Dallas, TX 75205, USA

surface, the escrow websites look different, but they often share similarities in page text or HTML structure. Yet another example is online Ponzi schemes called high-yield investment programs (HYIPs) [10]. The programs offer outlandish interest rates to draw investors, which means they inevitably collapse when new deposits dry up. The perpetrators behind the scenes then create new programs that often share similarities with earlier versions.

The designers of these scams have a strong incentive to keep their new copies distinct from the old ones. Prospective victims may be scared away if they realize that an older version of this website has been reported as fraudulent. Hence, the criminals make a more concerted effort to distinguish their new copies from the old ones.

While in principle the criminals could start all over from scratch with each new scam, in practice, it is expensive to recreate entirely new content repeatedly. Hence, things that can be changed easily are (e.g., service name, domain name, registration information). Website structure (if coming from a kit) or the text on a page (if the criminal's English or writing composition skills are weak) are more costly to change, so only minor changes are frequently made.

The purpose of this paper is to design, implement, and evaluate a method for clustering these 'logical copies' of scam websites. Section 2 gives a high-level overview of the combined-clustering process. In Section 3, we describe two sources of data on scam websites used for evaluation: fake escrow websites and HYIPs. Next, Section 4 details how individual website features such as HTML tags, website text, file structure, and image screenshots are extracted to create pairwise distance matrices comparing the similarity between websites. In Section 5, we outline two optimized combined-clustering methods that takes all website features into consideration in order to link disparate websites together. We describe a novel method of combining distance matrices by selecting the minimum pairwise distance. We then evaluate the method compared to other approaches in the consensus clustering literature and cybercrime literature to demonstrate its improved accuracy in Section 6. In Section 7, we apply the method to the entire fake escrow and HYIP datasets and analyze the findings. We review related work in Section 8 and conclude in Section 9.

2 Process for identifying replicated criminal websites

This paper describes a general-purpose method for identifying replicated websites. Figure 1 provides a high-level overview, which is now briefly described before each step is discussed in greater detail in the following sections.

1. *URL crawler:* raw information on websites is gathered.

2. *URL feature extraction:* complementary attributes such as website text and HTML tags are extracted from the raw data for each URL provided.
3. *Input attribute feature files:* extracted features for each website are saved into individual feature files for efficient pairwise distance calculation.
4. *Distance matrices:* pairwise distances between websites for each attribute are computed using the Jaccard distance metrics.
5. *Individual clustering:* hierarchical, agglomerative clustering methods are calculated using each distance matrix, rendering distinct clusterings for each input attribute.
6. *Combined matrices:* combined distance matrices are calculated using various individual distance matrix combinations.
7. *Ground truth selection:* criminal websites are manually divided into replication clusters and used as a source of ground truth.
8. *Cut height optimization:* ground truth clusters are used in combination with the Rand index to identify the optimal clustering cut height for each input attribute.
9. *Combined clustering:* hierarchical, agglomerative clustering methods are calculated using each combined distance matrix to arrive at any number of multi-feature clusterings.
10. *Top performer selection:* the Rand index is calculated for all clusterings against the ground truth to identify the top performing individual feature or combined feature set.

Step 1 is described in Section 3. Steps 2 and 3 are described in Section 4.1, while step 3 is described in Section 4.2. Finally, the clustering steps (5-10) are described in Section 5.

3 Data collection methodology

In order to demonstrate the generality of our clustering approach, we collect datasets on two very different forms of cybercrime: online Ponzi schemes known as HYIPs and fake escrow websites. In both cases, we fetch the HTML using wget. We followed links to a depth of 1, while duplicating the website's directory structure. All communications were run through the anonymizing service Tor [11].

3.1 Data source 1: online Ponzi schemes

We use the HYIP websites identified by Moore et al. in [10]. HYIPs peddle dubious financial products that promise unrealistically high returns on customer deposits in the range of 1% to 2% interest, compounded *daily*. HYIPs can afford to pay such generous returns by paying out existing depositors with funds obtained from new

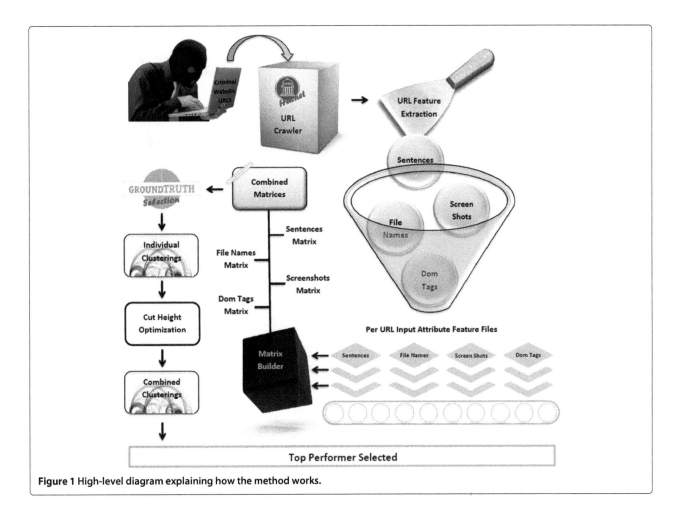

Figure 1 High-level diagram explaining how the method works.

customers. Thus, they meet the classic definition of a Ponzi scheme. Because HYIPs routinely fail, a number of ethically questionable entrepreneurs have spotted an opportunity to track HYIPs and alert investors to when they should withdraw money from schemes prior to collapse. Moore et al. repeatedly crawled the websites listed by these HYIP aggregators, such as hyip.com, who monitor for new HYIP websites as well as track those that have failed. In all, we have identified 4,191 HYIP websites operational between 7 November 2010 and 27 September 2012.

3.2 Data source 2: fake escrow websites

A long-running form of advanced-fee fraud is for criminals to set up fraudulent escrow services [9] and dupe consumers with attractively priced high-value items such as cars and boats that cannot be paid for using credit cards. After the sale, the fraudster directs the buyer to use an escrow service chosen by the criminal, which is in fact a sham website. A number of volunteer groups track these websites and attempt to shut the websites down by notifying hosting providers and domain name registrars. We identified reports from two leading sources of fake escrow

websites, aa419.org and escrow-fraud.com. We used automated scripts to check for new reports daily. When new websites are reported, we collect the relevant HTML. In all, we have identified 1,216 fake escrow websites reported between 07 January 2013 and 06 June 2013.

For both data sources, we expect that the criminals behind the schemes are frequently repeat offenders Figure 2. As earlier schemes collapse or are shut down, new websites emerge. However, while there is usually an attempt to hide evidence of any link between the scam websites, it may be possible to identify hidden similarities by inspecting the structure of the HTML code and website content. We next describe a process for identifying such similarities.

4 Identifying and extracting website features

We identified four primary features of websites as potential indicators of similarity: displayed text, HTML tags, directory file names, and image screenshots. These are described in Section 4.1. In Section 4.2, we explain how the features are computed in a pairwise distance matrix.

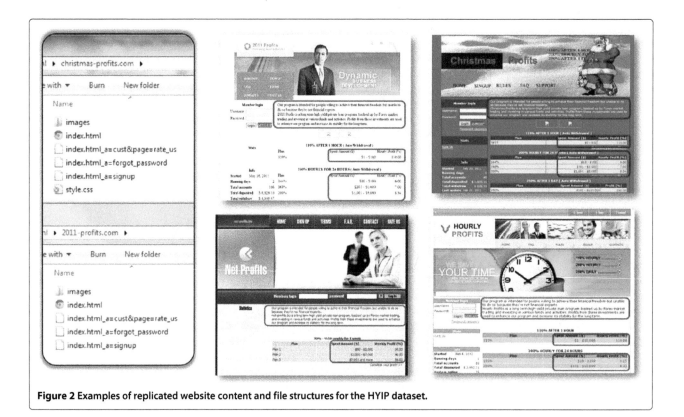

Figure 2 Examples of replicated website content and file structures for the HYIP dataset.

4.1 Website features

4.1.1 Website text

To identify the text that renders on a given web page, we used a custom 'headless' browser adapted from the WatiN package for C# [12]. We extracted text from all pages associated with a given website, then split the text into sentences using the OpenNLP sentence breaker for C#. Additional lower level text features were also extracted such as character n-grams, word n-grams, and individual words for similarity benchmarking. All text features were placed into individual bags by website. Bags for each website were then compared to create pairwise distance matrices for clustering.

4.1.2 HTML content

Given that cybercriminals frequently rely on kits with similar underlying HTML structure [13], it is important to check the underlying HTML files in addition to the rendered text on the page. A number of choices exist, ranging from comparing the document object model (DOM) tree structure to treating tags on a page as a set of values. From experimentation, we found that DOM trees were too specific, so that even slight variations in otherwise similar pages yielded different trees. We also found that sets of tags did not work well, due to the limited variety of unique HTML tags. We found a middle way by counting how often a tag was observed in the HTML files.

All HTML tags in the website's HTML files were extracted, while noting how many times each tag occurs. We then constructed a compound tag with the tag name and its frequency. For example, if the '<br>' tag occurs 12 times within the targeted HTML files, the extracted feature value would be '
12'.

4.1.3 File structure

We examined the directory structure and file names for each website since these could betray structural similarity, even when the other content has changed. However, some subtleties must be accounted for during the extraction of this attribute. First, the directory structure is incorporated into the file name (e.g., `admin/home.html`). Second, since most websites include a home or main page given the same name, such as `index.htm`, `index.html`, or `Default.aspx`, websites comprised of only one file may in fact be quite different. Consequently, we exclude the common home page file names from consideration for all websites. Unique file names were placed into bags by website, and pairwise distances were calculated between all websites under consideration.

4.1.4 Website screenshot images

Finally, screenshots were taken for each website using the Selenium automated web browser for C# [14]. Images were resized to $1,000 \times 1,000$ pixels. We calculated both vertical and horizontal luminosity histograms for each image. Image luminosity features and similarity measures were determined using the EyeOpen image library for C# [15]. During image feature extraction, the red, green, and blue channels for each image pixel were isolated to estimate relative luminance, and these values were then aggregated by each vertical and horizontal image pixel row to calculate two luminosity histograms for each image.

4.2 Constructing distance matrices

For each input attribute, excluding images, we calculated both the Jaccard and Cosine distances between all pairs of websites creating pairwise distance matrices for each input attribute and distance measure. During evaluation, it was determined that the Jaccard distance was the most accurate metric for successfully identifying criminal website replications.

The Jaccard distance between two sets S and T is defined as $1 - J(S, T)$, where

$$J(S, T) = \frac{|S \cap T|}{|S \cup T|}$$

Consider comparing website similarity by sentences. If website A has 50 sentences in the text of its web pages and website B has 40 sentences, and they have 35 sentences in common, then the Jaccard distance is $1 - J(A, B) = 1 - \frac{35}{65} = 0.46$.

Website screenshot images were compared for both vertical and horizontal similarity using luminosity histograms. The luminosity histograms for each matched image pair were compared for similarity by calculating the weighted mean between both the vertical and horizontal histograms. Next, both the average and maximum similarity values between histograms were empirically evaluated for clustering accuracy. Taking the average similarity score between the vertical and horizontal histograms performed best during our evaluation. Once the average vertical and horizontal similarity score was determined, then the pairwise image distance was calculated as 1 - the pairwise image similarity.

Distance matrices were created in parallel for each input attribute by 'mapping' website input attributes into pairwise matches, and then simultaneously 'reducing' pairwise matches into distances using the appropriate distance metric. The pairwise distance matrices were chosen as the output since they are the required input for the hierarchical agglomerative clustering process used during optimized clustering.

5 Optimized combined-clustering process

Once we have individual distance matrices for each input attribute as described in the previous section, the next step is to build the clusters. We first describe two approaches for automatically selecting cut heights for agglomerative clustering: *dynamic cut height*, which is unsupervised, and *optimized cut height*, which is supervised. Next, we compute individual clusterings based on each input attribute. Finally, we construct combined distance matrices for combinations of input attributes and cluster based on the combined matrices.

5.1 Cluster cut height selection

We use a hierarchical agglomerative clustering algorithm [16] to cluster the websites based on the distance matrices. During HAC, a cut height parameter is required to determine the dissimilarity threshold at which clusters are allowed to be merged together. This parameter greatly influences the clustering accuracy, as measured by the Rand index, of the final clusters produced. For instance, using a very high cut height or dissimilarity threshold would result in most websites being included in one giant cluster since a weak measure of similarity is enforced during the merging process.

Traditionally, a static cut height is selected based on the type of data being clustered. Because website input attributes can have very different similarities and still be related, we deploy two methods for automatically selecting the optimal cut heights, one unsupervised and one supervised. In instances where no dependable source of ground truth data is readily available, we use a *dynamic cut height* based on the algorithm used as described in [17]. While the dynamic cut height produces satisfactory results when no ground truth information is available, a better strategy is available where reliable sources of ground truth are present.

Using *optimized cut height*, the best choice is found using the Rand index as a performance measure for each possible cut height parameter value from 0.01 to 0.99. This approach performs clustering and subsequent Rand index scoring at all possible dendrogram height cutoffs using supervised cut height training on the ground truth data. The resulting cut height selected represents the dissimilarity threshold which produces the most accurate clustering results against the ground truth data according to the Rand index score. For example, fake escrow website HTML tags produce clusterings with the Rand index scores ranging from 0% to 97.9% accuracy while varying only the cut height parameter. Figure 3 shows fake escrow website HTML tags generating the highest Rand index score of 0.979 at a cut height of 0.73 with the Rand index score quickly descending back to 0 as the cut height is increased from 0.73 to 1.00. Other fake escrow website input attributes, such as sentences, file names, and images, produce their highest Rand index scores at differing cut height values (0.86, 0.67, and 0.29, respectively).

These results detailed in Section 6.2 demonstrate that the optimized cut height approach produces more accurate clusters than dynamic cut height selection, provided that suitable ground truth data is available to find the

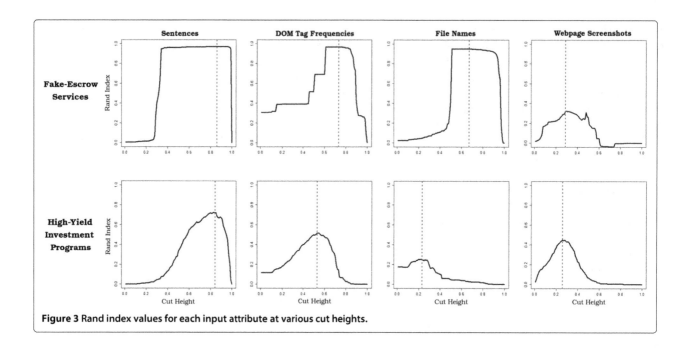

Figure 3 Rand index values for each input attribute at various cut heights.

recommended heights. Furthermore, we also note that the optimized cut height approach performs more consistently, selecting the same top performing input attributes during training and testing executions on both data populations.

5.2 Individual clustering

Because different categories of criminal activity may betray their likenesses in different ways, we need a general process that can select the best combination of input attributes for each dataset. We cannot know, *a priori*, which input attributes are most informative in revealing logical copies. Hence, we start by clustering on each individual attribute independently, before combining the input attributes as described below. It is indeed quite plausible that a single attribute better identifies clusters than does a combination. The clusters are selected using the two cut-height methods outlined above.

5.3 Best min combined clustering

While individual features can often yield highly accurate clustering results, different individual features or even different combinations of multiple features may perform better across different populations of criminal websites as our results will show. Combining multiple distance matrices into a single 'merged' matrix could be useful when different input attributes are important.

However, combining orthogonal distance measures into a single measure must necessarily be an information-lossy operation. A number of other consensus-clustering methods have been proposed [18-21], yet as we will demonstrate in the next section, these algorithms do not perform well when linking together replicated scam websites, often

yielding less accurate results than clusterings based on individual input attributes.

Consequently, we have developed a simple and, in practice, more accurate approach to combining the different distance matrices. We define the pairwise distance between two websites *a* and *b* as the *minimum* distance across all input attributes. The rationale for doing so is that a website may be very different across one measure but similar according to another. Suppose a criminal manages to change the textual content of many sentences on a website, but uses the same underlying HTML code and file structure. Using the minimum distance ensures that these two websites are viewed as similar. Figure 2 demonstrates examples of both replicated website content and file structures. The highlighted text and file structures for each website displayed are nearly identical. One could also imagine circumstances in which the average or maximum distance among input attributes was more appropriate. We calculate those measures, too but found that the minimum approach worked best and so only those results are reported.

We created combined distance matrices for all possible combinations of distance matrices. In the case of the four input attributes considered in this paper, that means, we produced 11 combined matrices (sentences and DOM tags, sentences and file structures, sentences and images, DOM tags and file structures, DOM tags and images, file structure and images, sentences and DOM tags and file structure, sentences and DOM tags and images, sentences and file structures and images, DOM tags and file structures and images, and sentences and DOM tags and file structures and images). In situations where many additional features are used, several specifically targeted feature combinations could also be identified for creating a limited number of combined distance matrices.

Combined clusterings are computed for each combined distance matrix using both cut-height selection methods. Ultimately, the top performing individual attribute or combination is selected based on the accuracy observed when evaluating the labeled training dataset.

6 Evaluation against ground truth data

One of the fundamental challenges of clustering logical copies of criminal websites is the lack of ground truth data for evaluating the accuracy of automated methods. Some researchers have relied on expert judgment to assess similarity, but most forego any systematic evaluation due to a lack of ground truth (e.g., [22]). We now describe a method for constructing ground truth datasets for samples of fake escrow services and high-yield investment programs.

We developed a software tool to expedite the evaluation process. This tool enabled pairwise comparison of website screenshots and input attributes (i.e., website text sentences, HTML tag sequences, and file structure) by an evaluator.

6.1 Performing manual ground truth clusterings

After the individual clusterings were calculated for each input attribute, websites could be sorted to identify manual clustering candidates which were placed in the exact same clusters for each individual input attribute's automated clustering. Populations of websites placed into the same clusters for all four input attributes were used as a starting point in the identification of the manual ground truth clusterings. These websites were then analyzed using the comparison tool in order to make a final assessment of whether the website belonged to a cluster. Multiple passes through the website populations were performed in order to place them into the correct manual ground truth clusters. When websites were identified but did not belong in their original assigned cluster, these sites were placed into the unassigned website population for further review and other potential clustering opportunities.

Deciding when to group together similar websites into the same cluster is inherently subjective. We adopted a broad definition of similarity, in which sites were grouped together if they shared most, but not all, of their input attributes in common. Furthermore, the similarity threshold only had to be met for one input attribute. For instance, HYIP websites are typically quite verbose. Many such websites contain three or four identical paragraphs of text, along with perhaps one or two additional paragraphs of completely unique text. For the ground truth evaluation, we deemed such websites to be in the same cluster. Likewise, fake escrow service websites might appear visually identical in basic structure for most of the site. However, a few of the websites assigned to the same cluster might contain extra web pages not present in the others.

We note that while our approach does rely on individual input attribute clusterings as a starting point for evaluation, we do not consider the final combined clustering in the evaluation. This is to maintain a degree of detachment from the combined-clustering method ultimately used on the datasets. We believe the manual clusterings identify a majority of clusters with greater than two members. Although the manual clusterings contain some clusters including only two members, manual clustering efforts were ended when no more clusters of greater than two members were being identified.

6.2 Results

In total, we manually clustered 687 of the 4,188 HYIP websites and 684 of the 1,220 fake escrow websites. The manually clustered websites were sorted by the date each website was identified, and then both datasets were divided into training and testing populations of 80% and 20%, respectively. The test datasets represented 20% of the most recent websites identified within both the fake escrow services and HYIP datasets. Both datasets were divided in this manner to effectively simulate the optimized combined-clustering algorithm's performance in a real-world setting.

In such a scenario, ground truth data would be collected for some period of time and used as training data. Once the training dataset was complete, Rand index optimized cut heights and top performing individual or combined input attributes would be selected using the training data. Going forward, the optimized cut heights would be used during optimized combined-clustering to cluster all new websites identified using the top performing individual or combined input attribute matrices. Chronologically splitting the training and test data in this manner is consistent with how we expect operators fighting cybercrime to use the method.

We computed an adjusted Rand index [23] to evaluate the combined-clustering method described in Section 5 against the constructed ground truth datasets using an optimized cut height which was determined from the training datasets. The optimized cut height was identified by empirically testing cut height values between 0.01 and 0.99 in increments of 0.01 against the training data. Figure 3 illustrates the Rand index values by input attribute at each of these intervals. The optimized Rand index value selected is indicated by the dotted line on each input attribute's chart. Finally, the cut heights selected during the training phase are used to perform optimized combined clustering against the testing data to assess how this technique might perform in the real-world setting previously described above. We also evaluated employing the unsupervised dynamic tree cut using the method described in [17] to determine an appropriate cut height along with other consensus-clustering methods for comparison. Rand index scores range from 0 to 1, where a score of 1 indicates a perfect match between distinct clusterings.

Table 1 shows the adjusted Rand index for both datasets and all combinations of input attributes using the dynamic and optimized-cut height combined-clustering methods. The first four rows show the Rand index for each individual clustering. For instance, for fake escrow services, clustering based on HTML tags alone using a dynamically determined cut height yielded a Rand index of 0.678 for the training population. Thus, clustering based on tags alone is much more accurate than by website sentences, file structure, or image similarity alone (Rand indices of 0.107, 0.094, and 0.068, respectively). When combining these input attributes, however, we see further

Table 1 Adjusted Rand index for different clusterings, varying the number of input attributes considered (best-performing clusterings italicized)

Scam websites	Dynamic cut height		Optimized cut height	
	Test	Train	Test	Train
Fake escrow services				
Sentences	0.107	0.289	*0.982*	*0.924*
DOM tags	0.678	*0.648*	0.979	0.919
File names	0.094	0.235	0.972	0.869
Images	0.068	0.206	0.325	0.314
S and D	*0.942*	0.584	*0.982*	*0.925*
S and F	0.120	0.245	0.980	0.895
S and I	0.072	0.257	0.962	0.564
D and F	0.558	0.561	0.979	0.892
D and I	0.652	0.614	0.599	0.385
F and I	0.100	0.224	0.518	0.510
S and D and F	0.913	0.561	0.980	0.895
S and D and I	0.883	0.536	0.971	0.673
S and F and I	0.100	0.214	0.975	0.892
D and F and I	0.642	0.536	0.831	0.772
S and D and F and I	*0.941*	0.536	0.971	0.683
High-yield investment programs				
Sentences	*0.713*	*0.650*	*0.738*	*0.867*
DOM tags	0.381	0.399	0.512	0.580
File names	0.261	0.299	0.254	0.337
Images	0.289	0.354	0.434	0.471
S and D	0.393	0.369	0.600	0.671
S and F	0.291	0.310	0.266	0.344
S and I	0.290	0.362	0.437	0.471
D and F	0.309	0.358	0.314	0.326
D and I	0.302	0.340	0.456	0.510
F and I	0.296	0.289	0.397	0.336
S and D and F	0.333	0.362	0.319	0.326
S and D and I	0.319	0.350	0.459	0.510
S and F and I	0.303	0.289	0.398	0.336
D and F and I	0.320	0.337	0.404	0.405
S and D and F and I	0.320	0.337	0.404	0.405

improvement. Clustering based on taking the minimum distance between websites according to HTML tags and sentences yield a Rand index of 0.942, while taking the minimum of all input attributes yields an adjusted Rand index of 0.941. Both combined scores far exceed the Rand indices for any of the other individual input attributes using a dynamically determined cut height.

Results on the test population, for fake escrow services, show that using the dynamic cut height method may not always produce consistent performance results. While the combined matrices achieve the highest Rand index during training, individual HTML tags outperformed all other input attributes by a large margin at 0.648 in the test population.

The optimized cut height algorithm, however, consistently demonstrates a more stable performance selecting the individual sentences matrix and the combined sentences and HTML tags matrix as the top performers in both the training and test populations.

Because cybercriminals act differently when creating logical copies of website for different types of scams, the input attributes that are most similar can change. For example, for HYIPs, we can see that clustering by website sentences yields the most accurate individual Rand index, instead of HTML tags as is the case for fake escrow services. We can also see that for some scams, combining input attributes does not yield a more accurate clustering. Clustering based on the minimum distance of all four attributes yields a Rand index of 0.405 on the optimized cut height's test population, far worse than clustering based on website sentences alone. This underscores the importance of evaluating the individual distance scores against the combined scores, since in some circumstances an individual input attribute or a combination of a subset of the attributes may fare better.

However, it is important to point out that the optimized cut height algorithm appears to more consistently select top performing input matrices and higher Rand index scores on all of the data we benchmarked against. Rand index scores dropped in both the fake escrow services and HYIP test datasets using a dynamically determined cut height (0.294 and 0.63, respectively). When using optimized combined clustering, however, this decrease was smaller in the fake escrow services test population at 0.057 while test results for the HYIP data actually improved from 0.738 to 0.867 for an increase of 0.129% or 12.9%.

We used several general-purpose consensus-clustering methods from R Clue package [24] as benchmarks against the our 'best min optimized-cut height' approach:

1. *'SE'* - implements 'a fixed-point algorithm for obtaining soft least squares Euclidean consensus partitions' by minimizing using Euclidean dissimilarity [19,24].

2. *'DWH'* - uses an extension of the greedy algorithm to implement soft least squares Euclidean consensus partitions [19,24].
3. *'GV3'* - utilizes a sequential unconstrained minimization technique (SUMT) algorithm which is equivalent to finding the membership matrix m for which the sum of the squared differences between $C(m) = mm'$ and the weighted average co-membership matrix $\sum_b w_b C(_m b)$ of the partitions is minimal [20,24].
4. *'soft/symdiff'* - given a maximal number of classes, uses an SUMT approach to minimize using Manhattan dissimilarity of the co-membership matrices coinciding with symdiff partition dissimilarity in the case of hard partitions [21,24].

Table 2 summarizes the best performing measures for the different combined- and consensus-clustering approaches. We can see that our 'best min optimized cut height' approach performs best. It yields more accurate results than other general-purpose consensus-clustering methods, as well as the custom clustering method used to group spam-advertised websites by the authors of [6].

7   Examining the clustered criminal websites
We now apply the dynamic cut-height clustering methods presented earlier to the entire fake escrow (considering sentences, DOM tags, and file structure) and HYIP datasets (considering sentences alone). The 4,191 HYIP websites formed 864 clusters of at least size two, plus an additional 530 singletons. The 1,216 fake escrow websites observed between January and June 2013 formed 161 clusters of at least size two, plus seven singletons.

7.1   Evaluating cluster size
We first study the distribution of cluster size in the two datasets. Figure 4(left panel) plots a CDF of the cluster

Table 2 The best performing measures for the different combined and consensus-clustering approaches (clusterings chosen by the method are italicized)

	Escrow	HYIPs
Minimum	0.683	0.405
Average	0.075	0.443
Max	0.080	0.623
Best min.	*0.985*	*0.867*
DISTATIS	0.070	0.563
Clue SE	0.128	0.245
Clue DWH	0.126	0.472
Clue GV3	0.562	0.508
Clue soft/symdiff	0.095	0.401
Click trajectories [6]	0.022	0.038

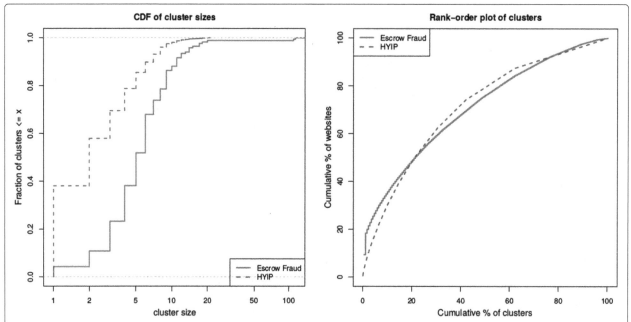

Figure 4 Evaluating the distribution of cluster size in the escrow fraud and HYIP datasets. Cumulative distribution function of cluster size (left panel). Rank order plot of cluster sizes (right panel).

size (note the logarithmic scale on the x-axis). We can see from the blue dashed line that the HYIPs tend to have smaller clusters. In addition to the 530 singletons (40% of the total clusters), 662 clusters (47% of the total) include between two and five websites. One hundred seventy-five clusters (13%) are sized between six and ten websites, with 27 clusters including more than ten websites. The biggest cluster included 20 HYIP websites. These results indicate that duplication in HYIPs, while frequent, does not occur on the same scale as many other forms of cybercrime.

There is more overt copying in the fake escrow dataset. Only seven of the 1,216 escrow websites could not be clustered with another website. Eighty clusters (28% of the total) include between two and five websites, but another 79 clusters are sized between six and 20. Furthermore, two large clusters (including 113 and 109 websites, respectively) can be found. We conclude that duplication is used more often as a criminal tactic in the fake escrow websites than for the HYIPs.

Another way to look at the distribution of cluster sizes is to examine the rank-order plot in Figure 4(right panel). Again, we can observe differences in the structure of the two datasets. Rank-order plots sort the clusters by size and show the percentages of websites that are covered by the smallest number of clusters. For instance, we can see from the red solid line the effect of the two large clusters in the fake escrow dataset. These two clusters account for nearly 20% of the total fake escrow websites. After that, the next biggest clusters make a much smaller contribution in identifying more websites. Nonetheless, the incremental

contributions of the HYIP clusters (shown in the dashed blue line) are also quite small. This relative dispersion of clusters differs from the concentration found in other cybercrime datasets where there is large-scale replication of content.

7.2 Evaluating cluster persistence
We now study how frequently the replicated criminal websites are re-used over time. One strategy available to criminals is to create multiple copies of the website in parallel, thereby reaching more victims more quickly. The alternative is to re-use copies in a serial fashion, introducing new copies only after time has passed or the prior instances have collapsed. We investigate both datasets to empirically answer the question of which strategy is preferred.

Figure 5 groups the ten largest clusters from the fake escrow dataset and plots the date at which each website in the cluster first appears. We can see that for the two largest clusters there are spikes where multiple website copies are spawned on the same day. For the smaller clusters, however, we see that websites are introduced sequentially. Moreover, for all of the biggest clusters, new copies are introduced throughout the observation period. From this, we can conclude that criminals are likely to use the same template repeatedly until stopped.

Next, we examine the observed persistence of the clusters. We define the 'lifetime' of a cluster as the difference in days between the first and the last appearance of a website

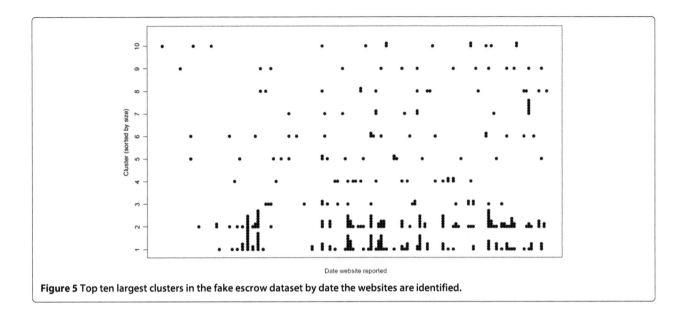

Figure 5 Top ten largest clusters in the fake escrow dataset by date the websites are identified.

in the cluster. For instance, the first reported website in one cluster of 18 fake escrow websites appeared on 2 February 2013, while the last one occurred on 7 May 2013. Hence, the lifetime of the cluster is 92 days. Longer-lived clusters indicate that cybercriminals can create website copies for long periods of time with impunity.

We use a survival probability plot to examine the distribution of cluster lifetimes. A survival function $S(t)$ measures the probability that a cluster's lifetime is greater than time t. Survival analysis takes into account 'censored' data points, i.e., when the final website in the cluster is reported near the end of the study. We deem any cluster with a website reported within 14 days of the end of data collection to be censored. We use the Kaplan-Meier estimator [25] to calculate a survival function.

Figure 6 gives the survival plots for both datasets (solid lines indicate the survival probability, while dashed lines indicate 95% confidence intervals). In the left graph, we can see that around 75% of fake escrow clusters persist for at least 60 days, and that the median lifetime is 90 days. Note that around 25% of the clusters remained active at the end of the 150-day measurement period, so we cannot reason about how long these most persistent clusters will remain.

Because we tracked HYIPs for a much longer period (Figure 6 (right)), nearly all clusters eventually ceased to be replicated. Consequently, the survival probability for even long-lived clusters can be evaluated. Twenty percent of the HYIP clusters persist for more than 500 days, while 25% do not last longer than 100 days. The median lifetime of HYIP clusters is around 250 days. The relatively long persistence of many HYIP clusters should give law enforcement some encouragement: because the

criminals reuse content over long periods, tracking them down becomes a more realistic proposition.

8 Related work

A number of researchers have applied machine learning methods to cluster websites created by cybercriminals. Wardman et al. examined the file structure and content of suspected phishing web pages to automatically classify reported URLs as phishing [7]. Layton et al. cluster phishing web pages together using a combination of k-means and agglomerative clustering [8].

Several researchers have classified and clustered web spam pages. Urvoy et al. use HTML structure to classify web pages, and they develop a clustering method using locality-sensitive hashing to cluster similar spam pages together [26]. Lin uses HTML tag multisets to classify cloaked web pages [27]. Lin's technique is used by Wang et al. [28] to detect when the cached HTML is very different from what is presented to the user. Finally, Anderson et al. use image shingling to cluster screenshots of websites advertised in email spam [5]. Similarly, Levchenko et al. use a custom clustering heuristic method to group similar spam-advertised web pages [6]. We implemented and evaluated this clustering method on the cybercrime datasets in Section 6. Der et al. clustered storefronts selling counterfeit goods by the affiliate structure driving traffic to different stores [29]. Finally, Leontiadis et al. group similar unlicensed online pharmacy inventories [22]. They did not attempt to evaluate against ground truth; instead they used the Jaccard distance and agglomerative clustering to find suitable clusters.

Neisius and Clayton also studied high-yield investment programs [13]. Notably, they estimated that a majority

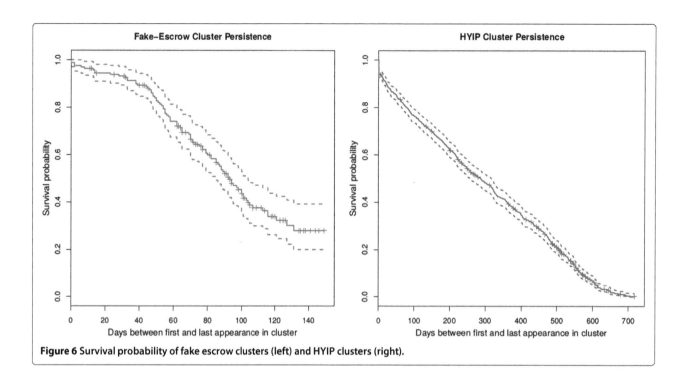

Figure 6 Survival probability of fake escrow clusters (left) and HYIP clusters (right).

of HYIP websites used templates licensed from a company called 'Goldcoders'. While we did observe some Goldcoder templates in our own datasets, we did not find them occurring at the same frequency. Furthermore, our clustering method tended to link HYIP websites more by the rendered text on the page rather than the website file structure.

Separate to the work on cybercriminal datasets, other researchers have proposed consensus clustering methods for different applications. DISTATIS is an adaptation of the STATIS methodology specifically used for the purpose of integrating distance matrices for different input attributes [30]. DISTATIS can be considered a three-way extension of metric multidimensional scaling [31], which transforms a collection of distance matrices into cross-product matrices used in the cross-product approach to STATIS. Consensus can be performed between two or more distance matrices by using DISTATIS and then converting the cross-product matrix output into into a (squared) Euclidean distance matrix which is the inverse transformation of metric multidimensional scaling [32].

Our work follows in the line of both of the above research thrusts. It differs in that it considers multiple attributes that an attacker may change (site content, HTML structure, and file structure), even when she may not modify all attributes. It is also tolerant of greater changes by the cybercriminal than previous approaches. At the same time, though, it is more specific than general

consensus clustering methods, which enables the method to achieve higher accuracy in cluster labelings.

9 Conclusions

When designing scams, cybercriminals face trade-offs between scale and victim susceptibility and between scale and evasiveness from law enforcement. Large-scale scams cast a wider net, but this comes at the expense of lower victim yield and faster defender response. Highly targeted attacks are much more likely to work, but they are more expensive to craft. Some frauds lie in the middle, where the criminals replicate scams but not without taking care to give the appearance that each attack is distinct.

In this paper, we propose and evaluate a combined-clustering method to automatically link together such semi-automated scams. We have shown it to be more accurate than general-purpose consensus-clustering approaches, as well as approaches designed for large-scale scams such as phishing that use more extensive copying of content. In particular, we applied the method to two classes of scams: HYIPs and fake escrow websites.

The method could prove valuable to law enforcement, as it helps tackle cybercrimes that individually are too minor to investigate but collectively may cross a threshold of significance. For instance, our method identifies two distinct clusters of more than 100 fake escrow websites each. Furthermore, our method could substantially reduce the workload for investigators as they prioritize which criminals to investigate.

Competing interests
The authors declare that they have no competing interests.

Acknowledgements
We would like to thank the operators of `escrow-fraud.com` and `aa419.org` for allowing us to use their lists of fake escrow websites. This work was partially funded by the Department of Homeland Security (DHS) Science and Technology Directorate, Cyber Security Division (DHS S&T/CSD) Broad Agency Announcement 11.02, the Government of Australia, and the SPAWAR Systems Center Pacific via contract number N66001-13-C-0131. This paper represents the position of the authors and not that of the aforementioned agencies.

References

1. T Moore, R Clayton, in *Second APWG eCrime Researchers Summit. eCrime '07*. Examining the impact of website take-down on phishing (ACM Pittsburgh, 2007)
2. D Florencio, C Herley, in *Second APWG eCrime Researchers Summit. eCrime '07*. Evaluating a trial deployment of password re-use for phishing prevention (ACM New York, 2007), pp. 26–36. doi:10.1145/1299015.1299018. http://doi.acm.org/10.1145/1299015.1299018
3. C Kanich, C Kreibich, K Levchenko, B Enright, G Voelker, V Paxson, S Savage, in *Conference on Computer and Communications Security (CCS)*. Spamalytics: an empirical analysis of spam marketing conversion (Alexandria, VA, 2008)
4. N Provos, P Mavrommatis, M Rajab, F Monrose, in *17th USENIX Security Symposium*. All your iFrames point to us, (2008)
5. DS Anderson, C Fleizach, S Savage, GM Voelker, in *Proceedings of 16th USENIX Security Symposium*. Spamscatter: Characterizing Internet scam hosting infrastructure (USENIX Association Berkeley, 2007), pp. 10–11014. http://dl.acm.org/citation.cfm?id=1362903.1362913
6. K Levchenko, A Pitsillidis, N Chachra, B Enright, M Félegyházi, C Grier, T Halvorson, C Kanich, C Kreibich, H Liu, D McCoy, N Weaver, V Paxson, GM Voelker, S Savage, in *Proceedings of the 2011 IEEE Symposium on Security and Privacy. SP '11*. Click trajectories: end-to-end analysis of the spam value chain (IEEE Computer Society Washington, DC, 2011), pp. 431–446. doi:10.1109/SP.2011.24. http://dx.doi.org/10.1109/SP.2011.24
7. B Wardman, G Warner, in *eCrime Researchers Summit, 2008*. Automating phishing website identification through deep MD5 matching (IEEE, 2008), pp. 1–7
8. R Layton, P Watters, R Dazeley, in *eCrime Researchers Summit (eCrime), 2010*. Automatically determining phishing campaigns using the uscap methodology, (2010), pp. 1–8. doi:10.1109/ecrime.2010.5706698
9. T Moore, R Clayton, *The Impact of Incentives on Notice and Take-down*. (ME Johnson, ed.) (Springer, 2008), pp. 199–223
10. T Moore, J Han, R Clayton, in *Financial Cryptography*. Lecture Notes in Computer Science, vol. 7397, ed. by Keromytis A D. The postmodern Ponzi scheme: Empirical analysis of high-yield investment programs (Springer, 2012), pp. 41–56. http://lyle.smu.edu/~tylerm/fc12.pdf
11. R Dingledine, N Mathewson, P Syverson, in *13th USENIX Security Symposium*. Tor: The second-generation onion router, (2004)
12. WatiN: Web application Testing in.Net. http://www.watin.org Accessed October 16, 2014
13. J Neisius, R Clayton, in *APWG Symposium on Electronic Crime Research*. Orchestrated crime: the high yield investment fraud ecosystem, (2014)
14. HQ Selenium. http://www.seleniumhq.org/ Accessed October 16, 2014
15. Similar images finder - NET Image processing in C# and RGB projections. https://similarimagesfinder.codeplex.com/ Accessed October 16, 2014
16. SC Johnson, Hierarchical clustering schemes. Psychometrika. **32**(3), 241–254 (1967)
17. P Langfelder, B Zhang, S Horvath, Defining clusters from a hierarchical cluster tree. Bioinformatics. **24**(5), 719–720 (2008). doi:10.1093/bioinformatics/btm563
18. H Abdi, AJ O'Toole, D Valentin, B Edelman, in *Computer Vision and Pattern Recognition - Workshops, 2005. CVPR Workshops. IEEE Computer Society Conference On*. Distatis: The analysis of multiple distance matrices, (2005), pp. 42–42. doi:10.1109/CVPR.2005.445
19. E Dimitriadou, A Weingessel, K Hornik, A combination scheme for fuzzy clustering. Int. J. Pattern Recogn. Artif. Intell. **16**(07), 901–912 (2002). doi:10.1142/S0218001402002052. http://www.worldscientific.com/doi/pdf/10.1142/S0218001402002052
20. AD Gordon, M Vichi, Fuzzy partition models for fitting a set of partitions. Psychometrika. **66**(2), 229–247 (2001). doi:10.1007/BF02294837
21. AV Fiacco, GP McCormick, *Nonlinear Programming: Sequential Unconstrained Minimization Techniques*, vol. 4, (Siam, 1990)
22. N Leontiadis, T Moore, N Christin, in *Proceedings of the Fourteenth ACM Conference on Electronic Commerce*. Pick your poison: pricing and inventories at unlicensed online pharmacies (ACM, 2013), pp. 621–638
23. WM Rand, Objective criteria for the evaluation of clustering methods. J. Am. Stat. Assoc. **66**(336), 846–850 (1971). doi:10.1080/01.621459.1971.10482356
24. K Hornik, A CLUE for CLUster ensembles. Journal of Statistical Software. **14**, 65–72 (2005)
25. EL Kaplan, P Meier, Nonparametric estimation from incomplete observations. J. Am. Stat. Assoc. **53**, 457–481 (1958)
26. T Urvoy, E Chauveau, P Filoche, T Lavergne, Tracking web spam with html style similarities. ACM Trans. Web. **2**(1), 3–1328 (2008). doi:10.1145/1326561.1326564
27. J-L Lin, Detection of cloaked web spam by using tag-based methods. Expert Syst. Appl. **36**(4), 7493–7499 (2009). doi:10.1016/j.eswa.2008.09.056. Available at, http://dx.doi.org/10.1016/j.eswa.2008.09.056
28. DY Wang, S Savage, GM Voelker, in *Proceedings of the 18th ACM Conference on Computer and Communications Security. CCS '11*. Cloak and dagger: dynamics of web search cloaking (ACM New York, 2011), pp. 477–490. doi:10.1145/2046707.2046763. Available at http://doi.acm.org/10.1145/2046707.2046763
29. MF Der, LK Saul, S Savage, Voelker G M, in *ACM SIGKDD Conference on Knowledge Discovery and Data Mining*. Knock it off: profiling the online storefronts of counterfeit merchandise (ACM, 2014)
30. H Abdi, LJ Williams, D Valentin, M Bennani-Dosse, Statis and distatis: optimum multitable principal component analysis and three way metric multidimensional scaling. Wiley Interdiscip. Rev.: Comput. Stat. **4**(2), 124–167 (2012). doi:10.1002/wics.198
31. S Krolak-Schwerdt, in *Data Analysis and Decision Support*. Studies in Classification, Data Analysis, and Knowledge Organization, ed. by D Baier, R Decker, and L Schmidt-Thieme. Three-way multidimensional scaling: formal properties and relationships between scaling methods (Springer, 2005), p. 82–90. doi:10.1007/3-540-28397-8_10. http://dx.doi.org/10.1007/3-540-28397-8_10
32. H Abdi, ed. by NJ Salkind. Encyclopedia of Measurement and Statistics (SAGE Publications, Inc, 2007), p. 598–605. doi:10.4135/9781412952644. http://dx.doi.org/10.4135/9781412952644

Laribus: privacy-preserving detection of fake SSL certificates with a social P2P notary network

Karl-Peter Fuchs[*], Dominik Herrmann, Andrea Micheloni and Hannes Federrath

Abstract

In this paper we present Laribus, a peer-to-peer network designed to detect local man-in-the-middle attacks against secure socket layer/transport layer security (SSL/TLS). With Laribus, clients can validate the authenticity of a certificate presented to them by retrieving it from different vantage points on the network. Unlike previous solutions, clients do not have to trust a central notary service nor do they have to rely on the cooperation of website owners. The Laribus network is based on a social network graph, which allows users to form notary groups that improve both privacy and availability. It integrates several well-known techniques, such as secret sharing, ring signatures, layered encryption, range queries, and a distributed hash table (DHT), to achieve privacy-aware queries, scalability, and decentralization. We present the design and core components of Laribus, discuss its security properties, and also provide results from a simulation-based feasibility study.

Keywords: Privacy; Anonymity; Man-in-the-middle attacks; SSL; P2P

1 Introduction

The Secure Sockets Layer (SSL) and Transport Layer Security (TLS) protocol suite [1,2] provides basic security mechanisms such as confidentiality, data integrity, and especially authentication (cf. [3] for a detailed treatment of SSL and its successor TLS). There have been various attempts to attack these protocols, i. e., to eavesdrop on a connection. Attacks on the security of SSL can be categorized into two classes: attacks from the first category exploit security flaws in the protocols, weaknesses in the construction of the cryptographic primitives used or implementation errors (e. g., the BEAST [4], CRIME, BREACH [5], and *Lucky Thirteen* [6] attacks; cf. [7,8] for a comprehensive overview). The second category of attacks, which we are interested in, attacks weaknesses in the *authentication model*.

SSL relies on a X.509 PKI [9] for the purpose of *authenticating* a remote entity's key. This protects clients from disclosing data to adversaries that impersonate a designated destination. Authentication is delegated to certification authorities (CAs) that issue certificates by cryptographically signing the public key of website owners, guaranteeing the authenticity of the association ⟨*public key, website*⟩ or, in some cases, ⟨*public key, website, organization*⟩.

In a 2010 study, the Electronic Frontier Foundation found that browsers from Microsoft and Mozilla are (in-)directly trusting more than 650 CAs [10]. Unfortunately, the X.509 model allows *any* CA to certify *any* domain [11]. It only takes a single CA to misbehave (by being hacked, tricked, bribed, or legally forced) to generate a seemingly valid *fake certificate*. Having obtained a fake certificate, an adversary can mount a man-in-the-middle (MitM) attack impersonating any website of his choice. The MitM attack goes undetected because the fake certificate contains a genuine signature and thus appears legitimate. MitM attacks typically affect only users in a confined part of the Internet (cf. Figure 1). The severity of this risk is demonstrated by security incidents involving the two CAs Comodo and DigiNotar. The attackers created fake certificates for high-profile sites (among them Google and Paypal) to intercept the SSL traffic of Internet users in Iran [12]. Solely relying on CAs for authenticating remote servers has shown to be fragile and insecure.

*Correspondence: fuchs@informatik.uni-hamburg.de
Department of Informatics, University of Hamburg, Vogt-Kölln-Str. 30, 22527 Hamburg, Germany

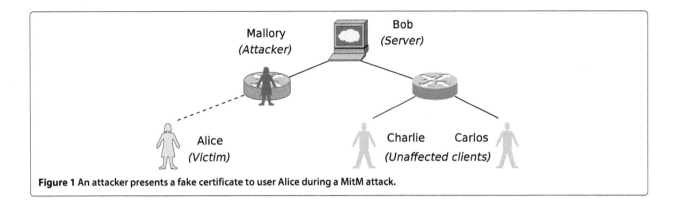

Figure 1 An attacker presents a fake certificate to user Alice during a MitM attack.

Previous proposals aim to fix the CA-based authentication approach either by relying on other hierarchical structures (e. g., the DNS tree) or by introducing *notary servers* that validate certificates on the user's behalf. Both approaches are subject to considerable limitations (cf. Section 2). In contrast, with *Laribus* (referring to guardian deities in ancient Roman religion), we propose that web clients should *collaborate* to validate certificates in a distributed manner. Our *contribution* consists of integrating well-known techniques to organize the clients in *a fully distributed peer-to-peer (P2P) network* that meets security, privacy, and availability expectations of web clients. Laribus provides users with the ability to *model trust relationships that reflect their social relationships*, i. e., users can choose to trust their *friends*, and not unknown organizations, with certificate validation. The P2P architecture of Laribus improves *scalability* and provides *blocking-resistance*. *Privacy-preserving query techniques* protect the user's surfing behavior. A distributed storage mechanism offers *resilience to client churn* and increased performance via *caching*. This paper extends our previously published work in [13], providing a more comprehensive survey of related efforts that aim to improve the security of certificate validation as well as a more detailed description of the privacy-preserving mechanisms of Laribus.

The rest of this paper is structured as follows. In Section 2, we review related work and motivate our design choices. We outline the architecture of Laribus in Section 3 and focus on the details of the cryptographic mechanisms involved in Section 4. We present results of an initial feasibility study in Section 5 and discuss limitations in Section 6. We conclude in Section 7.

2 Related work

The issues with SSL and the CA trust model have been known for years, and various proposals have appeared in the literature, suggesting to replace, amend, or complement the current system. Laribus is a combination and extension of techniques selected from the current state

of the art. It does not replace the existing PKI infrastructure but serves as an additional source of trust during certificate validation.

This section provides an overview of the most important research directions, outlining their benefits and limitations. A comprehensive discussion of previous work can be found in [14,15].

In Sections 2.1 and 2.2, we describe approaches that advocate to restrict the domains a CA may issue certificates for. In Section 2.3, we describe the *trust on first use* model. We proceed with proposals that rely on out-of-band information for certificate validation in Section 2.4. Another avenue of research focuses on the application of append-only data structures (cf. Section 2.5). Finally, in Section 2.6, we discuss existing work that relies on *notaries* that provide clients with a third-party perspective of a certificate.

2.1 Limiting the scope of CAs

One of the main limitations of the X.509 PKI is the fact that any CA can issue a certificate for any domain name. The large number of CAs that are trusted by default by common browsers constitutes a significant attack surface. In order to decrease the risk, CAs could be *restricted to specific top-level domains*. Karsten et al. [16] show that in practice most CAs provide online certificates for a small number of top-level domains and that the domains in most top-level domains use certificates from a small set of CAs only. Moreover, some CAs appear to operate for a single organization in a single country only. Browser vendors could incorporate this kind of information into their software in order to warn the user when a certificate for a domain is issued from a CA that has not issued certificates for the corresponding top-level domain so far.

Recent findings from Perl et al. indicate that the number of trusted CAs could be reduced considerably: based on scans of all publicly reachable web servers listening on port 443, they observed that 34% of the trusted CAs have not issued a single certificate yet [17]. They suggest to *remove the root certificates* of these CAs from the browser trust stores. However, this approach may have undesirable consequences for closed user groups that use non-public HTTPS sites that use a certificate of one of the deleted CAs. These users will see a warning message when they access their secure sites, which weakens the effectiveness of such warnings [18].

These two measures, limiting the scope of CAs as well as removing unnecessary certificates from the browser trust store, may help to decrease the likelihood of an adversary obtaining a fake certificate in practice. However, they cannot prevent MitM attacks reliably and have not been integrated into Laribus. Laribus is supposed to be a complementary certificate validation service that provides an additional layer of security. Therefore, it should be oblivious of the trust relationships within the existing PKI trust model.

2.2   Certificate pinning

A complementary solution to limiting the scope of CAs (i. e., limiting the domain names for which a CA may issue certificates) is *certificate pinning*, which approaches the problem from the perspective of domain name owners. Certificate pinning allows them to limit the CAs that are authorized to issue a certificate for a given domain.

Certificate pinning has been introduced by Google in its Chrome browser for a small set of Google domain names. As a predefined whitelist embedded in the browser software scales rather poorly, there are several ongoing efforts that try to provide operators of web servers with a means to publish certificate pins, either via HTTP headers [19] or via TLS extensions [20]. As these proposals require changes to the server as well as the client software, it will take time until they are widely adopted.

Domain name system (DNS)-based Authentication of Named Entities (DANE) [21] is an IETF standard that proposes to utilize the DNS infrastructure to store the pinning information. The operator of a web server can include DANE resource records for his domain that indicate the CAs that have issued its certificates or the fingerprint of the certificate itself.

DANE relies on an existing decentralized hierarchy, the DNS namespace, to authenticate website certificates. The security of this approach depends on the integrity of the data supplied via DNS, i. e., DNSSEC [22] is a mandatory prerequisite in DANE. As pointed out in [23], DANE would significantly reduce the risk of an MitM attack remaining undetected, since an adversary would have to compromise both, a CA and the respective authoritative DNS server. However, leveraging DNS has some limitations in practice: Firstly, only few DNS servers make use of DNSSEC so far and its widespread deployment has proven to be challenging [24]. Moreover, DANE requires changes to the resolver library on client machines as well as adoption by server operators. Finally, parts of the DNS

hierarchy are connected to the X.509 PKI infrastructure: A prominent example is Verisign itself, which maintains a certificate authority providing hundreds of thousands of SSL certificates [25]. At the same time, Verisign acts as a DNS registry for several top-level domains, among them .com and .net, which makes it a particularly weak spot.

DNS Certification Authority Authorization (CAA) [26] is a complementary proposal. CAA allows a server operator to include DNS records in a domain that specify the CAs that are allowed to issue certificates for that domain. CAA-compliant CAs are required to look up the respective CAA records and issue a certificate for the domain only if the CAA records indicate that they are authorized to proceed. A conceptual limitation of the CAA concept is that it assumes that all trusted CAs are implementing this policy. However, CAA cannot prevent an adversary that has gained access of the signing key of a CA from issuing fake certificates.

Certificate pinning may be an effective measure to detect MitM attacks. However, the aforementioned proposals may scale quite poorly: They have to be implemented by the administrators of each and every website (or CA). In contrast, one of the central design goals for Laribus consists in providing a *client-only solution* that enables clients to validate the certificate of any website without involving its operator.

2.3   Trust on first use

Advocates of the *trust on first use method (TOFU)* reject the idea of having to rely on a third-party-issuing certificates that have to be renewed periodically. Instead users are supposed to make a leap of faith, trusting and pinning the certificate that has been presented by a remote host during the very first connection attempt. This approach is familiar from its use in SSH and it also has been proposed for encrypted e-mails [27]. The application of the TOFU approach for SSL certificate validation has been proposed in [28]. An implementation of the concept is the certificate patrol browser extension [29].

However, certificate renewal is handled poorly in the TOFU trust model. It may be difficult for users to distinguish between the case of a certificate having been changed deliberately and legitimately by the operator of a remote host and the case of an MITM attack. Therefore, Laribus does not rely on the TOFU principle.

2.4   Incorporating out-of-band information

The following approaches try to establish secure connections without a set of fixed, potentially untrusted third parties.

Direct Validation of Certificates (DVCert) [30] allows a client to validate the authenticity of a server certificate without having to rely on third parties at all. DVCert leverages the fact that many websites can be personalized, i.e., users have to log in with application-level credentials (username and password). In DVcert, the fact that client and server know the user's credentials is exploited by the web server to prove to a connecting client that it is in fact talking to the desired web server and not to a man-in-the-middle.

However, first-time users that do not have an account at a web site yet cannot benefit from DVCert during registration. Moreover, DVCert is not suitable to secure sites that are available without any authentication at all. Finally, as with certificate pinning, DVCert has to be implemented in each and every website, which conflicts with our design goal to build a system that does not rely on any cooperation on the server side.

MonkeySphere [31] builds upon the PGP Web of Trust (WoT) concepts of a network of people who trust other people: Users who never met before can safely authenticate their identities due to the presence of a trust path in the network between them, established by friends who trust their friends, respectively. Whenever the MonkeySphere daemon encounters a self-signed or invalid certificate, it searches public key servers for a PGP key associated with that website's name. The certificate is trusted only if the daemon can construct a trust path from the user's key to the server's key. This approach could effectively abolish the need for CAs and allow users to trust self-signed certificates, also providing a theoretically sound way of trusting remote certificates and detecting MitM attacks.

However, MonkeySphere relies on the cooperation of the administrators of the webservers, which conflicts with our design goals: Clients can only validate the certificates of those servers, whose administrators have signed their certificates and uploaded them to a key server. Moreover, administrators have to ensure that their certificates are extensively connected with other users within the PGP Web of Trust to ensure that as many users as possible will be able to find a trust path to the server.

Strictly relying on trust paths between users and target servers may lead to bootstrapping issues: Users will only be able to validate server certificates with high probability, if PGP and MonkeySphere are widely adopted and all users actively contribute to the Web of Trust. However, so far, PGP suffers from poor adoption due to usability issues resulting from its intrinsic complexity.

In contrast, Laribus users can validate the certificate of any server at any time, even when the server is completely oblivious of Laribus. Moreover, bootstrapping Laribus may be easier because users do not have to establish trust paths from them to individual destination servers. In Laribus certificate validation is possible even if only a few small user groups (cliques based on real-world social relationships) participate in the system.

2.5 Append-only timelines

The following proposals advocate a publicly available log file containing all certificate transactions.

Sovereign keys [32] proposes to maintain a verifiable append-only data structure, which contains the history of all SSL-enabled domains. Server operators are supposed to push their authentication data (newly deployed certificates as well as blacklisted old certificates) to one of 20 redundant *Timeline Servers*. Clients interact with them to validate previously unseen certificates. The basic concept has been extended by the proposals *Certificate Transparency* [33] and *Transparent Key Integrity* [34].

Append-only data structure could indeed be the definitive answer to the trust problems in SSL, since attackers would have to publicly insert fake certificates into the data structure to be successful. However, append-only timelines have to be provided via a set of dedicated servers, they require the cooperation of web server administrators or CAs, and querying timeline servers may infringe the privacy of users, who provide the domain names they want to validate. Therefore, Laribus does not contain a permanent global timeline. Instead Laribus incorporates a distributed cache that contains recently validated certificates to improve its performance and availability.

2.6 Relying on notaries and peers

The following proposals advocate to validate certificates by relying on dedicated notary servers or on peers.

Perspectives [35] and its follow-up *Convergence* [36] employ a set of network servers (so-called notary servers) that fetch and store SSL certificates from Internet hosts. In order to validate a server certificate, users connect to one or more of the notary servers and ask them for the certificates they see from their vantage point. An attacker close to the client could then be easily detected by comparing the certificates provided by the notaries with the certificate the client received from the server (cf. Figure 2).

The notary model is based on the assumption that an attacker cannot interfere with both the connection of the users as well as the connection of (all the) queried network notaries. In the original design of Perspectives and Convergence, notaries are full-blown dedicated servers, which have to be maintained by their operators to be always up and running. As a result, there is only a limited number of them, i.e., more powerful man-in-the-middle adversaries may be able to attack a user as well as all queried notaries. In order to reduce the risk of such attacks, notaries can be spread over multiple autonomous systems (AS) as proposed in [37].

Moreover, users must put considerable trust into notaries. From a security perspective, users have to trust them not to lie (or collaborate with an adversary). From a privacy perspective, notaries have to be trusted to operate responsibly. Without any additional means, they learn all

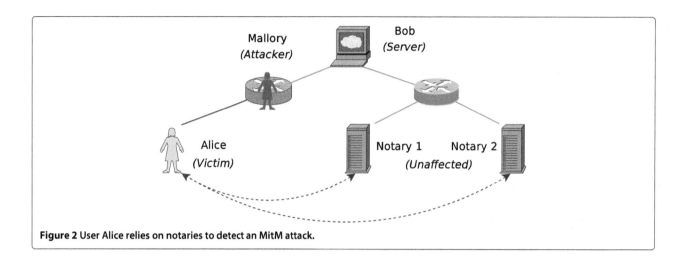

Figure 2 User Alice relies on notaries to detect an MitM attack.

of a user's visited SSL domains. Privacy can be increased by forwarding queries to notaries via the Tor network [38], which requires additional software on clients, though.

These privacy concerns are embraced by *DoubleCheck* [39], which suggests that whenever a client connects to a SSL web server it should retrieve its certificate additionally via the Tor network for comparison. An extension of this design is *DetecTor* [40], which suggests to retrieve each certificate over multiple Tor circuits using different exit nodes for increased trust. It also provides a prototypical implementation. However, using the Tor network for certificate validation may be problematic as users have to trust exit nodes, whose trustworthiness has proven to be questionable in the past [41,42].

While the *ICSI Notary* service [43] is similar in spirit to Perspectives and Convergence, it differs in two important aspects. Firstly, while other approaches either actively scan the Internet [10,44] to obtain certificates or request them from servers upon request, the ICSI Notary collects certificates *passively* by monitoring upstream traffic of various Internet sites. Secondly, the ICSI Notary service can be queried via DNS, which helps to protect the privacy of its users: The notary servers do not see the IP address of a client but only the IP address of their recursive name server. The authors suggest to use a third-party DNS resolver, such as Google Public DNS (8.8.8.8) so that no information about the location of a user is leaked to the notary. While this suggestion succeeds in providing sender anonymity against the notary service, it does not protect the privacy against the *recursive name server*, which can eavesdrop on the users' queries and thus learn which certificates a user wants to validate.

The concept of notaries has also been used in application areas other than SSL certificate validation. We are aware of notary- and peer-based proposals for HTTP queries as well as DNS queries. *Senser* [37] proposes to retrieve websites over multiple proxies in order to validate

that the content is not tampered with. However, the concept does not account for privacy, i. e., the selected proxies can observe the IP addresses of the clients as well as the URLs and the content of the websites a user visits. Regarding DNS queries, *DepenDNS* [45] suggests that DNS clients should send their lookup queries to multiple resolvers in order to detect cache poisoning attacks. DepenDNS is based on the cooperative name lookup systems CoDNS [46] and ConfiDNS [47], which advocate that DNS clients should send queries to each other in order to improve integrity, availability, and lookup performance. This peer-to-peer approach is embraced by *DoX* [48], which suggests that DNS resolvers should form a peer-to-peer network to cross-check the responses they obtain. However, all the aforementioned proposals neglect the issue of user privacy. Moreover, they do not implement mechanisms that allow users to express to what degree they are willing to trust any given peer or notary server.

The design of Laribus is derived from the concept of notaries. However, as one of our design goals is to provide a scalable *fully-distributed solution that does not require fixed entities*, we cannot rely on a constrained set of dedicated notary servers. In contrast, in Laribus, multiple clients collaborate to provide notary services.

3 The Laribus proposal

In this section, we will present an overview of the architecture of Laribus and the interactions of the involved components. We will start out with a naïve approach for client-based certificate validation in order to explain the issues that must be overcome. After that, we will explain how the design of Laribus addresses these challenges.

3.1 Shortcomings of a naïve approach

Given the initial scenario in Figure 1, Alice could ask one of the unaffected users, e. g., Carlos, to retrieve the certificate for the server she wants to connect to (Bob). If

Alice receives different certificates from Carlos and Bob, she can detect the MitM attack.

This naïve approach, however, has several shortcomings. First of all, it does not meet users' *security* expectations. Alice wants to be sure that Carlos is neither cooperating with Mallory and therefore not telling her the truth (Problem 1: intentionally false testimonies), nor that Carlos is unknowingly also affected by Mallory's attack (Problem 2: unintentionally false testimonies). Alice can solve the first problem by asking only friends she trusts to validate certificates. The second problem can be solved by asking users that are dispersed throughout the world, e. g., friends living in different countries.

Secondly, the naïve approach does not meet users' *privacy* expectations. If Alice asks her friends to retrieve certificates on her behalf, her friends will know which servers she connects to. While it is a reasonable assumption that her friends will honestly answer requests for certificates, they must be considered to be *curious*; spying on an acquaintance may be more attractive than snooping on a stranger. Security and privacy seem to be conflicting goals in this respect. Solutions for this dilemma do however exist: Alice could ask a client she trusts, but she doesn't know personally, e. g., a client run by a university. Alternatively, she could use a suitable privacy-enhancing technique to hide her identity, e. g., Tor [38].

Thirdly, the naïve approach does not meet users' *availability* expectations. Alice cannot assume that a friend is online every time she wants to validate a certificate. Typically, Alice will also not be willing to wait until a friend comes online again. This availability issue can either be resolved by caching recently obtained validation results or by resorting to delegate certificate validation to less trustworthy clients.

Finally, certificate validation must be *scalable*. Asking one's friends to validate certificates scales well under three assumptions. Firstly, users that *consume* validation services, i. e., requesting other clients to perform certificate validation on their behalf, do also offer validation services to others, i. e., there is no *free-riding*. Secondly, friends trust each other *mutually*, i. e., they are willing to consume and offer validation services among themselves. Thirdly, the available resources offered by a group of friends are sufficient to handle the aggregate query volume issued by all of its members. However, in reality, it is difficult to force users to honor these assumptions. Therefore, a practical system should be able to cope with unbalanced trust relationships as well as uneven resources and loads.

3.2 Layered network structure

Laribus is a decentralized, distributed peer-to-peer system comprised of clients that collaborate for certificate validation. Each client offers validation on behalf of others and each client can request validation by other clients.

The Laribus P2P network is structured into multiple layers of abstraction (cf. Figure 3). Clients are requested to explicitly point out their friends from the real world, to limit the influence of adversaries. These social relationships are captured in the *social network layer*, a directed graph that reflects the *friendship relations* expressed by the clients. The set of close friends of a user (also referred to as his *clique*), makes up his *trusted core* in Laribus. The resulting friendship graph is typically not fully connected. In fact, some parts of the graph may be isolated from the rest, e. g., in case of cliques that do not point out any friends apart from members of their trusted core. We assume that adversaries will be unable to enter the trusted core, because this typically involves establishing a close social relationship with users in the *real world*.

Apart from pointing out their friends, clients organize themselves into *notary groups*. Group memberships are reflected in the *notary group layer*. Clients within a group collaboratively act as a notary. The members of a notary

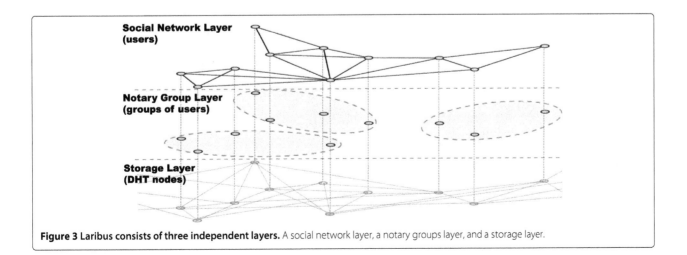

Figure 3 Laribus consists of three independent layers. A social network layer, a notary groups layer, and a storage layer.

group are not supposed to be *fully congruent* with the set of clients within a trusted core.

Finally, clients are expected to contribute resources for distributed storage of validation data. The *storage layer* consists of a global distributed hash table (DHT) based on Kademlia [49], in which Laribus stores all information regarding group memberships and trust relationships. Apart from providing decentralized storage, this layer serves as a cache to provide cheap access to the results obtained from previous certificate validations. Data stored in the DHT is cryptographically signed (cf. Section 4.4).

3.3   Interactions during certificate validation

Figure 4 extends the initial scenario by the components of Laribus. Alice connects to Bob's HTTPS website (Step A in Figure 4). We assume that Alice is subject to an MitM attack perpetrated by Mallory. Other Laribus users, such as members of notary groups 1, 2, and 3 are supposed to be unaffected by the MitM attack. Formally, Alice tries to connect to a server SRV and is presented with a fake certificate $cert_M$. Some unaffected clients are able to fetch the authentic certificate $cert_B$. In the following, we will only briefly sketch the relevant interactions. For conciseness, we will defer the treatment of the involved security and privacy techniques to Sections 3.5 and 3.7.

The straightforward way to validate certificates in Laribus is via the *direct queries* technique. A requestor,

Alice, sends a direct query to a notary group of her choice (Step B in Figure 4). She may choose a random group for this purpose, or a group containing one of her friends, asking members of the selected notary group to retrieve the certificate of SRV from their respective vantage points. The notary group exchanges the obtained certificates in order to reach a consensus about the certificate of SRV by means of a majority vote: The winning certificate is signed by the group's *notary signature* and returned to Alice (not shown). Alice validates the certificate presented to her by Bob by comparing it with the result obtained from the notary group.

Issuing direct queries for every certificate validation is inefficient. An alternative way for a client to validate certificates consists of retrieving certificates that have been obtained by other clients via direct queries with the *DHT Lookup* technique. Every time a notary group obtains a consensus about a server's certificate, it signs and stores it in the DHT (Step F in Figure 4, further discussed in Section 4.4). Instead of issuing a direct query, clients can look up both the unknown certificate's hash or hostname of SRV in the DHT (Step E). Summing up, in Laribus, a client performs the following steps to validate a certificate:

1. Alice performs a DHT lookup to determine whether $cert_M$ has been seen previously. If there are entries for $cert_M$, she retrieves them and (depending on how

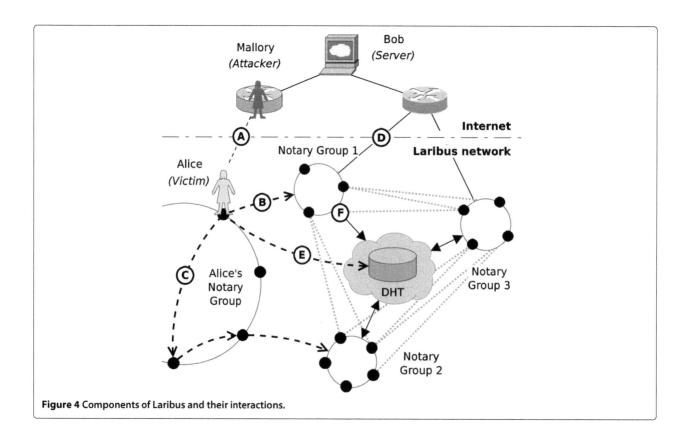

Figure 4 Components of Laribus and their interactions.

much she trusts the notary groups that stored the entries into the DHT) validates the certificate presented to her. If no trusted notary group has seen that particular certificate before, she proceeds with a direct query.

2. Alice contacts a number of notary groups with a direct query asking them to report what certificate server SRV is offering. The queried group's members connect to SRV and get $cert_B$, and then sign with a notary signature the fact of having seen $cert_B$ at the moment of fetching.

3. The queried notary groups store the obtained certificates in the DHT.

3.4 User-defined trust

Laribus bases its security upon the social network of its users. Like in the PGP Web of Trust, users are required to define social relationships, i. e., determine to which extent they trust particular users (*user trust level*).

Alice can assign the following *user trust levels* to a friend (Charlie):

Connection: Alice receives and processes Charlie's messages. The consequence is that Charlie gets to know Alice's IP address and connection times.

Direct query: Alice includes Charlie in the list of users she will (try to) send direct queries to. As a result, Charlie may learn about Alice's (group's) surfing habits.

Transitive trust: Alice trusts Charlie's friends to some extent and would receive and forward their messages. In consequence, if Charlie authenticates untrustworthy users, both Alice and Charlie are affected.

Group trust: Alice vouches for Charlie's inclusion into her group (however, Charlie cannot join the group until all members vote for his inclusion). If Charlie is an attacker, he can perform denial-of-service attacks against Alice's group, i. e., by not forwarding messages or not participating in creating notary signatures.

3.5 Security measures

In order to prevent outsiders from forging messages or launching impersonation attacks, Laribus clients make use of public-key cryptography for *message authentication* and identification purposes. Before connecting to the Laribus network for the first time, each client n_i creates a key pair (S_i, P_i, ID_i), where ID_i is a self-signed pseudonym, (ID_i, P_i) is the public key and S_i is the secret key. ID_i does not necessarily have to reveal the actual identity of a user, but friends should be able to discover each other based on these pseudonyms.

As direct queries are quite expensive, they could be used to mount denial of service attacks. Therefore, they cannot be issued anonymously but have to be authenticated by the requestor by a digital signature. This allows notary groups to reject queries received from misbehaving clients or to only accept queries from trusted groups. However, if clients sign direct queries themselves, validation requests can be linked and tracked back to their pseudonym. We will discuss ways to overcome this privacy issue in Section 3.7.1. Moreover, the certificate records stored within the DHT are also signed by the notary groups in order to guarantee their authenticity.

3.6 Availability measures

Given the P2P approach of Laribus, clients cannot be expected to be online at all times. We address this problem with three mechanisms: a ring signature scheme, a threshold signature scheme, and a DHT (i. e., the storage layer, cf. Section 3.2).

The *ring signature scheme* allows Alice to sign a direct query, i. e., to ask another notary group to retrieve a certificate even if Alice is the only (online) member of her group (cf. Section 4.1). With this scheme Alice can prove that she is a member of her group without disclosing her identity (cf. Section 3.7).

The purpose of the *threshold signature scheme*, called *notary signatures* in this paper (cf. Section 4.2.3), is to allow groups to sign replies to direct queries when only a subset of the group members is online. We propose to employ an efficient threshold scheme by Lesueur et al. [50].

The most important availability feature of Laribus is *the DHT*, which serves as a distributed cache. It contains a public *timeline* of the certificates seen by different groups at different locations. Since the DHT is distributed among *all* clients (i. e., independent from the social network and notary group structures), it assures availability of the signed records (i. e., the past validations) of a notary group, even if not a single member of that group is online (cf. Section 4.4). As every record is signed by a notary group before it is put into the DHT, relying on cached information does not introduce additional security issues. As Laribus is meant to complement the existing PKI infrastructure, checking for certificate revocation is out of the scope of the system. Clients have to rely on existing techniques such as certificate revocation lists or OCSP to ensure that they are not relying on stale validation information.

3.7 Privacy-preserving certificate validation

To meet the users' privacy expectations, i. e., to prevent that network nodes will get to know who wants to validate which certificates, we use well-known and approved techniques from the privacy-enhancing technologies research community. Laribus contains privacy-preserving mechanisms for both *direct queries* and *DHT lookups*.

3.7.1 Preserving privacy for direct queries

If Alice asked a notary group to validate a certificate directly (Step B in Figure 4), she could be easily identified by her IP address or by her signature of the direct query. To prevent identification via signatures, we use ring signatures, i. e., other notary groups can validate that *some member* of a certain group has signed a request, but not which member exactly (details follow in Section 4.1).

To obfuscate IP addresses, simple solutions like Convergence's approach to route requests via a low-latency anonymity system (Tor) could be employed. This approach however conflicts with our design goal of a decentralized solution and would be subject to performance problems of such anonymity systems [51]. To this end, we have designed a scheme that utilizes the group structure of our network to build anonymity sets. Before a request is sent to another notary group, it is passed around between the members of Alice's group (cf. Step C in Figure 4). As a result, members of other groups will not be able to get to know whether a request was initiated by the requesting host itself or whether the request was sent on behalf of another member of the group.

This mechanism offers privacy towards other groups (e. g., *Group 2* in Figure 4), but it cannot protect Alice from the members of her own group. To this end, we use a layered encryption scheme (cf. [52]). With the layered encryption scheme, Alice chooses *r hops* (i. e., friends) to forward her request (source routing). The layered encryption scheme hides the routing information required by her friends to relay the request. Each hop removes one layer of encryption and, if it is an intermediate node, receives the address of the *next hop* (i. e., the next group member), or the destination address (i. e., the address of the *destination group*) if it is the final hop. Details about the layered encryption scheme used in Laribus follow in Section 4.3.

3.7.2 Preserving privacy of DHT lookups

To meet the users' privacy requirements for DHT lookups, we use a *range query approach* [53]: Alice will not request a specific entry using its key, but instead a set of results by querying for a prefix that refers to a certain subtree within the DHT (cf. Figure 5).

As a result, an attacker that is able to observe this process will only get to know that Alice is interested in one of the records of the subtree, but not in which exactly. The security parameter k determines the size of the result set, which allows to balance performance and privacy (cf. [49] and Section 4.4).

4 Laribus cryptography mechanisms

In this section we will present details about the cryptographic mechanisms of Laribus, especially ring signatures, notary signatures and the layered encryption scheme. We describe how notary group key pairs are generated and (dynamically) shared as well as the structure and data format of the DHT.

4.1 Ring signatures

In Laribus, direct queries have to be signed as notary groups are not required to answer direct queries from any other group (cf. Section 3.5). However, we also want to provide privacy for direct queries (cf. Section 3.7.1). We use ring signatures to solve this problem [54,55]. Ring signatures allow a single member of a group to sign data (m) on behalf of all group members. The signer requires only his own private key (S_s) and the public keys of the other ring members (P_r) as input to create a signature.

To this end, given a signing scheme based on trapdoor one-way permutations (e. g., RSA), the signer constructs a *verification equation* $C_{k,v}(g_1(x_1), g_2(x_2), \ldots, g_r(x_r)) = z$ combining a hash of the data to be signed and the ring's public keys functions with trapdoor $g_1, g_2, \ldots, g_r$. The equation is infeasible to solve for all inputs without inverting any trapdoor function g_i (i. e., not possessing the relative secret key to a key in the ring), therefore, the signature proves the signer's membership in the ring. Only the signer can provide the solution to the equation as the trapdoor is available only to him [54].

4.2 Notary signatures

When Alice asks a notary group to retrieve a certificate on her behalf (*direct query*), the notary group has to sign its answer (*notary signature*) to guarantee authenticity (cf. Section 3.3). In contrast to the case of *ring signatures*, a majority of the notary group must participate to perform the signature. On the other hand, to meet the availability requirements of Laribus, we must ensure that notary signatures can be obtained even if some group members are offline. A suitable solution for this problem is *threshold cryptography* [56].

With *threshold cryptography*, a public/private key pair (P, S) can be jointly generated by n parties. After key generation, each party knows P and holds a share s_i of S, but no party knows S entirely. Signatures can be obtained as long as a *threshold t* of shares is available, i. e., t parties participate. However, t and n must be chosen before the distributed key generation is initialized, and cannot be changed afterwards. As a result, using a *standard $(t - n)$-*threshold scheme directly would require to generate a new key pair every time n changes, i. e., whenever a notary group is resized. Furthermore, the overhead for generating keys increases drastically with the number of nodes [57] and would thus be impractical for our case as we assume that groups may consist of up to about 15 (and at least 3) members.

To overcome this problem, we propose to use a dynamic scheme by Lesueur et al. [50] that allows share merging and splitting. After an initial key generation process (e. g.,

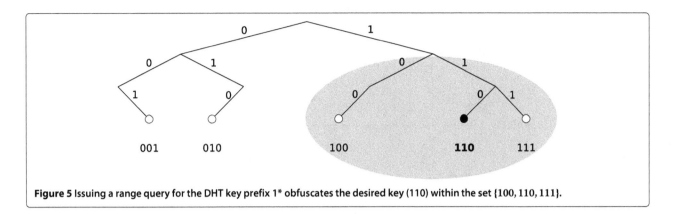

Figure 5 Issuing a range query for the DHT key prefix 1* obfuscates the desired key (110) within the set {100, 110, 111}.

to generate three shares) the number of shares can be adjusted to match the actual number of nodes. Furthermore, its performance is sufficient for larger group sizes, in fact even much larger than required for Laribus [50]. In the following, we will explain details about key generation, dynamic share handling, signing and notary group protection measures against Sybil attackers.

4.2.1 Key generation

To create a key pair for a notary group, we employ Boneh et al.'s efficient method of distributed RSA key pair generation [57]. The protocol allows a set of parties to construct an RSA modulus $N = pq = \sum p_i \sum q_i$ where N is publicly known, and each member N_i only knows about p_i and q_i, not about the factorization of N. To enable sharing of the secret key, they then calculate shares of $d = e^{-1} mod \varphi(N)$ for any given RSA encryption exponent e. Once each of the n group founders has obtained an initial share e_i of the secret d, to which we'll refer as S_G, the following holds: $\sum_{i=1}^{n} e_i = S_G$ [57]. In Laribus, we parameterize Boneh et al.'s method as a $(3-3)$-threshold scheme, i.e., a group will create three shares and all three shares are required to obtain a signature. To meet the security and availability requirements, the number of shares is adjusted with the protocol described in the next section.

4.2.2 Dynamic share handling

To dynamically assign shares to group members, we use the scheme of Lesueur et al. [50]. With this scheme, even though a group is composed of n members, the number E of shares can vary in respect to the number $t' \leq n$ of online members. The scheme allows to specify a fixed *ratio r* of nodes that are required to recover S_G (not a fixed *number* of nodes as in *classical* threshold schemes [50]). To achieve this, shares (e_i) are split and merged and may be replicated on different nodes. Nodes that are assigned the same share e_i compose a *sharing group*.

The share and merge operations require distributed sums and subtractions, since $split(e_i) = (e_{i_1}, e_{i_2})$ and $merge((e_j, e_k)) = e_{jk}$. To prevent an attacker from

reconstructing S_G from *old* shares, *old* shares must be rendered useless after each split and merge operation. To this end, if a newly created e_i is mixed with another share e_j, their owners collaboratively calculate $e_i := e_i - \Delta$ and $e_j := e_j + \Delta$, maintaining $\sum_{i=1}^{E} e_i = S_G$. Δ is a chosen random value that hides the original share (cf. [50]).

The ideal number of shares is $E = r \times t'$, with each sharing group composed of $g = \frac{1}{r}$ nodes knowing the same share [50]. We require clients to participate in merge operation only if the number of shares E would not fall under a minimum of $E_{min} = 3$. This way, at least three colluding attackers must be present in a group to recover S_G and forge notary signatures. In practice, when only three group members are online and one member wants to disconnect, the whole group is shut down. The last three shares are assigned to a third of the group members and stored in the DHT encryptedly. Nodes can recover the shares once they re-connect. The notary group ratio is set to $r = \frac{1}{2}$. We will motivate this choice in Section 5.

4.2.3 Obtaining a notary signature

In order to obtain a notary signature for a message D, there must be at least one member per *sharing group* available and willing to sign D, i.e., each share e_i is required for the signature computation. Following the signature protocol (cf. Figure 6), the group signature of D is $D^{S_G}[m]$. With the equality

$$D^{S_G}[m] = D^{(\sum_{i=1}^{E} e_i)}[m] = \left(\prod_{i=1}^{E} D^{e_i}[m] \right)[m]$$

the signature can be calculated collaboratively. One node per *sharing group* signs D with its share, i.e., calculates $s_i = D^{e_i}[m]$ and multiplies the result (mod m) with the result from the previous group (cf. Figure 6 and [50]).

4.2.4 Notary group protection measures

Like any other P2P system, Laribus has to address Sybil attacks that consist of a malicious user joining the network with multiple nodes and *fake* identities in order to

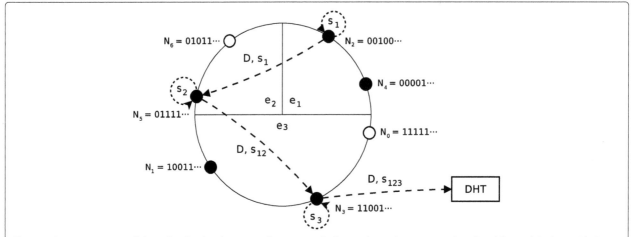

Figure 6 **A notary group collaborating for the signature of a message *D*.** One node per *sharing group* signs *D* and forwards it along with the calculated incremental product to the next *sharing group*. Shares are stored encryptedly in the DHT for offline nodes (empty circles).

control (large) parts of the network. We plan to employ Gatekeeper [58] as an admission control system to counter Sybil attacks. Gatekeeper uses a *ticket distribution algorithm* to detect attackers and is a suitable choice since, like Laribus, it is based on a social network and does not require users to have a global view of the network.

When a notary group decides about the inclusion of a new candidate (P_i, ID_i), already present members will take into account their own friendship relations (cf. Section 3.4) as well as Gatekeeper. If the new candidate passes both tests, his public key is collaboratively signed by the notary group and stored in the DHT to prove its membership. From that moment on, the candidate's NodeID in the group and DHT is fixed as $sig_{grp,inc}$. Table 1 shows the resulting data structure.

4.3 Layered encryption scheme

As mentioned in Section 3.7.1, direct queries in Laribus are protected by a layered encryption scheme and passed around between members of a notary group to obfuscate IP addresses (cf. Step C in Figure 4). To this end, whenever Alice wants to perform a direct query, she chooses r members of her group at random and establishes a shared secret s_r with each of the hops. The shared secrets are required by the hops involved to derive cryptographic keys for decryption and integrity validation of Alice's

query (*request direction*) and for encryption of the corresponding response, i.e., the requested certificate (*response direction*).

To reduce overhead, instead of an iterative channel construction as used in Tor [38], we employ a *none-interactive scheme* that requires only a single message to establish all shared secrets between Alice and the r hops. The scheme is based on the *Sphinx blinding logic* (cf. [59] and [60]): Instead of sending r shared secrets, a single element e of a cyclic group of prime order (satisfying the decisional Diffie-Hellman assumption) is used at each hop to derive the individual secrets. To prevent linkability, the element is *blinded* at each hop with a blinding factor derived from e. Figure 7 shows the operations performed by each hop.

A query consists of e, a header field h, a message authentication code (MAC) and a payload field n. When hop r receives a query, it uses its private key x_r to compute s_r (the shared secret). If s_r was seen before by r, the query is discarded (replay detection). Otherwise, hop r uses a key derivation function (KDF) initialized with s_r to derive $k_{MAC,r}$ and verify the integrity of the query. If the query is valid, another key ($k_{SYM,r}$) and an initialization vector (IV_r) is derived from s_r with KDF in order to decrypt h and n (i. e., to remove one layer of encryption). Further, r derives and stores a key ($k_{Response,r}$) and an initialization vector ($IV_{Response,r}$) from s_r with KDF that will be used

Table 1 **The inclusion of a node in a notary group**

Row type	Node	Timestamp
Inclusion	(P_i, ID_i)	t_x
Signature		
$sig_{grp,inc}$		

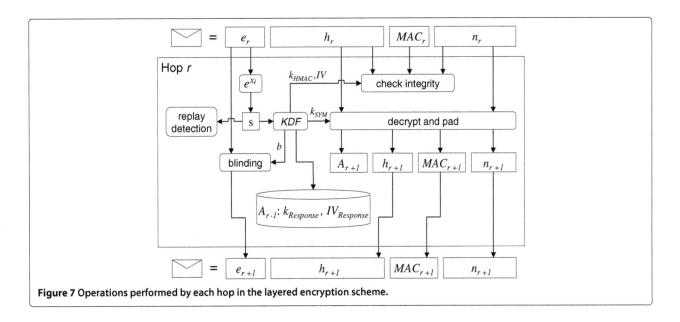

Figure 7 Operations performed by each hop in the layered encryption scheme.

later to encrypt the response for Alice's request (i. e., to add a layer of encryption).

If r is *not* the final hop, the decryption reveals the IP address of the next hop ($A_r + 1$) along with its header field, MAC and payload (h_{r+1}, MAC_{r+1} and n_{r+1}). In this case, hop r will pad the request with random data derived from s_r in order to maintain a constant message length (otherwise, the hops would get to know their position in the path), contact it with e_{r+1} (the blinded element for the next hop) and forward the resulting message to hop $r + 1$. The required blinding factor b is again derived from s_r with *KDF*.

If r *is* the final hop, the plaintext of n will reveal Alice's query along with padding and an identifier of the notary group the query is intended for. In this case, the final hop will retrieve the response from the intended notary group on behalf of Alice, pad it to a constant message length, encrypt it with $k_{Response,r}$ and forward the resulting ciphertext to the previous hop in the path (hop $r - 1$, *response direction*).

Each of the following $r - 1$ reply hops will add another layer of encryption with its corresponding key $k_{Response}$ derived and stored during query processing before. Since all keys, blinding factors etc. are derived from e, and e is chosen by Alice, she is able to create all those items locally and remove the layers of encryption added by the hops.

4.4 Certificate timeline and storage data format

To improve performance and availability of Laribus, clients can retrieve certificates signed by other groups, *certificate validation records* (CVR), from the DHT instead of issuing a direct query (cf. Section 3.3). The DHT stores $\langle key \rightarrow value \rangle$ pairs (cf. Table 2), where multiple values (i. e., CVRs) per key can be returned, e. g., records from different groups or from different times (*certificate timeline*). Laribus employs the Kademlia DHT [49], i. e., keys are truncated to 160 bits (cf. Table 2).

DHT lookups require either a hash of the certificate in question ($cert_X$) or a hash of the domain name ($\mathcal{SRV}_X$, cf. Section 3.3), i. e., the DHT stores two different keys for CVR lookups (cf. Table 2). As mentioned in Section 3.7.2, to meet the users' privacy requirements, clients may request a subtree of the DHT by submitting only a prefix with $160 - k$ bits (*range query*), i. e., they will receive all CVRs with a key that starts with the prefix.

The data format of a CVR is shown in Table 3. The row type *validation* separates *blacklisted* from *whitelisted* CVRs. The *certificate* field identifies the certificates by their SHA_{256} hash. The row type *server* consists of $\mathcal{SRV} = \langle hostname, port \rangle$ values that identify the server which offered $cert_X$. The *timestamp* field states when $cert_X$ was validated. All CVR fields are signed with the respective notary group's signature (sig_{grp}).

Table 2 The stored $cert_X$ validation records in the DHT

DHT keys		
$SHA_{256}(cert_X)[0 \cdots 159]$	$\Longrightarrow$	CVR
$SHA_{256}(\mathcal{SRV}_X)[0 \cdots 159]$	$\Longrightarrow$	

Table 3 Certificate validation record storage format

Row type	Certificate	Server	Timestamp
Validation	$SHA_{256}(cert_X)$	$\mathcal{SRV}_X$	t_x

Signature
sig_{grp}

5 Evaluation

The goal of this section is to provide an initial feasibility study of Laribus. We focus on the computational cost of cryptographic processes as well as availability aspects.

5.1 Cryptographic processes

Laribus makes use of four cryptographic schemes: Distributed key generation (cf. Section 4.2.1), notary signatures (cf. Section 4.2.3), ring signatures (cf. Section 4.1) and a layered encryption scheme (cf. Section 4.3).

The *distributed key generation* scheme is by far the most expensive sub-protocol of Laribus. It requires several rounds of private distributed computation, e. g., to generate an RSA modulus and for biprimality testing. However, key generation is performed only once per group, when a new group is initialized. Given the results of Congos et al. [61], generating a 2,048 bit key that consists of three shares can be expected to be finished in less than 4 min on commodity hardware and with a total network traffic of less than 25 Mbyte. As this process is required only once per group and has no strong real-time requirements, we expect no practical limitations no matter if keys are generated in a LAN or via Internet.

The *notary signature* scheme consists of share assignment and distribution and the signing process itself. The distribution of shares is not expensive, as it only consists of distributed sums and subtractions (cf. Section 4.2.2 and [50]). The signing process requires a single *normal* signature per sharing group, as well as a simple multiplication of the resulting signatures (cf. Section 4.2.3 and [50]). The overhead of both processes seems negligible.

The *ring signature scheme* [55] is practical for our scenario as well: It requires only between n and $2n$ modular multiplications, where n is the group size and can be performed locally by a single node (cf. Section 4.1).

The *layered encryption scheme* of Laribus (cf. Section 4.3) requires essentially $2r$ public key operations to create a message (r is the number of hops) and again two public key operations on each of the r hops (i. e., group members) that forward the message for the Sphinx *blinding logic* and the computation of the shared secrets [59]. It can be used in conjunction with the very efficient Curve25519 elliptic curve library [62]. Results of a recent study [63] indicate that the delay introduced by Sphinx and the relaying of messages should be well below 1 s.

In conclusion, we do not expect performance problems due to cryptographic overhead. The only sub-protocol of Laribus that introduces considerable delay is the distributed key generation, which takes place only once a group is initialized.

5.2 Availability aspects

Whether a group is operational (i. e., it can answer direct queries, for instance) depends on three factors: the group size n, the number of online nodes necessary to recover the group secret (*threshold t'*) and the user behavior (i. e., online and offline times). We have performed a simulation-based study to determine adequate values for n and t' and to assess whether these values are indeed practical or not. Source code and configuration files will be made available by the authors on request.

Since Laribus is not deployed yet, we have to estimate the *user behavior* of clients. We model four different types of users: *casual, normal, office,* and *power users. Casual users* connect to the Internet with short session times (on average, 10 min per session) during daytime (between 8:00 and 21:00) and spend 60 min on the Internet per day on average. *Normal users* are connected 5 h per day on average, split into two sessions, one in the morning (around 10:00) and evening (around 19:00). *Office users* connect between 9:00 and 10:00 and end their session between 17:00 and 18:00. *Power users* are either running a server or leaving their computer online most of the day, with 4 h of *downtime* per day on average. User connection times and session durations are sampled from a Gaussian distribution (standard deviation 0.5), except for casual and power users, whose connection times are drawn uniformly from the [8, 21] and [0, 24] hour ranges, respectively. We assume that Laribus is run as a system service, i. e., that clients are available whenever a user is connected to the Internet.

Figures 8, 9, and 10 show the *success percentage p* for different group sizes n, thresholds t' and (mixes of) user types. The *success percentage* is defined as the probability that, whenever at least one node of a notary group is online, the group is operational (i. e., it can perform a notary signature), i. e., at least t' of its nodes are online.

Figures 8 and 9 present the success ratios of groups with uniform type of users, respectively *normal* and *power*

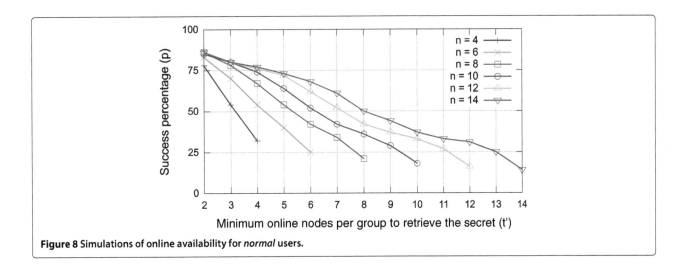

Figure 8 Simulations of online availability for *normal* users.

users. Figure 10 shows results for a more realistic case with mixed user types, i.e., 80% normal and office users and 20% casual and power users. As we can see from Figures 8 and 9, user behavior has a strong influence on the *success percentage*. The results for *normal users* (Figure 8) suggest that for $p = 50\%$ and $n = 6$, $t' \approx 0.7n$ would be a reasonable choice ($\frac{t'}{n} = \frac{4}{6} \approx 0.7$), while the results for *power users* (Figure 9) suggest $t' \approx 0.9n$. The simulation of the most realistic case, the mixed case (Figure 10), suggests $t' \approx 0.5n$. As expected, larger groups can tolerate a bigger fraction of offline nodes for the desired *success percentage* of 50%. For instance, a group with $n = 14$ nodes can tolerate nine offline nodes in the mixed case, which is about 64%, while a group with $n = 6$ nodes can tolerate only about three offline nodes, i.e., about 50% (cf. Figure 10).

In conclusion, the results suggest that $t' \approx \frac{n}{2}$ is a reasonable choice, if $n \geq 6$, i.e., groups should consist of at least 6 members to be operational in 50% of cases.

6 Limitations and discussion

In this section, we will discuss limitations and challenges of Laribus. We focus on the attacker model as well as practical problems, performance tradeoffs, and bootstrapping.

Laribus cannot protect against attackers that control large parts of the Internet. By design, and like any other notary-based MitM detection approach, *Laribus can solely detect local attacks*, i.e., the majority of notaries must not be affected by an attack and must be able to retrieve valid certificates. Attacks that affect a single country (e.g., a repressive regime) or continent can be detected as long as notaries from different parts of the world are available. Moreover, strong attackers may try to block all traffic pertaining to certificate validation. While this is straightforward given static, centralized notaries, Laribus is less vulnerable to blocking due to its decentralized architecture.

A general problem of collaborative distributed certificate validation is that some hosts and especially

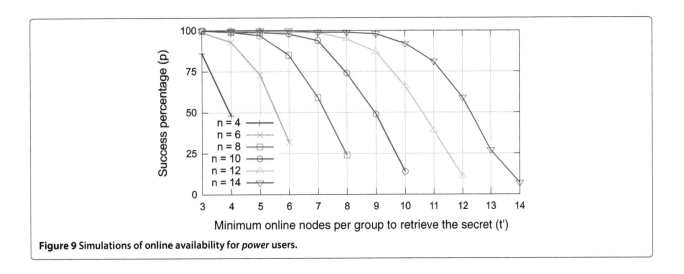

Figure 9 Simulations of online availability for *power* users.

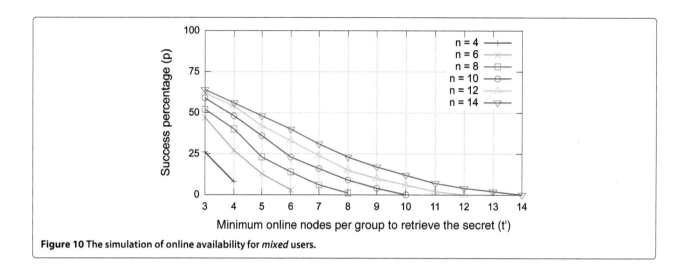

Figure 10 The simulation of online availability for *mixed* users.

content distribution networks (CDNs) *use different valid certificates for the same host.* As a result, a 1:1-comparison of certificates is not appropriate. However, since the *timeline* of seen certificates of Laribus allows to store several certificates for a host (cf. Section 4.4), clients can still judge the validity of a certificate by the number of notaries that have seen the same certificate.

Newly issued or renewed certificates cannot be answered with DHT lookups as the *timeline* will not contain any records for them. In this case direct queries (cf. Section 3.3) have to be issued, i.e., enough notaries that the client trusts have to be available.

The results of our initial feasibility study suggest that groups should consist of at least six members to be operational in 50% of cases (cf. Section 5.2). Composing a group of at least six friends should not be a problem in practice. An average 50% availability of a notary group should be practical as well, especially since the storage and caching mechanisms of the DHT do allow to access the *timeline* of the certificates seen by different groups even if all members of those groups are offline. Further, previous studies indicate that the popularity of web hosts follows a power-law distribution [64], i.e., a small set of popular hosts is responsible for the vast majority of all requests, while the *long tail* of remaining hosts is requested rarely. Thus, we expect that the DHT's cache hit ratio will be high; direct queries will not be needed in most cases. Our analysis of the cryptographic processes of Laribus showed that *cryptographic overhead is moderate*, except for distributed key generation which is required only during initialization (cf. Section 5.1).

In conclusion, results for both availability and performance are quite promising. They indicate that a Laribus deployment would indeed be practical. However, future work should focus on analyzing the cache hit ratio using different caching strategies (such as 'most recently used' or based on a time-to-live value like in DNS) and the

resulting user-perceived latencies. The results would be of particular interest for the parameterization of Laribus, especially the security parameter k of the range query protection mechanism (cf. Section 3.7.2).

To offer adequate performance and availability during the initial deployment of Laribus, we suggest to *bootstrap the network* with a set of dedicated servers operated by different universities around the world until enough users participate. In fact, a permanent operation of these servers could be an option as well as it would allow to combine the benefits of P2P (especially blocking resistance) and client-server solutions and thus further increase the attractiveness of Laribus. Furthermore, snapshots of the *timeline* (including group signatures) could be mirrored and made publicly available for all users on the Internet. This resembles the approach of *Sovereign Keys* (cf. Section 2 and [32]) and would also help to reduce lookup latencies as well as the size of the DHT.

7 Conclusions

In this paper, we presented Laribus, a social peer-to-peer network that addresses the problem of man-in-the-middle attacks on SSL. Laribus integrates approved techniques from current state-of-the-art solutions and combines them with well-known proposals from the privacy enhancing technologies research community to improve both privacy and availability.

To the best of our knowledge, Laribus is the first fully distributed solution for the detection of fake SSL certificates. It does not require cooperation of website owners and is blocking-resistant due to its decentralized architecture. Further, clients do not have to trust a central notary service. The Laribus architecture is fundamentally different from previous solutions since users can model trust relationships that reflect their social relationships and may create virtual notaries that consist of their friends. The resulting groups of friends are utilized both as anonymity sets and to increase availability.

Our initial evaluation results are promising and suggest that Laribus is feasible. Future work will focus on an implementation of its components as well as an in-depth analysis of the effectiveness of caching and user-perceived latencies in order to prepare the practical deployment of Laribus.

Competing interests
The authors declare that they have no competing interests.

Acknowledgements
The authors are grateful to the anonymous reviewers for their constructive feedback and insightful comments. A preliminary version of this article has been published in the ARES 2013 proceedings [13].

References

1. T Dierks, E Rescorla, *The Transport Layer Security (TLS) Protocol Version 1.2 RFC 5246*. (IETF, Fremont, CA, USA, 2008)

2. A Freier, P Karlton, P Kocher, *The Secure Sockets Layer (SSL) Protocol Version 3.0 RFC 6101*. (IETF, Fremont, CA, USA, 2011)

3. E Rescorla, *SSL and TLS: Designing and Building Secure Systems*. (Addison-Wesley, Boston, Toronto, Paris, 2001)

4. J Rizzo, T Duong, Here Come The XOR Ninjas. Unpublished manuscript (2011). http://netifera.com/research/beast/beast_DRAFT_0621.pdf

5. Y Gluck, N Harris, A Prado, BREACH: Reviving THE CRIME Attack. Unpublished manuscript (2013). http://breachattack.com/resources/BREACH%20-%20SSL,%20gone%20in%2030%20seconds.pdf

6. NJ AlFardan, KG Paterson, in *IEEE Symposium on Security and Privacy (S&P 2013), Berkeley, CA, USA, May 19–22, 2013, Proceedings*. Lucky Thirteen: Breaking the TLS and DTLS Record Protocols (IEEE New York, NY, USA, 2013), pp. 526–540

7. C Meyer, J Schwenk, Lessons Learned From Previous SSL/TLS Attacks – A Brief Chronology Of Attacks And Weaknesses. Cryptology ePrint Archive, Report 2013/049 (2013). http://eprint.iacr.org/2013/049/20130201:021008

8. C Meyer, J Schwenk, in *Information Security Applications – 14th International Workshop (WISA 2013), Jeju Island, Korea, August 19–21, 2013, Revised Selected Papers*, Lecture Notes in Computer Science, ed. by Y Kim, H Lee, and A Perrig. SoK: Lessons Learned from SSL/TLS Attacks, vol. 8267 (Springer Berlin Heidelberg, 2013), pp. 189–209

9. D Cooper, S Santesson, S Farrell, S Boeyen, R Housley, W Polk, *Internet X.509 Public Key Infrastructure Certificate and Certificate Revocation List (CRL) Profile, RFC 5280*. (IETF, Fremont, CA, USA, 2008)

10. Electronic Frontier Foundation, EFF SSL Observatory. https://www.eff.org/observatory. accessed 2014-03-14

11. C Soghoian, S Stamm, in *Financial Cryptography and Data Security – 15th International Conference (FC 2011), Gros Islet, St. Lucia, February 28 – March 4, 2011, Revised Selected Papers*. Lecture Notes in Computer Science, ed. by G Danezis. Certified Lies: Detecting and Defeating Government Interception Attacks Against SSL, vol. 7035 (Springer Berlin Heidelberg, 2012), pp. 250–259

12. N Leavitt, Internet Security Under Attack: The Undermining of Digital Certificates. IEEE Computer. **44**(12), 17–20 (2011)

13. A Micheloni, K-P Fuchs, D Herrmann, H Federrath, in *International Conference on Availability, Reliability and Security (ARES 2013), Regensburg, Germany, September 2–6, 2013, Proceedings*. Laribus: Privacy-Preserving Detection of Fake SSL Certificates with a Social P2P Notary Network (IEEE New York, NY, USA, 2013), pp. 1–10

14. J Clark, PC van Oorschot, in *IEEE Symposium on Security and Privacy (S&P 2013), Berkeley, CA, USA, May 19–22, 2013, Proceedings*. SoK: SSL and HTTPS: Revisiting Past Challenges and Evaluating Certificate Trust Model Enhancements (IEEE New York, NY, USA, 2013), pp. 511–525

15. H Tschofenig, E Lear, *Evolving the Web Public Key Infrastructure. Internet Draft*. (IETF, Fremont, CA, USA, 2013). http://tools.ietf.org/html/draft-tschofenig-iab-webpki-evolution-01

16. J Kasten, E Wustrow, JA Halderman, in *International Conference on Financial Cryptography and Data Security (FC 2013), Okinawa, Japan, April 1–5, 2013, Revised Selected Papers*. Lecture Notes in Computer Science, ed. by A-R Sadeghi. Cage: Taming Certificate Authorities by Inferring Restricted Scopes, vol. 7859 (Springer Berlin Heidelberg, 2013), pp. 329–337

17. H Perl, S Fahl, M Smith, in *18th International Conference on Financial Cryptography and Data Security (FC 2014), Barbados, March 3—7, 2014, Proceedings*. You Won't Be Needing These Any More: On Removing Unused Certificates From Trust Stores, (2014)

18. J Sunshine, S Egelman, H Almuhimedi, N Atri, LF Cranor, in *USENIX Security Symposium, Montreal, Canada, August 10–14, 2009, Proceedings*. Crying Wolf: An Empirical Study of SSL Warning Effectiveness (USENIX Association Berkeley, CA, USA, 2009), pp. 399–416

19. C Evans, C Palmer, R Sleevi, *Public Key Pinning Extension for HTTP. Internet Draft*. (IETF, Fremont, CA, USA, 2014). http://tools.ietf.org/html/draft-ietf-websec-key-pinning-11

20. M Marlinspike, T Perrin, *Trust Assertions for Certificate Keys. Internet Draft*. (IETF, Fremont, CA, USA, 2013). http://tools.ietf.org/html/draft-perrin-tls-tack-02

21. P Hoffman, J Schlyter, *The DNS-Based Authentication of Named Entities (DANE) Transport Layer Security (TLS) Protocol: TLSA. RFC 6698*. (IETF, Fremont, CA, USA, 2012)

22. R Arends, R Austein, M Larson, D Massey, S Rose, *DNS Security Introduction and Requirements RFC 4033*. (IETF, Fremont, CA, USA, 2005)

23. E Osterweil, B Kaliski, M Larson, D McPherson, in *Workshop on Securing and Trusting Internet Names (SATIN 2012), March 22–23, 2012, Teddington, UK, Proceedings*. Reducing the X.509 Attack Surface with DNSSEC's DANE, (2012). http://conferences.npl.co.uk/satin/papers/satin2012-Osterweil.pdf

24. H Yang, E Osterweil, D Massey, S Lu, L Zhang, Deploying Cryptography in Internet-scale Systems: A Case Study on DNSSEC. Dependable and Secure Computing, IEEE Transactions on. **8**(5), 656–669 (2011)

25. VeriSign, Licensing Verisign Certificates. Technical Report (2005). http://www.verisign.com/static/001496.pdf

26. P Hallam-Baker, R Stradling, *DNS Certification Authority Authorization (CAA) Resource Record. RFC 6844*. (IETF, Fremont, CA, USA, 2013)

27. W Koch, M Brinkmann, STEED – Usable End-to-End Encryption. Unpublished manuscript (2011). http://g10code.com/docs/steed-usable-e2ee.pdf

28. GX Toth, T Vlieg, Public Key Pinning for TLS – Using a Trust on First Use Model. Technical report, University of Amsterdam (2013). http://www.delaat.net/rp/2012-2013/p56/report.pdf

29. Certificate Patrol Homepage. http://tg-x.net/code/certpatrol. accessed 2014-03-14

30. I Dacosta, M Ahamad, P Traynor, in *European Symposium on Research in Computer Security (ESORICS 2012), Pisa, Italy, September 10–12, 2012, Proceedings*. Lecture Notes in Computer Science, ed. by S Foresti, M Yung, and F Martinelli. Trust No One Else: Detecting MITM Attacks against SSL/TLS without Third-Parties, vol. 7459 (Springer Berlin Heidelberg, 2012), pp. 199–216

31. The Monkeysphere Project. http://web.monkeysphere.info/. accessed 2014-03-14

32. The Sovereign Keys Project. https://www.eff.org/sovereign-keys. accessed 2014-03-14

33. B Laurie, A Langley, E Kasper, *Certificate Transparency. RFC 6962*. (IETF, Fremont, CA, USA, 2013)

34. TH-J Kim, L-S Huang, A Perrig, C Jackson, V Gligor, Transparent Key Integrity (TKI): A Proposal for a Public-Key Validation Infrastructure. Technical Report CMU-CyLab-12-016, Carnegie Mellon University (July 2012). https://www.cylab.cmu.edu/files/pdfs/tech_reports/CMUCyLab12016.pdf

35. D Wendlandt, DG Andersen, A Perrig, in *USENIX Annual Technical Conference, Boston, MA, USA, June 22–27, 2008, Proceedings*. Perspectives: Improving SSH-style Host Authentication with Multi-Path Probing (USENIX Berkeley, CA, USA, 2008), pp. 321–334

36. The Convergence Project. http://convergence.io/. accessed 2014-03-14

37. J Wilberding, A Yates, M Sherr, W Zhou, in *Annual Computer Security Applications Conference (ACSAC '13), New Orleans, LA, USA, December 9-13, 2013, Proceedings*, ed. by CNP Jr. Validating Web Content with Senser (ACM New York, NY, USA, 2013), pp. 339–348

38. R Dingledine, N Mathewson, PF Syverson, in *USENIX Security Symposium, August 9–13, 2004, San Diego, CA, USA, Proceedings*. Tor: The Second-Generation Onion Router (USENIX Berkeley, CA, USA, 2004), pp. 303–320

39. M Alicherry, AD Keromytis, in *IEEE Symposium on Computers and Communications (ISCC 2009), July 5–8, Sousse, Tunisia, Proceedings*. DoubleCheck: Multi-path Verification Against Man-in-the-Middle Attacks (IEEE New York, NY, USA, 2009), pp. 557–563

40. K Engert, DetecTor (version 1.02 2013). http://detector.io/DetecTor.pdf accessed 2014-03-14

41. D McCoy, KS Bauer, D Grunwald, T Kohno, DC Sicker, in *Privacy Enhancing Technologies, 8th International Symposium (PETS 2008), Leuven, Belgium, July 23–25, 2008, Proceedings*. Lecture Notes in Computer Science, ed. by N Borisov, I Goldberg. Shining Light in Dark Places: Understanding the Tor Network, vol. 5134 (Springer Berlin Heidelberg, 2008), pp. 63–76

42. P Winter, R Köwer, M Mulazzani, M Huber, S Schrittwieser, S Lindskog, E Weippl, in *Privacy Enhancing Technologies, 14th International Symposium (PETS 2014), Amsterdam, The Netherlands, July 16–18, 2014, Proceedings*. Lecture Notes in Computer Science, ed. by E De Cristofaro, SJ Murdoch. Spoiled Onions: Exposing Malicious Tor Exit Relays, vol. 8555 (Springer Berlin Heidelberg, 2014), pp. 304–331

43. B Amann, M Vallentin, S Hall, R Sommer, *Extracting Certificates from Live Traffic: A Near Real-Time SSL Notary Service. Technical Report TR-12-014*. (International Computer Science Institute, Berkeley, CA, USA, 2012). http://www.icsi.berkeley.edu/pubs/techreports/ICSI_TR-12-014.pdf

44. R Holz, T Riedmaier, N Kammenhuber, G Carle, in *European Symposium on Research in Computer Security (ESORICS 2012), Pisa, Italy, September 10–12, 2012, Proceedings*. Lecture Notes in Computer Science, ed. by S Foresti, M Yung, and F Martinelli. X.509 Forensics: Detecting and Localising the SSL/TLS Men-in-the-Middle, vol. 7459 (Springer Berlin Heidelberg, 2012), pp. 217–234

45. H-M Sun, W-H Chang, S-Y Chang, Y-H Lin, in *Cryptology and Network Security, 8th International Conference (CANS 2009), Kanazawa, Japan, December 12–14, 2009, Proceedings*. Lecture Notes in Computer Science, ed. by JA Garay, A Miyaji, and A Otsuka. DepenDNS: Dependable Mechanism against DNS Cache Poisoning, vol. 5888 (Springer Berlin Heidelberg, 2009), pp. 174–188

46. K Park, VS Pai, LL Peterson, Z Wang, in *Symposium on Operating System Design and Implementation (OSDI 2004), San Francisco, California, USA, December 6–8, 2004, Proceedings*. CoDNS: Improving DNS Performance and Reliability via Cooperative Lookups (USENIX Association Berkeley, CA, USA, 2004), pp. 199–214

47. L Poole, VS Pai, in *USENIX Annual Technical Conference, Boston, MA, USA, June 22–27, 2008, Proceedings*. ConfiDNS: Leveraging Scale and History to Detect Compromise (USENIX Berkeley, CA, USA, 2008), pp. 99–112

48. L Yuan, K Kant, P Mohapatra, C-N Chuah, in *International Conference on Communications (ICC 2006), Istanbul, Turkey, 11-15 June 2006, Proceedings*. DoX: A Peer-to-Peer Antidote for DNS Cache Poisoning Attacks (IEEE New York, NY, USA, 2006), pp. 2345–2350

49. P Maymounkov, D Mazières, in *Peer-to-Peer Systems, First International Workshop (IPTPS 2002), Cambridge, MA, USA, March 7–8, 2002, Revised Papers*. Lecture Notes in Computer Science. Kademlia: A Peer-to-Peer Information System Based on the XOR Metric, vol. 2429 (Springer Berlin Heidelberg, 2002), pp. 53–65

50. F Lesueur, Mé, VVT Tong, in *Resilient Networks and Services, Second International Conference on Autonomous Infrastructure, Management and Security (AIMS 2008), Bremen, Germany, July 1–3, 2008, Proceedings*. Lecture Notes in Computer Science. A Distributed Certification System for Structured P2P Networks, vol. 5127 (Springer Berlin Heidelberg, 2008), pp. 40–52

51. R Dingledine, SJ Murdoch, Performance Improvements on Tor, or, Why Tor is Slow and What We're Going to Do About It. Unpublished manuscript (2009). https://svn.torproject.org/svn/projects/roadmaps/2009-03-11-performance.pdf

52. D Chaum, Untraceable electronic mail, return addresses, and digital pseudonyms. Communications of the ACM. **24**(2) (1981)

53. Y Lu, G Tsudik, in *International Conference on Peer-to-Peer Computing (P2P 2010), Delft, The Netherlands, 25–27 August 2010, Proceedings*. Towards Plugging Privacy Leaks in the Domain Name System (IEEE New York, NY, USA, 2010), pp. 1–10

54. RL Rivest, A Shamir, Y Tauman, in *Advances in Cryptology (ASIACRYPT 2001), 7th International Conference on the Theory and Application of Cryptology and Information Security, Gold Coast, Australia, December 9–13, 2001, Proceedings*. Lecture Notes in Computer Science, ed. by C Boyd. How to Leak a Secret, vol. 2248 (Springer Berlin Heidelberg, 2001), pp. 552–565

55. RL Rivest, A Shamir, Y Tauman, in *Theoretical Computer Science, Essays in Memory of Shimon Even*. Lecture Notes in Computer Science, ed. by O Goldreich, AL Rosenberg, and AL Selman. How to Leak a Secret: Theory and Applications of Ring Signatures, vol. 3895, vol. 3895 (Springer Berlin Heidelberg, 2006), pp. 164–186

56. A Shamir, How to share a secret. Commun. ACM. **22**(11), 612–613 (1979)

57. D Boneh, MK Franklin, in *Advances in Cryptology (CRYPTO '97), 17th Annual International Cryptology Conference, Santa Barbara, California, USA, August 17–21, 1997, Proceedings*. Lecture Notes in Computer Science. Efficient Generation of Shared RSA Keys (Extended Abstract), vol. 1294 (Springer Berlin Heidelberg, 1997), pp. 425–439

58. DN Tran, J Li, L Subramanian, SSM Chow, in *International Conference on Computer Communications (INFOCOM 2011), Joint Conference of the IEEE Computer and Communications Societies, 10–15 April 2011, Shanghai, China, Proceedings*. Optimal Sybil-Resilient Node Admission Control (IEEE New York, NY, USA, 2011), pp. 3218–3226

59. G Danezis, I Goldberg, in *IEEE Symposium on Security and Privacy (S&P 2009), 17–20 May 2009, Oakland, California, USA, Proceedings*. Sphinx: A Compact and Provably Secure Mix Format (IEEE New York, NY, USA, 2009), pp. 269–282

60. A Kate, I Goldberg, in *Financial Cryptography and Data Security, 14th International Conference (FC 2010), Tenerife, Canary Islands, January 25–28, 2010, Revised Selected Papers*. Lecture Notes in Computer Science, ed. by R Sion. Using Sphinx to Improve Onion Routing Circuit Construction, vol. 6052 (Springer Berlin Heidelberg, 2010), pp. 359–366

61. T Congos, F Lesueur, in *Workshop on Security and Trust Management (STM 2009), Proceedings*. Electronic Notes in Theoretical Computer Science. Experimenting with Distributed Generation of RSA Keys (Elsevier Saint-Malo, France, 2009)

62. DJ Bernstein, in *Public Key Cryptography – 9th International Conference on Theory and Practice of Public-Key Cryptography (PKC 2006), New York, NY, USA, April 24–26, 2006, Proceedings*. Lecture Notes in Computer Science. Curve25519: New Diffie-Hellman Speed Records, vol. 3958 (Springer Berlin Heidelberg, 2006), pp. 207–228

63. K-P Fuchs, D Herrmann, H Federrath, in *European Symposium on Research in Computer Security (ESORICS 2012), Pisa, Italy, September 10–12, 2012, Proceedings*. Lecture Notes in Computer Science, ed. by S Foresti, M Yung, and F Martinelli. Introducing the gMix Open Source Framework for Mix Implementations, vol. 7459 (Springer Berlin Heidelberg, 2012), pp. 487–504

64. J Jung, E Sit, H Balakrishnan, R Morris, DNS Performance and the Effectiveness of Caching. Networking, IEEE/ACM Transactions on. **10**(5), 589–603 (2002)

13

ADLU: a novel anomaly detection and location-attribution algorithm for UWB wireless sensor networks

Eirini Karapistoli[*] and Anastasios A Economides

Abstract

Wireless sensor networks (WSNs) are gaining more and more interest in the research community due to their unique characteristics. Besides energy consumption considerations, security has emerged as an equally important aspect in their network design. This is because WSNs are vulnerable to various types of attacks and to node compromises, and as such, they require security mechanisms to defend against them. An intrusion detection system (IDS) is one such solution to the problem. While several signature-based and anomaly-based detection algorithms have been proposed to date for WSNs, none of them is specifically designed for the ultra-wideband (UWB) radio technology. UWB is a key solution for wireless connectivity among inexpensive devices characterized by ultra-low power consumption and high precision ranging. Based on these principles, in this paper, we propose a novel anomaly-based detection and location-attribution algorithm for cluster-based UWB WSNs. The proposed algorithm, abbreviated as ADLU, has dedicated procedures for secure cluster formation, periodic re-clustering, and efficient cluster member monitoring. The performance of ADLU in identifying and localizing intrusions using a rule-based anomaly detection scheme is studied via simulations.

Keywords: Wireless sensor networks; UWB radio technology; Security in UWB WSNs; Anomaly-based detection; Attack attribution; Ranging attacks

1 Introduction

A wireless sensor network is a network of cheap and simple processing autonomous devices (called sensor nodes) that are spatially distributed in an area of interest in order to cooperatively monitor physical or environmental phenomena. Mostly based on non-renewable resources, such as batteries, wireless sensor networks (WSNs) call for robust and energy-efficient solutions both at the software and hardware levels. Undoubtedly, the IEEE 802.15.4-2011 standard [1] for low-rate wireless personal area networks (LR-WPANs) is a valuable candidate for the energy-constrained WSNs. The standard defines the physical (PHY) and medium access control (MAC) layers. Among the available PHY options, the impulse radio ultra-wideband (IR-UWB) PHY (formerly defined in the IEEE 802.15.4a-2007 standard) has several advanced

properties, such as built-in ranging capabilities, low duty cycle, low probability of detection, and robustness against interference, appointing it an ideal information carrier for communication among the sensor network devices [2].

From an application's point of view, the driving force behind research in WSNs is to develop systems that can operate unattended for large periods. Besides energy consumption considerations, the unattended nature of the deployed WSNs raises administration problems and appoints the security as an additional critical element in the network design [3]. As identified in [4-6], WSNs are susceptible to various types of attacks or to node compromises that exploit known and unknown vulnerabilities of protocols, software, and hardware, and threaten the security, integrity, authenticity, and availability of data that reside in these networked systems.

UWB transmissions offer a potentially robust physical layer security for WSNs as a consequence of their large bandwidth. Indeed, WSNs that rely on UWB radio signals are somewhat inherently more secure, because

*Correspondence: ikarapis@uom.gr
Interdepartmental Programme of Postgraduate Studies in Information Systems, University of Macedonia, Egnatias 156, Thessaloniki 54006, Greece

the low output power and short pulses of these signals make their transmissions to appear as white noise from a distance. Nevertheless, UWB signals could potentially be sniffed by a determined attacker who is located close to the transmitter, enabling the latter to launch an attack against the WSN [7,8]. Therefore, even this class of WSNs requires that security mechanisms are implemented at every layer of the sensor network protocol stack.

Currently, research on providing security solutions for WSNs has mainly focused on key management [9], authentication, and secure routing [10], as well as secure services including secure localization [11] and secure aggregation [12]. A few secure ranging and localization protocols were specifically designed for protecting the integrity of ranging and for addressing location-related attacks in UWB WSNs [13-16]. Signaling schemes have also been proposed to improve physical layer security of UWB systems [8]. Finally, a number of routing and clustering protocols attempt to address networking issues in UWB WSNs [17], lacking however advanced security features in their design.

In general, most of the security protocols mentioned above can cope with weak, external attackers. However, strong, internal attackers, which managed to penetrate the first perimeter of defense (for instance through tampering sensor nodes [18]), can only be dealt with using intrusion detection systems (IDSs). Various signature-based and anomaly-based IDS architectures have been proposed for flat and hierarchical WSNs [19]. However, the energy constraints and scalability issues in WSNs dictate the use of an hierarchical anomaly-based detection model for IDS [20]. In this grouping technique, the essential operation is to select a set of cluster heads (CHs) among the nodes in the network and to cluster the rest of the nodes with them. Cluster heads are responsible for coordination among the nodes inside their clusters (intra-cluster data gathering) and for forwarding the collected data to the sink node, usually after efficiently aggregating them. With regard to anomaly detection, cluster heads are also tasked with intrusion detection functions, such as collecting intrusion alarms from their cluster members (CMs). Additionally, the cluster head nodes may also detect attacks against other cluster head nodes of the network, since they constitute the backbone of the routing infrastructure.

While a number of anomaly-based detection systems (ADSs) have been proposed for hierarchical, cluster-based WSNs [19-21], to the best of our knowledge, none of them is specifically designed for the emerging UWB transmission technology. The ultra-wideband nature of this PHY and its high precision ranging capability (1-m accuracy and better [22]) enable the ADS not only to detect a malicious behavior, but also to localize the anomaly

by relying on internal tools, namely on accurate time-of-arrival (TOA)-based UWB distance measurements.

Accordingly, the present work contributes to the area of wireless sensor network security by proposing a novel anomaly-based detection and location-attribution algorithm for cluster-based UWB WSNs, named ADLU. The proposed algorithm has dedicated procedures for secure cluster formation, periodic re-clustering, and efficient cluster member monitoring. Furthermore, it exploits the peculiar characteristics of the UWB PHY defined in the IEEE 802.15.4 standard [1] in order to facilitate the anomaly detection and location attribution processes. To help address the security challenges, ADLU offers the following contributions:

- It defines a novel, trust-aware leader election metric that makes the leader election process of clustering immune to ranging attacks.
- It introduces a monitoring mechanism for both the cluster members and the cluster heads.
- It specifies a rule-based detection engine that accurately analyzes data packets to detect signs of sensor network anomalies.
- It encapsulates a UWB time-of-arrival triangulation of ranges technique that adds location-attribution capabilities to the algorithm.

ADLU is different from existing works in several other ways. Firstly, it does not rely on a special type of hardware, i.e., global positioning system (GPS) devices, to perform the localization task. Moreover, it does not require heavy communication among the nodes, since the decision making and node revocation processes follow the low overhead hierarchical network model.

The remainder of the paper is organized as follows. In Section 2, existing anomaly detection algorithms developed for cluster-based WSNs are outlined. A detailed description of the ADLU algorithm is provided in Section 3. Section 4 illustrates the obtained simulation results, followed by detailed reports. Finally, conclusions are given in Section 5.

2 Related work

The issue of anomaly detection in hierarchical, cluster-based WSNs has been addressed by several scientific works. According to a recent study [20], the developed ADSs can be categorized based upon the incorporated anomaly detection pattern. The detection pattern is basically linked to who takes charge of carrying out the data processing procedure of anomaly detection. There are basically three available options, which are highlighted in Figure 1. First, the cluster head is responsible for the processing and decision making alone [23]. Second, the cluster head and cluster members cooperate to accomplish

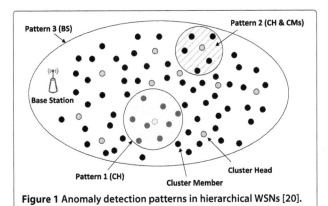

Figure 1 Anomaly detection patterns in hierarchical WSNs [20].

this [24-27]. Third, this procedure is carried out by a central authority, namely, the base station (BS) [28,29].

More specifically, in the protocol of the first detection pattern [23], the cluster head depends on the alarms or data received from the cluster members to determine whether a node is malicious. Thus, the cluster members, except collecting the input data sets, neither participate in the data processing procedure nor contribute to the procedure of analysis and decision. However, this clearly leads to the overuse of energy in the cluster heads. Moreover, the decision making procedure depends on the validity of the incoming data. If this data is falsified by a compromised node, the cluster head will not take the right decision [30].

The second and third detection patterns seem to balance the nodes' energy dissipation more reasonably. For instance, in [26] and [25], the cluster head is taking care of its cluster members, whereas a part of the cluster members are activated for monitoring the cluster head. By letting the cluster head be attended, one increases the security, as he or she meets the 'trust-no-node' requirement [31]. In [26], the authors by employing the self-organizing map (SOM) neural network algorithm and the K-means clustering algorithm at the same time, they raise massive computation burdens. Similarly in [25], the kernel density estimator, on which this detection scheme relies, requires massive information exchange between the sensor nodes, or equivalently, smart strategies to reduce the communication cost.

To reduce the energy overheads, the genetic algorithm (GA)-based scheme presented in [28] benefits from the hierarchical structure of the network arranging the primary computing tasks to the base station (recall that the base station has much softer limitations for power and computation). While this scheme is not directly concerned with detection, however, it could assist detection schemes in advancing their performance and efficiency by optimizing, for instance, the placement of the monitoring nodes. The limitation of this scheme is that GA

suffers from exponential time increase if the network's scale grows.

From the above analysis, it becomes apparent that extensive work has been done in the area of anomaly-based detection for cluster-based WSNs. However, none of the proposed network-based ADS architectures can be directly applied to IEEE 802.15.4-compliant WSNs operating under the UWB PHY since they do not take into account the UWB technology strengths and limitations. Therefore, in this paper, we move towards that direction by proposing a modular, robust, and lightweight ADS architecture specifically designed for this class of wireless sensor networks.

3 Anomaly detection and localization in UWB wireless sensor networks

3.1 Basic concept and model assumptions

As already revealed, the energy constraints in WSNs dictate the use of a hierarchical model for anomaly detection. In order to partition the network into clusters and determine the cluster heads, a cluster formation protocol is executed first. Towards securing the leader election mechanism of this protocol, a new trust-aware leader election metric is defined. After the clusters are formed and a specific number of rounds is reached, called *repetition period* (RP), ADLU redistributes the role of the CH. One round is assumed to be completed when all cluster members (at maximum N_u) have exchanged a packet with their CH. Since each cluster may have a different number of cluster members, a total number of N_u exchanges is assumed so that all clusters begin and end their rounds in exactly the same time. ADLU adopts the concept of cluster member limitation, i.e., a maximum number of N_u nodes is set that can be members of a CH, so as to avoid high-energy transmissions and to bound the induced interference.

3.1.1 Exploiting the ranging capability of the 802.15.4 standard

Towards providing anomaly detection and localization functionalities, ADLU exploits the peculiar characteristics of the IEEE 802.15.4 UWB PHY and most importantly its capability at providing high precision ranging [1]. This feature is an enabler for our anomaly detection and location-attribution algorithm. Ranging in IEEE 802.15.4 standard is an optional capability achieved through support of a number of specific PHY capabilities as well as defined MAC behaviors and protocols. The mandatory ranging protocol is the two-way ranging (TWR) depicted in Figure 2, which allows for ranging measurements based on the round trip delay between two stations, without the need for a common time reference [22]. In this scheme, the ranging-capable device (RDEV) A begins the session by sending a range request packet[a] to node B. Then, node B waits a time τ, known to both devices, to send a request

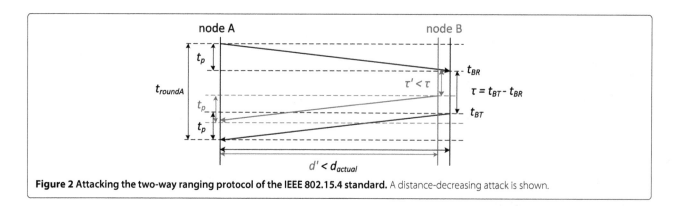

Figure 2 Attacking the two-way ranging protocol of the IEEE 802.15.4 standard. A distance-decreasing attack is shown.

back to node A. Based on that packet, node A can measure the round-trip time, $t_{\text{roundA}} = t_p + \tau$, and extract the one-way time-of-flight, t_p, with respect to its own reference time.

3.1.2 Vulnerability of the two-way ranging protocol
In localizing anomalies, trustworthy distance measurements are necessary. According to a recent study [32], however, the two-way ranging protocol of the UWB PHY is vulnerable to ranging attacks. A compromised node B may tamper its processing time as τ' in order to manipulate the distance measurement and cheat node A about its distance (see Figure 2 for an explanation). Hence, in making the UWB distance measurements immune to ranging attacks, even in the presence of an adversary interfering with the ranging process, ADLU adopts the PHY hacks proposed in [32], which include an energy detection (ED) countermeasure and convolutional plus time-hopping code patches.

Next, we describe the ADLU algorithm in detail. Within our model, we assume that no node can be fully trusted since no pre-existing distributed trust model exists. Moreover, we assume that a number of legitimate nodes are tampered with and reprogrammed for an adversary's purpose, i.e., in order to launch an attack against the clustering protocol. While an adversary can completely take over the nodes, we assume that such an adversary cannot outnumber legitimate nodes by replicating captured ones or introducing new ones in sufficiently many parts of the network.

3.2 Detailed protocol description
The ADLU algorithm uses a round-based approach towards cluster formation and anomaly detection. At the end of each round (RP), the network is re-clustered and new cluster heads are assigned. A monitoring mechanism is introduced to assist the analysis and decision making process of anomaly detection. Finally, anomalies are localized using a geometric, *trilateration* technique. The different phases of the ADLU algorithm are analyzed below.

3.2.1 Phase 1: secure leader election and cluster formation
In order to establish the clusters, a modified version of the *energy-aware self-organizing clustering* (EASOC) algorithm [33] is used. This protocol is a *leader-first* clustering protocol developed for UWB wireless sensor networks. This means that the cluster heads are elected first, based on an *energy-aware interference factor* (EAIF) shown in Equation (1) and then other nodes join these cluster heads forming a multi-cluster network.

$$\text{EAIF}_i = \frac{\frac{1}{N_i}\sum_{k=1}^{N_i} D_{ik}^\alpha}{E_i^{\text{res}}}. \tag{1}$$

This protocol, however, does not offer the security we need when electing the cluster heads, because internal attackers that do not follow the protocol semantics can lie about their distance or their residual energy to make themselves elected as cluster heads, thus giving them the chance to launch severe attacks. This vulnerability is dealt with by modifying the leader election protocol (LEP). In securing the LEP protocol, a new leader election metric is introduced: the *secure leader election indicator* (SLEI). For a node i with N_i neighbors, its SLEI_i is computed as follows:

$$\text{SLEI}_i = \text{EAIF}_i \cdot W_i = \frac{\frac{1}{N_i}\sum_{k=1}^{N_i} D_{ik}^\alpha}{E_i^{\text{res}}} \cdot \frac{1}{N_i}\sum_{k=1}^{N_i} \theta_{ki}, \tag{2}$$

where D_{ik} is the distance between node i and its kth neighbor, α is the path loss exponent, E_i^{res} is the residual energy of node i, W_i is a weight ranging from 0 to 1, and $\theta_{ki} \in [0, 1]$ is a trust value assigned to node i by its peers. The rationale behind this definition is that when all nodes have the same EAIF_i, we should select the nodes with the highest weighted trust, W_i. Nodes that have lower weighted trusts are avoided from becoming cluster heads, even though they may have higher EAIF_i (note that the EAIF indicator is upper bounded).

Basically, the clustering algorithm in [33] follows four steps towards dividing the network into clusters and defining the cluster heads. The *first step* consists of the exchange of ranging-enabled beacons between the neighbor nodes and the computation of the $EAIF_i$ indicator. In the *second step*, each node floods the network with a table containing its closest N_u neighbors, and its locally computed $EAIF_i$, which maybe falsified if node i is malicious.

Hence, within ADLU, we modify this. Each node floods the network with a table containing its $EAIF_i$ value and the trust values θ_{ik} this node assigns to its closest N_u neighbors. The trust metric is initialized to 1 and is updated every time a node enters the 'monitoring and trust update' phase. Trust updates are based on the trustworthiness of a node. We classify the trustworthiness into three grades: *trust*, *distrust*, and *uncertain*, valued as 1, 0, and 0.5, respectively. Hence, if node i behaves maliciously, the trust values assigned to this node by its monitoring neighbors, θ_{ki}, will be decreased using a *two-step strategy*: from 1 to 0.5 and then to 0. Accordingly, W_i and $SLEI_i$ will be decreased. At the end of this step, every node constructs a table of N entries, one for every node in the network. Hence, all nodes have exactly the same global knowledge of the network status.

In the *third step*, ADLU's secure LEP protocol begins. The node with the maximum $SLEI_i$ is marked as cluster head, and all its neighbors, N_u at maximum, are removed from the table. This procedure continues until there is no node left to be examined that is not a cluster head. After the cluster heads have been marked, every other node selects the closest one and joins its cluster. In the *fourth step*, the cluster heads and their cluster members exchange data. The cluster heads then forward the collected data to the BS. When a predefined number of data exchanges is reached, namely RP, the entire procedure starts from the beginning. In each RP, the cluster heads will probably be different from the previous ones, and in this way, the energy-consuming role of the cluster head is reassigned among the nodes of the network, resulting in a more uniform energy consumption. We do not oversee the cases where a malicious node is elected as cluster head, especially during the network setup when no prior knowledge exists. This is the reason why we introduce a mechanism to monitor the activity of the cluster heads as well.

3.2.2 Phase 2: monitoring and trust update

The next problem we must deal with is the determination of the nodes that will run the ADS, i.e., how many and which nodes should be on duty to detect misbehaviors. In monitoring the cluster members, the intrusion detection function is activated on the cluster heads. If after an interval equal to a *monitoring period* (MP) (measured in rounds) a cluster member is judged to be abnormal by its cluster head, it is revoked. In doing so, the trust value of the malicious node as seen by its cluster head is updated (reduced) and is broadcasted as an alarm message to all cluster member nodes.

Cluster heads on the other hand are monitored by their cluster members. Cluster head monitoring is necessary to assure that even in the case the LEP protocol fails, malicious cluster heads that went undetected do not retain this role for long. A part of the cluster members, three in total, are activated for monitoring and jointly making final decisions on the maliciousness of their CH. In each MP, the cluster member nodes with the second, third, and fourth in succession biggest $SLEI_i$ values compose the monitoring team of the CH (recall that the CH has the highest $SLEI_i$ value within its cluster). If after the MP interval half of these nodes indicate that the cluster head is malicious (majority vote rule), then the cluster head is revoked by the monitoring team. In revoking a malicious cluster head, each member of the monitoring team broadcasts an alarm message containing the reduced trust value of the malicious cluster head, as well as its new $EAIF_i$ value (recall that a change in the $EAIF_i$ value is reflected on the $SLEI_i$ value; hence, this information would allow different cluster member nodes to probably monitor the cluster head in the next MP intervals). Following the identification and revocation of the malicious CH, another cluster head, among the cluster members, is elected. In this re-clustering process, the node with the new highest $SLEI_i$ value in the attacked cluster becomes its cluster head. This node may retain the role of the CH until the next RP round, unless it is marked as malicious by its cluster members.

With a majority rule being applied when monitoring the activity of a cluster head, if a node from the monitoring team is compromised and issues a false alarm trying to revoke a legitimate cluster head, it would have no effect because the majority would prevail. However, since the majority-vote rule represents a cooperative anomaly-detection scheme, there might be the case that multiple malicious nodes with high $SLEI_i$ values obtain the role of the monitoring team inside a cluster, enabling them to deceive the majority-vote rule and to revoke a legitimate CH. This situation is identified by the simulation results depicted in Section 4.2 and is indicated with a drop in the detection accuracy of the ADLU algorithm when 40% or more of the nodes behave maliciously. However, this is a highly hostile condition and cannot be dealt effectively by any cooperative anomaly-detection scheme.

3.2.3 Phase 3: anomaly detection and localization

Our network-based ADS detects anomalies based on the packets that it monitors. Each node running the ADS stores a data structure for each collected packet. Then, each data structure is evaluated according to the sequence of rules defined in Table 1 (please note that jamming attacks are not considered in our study). This means that within ADLU, we employ a rule-based approach to anomaly detection. Rule-based detection appears to be

Table 1 Rule definition

Rule description	Detection metric	Attack detected
When a packet is not forwarded as it should, increase a counter. When this counter reaches a threshold t after MP rounds, raise an alarm.	Packet drop rate	Selective forwarding and black hole attacks [34]
When a packet does not originate from a node with a distance no longer than the radio range of a single hop, raise an alarm.	Packet origin address	Hello flood and sinkhole attacks [35]
When the distance measurements between multiple, at least two, distinct nodes match, raise an alarm.	Distance matching criterion	Sybil [36] attacks

very attractive in the context of WSNs in the essence that the detection speed and complexity certainly benefits from the absence of an explicit training procedure required, for example, in data mining approaches [20]. In rule-based detection, the anomaly detector uses predefined rules to classify data points as anomalies or normalities. While monitoring the network, these rules are selected appropriately and applied to the monitored data packets. A data packet is discarded after being tested against all rules without violating any of them. On the contrary, if a violation of any of these rules occurs or equivalently if the rules defining an anomaly are satisfied, an anomaly is declared and an alarm will be raised. An alarm generated by a cluster head indicates that a cluster member is an intruder and needs to be revoked. Similarly, if the independent alarms raised by the monitor nodes of a cluster head satisfy the majority-vote rule, then this cluster head is revoked and a new cluster head, among the cluster members, is elected.

Each time an untrustworthy node is revoked (the revocation is indicated by a broadcast alarm message), an UWB ranging-based localization algorithm is executed to identify the location of the attacker. The location-finding algorithm is composed of two steps: *ranging* and *localization* [37]. The ranging process is the action of estimating the distance between two devices. Localization is the mechanism of finding the exact location of a given node by utilizing three or more range estimates. As already analyzed, among the available ranging techniques defined by the IEEE 802.15.4 standard [1], within ADLU, the range estimates are obtained using the two-way time-of-arrival technique depicted in Figure 2. Regarding the localization process, ADLU adopts the time-of-arrival triangulation of ranges technique defined by the standard. This technique applies to the general network lacking synchronization between devices and/or *a priori* organization, and assumes that three ranges $d_1 = c \times t_1$, $d_2 = c \times t_2$, and $d_3 = c \times t_3$ are gathered from three 'anchor devices' $i = 1, 2, 3$ with locations (x_i, y_i) (see Figure 3 for a geometry of this technique). The role of the three anchor nodes is assigned to those cluster member nodes that within the given MP interval have been elected to monitor the CH.

Following the assignment of the anchor nodes, the coordinates of the target node in the 2D space are computed by solving a linear least-squares (LLS) problem, which translates to finding the intersection of three circles. As soon as the x, y coordinates of the malicious node are determined, the anchor nodes are then responsible for forwarding this information to the BS to enable the system administrators and the security professionals to take countermeasures. In doing so, they first transmit the location information to the CH. Then, the CH forwards this information to the BS either directly (if the BS is within range) or via multiple hops (inter-cluster routing). Since, there might be the case that the CH is the malicious node the anchor nodes were monitoring and for which they initiated the localization process, then in this case, the anchor nodes will have to wait for the new CH to be elected before transmitting this critical data to the legitimate one. The three phases of the ADLU algorithm are summarized in algorithmic form within Algorithm 1.

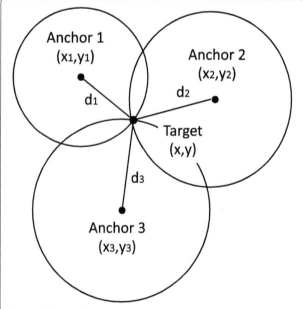

Figure 3 Time-of-arrival triangulation of ranges to determine location (Adapted from [1]).

Algorithm 1 The ADLU algorithm

{ *Phase 1: Secure Leader Election and Cluster Formation*}
for each node i in the network **do**
    Step 1: exchange a ranging-enabled beacon with all its neighbors (closest N_u)
    Step 1: calculate its $EAIF_i$ indicator
    Step 2: flood the network with the table {node_ID i, $EAIF_i$, $\theta_{ik} = 1, \forall$ neighbors k}
end for
Step 2: construct a table from the received messages
for each node i in the table run the LEP protocol **do**
    if nodes are left in the table **then**
        Step 3: mark node with the maximum $SLEI_i$ as cluster head (CH)
        Step 3: delete the neighbors of this CH from table (N_u at most)
    end if
end for
for each node left in the table **do**
    Step 4: node i joins the closest CH
end for
Step 4: cluster members (CMs) exchange data with their CH

if Rounds > repetition period, RP **then**
    start from the beginning (**Step 1**)
end if
{ *Phase 2: Monitoring & Trust Update* }
for each node i in the network **do**
    if node i is the CH **then**
        start monitoring your CMs
        if Rounds > monitoring period, MP **then**
            collect data, update, if necessary, the trust values, θ_{ik}, and execute **Phase 3**
        end if
    else
        select the cluster member nodes with the 2nd, 3rd, and 4th in succession biggest $SLEI_i$ values, and start to monitor the CH
        if Rounds > MP **then**
            collect data, update, if necessary, the trust value θ_{ki} of the CH, and execute **Phase 3**
            update, if necessary, the members of the CH's monitoring team based on the updated $EAIF_i$ values of current monitoring nodes
        end if
    end if
end for
{ *Phase 3: Anomaly Detection and Localization* }
Apply rules on the collected data packets
if Rules are satisfied **then**
    Step 1: Declare the anomaly and start node revocation
    Step 2: Execute the time-of-arrival triangulation of ranges algorithm to localize the malicious node
else
    Discard the packet and continue operation
end if

---

4 Performance evaluation

We used a custom-developed simulation tool implemented in C++ to evaluate the performance of the ADLU algorithm. As stated earlier, comparison of our algorithm with classical, cluster-based ADSs would not be appropriate, as they do not take into account the UWB technology limitations and strengths. We only compare the ADLU algorithm with its ancestor, the EASOC algorithm [33], in an attempt to evaluate the energy and communication overhead it incurs to a clustering algorithm that does not implement the detection and location-attribution engines of the ADLU algorithm.

With regard to the network topology, 100 nodes were randomly placed inside a square area of 100×100 m^2 (the BS was placed at the center). The cluster member-limitation parameter, N_u, was set to 10^b. Cluster member nodes where generating packets with an interarrival time equal to two packets per second. We chose to vary the monitoring period and the repetition period as follows: MP $= \{1, 2, 3\}$ rounds and RP $= \{80, 140\}$ rounds. The UWB PHY parameters are summarized in Table 2. All the presented results were averaged over 20 simulation runs.

We simulated a security-oriented application supporting sink-based reporting, that is to say, traffic flowing from the leaf nodes to the BS (typical case of a sensor network). Randomly selected intelligent adversaries include themselves in the network by replicating legitimate (captured) nodes and start launching an attack, as reflected in Table 1. In case of selective forwarding attacks, a malicious node selectively drops packets with a probability p_d. When $p_d = 1.0$, the attacker is executing a black hole attack.

Three metrics were used to evaluate the efficiency of the ADLU algorithm. These are as follows:

1. The *communication overhead*, defined as the ratio of the total communication overhead in a system that incorporates our detection algorithm against a system that does not
2. The *percentage reduction in network lifetime*, resulting from the incorporation of our detection algorithm
3. The *detection accuracy*, defined as the ratio of the detected attacks to the total number of detected and undetected attacks
4. *False negative rate*, defined as the rate at which events are not flagged intrusive by the detector, although the attack exists.

4.1 Energy and communication overhead

We begin by analyzing the communication overhead of two systems, one incorporating the ADLU algorithm and its anomaly detection and location-attribution engines, and one that does not, namely the EASOC algorithm.

Table 2 UWB PHY parameters

Property	Value
PHY option	IEEE 802.15.4 UWB PHY
Frequency band	Channel {0} with $f_c = 499.2$ MHz and BW = 499.2 MHz
Data rate	0.85 Mbs (mandatory data rate)
Rate-dependent and	mean PRF = 15.60 MHz, $T_{dsym} = 1,025.64$ ns,
Timing-related parameters	$T_{psym} = 993.6$ ns, $N_{sync} = 64$ symbols, $N_{sfd} = 8$ symbols
Power	36.5 μW (FCC limit for $\approx$ 0.5-GHz bandwidth)
Communication range	20 m
DATA packet length	1,038 symbols (+ 64 symbols for SYNC trailer)
Ranging support	TW-TOA (mandatory ranging)
Channel access	UWB preamble sense based on the SHR of a frame
	(clear channel assessment - CCA Mode 5)

Their ratio is denoted as the relative communication overhead. To simulate this scenario, we chose at random a number of network nodes, and we programmed them to selectively launch one of the attacks depicted in Table 1. With regard to selective forwarding attacks (launched only by cluster heads), the attacker was dropping packets with a probability $p_d = 30\%$. When $p_d = 100\%$, the attacker was executing a black hole attack. We set the threshold value for the percentage of packets being dropped over an interval MP to be $t = 20\%$. Above this threshold, an alarm was generated and node revocation was initiated. Packets dropped at a lower rate were attributed to other factors, such as collisions or node failures and did not produce an intrusion alert. For all other types of attack, distance-related rules are responsible for raising an alarm.

In Figure 4a, the curves show that the relative communication overhead increases smoothly as the percentage of malicious nodes increases. This is because more packet exchanges occur following the introduction, identification, and revocation of an increasing number of adversaries. In all cases, however, the communication overhead

is kept at very low ratios, as low as 0.050 and 0.042 for RP = 80 and 140 rounds, respectively. A smaller RP value causes a slightly higher increase to the relative communication overhead, notably because of the slightly higher number of packets being broadcasted as a result of the shorter network re-clustering phase. As expected, the communication overhead is extremely low when the network contains no malicious nodes. No curves are shown with regard to the changing value of the monitoring period, MP. This is because the MP interval by relating to the decision making window of the monitoring phase mostly affects the detection accuracy of the ADLU algorithm.

Figure 4b illustrates the percentage reduction in network lifetime when common sensor nodes run our anomaly detection and location attribution algorithm. Once again, the results illustrate that as the percentage of malicious nodes inside the network increases, the reduction in the network lifetime increases. As the curves highlight, the reduction is slightly higher when RP is equal to 80. As mentioned earlier, smaller RP values cause a slightly higher increase to the relative communication overhead, which also translates to an increase in the

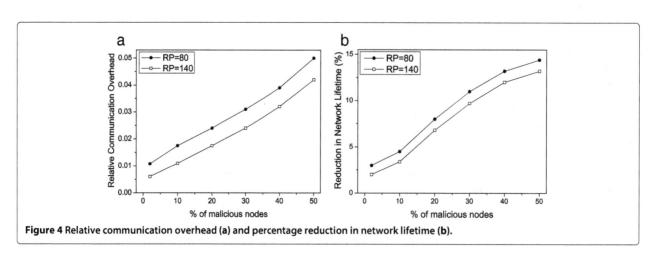

Figure 4 Relative communication overhead (**a**) and percentage reduction in network lifetime (**b**).

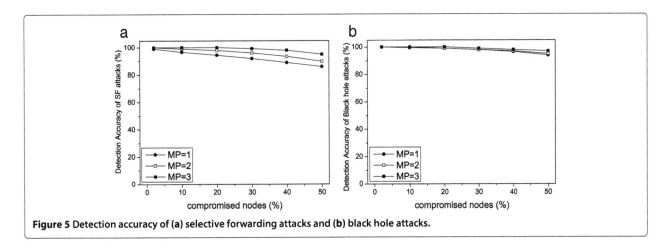

Figure 5 Detection accuracy of **(a)** selective forwarding attacks and **(b)** black hole attacks.

energy dissipation of the nodes. Overall, the network lifetime decreases by as high as 14.4% when RP = 80 rounds, and by 13.2% when RP = 140 rounds. The relatively small reduction observed in both cases is due to the fact that within ADLU, the nodes rotate the energy-consuming roles of the CH and that of the monitoring team, and as such, the energy dissipation is uniformly distributed among the network nodes. Since the network lifetime is in comparative levels when compared to a system that does not incorporate our anomaly detection algorithm, this fact can justify the installation of our ADS on the sensor nodes.

4.2 Detection accuracy and false-negative rate
The rest of the figures evaluate the detection accuracy of the ADLU algorithm against the attacks of Table 1 and the false-negative rates that it achieved. In the subsequent simulations, and more specifically in each attack scenario presented next, there was always one single type of attacker, which was varied in each simulation.

As an overall observation, we can say that the variation of MP solely affects the detection accuracy of the selective forwarding and black hole attacks illustrated

in Figure 5a,b. This happens because these attacks are assessed over a time window, and therefore, their detection accuracy is affected by the monitoring interval, MP. Recall that the interval MP relates to the time window that a monitor node has in order to gather packets and analyze them for signs of intrusion. Since less packets are being collected as a result of the smaller MP interval and given that packets are dropped probabilistically, there might be the case that during a monitoring interval, the dropped packets are less than $t = 20\%$, and hence, no alarm is produced, generating false negatives (see Figure 6a). This is less probable to happen when the value of MP gets bigger or when nodes launch black hole attacks, i.e., $p_d = 100\%$. In the latter case depicted in Figure 5b, the probability that the dropped packets during an MP interval are less than t, which results in a false negative, is close to zero, and hence, the accuracy in detecting this attack is close to 100% (this is also shown in Figure 6b).

Figure 7a illustrates the detection accuracy of hello flood attacks (similar curves are obtained when the attacker launches a sinkhole attack). In examining these attacks, we chose to vary the accuracy in the UWB

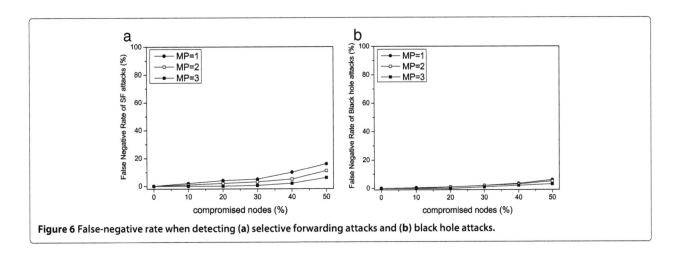

Figure 6 False-negative rate when detecting **(a)** selective forwarding attacks and **(b)** black hole attacks.

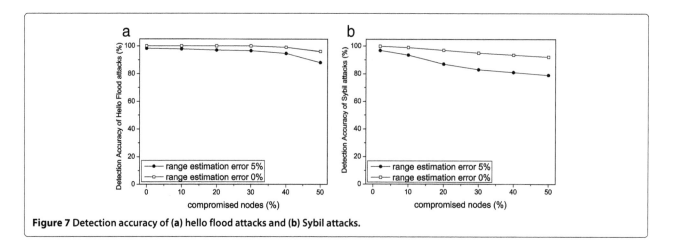

Figure 7 Detection accuracy of **(a)** hello flood attacks and **(b)** Sybil attacks.

distance measurements resembling ranging attacks that went undetected. When the range estimation error ϵ_r is equal to 0%, the detection was always close to 100%, notably because of the rule being applied to detect this kind of attack. Another factor that keeps the detection levels high in this case is that these attacks are not mistaken with occasional network or communication failures, as the previous attack category, and as such, fewer false negatives are generated as shown in Figure 8a. However, an increase in the number of misdetections is obtained in two cases. Firstly, when half or more of the network nodes behave maliciously. In this case, the majority-vote rule being applied fails to prevail. Secondly, when inaccuracies are introduced in the UWB range estimates, namely, when ϵ_r is up to 5%. Recall that in these attacks, the rule being applied depends on the distance measurements. Hence, when range estimation errors exist, the detection effectiveness of the ADLU algorithm drops.

Similar to the previous attack scenario, the accuracy in detecting Sybil attacks depends on the accuracy of the UWB distance measurements. As shown in Figure 7b, the detection accuracy of Sybil attacks ranges between 99%

and 78.8%. The drop in the detection accuracy is higher when compared to the previous attack scenario. This is actually an indication of the higher dependence between the rule being applied to detect this kind of attack and the distance estimation error, ϵ_r. Apparently, the distance-matching criterion could not be satisfied when inaccuracies in the range estimates, ϵ_r, are introduced. Following this observation, we then relaxed the matching criterion and adjusted the rule, taking into account errors in the distance estimation in the order of 2%. By doing this, we slightly reduced the number of generated false negatives (see Figure 8b).

5 Conclusions

In this paper, we presented an anomaly detection and localization algorithm specifically designed for hierarchical, cluster-based UWB wireless sensor networks. A novel, trust-aware leader election metric was defined to secure the algorithm's cluster formation protocol. The simulation results showed that the proposed algorithm achieves high detection accuracy and low false-negative rates while maintaining the communication overhead at low levels.

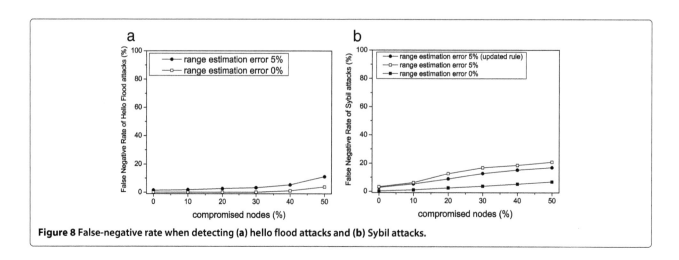

Figure 8 False-negative rate when detecting **(a)** hello flood attacks and **(b)** Sybil attacks.

In the future, we intend to examine the effectiveness of the ADLU algorithm in detail by considering larger networks as well as the presence of malicious nodes heavily interfering with the UWB ranging process.

Endnotes

[a]The packets used for ranging estimation are standard packets, with the only difference being the value of a specific bit in the PHY header (PHR) called the 'ranging bit', which is set by the transmitting PHY for frames intended for ranging. A UWB frame with the ranging bit set to 1 is called a ranging frame (RFRAME). There is nothing else, beyond the ranging bit, that makes an RFRAME unique. RFRAMEs can carry data or can even be acknowledgments.

[b]Note that the choice of the N_u parameter may affect the operation of ADLU. As such, we have run multiple simulation tests to fine-tune this metric prior to selecting its final value.

Competing interests
The authors declare that they have no competing interests.

Acknowledgements
This work was performed within the framework of the Action 'Supporting Postdoctoral Researchers' of the Operational Programme 'Education and Lifelong Learning' (Actions Beneficiary: General Secretariat for Research and Technology, GSRT), and is co-financed by the European Social Fund (ESF) and the Greek State.

References

1. IEEE, *IEEE 802.15.4™-2011*: IEEE Standard for Local and Metropolitan Area Networks–Part 15. 4: Low-Rate Wireless Personal Area Networks (LR-WPANs). (IEEE, Piscataway, 2011)
2. E Karapistoli, FN Pavlidou, I Gragopoulos, I Tsetsinas, An overview of the IEEE 802.15.4a Standard. Commun. Mag. IEEE. **48**(1), 47–53 (2010)
3. N Sastry, D Wagner, Security considerations for IEEE 802.15.4 networks. Paper presented at the 3rd ACM workshop on wireless security (WiSe), Philadelphia, PA, USA, 1 Oct 2004, pp. 32–42
4. C Karlof, D Wagner, Secure routing in wireless sensor networks: Attacks and countermeasures. Paper presented at the first IEEE international workshop on sensor network protocols and applications, Anchorage, AK, USA 11 May 2003, pp. 113–127
5. D Martins, H Guyennet, Wireless sensor network attacks and security mechanisms—A short survey. Paper presented at 13th international conference on network-based information systems (NBiS), Takayama, Japan, 14–16 Sept 2010, 313–320
6. K Xing, S Srinivasan, M Rivera, J Li, X Cheng, ed. by SCH Huang, D MacCallum, and D-Z Du, Attacks and countermeasures in sensor networks: A survey, in *Network Security* (Springer, New York, 2010), pp. 251–272
7. S Ghose, R Bose, Physical layer security in UWB networks. Paper presented at the IEEE international conference on microwaves, communications, antennas and electronics systems (COMCAS), Tel Aviv, 7–9 Nov 2011, pp. 1–5
8. M Ko, D Goeckel, Wireless physical-layer security performance of UWB systems. Paper presented at the military communications conference (MILCOM), San Jose, CA, USA 31 Oct–3 Nov 2010, pp. 2143–2148
9. SA Camtepe, B Yener, Key distribution mechanisms for wireless sensor networks: A survey. Technical report, Rensselaer Polytechnic Institute, 2005
10. E Shi, A Perrig, Designing secure sensor networks. IEEE Wireless Commun. Mag. **11**(6), 38–43 (2004)
11. L Lazos, R Poovendran, SeRLoc: Robust localization for wireless sensor networks. ACM Trans. Sensor Netw. (TOSN). **1**, 73–100 (2005)
12. S Roy, M Conti, S Setia, S Jajodia, Secure data aggregation in wireless sensor networks. IEEE Trans. Inf. Forensics Secur. **7**(3), 1040–1052 (2012)
13. M Flury, M Poturalski, P Papadimitratos, JP Hubaux, JY Le Boudec, Effectiveness of distance-decreasing attacks against impulse radio ranging. Paper presented at the third ACM conference on wireless network security (WiSec). Hoboken, NJ, USA, 22–24 March 2010, pp. 117–128
14. N Tippenhauer, S Capkun, ID-based secure distance bounding and localization. ESORICS. **5789**, 621–636 (2010)
15. Y Wang, X Ma, G Leus, An UWB ranging-based localization strategy with internal attack immunity. ICUWB. **2**, 1–4 (2010)
16. Y Zhang, W Liu, Y Fang, D Wu, Secure localization and authentication in ultra-wideband sensor networks. IEEE J. Select. Areas Commun. **24**(4), 829–835 (2006)
17. YH Jazyah, M Hope, ed. by D Taniar, O Gervasi, B Murgante, E Pardede, and BO Apduhan, A review of routing protocols for UWB MANETs, in *Proceedings of the 2010 International Conference on Computational Science and Its Applications, Part III* (Springer, Berlin, 2010), pp. 228–245
18. A Becher, Z Benenson, M Dornseif, ed. by J Clark, R Paige, Polack F, and P Brooke, Tampering with motes: Real-world physical attacks on wireless sensor networks, in *Security in Pervasive Computing, Lecture Notes in Computer Science, vol. 3934* (Springer, Berlin, 2006), pp. 104–118
19. A Farooqi, F Khan, ed. by Slezak D, T Kim, AC Chang, T Vasilakos, M Li, and Sakurai Kouichi, Intrusion detection systems for wireless sensor networks: A survey, in *Communication and Networking, vol. 56* (Springer, Berlin, 2009), pp. 234–241
20. M Xie, S Han, B Tian, S Parvin, Anomaly detection in wireless sensor networks: A survey. J Netw. Comput. Appl. **34**(4), 1302–1325 (2011)
21. V Chandola, A Banerjee, V Kumar, Anomaly detection: A survey. ACM Comput. Surv. **41**(3), 15:1–15:58 (2009)
22. Z Sahinoglu, S Gezici, Ranging in the IEEE 802.15.4a Standard. Paper presented at the IEEE annual conference on wireless and microwave technology (WAMICON), Clearwater Beach, FL, USA, 4–5 Dec 2006, pp. 1–5
23. CC Su, KM Chang, YH Kuo, MF Horng, The new intrusion prevention and detection approaches for clustering-based sensor networks. WCNC. **4**, 1927–193 (2005)
24. S Rajasegarar, C Leckie, M Palaniswami, J Bezdek, Distributed anomaly detection in wireless sensor networks. Paper presented at the 10th IEEE international conference on communication systems (ICCS), Singapore, 30 Oct–2 Nov 2006, pp. 1–5
25. S Subramaniam, T Palpanas, D Papadopoulos, V Kalogeraki, D Gunopulos, Online outlier detection in sensor data using non-parametric models. Paper presented at the 32nd international conference on very large data bases (VLDB), Seoul, South Korea, 12–15 Sept 2006, pp. 187–198
26. H Wang, Z Yuan, C Wang, Intrusion detection for wireless sensor networks based on multi-agent and refined clustering. CMC. **3**, 450–454 (2009)
27. YY Zhang, W-C Yang, K-B Kim, M-S Park, Inside attacker detection in hierarchical wireless sensor network. Paper presented at the 3rd international conference on innovative computing information and control (ICICIC). Dalian, Liaoning, 18–20 June 2008, pp. 594–594
28. K Rahul, H Liu, HH Chen, Reduced complexity intrusion detection in sensor networks using genetic algorithm. Paper presented at the IEEE international conference on communications, Dresden, Germany, 14–18 June 2009, pp 1–5
29. S Rajasegarar, C Leckie, M Palaniswami, J Bezdek, Quarter sphere based distributed anomaly detection in wireless sensor networks. Paper presented at the IEEE international conference on communications, Glasgow, 24–28 June 2007, pp. 3864–3869
30. IM Atakli, H Hu, Y Chen, WS Ku, Z Su, Malicious node detection in wireless sensor networks using weighted trust evaluation. Paper presented at the spring simulation multiconference (SpringSim), Ottawa, Canada, 14–17 Apr 2008, pp 836–843
31. I Krontiris, T Dimitriou, FC Freiling, Towards intrusion detection in wireless sensor networks. Paper presented at the 13th European wireless conference, Paris, France, 1–4 Apr 2007
32. M Poturalski, M Flury, P Papadimitratos, JP Hubaux, JY Le Boudec, Distance bounding with IEEE 802.15.4a: Attacks and countermeasures. IEEE Trans. Wireless Commun. **10**(4), 1334–1344 (2011)

33. G Koltsidas, E Karapistoli, FN Pavlidou, An energy-aware self-organizing clustering algorithm for UWB wireless sensor networks. Paper presented at the IEEE 19th international symposium on personal, indoor and mobile radio communications (PIMRC). Cannes, 15–18 Sept 2008, pp. 1–5

34. L Bysani, A Turuk, A survey on selective forwarding attack in wireless sensor networks. Paper presented at the international conference on devices and communications (ICDeCom), Mesra, Algeria, 24–25 Feb 2011, pp. 1–5

35. I Krontiris, T Giannetsos, T Dimitriou, Launching a sinkhole attack in wireless sensor networks: The intruder side. Paper presented at the IEEE international conference on wireless and mobile computing, networking and communication, Avignon, France, 12–14 Oct 2008, pp. 526–531

36. J Newsome, E Shi, D Song, A Perrig, The Sybil attack in sensor networks: Analysis defenses. Paper presented at the third international symposium on information processing in sensor networks. Berkeley, California, USA, 26–27 Apr 2004, pp. 259–268

37. S Gezici, Z Tian, G Giannakis, H Kobayashi, A Molisch, H Poor, Z Sahinoglu, Localization via ultra-wideband radios: A look at positioning aspects for future sensor networks. Signal Process Mag. IEEE. **22**(4), 70–84 (2005)

14

MUSE: asset risk scoring in enterprise network with mutually reinforced reputation propagation

Xin Hu[1]*, Ting Wang[1], Marc Ph Stoecklin[2], Douglas L Schales[1], Jiyong Jang[1] and Reiner Sailer[1]

Abstract

Cyber security attacks are becoming ever more frequent and sophisticated. Enterprises often deploy several security protection mechanisms, such as anti-virus software, intrusion detection/prevention systems, and firewalls, to protect their critical assets against emerging threats. Unfortunately, these protection systems are typically 'noisy', e.g., regularly generating thousands of alerts every day. Plagued by false positives and irrelevant events, it is often neither practical nor cost-effective to analyze and respond to every single alert. The main challenges faced by enterprises are to extract important information from the plethora of alerts and to infer potential risks to their critical assets. A better understanding of risks will facilitate effective resource allocation and prioritization of further investigation. In this paper, we present MUSE, a system that analyzes a large number of alerts and derives risk scores by correlating diverse entities in an enterprise network. Instead of considering a risk as an isolated and static property pertaining only to individual users or devices, MUSE exploits a novel *mutual reinforcement principle* and models the dynamics of risk based on the interdependent relationship among multiple entities. We apply MUSE on real-world network traces and alerts from a large enterprise network consisting of more than 10,000 nodes and 100,000 edges. To scale up to such large graphical models, we formulate the algorithm using a distributed memory abstraction model that allows efficient in-memory parallel computations on large clusters. We implement MUSE on Apache Spark and demonstrate its efficacy in risk assessment and flexibility in incorporating a wide variety of datasets.

Keywords: Risk scoring; Enterprise network; Reputation propagation

Introduction

Mitigating and defending against ever more frequent and sophisticated cyber attacks are often top priorities for enterprises. To this end, a plethora of detection and prevention solutions have been developed and deployed, including anti-virus software, intrusion detection/prevention systems (IDS/IPS), blacklists, firewalls, and so on. With these state-of-the-art technologies capturing various types of security threats, one would expect that they are very effective in detecting and preventing attacks. In reality, however, the effectiveness of these systems often fall short. The increasingly diversified types of cyber attacks, coupled with increasing

collection of applications, hardware configurations, and network equipments, have made the enterprise environment extremely 'noisy'. For example, IDS/IPS systems regularly generate over 10,000 alerts every day. Majority of them turn out to be false positives. Even true alerts are often triggered by low level of threats such as brute-force password guessing and SQL injection attempts. Although the suspicious nature of these events warrants the reports by IPS/IDS systems, their excessive amount often only made the situation even more noisy.

Digging into the haystack of alerts to find clues to actual threats is a daunting task that is very expensive, if not impossible, through manual inspection. As a result, most enterprises practically only have resources to investigate a very small fraction of alerts raised by IPS/IDS systems. Vast majority of others are stored in a database merely for forensic purposes and inspected only after significant incidents have been discovered or critical assets have

*Correspondence: huxin@us.ibm.com
[1] Security Research Department, IBM T.J. Watson Research Center, 1101 Kitchawan Rd, Yorktown Heights, NY, USA
Full list of author information is available at the end of the article

already been severely damaged, e.g., security breaches and data leakage. However, even those small fraction of true positive alerts (e.g., device compromise, virus infection on a user's computer) are often too voluminous to become security analysts' top priority. In addition, these alerts are often considered as low level of threats and pose far less risks to the enterprises comparing with more severe attacks, such as server compromise or sensitive data leakage. Evidently, a more effective solution is to better understand and rank potential risks associated with these alerts so that analysts can effectively prioritize and allocate resources for alert investigation.

In a typical enterprise environment, as shown in Figure 1, there are different sets of entities: servers, devices, users, credentials, and (high-value) assets (e.g., databases, business processes). The connections between these entities represent their intuitive relationships; for example, a user may own multiple devices, a device may connect to different types of servers and internal databases, a device may be associated with multiple user accounts with different credentials, etc. We note that the reputation of these entities provide valuable indicators into their corresponding risks and are important factors to rank various security incidents associated with these entities e.g., IPS/IDS alerts and behavior anomalies. More importantly, an entity's reputation and the risk it may produce are not restricted to each individual entity. In fact, multiple entities are often tied together in a mutually reinforcing relationship with their reputation closely interdependent with each other.

In this work, we develop MUSE (Mutually-reinforced Unsupervised Scoring for Enterprise risk), a risk analysis framework that analyzes a large amount of security alerts

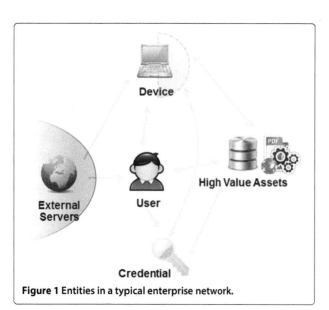

Figure 1 Entities in a typical enterprise network.

and computes the reputation of diverse entities based on various domain knowledge and interactions among these entities. Specifically, MUSE models the interactions with composite, multi-level bipartite graphs where each pair of entity types (e.g., a user and a device) constitute one bipartite graph. MUSE then applies an iterative propagation algorithm on the graphic model to exploit the mutual reinforcement relationship between the connected entities and derive their reputation and risk score simultaneously. Finally, with the refined risk scores, MUSE is able to provide useful information such as ranking of low-reputation entities and potential risks to critical assets, allowing security analysts to make an informed decision as to how resources can be prioritized for further investigation. MUSE will also provide greater visibility into the set of alerts that are responsible for an entity's low reputation, offering insights into the root cause of cyber attacks.

The main contributions of this work include: 1) a mutual reinforcement framework to analyze the reputation and the risk of diverse entities in an enterprise network, 2) a scalable propagation algorithm to exploit the networking structures and identify potential risky entities that may be overlooked by a discrete risk score, 3) a highly flexible system that can incorporate data sources in multiple domains, 4) implementation of MUSE that takes advantage of recent advances in distributed in-memory cluster computing framework and scales to very large graphic models, and 5) evaluations with real network traces from a large enterprise to verify the efficiency and efficacy of MUSE.

Risk and reputation in a multi-entity environment

In the following sections, we will present the design and the architecture of MUSE. We will first formulate the problem of risk and reputation assessment in enterprise network and then discuss specific domain knowledge and intuition that are crucial for solving the problem.

Problem formulation

In a typical enterprise environment, there are multiple sets of connected entities. Specifically, we consider five distinct types of entities as depicted in Figure 1: users $\mathcal{U}$, devices $\mathcal{D}$, credentials $\mathcal{C}$, high value assets $\mathcal{A}$, and external servers $\mathcal{S}$. These entities are often related in a pairwise many-to-many fashion. For example, a device can access multiple external servers. A user may own several devices e.g., laptops and workstations, while one device (e.g., server clusters) can be used by multiple users.

We model the interconnection between entities as a composite bipartite graph $G = (V, E)$, schematically shown in Figure 2. In G, vertices $V = \{\mathcal{U}, \mathcal{D}, \mathcal{C}, \mathcal{A}, \mathcal{S}\}$ represent various entities. Edges $E = \{\mathcal{M}_{\mathcal{DS}}, \mathcal{M}_{\mathcal{DU}}, \mathcal{M}_{\mathcal{DA}}, \mathcal{M}_{\mathcal{UC}}, \mathcal{M}_{\mathcal{DC}}\}$ of bipartite graphs represent their

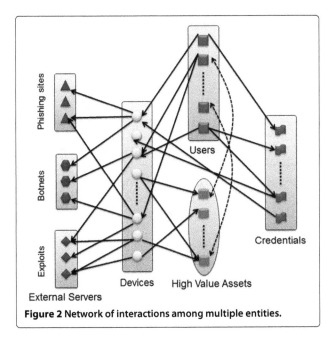

Figure 2 Network of interactions among multiple entities.

- **Device reputation** $p_d = P_d(x_{NR})$ represents the probability that a device may have been infected or compromised and thus under control of adversaries.
- **User reputation** $p_u = P_u(x_{NR})$ indicates how suspiciously a user behaves, e.g., an unauthorized access to sensitive data.
- **Credential reputation** $p_c = P_c(x_{NR})$ denotes the probability that a credential may have been leaked to the adversaries and thus making any servers associated with the credential vulnerable.
- **High-value asset reputation** $p_a = P_a(x_{NR})$ denotes the asset's probability of being risky; for instance, a confidential database being accessed by unauthorized users, exfiltration of sensitive data, etc.

As there is a natural correlation between reputation and risk (e.g., less reputable entities generally pose high risks), we define an entity's risk as $P(x_R) = (1 - P(x_{NR}))$ weighted by the importance of the entity, such that a high-value asset will experience a large increase in its risk score even with a small decline in its reputation. With these definitions, the goal of MUSE is to aggregate large amounts of security alerts, determine the reputation of each entity by exploiting their structural relationships in the connectivity graph, and finally output a ranked list of risky entities for further investigation. In the next section, we will describe the mutual reinforcement principle [1] that underlies MUSE.

Mutual reinforcement principle

The key observation of MUSE is that entities' reputation and risk are not separated; instead, they are closely correlated and interdependent. Through interacting with each other, an entity's reputation can impact on the risk associated with its neighbors, and at the same time, the entity's risk can be influenced by the reputation of its neighbors. For example, a device is likely to be of low reputation 1) if the server it frequently visits are suspicious or malicious e.g. Botnet C&C, Phishing, or malware sites, 2) if the users using the device have bad reputation, and 3) if the credentials used to log into the device have high risks of being compromised, leaked, or even used by an unauthorized user. Similarly, a credential's risk of being exposed will increase if it has been used by a less reputable user and/or on a device that exhibits suspicious behavior patterns. Along the same line, a user will have low reputation if she owns several low-reputation devices and credentials. Last but not least, a high-value asset or the sensitive data stored in internal databases are likely to be under a significant risk e.g., data exfiltration if they have been accessed by multiple low-reputation devices that also connect to external malicious servers. We describe these mutually dependent relationships more formally in our multi-layer mutual reinforcement framework, using the following set

relationships, where $\mathcal{M}_{DS}$ is the $|\mathcal{D}|$-by-$|\mathcal{S}|$ matrix containing all the pairwise edges, i.e., $\mathcal{M}_{DS}(i,j) > 0$ if there is an edge between device d_i and external server s_j. The value of $\mathcal{M}_{DS}(i,j)$ denotes the edge weight derived from the characteristics of the relationship, such as the number of connections, the number of bytes transmitted, duration, and so on. Similarly, $\mathcal{M}_{DS}$, $\mathcal{M}_{DU}$, $\mathcal{M}_{DA}$, $\mathcal{M}_{UC}$, and $\mathcal{M}_{DC}$ are the matrices of the pairwise edges representing the association of their respective entities.

Next, we define the risk and the reputation of different entities more precisely. We treat each entity as a random variable X with a binary class label $X = \{x_R, x_{NR}\}$ assigned to it. Here, x_R is a risky (or bad) label, and x_{NR} is a non-risky (or good) label. A probability distribution P is defined over this binary class, where $P(x_R)$ is the probability of being risky and $P(x_{NR})$ is the probability of being non-risky. By definition, the sum of $P(x_R)$ and $P(x_{NR})$ is 1. We use this probabilistic definition because it encompasses a natural mapping between $P(x_{NR})$ and the general concept of reputation, i.e., an entity with a high probability of being good (or non-risky) is expected to have high reputation. In addition, it accepts different types of entities to incorporate specific domain knowledge into the reputation computation considering their respective characteristics, e.g.,

- **External server reputation** $p_s = P_s(x_{NR})$ indicates the server's probability of being malicious and infecting the clients connecting to it. Notice that a low reputation p_s means high probability of being malicious.

of equations governing the server reputation p_s, device reputation p_d, user reputation p_u, credential reputation p_c, and high-value asset reputation p_a.

$$p_d \propto \omega_{ds} \sum_{d \sim s} m_{ds} p_s + \omega_{du} \sum_{d \sim u} m_{du} p_u + \omega_{dc} \sum_{d \sim c} m_{dc} p_c$$

$$p_u \propto \omega_{du} \sum_{d \sim u} m_{du} p_d + \omega_{uc} \sum_{u \sim c} m_{uc} p_c$$

$$p_c \propto \omega_{uc} \sum_{u \sim c} m_{uc} p_u + \omega_{dc} \sum_{d \sim c} m_{dc} p_d$$

$$p_a \propto \omega_{da} \sum_{d \sim a} m_{da} p_d + \omega_{ua} \sum_{u \sim a} m_{ua} p_u + \omega_{ca} \sum_{c \sim a} m_{ca} p_c,$$

where $d \sim s$, $d \sim u$, etc. represent edges connecting device d with server s and user u, etc., $\propto$ means 'proportional to', ω_{ij} indicates the weights associated with edges and reputation types, and m_{ij} is the value in the connectivity matrices. Next, we exploit this mutual reinforcement principle in the bipartite graph network to simultaneously estimate the reputation and the risk using the propagation algorithm described in the next section.

Reputation propagation algorithm

Specifically, we employ the principle of belief propagation (BP) [2] on the large composite bipartite graph G to exploit the link structure and efficiently compute the reputations for all entities. Belief propagation is an iterative message passing algorithm on general graphs and has been widely used to solve many graph inference problem [3], such as social network analysis [1], fraud detection [4], and computer vision [5].

BP is typically used for computing the marginal distribution (or so-called 'hidden' distribution) for the nodes in the graph, based on the prior knowledge (or 'observed' distribution) about the nodes and from its neighbors. In our case, the algorithm infers the probabilistic distribution of an entity's reputation in the graph based on two sources of information: 1) the prior knowledge about the entity itself and 2) information about the neighbor entities and relationship between them. The inference is accomplished by iteratively passing messages between all pairs of entities n_i and n_j. Let $m_{i,j}$ denote the 'message' sent from i to j. The message represents i's influence on j's reputation. One could view it as if i, with a certain probability of being risky, passes some 'risk' to j. Additionally, the prior knowledge about i (e.g., importance of the assets and a user's anomalous behavior) is expressed by *node potential function* $\phi(i)$ which plays a role in determining the magnitude of the influence passed from i to j. In details, edge $e_{i,j}$ is associated with message $m_{i,j}$ (and $m_{j,i}$ if the message passing is bi-directional). The outgoing message from i to neighbor j is updated at each iteration based on the

incoming messages from i's other neighbors and node potential function $\phi(i)$ as follows.

$$m_{i,j}(x_j) \leftarrow \sum_{x_i \in \{x_R, x_{NR}\}} \phi_i(x_i) \psi_{ij}(x_i, x_j) \prod_{k \in N(i) \setminus j} m_{k,i}(x_i) \tag{1}$$

where $N(i)$ is the set of i's neighbors, and $\psi_{i,j}$ is the *edge potential* which is a transformation function defined on the edge between i and j to convert a node's incoming messages into its outgoing messages. Edge potential also controls how much influence can be passed to the receiving nodes, depending on the properties of the connections between i and j (e.g., the number of connections and volume of traffic). $\psi(x_i, x_j)$ is typically set according to the transition matrix shown in Table 1, which indicates that a low-reputation entity (e.g. a less reputable user) is more likely to be associated with low-reputation neighbors (e.g. compromised devices). The algorithm runs iteratively and stops when the entire network is converged with some threshold T, i.e., the change of any $m_{i,j}$ is smaller than T, or a maximum number of iterations are done. Convergence is not theoretically guaranteed for general graphs; however, the algorithm often does converge for real-world graphs in practice. At the end of the propagation procedure, each entity's reputation (i.e. marginal probability distribution) is determined by the converged messages $m_{i,j}$ and the node potential function (i.e. prior distribution).

$$p(x_i) = k \phi_i(x_i) \prod_{j \in N(i)} m_{j,i}(x_i); \quad x_i \in \{x_R, x_{NR}\} \tag{2}$$

where k is the normalization constant.

Incorporating domain knowledge

One of the major challenges in adopting a BP algorithm is to properly determine its parameters, particularly, the node potential and the edge potential function. In this section, we briefly discuss how we leverage the available data sources in a typical enterprise network and incorporate specific domain knowledge (unique to each entity type) to infer the parameters.

Characteristics of external servers $\mathcal{S}$

We develop an intrusion detection system that leverages several external blacklists to inspect all the HTTP traffic. It flags different types of suspicious web servers to which internal devices try to connect; this which allows us to

Table 1 Edge potential function

$\psi(x_i, x_j)$	$x_i = x_{NR}$	$x_i = x_R$
$x_j = x_{NR}$	$0.5 + \epsilon$	$0.5 - \epsilon$
$x_j = x_R$	$0.5 - \epsilon$	$0.5 + \epsilon$

assign the node potential function according to the maliciousness of the external servers. Specifically, we classify suspicious servers into the following five types:

- *Spam websites*: servers that are flagged by external spam blacklists like Spamhaus, SpamCop, etc.
- *Malware websites:* servers that host malicious software including virus, spyware, ransomware, and other unwanted programs that may infect the client machine.
- *Phishing websites:* servers that try to purport to be popular sites such as bank sites, social networks, online payment, or IT administration sites in order to lure unsuspecting users to disclose their sensitive information e.g., user names, passwords, and credit card details. Recently, attackers started to employ more targeted spear phishing attacks which use specific information about the target to increase the probability of success. Because of its potential to cause severe damage, we assign a high risky value to its node potential.
- *Exploit websites:* servers that host exploit toolkits, such as Blackhole and Flashpack, which are designed to exploit vulnerabilities of the victims' web browsers and install malware on victims' machines.
- *Botnet C&C servers:* are connected with bot programs to command instructions, update bot programs, or to extrude confidential information. If an internal device makes an attempt to connect to any known botnet C&C servers, the device is likely to be compromised. In addition to blacklists (e.g., Zeus Tracker), we also design models to detect fast fluxing and domain name generation botnets based on their distinct DNS request patterns.

Using the categorization of suspicious servers, we determine initial node potential values according to the severity of their categories. We assign $(\phi(x_R), \phi(x_{NR})) = (0.95, 0.05)$ for the high-risk types, such as botnets and exploit servers. For the medium-risk (Phishing and malware) and low-risk (Spam) types, we assign $(0.75, 0.25)$ and $(0.6, 0.4)$, respectively.

Characteristics of internal entities $\mathcal{D}, \mathcal{U}, \mathcal{C}, \mathcal{A}$

For internal entities, e.g., devices, users, credentials, and assets, rich information can be obtained from the internal asset management systems and IPS/IDS systems. Available information include device's status (e.g., OS version, patch level), device behavior anomalies (e.g., scanning), suspicious user activities (e.g., illegal accesses to sensitive data, multiple failed login attempts), and credential anomalies (e.g., unauthorized accesses). For instance, from the IPS system deployed in our enterprise network, we are able collect over 500 different alert types, most of

which are various attack vectors such as SYN port scan, remote memory corruption attempts, bruteforce logon, XSS, SQL injection, etc. Based on these information, we adjust node potential for the internal entities by assigning a severity score (1 to 3 for low, medium, and high-risk alerts)to each type of suspicious activities exemplified above and summing up the severities of all suspicious activities associated with an entity i to get total severity S_i. Since an entity i may be flagged multiple times for the same or different types of suspicious behaviors, to avoid being overshadowed by a few outliers, we transform the aggregated severity score using the sigmoid function

$$P_i = \frac{1}{1 + \exp(-S_i)}$$

The node potential for i is then calculated as $(\phi(x_R), \phi(x_{NR})) = (P_i, 1 - P_i)$. The key benefit of using a sigmoid function is that if no alerts have been reported for an entity (e.g. $S_i = 0$), its initial node potential will automatically be set to $(0.5, 0.5)$ i.e. equal probability of being risky and non-risky, implying that no prior information exist for the particular entity.

Although the parameters in MUSE require some level of manual tuning by domain experts, it is valuable to security analysts in several aspects. First, the output of MUSE is the ranking of high-risk entities whose absolute risk values are less important. As long as the parameters are assigned based on reasonable estimation of the severities of different types of alerts, MUSE will able to derive a ranking of entities based on their potential risks, thus providing useful information to help analysts prioritize their investigation. Second, MUSE offers the flexibility to incorporate diverse types of entities and thus can be easily adapted in a wide variety of other domains. Finally, it is possible to automatically learn the appropriate parameter values through machine learning techniques, provided that proper labeled training sets are available. We leave this as our plan for future exploration.

Scale up propagation algorithm to big data

Another major challenge of applying BP algorithm in a large enterprise network is the scalability. Even though BP itself is a computationally efficient algorithm: the running time scales quadratically with the number of edges in the graph, for large enterprises with hundred of thousands nodes and edges, the computation cost can become significant. To make the MUSE practical for large-scale graphic models, we observe that the main computation in belief propagation is *localized*, i.e. message passing is performed between only a specific node and its neighbors. This means that the computation can be efficiently parallelized and distributed to a cluster of machines.

One of the most prominent parallel programming paradigms is MapReduce, popularized by its open-source implementation of Apache Hadoop [6]. MapReduce framework consists of the map and the reduce stage that are chained together to perform complex operations in a distributed and fault-tolerant fashion. However, MapReduce is notoriously inefficient for *iterative* algorithms where the intermediate results are reused across multiple rounds of computations. Due to the lack of abstraction for leveraging distributed memory, the only way to reuse data across two MapReduce jobs is to persist them to an external storage system e.g. HDFS and load them back via another Map job. This incurs substantial overheads due to disk I/O and data synchronization which can dominate the execution times. Unfortunately, the BP algorithm underlying MUSE is a typical example of iterative computation where the same set of operations i.e. message update in Equation 1 are repeatedly applied to multiple data items. As a result, instead of MapReduce, we leverage a new cluster computing abstraction called Resilient Distributed Datasets (RDDs) [7] that achieves orders of magnitude performance improvement for iterative algorithms over existing parallel computing frameworks[a].

RDDs are parallel data structures that are created through deterministic operations on data in stable storage or through transformations from other RDDs. Typical transformations include map, filter, join, reduce, etc. The major benefit of RDDs is that it allows users to explicitly specify which intermediate results (in the form of RDDs) they want to reuse in the future operations. Keeping those persistent RDDs in memory eliminates unnecessary and expensive disk I/O or data replication across iterations, thus making it ideal for iterative algorithms. To abstract BP algorithm into RDDs, our key observation is that the message update process Equation 1 can be more efficiently represented by RDDs on an induced *line graph* from the original graph which represents the adjacencies between edges of original graph. Formally, given a directed graph $G = (V, E)$, a directed *line graph* or *derived graph* $L(G)$ is a graph such that:

- each vertex of $L(G)$ represents an edge of G. We use following notations to denote vertices and edges in G and $L(G)$: let $i, j \in V$ denote two vertices in the original graph G, we use (i, j) to represent the edge in G and the corresponding vertex in $L(G)$
- two vertices of $L(G)$ are adjacent if and only if their corresponding edges share a common endpoint ('are incident') in G and they form a length two directed path. In other words, for two vertices (i, j) and (m, n) in $L(G)$, there is an edge from (i, j) to (m, n) if and only if $j = m$ in the original G.

Figure 3 shows the conversion of original graph G to its directed line graph. Since an edge $(i, j) \in E$ in the original graph G corresponds to a node in $L(G)$, the message

passing process in Equation 1 is essentially an iterative updating process of a node in $L(G)$ based on all of this node's adjacent nodes. On each iteration, each node in $L(G)$ sends a message (or influence) $m_{i,j}$ to all of its neighbors and at the same time, it updates its own message based on the message it received from the neighbors. This can be easily described in RDDs as follows:

Algorithm 1 Message passing algorithm using RDDs

1: // Load line graph $L(G)$ as an RDD of (srcNode, dstNode) pair

2: links = RDD.textFile(graphFile).map(split).**persist()**

3:

4: // load initial node potential function in original graph G as (node, ϕ_i) pairs

5: potentials = RDD.textFile(potentialFile).map(split) **.persist()**

6:

7: messages = // initialize RDD of messages as (Node, $m_{i,j}$) pairs

8:

9: **for** iteration **in** xrange(ITERATIONS):

10:     // Build an RDD of (dstNode, m_{src}) pairs with messages sent by all node to dstNode

11:     MsgContrib = links.join(messages).map(

12:                     lambda(srcNode, (dstNode, m_{src}): (dstNode, m_{src}))

13:

14:     // Multiplication of all incoming messages by dstNode

15:     AggContrib = MsgContrib.reduceByKey(labmda (m_1, m_2): $m_1 * m_2$)

16:

17:     // Get New updated Messages for the next iteration

18:     messages = potentials.join(AggContrib).map(

19:                     labmda(dstNode, (ϕ_i, m_{agg})): $\phi_i * \psi_{i,j} * m_{agg}$)

20:

21: //After iterations, compute final belief according to Eq. 2

22: belief = potentials.join(messages).mapValues(lambda (ϕ_i, m_{agg}): $k * \phi_i * m_{agg}$)

23:

24: // and save to external storage

25: belief.saveAsTextFile("Beliefs.txt")

The above algorithm leads to the RDD lineage graph in Figure 4. On each iteration, the algorithm create a new *messages* dataset based on the aggregated contributions *AggContrib* and *messages* from previous iteration as well as the static *links* and *potential* datasets that are persisted

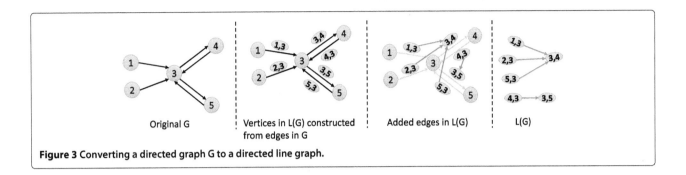

Figure 3 Converting a directed graph G to a directed line graph.

| Original G | Vertices in L(G) constructed from edges in G | Added edges in L(G) | L(G) |

in memory. Keeping these static datasets and intermediate *messages* in memory and making them readily available in the subsequent iterations avoids unnecessary I/O overhead and thus significantly speed up the computation.

Evaluation
Datasets
We evaluated MUSE with datasets collected from multiple data sources in the entire USNorth IBM network. The data sources included DNS messages from local DNS servers, network flows from edge routers, proxy logs, IPS alerts, and HTTP session headers (for categorization of websites). The size of the raw data per day was about 200 GB and the average data event rates are summarized in Table 2.

Experiment results
We first evaluate MUSE using data collected over 1 week period of time. The resulting graph consists of 11,790 nodes and 44,624 edges. The number of different entity types[b] are shown in Table 3.

We applied MUSE to the graph, and our algorithm converged at the 5th iteration. We manually inspected top ranked entities (i.e., with higher $P(x_R)$) in each entity type and were able to confirm that they were all suspicious or malicious entities including infected devices, suspicious users, etc. Here, we show one example of user reputation among our findings. We selected five top risky users based on the output of MUSE. Figure 5 shows their risk values at each iteration. Note that all the users started with neutral score (0.5, 0.5), meaning that these users had not been flagged by anomalous behaviors. However, due to their interaction with low-reputation neighbors, their associated risks increased. Further investigation showed that user332755 owned five devices which made 56 times of connections to spam websites, four times of connections to malware websites, and two times of connections to exploit websites during our monitoring period. user332755 inherited low reputation from his neighbors including the user's devices, causing his risk to quickly rise to the top.

We also measured the running time of MUSE at each iteration against different size of the graph in terms of the number of edges. Experiments are performed in a server blade with 2.00 GHz Intel(R) Xeon(R) CPU and 500 G memory (the memory usage of MUSE is less than 1 G). The experiment results are shown in Figure 6. From the figure, one can see that BP is efficient in handling small-to-medium-sized graphic models. Even for 1 week worth of traffic data, MUSE is able to finish each iteration in less than 1 min. However, we also notice that the running

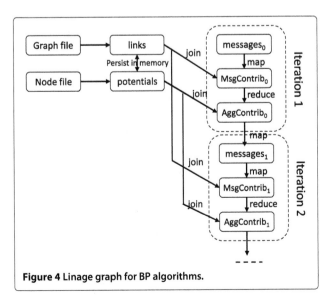

Figure 4 Linage graph for BP algorithms.

Table 2 Average traffic rate for IBM US North network

Data type	Data rate
Firewall logs	950 M/day
DNS messages	1,350 M/day
Proxy logs	490 M/day
IPS/IDS events	4 M/day
Overall:	2.5 billion events/day

Table 3 Number of different entities for one week data

Server					Device	User	Assets
Spam	Malware	Phishing	Exploit	Botnet			
5,500	124	10	26	16	3,823	2,191	100

time quadratically increases with the number of edges, which can be a bottleneck to handle large graphs as we will demonstrate in the next section.

Scalability of MUSE using RDDs

To compare the scalability of non-parallelized BP algorithm with that of the distributed version using RDDs abstraction, we collected half month worth of network traffic to stress test MUSE. The resulting graph consists of 24,706 nodes and 123,380 edges. The number of different entities are listed in Table 4. As a baseline benchmark, we ran the non-distributed version of MUSE against this large dataset for five iterations on the same server blade. The overall experiment took 1,641 s to finish and each iteration on average required 328 s.

We implement a distributed version of MUSE on Apache Spark [8] which is the open source implementation of RDDs. We deploy Spark on our blade center with three blade servers. We vary the number of CPU cores available for the Spark framework from 10 to 30 and submit the same workload to it. Figure 7 illustrates the comparison results. From the figure, we can notice that MUSE is able to leverage RDDs' in-memory cluster computing framework to achieve 10× to 15× speed up. For instance, with 30 CPU cores, MUSE is able to complete five iterations in 104 s with each iteration requiring less than 20 s. Although the algorithm does not scale linearly with the number of cores due to fixed I/O and communication overhead, the results demonstrate that with

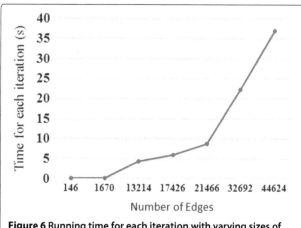

Figure 6 Running time for each iteration with varying sizes of graphs.

moderate hardware configuration, MUSE is scalable and practical for large enterprise networks.

Related work

With the cyber threats rapidly evolving towards large-scale and multi-channel attacks, security becomes crucial for organizations of varying types and sizes. Many traditional intrusion detection and anomaly detection methods are focused on a single entity and applied rule-based approaches [9]. They were often too noisy to be useful in practice [10]. Our work is inspired by the prominent research in the social network area that used a link structure to infer knowledge about the network properties. Previous work demonstrated that social structure was valuable to find authoritative nodes [11], to infer individual identities [12], to combat web spam [13], and to detect security fraud [14]. Among various graph mining algorithms, the belief propagation algorithm [2] has been successfully applied in many domains, e.g., detecting fraud [4], accounting irregularities [15], and malicious software [3]. For example, NetProbe [4] applied a BP algorithm to the eBay user graph to identify subgraphs of fraudsters and accomplices.

Conclusion

In this paper, we proposed MUSE, a framework to systematically quantify and rank risks in an enterprise network. MUSE aggregated alerts generated by traditional IPS/IDS on multiple data sources, and leveraged the link structure

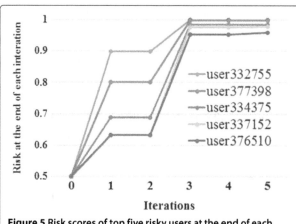

Figure 5 Risk scores of top five risky users at the end of each iteration.

Table 4 Number of different entities for half a month data

Server					Device	User	Assets
Spam	Malware	Phishing	Exploit	Botnet			
8,924	171	103	33	22	10,809	4,527	116

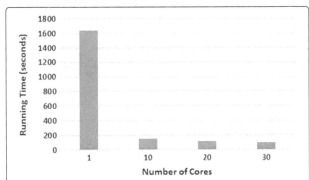

Figure 7 Comparison of running time between non-distributed MUSE and distributed version implemented using RDDs.

among entities to infer their reputation. The key advantage of MUSE was that it derived the risk of each entity not only by considering its own characteristics but also by incorporating the influence from its neighbors. This allowed MUSE to pinpoint a high-risk entity based on its interaction with low-reputation neighbors, even if the entity itself was benign. By providing risk rankings, MUSE helps security analysts to make an informed decision on allocation of resources and prioritization of further investigation to develop proper defense mechanisms at an early stage. We have implemented and tested MUSE on real world traces collected from large enterprise network, demonstrating that the efficacy and scalability of MUSE.

Endnotes

[a]10x-100x speedup as compared to Hadoop [8].

[b]Due to the privacy issues, we were not able to include authentication logs to incorporate user credentials in our experiments.

Competing interests
The authors declare that they have no competing interests.

Acknowledgements
This research was sponsored by the U.S. Army Research Laboratory and the U.K. Ministry of Defense and was accomplished under Agreement Number W911NF-06-3-0001. The views and conclusions contained in this document are those of the author(s) and should not be interpreted as representing the official policies, either expressed or implied, of the U.S. Army Research Laboratory, the U.S. Government, the U.K. Ministry of Defense, or the U.K. Government. The U.S. and U.K. Governments are authorized to reproduce and distribute reprints for government purposes notwithstanding any copyright notation hereon.

Author details
[1]Security Research Department, IBM T.J. Watson Research Center, 1101 Kitchawan Rd, Yorktown Heights, NY, USA. [2]IBM Zurich Research Lab, Saumerstrasse 4, 8803 Ruschlikon, Switzerland.

References
1. J Bian, Y Liu, D Zhou, E Agichtein, H Zha, in *Proceedings of WWW '09*. Learning to recognize reliable users and content in social media with coupled mutual reinforcement (ACM New York, 2009)
2. JS Yedidia, WT Freeman, Y Weiss, in *Exploring Artificial Intelligence in the New Millennium, Volume 8*. Understanding belief propagation and its generalizations (Morgan Kaufmann Publishers Inc., San Francisco, 2003), pp. 236–239
3. DH Chau, C Nachenberg, J Wilhelm, A Wright, C Faloutsos, in *SIAM International Conference on Data Mining*. Polonium: tera-scale graph mining and inference for malware detection, (2011)
4. S Pandit, DH Chau, S Wang, C Faloutsos, in *International Conference on World Wide Web*. Netprobe: a fast and scalable system for fraud detection in online auction networks (ACM New York, 2007)
5. PF Felzenszwalb, DP Huttenlocher, Efficient belief propagation for early vision. Int. J. Comput. Vis. **70**, 41–54 (2006)
6. AS Foundation, Apache Hadoop. http://hadoop.apache.org/
7. M Zaharia, M Chowdhury, T Das, A Dave, J Ma, M McCauley, MJ Franklin, S Shenker, I Stoica, in *Proceedings of the 9th USENIX Conference on Networked Systems Design and Implementation*. Resilient distributed datasets: a fault-tolerant abstraction for in-memory cluster computing (USENIX Association San Jose, 2012), pp. 2–2
8. AS Foundation, Apache Spark Lightning-fast cluster computing. https://spark.apache.org/
9. P Garcia-Teodoro, J Diaz-Verdejo, G Maciá-Fernández, E Vázquez, Anomaly-based network intrusion detection: techniques, systems and challenges. Comput. Secur. **28**, 18–28 (2009)
10. J Viega, *Myths of Security*. (O'Reilly Media, Inc, Sebastopol, 2009)
11. JM Kleinberg, Authoritative sources in a hyperlinked environment. J. ACM. **46**(5), 604–632 (1999)
12. S Hill, F Provost, The Myth of the double-blind review?: Author identification using only citations. ACM SIGKDD Explorations Newsl. **5**(2), 179–184 (2003)
13. Z Gyöngyi, H Garcia-Molina, J Pedersen, in *Intl Conference on Very Large Data Bases*. Combating Web Spam with Trustrank (VLDB Endowment Toronto, 2004)
14. J Neville, O Simsek, D Jensen, J Komoroske, K Palmer, H Goldberg, in *ACM Conference on Knowledge Discovery and Data Mining*. Using relational knowledge discovery to prevent securities fraud (ACM New York, 2005)
15. M McGlohon, S Bay, MG Anderle, DM Steier, C Faloutsos, in *ACM Conference on Knowledge Discovery and Data Mining*. SNARE: a link analytic system for graph labeling and risk detection (ACM New York, 2009)

15

Error correcting codes for robust color wavelet watermarking

Wadood Abdul[1], Philippe Carré[1*] and Philippe Gaborit[2]

Abstract

This article details the conception, design, development and analysis of invisible, blind and robust color image watermarking algorithms based on the wavelet transform. Using error correcting codes, the watermarking algorithms are designed to be robust against intentional or unintentional attacks such as JPEG compression, additive white Gaussian noise, low pass filter and color attacks (hue, saturation and brightness modifications). Considering the watermarking channel characterized by these attacks, repetition, Hamming, Bose Chaudhuri Hocquenghem and Reed-Solomon codes are used in order to improve the robustness using different modes and appropriate decoding algorithms. The article compares the efficiency of different type of codes against different type of attacks. To the best of our knowledge this is the first time that the effect of error-correcting codes against different attacks are detailed in a watermarking context in such a precise way: describing and comparing the effect of different classes of codes against different type of attacks. This article clearly shows that list decoding of Reed-Solomon codes using the algorithm of Sudan exhibits good performance against hue and saturation attacks. The use of error correcting codes in a concatenation mode allows the non-binary block codes to show good performance against JPEG compression, noise and brightness attacks.

1 Introduction

Watermarking provides a possible solution to ensure and safeguard copyright and intellectual property rights for online multimedia content. The watermarking of color images raises the issues of robustness against intentional or unintentional attacks; the invisibility with respect to the human visual system (HVS); the maximum allowable information that can be inserted into the image and the security of the watermark. The watermarking algorithms must be designed in order to cater for these requirements. In this article, we will discuss and propose effective solutions for the issue of robustness related to color image watermarking.

Robustness to intentional attacks is a main issue for color image watermarking where the inserted watermark can be removed or manipulated to such an extent that the attribution of a watermark to a particular individual or image is difficult or impossible. The robustness of watermarking algorithms can also be affected by unintentional attacks which can result from a change in color space or common signal distortions.

The watermarking problem is considered analogous to the transmission of a signal over a noisy channel and the underlying characteristics of the channel are defined by the different attacks. Error correcting codes have been widely used to protect the signature (identification of a buyer/seller or transaction) of an image for watermarking applications. The robustness performance of our wavelet based watermarking algorithm (presented in Section 2), which uses the relation between wavelet color coefficients, is enhanced with the help of error correcting codes. The robustness improvement against attacks such as JPEG compression, additive white Gaussian noise, low pass filtering and color attacks (hue, saturation and brightness modifications) is demonstrated using different families and modes of error correcting codes. We explore and demonstrate the use and effectiveness of the concatenation of repetition codes, Hamming codes and BCH codes to enhance the robustness of the watermarking algorithm. Reed-Solomon codes are also used in a standalone manner using list decoding algorithm of Sudan [1] to correct errors resulting from attacks which can

---

*Correspondence: carre@sic.univ-poitiers.fr
[1] Laboratory SIC-XLIM, University of Poitiers, bat. SP2MI, av. Marie et Pierre Curie, 86960, Chasseneuil Cédex, France
Full list of author information is available at the end of the article

induce burst errors. Generally watermarking algorithms use bounded distance decoding algorithms for different error correcting codes along with the concatenation of these codes with each other [2-5]. We compare the performance of list decoding of Reed-Solomon codes with bounded distance decoding algorithms of repetition, Hamming, BCH, and the concatenation of these codes. Relatively recent developments [1,6] in the field of error correcting codes, for decoding Reed-Solomon codes, have made it possible to correct errors beyond the conventionally used bounded distance algorithms. As code rates tends towards 0, the list decoding of Reed-Solomon codes shows asymptotic improvement in performance over the bounded distance algorithms. As generally [5,7,8] the codes rates for watermarking schemes rates are very low, we can therefore employ this asymptotic improvement to our advantage.

These different error correcting codes exhibit different performance when the watermarked image is attacked. As the image and the attack have different characteristics we give the best error correcting code against the different types of attacks. We intend to find out the relationship between the different attack types and the protection provided by the error correcting codes. Our main focus in the robustness analysis is to provide suitable countermeasures against color attacks. Detailed analysis is carried out for the robustness issue against the attacks under consideration using the different modes and families of the error correcting codes.

Moreover, as watermarking algorithms do not usually consider color attacks and counter measures to protect the color images against such attacks have not been explored in earlier study. One of the objectives of this article is to study color attacks and propose adequate robustness measures.

In this study, our contribution is twofold. We first propose in Section 2, a wavelet based color image watermarking algorithm, with enhanced invisibility. The insertion is intended to keep the watermark invisible and the blind detection is performed without using the original (unwatermarked) image. In Section 3, we present the error correcting codes along with their use in the watermarking process. The last section studies the effectiveness of the codes against different types of attack.

2 Color image watermarking algorithm based on the wavelet transform

In this section, we want to describe the design of invisible color image watermarking schemes in terms of human perception of change and image quality degradation proposed by the authors. After, we also intend to improve the robustness performance of invisible color image watermarking algorithms so that such algorithms can resist intentional or unintentional attacks.

To cater for the requirements of invisibility and robustness, watermarking techniques employ the spatial and transform domains [9-13]. In general, the insertion of the watermark in the spatial domain has low complexity but also low robustness to attacks originating from the transform domains, such as JPEG compression, or for example median filtering. We could choose the band of frequencies in the multiresolution domain, thus giving us more control as to where to place the watermark. It is also important to note that these algorithms also differ in other aspects such as the way the watermark is prepared and inserted.

This article deals withe transform domain watermarking algorithm. Such algorithms employ discrete Fourier transform (DFT) [14-17], discrete cosine transform (DCT) [18-21], discrete wavelet transform (DWT) [22-27] and the contourlet transform (CT) [8] to insert the watermark with the best compromise between the invisibility, robustness and capacity criteria.

It is known that robustness against image distortion is enhanced if the watermark is placed in perceptually significant parts of the image. This contrasts with one of the requirements of an invisible watermarking algorithm, the embedded watermark should be invisible to the human visual system (HSV). Watermarking techniques have to be developed taking into account the masking properties of the HVS. Some characteristics of the HVS with respect to watermarking are highlighted in the literature [28,29]. These characteristics include frequency sensitivity, that is the difference sensitivity of the human eye to sine wave gratings at different frequencies; luminance sensitivity, that is the different sensitivity of the eye to a noise signal on a constant background, depending on the average value of the background luminance and on the level of the noise luminance; and contrast masking, which refers to the perception of a signal in presence of a masking stimulus, and which depends on the relative spatial frequency, location and orientation. For example, an approach [30] based on the Fourier transform insists that interoperability between the HVS model and the watermark embedding may not be optimal and the DCT and DWT domains do not allow the implementation of a suitable HVS model. Another important observation is that the CSF is not adapted to predict invisibility for complex signals such as natural images, essentially because the HVS is modeled by a single channel. Based on psychovisual experiments, they have derived a perceptual channel decomposition (PCD).

The algorithm presented during the course of this study is based on the wavelet transform. In the case of the DFT any change in the transform coefficients affects the entire image but in the case of the wavelet transform we have the additional spatial description of the image. Another great advantage is that we can adapt the watermark insertion according to the local image information. The DCT is non adaptive to the image as the different levels of information could not be extracted and only the frequency information is present. Whereas transform domains such as the DWT map an image into the spatial-temporal domain. As a typical natural image is dominated by low frequency components, the energy concentration in corresponding coefficients could be efficiently exploited to insert the watermark. Those low frequencies represent the overall shapes and outlines of features in the image, and its luminance and contrast characteristics. High frequencies represent sharpness in the image, but contribute little spatial-frequency energy. The main advantage of the DWT and the CT is that we can choose the band of frequencies and the spatial and frequential combinations which are most suitable to carry the watermark. Our later discussion will be limited to the DWT.

The watermarking algorithms discussed, designed and implemented in this article belong to the class of blind algorithms [12,19,31-44] which means that (unlike the non-blind watermarking algorithms [45,46]) the originally image is not consulted at the time of the detection or decoding of the watermark.

One can mention mainly three insertion methods, each of them can be applied on pixels in the spatial domain, or on coefficients in any transform domain: LSB modification, Spread Spectrum and the Quantization Index Modulation. One such invisible watermarking algorithm uses LSB modifications of any color or grey-scale image [9]. The algorithm uses m-sequences due to their good auto-correlation properties and pseudo-random nature. The algorithm embeds the m-sequence on the LSB of the image. The watermark is decoded by comparing the LSB bit pattern with a stored counterpart. The Spread Spectrum techniques are well known in Communications for their low SNR operations. A message bit is "spread" using a pseudo-random unit vector. To decode, a scalar correlation is computed and the final decision is computed with a maximum likelihood decision rule. Lastly, the quantization index modulation is a generalization of LSB embedding. At each position, the quantizer Q_i is selected according to the message value $m = i$. To decode, the distances between the signal value and all the quantizer are computed and the smallest distance is selected.

The wavelet based color image watermarking algorithm presented in this Section is used to test the robustness improvement achieved by the incorporation of the different modes and families of error correcting codes. The signature is the information we want to embed into the image, it identifies uniquely the person who intends to watermark the image or a transaction. The watermark is the information that we actually embed into the image, it could be the same as the signature, or it could be processed. In our case, we pass the signature through an encoding procedure to make the watermark robust and invisible.

2.1 The watermark construction

The initial matrix or the signature is constructed by a random number generator according to the user specified parameters. After we apply the encoding scheme to construct the watermark which is then embedded into the image with certain limitations depending on image size and user defined parameters. The signature size is chosen to be 8×8 as it corresponds to a compromise between a sufficient size for a copyright application and a minimum robustness.

In the literature, we have many options to construct the final watermark from the initial matrix. For the purpose of illustration let us consider the very basic encoding scheme—the repetition codes. This signature or the initial matrix is repeated four times into an intermediate matrix which is again repeated according to the image capacity.

The human visual system is sensitive to changes in the lower frequencies as they are associated to the more significant characteristics of the image. The higher frequencies give the details of the image but changes in the higher frequencies could be easily eliminated by a low pass filter. Therefore the proposed algorithm uses middle frequencies for the insertion of the mark as both invisibility and robustness against low pass filter attacks is required in such an algorithm.

2.2 Wavelet decomposition

The wavelet decomposition is applied to each color component R, G, and B. The wavelet decomposition gives us the decomposition of the signal into different frequency bands. This decomposition is done by a filter bank in such a way that we split the low frequency band into small segments in order to separate all the components of the signal and we split the higher frequency bands into large segments as they contain less information. We embed the mark into middle frequencies as the higher frequencies could be simply eliminated by a low pass filter and the lower frequencies carry the overall form of the image and changing these lower frequencies may make the watermark visible.

2.3 Vector definition

The wavelet decomposition gives us the wavelet coefficients to the level/scale L associated to a middle frequency band. From these coefficients the vectors are defined

$$(\vec{V}_a[n,m])_{0<(n,m)<\frac{N}{2^L}}. \tag{1}$$

Such that,

$$\vec{V}_a[n,m] = \{d_{1,L}^a[n,m], d_{2,L}^a[n,m], d_{3,L}^a[n,m]\}. \quad (2)$$

With $a = \{R, G, B\}$, $[n, m]$ representing the coordinates, and $(d_{j,L})_{j=1,2,3}$ the sub-bands of the wavelet decomposition at the Lth level, as shown in Figure 1. The top right side of the Figure 1 (after wavelet decomposition) corresponds to the result of a low pass operation and the corresponding detail bands generated by the sub band filtering operation for the red color component. This process is repeated for each of the following wavelet decompositions until we reach the Lth level where we are interested to insert the watermark. Then the vectors are defined for each of the color component. The bottom part of Figure 1 shows the vector definition for the red color component at scale $L = 1$ and position $[n, m]$. Here $(d_{1,L})$ (resp., $(d_{2,L})$ and $(d_{3,L})$) corresponds to the horizontal (resp., vertical and diagonal) details of the image.

The maximum information (capacity) that can be embedded using the watermarking scheme is calculated using $\frac{D_x}{2^L} * \frac{D_y}{2^L}$, where D_x and D_y are the horizontal and vertical dimensions of the image and L is the level of the wavelet decomposition where we are interested to insert the watermark M.

2.4 Watermark insertion

In order to define the insertion process, we propose to adapt the QIM principle to vectorial case. For this, we will introduce a modification rule of color wavelet coefficients. As we have said the QIM uses a quantizer that is a function that maps a value to the nearest point belonging to a class of pre-defined discontinuous points. For non-adaptive QIM, the quantization step size is independent of the content. However, it is well known that the ability to perceive a change depends on the content. For example, the HVS is much less sensitive to changes in heavily textured regions and much more sensitive to changes in uniform regions. Moreover, the coefficient modifications and QIM process pose some challenges when applied generally to the color domain.

To account for this, we propose to use a method to automatically adapt the quantization step size at each sample. First, the step value is controlled by the wavelet coefficients that measure the spatial local activity. Second, the watermark insertion process is based upon moving one of the three color vectors (R, G, and B). A better candidate is defined in order to minimize the distortion at each insertion space.

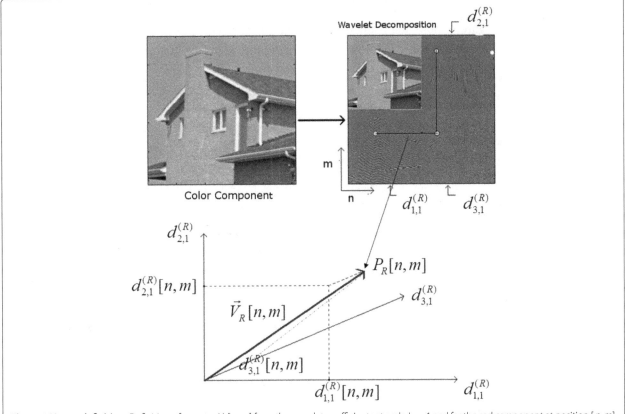

Figure 1 Vector definition. Definition of a vector $V_R[n,m]$ from the wavelet coefficients at scale $L = 1$ and for the red component at position $[n,m]$.

For each coordinate, we have to define one vector $\vec{V}_M$ that denotes the vector to be watermarked, and two reference vectors $\vec{V}_{vref1}$ and $\vec{V}_{vref2}$. $\vec{V}_M$, $\vec{V}_{vref1}$, and $\vec{V}_{vref2}$ are selected with respect of the correspondence to the following equations

$$\|P_{\text{ref1}} - P_{\text{ref2}}\|^2 = \max_{(a,b) \in \{R,G,B\}_{a \neq b}} \|P_a - P_b\|^2; \ P_M = P_c.$$

(3)

With $c \in \{R, G, B\}$, $c \neq a$ and $c \neq b$

Figure 2 shows that P_{ref1} and P_{ref2} are the most distant points from each pair of points and that is why P_R is chosen as P_M. Here P_x refers to the extreme point of the vector $\vec{V}_x$. P_M corresponds to $\vec{V}_M$ which is marked with the contents of the watermarking matrix M.

The watermarking convention is presented in Figure 3, where the watermarked vector $\vec{V}_{M,W}$, that corresponds to the original vector $\vec{V}_M$.

After watermarking, if $\vec{V}_M$ denotes $\vec{V}_R$, then:

- if $M[n, m] = 0$, then $\vec{V}_{R,W}[n, m]$ will be nearer to $\vec{V}_G[n, m]$ than $\vec{V}_B[n, m]$,
- else $\vec{V}_{R,W}[n, m]$ will be nearer to $\vec{V}_B[n, m]$ than $\vec{V}_G[n, m]$.

One of the most important possibilities lies on the ability of tuning the $P_{M,W}$ shift in order to limit the visual degradations on the image. Figure 4 shows the possible shifts of $P_{M,W}$. Two cases are considered, *Shift 1* and *Shift 2*. The limit of the two possible modifications is the median line between P_{ref1} and P_{ref2}. To be more robust, we define around this line a particular area (Figure 4) such that after the watermarking if $P_{M,W}$ is in this area, it has to be moved out by increasing the strength of the insertion process. The border of this area can be equivalent to $\pm 5\%$ of the distance between P_{ref1} and P_{ref2}.

With this approach, there exist two cases of *Shift*. In the first case, P_M is already nearest to P_{ref1} and the possible positions of $P_{M,W}$ after watermarking belongs to the segment $\vec{P}_M P_{\text{ref1}}$ (if P_M is out of the median area). In the

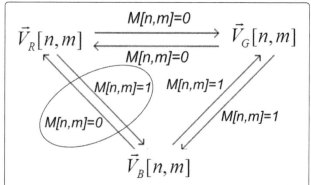

Figure 3 Watermarking convention. Example of watermarking convention.

second case, P_M is not already nearest to P_{ref1} and we create an intermediate point P_{int}, defined by:

- $\vec{P}_M P_{\text{int}}$ is parallel to $\vec{P}_{\text{ref1}} P_{\text{ref2}}$,
- P_{int} is located at the border of the median area (the distance between P_{int} and the median line must be equivalent to 5% of the distance between P_{ref1} and P_{ref2}).

Then, the possible positions of $P_{M,W}$ belongs to the segment $\vec{P}_{\text{int}} P_{\text{ref1}}$. For the *Case 1*, where P_M is the initial point of $P_{M,W}$, and for the *Case 2*, where P_{int} is the initial point of $P_{M,W}$, the watermark is defined by:

$$\vec{V}_{M,W}[n, m] = \vec{V}_{\text{refi}}[n, m]$$
$$- (1 - F_a[n, m]).(\vec{V}_{\text{refi}} - \vec{V}_S[n, m]),$$

(4)

where $i = \{1, 2\}$, $a = \{R, G, B\}$, $0 \leq F_a[n, m] \leq 1$, $S = \{M; int\}$ and F_a represents the weighted matrix for watermarking for each location $[n, m]$.

- If $F_a[n, m] = 0$, the force of insertion is minimum.
- If $F_a[n, m] = 1$, the force of insertion is maximum and $P_{M,W}$ is superposed on P_{refi}.

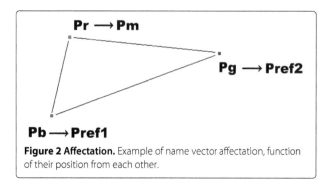

Figure 2 Affectation. Example of name vector affectation, function of their position from each other.

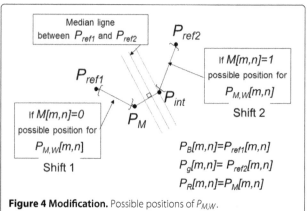

Figure 4 Modification. Possible positions of $P_{M,W}$.

In the case of maximum force of insertion $F_a = 1$, a conflict problem is highlighted, as shown on Figure 3 with a circle. It is observed that the bit value between P_R and P_B can be different: M can receive 0 or 1. This means that, in the detection step, the vector identification (V_R, V_R, and V_R to $\vec{V}_M$, $\vec{V}_{ref1}$, and $\vec{V}_{ref2}$) could be false. Thus, to avoid this configuration, F_a must be set inferior to 1.

The modification operation is applied on the whole host image in the wavelet domain. The last step in the watermark insertion process is the reconstruction of the image in to the spatial domain by inverse wavelet transform.

2.5 Watermark extraction

The first step of the extraction process consists also in a decomposition of the image with the same wavelet basis used in the insertion step. The watermark M_D is detected by measuring the largest distance between $||\vec{V}_{vref1} - \vec{V}_M||$ and $||\vec{V}_{vref2} - \vec{V}_M||$. Following the convention used in insertion, the watermark is thus reconstructed, bit by bit. The signature S_D is obtained by making an average and a binarization that corresponds to the coding method used for the creation of the mark M. In order to decide if S_D corresponds to S, a threshold is fixed to accept an extracted signature. This threshold is based on the acceptable level of bit error rate for the watermarking system.

Based on this we can define an acceptance threshold which decides as to whether to accept the detected watermark or to reject it. The different modes and families of error correcting codes, discussed in Section 3 help to lower this acceptance threshold, thus increasing the robustness of the watermarking scheme.

3 How to improve robustness with error correcting codes

Lots of research has been carried out to improve the robustness of a watermarked image where the use of error correcting codes to protect the signature is the most highlighted [2-5]. The watermarking problem is synonymous to the transmission of a signal over a noisy channel, where the image is considered to be the channel, the attacks are considered to be noise signals and the signature is considered to be the signal to be transmitted in the form of the watermark.

This section deals with the investigation of the performance capabilities of different error correcting schemes employed for a digital color image watermarking application based on the discrete wavelet transform. We worked on improving the robustness of the signature with the help of four families of error correcting codes. These four families of error correcting codes give different response when tested against different attacks on watermarked images. This is so because each of the attacks modifies the watermarked image in a diverse way and the properties exhibited by the error correcting codes are different

against different error types (burst errors or random errors). To counter this problem we have employed repetition codes (presented at the first section), Hamming codes [47], Bose Chaudhuri Hocquenghem (BCH) codes [48] and Reed-Solomon codes [49].

In the literature different types of error correcting schemes for the watermarking problem are proposed. For example since 1998 Wang et al. use Hamming codes [50], Perreira et al. study the BCH codes for watermarking applications [51], some were hybrids between for example BCH and repetition codes [4]. Finally, some articles suggest using convolutional codes for watermarking [52,53]. Some compared different types of coding schemes, e.g., Reed Solomon, BCH and repetition codes [3].

What makes our study original is that we describe and compare the effect of different classes of codes against different type of real image attacks, we include different codes and the list decoding scheme in a color watermarking complete process. With this study, we propose to describe the errors introduced by different attacks and thus to illustrate the connection of a particular attack with a particular error correcting scheme in the context of our color wavelet algorithm. Since, there is a relationship between the contents of an image and the error nature attack, the result section analyzes the different results with empirical observation and provides intuitive explanations.

We adopted a rigorous testing process where we tested the robustness of different watermarked images with multiple signatures. We employed some standard attacks which include color attacks, filtering attacks, noise attacks and image compression attacks. The scheme had already been tested against some of these attacks with the use of repetition codes [5]. It proved to be robust against these attacks to a certain extent. We wished to explore the effectiveness of other error correcting codes against these attacks.

The different error correcting codes are tested using the wavelet based color image watermarking scheme presented in Section 2. Then using some possible attacks the robustness obtained using the different families and modes of error correcting codes is shown and the results are presented in Section 4.

3.1 Characteristics of the watermarking channel

Due to the requirement of watermark invisibility, the watermarks are weakly inserted in to the image. This makes the watermark signal prone to errors or attacks. The watermark channel is very noisy due to the different types of intentional or unintentional attacks. We consider the problem of watermark robustness against different errors or attacks analogous to the transmission of a signal over a noisy channel. To correctly transmit a signal over a noisy channel error correcting codes are used to protect the signal from the effects of the channel.

The characteristics of the watermarking channel depend upon the type of attacks experienced by the watermarked image. Like in the transmission of a signal over a noisy channel, error correcting codes are used to protect the signature in the form of a watermark so that the effects of the channel are reduced or minimized. The underlying characteristics of an image, e.g., the texture and color information also determine the effect an attack has on the watermarked image. The watermarking algorithm and the type and mode of error correcting codes also play an important role in defining the combined performance of robustness and invisibility.

The characteristics of the watermarking channel are primarily determined by the different attacks. We consider JPEG compression, additive white Gaussian noise, low pass filter, hue, saturation, and brightness as the underlying characteristics of the watermarking channel. Each of the different error correcting codes presented in the following Section exhibit different properties against these attacks.

The watermarking channel is characterized by very high error rates. To correct these errors we use different error correction schemes. Four families of error correcting schemes are used in our study to enhance the robustness of the watermark—repetition codes, Hamming codes, BCH codes and Reed-Solomon codes. We explore the use and effectiveness of the concatenation of these different families of error correcting codes to enhance the robustness of the watermarking scheme.

We employ a concatenation model where two of these error correcting codes are concatenated so that the two error correcting codes can facilitate one another. The outer error correcting codes are a second version of the repetition codes: the watermark is built up from some repetitions of the signature. The outer error help in reducing the error rates so that the inner error correcting codes (repetition, Hamming, or BCH) could then further reduce the errors so that the decision that the received watermark is valid or not could be taken.

Error correcting codes are expressed in the following article in the form of (n, k, d), where n is the length of the code, k is the dimension and d is the minimum Hamming distance between any pair of different codewords. The Hamming distance, H_d is based on the Hamming weight

of a codeword c given by $H_w(c)$, the number of non zero elements in a vector. The Hamming distance H_d between two codewords is the number of elements in which they differ. The minimum Hamming distance d, between any two different codewords defines the error correcting capability of the particular error correcting code. An (n, k, d) error correcting code is capable of correcting t errors where $t < \frac{d}{2}$.

3.2 Concatenated error correcting codes

As we have said, the robustness of the watermarking scheme could be improved by concatenating these codes using signature repetition codes as outer codes and bit repetition, Hamming or BCH codes as inner codes. The outer coding is adaptive and is in accordance to the size of the image and user parameters, it is always repetition coding as shown in Figure 5.

At the receiver side an exact opposite procedure is applied to decode the signature from the watermark, i.e., we decode the watermark using repetition decoding first and then we decode the resulting information using repetition, Hamming or BCH decoding and we have the signature.

Such a concatenation mode has been selected because error correcting codes cannot display their potential unless the error rate induced by the channel is reduced below a critical value which brings about the possibility of first improving the channel error rate via repetition coding to an acceptable level, before any further decoding. The watermark channel may have to operate at very high bit error rates and codes such as BCH stop bringing in any advantage while the repetition codes continue with their modest protection. However concatenation of repetition and BCH codes is a way to improve the decoding performance when the error rates are high [3]. The BCH codes can correct up to $t = \lfloor (d - 1)/2 \rfloor$ errors, all errors exceeding t may cause the decoder to decode erroneously. The repetition codes display better characteristics than BCH under high error rates. This could be seen in Section 4.2 (noise attack) where the repetition codes perform much better than the BCH (63,16,23) codes when the SNR < 2.

As mentioned in the introduction Reed-Solomon codes are used in a standalone mode to correct burst errors.

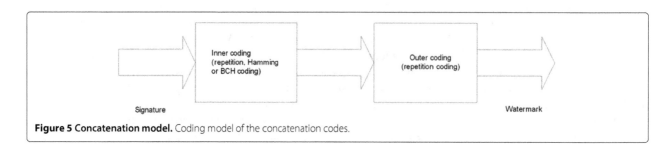

Figure 5 Concatenation model. Coding model of the concatenation codes.

The decoding of Reed-Solomon codes is carried out using list decoding algorithms [1,6]. The list decoding algorithms offer enhanced performance over bounded distance algorithms when the code rates are low.

3.3 Repetition codes

Repetition codes are used to construct the watermark from the signature and they are expressed in the form of (n, k, d). They are always used as $(n, 1, n)$ where each codeword is repeated n number of times. The repetition codes are used as inner codes in the construction of the watermark. They are also used as outer codes in all cases. The decoding of the repetition codes is always done using a mean operation on the received codeword to distinguish between a 0 or a 1.

3.4 Hamming codes

Hamming codes are linear block codes. For an integer $m > 1$, we have the following representation for the binary Hamming codes in the form $(n, k, d) = (2^m - 1, 2^m - 1 - m, m)$.

For $m = 3$, we have $(7, 4, 3)$ Hamming error correcting codes. These Hamming codes encode 4 bits of data into 7 bit blocks (a Hamming code word). The extra 3 bits are parity bits. Each of the 3 parity bits is parity for 3 of the 4 data bits, and no 2 parity bits are for the same 3 data bits. All of the parity bits are even parity. The $(7, 4, 3)$ Hamming error correcting code can correct 1 error in each of the Hamming codeword.

When we multiply the received codeword with the parity check matrix we get the corresponding parity ranging from 000 to 111. These three bits give us the error location. 000 indicating that there were no errors in transmission and the rest from 001 to 111 indicate the error location in our seven bit received codeword. Here we can correct one error according to $t = \lfloor (d - 1)/2 \rfloor$ as the minimum Hamming distance between our code words is $7 - 4 = 3$, we have 1 as the number of correctable errors. Now we have the error location, we could simply flip the bit corresponding to the error location and the error will be corrected. Then we discard the parity bits from position one, two and four we have our received data words. Hamming Codes are perfect 1 error correcting codes. That is, any received word with at most one error will be decoded correctly and the code has the smallest possible

size of any code that does this. The Hamming codes that we used could correct 1 error in each codeword. There was a need to test other types of codes which can correct more errors. We selected the BCH codes which are explained in the following section.

3.5 Bose Chaudhuri Hocquenghem (BCH) codes

BCH codes are cyclic block codes such that for any positive integers $m \geq 3$ and t with $t \leq 2^{m-1} - 1$, there is a BCH codes of length $n = 2^m - 1$ which is capable of correcting t error and has dimension $k = n - m * t$.

Let C be a linear block code over a finite field F of block length n. C is called a cyclic code, if for every codeword $c = (c_1, \ldots, c_n)$ from C, the word $(c_n, c_1, \ldots, c_{n-1})$ in F^n obtained by a cyclic right shift of components is also a codeword from C.

We have selected the BCH$(15, 7, 5)$ and the BCH$(63, 16, 23)$ error correcting codes for the purpose of our experimentation. The BCH$(63, 16, 23)$ is in line with our algorithm testing parameters since the size of our initial matrix is 8×8 bits.

3.6 Reed-Solomon codes

Reed-Solomon codes [49,54] are q-ary $[n, k, d]$ error correcting codes of length n, dimension k and Hamming minimum distance d equal to $n - k + 1$. These codes can decode in a unique way up to $\frac{n-k}{2}$ errors, and there exists the possibility to decode them beyond the classical bounded radius $\frac{n-k}{2}$. Usually these codes are considered over the Galois field $GF(p^m)$ (for p a prime) and have parameters $[p^m - 1, p^m - 1 - 2t, 2t + 1]$. In particular the case $p = 2$ is often considered for applications since in that case any symbol of the code can be described with m bits. It is also possible either by considering less coordinates in their definition, either by shortening them, to construct Reed-Solomon codes over $GF(p^m)$ with parameters $[p^m - 1 - s, p^m - 1 - 2t - s, 2t + 1]$, which can be decoded in the same way that non shortened Reed-Solomon codes.

Reed-Solomon codes are particularly useful against burst noise. This is illustrated in the following example.

Consider an $(n, k, d) = (40, 11, 30)$ Reed-Solomon code over $GF(2^6)$, where each symbol is made up of $m = 6$ bits as shown in Figure 6. As $d = 30$ indicates that this code can correct any $t = 14$ symbol error in a block

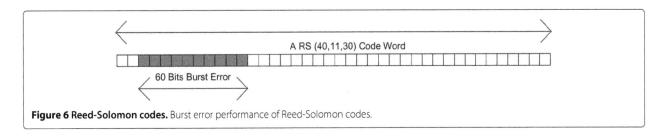

Figure 6 Reed-Solomon codes. Burst error performance of Reed-Solomon codes.

of 40. Consider the presence of a burst of noise lasting 60 bits which disturbs 10 symbols as highlighted in Figure 6. The Reed-Solomon $(40, 11, 30)$ error correcting codes can correct any 14 symbol errors using the bounded distance decoding algorithm without regard to the type of error induced by the attack . The code corrects by blocks of 6 bits and replaces the whole symbol by the correct one without regard to the number of bits corrupted in the symbol, i.e., it treats an error of 1 bit in the symbol in the same way as it treats an error of 6 bits of the symbol—replacing them with the correct 6 bit symbol. This gives the Reed-Solomon codes a tremendous burst noise advantage over binary codes. In this example, if the 60 bits noise disturbance can occur in a random fashion rather than as a contiguous burst, that could effect many more than 14 symbols which is beyond the capability of the code.

In the watermarking channel, the errors, characterized by the different attacks, occur in random or burst manner. Depending on the placement of the watermark in an image and the use of error correcting codes, the robustness of the signature can be increased against the attacks.

For Reed-Solomon codes the conventionally used, bounded distance decoding algorithms correct up to $t = \lfloor (n - k)/2 \rfloor$ symbol errors as shown in the above example. Using list decoding, Sudan [1] and later Guruswami-Sudan [6] showed that the error correcting capability of Reed Solomon could be improved to $t_S = n - \sqrt{2kn}$ and $t_{GS} = n - \sqrt{nk}$ respectively.

3.7   List decoding of Reed-Solomon codes

It is well known that for a linear code $[n, k, d]_q$ over the field $GF(q)$, of length n, dimension k and distance d, it is possible to decode the code in a unique way up to a number of errors: $t = [(d - 1)/2]$. Now what happens if the number of errors is greater than t? Clearly there will always be cases where a unique decoding will not occur. For instance if d is odd and a codeword c has weight d, any element x of weight $(d + 1)/2$ (which support the set of non zero coordinates) is included in the support of c, will be at distance $(d + 1)/2$ of two codewords: x and $(0, 0, \ldots, 0)$, which gives two possibilities for decoding. Meanwhile if one considers a random element of weight $(d + 1)/2$ the probability that such a situation occurs is very unlikely. A closer look at probabilities leads to the fact that in fact even for larger t (but with t bounded by a certain bound, called the Johnson bound) the probability of a random element to be incorrectly decoded is in fact very small.

The idea of list decoding is that for $t > (d - 1)/2$ a list decoding algorithm will output a list of codewords rather than a unique codeword. List decoding was introduced by Elias [55], but the first usable algorithm for a family of codes, the Reed Solomon codes, was proposed by Sudan in [1], later the method was improved by Guruswami and Sudan [6].

The list decoding method is a very powerful method but it is slower than classical algorithms which decode less errors. For usual context in coding theory the decoding speed is a very important factor since one wants to optimize communications speed, but there exist contexts in which the use of such a decoding is not as important since the use of the algorithm is only causal in the overall process. This is for instance the case in cryptography and in traitor tracing schemes [56] where list decoding algorithms are used when one wants to search a corrupted mark (which does not occur all the time).

The principle of the algorithm is a generalization of the classical Welch-Berlekamp algorithm, the algorithm works in two steps: first construct a particular bivariate polynomial $Q(x, y)$ over $GF(q)$ and then factorize it for finding special factors. These factors lead to a list of decoded codewords.

The first algorithm by Sudan permits (for $k/n < 1/3$) to decode up to $n - \sqrt{2kn}$ errors rather than $n/2$ for classical algorithms. This method is based on Lagrange interpolation.

The list decoding algorithm of Sudan [1,57] is detailed in the following steps

For a received codeword $r = (r_1, r_2, \ldots, r_n)$ and a natural number

$$t_S < n \frac{l}{l+1} - \frac{l}{2}(k - 1) \tag{5}$$

and for

$$\frac{k}{n} < \frac{1}{l+1} + \frac{1}{n} \tag{6}$$

1. Solve the following system of linear equations

$$\sum_{j=0}^{l} \begin{bmatrix} r_1^j & \cdots & 0 & 0 \\ 0 & r_2^j & \cdots & 0 \\ \vdots & \vdots & \ddots & 0 \\ 0 & 0 & \cdots & r_n^j \end{bmatrix} \begin{bmatrix} 1 & x_1 & \cdots & x_1^{l_j} \\ 1 & x_2 & \cdots & x_2^{l_j} \\ \vdots & \vdots & \cdots & \vdots \\ 1 & x_n & \cdots & x_n^{l_j} \end{bmatrix} \begin{bmatrix} Q_{j,0} \\ Q_{j,1} \\ Q_{j,2} \\ \vdots \\ Q_{j,l_j} \end{bmatrix} = \begin{bmatrix} 0 \\ 0 \\ 0 \\ \vdots \\ 0 \end{bmatrix}, \tag{7}$$

where $l_j = n - 1 - t_G - j(k - 1)$.

2. Put

$$Q_j(x) = \sum_{r=0}^{l_j} Q_{j,r} x^r$$

and

$$Q(x, y) = \sum_{j=0}^{l} Q_j(x) y^j.$$

3. Find all factors of $Q(x, y)$ of the form $(y - f(x))$ with degree $(f(x)) < k$.

4. A list of factors $f(x)$ that satisfy the following is obtained

$$H_d((f(x_1), f(x_2), \ldots, f(x_n)), (r_1, r_2, \ldots, r_n)) \leq t_G$$

5. Calculate $f(x)$ over the encoding elements to obtain the corrected codeword $(c_1, c_2, c_3, \ldots, c_n)$.

The second method of Guruswami and Sudan [6,57] permits to decode up to $n - \sqrt{kn}$ errors, but is trickier to use since it is based on Hermite bivariate interpolation and on the notion of Hasse derivative.

For a bivariate polynomial:

$$Q(x, y) = \sum_{a=0}^{\infty} \sum_{b=0}^{\infty} q_{a,b} x^a y^b,$$

the Hasse derivative for the point (a', b') is defined as:

$$Q^{[a',b']}(x, y) = \sum_{a \geq a', b \geq b'} \binom{a}{a'} \binom{b}{b'} q_{a,b} x^{a-a'} y^{b-b'}.$$

In practice the hard step of decoding is finding the polynomial $Q(x, y)$. It can be done in cubic complexity in an elementary (but slow) way by the inversion of a matrix, or also in quadratic complexity but with a more hard to implement method [58].

The Guruswami-Sudan list decoding algorithm detailed in [1,57] could be summarized in the following three steps

1. For a received word $(r_1, r_2, r_3, \ldots, r_n)$ and encoding elements $(x_1, x_2, x_3, \ldots, x_n)$ belonging to a Galois Field, solve for $Q_{a,b}$ the system of homogeneous linear equations

$$\sum_{a \geq h, b \geq u} \binom{a}{h} \binom{b}{u} Q_{a,b} x_i^{a-h} r_i^{b-u} = 0, \qquad (8)$$

where $h + u < s, i = 1, 2, \ldots, n$, and s is a natural number.
$Q_{a,b} = 0$ if $l > a$ or $b > l_a$ where
$l_a = s(n - t_{GS}) - 1 - a(k - 1)$ and l and s are the list size and multiplicity factor [6,57] for the Reed-Solomon code. Where

$$t_{GS} = \frac{n(2l - s + 1)}{2(l + 1)} - \frac{l(k - 1)}{2s} \qquad (9)$$

and

$$\frac{k}{n} \leq \frac{1}{n} + \frac{s}{l + 1} \qquad (10)$$

2. Put $Q_j(x) = \sum_{u=0}^{l_j} Q_{j,u} x^u$ and consequently $Q(x, y) = \sum_{j=0}^{l} Q_j(x) y^j$.

3. Find all factors of $Q(x, y)$ of the form $(y - f(x))$ with $degree(f(x)) < k$, and then calculate $f(x)$ over the

encoding elements to obtain the corrected codeword $(c_1, c_2, c_3, \ldots, c_n)$.

The performance of Guruswami-Sudan algorithm is better than the algorithm proposed by Sudan when the code rate $R = k/n$ is high. When the code rate is very low they have similar performance. The performance of both the list decoding algorithms shows clear improvement over the bounded distance (BD) algorithms when the code rate is low. We exploit this property of the list decoding algorithms to encode the signature in to the watermark. The improvement of performance is shown in Figure 7.

We select the Sudan's algorithm for the purpose of decoding as the code rate $R < 1/3$ for the watermarking scheme presented in Section 2 [5] for a signature size of 64 bits and the actual performance gain by the Guruswami-Sudan over the Sudan algorithm is not significant. The parameters used to demonstrate the performance of the Reed-Solomon codes are RS $(40, 11, 30)$, RS $(127, 9, 119)$, and RS $(448, 8, 441)$ and the code rates for these three cases are 0.275, 0.071, and 0.018 respectively. Therefore it is useless to use the high complexity Guruswami-Sudan algorithm as for the code rates are very low for the given cases and Sudan algorithm has similar performance, specially for RS $(127, 9, 119)$ and RS $(448, 8, 441)$, as seen in Figure 7.

According to the properties of the different codes, we are now going to study the integration of these tools in our color watermarking process.

4 Tests and results

For the tests we have used 15 images of different types and sizes (256×256, 512×512, and 1024×1024). In this article, we focus on the largest images 1024×1024 shown in Figure 8. Each image is marked with 5 different signatures where the signature size is 64 bits. This made us independent of the signature and helped us to measure

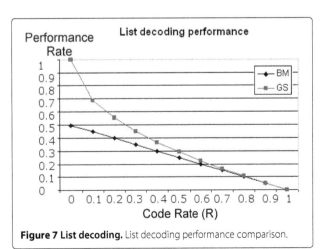

Figure 7 List decoding. List decoding performance comparison.

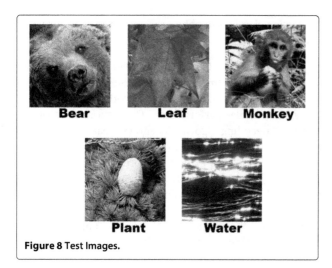

Figure 8 Test Images.

certain robustness. The attack types under study are JPEG compression, noise, low pass filter, hue, saturation and brightness attack. Then corresponding graphs show average performance of the error correcting codes, BER (bit error rate) against the attack type for the different image sizes. Bit error rate (BER) is used to measure the performance of the error correcting codes BER $= \frac{B_E}{B_T}$, where B_E is the number of erroneous bits received for each attacks and B_T is the total number of bits of the signature.

In the following figures, the graphs represent the parameter of the attack on the x-axis and on the y-axis the bit error rate is shown. The graphs show the average for each of the tested image size and error correcting codes against each of the attacks.

4.1 JPEG compression

Due to the lossy JPEG compression we lose the higher frequency components which results in blurring of the image. As the watermarking algorithm embeds the watermark in middle frequencies, the attack does not completely remove the watermark at low levels. Blurring

and blocking effects can be noticed in attacked images with a higher compression level causing random errors in the watermark.

We tested our method against JPEG attack by starting off the compression from a quality level of 1% to a quality level of 96% with a step size of 5% as one could see in Figure 9a.

In general, we can say that our watermarking method is robust against JPEG compression where the compression level is up to 50%. If the compression level of the image is reduced beyond 50% then the image is quite degraded. This is so because the JPEG compression starts to compress middle frequencies where the watermark resides.

If the quality level is reduced beyond 50% then we observe loss of high frequency information, artifacts on subimage boundaries and localized stronger artifacts. The loss of high frequency information has no effect, but the localized artifacts have influence to some wavelet coefficient values. Due to the relationship between the contents of an image and the position of the artifacts, the effects of the errors induced by the JPEG compression on the wavelet coefficients are random in nature.

Given the random comportment of the errors induced by the JPEG compression, the BCH codes show the best performance in all cases of image size, with and without the extra protection of repetition codes, and the Reed-Solomon codes give the worst performance due to the random nature of the attack.

As we have said, there is also a relationship between the contents of an image and the attack applied. The dependability of this relationship and the type of error correcting codes used is also significant. The test images have different distribution of frequency content. The watermarking scheme uses these characteristics to insert the watermark. The robustness of these images using Reed-Solomon codes against JPEG compression is shown in Figure 9b.

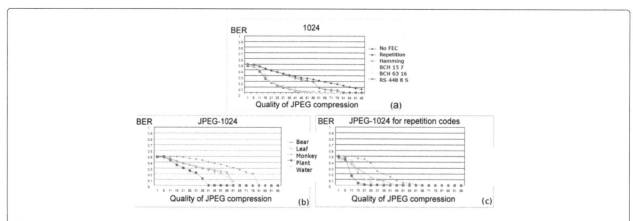

Figure 9 JPEG compression attack. (a) Comparison of coding schemes against JPEG compression for image size 1024 × 1024; **(b)** Comparison of different images for RS codes; **(c)** Comparison of different images for repetition codes.

The effect of the use of the different types of error correcting codes and the relationship between the type of image used for the JPEG compression attack could be observed while considering repetition codes and Reed-Solomon codes. Let us consider repetition codes for the same images. In the results shown in Figure 9b,c we can notice the difference in performance of the repetition codes and Reed-Solomon codes for the same images. It is observed that the repetition codes protect the same images at higher compression levels than the Reed-Solomon codes but with the same sensibility to the characteristics of the image.

Notice the difference in robustness of a compression factor of 40 for the image *Bear* and the image *Plant* shown in Figure 8. This difference in performance for the two images is due to their characteristics, the manner in which watermarking scheme exploits these characteristics to insert the watermark and how these locations are effected by the attack. The frequency contents of the image Bear are generally high, very sensitive to the compression scheme. Whereas the figure Plant has relatively lower frequency content and has important discontinuities. The watermarking scheme uses middle frequencies to insert the watermark and the JPEG compression attack will first remove any high frequencies in an image, this explains the observed results.

To conclude, the analysis of robustness against JPEG compression using the different families of error correcting codes shows that the image play a very important role for the overall robustness of the watermarking algorithm, and also shows that different error correcting codes have different performance against the different attacks for every type of image. We consider that Color watermarking scheme with BCH codes is usually robust to JPEG compression.

4.2 Additive white Gaussian noise

The type of noise that we introduce into the image is additive white Gaussian noise (AWGN). The insertion of the noise or the attack is completely random in nature and there are no bursts of noise. The x-axis in the Figure 10a shows the signal to noise ratio (SNR) and the y-axis

shows the bit error rate. The AWGN is distributed uniformly through the image and due to the randomness of the attack the wavelet coefficients are effected uniformly. The difference in the performance of the Reed-Solomon codes and the others is evident as all other codes except the Reed-Solomon codes are more capable to correct the random errors.

4.3 Low pass filtering

The low pass filter gives a blurring effect to an image as it filters out high frequency components from the image. The watermark is robust against low pass filtering as it is not embedded into high frequencies. The error correcting codes perform equally well for the low pass filter attack, the bit error rate is 0 (Figure 10b) except for some cases of large filter dimensions (9 × 9) and no code protection. This is because the low pass filter starts filtering frequencies where the watermark is embedded but the error correcting codes provide enough robustness so that this error remains negligible. This robustness against low pass filter is a generic feature of transform domain watermarking schemes as usually transform domain watermarking schemes do not insert the mark in high frequencies.

One of the main objectives of this article is to highlight the effects of modification of the color components for watermarking schemes and provide effective robustness against color attacks. We will now discuss some of these color attacks and effective counter measures using error correcting codes.

4.4 Hue

The term hue describes the distinct characteristics of color that distinguishes red from yellow and yellow from blue. These hues are largely dependent on the dominant wavelength of light that is emitted or reflected from an object. Hue is the angle between the color vector associated with the pixel and a color vector taken anywhere on the plan orthogonal to grey axis and which sets the reference zero Hue angle. This reference Hue value is often taken to represent the red color vector, so we decided arbitrarily to associate the red color vector and gave it a

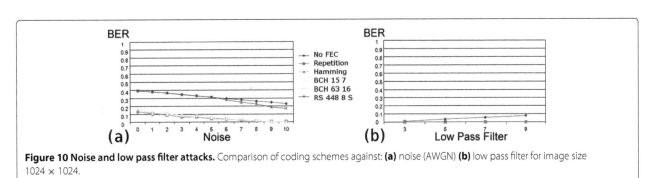

Figure 10 Noise and low pass filter attacks. Comparison of coding schemes against: **(a)** noise (AWGN) **(b)** low pass filter for image size 1024 × 1024.

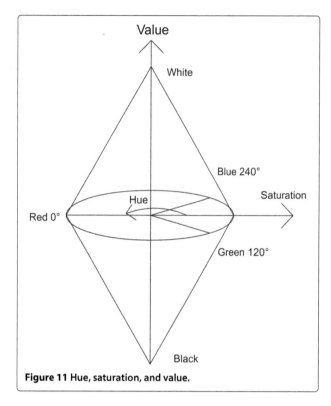

Figure 11 Hue, saturation, and value.

zero Hue value (Figure 11). Hue is the angle between this reference color vector and the color vector.

The scheme is not very resistant against changes in hue because they effect directly the color vectors that we use in the watermarking process.

In general, all the coding schemes except the Reed-Solomon codes give almost the same results as the error rates are beyond their error correcting capacity. To characterize the noise introduced by hue modification, we can say that changes in hue affect all coefficients representing a particular color similarly and this would have hue effect in blocks.

This is in accordance with the block design of Reed-Solomon codes which help protect the watermark to a certain limit. The progressive improvement of the performance of Reed-Solomon codes could be seen in Figure 12, where reasonable changes modulo 180° are correctable when using RS(448, 8, 441). The little resistance to the changes in hue is provided by list decoding of Reed-Solomon codes as changes in hue effect all the color components at the same time, consequently effecting the wavelet coefficients, where the watermark has been inserted.

Even Reed-Solomon codes are not able to resist the hue attack if the force of the attack is increased (the changes in hue are increased) as the blocks of Reed-Solomon codes and the blocking effect of changes in hue do not cater for exactly the same wavelet color vectors.

4.5 Saturation

Saturation is the measure of color intensity in an image, the Saturation is the distance between the color vector and the grey axis (Figure 11). The less saturated the image, the more washed-out it appears until finally, when saturation is at -100, the image becomes a monochrome or grayscale image and as the saturation increases the colors become more vivid until they no longer look real.

The negative saturation poses no problem to any of our error correction schemes except for a value of -100 but then the image is just a grayscale image. Now the image is desaturated and all the color planes have the same values and there is no difference between the different color vectors. Therefore the watermarking algorithm is not able to decode the watermark. When the image is not completely desaturated then the difference between the wavelet color coefficients is changed in relative proportion to the changes in saturation and the watermarking algorithm is able to decode the signature without the help of error correcting.

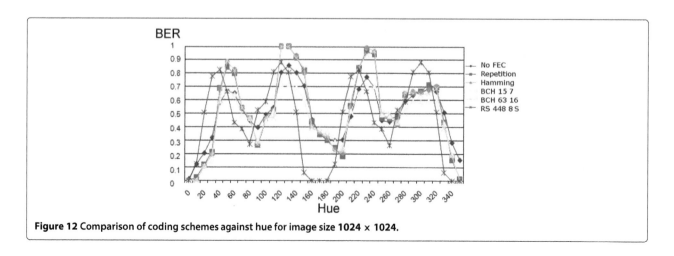

Figure 12 Comparison of coding schemes against hue for image size 1024 × 1024.

On the positive side, except the list decoding of Reed-Solomon codes, the coding schemes start giving a significant number of errors when the change in saturation exceeds a value of about 30.

As for the previous hue attack, the saturation attacks has effect in blocks. In fact, the saturation on the positive side might not effect the watermark if the change in saturation does not effect the color vectors strongly. But if the change in saturation effects the color components beyond a certain limit, then the error correcting codes are not able to provide robustness for these high levels. This is the case where the pixels values go out of bounds after processing. To take care of the R, G, and B values exceeding the bound, this problem is tackled by clipping the out of boundary values to the bounds. Clipping the values to the bounds create undesirable shift of hue and as in the previous section affect all coefficients representing a particular color similarly and this would have effect in blocks. This is in accordance with the block design of Reed-Solomon codes. The performance improvement using the Reed-Solomon codes is evident in Figure 13a, where the BER < 0.1. Furthermore if the image is saturated beyond a value of 60, it ceases to have a commercial value as natural images are not saturated to such values on the positive side.

The saturation attack, like the other attacks, has dependency on the contents of the image and the robustness measure applied to protect the watermark. The BER increase in Figure 13a for high saturation values is due to the image *Leaf* and image *Monkey* (Figure 8) as shown in Figure 13b and it is not attributed entirely to the incapability of list decoding of Reed-Solomon codes to decode the watermark for highly saturated images. For example, the original image Leaf is highly saturated and the modification of the saturation is quickly associated with R, G, and B values exceeding the bound.

4.6 Brightness

The brightness of a color measures the intensity of light per unit area of its source. We consider that brightness is the norm of the color's orthogonal projection vector on the grey axis (Figure 11). It is enough to say

that brightness runs from very dim (dark) to very bright (dazzling).

Our scheme resists the modification in brightness in the negative side to the extent of −90, where the image is hardly invisible. On the positive side at a value after 40 none of the schemes could correct the errors but then the image is degraded to such an extent that it is no longer useful.

The modification of the Brightness distorts the saturation as a side effect and the effect of saturation change is more significant when the change in luminance is important. Contrary to the others attacks, it may be more difficult to fully characterize this transform. The attack impact will depend on a significant number of factors (the parameter of the modification, the saturation value, the intensity value). Furthermore, the modification of the brightness may be considered as a random degradation dependent on the characteristics of the image.

In general, all the coding schemes except the Reed-Solomon codes give almost the same results as the error rates are beyond their error correcting capacity and give better performance than RS code for large size images (Figure 14a). Moreover, the response of individual watermarked images is also dependent on the characteristics of the image as shown in Figure 14b. For example, using Reed-Solomon codes, the figure "Bear" has the same robustness as for other error correcting codes, this image is unsaturated. The rest of the images have different robustness.

The results and the special cases discussed in this section show that the characteristics of the image, the watermarking scheme, the use of error correcting codes and the effects of the attack all play a very important role determining the robustness for watermarking schemes. Each of these characteristics has to be considered separately and also the relationship between each of these issues is to be considered while determining the robustness performance of watermarking schemes.

On the whole, we can say that the strategy we propose based on wavelet domain and error correcting codes (with judicious choices) perform well for the different attacks.

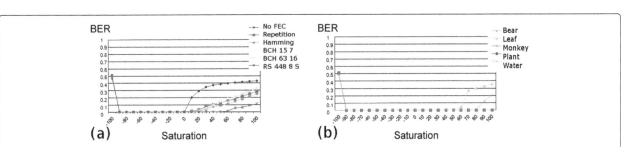

Figure 13 Saturation attack. (a) Comparison of coding schemes against saturation; **(b)** Comparison of different images against saturation for image size 1024 × 1024.

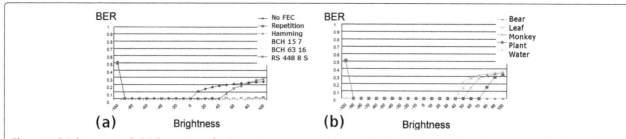

Figure 14 Brightness attack. (a) Comparison of coding schemes against brightness; **(b)** Comparison of different images against brightness for image size 1024 × 1024.

5   Conclusion

It is general knowledge that no digital image watermarking scheme is robust against all types of attacks. The purpose of this article is to be able to evaluate the performance of the error correcting codes with reference to each attack type.

The first contribution is to adapt the QIM principle to vectorial case with a watermark insertion process based upon moving one of the three color vectors (R, G, and B). This process, associated with the Wavelet decomposition is defined in order to minimize the color distortion .

The second contribution concerns the investigation of the performance capabilities of different error correcting schemes employed for a digital color image watermarking application based on the discrete wavelet transform. We have worked on improving the robustness of the signature with the help of four families of error correcting codes. We have described and compared the effect of different classes of codes against different type of real image attacks, we have included different codes and the list decoding scheme in a color watermarking complete process. For this, we have analyzed the errors introduced by different attacks and highlighted the connection of a particular attack with a particular error correcting scheme in the context of our color wavelet algorithm.

The results shown in this article confirm that the approach of using error correcting codes as a tool to enhance the robustness of watermarking schemes. During the course of this study, we observed that the use of different types of error correcting codes give different robustness to the inserted watermark. This robustness to the different types of attacks depends upon the underlying characteristics of the image.

It was observed that the four different families of error correcting codes exhibit different characteristics when different attacks are applied to different watermarked images. In general, the BCH(63, 16, 23) outperform the other error correcting codes used to evaluate the bounded distance algorithms but when the error rates are very high then the repetition codes continue to give modest performance. This is of no great advantage as the image is quite degraded in such cases.

This property of the repetition codes helps in the concatenation model and they are always used as the outer error correction codes. It was also observed that the concatenation model used in the course of this study is very useful in terms of reducing the error rate so that the inner error correcting codes can correct the errors at a lower error rate. We conclude that in general the BCH(63, 16, 23) (using with the repetition codes and the concatenation model) give us the best performance against attacks which induce errors in a random manner.

The list decoding of Reed-Solomon codes using Sudan's algorithm was used to further enhance the robustness of the watermarking scheme. We obtain very good results especially for codes with low rates. An important consequence of using the method is that when the code rate k/n tends to 0 the algorithm can decode asymptotically $n\left(1 - \sqrt{\frac{2k}{n}}\right)$ errors which means that the proportion of potential errors tends to 1.

The list decoding of Reed-Solomon codes shows better performance for color attacks, specially hue and saturation, where the pixels values go out of bounds after processing and have effect in blocks. The performance against noise and JPEG compression is not good because of the complete and semi-random nature of the two attacks, respectively. The low pass filtering does not effect the watermark as the watermark is inserted in middle frequencies and all error correcting schemes encounter minimal errors even for the large filter size of 9 × 9, which significantly degrades the quality of an image.

To conclude, we will once again underline the fact that our discrete wavelet transform based color image watermarking scheme is very useful itself to protect the watermark. It uses middle frequencies and local image characteristics; this makes it robust to a certain extent against low pass filter attack and JPEG compression. The error correcting codes add further robustness to the cases where the scheme is not inherently robust, as shown during the course of this article. Our results show that some codes are better than others for different types of attacks. Each attack modifies the image in a different way depending on the characteristics of the image. The error correcting codes can correct certain error types and depending upon their own construction the error correcting codes could be beneficial in the case of burst or random noise. Based on the above, it is inferred that for a precise scenario and thus associated with a given restricted set of attacks, we can choose the adapted error correcting codes with our wavelet transform based color image watermarking scheme.

In future study, we will study the invisibility issue of the watermarking algorithm. The use of the image characteristics have a very significant role to play in determining the robustness performance of a particular watermarking scheme and the method used to enhance the robustness or invisibility of the inserted watermark. The actual study is dedicated to the efficient insertion of the watermark inside an image depending upon the characteristics of the image, hence increasing the robustness and reducing the degradation of image quality due to watermark insertion.

Competing interests

The authors declare that they have no competing interests.

Author details

[1]Laboratory SIC-XLIM, University of Poitiers, bat. SP2MI, av. Marie et Pierre Curie, 86960, Chasseneuil Cédex, France. [2]MLaboratory DMI-XLIM, University of Limoges, 123, av. A. Thomas, 87060, Limoges, France.

References

1. M Sudan, Decoding of Reed-Solomon codes beyond the error correction bound. J. Complex. **12**, 180–193 (1997)
2. J Darbon, B Sankur, H Maitre, Error correcting code performance for watermark protection. Secur. Watermark. Multimedia Contents 3 SPIE. **4314**, 663–672 (2001)
3. N Terzija, M Repges, K Luck, W Geisselhardt, in *Visualization, Imaging, and Image Processing*. Digital image watermarking using discrete wavelet transform: performance comparison of error correcting codes (Acta press, 2002)
4. S Baudry, J Delaigle, B Sankur, B Macq, H Maitre, Analyses of error correction strategies for typical communication channels in watermarking. Signal Process. **81**, 1239–1250 (2001)
5. A Parisis, P Carre, C Fernandez-Maloigne, N Laurent, Color image watermarking with adaptive strength of insertion. IEEE ICASSP. **3**, 85–88 (2004)
6. V Guruswami, M Sudan, Improved decoding of Reed-Solomon codes and algebraic geometry codes. IEEE Trans. Inf. Theory. **45**, 1755–1764 (1999)
7. W Abdul, P Carre, P Gaborit, in *Proceedings of SPIE Media Forensics and Security XII*, vol. 75410U. Human visual system-based color image steganography using the contourlet transform, (2010)
8. W Abdul, P Carre, H Saadane, P Gaborit, in *IEEE ICIP*. Watermarking using multiple visual channels for perceptual color spaces, (2010), pp. 2597–2600
9. R van Schyndel, A Tirkel, C Osborne, in *International Conference on Image Processing*, vol. 2. A digital watermark, Austin Texas, 1994), pp. 86–90
10. R Wolfgang, E Delp, in *International Conference on Images Processing*. A watermark for digital images, Lausanne, 1996), pp. 219–222
11. A Tirkel, G Rankin, R Van Schyndel, W Ho, N Mee, C Osborne, Electronic watermark. Digital Image Comput. Technol. Appl. (DICTA93), 666–673 (1993)
12. J Liu, S Chen, Fast two-layer image watermarking without referring to the original image and watermark. Image Vision Comput. **19**(14), 1083–1097 (2001)

13. M Queluz, Spatial watermark for image content authentication. J. Electron. Imag. **11**, 275 (2002)
14. A De Rosa, M Barni, F Bartolini, V Cappellini, A Piva, in *Information Hiding*, vol. 3657. Optimum decoding of non-additive full frame DFT watermarks, San Jose, 2000), pp. 159–171
15. E Ganic, SD Dexter, AM Eskicioglu, Eskicioglu, in *Proceedings of SPIE: Security, Steganography, and Watermarking of Multimedia Contents VII*, vol. 5681. Embedding multiple watermarks in the DFT, domain using low and high frequency bands, (2005), pp. 175–184
16. X Kang, J Huang, Y Shi, Y Lin, A DWT-DFT composite watermarking scheme robust to both affine transform and JPEG compression. 13. **8**, 776–786 (2003)
17. V Solachidis, L Pitas, Circularly symmetric watermark embedding in 2-D DFT domain. IEEE Trans. Image Process. **10**(11), 1741–1753 (2001)
18. F Alturki, R Mersereau, in *Proceedings of the Acoustics, Speech, and Signal Processing, 2000 on IEEE International Conference*, vol. 04. An oblivious robust digital watermark technique for still images using DCT phase modulation, Washington, 2000), pp. 1975–1978
19. A Briassouli, P Tsakalides, A Stouraitis, *Hidden messages in heavy-tails: DCT-domain watermark detection using alpha-stable models*, vol. 7, (2005)
20. JR Hernndez, M Amado, F Prez-Gonzlez, DCT-domain watermarking techniques for still images: detector performance analysis and a new structure. IEEE Trans. Image Process. **9**(1), 55–68 (2000)
21. S Lin, C Chin, A robust DCT-based watermarking for copyright protection. IEEE Trans. Consumer Electron. **46**, 415–421 (2000)
22. Z Zhuancheng, Z Dianfu, Y Xiaoping, A robust image blind watermarking algorithm based on adaptive quantization step in DWT. J. Image Graph. **11**(6), 840–847 (2006)
23. S Agreste, G Andaloro, D Prestipino, L Puccio, An image adaptive, wavelet-based watermarking of digital images. J. Comput. Appl. Math. **210**(1–2), 13–21 (2007)
24. M Barni, F Bartolini, A Piva, Improved wavelet based watermarking through pixel-wise masking. IEEE Trans. Image Process. **10**, 783–791 (2001)
25. Z Fan, Z Hongbin, in *EUSIPCO. Conference*. Wavelet domain watermarking capacity analysis, (Vienna, 2004), pp. 1469–1472
26. J Wang, G Liu, Y Dai, J Sun, Z Wang, S Lian, Locally optimum detection for Barni's multiplicative watermarking in DWT domain. Signal Process. **88**, 117–130 (2008)
27. X Xia, C Boncelet, G Arce, Wavelet transform based watermark for digital images. Optics Exp. **3**(12), 497–511 (1998)
28. A Piva, M Barni, F Bartolini, in *Proc. of SPIE Mathematics of Data/Image Coding, Compression, and Encryption*, vol. 3456, ed. by Schmalz. Copyright protection of digital images by means of frequency domain watermarking, (San Diego, 1998), pp. 25–35
29. F Bartolini, M Barni, V Cappellini, A Piva, in *Proceedings of 5th IEEE International Conference on Image Processing ICIP*, vol. I. Mask building for perceptually hiding frequency embedded watermarks, (Chicago, 1998), pp. 450–454
30. F Autrusseau, PL Callet, A robust watermarking technique based on qunatization noise visibility thresholds. Signal Process. **87**(6), 1363–1383 (2007)
31. A Piva, M Barni, F Bartolini, V Cappellini, in *IEEE International Conference on Image Processing*. Dct-based watermark recovering without resorting to the uncorrupted original image, (Santa Barbara, 1997), pp. 520–523
32. S Pereira, T Pun, Robust template matching for affine resistant image watermarks. IEEE Trans. Image Process. **9**, 1123–1129 (2000)
33. DD Vleeschouwer, CD Vleeschouwer, B Macq, Watermarking algorithm based on a human visual model. Signal Process. **66**, 319–335 (1998)
34. A Piva, M Barni, F Bartolini, V Cappellini, in *IEEE International Conference on Image Processing*. DCT-based watermark recovering without resorting to the uncorrupted original image, (Santa Barbara, 1997), pp. 520–523
35. H Qiang, M Hong, *Blind watermark algorithms based on HVS in DCT domain*, vol. 3, (2005)
36. L Xudong, *Blocked DCT and quantization based blind image watermark algorithm*, vol. 21, (2006)
37. W Jin-wei, D Yue-wei, W Zhi-quan, *Blind watermark scheme replacing middle frequency coefficients in DCT domain*, (2005)
38. X Cong, A new blind watermark embedding detection scheme based on DCT, vol. 2, (2004)

39. L Chen, M Li, in *7th World Congress on Intelligent Control and Automation.* An effective blind watermark algorithm based on DCT, (Chongqing, 2008), pp. 6822–6825

40. X Li, *Blocked DCT quantization based blind image watermark algorithm,* vol. 32, (2006)

41. M Jun, S Jiang-hai, *A blind watermark embedding detection scheme based on DCT apply to core image,* vol. 4, (2006)

42. Q Yuan, H Yao, W Gao, S Joo, in *Proceedings 2002 IEEE International Conference on Multimedia and Expo, 2002. ICME'02,* vol. 2. Blind watermarking method based on DWT middle frequency pair, (Lausanne, 2002), pp. 473–476

43. L Ting, Y Weiyan, *A digital watermarking technique for color images based on DWT and HVS,* (2003)

44. Y Zhang, Blind watermark algorithm based on HVS and RBF neural network in DWT domain. WSEAS Trans. Comput. **8**, 174–183 (2009)

45. S Joo, Y Suh, J Shin, H Kikuchi, S Cho, A new robust watermark embedding into wavelet DC components. ETRI J. **24**(5), 401–404 (2002)

46. G El-Taweel, H Onsi, M Samy, M Darwish, Secure and non-blind watermarking scheme for color images based on DWT. GVIP Special Issue Watermarking. **5**, 1–5 (2007)

47. RW Hamming, Error detecting and error correcting codes. Bell Syst. Tech. J. **29**(2), 147–160 (1950)

48. R Bose, D Ray-Chaudhuri, On a class of error correcting binary group codes. Inf. Control. **3**, 68–79 (1960)

49. IS Reed, G Solomon, Polynomial codes over certain finite fields. SIAM J. Appl. Math. **8**, 300–304 (1960)

50. J Wang, G Wiederhold, in *Proceedings of SPIE,* vol. 3528. WaveMark: digital image watermarking using Daubechies' wavelets and error correcting coding, (Boston, 1998), pp. 432–439

51. S Pereira, T Pun, in *Information Hiding,* vol. 1768. Fast robust template matching for affine resistant image watermarks, (Dresden, 2000), pp. 199–210

52. B Verma, S Jain, D Agarwal, A Phadikar, A new color image watermarking scheme. Infocomp. J. Comput. Sci. **5**(2), 37–42 (2006)

53. M Schlauweg, D Prufrock, E Muller, in *Proceedings of the 9th international conference on Information hiding,* vol. 4567. Soft feature-based watermark decoding with insertion/deletion correction, (Saint Malo, 2007), pp. 237–251

54. B Sklar, *Digital Communications: Fundamentals and Applications.* (Prentice Hall, Upper Saddle River, 2001)

55. P Elias, *List decoding for noisy channels. Tech. rep., Technical Report 335.* (Research Laboratory of Electronics, MIT, 1957)

56. A Silverberg, J Staddon, J Walker, *Efficient traitor tracing algorithms using list decoding,* (2001). http://eprint.iacr.org/2001/016

57. J Justesen, T Høholdt, *A course in error-correcting codes,* (2000)

58. P Gaborit, O Ruatta, Efficient interpolation for algebraic list decoding. IEEE Int. Symp. Inf. Theory ISIT, 143–147 (2006)

16

A survey on security attacks and countermeasures with primary user detection in cognitive radio networks

José Marinho[1,2], Jorge Granjal[2,3*] and Edmundo Monteiro[2,3]

Abstract

Currently, there are several ongoing efforts for the definition of new regulation policies, paradigms, and technologies aiming a more efficient usage of the radio spectrum. In this context, cognitive radio (CR) emerges as one of the most promising players by enabling the dynamic access to vacant frequency bands on a non-interference basis. However, the intrinsic characteristic of CR opens new ways for attackers, namely in the context of the effective detection of incumbent or primary users (PUs), the most fundamental and challenging requirement for the successful operation of CR networks. In this article, we provide a global and integrated vision of the main threats affecting CR environments in the context of the detection of primary users, with a particular focus on spectrum sensing data falsification and primary user emulation attacks. We also address solutions and research challenges still required to address such threats. Our discussion aims at being complete and self-contained, while also targeting readers with no specific background on this important topic of CR environments. It is, as far as our knowledge goes, the first work providing a global and clear vision of security threats and countermeasures in the context of primary user detection in CR.

Keywords: Security in cognitive radio; Primary user detection; Primary user emulation; Spectrum sensing falsification

1 Review

1.1 Introduction

The radio spectrum is a finite resource currently experiencing a tremendous increase in demand and, consequently, growing in scarcity. This trend will continue in the future as the number of deployed wireless technologies and devices increases, the same applying to the bandwidth requirements. Additionally, the few existing license-free radio frequencies, such as the industrial, scientific, and medical (ISM) bands, are often overcrowded, especially in densely populated areas. This situation results in contention and interference, and, consequently, in significant performance degradation. Despite such aspects, we can also observe that the majority of the licensed radio spectrum remains unused or underutilized independently of time and location, resulting in numerous vacant spectrum bands [1]. This inefficient usage of the spectrum

results directly from the current spectrum regulation policies, which divide the spectrum into static licensed and unlicensed frequencies. The definition of more flexible regulation policies and the development of related and innovative technologies will change this paradigm, with cognitive radio (CR) emerging as one of the key enablers in this context [1,2].

A CR device is intended to possess the capability to observe and learn from its environment, and to dynamically and autonomously adjust transmission parameters such as the operating frequency and transmission power, in order to increase its performance on a non-interference basis. A key component of the CR paradigm is the usage of software-defined radios (SDR), radio communication systems with components implemented in software rather than in hardware. We currently verify an increasing availability of SDR platforms, which are employed in the context of the development of new platforms and research proposals in the area of CR. Through a dynamic spectrum access (DSA) approach [1], CR users, also designated as secondary users (SUs), are able to opportunistically and intelligently access the spectrum holes in a transparent

* Correspondence: jgranjal@dei.uc.pt
[2]DEI-UC - Department of Informatics Engineering, University of Coimbra, Pólo II - Pinhal de Marrocos, 3030-290 Coimbra, Portugal
[3]CISUC - Centre for Informatics and Systems of the University of Coimbra, Pólo II - Pinhal de Marrocos, 3030-290 Coimbra, Portugal
Full list of author information is available at the end of the article

way to the primary users (PUs) and without causing them any harmful interference. The accurate location of spectrum holes appears thus as the most challenging and fundamental issue in CR environments.

It is well assumed in the literature that approaches for the localization of vacant spectrum bands based exclusively on local sensing and learning do not offer satisfactory results [3,4]. The main reasons are missed PU detection and false alarm probabilities, which are inherent to any kind of sensing hardware and may also result from adverse propagation effects such as multipath fading and shadowing. This implies that in practice any spectrum decision must be made taking into account several sources of information. For instance, a fusion rule might be applied to the sensing reports of several SUs and to geo-location data, if available. In this context, the usage of spurious data is a serious threat which can lead to wrong spectrum decisions and, in consequence, to an inefficient protection of PUs (i.e., due to missed detections) or to an inefficient, suboptimal, or unfair usage of the spectrum (i.e., due to false alarms).

The normal operation of a CR environment depends greatly on the effectiveness of the mechanisms designed to perform spectrum analysis and decision on the SUs. Those mechanisms aim to decide on the availability of spectrum space for the purpose of allowing the SUs to transmit but in practice may be affected by erroneous or falsified data. Erroneous spectrum availability data may be due to hardware imperfections and adverse propagation effects or, on the other hand, to security attacks, particularly data falsification and PU emulation, as we discuss throughout this survey. Attackers with malicious intents may report the opposite of their observations in order to disrupt the operation of the CR network (i.e., reduce the protection of PUs or spectrum usage efficiency). On the other hand, attackers with greedy or selfish intents may positively report the presence of PU activity in order to gain exclusive access to the spectrum. Globally, malicious and greedy attackers have the common objective of causing denial of service (DoS) to legitimate SUs [5]. In Table 1, we summarize the main motivations for attacks against normal CR operations.

The protection against the usage of spurious information in the context of PU detection is of major importance in CR environments and the main focus of our discussion in the survey. Overall, any threat against the normal functioning of mechanisms designed to guarantee detection of PU activity or spectrum availability is potentially disruptive of normal CR operations. Our goal is also to discuss how such threats are addressed by current technological solutions and to identify open issues in this context. Despite the existence of several published works on security issues related to CR environments [6-11], none of them specifically provides a global and clear vision of security threats against normal PU detection in CR environments, together with the available countermeasures and open research challenges, as we address in this survey. Our discussion seeks to provide a detailed discussion on the impact of such threats to the normal operation of CR environments and on how research is dealing with them, both in respect to current proposals and challenges to be faced by future research efforts.

The survey proceeds as follows. Section 1.2 identifies the CR scenarios that contextualize our discussion on security throughout the paper. Section 1.3 discusses the main security requirements and threats applying to CR environments, and in Section 1.4, we discuss the risks that can affect the effectiveness of PU detection as well as existing research proposals in this context. Finally, Section 2 concludes the paper and identifies the existing research challenges in this area.

1.2 Cognitive radio networks

A network employing CR technology may adopt a centralized or distributed architecture, as illustrated in Figure 1. With a centralized approach or infrastructure-based CR network, spectrum decisions are performed and coordinated by a central entity (e.g., a base station) based on the fusion of sensing results collected from several SUs or dedicated sensors. This approach therefore enables a centralized cooperative sensing scheme. The central entity can additionally rely on geo-location databases providing the coordinates of known primary transmitters (e.g.,

Table 1 Characterization of attacks against the normal functioning of CR networks

Motivations	Attack goals	Attack approaches	Attack effects
Greedy/selfish	Maximize the communication performance of the attacker.	Make the SUs believe that vacant portions of the spectrum are busy (i.e., induce false alarms) and access them exclusively.	A global decrease on spectrum sharing efficiency and usage fairness.
Malicious	Disrupt the performance and operations of the SUs and/or PUs.	Make the other SUs believe that vacant portions of the spectrum are busy.	A decrease in spectrum usage efficiency and, therefore, in the performance of the affected SUs.
		Make the SUs believe that busy portions of the spectrum are idle (missed detections).	A decrease in the protection of the affected PUs against interferences caused by (erroneous) SU transmissions.

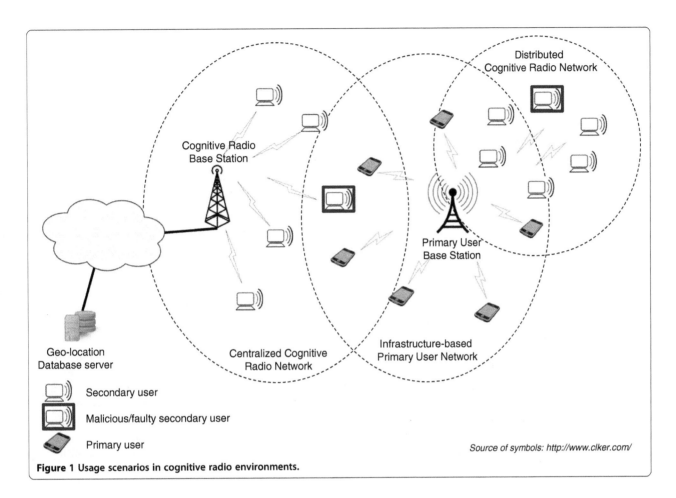

Secondary user

Malicious/faulty secondary user

Primary user

Source of symbols: http://www.clker.com/

Figure 1 Usage scenarios in cognitive radio environments.

television transmitter towers) and their respective regions of potential interference. This is the approach adopted in the recent IEEE 802.22 standard [12], which targets CR operations over television frequency bands (54 to 862 MHz) in order to enable the deployment of wireless regional networks. IEEE 802.22 uses both spectrum sensing and geo-location databases for the detection of spectrum holes, with regulatory bodies being responsible for the maintenance of the information describing the locations of the primary systems. When this information is not available, all the television channels are considered potential opportunities and only sensing is used.

In distributed or *ad hoc* CR networks [13], each SU supports its own spectrum decisions based on local observation and learning. With a cooperative scheme, each SU also considers the signaling information provided by its neighbors (e.g., sensing reports), therefore acting as a data fusion center. Cooperative schemes have more communication overhead than non-cooperative solutions but may result in higher spectrum usage efficiency and sensing accuracy [4]. We also note that, although the distributed CR network illustrated in Figure 1 follows a one-hop approach, given that every SU is in the transmission range of each other, multi-hop approaches are also possible.

As Celebi and Arslan [14] state, centralized and distributed approaches are the two extreme cognition limits between which various approaches can be developed. For instance, a CR mesh network may be considered, where spectrum decision is performed by several mesh gateways or by the SUs themselves (as with a pure distributed approach), with optional usage of geo-location databases accessible through the gateways. In order to support our following discussion on security in the context of CR environments, in Figure 1 we also illustrate the presence of SUs which are supposed to be malicious, faulty, or both. For the sake of realism, in practice we must also consider that any sensing device is characterized by non-null missed detection and false alarm probabilities, which may occasionally influence erroneous decisions.

1.3 Cognitive radio security threats and requirements

Security threats against CR networks may be motivated not only by the wireless nature of such communication environments (and that are in fact inherent of any wireless communications technology) but also by the employment of specific cognitive operations. In Figure 2,

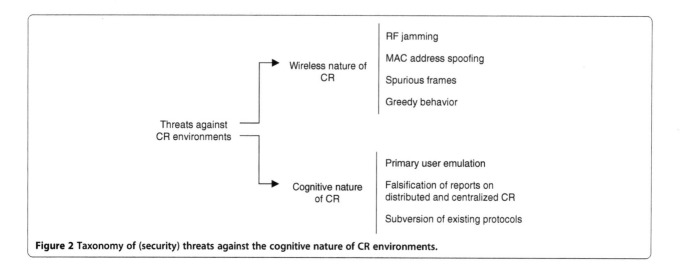

Figure 2 Taxonomy of (security) threats against the cognitive nature of CR environments.

we illustrate a taxonomy of the security threats against CR environments, considering such two different and complementary perspectives.

Given its wireless nature, CR environments may be open to attacks against wireless communications, particularly at the physical and medium access control (MAC) layers. For example, radio frequency (RF) jamming may target the physical layer and disrupt the network operations. Attacks at the MAC layer may include address spoofing, transmission of spurious MAC frames, and greedy behavior by cheating on the back off rules established by the MAC protocol. On the other hand, security concerns due to the cognitive nature of CR networks motivate the development of mechanisms to protect both primary and secondary users [15] and are the main focus of our discussion in this survey.

In CR environments, a SU can be fooled by malicious elements of its environment, as it relies on observation and possibly on cooperation for spectrum decision and learning. Among various types of threats, two assume particular importance on CR environments and motivate our analysis throughout the survey: *PU emulation* and *data falsification* attacks. Data falsification attacks in the context of CR networks may involve for example the reporting of false spectrum sensing data, as we discuss in detail later. Security threats that are out of the scope of our discussion may include attacks aiming the installation of malicious code in the cognitive radio devices, with the goal of subverting existing CR protocols. Such protocols are expected to assure that only vacant channels are accessed by the SUs and that the channels are evacuated by the SUs upon the return of PU activity.

Looking more closely at the problems of PU emulation and spectrum sensing data falsification, a PU emulation attack allows an attacker to mimic a PU in order to force other CR users to vacate a specific frequency band and consequently cause the disruption of the network's operations and unfairness on spectrum sharing. We may also note that this attack is specific to CR networks. On the other hand, the falsification of reports in cooperative schemes consists in providing false information to the neighbors or to a data fusion center and affects the effectiveness of spectrum decision. In Table 2, we identify the applicability, the effects, and possible approaches or countermeasures against primary user emulation and spectrum sensing data falsification attacks. Our discussion throughout the survey explores in detail the aspects described in this table.

Many existing CR proposals employ statistics collected about the observed PU activity, in order to learn and make predictions based on beliefs that result from current and past observations. In this context, manipulated and faulty data may lead to what Clancy and Goergen [16] designate as belief-manipulation attacks. In fact, learning capabilities (e.g., based on neural and evolutionary algorithms) not only result in great benefits to CR scenarios but also offer new opportunities for attackers. Any manipulation may potentially affect future spectrum selections, as the SUs employ all their experiences in order to derive long-term behavior. This also implies that learned beliefs should never be permanent. In non-cooperative networks, an attack against a SU does not affect the others, since every SU is able to make its own spectrum sensing and spectrum decisions. On the contrary, when a cooperative or centralized scheme is employed, an attack to a single device may affect the outcome of the entire CR network. Overall, intentional and unintentional anomalies may result in a decrease in terms of the performance of PU protection and spectrum usage, and in spectrum access unfairness among the various SUs. Security is thus of prime importance for the normal functioning of CR network operations, as we proceed to discuss.

Table 2 Attacks against CR environments and applicable countermeasures

Attack	Applicability	Effects	Countermeasures
PU emulation	CR networks based on non-cooperative schemes. Note: in such environments an attack against a specific SU may only affect that SU.	False alarms due to fake signals. The affected SUs are denied access to the affected spectrum holes due to greedy or malicious motivations, and, therefore, their performances are likely to decrease.	Sensing techniques that consider *a priori* known characteristics of the legitimate PU signals. Solutions based on capabilities such as location determination techniques and access to geo-location information about *a priori* known PUs.
Spectrum sensing data manipulation/ falsification	CR networks based on cooperative schemes. Note: in such environments, attacks against a single SU may affect several SUs or the entire network.	Cooperative spectrum sensing accuracy decreases due to the propagation of false alarms and/or missed detections that are forged.	Solutions for providing characteristics such as mutual authentication, data integrity, and data encryption.
		If learning is considered, the behavior of the SUs is likely to suffer a negative impact on the long-term basis due to the usage of manipulated data in the learning process.	Outlier detection techniques.
		Malicious attacks may impact on PUs by inducing missed detections.	Approaches based on the exploration of spectrum spatial correlation and location techniques.
		Malicious and greedy attacks may impact the performance of the SUs by inducing false alarms.	Schemes that enable determining the trustiness of the SUs and, therefore, dropping reports from untrustworthy sources. Deployment of dedicated trusty sensors. Usage of mechanisms to selectively forget past information in order to make beliefs and learning outputs temporary.

1.4 Approaches to attack-tolerant primary user detection on CR environments

Various security threats are transversal to wireless environments and may consequently also affect CR applications and communication mechanisms. For example, a beacon falsification attack in IEEE 802.22 environments may allow the transmission of false spectrum or geo-location information to users, allowing the subversion of normal spectrum space access and usage rules. As in most wireless environments, well-known security solutions may be of help in circumventing many of such attacks in CR networks. In this context, the security layer 1 as defined in IEEE 802.22 defines encryption and authentication mechanisms offering protection for geo-location information as reported by the SUs using the co-existence beacon protocol (CBP).

Other than the employment of classic cryptographic approaches to support security mechanisms designed for CR environments, we may note that the most important challenges to research and standardization work regarding security reside in the design of security solutions to cope with the threats that are inherent to the cognitive nature of such environments, as previously discussed [17]. Such threats may potentially challenge the main goal of CR, which is the usage of the available radio spectrum space in a fair and optimal way, while preserving primary or incumbent transmitters from interferences. We proceed with a discussion on how such threats may be approached, with a particular focus on a fundamental mechanism of CR: the effective detection of primary user activity and spectrum opportunities.

1.4.1 Attacks against cooperative sensing

Spectrum sensing is a fundamental mechanism of CR networks and, in this context, one major problem to avoid is the designated hidden PU problem. This problem occurs when a SU cannot sense the activity of a PU it interferes with, i.e., when it is out of the coverage area of the PU or when sensing is affected by well-known adverse effects in wireless communications, in particular multipath fading and shadowing. For instance, in Figure 1 the PU base station is a hidden PU, in the perspective of the three nodes of the distributed CR network that are out of its coverage area, while having transmission ranges that overlap it. In practice, we must consider that sensing can also be erroneous due to inherent hardware imperfections, and consequently the usage of spectrum occupancy information obtained exclusively from local sensing might not achieve satisfactory results. In this context, cooperative or collaborative sensing is considered an effective means to increase the efficiency of PU detection in CR environments. However, it also creates new security vulnerabilities, as we proceed to discuss in greater detail.

1.4.1.1 Data fusion: a key enabler for cooperative sensing In collaborative sensing schemes, the final

decision regarding spectrum access is based on the fusion of sensing data from multiple SUs. In particular, the fusion process may be centrally achieved by a common data fusion center, or in alternative be implemented in a distributed manner, as illustrated in Figure 3. In the distributed approach, each SU acts as both a sensing and a fusion center, by collecting reports from its neighbors and performing data fusion and decisions individually. Distributed approaches are usually preferable, as a centralized fusion center in practice represents a single point of failure against the operability of the entire CR network. On the other hand, the required transmission

of collaborative information may result in overhead. In their work about compressive spectrum sensing, Chen et al. [18] approach this problem by considering that the SUs only transmit part of the available sensing information as a strategy to reduce overhead. Lo and Akyildiz [19] also identify and address other possible overhead causes and effects that limit gains in collaborative sensing.

With the goal of reporting their sensing results, each SU in the context of a cooperative approach can either follow a hard-decision or a soft-decision approach. With hard-decision, each SU reports its decision in a binary form (i.e., channel is busy or idle), while with soft-decision

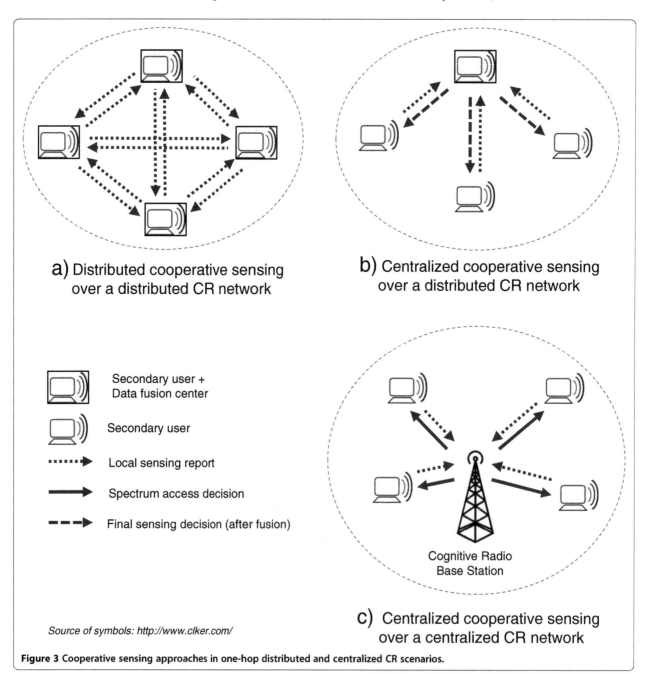

a) Distributed cooperative sensing over a distributed CR network

b) Centralized cooperative sensing over a distributed CR network

Secondary user + Data fusion center

Secondary user

Local sensing report

Spectrum access decision

Final sensing decision (after fusion)

Cognitive Radio Base Station

c) Centralized cooperative sensing over a centralized CR network

Source of symbols: http://www.clker.com/

Figure 3 Cooperative sensing approaches in one-hop distributed and centralized CR scenarios.

they report the sensed energy levels. In terms of sensing performance, Wang et al. [20] discuss that hard-decision performs almost the same as soft-decision when cooperative users face independent fading (e.g., when the SUs are not nearby each other). Additionally, we may note that hard-decision reduces the overhead in reporting sensing results [21]. Concerning soft-decision, Clouquer et al. [22] conclude that it is superior to hard-decision when fault-tolerance is not required or when sensors are highly reliable and fault-free.

Various approaches have been proposed regarding the fusion of sensing outputs in CR environments. Three common fusion approaches are implemented in the form of the OR-rule, the AND-rule, and the voting-rule. The OR-rule considers that PU activity is present if detected by at least one sensor, while the AND-rule requires that all participating sensors detect activity from the PU. With the voting-rule, a PU is declared to be present if more than a given fraction of the sensors are able to detect its activity [15]. In general terms, the OR-rule is the most commonly used approach, especially when a hard-decision approach is followed. In particular, Clouquer et al. [22] consider that this rule achieves the best performance in the presence of a hard decision. However, when the OR-rule is applied, the potential impact of the false spectrum access denial problem (i.e., when access is denied despite the SU being out of the region of potential interference) increases as the number of CRs increases [23].

Nasipuri and Li [24] propose a hard-decision process in which the decisions are performed by comparing the number of positive local decisions against a threshold (e.g., it results in the OR-rule if the threshold is equal to one). Other approaches are also possible, for example, the average fusion rule computes the average of the sensing outputs and compares it against a given threshold [22]. Malady and Silva [23] propose a centralized soft-decision approach employing a rule that computes a weighted sum of the signal strengths reported by the sensing SUs, again with the channel being considered busy if the computed value is greater than a particular threshold. Fatemieh, Chandra, and Gunter [25] discuss that the usage of a statistical median provides results that are more robust to excessively high or low reports by malicious or deeply faded nodes than when using a mean value. In their proposal, they jointly employ both estimators in order to achieve a mix of accuracy (mean) and robustness (median) in the decision process.

1.4.1.2 Security issues in the context of cooperative sensing
As the final decision in collaborative sensing results from the combination of multiple sensing results, new opportunities emerge for attackers that are able to send manipulated sensing data. This is a major concern and one of the most fundamental security challenges

that must be addressed before considering any collaborative sensing proposal to be feasible in practical terms and, in consequence, to fully achieve the benefits of CR [26]. Furthermore, as a SU might use experience learned from past to reason new behaviors and to anticipate future actions, non-detected attackers or faulty nodes may cause an impact on behavior on a long-term basis [27]. Despite this, the security aspects of spectrum sensing have in general received very little attention from research [28,29]. As previously discussed, in this context, one must also consider the likelihood of well-behaved SUs occasionally sending wrong sensing reports due to the uncertainty of the sensing environment and also to hardware imperfections. We note that cooperation in CR environments is not limited to the sharing of sensing reports. For example, it may involve the exchange of statistical data for cooperative learning. Therefore, the remainder of our discussion and the content of Figure 3 can be generalized to the exchange and fusion of generic data.

In general terms, reliable inputs (or inputs from reliable SUs) must be appropriately filtered and accepted prior to the execution of the fusion and decision processes. One of the possible strategies may consist in the utilization of a combination of mutual authentication, data integrity protection, and data encryption in order to restrict data inputs only to those from trustworthy users and consequently prevent illegitimate manipulation of data [16]. The work of Rifà-Pous and Garrigues [30] and also the IEEE 802.22 standard apply in this context. For example, IEEE 802.22 defines the secure control and management protocol (SCMP), a security mechanism derived from IEEE 802.16, providing authentication, authorization, message integrity, confidentiality, and privacy. SCMP guarantees that only authorized devices can access the network and that a device generating spurious data can be unauthorized by the base station. Additionally, if a geo-location database and localization techniques are used, it is also possible to compare the estimated position of an authenticated transmitter and its *a priori* known location. Rifà-Pous and Garrigues [30] propose a centralized solution that enables a fusion center to validate the identity of the SUs and authenticate their sensing reports and is appropriate for large CR networks. This solution uses cryptographic signatures based on simple hash functions and symmetric keys and requires the fusion center and the SUs to hold valid certificates.

For the detection of spurious sensing data, the most commonly used approach is outlier detection [26], also designated as anomaly or deviation detection. In a given set of values, an outlier corresponds to data that appears to be inconsistent with the remaining values. One of the main difficulties in outlier detection consists in preventing normal data from being erroneously classified as an outlier. There are simple and straightforward outlier detection techniques that may be employed during the fusion process, for example, ignoring extremely low or high sensing reports, or the m largest and m smallest reported values. However, with such solutions, meaningful values may be dropped and, consequently, accuracy reduced. Choosing the threshold value (i.e., the value for m or the predefined high and low levels) is not a trivial task. Ideally, it should be dynamically learned and adjusted without any *a priori* knowledge [31]. The work of Chen, Song, and Xin [32] is an example of a solution that uses more complex statistics for detecting spurious sensing data in cooperative sensing. However, in this work the authors assume that the locations of PUs are known to all SUs and that each SU is also location-aware, aspects which might limit the practicality of this proposal.

Several authors consider in their proposals that the number of malicious and faulty nodes cannot be greater than the number of properly behaving and honest working nodes. For instance, Min, Shin, and Hu [33] assume in their work that at least two thirds of the nodes are well behaving. On the contrary, Wang and Chen [34] propose a data fusion scheme for centralized CR networks that tolerates a high percentage of malicious SUs. This strength results from allowing the data fusion center to also sense the spectrum and use its own outcomes to assess the honesty of the SUs. In order to consider statistical, sporadic, and transient phenomena (e.g., false alarm probabilities), recent historical values may also be considered. For example, the proposal in the work of Li and Han [35] aims at finding the outlier users that are far from most SUs in the history space in terms of the reported values.

It must be noted that spectrum status is usually assumed to be correlated for SUs in close proximity and, in this context, spatial correlation can also be explored. A SU is thus very likely to have an erroneous sensing decision if most nearby SUs have the opposite decision (i.e., it is an outlier), as discussed by Zhang, Meratnia, and Havinga [31]. Therefore, the distinction between genuine and spurious data is based on the assumption that faulty or falsified reports are likely to be unrelated with neighboring data (i.e., spatially unrelated), while accurate sensing reports from neighboring sensors are likely to be (spatially) correlated [31]. This results in the commonly used nearest neighbor-based approaches or distance-based clustering approaches (i.e., sensors in close proximity are grouped into clusters). For instance, Min, Shin, and Hu [33] propose a collaborative sensing protocol in which sensors in close proximity are grouped in a cluster, with the purpose of safeguarding collaborative sensing. The sensors report their energy-detector's output along with their location information to the fusion center at the end of each

sensing period. This work thus considers the spatial correlation in received signal strengths among nearby sensors. Chen, Song, Xin, and Alam [36] follow a similar approach, as they also explore spatial correlation of received signal strengths among nearby SUs, with the purpose of detecting malicious SUs in cooperative spectrum sensing. This proposal also includes a neighborhood majority-voting rule.

The work of Nasipuri and Li [24] is another example that can be mentioned in this context, and its proposed fusion rule includes a clustering metric. In this proposal, location information from collaborative sensors is employed in order to determine the proximity of sensors that have similar observations. The proposal of Chen et al. [29] also considers geographical information, as it is based on a spatial correlation technique. Defining which SUs are in close proximity remains a challenging issue in the context of the successful exploration of spatial correlation and requires appropriate geo-location techniques [37].

The detection of outliers can also be a means to dynamically determine the reputation levels of the SUs, i.e., for drawing conclusions about the quality of the information they report. As indicated in Table 2, this approach enables the use of trust-based security schemes that may, for instance, attribute more relevance to the reports of more trustworthy SUs (e.g., through a weighted mean-based fusion scheme in which different weights are adaptively assigned to the SUs according to their reputation levels) [6,29,33,38] or ignore the sensing reports from SUs with reputation values under a defined threshold [21,34,39,40]. Globally, when a SU reports sensing data not tagged as an outlier, its reputation is increased. In the opposite scenario, when a SU frequently sends reports inconsistent with the final decision [38], its reputation value is decreased. Through this reinforcement-based approach, past reports are therefore considered for the computation of decisions. Examples of schemes following this approach may be found in the collaborative sensing solutions proposed by Wang et al. [20], Wang and Chen [34], and by Zeng, Paweczak, and Cabric [21]. In the former, the nodes are classified either as honest or as malicious, with all nodes initially assumed to be honest. The later proposal describes a similar dynamic reputation-based approach, in which the SUs can be in three possible states: discarded, pending, and reliable. Initially, only a predefined set of trusted nodes is considered reliable. Concerning the proposal of Wang and Chen [34], which also consists in a trust-based data fusion scheme, it targets centralized CR networks and aims at tolerating a high percentage of malicious SUs. We note that some authors consider that the soft-decision approach presents more potential to support the implementation of reputation-based security solutions [21]. We cannot also ignore the possibility of an attacker being intelligent enough in order to know the internal workings of the fusion rule. In this scenario, the attacker could adapt and start behaving honestly anytime its reputation level drops below a defined threshold [6,32]. Tingting and Feng [41] describe an attacker of this type as a hidden malicious user.

An alternative approach is to assume that nodes from a given set are reliable (e.g., access points, base stations, or specific SUs) [5,21]. Such an assumption may provide an increase in the performance of collaborative sensing, for example, by initially considering only reports from reliable nodes. Yang et al. [37] propose a sensing service model that employs dedicated wireless spectrum sensing networks providing spectrum sensing as a service, which include a large number of low-cost, well-designed, and carefully controlled sensors. Zhang, Meratnia, and Havinga [31] state that the existing outlier detection techniques do not consider node mobility or dynamically changing topologies and, as such, should be based on decentralized approaches (i.e., performed locally such as in distributed cooperative sensing) in order to keep the communication overhead, memory, and computational costs low, while enhancing scalability. The same authors also state that the outlier detection operations must be performed online and without any *a priori* information, given that it may be difficult to pre-classify normal and abnormal sensing data in distributed CR environments in terms of PU activity.

1.4.2 Primary user emulation in CR environments

Primary user emulation attacks in CR environments aim at forcing SUs to avoid using specific frequency bands and, therefore, may cause the same adverse effect as always reporting a channel to be busy with cooperative sensing schemes, as described in Table 2. This threat is materialized through the transmission of fake PU signals and does not necessarily require the attackers to participate in any underlying cooperative scheme. Thus, a PU emulation attacker does not aim at causing interference to PUs and, according to Araujo et al. [42], PU emulation is the most studied attack against CR.

Various approaches may be followed to achieve PU detection, namely energy detection, feature detection, and matched filtering [4]. The detection of PU activity through energy detection is the mostly used approach, namely due to its simplicity of implementation and because it does not require any *a priori* information about each PU transmission characteristics [4,20,43]. This detection scheme checks the received power against a given threshold and does not investigate any particular characteristic of the signals. However, energy detection also facilitates attacks from non-sophisticated adversaries, given the simplicity of generating a signal with a particular energy level in the same frequency as the PU. In fact, it is the most susceptible detection scheme to PU emulation attacks [43]. The employment of more advanced spectrum sensing methods also does not provide effective protection against security attacks, as they simply require more sophisticated attackers.

We must also consider the possibility of attackers being able to predict which channels will be used by the SUs and emulate PU activity on those specific channels, increasing significantly the effectiveness of the attacks [44]. In fact, a PU emulation attack can result in a DoS attack to a legitimate SU when the attacker has enough intelligence to transmit a fake signal on the selected channel any time that SU performs sensing [45]. We note that it is not reasonable or efficient for an attacker to emulate PU activity continuously due to energy concerns [46]. Therefore, an attacker should have sensing and learning capabilities similarly to the SUs. Naqvi, Murtaza, and Aslam [45] define a smart PU emulation attacker as one that emulates PU activity exclusively during sensing times in the CR network. A greedy attacker uses the channel after it was sensed as busy by the legitimate SUs it successfully fooled, while a malicious attacker remains silent. Haghighat and Sadough [46] define a smart attacker as an attacker that only transmits fake signals during the absence of PU activity. In their work, they also show that a smart attacker produces the same level of disruption as when transmitting continuously, although at the expense of less energy spent. In their work, Yu et al. [47] state that a successful PU emulation attack requires the attackers to be able to track and learn the characteristics of primary signals and avoid interfering with the primary network. In this context, features and approaches other than spectrum sensing are required to identify PU emulation attacks, as we proceed to discuss.

1.4.2.1 Location- and distance-based approaches

Most existing proposals address the detection of PU emulation attacks by estimation of the location of the transmitters and comparing it with the *a priori* known locations of the legitimate PUs, as in IEEE 802.22 through the access to geo-location databases [5,6,43,44,48,49]. If the estimated location of an emitter deviates from the known locations of the PUs, then the likelihood of this being a PU emulation attacker increases. Therefore, it is usual to assume that each SU is equipped with a positioning device enabling self-positioning capabilities [41,43,49], in particular using Global Position System (GPS) for absolute location information (i.e., defining the position in a system of coordinates) [14,50]. However, GPS presents various limitations, as it may not be available for all nodes in the network, is not appropriate for indoor usage, is inefficient in terms of power consumption, and may represent an additional cost not always supportable [51,52]. Despite such difficulties, Celbi and Arslan [14] state that location awareness is an essential characteristic of SUs and that they should be able to realize seamless positioning and interoperability between different positioning systems.

Having the locations of the legitimate PUs known to all the SUs is a linear task in the absence of PU mobility, such as with television towers or cellular base stations, and considering that geo-location databases are available. However, such requirements may be either challenging or impossible in many CR scenarios. Idoudi, Daimi, and Saed [53] state that existing solutions against PU emulation attacks do not handle PU and SU mobility appropriately. For example, Yuan et al. [44] only consider the possibility of television transmitters in their proposal, i.e., PUs with fixed and known PU locations. The cooperative solution that is proposed by León, Hernández-Serrano, and Soriano [54], which specifically targets centralized IEEE 802.22 networks, is based on the same assumption and thus cannot cope with the emulation of PUs that have unknown locations (e.g., wireless microphones), despite its ability to precisely determine the locations of received signals. Blesa et al. [55] state that countermeasures based on geo-location are not appropriate for scenarios with mobile PUs and SUs, and, according to Araujo et al. [42], mobile attackers can take advantage of their mobility in order to remain undetected. We note that Peng, Zeng, and Zeng [56] propose what they argue to be the first PU emulation detection solution considering mobile attackers. Xin and Song [5] present a PU emulation attack detection scheme, designated as Signal Activity Pattern Acquisition and Reconstruction System (SPARS), which does not use any *a priori* knowledge of PUs. They argue that, in contrast with existing solutions on PU emulation detection, SPARS can be applied to all types of PUs.

The accurate determination of the location of the transmitter of a given signal in relative terms (i.e., when compared to the position of the receiving SU) is in general a challenging task. Several practical mechanisms have been proposed for wireless nodes to perform direct distance measurements [57], and the most common current approach is to derive the distance between the transmitter and the receiver based on the signal strengths (RSS) of the received signals [37]. This computation requires knowledge about the emitter's transmission power, the usage of an accurate propagation model, and a statistical model of phenomena such as background noise [22]. We may however consider such methods to be limited in terms of accuracy, as the measured values can fluctuate even in small areas due to numerous adverse factors, such as fading or the presence of obstacles [50]. Other approaches are possible for automated distance determination, such as having the nodes equipped with

arrays of directional antennas that enable determining the angles of arrival (AoA) of the received signals using trigonometric techniques [57]. When compared to the usage of RSS, this approach has the advantage of not requiring any *a priori* knowledge about the transmission power used by the transmitter, being more precise, and enabling the determination of relative positions instead of merely the distances to PUs. In particular, if a node is equipped with a minimum of two antennas, the location of the emitter of a signal can be computed by the cross point of two lines with the corresponding incoming angles. Nevertheless, we may observe that RSS is still the prime candidate for range measurements, mainly due to its simplicity and low cost.

The estimation of the distances to the transmitters of the received signals using RSS values is employed by most of the existing proposals addressing the detection of PU emulation attacks [56]. However, as the transmission power of attackers is not known by the SUs and can vary over time if they have power control capabilities, estimating the distance to the sources of the signals requires additional features. A possible approach consists in deploying an additional network of sensors to cooperatively determine the locations of the transmitters and, therefore, of the potential PU emulation attackers, such as in the proposal of Chen, Park, and Reed [48]. In this context, Jin, Anand, and Subbalakshmi [43] also discuss that most existing proposals assume this type of approach for the localization of malicious nodes.

The proposal of Yuan et al. [44], designated as belief propagation, is also based on RSS and on the comparison of the location of suspect attackers with the *a priori* known locations of the legitimate PUs. However, Yuan et al. [44] propose an alternative solution that intends to detect PU emulation attacks regardless of the locations and transmission powers of the attackers. This proposal avoids the utilization of an additional sensor network and of expensive hardware, does not require estimating the exact location of PU emulation suspects, and assumes a simple energy detection approach. As the SUs have no idea about the transmission power of the potential attacker and the distance to it, a cooperative scheme enables each SU to compare the distribution of the observed RSS values in order to estimate the locations of the suspect transmitters and build a belief about a particular sender being an attacker or not. These beliefs are iteratively exchanged and updated among the various SUs. After convergence, if the mean of the final beliefs is below a defined threshold, the source of the signal is considered to be an attacker. In this case, all the SUs are informed about the characteristics of the PU emulation attacker and ignore its activity. Despite the interest of belief propagation approaches, we also observe that they usually lack validation in real implementation scenarios, and that may be costly from the point of view of the number of observations that a secondary user may be required to perform.

The proposal of Jin, Anand, and Subbalakshmi [43] is another example that assumes neither advanced features from the SUs nor the usage of sensor nodes dedicated to assist in determining the source locations of the received signals. As in various existing proposals, this work considers that energy detection is used and that the locations of the PUs are known to all the SUs. On the contrary of Yuan et al. [44], in this proposal there is no cooperation between the SUs and, therefore, no propagation of local beliefs concerning PU emulation attacks. Jin, Anand, and Subbalakshmi [43] propose the utilization and combination of two hypothesis tests in order for each SU to detect PU emulation attacks. A Neyman-Pearson composite hypothesis test [43] enables a secondary user to distinguish between a legitimate PU and an attacker, considering some constraints on the miss probability of a positive detection. An alternative approach is also discussed, based on the usage of a Wald's sequential probability test enabling a secondary user to set thresholds for both false alarm and miss probabilities, possibly at the cost of more radio observations required to arrive at a decision.

1.4.2.2 Cryptographic approaches Regarding PU detection, it is important to note that other methods not based on any *a priori* knowledge on the location of PUs can be developed, in particular by integrating security-related data with signals from primary users. Possible directions consist in including cryptographic signatures within such signals, or using integrity and authentication mechanisms for communications between primary and secondary CR users. In the context of practical CR applications, such approaches must guarantee compatibility with regulatory decisions such as those from the Federal Communications Commission (FCC), which states that the utilization of available spectrum by SUs should be possible without requiring any modification to the incumbent users and their signals. Therefore, PU authentication is a challenging issue and existing proposals are subject to practical limitations [53]. Kim, Chung, and Choo [58] discuss that this restriction limits the accuracy of secure distributed spectrum sensing schemes in CR networks. For example, the proposal of Borle, Chen, and Du [59] employs a physical layer authentication scheme based on cryptographic signatures to address PU emulation attacks. The proposed scheme is transparent to the primary receivers but inevitably requires some level of modification to the primary transmitters. The PU emulation attack defense solution that Alahmadi et al. [60] propose targets digital television networks and also requires modifying the primary transmitters, such that they generate reference signals encrypted through the Advanced Encryption Standard (AES) algorithm.

The authors state that their approach only requires equipping the primary transmitters with a commercially available AES chip, while we note that the SUs and the PUs must also have a shared secret, so further work in the context of key management should be addressed.

In the context of the cryptographic approaches, Liu, Ning, and Dai [61] propose the integration of signatures with RSS information by employing a helper node that is physically close to the PU, in order to enable the SUs to verify transmissions from the PU and decide on its legitimacy. This proposal integrates cryptographic signatures and wireless link signatures derived from physical radio channel characteristics (such as channel impulse responses). A SU may thus verify the signatures carried by the helper node's signals and thus obtain the helper node's (authenticated) link signatures from which it may derive the legitimacy of the primary node's transmissions. We may again consider that the limitation of this approach may be in the cost of the usage and deployment of dedicated helper nodes, particularly considering that its physical proximity to a PU is an important requirement of the effectiveness of this approach.

We finally note that detecting PU emulation must not be considered to be an end by itself. Countermeasure solutions must be developed in order to invalidate the effects and goals of such attacks and preferentially to prevent their occurrence by building security at the foundations of CR environments. This is probably the most challenging and unexplored issue in this context. Nevertheless, most existing works on PU emulation attack only target its detection [45]. Actually, the foundations of the CR paradigm inherently enable the SUs to circumvent PU emulation attacks even when they are not detected. That is, with CR, a SU determines which channels are busy and selects one of them if any exists. Upon the detection of activity on a channel being used for secondary transmission, either it is a primary or fake signal, the secondary transmitter must go through a spectrum handoff process (i.e., transmission is interrupted and resumed on a new channel) [47]. Therefore, according to Xin and Song [5], it is not really relevant for a SU to determine if a busy channel results from legitimate PU traffic or any emulation attack, since it reacts similarly. Xin and Song [5] also state that when an attacker realistically mimics the activity pattern of the PUs, the resulting interference is tolerable by the CR network. That is, CR has been designed to cope with a mild disruption from PUs and, therefore, they can tolerate PU emulation attacks that cause similar types of disruption. However, we note that this CR native feature is not effective when a PU emulation attack is performed by an intelligent attacker that has knowledge about the internals of the CR networks, i.e., that can guess the next channel to be selected by a SU, or when the attack is launched on different channels simultaneously by coordinated malicious nodes [5,53]. Under such circumstances, service disruption of SUs due to busy channels considerably increases and might result in DoS when the affected SUs fail in finding a vacant channel [47,53].

Concerning smart PU emulation attacks [45,46], malicious attackers remain silent during secondary transmission slots in order to save energy, and greedy attackers use the channel if it is effectively vacant (i.e., without PU traffic). Based on this assumption, Naqvi, Murtaza, and Aslam [45] propose a strategy that enables detecting and mitigating malicious PU emulation attacks. Their solution is based on allowing the SUs to perform sensing at random intervals other than the regular ones, i.e., when the attacker is supposedly quiet. That is, a SU senses the intended channel out of the sensing periods expected by the attacker and uses the remaining time slot to transmit data if the channel is actually vacant. According to Naqvi, Murtaza, and Aslam [45], their proposal is the only one that, beyond identifying PU emulation attacks, also provides countermeasures against this type of threat. Yu et al. [47] suggest that the utilization of a guard channel is a simple but effective solution to mitigate the effect of PU emulation attacks in CR networks. They also propose a defense strategy that includes reserving a portion of channels for spectrum handoff in order to reduce the resulting rate of secondary service disruption.

2 Conclusions

Cognitive radio is a highly multidisciplinary area currently attracting numerous research efforts, which provides a large number of challenges regarding security and accurate sensing [62]. As previously discussed, this survey is focused particularly on security in the context of primary user detection, particularly in what concerns two major types of attacks: primary user emulation and spectrum sensing data falsification. The importance of such attacks is also related to the fact that they may in fact compromise the feasibility of CR solutions and applications. As in other communication approaches, we may expect security to represent a fundamental enabling factor of future CR applications.

As discussed throughout the survey, in practical terms, improvements and new solutions are required to properly address the described security threats. Despite the usefulness and interest of most of the proposals previously discussed, many of them are not practical from a deployment point of view. For instance, many current proposals require the deployment of additional sensors (helping devices) or the comparison of observations against characteristics known a priori, particularly the locations of the PUs. The cost of such solutions, the unavailability of location information, or the lack of

accuracy of the positioning mechanisms may complicate the design and effectiveness of new security approaches. Also, the assumption about the primary users' locations being known a priori may be both simplistic and unrealistic. In our point of view, these are the main issues still open regarding the identification of attacks against the detection of PU activity, one major open issue regarding security in CR environments.

Recent technologies such as IEEE 802.16 Worldwide Interoperability for Microwave Access (WIMAX) are expected to contribute to increase the number of mobile primary users in a near future, and in consequence mobility and variable topologies will be a reality in many environments. In consequence, advanced security solutions not assuming a priori knowledge of the location of the PUs must be investigated and properly evaluated in real deployment environments. On the other hand, in scenarios where such information may be available, security may benefit from the utilization of cost-effective and accurate positioning techniques.

In terms of security, distributed CR networks may provide a better approach than centralized approaches, despite complicating the design of appropriate mechanisms. By allocating spectrum and security decisions to several SUs, the risk of DoS attacks against a single point of failure (i.e., the central entity) is eliminated. In this context, clustering schemes may be an intermediate alternative, with each cluster having its own central entity (i.e., decision and fusion center) and the SUs being able to elect another central entity or migrate to another cluster in case of failure or attack.

Future developments on security for CR network environments may also involve standardization efforts in the context of normalization entities workforces, such as the European Telecommunications Standards Institute (ETSI) Reconfigurable Radio Systems (RRS) Technical Committee (TC). This TC is currently active in the standardization of CR systems and also in the addressing of security threats [62]. In the same context as IEEE 802.22, the European Computer Manufacturers Association (ECMA)-392 workgroup aims at designing mechanisms to enable wireless devices to exploit the white spaces in the television frequency bands. Soto and Nogueira [17] state that, despite recently proposed protocols, architectures, and standards already including security (e.g., see IEEE 802.11 SCMP in Section 1.4), they use conventional techniques that are not sufficient to prevent CR networks from the attacks described in this survey. We also believe that reviewing existing limitations in normalization activities, such as FCC specifying that no modifications are allowed on primary networks, can contribute to make identifying PU emulation attacks less challenging, even when PUs are mobile and not known a priori.

As for the current Internet architecture and communications technologies, we may expect research and standardization work to provide equally important contributions in the addressing of security in future open CR environments. Overall, primary user detection will subsist as a fundamental network operation, and security will certainly be required to provide appropriate protection against the usage of spurious information, which can otherwise compromise the applicability of CR.

Competing interests
The authors declare that they have no competing interests.

Acknowledgements
The authors would like to acknowledge the support of project Intelligent Computing in the Internet of Services (iCIS; reference CENTRO-07-0224-FEDER-002003).

Author details
[1]Instituto Politécnico de Coimbra, ISEC, DEIS, Rua Pedro Nunes - Quinta da Nora, 3030-199 Coimbra, Portugal. [2]DEI-UC - Department of Informatics Engineering, University of Coimbra, Pólo II - Pinhal de Marrocos, 3030-290 Coimbra, Portugal. [3]CISUC - Centre for Informatics and Systems of the University of Coimbra, Pólo II - Pinhal de Marrocos, 3030-290 Coimbra, Portugal.

References
1. IF Akyildiz, WY Lee, MC Vuran, S Mohanty, NeXt generation/dynamic spectrum access/cognitive radio wireless networks: a survey. Comput. Netw. 50(13), 2127–2159 (2006)
2. J Mitola, G Maguire, Cognitive radio: making software radios more personal. IEEE Personal Commun. 6(4), 13–18 (1999)
3. L Lu, X Zhou, U Onunkwo, GY Li, Ten years of research in spectrum sensing and sharing in cognitive radio. EURASIP J. Wirel. Commun. Netw. 2012(1), 1–16 (2012)
4. J Marinho, E Monteiro, Cognitive radio: survey on communication protocols, spectrum decision issues, and future research directions. Wireless Net. 18(2), 147–164 (2012)
5. C Xin, M Song, Detection of PUE attacks in cognitive radio networks based on signal activity pattern. IEEE Transact. Mobile Comput. 13(5), 1022–1034 (2014)
6. A Fragkiadakis, E Tragos, I Askoxylakis, A survey on security threats and detection techniques in cognitive radio networks. IEEE Commun. Surveys Tutorials 15(1), 428–445 (2013)
7. A Attar, H Tang, AV Vasilakos, FR Yu, VCM Leung, A survey of security challenges in cognitive radio networks: solutions and future research directions. Proceedings IEEE 100(12), 3172–3186 (2012)
8. G Baldini, T Sturman, AR Biswas, R Leschhorn, G Godor, M Street, Security aspects in software defined radio and cognitive radio networks: a survey and a way ahead. IEEE Commun. Surveys Tutorials 14(2), 355–379 (2012)
9. AC Sumathi, R Vidhyapriya, Security in Cognitive Radio Networks - A Survey. 12th International Conference on Intelligent Systems Design and Applications, ISDA 2012, 2012, pp. 114–118
10. W El-hajj, H Safa, M Guizani, Survey of security issues in cognitive radio networks. J. Internet Tech. 12(2), 181–198 (2011)
11. O León, J Hernández-Serrano, M Soriano, Securing cognitive radio networks. Int. J. Commun. Systems 23(5), 633–652 (2010)
12. IEEE 802.22 WRAN WG Website. http://www.ieee802.org/22/. Accessed 31 July 2012.
13. P Ren, Y Wang, Q Du, J Xu, A survey on dynamic spectrum access protocols for distributed cognitive wireless networks. EURASIP J. Wirel. Commun. Netw. 2012(60), 1–21 (2012)
14. H Celebi, H Arslan, Utilization of location information in cognitive wireless networks. IEEE Wireless Commun. 14(4), 6–13 (2007)
15. AN Mody, R Reddy, T Kiernan, TX Brown, Security in Cognitive Radio Networks: An Example Using the Commercial IEEE 802.22 Standard. IEEE Military Communications Conference, MILCOM 2009, 2009, pp. 1–7
16. TC Clancy, N Goergen, Security in Cognitive Radio Networks: Threats and Mitigation. IEEE 3rd International Conference on Cognitive Radio Oriented Wireless Networks and Communications, CrownCom 2008, 2008, pp. 1–8
17. J Soto, M Nogueira, A framework for resilient and secure spectrum sensing on cognitive radio networks. Comput. Netw. 79, 313–322 (2015)
18. J Chen, L Jiao, J Wu, X Wang, Compressive spectrum sensing in the cognitive radio networks by exploiting the sparsity of active radios. Wireless Net 19(5), 661–671 (2013)
19. B Lo, I Akyildiz, Reinforcement learning for cooperative sensing gain in cognitive radio ad hoc networks. Wireless Net 19(6), 1237–1250 (2013)
20. W Wang, H Li, Y Sun, Z Han, Securing collaborative spectrum sensing against untrustworthy secondary users in cognitive radio networks. EURASIP J. Adv. Sig. Pr. 2010, 1–15 (2010)
21. K Zeng, P Paweczak, D Cabric, Reputation-based cooperative spectrum sensing with trusted nodes assistance. IEEE Commun. Letters 14(3), 226–228 (2010)
22. T Clouqueur, P Ramanathan, KK Saluja, KC Wang, Value-fusion versus decision-fusion for fault-tolerance in collaborative target detection in sensor networks. Proceedings of the Fourth International Conference on Information Fusion, 2001, pp. 25–30
23. AC Malady, C Silva, Clustering methods for distributed spectrum sensing in cognitive radio systems. IEEE Military Commun. Conference MILCOM 2008, 1–5 (2008)
24. A Nasipuri, K Li, Collaborative Detection of Spatially Correlated Signals in Sensor Networks. Proceedings of the 2005 International Conference on Telecommunication Systems Modeling and Analysis, 2005, pp. 17–20
25. O Fatemieh, R Chandra, CA Gunter, Secure Collaborative Sensing for Crowd Sourcing Spectrum Data in White Space Networks. IEEE Symposium on New Frontiers in Dynamic Spectrum, 2010, pp. 1–12
26. B Khaleghi, A Khamis, FO Karray, SN Razavi, Multisensor data fusion: a review of the state-of-the-art. Info Fusion 14(1), 28–44 (2013)
27. JL Burbank, Security in cognitive radio networks, The required evolution in approaches to wireless network security. 3rd International Conference on Cognitive Radio Oriented Wireless Networks and Communications, CrownCom 2008, 2008
28. R Chen, JM Park, YT Hou, JH Reed, Toward secure distributed spectrum sensing in cognitive radio networks. IEEE Commun. Magazine 46(4), 50–55 (2008)
29. CY Chen, YH Chou, HC Chao, CH Lo, Secure centralized spectrum sensing for cognitive radio networks. Wireless Net 18(6), 667–677 (2012)
30. H Rifà-Pous, C Garrigues, Authenticating hard decision sensing reports in cognitive radio networks. Comput. Netw. 56(2), 566–576 (2012)
31. Y Zhang, N Meratnia, P Havinga, Outlier detection techniques for wireless sensor networks: a survey. IEEE Commun. Surveys Tutorials 12(2), 159–170 (2010)
32. C Chen, M Song, CS Xin, CoPD: a conjugate prior based detection scheme to countermeasure spectrum sensing data falsification attacks in cognitive radio networks. Wireless Net 20(8), 2521–2528 (2014)
33. AW Min, KG Shin, X Hu, Attack-tolerant distributed sensing for dynamic spectrum access networks. 17th IEEE International Conference on Network Protocols, ICNP 2009, 2009, p. 294
34. J Wang, IR Chen, Trust-based data fusion mechanism design in cognitive radio networks. 2014 IEEE Conference on Communications and Network Security, CNS, 2014, pp. 53–59
35. H Li, Z Han, Catching Attacker(s) for Collaborative Spectrum Sensing in Cognitive Radio Systems: An Abnormality Detection Approach (Spectrum, IEEE Symposium on New Frontiers in Dynamic, 2010), pp. 1–12
36. C Chen, M Song, C Xin, M Alam, A robust malicious user detection scheme in cooperative spectrum sensing. 2012 IEEE Global Communications Conference, GLOBECOM, 2012, pp. 4856–4861
37. Y Yang, Y Liu, Q Zhang, L Ni, Cooperative boundary detection for spectrum sensing using dedicated wireless sensor networks. IEEE International Conference on Computer Communications, INFOCOM, 2010, pp. 1–9
38. M Atakli, H Hu, Y Chen, WS Ku, Z Su, Malicious node detection in wireless sensor networks using weighted trust evaluation. Proceedings of the 2008 Spring Simulation Multiconference, 2008, p. 836
39. T Suen, A Yasinsac, Peer identification in wireless and sensor networks using signal properties. IEEE International Conference on Mobile Adhoc and Sensor Systems Conference, 2005
40. J Li, Z Feng, Z Wei, Z Feng, P Zhang, Security management based on trust determination in cognitive radio networks. EURASIP J. Adv. Sig. Pr 2014(1), 1–16 (2014)
41. L Tingting, S Feng, Research on hidden malicious user detection problem. Sec. Commun. Net. 7(6), 958–963 (2014)

42. A Araujo, J Blesa, E Romero, D Villanueva, *Security in cognitive wireless sensor networks. Challenges and open problems. EURASIP Journal on Wireless Communications and Networking 2012*, 2012

43. Z Jin, S Anand, KP Subbalakshmi, Mitigating primary user emulation attacks in dynamic spectrum access networks using hypothesis testing mobile computing and communications. ACM SIGMOBILE Mobile Comput. Commun. Rev **13**(2), 74–85 (2009)

44. Z Yuan, D Niyato, H Li, JB Song, Z Han, Defeating primary user emulation attacks using belief propagation in cognitive radio networks. IEEE J. Selec. Areas Commun **30**(10), 1850–1860 (2012)

45. B Naqvi, S Murtaza, B Aslam, *A mitigation strategy against malicious primary user emulation attack in cognitive radio networks. 2014 IEEE International Conference on Emerging Technologies, ICET*, 2014, pp. 112–117

46. M Haghighat, SMS Sadough, *Smart primary user emulation in cognitive radio networks: defence strategies against radio aware attacks and robust spectrum sensing. Transactions on Emerging Telecommunications Technologies 2014*, 2014. doi:10.1002/ett.2848

47. R Yu, Y Zhang, Y Liu, S Gjessing, M Guizani, Securing cognitive radio networks against primary user emulation attacks. arXiv preprint arXiv **1308**, 6216 (2013)

48. R Chen, JM Park, JH Reed, Defense against primary user emulation attacks in cognitive radio networks. IEEE J. Selec. Areas Com **26**(1), 25–37 (2008)

49. R Chen, JM Park, *Ensuring Trustworthy Spectrum Sensing in Cognitive Radio Networks. 1st IEEE Workshop on Networking Technologies for Software Defined Radio Networks, SDR '06*, 2006, pp. 110–119

50. D Niculescu, Positioning in ad hoc sensor networks. IEEE Net **18**(4), 24–29 (2004)

51. F Franceschini, M Galetto, D Maisano, L Mastrogiacomo, A review of localization algorithms for distributed wireless sensor networks in manufacturing. Int. J. Comput. Integ. Manufac **22**(7), 698–716 (2009)

52. B Xiao, H Chen, S Zhou, *A walking beacon-assisted localization in wireless sensor networks. IEEE International Conference on Communications, ICC'07*, 2007, pp. 3070–3075

53. H Idoudi, K Daimi, M Saed, *Security Challenges in Cognitive Radio Networks. Proceedings of the World Congress on Engineering*, 2014

54. O León, J Hernández-Serrano, M Soriano, Cooperative detection of primary user emulation attacks in CRNs. Comput. Netw. **56**(14), 3374–3384 (2012)

55. J Blesa, E Romero, A Rozas, A Araujo, PUE attack detection in CWSNs using anomaly detection techniques. EURASIP J. Wireless Com. Net. **2013**(1), 1–13 (2013)

56. P Kai, Z Fanzi, Z Qingguang, *A New Method to Detect Primary User Emulation Attacks in Cognitive Radio Networks. 3rd International Conference on Computer Science and Service System, CSSS 2014*, 2014, pp. 674–677

57. C Savarese, JM Rabaey, J Beutel, *Location in distributed ad-hoc wireless sensor networks. IEEE International Conference on Acoustics, Speech, and Signal Processing, ICASSP'01*, 2001, pp. 2037–2040

58. M Kim, MY Chung, H Choo, VeriEST: verification via primary user emulation signal-based test for secure distributed spectrum sensing in cognitive radio networks. Sec. Com. Net **5**(7), 776–788 (2012)

59. KM Borle, B Chen, W Du, *A physical layer authentication scheme for countering primary user emulation attack* (IEEE International Conference on Acoustics, Speech and Signal Processing, ICASSP, 2013), pp. 2935–2939

60. A Alahmadi, M Abdelhakim, J Ren, T Li, Defense against primary user emulation attacks in cognitive radio networks using advanced encryption standard. IEEE Transac. Info. Forensics Sec **9**(5), 772–781 (2014)

61. Y Liu, P Ning, H Dai, *Authenticating Primary Users' Signals in Cognitive Radio Networks via Integrated Cryptography and Wireless Link Signatures. 2010 IEEE Symposium on Security and Privacy*, 2010, pp. 286–301

62. VT Nguyen, F Villain, YL Guillou, Cognitive radio RF: overview and challenges. VLSI Design **2012**, 1–13 (2012). doi:10.1155/2012/716476

17

PeerShark: flow-clustering and conversation-generation for malicious peer-to-peer traffic identification

Pratik Narang[1][*], Chittaranjan Hota[1] and VN Venkatakrishnan[2]

Abstract

The distributed and decentralized nature of peer-to-peer (P2P) networks has offered a lucrative alternative to bot-masters to build botnets. P2P botnets are not prone to any single point of failure and have been proven to be highly resilient against takedown attempts. Moreover, smarter bots are stealthy in their communication patterns and elude the standard discovery techniques which look for anomalous network or communication behavior. In this paper, we present a methodology to detect P2P botnet traffic and differentiate it from benign P2P traffic in a network. Our approach neither assumes the availability of any 'seed' information of bots nor relies on deep packet inspection. It aims to detect the *stealthy* behavior of P2P botnets. That is, we aim to detect P2P botnets when they lie dormant (to evade detection by intrusion detection systems) or while they perform malicious activities (spamming, password stealing, etc.) in a manner which is not observable to a network administrator.

Our approach `PeerShark` combines the benefits of flow-based and conversation-based approaches with a two-tier architecture, and addresses the limitations of these approaches. By extracting statistical features from the network traces of P2P applications and botnets, we build supervised machine learning models which can accurately differentiate between benign P2P applications and P2P botnets. `PeerShark` could also detect *unknown* P2P botnet traffic with high accuracy.

Keywords: Botnets; Peer-to-peer; Machine learning; Security

1 Introduction

The past decade has seen the immense rise of the peer-to-peer (P2P) computing paradigm. In the beginning of the twenty-first century, the P2P architecture attracted a lot of attention of developers and end-users alike, with the share of P2P over the Internet in different continents being reported to be in the range of 45% to 70% [1]. As an increasing number of users got access to powerful processors, large storage spaces, and increasing bandwidths, P2P networks presented a great opportunity to share and mobilize resources.

Peer-to-peer overlay networks are distributed systems consisting of interconnected nodes which self-organize into network topologies. They are built with specific purposes of sharing resources such as content, CPU cycles, storage, and bandwidth. P2P networks have the ability to accommodate a transient population of nodes while maintaining acceptable connectivity and performance. They also operate without requiring the intermediation or support of a global centralized server or authority [2]. The construction of P2P networks is on the top of IP layer, typically with a decentralized protocol allowing 'peers' to share resources. The immense success of P2P applications is primarily attributed to the ease of resource sharing provided by them - be it in the form of music, videos, files (BitTorrent), or sharing of computing resources (SETI @ home project). Apart from these, P2P paradigm has also been widely deployed for IPTV (LiveStation) and voice over IP-based services (Skype[a]).

However, the P2P paradigm has been plagued with issues of privacy, security, and piracy to name a few [3-5]. Such issues, coupled with the advent of other popular content-sharing platforms (like YouTube and Netflix)

*Correspondence: p2011414@hyderabad.bits-pilani.ac.in
[1] BITS-Pilani, Hyderabad Campus, Hyderabad, Telangana 500078, India
Full list of author information is available at the end of the article

have led to decline in the share of P2P applications over the Internet to a mere 10% [6].

As P2P networks are inherently modeled without any centralized server, they lack a single point of failure [7]. This resilience offered by P2P networks has also attracted the attention of adversaries in the form of bot-masters (a.k.a. bot-herders). A 'bot' is a computer program which enables the operator to remotely control the infected system where it is installed. A network of such compromised end-hosts under the remote command of a master (i.e., the bot-master) is called a 'Botnet'. The ability to remotely command such bots coupled with the sheer size of botnets (numbering to tens of thousands of bots) gives the bot-masters immense power to perform nefarious activities. Botnets are employed for spamming, Bitcoin mining, click-fraud scams, distributed denial of service (DDoS) attacks, etc. on a massive scale, and generate millions of dollars per year in revenue for the bot-master [8]. Botnets are being touted as the largest threat to modern networks [9].

Botnets can either adopt a centralized or a distributed architecture for their command-and-control (C&C) communications. Earlier botnets were known to be centralized (e.g., Spybot, R-bot, Gaobot, etc.), and commonly used IRC or HTTP to receive commands from a single bot-master. But they suffer from a single point-of-failure since bringing down the bot-master effectively brought down the entire botnet. The distributed and decentralized P2P infrastructure has offered a lucrative alternative to bot-masters to build botnets which are not prone to any single point-of-failure. They have also proven to be highly resilient against takedown attempts [10].

Detection of P2P botnets by analysis of their network behavior has frequently utilized 'flow-based' approaches. Owing to certain limitations of these approaches in identifying modern P2P applications (discussed in Section 2.2), alternatives have been proposed in the form of super-flow-based and conversation-based approaches. However, these approaches are not yet mature and suffer from several drawbacks.

To this end, we present PeerShark, with a 'best of both worlds' approach utilizing flow-based approaches as well as conversation-based approaches in a two-tier architecture. PeerShark can differentiate between benign P2P traffic and malicious (botnet) P2P traffic, and also detect *unknown* P2P botnets with high accuracy. We envision PeerShark as a 'P2P-aware' assistant to network administrators wanting to segregate unwanted P2P traffic and detect P2P botnets.

PeerShark does not assume the availability of any 'seed' information of bots through blacklist of IPs. It does not rely on deep packet inspection (DPI) or signature-based mechanisms which are rendered useless by botnets/applications using encryption. It aims to detect the stealthy behavior of P2P botnets, that is, when they lie dormant in their rally or waiting stages (to evade intrusion detection systems which look for anomalous communication patterns) or while they perform malicious activities (spamming, password stealing, etc.) in a manner which is not observable to a network administrator.

PeerShark begins with the *de facto* standard 5-tuple flow-based approach and clusters flows into different categories based on their behavior. Within each cluster, we create 2-tuple 'conversations' from flows. Conversations are oblivious to the underlying flow definition (i.e., they are port- and protocol-oblivious) and essentially capture the idea of *who is talking to whom*. For all conversations, statistical features are extracted which quantify the inherent 'P2P' behavior of different applications, such as the duration of the conversation, the inter-arrival time of packets, the amount of data exchanged, etc. Further, these features are used to build supervised machine learning models which can accurately differentiate between benign P2P applications and P2P botnets.

To summarize our contributions:

- A 'best of both worlds' for P2P botnet detection which combines the advantages of flow-based and conversation-based approaches, as well as overcomes their limitations.
- Our approach relies only on the information obtained from the TCP/UDP/IP headers. Thus, it does not require DPI and cannot be evaded by payload-encryption mechanisms.
- Our approach can effectively detect activity of *stealthy* P2P botnets even in the presence of benign P2P applications in the network traffic.
- We extensively evaluate our system PeerShark with real-world P2P botnet traces. PeerShark could also detect *unknown* P2P botnets (i.e., those not used during the training phase) with high accuracy.

In the next section, we give a brief background of P2P botnets (Section 2.1) and discuss past efforts on P2P botnet detection (Section 2.2). In Section 3, we discuss the system design of PeerShark. Section 4 gives the details of design choices and implementation of PeerShark, followed by its evaluation in Section 5. In Section 6, we discuss about the limitations and possible evasions of PeerShark, and briefly mention about multi-class classification. We conclude in Section 7.

2 Background and related work
2.1 Background

A number of P2P-based botnets have been seen over the past decade, and a few of them have been taken down only recently with the combined effort of multiple nations. The massive Citadel botnet (a variant of the Zeus (or

'Gameover') P2P botnet) is believed to have stolen more than US $500 million from bank accounts over 18 months. It was reported in the past year that the 88% of the botnet has been taken down by the combined efforts of Microsoft and several security agencies and authorities of more than 80 countries [11]. However, recent reports claim that the botnet is on the rise again with a tweaked version being used to target a small number of European banks [12]. A variant of the Zeus P2P botnet also targeted Nokia phones using Symbian OS [13]. The botnet operated by installing a malware on the smart phone (via drive-by download from infected websites), which was used to steal the username-password credentials of the victim's online bank account transactions. The stolen details were forwarded to the bot-master.

Storm, a state-of-the-art botnet of its time, was known to comprise of at least a few million 'bots' when at its peak. It was involved in massive spamming activities in early 2007. Even the anti-spamming websites which targeted Storm came under a DDoS attack by the botnet [14]. Researchers have confirmed that the Waledac botnet is an improved version of the Storm botnet [15]. Waledac was capable of sending about 1.5 billion spam messages a day. It also had the capabilities to download and execute binaries and mine the infected systems for sensitive data. It was taken down in the year 2010.

A P2P bot's life cycle consists of the following stages:

- Infection stage, during which the bot spreads (this might happen through drive-by downloads, a malicious software being installed by the end-user, infected USB sticks, etc.)
- Rally stage, where the bot connects with a peer list in order to join the P2P network
- Waiting stage, where the bot waits for the bot-master's command (and does not exhibit much activity otherwise)
- Execution stage, in which it actually carries out a command, such as a denial of service (DoS) attack, generate spam emails, etc.

To evade detection by intrusion detection systems (IDSs) and firewalls, botnets tend to keep their communication patterns (with the bot-master or other bots) quite stealthy. IDSs and Firewalls, which rely on anomalous communication patterns to detect malicious behavior of a host, are not very successful in detecting such botnets. Generating little traffic, such bots 'lie low' and thus pass under the radars of IDSs/firewalls.

With the advent of the Internet of Everything, the possibility of malware taking control of 'smart' appliances such as television, air-conditioners, refrigerators, etc. will not be limited to theory. In fact, there have been recent reports of 'smart' refrigerators and cars being hacked, and

wi-fi-enabled LED bulbs having security weaknesses [16]. As the creators of botnets continue to adopt innovative means in creating botnets, detection of stealthy botnets continues to be a challenging paradigm.

2.2 Related work

Most prior work has either focused on P2P traffic classification from the perspective of a more general problem of Internet traffic classification [17-19], or has given special attention to detection of botnets (centralized or distributed) in Internet traffic [20-22]. The challenging context of detection of stealthy P2P botnets in the presence of benign P2P traffic has not received much attention.

Initial work on detection of P2P botnets involved signature-based and port-based approaches [23]. Solutions such as BotMiner [20] rely on DPI which can easily defeated by bots using encryption. Some of the recent work has used supervised [24,25] and unsupervised [26,27] machine learning approaches and other statistical measures [28]. PeerRush [24] created 'application profile' from the network traces of multiple P2P applications. Their work utilized payload sizes and inter-packet delays to categorize the exact P2P application running on a host. The approach of Zhang et al. [26,27] used 'control flows' of P2P applications to extract statistical fingerprints. P2P bots were identified based on certain features like fingerprint similarity, number of overlapping contacts, persistent communication, etc. However, their work can detect P2P bots inside a network only when there are multiple infected nodes belonging to the same botnet. Yen and Reiter [28] attempt to segregate P2P bots from benign P2P apps based on metrics like the volume of data exchanged and number of peers contacted. Unfortunately, their features are not sufficient to correctly differentiate P2P bots and apps. Furthermore, their approach fails to detect bots when bots and apps run on the same machine.

Most of the past works have employed the classical 5-tuple categorization of network flows. Packets were classified as 'flows' based on the 5-tuple of source IP, source port, destination IP, destination port, and transport layer protocol. Flows have bidirectional behavior, and the direction of the flow is decided based on the direction in which the first packet is seen. This traditional definition of flows has been greatly employed and has seen huge success in the problems of Internet traffic classification [29] and even in the early days of P2P traffic classification [30]. This definition relies on port number and transport layer protocol. The latest P2P applications as well advanced P2P bots are known to randomize their communication port(s) and operate over TCP as well as UDP. Such applications will not be well-identified by these traditional approaches. Since such a behavior is characteristic of only the latest variants of P2P applications (benign or malicious), it is obvious that past research did not touch upon this aspect.

In response to this, a recent work [22] has used the 2-tuple 'super-flows' based approach with a graph-clustering technique to detect P2P botnet traffic. Although authors in [22] presented interesting insight and obtained good accuracy in detecting the traffic of two P2P botnets, their approach has certain limitations. Their work evaluates the detection of P2P botnets only with regular web traffic (which was not analyzed for the presence or absence of regular P2P traffic). This is a serious limitation because P2P botnet traffic (quite obviously) exhibits many similarities to benign P2P traffic. Furthermore, graph-based approaches work on a 'snapshot' of the network. P2P networks have high 'churn-rate' (joining and leaving of peers). Since the network is changing fast, any solution suggested for a 'snapshot' of the network would quickly become obsolete. Thus, their approach would fail in the presence of benign P2P traffic. Distinguishing between hosts using regular P2P applications and hosts infected by a P2P botnet would be of great relevance to network administrators protecting their network.

Another recent work [31] has seen the use of 'conversation-based' approach in the P2P domain, but for a different problem, namely, the detection of overlapping P2P communities in Internet backbone. Their work does not focus on identification of any specific P2P application—whether malicious or benign.

A preliminary version of our work [32] adopted conversation-based approach for the detection of P2P botnets. In [32], we looked for high-duration and low-volume conversations in order to separate P2P bots from apps and used their timing patterns as a distinguishing feature for categorization of different P2P apps and bots. None of the past works employing super-flow or conversation-based approaches ([22,31,32]) address an inherent drawback of these approaches: they fail to detect botnet activity if P2P bots and apps are running on the same machine (which might be a rare scenario, but cannot be ruled

out nonetheless). This is because conversations (or super-flows) try to give a bird's eye view of the communications happening in the network and thus miss certain finer details.

3 System design

3.1 System overview
P2P botnets engage in C&C using custom or well-known P2P protocols. As a result, their traffic can blend with benign P2P traffic flowing in a network and thus pass undetected through IDSs or firewalls.

`PeerShark` uses a two-tier approach to differentiate P2P botnets from benign P2P applications. The first phase clusters P2P traffic-flows based on the differing behavior of different applications. In the second phase, conversations are created from flows within each cluster. Several statistical features are extracted from each conversation and are used to build supervised machine learning models for the detection of P2P botnets. In Section 5, we will evaluate the effectiveness of our detection scheme with traces of known and *unknown* (i.e., not used in the training phase) P2P botnets.

Figure 1 gives the architecture of `PeerShark`. The system design of `PeerShark` is explained here:

3.2 Flow-clustering phase
Flow-based analysis has been the *de facto* standard for Internet traffic classification and has yielded great success in the past [29,30]. Typically, 'flows' are constructed based on the 5-tuple: `<Src. IP, Dest. IP, Src. port, Dest. port, Proto>` (where 'Src.' stands for 'source', 'Dest.' stands for 'destination', and 'Proto' implies the transport layer protocol (TCP or UDP)). The direction of the flow is determined by the direction in which the first packet is seen. An important difference between flows of P2P applications and traditional client-server applications is that P2P traffic is inherently bi-directional in nature.

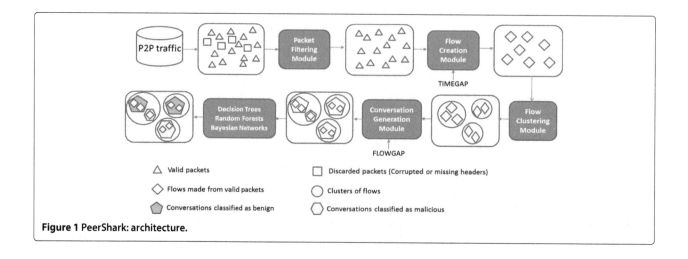

Figure 1 PeerShark: architecture.

This differentiating factor has been leveraged by some recent works [24,25] as well.

We leverage the bidirectional behavior of P2P traffic to segregate flows into different clusters based on their differing behavior. The correct classification (in terms of benign or malicious application) is not a concern at this point. At this stage, we want to separate flows into different clusters based on their behavior. As an example, we observed a peculiar behavior in the network traces of the Zeus botnet. Flows between two hosts switched between TCP and UDP. However, the communication over TCP was always fast but short-lived (a few hundred packets exchanged within a matter of seconds), while communication over UDP was stealthy and long-lived (two or three packets exchanged in half-an-hour duration). At this stage of flow clustering, these differing flows of Zeus are expected to get separated into different clusters.

For the purpose of clustering, we extract a five-feature vector for every flow: Protocol, Packets per second (f/w), Packets per second (b/w), Avg. Payload size (f/w), and Avg. Payload size (b/w), with 'f/w' and 'b/w' signifying the forward and the backward direction of the flow, respectively. The primary motivation behind the choice of these features is to exploit the bidirectional nature of P2P traffic and separate flows based on their 'behavior' in terms of the transport layer protocol used and packets and payload exchanged. A more detailed discussion on the choice of features and clustering algorithm will follow in Section 4.

3.3 Conversation-generation phase

Once a bot-master infects a particular machine, it is in the prime interest of the bot-master to not lose connectivity with his bots. The bot-peers near to each other in the P2P overlay network maintain regular communication amongst themselves to check for updates, to exchange commands, and/or to check if the peer is alive or not. If such messages are exchanged very frequently, the bots are at a risk of getting detected by IDS/firewalls monitoring the network. Hence, the communication between the bot-master and his bots, or that of bots amongst themselves, is expected to be low in volume (note here that this usually corresponds to the rally and waiting stages; 'execution' stage can be aggressive or stealthy depending upon the activity for which the bots are used; DDoS attack can be quite aggressive, while password stealing may remain stealthy).

Since certain botnets (and even benign P2P applications) are known to randomize their port numbers over which they operate, the classical 'flow' definition will not be able to give a clear picture of the activity a host is engaged in. The traditional 'flow' definition will create multiple flows out of what is actually a single conversation happening between two such peers (although happening on different ports) and thus give a false view of the communications happening in the network. To get a bird's eye view of the *conversations* happening between the P2P, hosts can be beneficial for a network administrator to hunt for malicious conversations between the bots.

As has been explained before, the present works utilizing conversation-based (or super-flow based) approaches [22,32] did not have the capabilities to detect a system infected by a P2P bot if it is running benign P2P applications as well. The main reason behind this flaw was that conversations attempt to provide a bird's eye view of the network activity to the network administrator but miss out certain finer details: since all flows between two IPs are aggregated into a single conversation, this approach will create a single conversation for two IPs having malicious as well as benign flows between them and thus fail to detect the malicious traffic. To combat this drawback, we use flow-clustering in the first phase which separates flows into different clusters based on their differing behavior. By this, we attempt to perform a coarse separation of P2P apps and bots based on their differing behavior.

In the second phase, we create conversations from flows *within each cluster*. Note that in our previous work and in other works, conversations were created by aggregating all flows/conversations between IP1 and IP2 into a single 'conversation'. Here, we limit conversation creation to the flows within each cluster. Since flows within the same cluster have similar behavior, we are creating conversations out of only those flows which show similar behavior. Thus, the drawback of aggregating *all* flows/conversations between two IPs into a single conversation (and thus missing out finer details) is addressed.

Furthermore, all P2P applications—whether malicious or benign—operate with their 'app-specific' *control messages* which are used by peers to connect to the P2P network, make file searches, leave the network, etc. Since each application has its own specific control messages, we exploit the timing patterns of these control messages to differentiate between P2P applications by considering the median value of the *inter-arrival time* of packets for each P2P application. Moreover, as has been explained before, bot traffic tends to be stealthy. Hence, bot conversations are expected to have higher inter-arrival time of packets than benign P2P conversations.

In summary, after creating conversations from flows, we extract four statistical features from each conversation:

1. The duration of the conversation
2. The number of packets exchanged in the conversation
3. The volume of data exchanged in the conversation
4. The median value of the inter-arrival time of packets in that conversation

These features are then used to build supervised machine learning models to differentiate between benign and malicious P2P traffic. More details will follow in the next section.

4 Design choices and implementation details

In this section, we present the implementation aspects and design choices of `PeerShark` in detail:

4.1 Data

This work uses data of benign P2P applications and P2P botnets obtained from two different sources. The data of four benign P2P applications, namely uTorrent, eMule, Vuze, and Frostwire, and the data of three P2P botnets, namely Storm, Waledac, and Zeus, was obtained from the University of Georgia [24]. The data for P2P applications was generated by the authors in [24] by running those applications in their lab environment for a number of days, using AutoIt scripts to simulate human-user activity on the P2P hosts. The data of P2P botnets corresponds to real-world traces obtained by them from third parties. The dataset of P2P botnet Nugache also corresponds to real-world traces obtained from authors of [33]. Altogether, we used four bots and four apps for this work.

As explained in the previous section, network traces of each application were parsed to create flows and further generate conversations (more details will follow in this section). The conversations thus obtained were labeled to create a 'labeled dataset' for training and testing purposes. For all conversations corresponding to P2P applications, we use the label 'benign'.

In the network traces of each of the P2P botnets, there are certain 'known malicious hosts' (Storm had 13, Waledac had 3, Zeus had 1, and Nugache had 4 'known malicious hosts'). However, it is not known whether the other IP addresses seen in the network traces are benign or malicious[b]. Hence, in order to create a 'ground truth' for our evaluation, we treat a conversation as 'malicious' if either of the IPs (either source or destination) is known to be 'malicious'. If none of the IPs in the conversation are known to be malicious, we treat that conversation as benign. Full details of this dataset are given in Table 1. Our training/testing datasets are representative of the real-world where the majority of traffic flowing in any network is benign. Our datasets contain more than 90% benign traffic.

4.2 Packet filtering module

`PeerShark` operates on a dump of network traces. The first module takes network logs in the form of raw packet data (`pcap` files) as input and parses them using the `Libpcap` library. The module reads each packet and isolates those which have a valid IPv4 header. For the purpose

Table 1 Dataset details

Name	Number of flows	Number of conversations	Purpose
eMule	413,995	293,704	Train/Test
uTorrent	1,409,291	458,624	Train/Test
Vuze	1,207,963	603,145	Train/Test
Frostwire	890,300	234,335	Train/Test
Storm	95,316	59,157	Train/Test
Waledac	81,778	5,765	Train/Test
Zeus	43,593	2,751	Unseen test
Nugache	51,428	49	Unseen test

of data sanitization, all packets without a valid IPv4 header are deemed invalid and discarded. The packets are further filtered to retain only those packets which have a valid TCP or UDP header and a non-zero payload. From each packet, the Timestamp, Source IP, Source port, Destination IP, Destination port, and Payload size are extracted and stored for future use. In addition to these, we also extract the TCP flags (SYN, ACK, RST, FIN etc.) for all TCP packets.

This module is algorithmically explained in Algorithm 1.

Algorithm 1 Packet filtering module

1: **procedure** FILTERPACKETS(packetCapture)
2:     *ArrayList < ModifiedPkt > filteredPkts*;
3:     **for** Packet *p* in *packetCapture* **do**
4:         *time ← p.getTimestamp()*;
5:         **if** *p* has IPHeader **then**
6:             *ip ← p.getIPHeader()*;
7:             *IP1 ← ip.getSourceIP()*;
8:             *IP1_port ← ip.getSourcePort()*;
9:             *IP2 ← ip.getDestIP()*;
10:             *IP2_port ← ip.getDestPort()*;
11:             **if** *p* has TCPheader or UDPheader **then**
12:                 *header ← p.getTransportHeader()*;
13:                 *pSize ← header.getPayloadSize()*;
14:                 **if** payloadSize not null or zero **then**
15:                     *nextPkt ← ModifiedPkt(IP1, IP1_port,*
16:                             *IP2, IP2_port, pSize, time)*;
17:                     *filteredPkts.add(nextPkt)*;
18:                 **end if**
19:             **end if**
20:         **end if**
21:     **end for**
22:     return *filteredPackets*;
23: **end procedure**

4.3 Flow creation module

The output of the packet filtering module is fed into this module to generate bidirectional flows. Each flow is identified by <Src. IP, Dest. IP, Src. port,

`Dest. port, Proto>`, as explained before. All packets corresponding to a 5-tuple are gathered and sorted based on timestamp. Flows are created based on the 5-tuple and a `TIMEGAP` value. `TIMEGAP` is defined as the maximum permissible inter-arrival time between two consecutive packets in a flow, beyond which we mark the latter packet as the beginning of a new flow. For TCP flows, in addition to `TIMEGAP` criteria, we initiate a flow only after the regular TCP three-way handshake has been established. The termination criteria for a TCP flow is met either by `TIMEGAP` or the TCP close connection sequence (in terms of `FIN` packets or `RST` packets), whichever is encountered first. In case of UDP's (virtual) flows, only the `TIMEGAP` can be employed. The module is explained algorithmically in Algorithm 2 (TCP connection establishment or termination sequences are skipped from the algorithm for the sake of brevity).

Note that `TIMEGAP` is a 'tunable' parameter, which must be decided by a network administrator based on his understanding of his network. From our experiments, we observed that a high `TIMEGAP` value was more suitable since many bots exchanged very few packets after long intervals of time. A low `TIMEGAP` value would imply just one or two packets per flow, which will be useless to extract any useful statistical metrics. We used a `TIMEGAP` value of 2,000 seconds.

Algorithm 2 Flow creation module

1: **procedure** CREATEFLOWS(filteredPackets)
2:     *ArrayList < Flow > initFlowList;*
3:     *ArrayList < PacketGroup > pgList;*
4:     *pgList ← filteredPkts.groupPktsBy5tuple();*
5:     **for** PacketGroup *pg* in *pgList* **do**
6:         sort packets in *pg* by timestamp;
7:         *nextFlow ← Flow(NULL);*
8:         **for** Packet *p* in *pg* **do**
9:             **if** *p.timestamp* between
10:                 (nextConv.start - TIMEGAP) &&
11:                 (nextConv.end + TIMEGAP) **then**
12:                     *nextFlow.addPacket(p);*
13:             **else**
14:                     *nextFlow ← Flow(p);*
15:                     *initFlowList.add(nextFlow);*
16:             **end if**
17:         **end for**
18:     **end for**
19:     return *initFlowList;*
20: **end procedure**

For every flow, a number of statistical features are extracted, such as:

1. Transport layer protocol
2. Avg. payload (forward and backward)
3. Total payload exchanged
4. Packets per second (forward and backward)
5. Bytes per second (forward and backward)
6. Total number of packets exchanged
7. Duration of the flow
8. Median of inter-arrival time of packets

Some of these are utilized for the flow clustering module, while some are retained for later use in the conversation generation module.

4.4 Flow clustering module

The flow clustering module aims to separate flows into different clusters based on their differing behavior. In order to keep our approach suitable for large networks, the choice of a fast clustering algorithm was necessary. At the same time, we would want the number of clusters to be chosen automatically as per the behavior seen in the data. To this end, we use the X-means clustering algorithm [34]. X-means algorithm is a variant of K-means which scales better and does not require number of clusters to be supplied by the user.

Clustering is an unsupervised learning approach. But since we had a labeled dataset available to us, we adopted the route of classes-to-clusters evaluation. In classes-to-clusters evaluation, the class label is initially ignored and the clusters are generated. Then, in a test phase, class labels are assigned to clusters based on the majority value of the class attribute in that cluster. Further, the classification error is computed, which gives the percentage of data points belonging to the wrong cluster. This classification error gives us a rough idea of how close the clusters are to the actual class labels of the instances.

Since the transport layer protocol naturally distinguishes between TCP and UDP flows, it was a natural choice for a feature to be used for clustering. In order to choose the rest of the features, we began with a superset S_n of n pair of features which represent bidirectional behavior of flows, such as: bytes per second (forward) & bytes per second (backward), packets per second (forward) & packets per second (backward), avg. payload (forward) & avg. payload (backward), etc. We computed the classification error obtained from classes-to-cluster evaluation with S_n and recomputed it for all S_{n-2} sets by removing one pair of features at a time (note that all features occur in pairs of 'forward' and 'backward'). The classification errors for S_n and all sets of S_{n-2} were compared. The set with the lowest classification error was chosen. If that set was S_n, the computation terminated. Else, the set S_{n-2} with lowest classification error was chosen, and the process was repeated until the classification error did not drop further.

The final set of features thus obtained were: `protocol, packets per second (f/w), packets per second (b/w), avg. payload size (f/w),` and `avg. payload size (b/w)`.

The classification error obtained with these features was 50.1163%. Irrespective of the number of features used, the X-means algorithm always created four clusters from the training data. Since our dataset is a representative dataset with the 4 P2P apps having the majority of instances, an outcome of four clusters was quite expected.

4.5 Conversation generation module

Within each cluster, the flows created previously are aggregated into conversations. Conversations are generated for a `FLOWGAP` value as desired by a network administrator. Flows between two IPs are aggregated into a single conversation if the last packet of flow 1 and first packet of flow 2 occur within the `FLOWGAP` time. Here, the network administrator is given the flexibility to mine data for the time period desired by him, say 2 h, 24 h, etc., thus giving him visibility into the network logs as required. Such flexibility is especially valuable for bots which are *extremely stealthy* in their communication patterns and exchange as low as a few packets every few hours. For this evaluation, the value being used is 1 h. This module is explained algorithmically in Algorithm 3.

Algorithm 3 Conversation generation module

1: **procedure** ConvoGeneration(initFlowList, FLOWGAP)
2:    $ArrayList < Conversation > ConvoList$;
3:    $ArrayList < ConversationGroup > cgList$;
4:    $cgList \leftarrow initFlowList.groupByIPpair()$;
5:    **for** ConversationGroup cg in $cgList$ **do**
6:        sort IPpairs in cg by timestamp;
7:        $nextConvo \leftarrow Conversation(NULL)$;
8:        **if** $cg.timestamp$ between
9:            $(nextConvo.start - FLOWGAP)$ &&
10:           $(nextConvo.end + FLOWGAP)$ **then**
11:               $nextConvo.addConvo(cg)$;
12:       **else**
13:               $nextConvo \leftarrow Conversation(cg)$;
14:               $ConvoList.add(nextConvo)$;
15:       **end if**
16:   **end for**
17:   return $ConvoList$;
18: **end procedure**

Using the features extracted from every flow, we extract fresh features for every conversation: number of packets, conversation volume (summation of payload sizes), conversation duration, and the median value of inter-arrival time of packets in the conversation. The reasons behind choosing these features have already been explained in the previous section.

The median of inter-arrival time of packets was observed to be a better metric than the mean because `PeerShark` aggregates several flows into a single conversation as per the `FLOWGAP` value supplied. In such a scenario, it is quite possible that flow 1 and flow 2 get merged into a single conversation while the last packet of flow 1 and first packet of flow 2 occur several minutes (or even hours) apart. This will skew the mean value, and the use of median value was found to be more suitable from our experiments.

5 Results and evaluation

5.1 Training and testing datasets

The labeled data of all four P2P apps along with Storm and Waledac was used for training and testing purposes. Altogether, the dataset contained 1,654,730 conversations (1,589,808 benign and 64,922 malicious). This dataset was split into training and testing datasets in a 2:1 ratio. The training dataset had 1,092,122 conversations (1,049,242 benign and 42,880 malicious), and the test split contained 558,348 conversations (540,566 benign and 22,042 malicious). The training as well as test splits contain more than 90% benign data. Although such class imbalance makes the task of detecting P2P botnets more challenging, this ratio is representative of the real-world scenario where majority of traffic flowing in a network is benign.

After building the models on the training set and testing them with the test set, we evaluate our models against *unseen* botnet datasets (i.e., not used in training) of Zeus and Nugache. Since the network traces of Zeus contain only one 'known malicious host', they are not adequate to train detection models. Similarly, although traces of Nugache contain data of four malicious hosts, the dataset is very small (see Table 1) and thus not suitable to build detection models. Nevertheless, they can be used to evaluate `PeerShark`'s capability on profiling unknown P2P bots.

5.2 Classifiers

The training and testing of our models was performed using the Weka machine learning suite [35].

Our training and testing dataset contains a high 'class imbalance' towards the benign class. This imbalance was kept on-purpose in order to have a dataset representative of real Internet traffic. Hence, we need to utilize learning algorithms which can handle class imbalance. Moreover, the classifiers must be fast to train. We use J48 decision trees, which are simple to train and fast classifiers and can handle class imbalance problems well.

Second, we use random forests. Random forests create an ensemble of decision trees and output the final class that is the mode of the classes output by individual trees. It randomly chooses a set of features for classification for each data point and uses averaging to select the most important features. It can effectively handle overfitting of data and run efficiently on large datasets.

Along with tree-based classifiers, we use a stochastic learning algorithm—Bayesian network. Bayesian networks are probabilistic graphical models that can handle class imbalance, missing data and outliers quite well. They can also identify relationships amongst variables of interest.

Ten-fold stratified cross-validation was used over the training dataset to build detection models with these classifiers. The models were tested with the test dataset. These results are presented in Table 2.

5.3 Evaluation metrics

We use established metrics such as precision, recall, and false positive rate for evaluation of our approach. We briefly define them here:

- *Precision* is the ratio of the number of relevant records retrieved to the total number of relevant and irrelevant records retrieved. It is given by $\frac{TP}{TP+FP}$.
- *Recall* (or true positive rate) is the ratio of the number of relevant records retrieved to the total number of relevant records in the complete dataset. It is given by $\frac{TP}{TP+FN}$.
- *False positive rate* is given by the total number of false positives over the total number of true negatives and false positives. It can be expressed mathematically as $\frac{FP}{FP+TN}$.

TP stands for true positive, TN stands for true negative, FP stands for false positive, and FN stands for false negative.

As the results in Table 2 show, PeerShark could consistently detect P2P bots with high accuracy and very low false positives. We emphasize that these results are over the test set and not the training data. All three classifiers achieved high precision and recall. Since the train and test datasets have higher number of 'benign' instances, benign traffic is naturally classified with much higher accuracy. However, even in the presence of more than 90% benign traffic, false positive rate for the 'malicious' class (i.e., benign conversations incorrectly classified as malicious) was quite low. This is important for any malicious

traffic classifier since it must not create false alarms by classifying benign traffic as malicious.

5.4 Testing on unseen data

To further evaluate the effectiveness of PeerShark on profiling new and unseen P2P botnet traffic, we use the three models trained above and test them against the conversations of Zeus and Nugache which were not used in training the models. It is evident from the results presented in Table 3 that the approach adopted by PeerShark is effective and generic enough to detect unseen P2P botnets with high accuracy.

An ardent reader may note that the detection accuracy achieved for the validation set of Nugache and Zeus is higher than that of the test set composed of Storm and Waledac. We would like to make two points in this regard. Firstly, our training and testing datasets were highly variegated, being composed of four benign P2P applications and two P2P botnets, with a huge number of flows/conversations of each and the proportion of benign traffic being more than 90%. With such variety, the results presented by us are indicative of what one might expect in a real-world scenario. But we did not have the same luxury with the validation datasets. Had there been more variety in the network traces of Nugache and Zeus, it is quite possible that the detection rate would have been slightly lower.

Secondly, we made an interesting observation in the network traces of Storm and Nugache. Nugache and Storm have been hailed as cousins [36]. Nugache which became well known amongst analysts has a 'TCP port 8 botnet' [37] since it used the unassigned port 8 over TCP for several communications. However, while examining the network traces of Storm, we observed some activity over TCP on port 8. This is not a typical behavior of Storm. We suspect that these hosts believed to have been infected by Storm also had Nugache infection on them (although we do not have the facility to verify this). This could possibly explain high detection rate for Nugache.

6 Discussion

6.1 Possible evasions

PeerShark clusters flows based on their behavior and then forms conversations from the flows within a cluster. Since it employs both approaches, PeerShark overcomes many limitations of past efforts. P2P bots which

Table 2 Performance of classifiers on test data

Class	Decision trees			Random forests			Bayesian network		
	Precision	Recall	FP rate	Precision	Recall	FP rate	Precision	Recall	FP rate
Malicious	95.3%	93.4%	0.2%	95.3%	94.9%	0.2%	91.9%	88.4%	0.3%
Benign	99.7%	99.8%	6.6%	99.8%	99.8%	5.1%	99.5%	99.7%	11.6%

Table 3 Performance of classifiers on unseen P2P botnets

	Decision trees			Random forests			Bayesian network		
	Classified malicious	Classified benign	Accuracy (%)	Classified malicious	Classified benign	Accuracy (%)	Classified malicious	Classified benign	Accuracy (%)
Zeus	2,696	55	98%	2,717	34	98.76%	2,660	91	96.69%
Nugache	42	7	85.71%	43	6	87.76%	48	1	97.96%

randomize port numbers and switch between TCP/UDP distort the network administrator's view of the actual communication happening between two hosts. Flow-based techniques are insufficient for such cases. The conversation-generation scheme adopted by PeerShark can effectively address this issue by aggregating flows of the same cluster into a single conversation. Previous works employing conversation-based approaches could not separate P2P bots and apps on the same machine. By segregating flows into different clusters based on their behavior, the approach adopted by PeerShark can effectively separate P2P bot and app traffic running on the same machine.

However, in order to differentiate between benign and malicious P2P traffic, PeerShark relies on 'behavioral' differences in the flows/conversations of P2P bots and apps. If two bot-peers mimic a benign P2P application, our system may fail in detecting them accurately. To elaborate more on this, consider the following scenario: a bot-master could configure his bots to engage in occasional file-sharing activity with each other on a regular P2P network (like eMule, uTorrent, etc.). Seeing such benign-like activity on a host, PeerShark is likely to mis-classify the flows/conversations between them as 'benign'. But, since occasional file-sharing by bots involves network bandwidth usage (and, say, accompanying monetary charges), such an activity has the likelihood of getting noticed by the owner of the system or a network administrator and is thus fraught with risks for the bot-master. Nonetheless, we admit that it is possible for bot-masters to design smarter bots which mimic benign-like behavior and/or add noise (or randomness) to their communication patterns and thus evade the present detection mechanism of PeerShark. Authors in [38] argue on a similar case by building a botnet with Skype and validate their assertions with simulations.

Furthermore, assume the case of a peer A which is engaged in P2P file sharing with a benign peer B, but is also covertly a part of a botnet and is engaged in exchanging command-and-control with a malicious peer C. PeerShark will see these as two conversations, namely A to B and A to C. Since PeerShark regards a conversations as 'malicious' even if either of the IPs (source or destination) is malicious, A to C is identified as 'malicious' without hesitation. But since the conversation between A

and B also involves one malicious peer (namely A), this conversation will also be tagged as 'malicious'. Although it is a limitation on the part of PeerShark to regard that peer B is engaged in a malicious conversation, it is not a serious shortcoming. Since peer B is, as a matter of fact, conversing with a peer which has been compromised, it runs high risk of being infected in the future. Thus, raising an alarm for conversations between A and B (apart from those between A and C) is not completely unwarranted.

Finally, as described in the packet filtering module (Section 4), PeerShark discards all packets having a zero payload. This was necessary to remove corrupted packets and sanitize the network traces obtained from authors in [24]. However, such an approach has an inherent drawback of dropping all legitimate packets with zero payload, such as TCP connection establishment (SYN) packets. It can be exploited by an active adversary who may use zero payload TCP packets (SYN or ACK packets) to exchange simple commands between bots.

6.2 A note on multi-class classification

In the preliminary version of our work [32], we had attempted a multi-class classification approach which could categorize the exact P2P application running on a host. Initially, we attempted multi-class classification for this work as well. The detection accuracy and false positive rate for P2P botnets was nearly the same as that of binary classification approach. However, *within* the benign P2P applications, we saw a false positive rate of 2% to 10%. Although in terms of percentage, the false positive rate is not high, it comes up to thousands of conversations in terms of the actual number of conversations. In particular, we saw many misclassified conversations between Vuze and Frostwire. Such misclassification may be attributed the fact that the majority of our benign P2P data consists of 'torrent' based applications. uTorrent, Vuze, and Frostwire are all 'torrent' based (while eMule is not). Thus, it is quite natural that conversations of one torrent-based app were misclassified as that of another. However this distribution is representative of the real world where the share of P2P in Internet traffic is dying, and BitTorrent is the only aspect of P2P which continues to dominate [6].

New P2P botnets continue to be seen every year. Many of these are just variants or 'tweaks' of older ones. For example, Citadel used a tweaked variant of Zeus [12]. A multi-class approach will only be able to correctly classify those botnets for which it has been trained. It will either miss new variants or call them as 'unknown' (as in [24]). Rather than calling a variant of an old botnet as 'unknown', we find a binary classification approach more suitable. Further, since a multi-class or binary-class approach had little impact on the detection accuracy of P2P botnets, we decided to go in favor of a simpler and intuitive binary approach.

However, in a specific case where a network administrator needs to profile the exact P2P application running on a host, multi-class classification is the only solution. For the interested reader, we briefly share our experimental findings in this regard with respect to Gaussian mixture models (GMMs) [39]. In the flow-clustering phase elaborated previously, we explained the use X-means algorithm, which is a variant of K-means for the purpose of clustering flows. X-means reported four clusters in the data, which corresponded to the four benign P2P applications. As noted earlier, this was quite natural since more than 90% of the flows belong to P2P applications. Moreover, we also got large false positives amongst the benign P2P applications, indicating that their data points lie in overlapping clusters. GMMs are a natural choice in such cases since they are well known for clustering problems involving overlapping clusters. We repeated the flow-clustering experiments with the entire dataset (all eight applications) using GMMs with the optimization approach of expectation-maximization (EM) [40]. The flow-clustering phase with GMMs generated seven clusters for the eight applications, with each application except Storm having a cluster where it was dominantly present (clusters of Storm and Waledac overlapped). However, we observed that GMMs with EM is an *extremely slow* clustering approach. X-means outperforms GMMs by hundreds of times. X-means did not require number of clusters as an input, whereas GMMs with EM does. Thus, we did not find it suitable for PeerShark. Since this approach is not the mainstay of PeerShark, we do not spend more time on it. But an interested reader can leverage from the ability of GMMs and EM to separate overlapping clusters.

7 Conclusions

In this paper, we presented our system PeerShark, which uses a 'best of both worlds' approach by combining flow-based and conversation-based approaches to accurately segregate P2P botnets from benign P2P applications in network traffic. PeerShark clusters flows based on statistical features obtained from their network behavior and then creates conversations between the flows in the same cluster. Using several statistical features extracted from each conversation, we build supervised machine learning models to separate P2P botnets from benign P2P

applications. With the models built on three classifiers, PeerShark could consistently detect P2P botnets with a true positive rate (or recall) ranging between 88% to 95% and achieved a low false positive rate of 0.2% to 0.3%. PeerShark could also detect unseen and unknown P2P botnet traffic with high accuracy.

As a part of work in progress, we are extending our approach with a distributed model for data collection where data collectors sit closer to the nodes inside the network (say at wi-fi access points). This will give greater visibility of the network traffic which occurs over LAN and never touches the backbone router of an enterprise. Such insight can be very valuable for detecting P2P bots inside a network perimeter which try to evade detection by maintaining connectivity with each other over LAN in a P2P fashion and limit the conversations with the outside world via one or two designated peers only (as seen in Stuxnet[c]).

Endnotes

[a] Skype has now moved to a cloud-based architecture [41].

[b] Personal communication with Babak Rahbarinia (November 2013) [24] w.r.t Storm, Waledac and Zeus.

[c] See [42] for details.

Competing interests
The authors declare that they have no competing interests.

Acknowledgements
This work was supported by grant number 12(13)/2012-ESD for scientific research under Cyber Security area from the Department of Information Technology, Govt. of India, New Delhi, India.

Author details
[1] BITS-Pilani, Hyderabad Campus, Hyderabad, Telangana 500078, India.
[2] University of Illinois at Chicago, Chicago, IL 60607, USA.

References

1. Ipoque Internet study 2008/2009. http://www.ipoque.com/en/resources/internet-studies. Accessed 4 Jan 2014
2. S Androutsellis-Theotokis, D Spinellis, A survey of peer-to-peer content distribution technologies. ACM Comput. Surv. **36**(4), 335–371 (2004)
3. P Kopiczko, W Mazurczyk, K Szczypiorski, Stegtorrent: a steganographic method for the p2p file sharing service, in *Proceedings of the 2013 IEEE Security and Privacy Workshops (SPW '13)* (IEEE Computer Society Washington, DC, USA, 2013), pp. 151–157
4. R-A Shang, Y-C Chen, P-C Chen, Ethical decisions about sharing music files in the p2p environment. J. Bus. Ethics. **80**(2), 349–365 (2008)
5. T Isdal, M Piatek, A Krishnamurthy, T Anderson, Privacy-preserving p2p data sharing with oneswarm, in *Proceedings of the ACM SIGCOMM 2010 Conference*, vol. 40 (ACM New York, NY, USA, 2010), pp. 111–122
6. Sandvine Global Internet Phenomena Report 2013. https://www.sandvine.com/trends/global-internet-phenomena/. Accessed 4 Jan 2014
7. J Buford, H Yu, EK Lua, *P2P Networking and Applications*. (Morgan Kaufmann Publishers Inc., San Francisco, 2008)
8. C Kanich, N Weavery, D McCoy, T Halvorson, C Kreibichy, K Levchenko, V Paxson, GM Voelker, S Savage, Show me the money: characterizing spam-advertised revenue, in *Proceedings of the 20th USENIX Conference on Security, (SEC'11)* (USENIX Association Berkeley, CA, USA, 2011), pp. 15–15

9. Microsoft Security Intelligence Report, Volume 9, January-June 2010. http://www.microsoft.com/security/sir/. Accessed 1 Feb 2014

10. C Rossow, D Andriesse, T Werner, B Stone-Gross, D Plohmann, CJ Dietrich, H Bos, Sok: P2PWNED - modeling and evaluating the resilience of peer-to-peer botnets, in *Security and Privacy (SP), 2013 IEEE Symposium On* (IEEE Computer Society Washington, DC, USA, 2013), pp. 97–111

11. D Fisher, 88 percent of Citadel botnets down. http://threatpost.com/microsoft-88-percent-of-citadel-botnets-down/101503. Accessed 9 Jan 2014

12. D Drinkwater, Gameover trojan rises from the dead. http://www.scmagazineuk.com/gameover-trojan-rises-from-the-dead/article/357964/. Accessed 20 Jul 2014

13. T Greene, ZeuS botnet has a new use: stealing bank access codes via SMS. http://www.networkworld.com/news/2010/092910-zeus-botnet-sms-banks.html. Accessed 9 Jun 2013

14. J Stewart, Storm worm DDoS attack. http://www.secureworks.com/cyber-threat-intelligence/threats/storm-worm/. Accessed 1 Feb 2014

15. A Lelli, Waledac botnet back on rise. http://www.symantec.com/connect/blogs/return-dead-waledacstorm-botnet-back-rise. Accessed 1 Feb 2014

16. J Leyden, Fridge hacked. Car hacked. Next up, your light bulbs. http://www.theregister.co.uk/2014/07/07/wifi_enabled_led_light_bulb_is_hackable_shocker/. Accessed 12 Jul 2014

17. S Sen, O Spatscheck, D Wang, Accurate, scalable in-network identification of p2p traffic using application signatures, in *Proceedings of the 13th International Conference on World Wide Web (WWW '04)* (ACM New York, NY, USA, 2004), pp. 512–521

18. J Li, S Zhang, Y Lu, J Yan, Real-time p2p traffic identification, in *Global Telecommunications Conference, 2008. IEEE GLOBECOM 2008* (IEEE, USA, 2008), pp. 1–5

19. M Iliofotou, H-C Kim, M Faloutsos, M Mitzenmacher P Pappu, G Varghese, Graph-based p2p traffic classification at the internet backbone, in *Proceedings of the 28th IEEE International Conference on Computer Communications Workshops (INFOCOM'09)* (IEEE Press Piscataway, NJ, USA, 2009), pp. 37–42

20. G Gu, R Perdisci, J Zhang, W Lee, *Botminer: clustering analysis of network traffic for protocol- and structure-independent botnet detection*. (USENIX Association, Berkeley, CA, USA, 2008), pp. 139–154

21. J François, S Wang, R State, T Engel, Bottrack: tracking botnets using netflow and pagerank, in *Proceedings of the 10th International IFIP TC 6 Conference on Networking - Volume Part I NETWORKING'11* (Springer Berlin, Heidelberg, 2011), pp. 1–14

22. H Hang, X Wei, M Faloutsos, T Eliassi-Rad, Entelecheia: detecting p2p botnets in their waiting stage, in *IFIP Networking Conference, 2013* (IEEE USA, 2013), pp. 1–9

23. R Schoof, R Koning, Detecting Peer-to-peer Botnets. University of Amsterdam (2007). University of Amsterdam. Technical report

24. B Rahbarinia, R Perdisci, A Lanzi, K Li, Peerrush: mining for unwanted p2p traffic, in *Detection of Intrusions and Malware, and Vulnerability Assessment* (Springer Berlin, Heidelberg, 2013), pp. 62–82

25. P Narang, JM Reddy, C Hota, Feature selection for detection of peer-to-peer botnet traffic, in *Proceedings of the 6th ACM India Computing Convention (Compute '13)* (ACM New York, NY, USA, 2013), pp. 16:1–16:9

26. J Zhang, R Perdisci, W Lee, U Sarfraz, X Luo, Detecting stealthy p2p botnets using statistical traffic fingerprints, in *Proceedings of the 2011 IEEE/IFIP 41st International Conference on Dependable Systems & Networks (DSN '11)* (IEEE Computer Society Washington, DC, USA, 2011), pp. 121–132

27. J Zhang, R Perdisci, W Lee, X Luo, U Sarfraz, Building a scalable system for stealthy p2p-botnet detection. IEEE Trans. Inf. Forensics Security. **9**(1), 27–38 (2014)

28. T-F Yen, MK Reiter, Are your hosts trading or plotting? Telling p2p file-sharing and bots apart, in *Proceedings of the 2010 30th International Conference on Distributed Computing Systems (ICDCS '10)* (IEEE Computer Society Washington, DC, USA, 2010), pp. 241–252

29. T Karagiannis, K Papagiannaki, M Faloutsos, Blinc: multilevel traffic classification in the dark, in *SIGCOMM Comput. Commun. Rev., vol. 35* (ACM New York, NY, USA, 2005), pp. 229–240

30. T Karagiannis, A Broido, M Faloutsos, K Claffy, Transport layer identification of p2p traffic, in *Proceedings of the 4th ACM SIGCOMM Conference on Internet Measurement (IMC '04)* (ACM New York, NY, USA, 2004), pp. 121–134

31. L Li, S Mathur, B Coskun, Gangs of the internet: towards automatic discovery of peer-to-peer communities, in *Communications and Network Security (CNS), 2013 IEEE Conference On* (IEEE USA, 2013), pp. 64–72

32. P Narang, S Ray, C Hota, VN Venkatakrishnan, Peershark: detecting peer-to-peer botnets by tracking conversations, in *Proceedings of the 2014 IEEE Security and Privacy Workshops (SPW'14)* (IEEE Computer Society Washington, DC, USA, 2014). in press

33. MM Masud, J Gao, L Khan, J Han, B Thuraisingham, Mining concept-drifting data stream to detect peer to peer botnet traffic (2008). Univ. of Texas at Dallas Technical Report# UTDCS-05- 08

34. D Pelleg, AW Moore, X-means: extending k-means with efficient estimation of the number of clusters, in *Proceedings of the Seventeenth International Conference on Machine Learning (ICML '00)* (Morgan Kaufmann Publishers Inc. San Francisco, CA, USA, 2000), pp. 727–734

35. M Hall, E Frank, G Holmes, B Pfahringer, P Reutemann, IH Witten, The WEKA data mining software: an update. ACM SIGKDD Explor. Newslett. **11**(1), 10–18 (2009)

36. D Fisher, Storm, Nugache lead dangerous new botnet barrage. http://searchsecurity.techtarget.com/news/1286808/Storm-Nugache-lead-dangerous-new-botnet-barrage. Accessed 20 Jul 2014

37. S Stover, D Dittrich, J Hernandez, S Dietrich, Analysis of the storm and nugache trojans: p2p is here. USENIX; login. **32**(6), 18–27 (2007)

38. A Nappa, A Fattori, M Balduzzi, M Dell'Amico, L Cavallaro, Take a deep breath: a stealthy, resilient and cost-effective botnet using skype, in *Detection of Intrusions and Malware, and Vulnerability Assessment* (Springer Berlin, Heidelberg, 2010), pp. 81–100

39. D Reynolds Gaussian mixture models, in *Encyclopedia of Biometrics*, ed. by S Li, A Jain (Springer, 2009), pp. 659–663

40. TK Moon, The expectation-maximization algorithm. IEEE Signal Processing Mag. **13**(6), 47–60 (1996)

41. M Gillett, Skype's cloud-based architecture. http://blogs.skype.com/2012/07/26/what-does-skypes-architecture-do/. Accessed 3 Jul 2014

42. LO Murchu, Stuxnet P2P component. http://www.symantec.com/connect/blogs/stuxnet-p2p-component. Accessed 12 Feb 2014

18

Conflict detection in obligation with deadline policies

Nada Essaouini[1,2*], Frédéric Cuppens[1], Nora Cuppens-Boulahia[1] and Anas Abou El Kalam[2]

Abstract

Many papers have already provided models to formally specify security policies. In this paper, security policies are modeled using deontic concepts of permission and obligation. Permission rules are used to specify access control policies, while obligation rules are useful to specify other security requirements corresponding to usage control policies as the availability of information in its allotted time. However, when both permission and obligation concepts are used to express security policies, several different types of conflict can be raised and should be detected and managed. We are interested in this work in managing conflicts between obligations with deadlines and permissions. Thus, we first begin by formally defining the conflicting situations using the situation calculus. Afterwards, we provide an algorithm for searching a plan of actions, when it exists, which fulfills all the active obligations in a given situation in their deadlines with respect to the permission rules. The length of the plan is set in advance and can be calculated in the case where the sets of actions and fluents are finite to ensure the decidability of the solution search. Furthermore, in the plan search, the choice of the execution time of the elected actions obeys to equations and inequalities which need to be solved. For this purpose, we need a component allowing these equations and inequalities resolution. To illustrate our approach, we take an example inspired from existing laws in hospitals regulating deadlines for completion of patient medical records. The example is formally specified in our language and implemented in ECRC Common Logic Programming System ECLIPSE 3.5.2, which is equipped with Simplex algorithm for solving linear equations and inequalities over the reals. In the implementation, we show how the plan search can be optimized through the use of some heuristics and make some evaluation tests.

Keywords: Security policy; Conflict detection; Obligation with deadline; Situation calculus

Introduction

A security policy is often defined as permission, prohibition, obligation, and exemption rules. Permission and prohibition rules are used to specify access control policies. Obligation and exemption rules are useful to specify other security requirements corresponding to usage control policies [1,2]. In the usage control literature, two different types of obligation are generally considered called system obligation and user obligation [3]. When the security policy includes user obligation, these obligations should be associated with deadlines. When these obligations are activated, these deadlines provide the user with some time to enforce the obligation before violation occurs.

The application of these rules to the same object may lead to conflicting situations. Preliminary work on the classification of conflicts are reported in [4], where several types of conflicts have been defined (see also [5,6]). Benferhat et al. [7] presents an approach based on possibilistic logic to deal with conflicts in prioritized security policies. However, there is another type of conflict which is not managed yet, namely, the conflict between obligations with deadlines. This kind of conflict could happen in the case of overlapping deadlines. For example: (i) The doctor is obliged to fill in the summary sheet within 1 h after the patient leaves. (ii) The surgeon must be vigilant in the operating room. If the doctor is a surgeon and he is in the operating room during a patient's leaving, and if the duration of the surgery ends 2 h after the patient's leaving, the surgeon cannot fill in the summary sheet of the patient because the surgery could end after the deadline associated with filling the summary sheet. Thus, there may be

---

*Correspondence: nada.essaouini@telecom-bretagne.eu
[1]Télécom Bretagne, 2 rue Châtaigneraie, Cesson Sévigné Cedex 3, France
[2]Cadi Ayyad University, ENSA, Boulevard Abdelkrim Al Khattabi, Marrakesh, Marrakesh 40000, Morocco

situations where it is impossible to meet certain obligation requirements of the security policy before their deadlines.

Conflicts between obligations with deadline are more complex to detect and manage. We need a model which manages how the information system evolves over the time. In this paper, we use a language based on deontic logic to specify security policies that include obligations with deadline. The advantage of deontic logic is that it provides means to consistently reason about deontic concepts as obligation and permission. Then, we suggest an approach based on the sequential temporal situation calculus [8] to give semantic to our language. The Situation Calculus allows us to analyze decidability and complexity of several useful problems:

- Temporal projection problem [9]: asks whether a formula holds after a sequence of actions is performed in the initial situation. This is useful to decide which rule can be applied to a given situation and detect violation.
- Planning [10]: given a goal formula, planning consists in finding a sequence of actions so that the goal is satisfied after executing this sequence of actions. We show how to detect, using planning task, if there is conflict between obligation with deadline rules. Then, we introduce the concept of legal plan to detect conflict between obligation and permission rules.

To illustrate our approach, we take the example of completion of medical records inspired from existing laws in hospitals [11]. This completion is regulated by obligation rules with deadline. Each rule specifies the associated deadline to complete each document in the patient record. Any latency on writing patient record could affect the information availability time for each patient which negatively impacts the quality of provided care. This has led some hospitals to specify sanctions when these deadlines are not respected, see for example the Ontario regulations [11]. The example shows a real need to have obligations with deadline in security policy and a real need to manage the conflicts between them.

The present work is an extended version of a previous conference paper [12]. The main contributions with respect to this extended version are the following:

- The initial proposed formalism is extended with two new modalities for expressing permissions and system obligations.
- Managing permissions induces a new type of conflict which occurs when it is impossible to find a sequence of permitted actions which leads to a situation where obligations are fulfilled in their deadlines. We formally define the situations which correspond to such conflicts by introducing the concept of a legal plan.

- The algorithm for detection of conflict between obligations with deadline initially proposed in the previous paper is extended to allow the detection of conflicts between permissions and obligations with deadlines.
- The previous implementation is extended to support the search for a legal plan. And finally, we made some evaluation tests and propose some optimization tools using heuristics.

This article is organized as follows. In Section 1, we give a motivation example. Section 2 presents the situation calculus. Section 3 explains how to define security policies that include obligations with deadline. This model is based on deontic logic, and a security policy is viewed as a set of deontic norms. Section 5 extends situation calculus to formally derive which actual norms apply in a given situation. In this section, we also formally define when an obligation with deadline is violated. Section 5 shows how to detect the presence of conflicting norms in the policy. In Section 6, we give the specification of the motivation example. In Section 7, we make the implementation of our model using the programming language GOLOG [13]. In this section, we make assessment on different situations that we built to simulate our model on the use case and discuss some performance evaluation. The related work is presented in Section 8. Finally, we present the conclusion and perspectives.

1 Motivation example

In the medical community, patient's record contains information about care provided to the patient during his stay in the hospital. The medical records are regulated by hospitals through legal texts [11]. These laws specify, in particular, the time given to doctors to complete patient records assigned to them. In hospitals where medical records are digitally stored, these rules may be expressed as obligations with deadlines. These rules aim to ensure the availability of medical information in expected time. In this section, we describe the impact of availability of medical information in expected time on the quality of patient care, and we give an example of obligations with deadline concerning completion of medical records.

1.1 Impact of deadlines to complete medical records on the availability of information

Studies have shown that patient care can be improved by timely sending a complete and accurate information on patient hospitalization to the practitioner [14-17]. In contrast, a breakdown of communication, due to delays in the transfer of information or incomplete information, can have serious consequences. For example, the physician who does not have access to the summary sheet of a patient hospitalization prepared by acute care services is in an uncomfortable situation when the patient's life is in danger. Despite what has been raised by these studies on the importance of time when transferring patient information, other studies have noticed that in practice, there is a lag in the transfer of this information. Some of these studies noticed a significant delay between the time when the patient receives his leave and when the generalist physician received the advice [18,19]. Therefore, the hospitals are required to establish regulations so that the medical records are filled timely to ensure continuity of patient care. In what follows, we give some examples of rules concerning the deadline assigned to doctors to complete certain elements of patient's records.

1.2 Rules regarding the completion of patient's medical record

The law on public hospitals specifies that medical records must be filled for any person registered or admitted to a health facility [11]. Also, it specifies the elements that a medical record must contain. The law may specify the deadline given to doctors so that each element is present in the patient's record, and the appropriate measures when these deadlines are not respected, see for example the Ontario regulations [11]. Among the documents that must be found in the medical records are as follows: summary sheet, admission note, medical observation, operating protocol, and discharge note. The time to make these documents present in the folder of the user differs from one document to the other:

- The medical summary/summary sheet: When a doctor authorizes the patient assigned to him to leave the hospital, he must complete the medical summary of this patient before this latter leaves the hospital.
- Admission note: The doctor must complete the admission note of the patient assigned to him when he is admitted in the hospital within 30 min following his admission.
- Medical observation: The doctor must complete the medical observation of the patient assigned to him when he is admitted in the hospital within 40 min following his admission.
- Operating Protocol: The doctor who did a surgery for a patient assigned to him must complete the operating protocol of this patient within 100 min following the intervention.
- Discharge note: If a doctor authorizes the patient assigned to him to leave the hospital, he must complete his discharge note. The discharge note must be completed before the patient's leaving.

2 Situation calculus

The situation calculus [20] is a second-order logic language specially designed to represent the change in dynamic worlds. The ontology and axiomatization of the sequential situation calculus was extended to include time [8], concurrency, and natural actions [21]. However, in all cases, the basic elements of language are actions, situations, and fluents. The situation language used in this paper is described below.

2.1 The language

The language consists of the following ontology:

- All changes in the world are the results of actions. They are designated by terms of first-order logic. To represent the time in the situation calculus, we add a time argument in all instantaneous actions which is used to specify the exact time or time range in which the actions occur in world history. For example, $sign(Jean, dischargeNote(Mary), 100)$ is the instantaneous action of signing the discharge note of $Mary$ by $Jean$ at the moment 100. The actions are instantaneous, but we can express actions with duration. For example, consider the following two instantaneous actions, $startConsultation(d, p, t)$, meaning d starts consultation of p at time t, and $endConsultation(d, p, t')$, meaning d ends consultation of p at time t'. The fluent $inConsultation(p, s)$, expressing the patient p is in consultation in the situation s, turns from false to true if there exists a time t and doctor d when the action $startConsultation(d, p, t)$ is performed, and turns to false if there exists a time t' when the action $endConsultation(d, p, t')$ is performed. Thus, in situations where fluent $inConsultation(p, s)$ is true, we can describe the properties of the world, such as the heartbeat of p per unit time, as a function of time that must be true during advancement of consultation.
- A possible history of the world, which is a sequence of actions is represented by the first-order terms denoted $situation$. The constant S_0 is the initial situation.
- There is a binary function symbol do; $do(\alpha, s)$ denotes the situation resulting from the execution of the action α in the situation s. For example, $do(write(Jean, dischargeNote(Mary), 5),$ $do(write(Jean, consultationReport(Mary), 8),$ $do(write(Jean, admissionNote(Mary), 10), S_0)))$ is the situation indicating the history of the world which consists of the execution of the sequence of actions $[write(Jean, admissionNote(Mary), 10), write(Jean, consultationReport(Mary), 8), write(Jean, dischargeNote(Mary), 5)]$.
- $Fluents$ describing the facts of a state. There are two types of fluents: $relational\ fluents$ and $functional\ fluents$. Relational fluents are symbols of predicates

which take a term of type *situation* as the last argument, which their truth values may vary from one situation to another. For example, *inConsultation(Mary, s)*, means that *Mary* is in consultation at situation *s*. Functional fluents are denoted by function symbols that take a situation as the last argument, which the truth of their function values changes from one situation to another. For example, *heartbeat(Mary, s)* denotes the number of heartbeats of *Mary* in situation *s*.

- There are also symbols of predicates and functions (including constants) denoting relations and functions independent of situations.
- A particular binary predicate symbol <, defines a strict order relation on situations; $s < s'$ means that we can reach s' by a sequence of actions starting from *s*. For instance, $\text{do}(a_2, \text{do}(a_1, S_0)) < \text{do}(a_4, \text{do}(a_3, \text{do}(a_2, \text{do}(a_1, S_0))))$.
- A second particular binary predicate symbol *Poss*, defines when an action is possible. $Poss(a, s)$ means that the action *a* can be executed in the situation *s*.
- A function symbol *time*: *time(a)* denotes the time when the action *a* occurs.
- A function symbol *start*: *start(s)* denotes the start time of the situation *s*.

2.2 Fundamental axioms

The basic axioms for the situation calculus, as defined in [22] and [23] are as follows:

- The second-order induction axiom:

$$(\forall P). [P(S_0) \wedge (\forall a, \sigma)(P(\sigma) \rightarrow P(do(a, \sigma)))] \rightarrow (\forall \sigma) P(\sigma)$$

The induction axiom says that to prove that property *P* is true in all situations, it is sufficient to prove that *P* is true in the initial situation S_0 (initialization step) and for all actions *a* and situations σ, if *P* is true in the situation σ, then *P* is still true in the situation $do(a, \sigma)$ (induction step). The axiom is necessary to prove properties true in all situations [24].

- The unique name axioms:

$$S_0 \neq \text{do}(a, s),$$
$$\text{do}(a, s) = \text{do}(a', s') \rightarrow a = a' \wedge s = s'$$

- Axioms that define an order relation < on situations:

$$\neg s < S_0,$$
$$s < \text{do}(a, s') \leftrightarrow (Poss(a, s') \wedge \text{start}(s') \leq \text{time}(a) \wedge s \leq s').$$

- The axiom: $\text{start}(\text{do}(a, s)) = \text{time}(a)$.

In addition to the axioms described above, we need to describe a class of axioms when we formalize an application domain:

- *Action precondition axioms*, one for each action:

$$Poss(A(\vec{x}, t), s) \leftrightarrow \phi(\vec{x}, t, s),$$

where $\phi(\vec{x}, t, s)$ characterizes the preconditions of the action *A*, it is any first-order formula with free variables among $\vec{x}$, *t*, and whose only term of sort of *situation* is *s*.
For example, a patient can leave the hospital if he is in the hospital.

$$Poss(leave(p, t), s) \leftrightarrow \text{inpatient}(p, s)$$

Using predicate poss(a), we can then recursively specify that a given situation *s* is executable.

Executable(s) $\leftrightarrow$
$(\forall a, s') . \text{do}(a, s') \leq s \rightarrow (Poss(a, s') \wedge \text{start}(s') \leq \text{time}(a)).$

- *Successor state axioms*, one for each fluent. These axioms characterize the effects of actions on fluents and they embody a solution to the frame problem[a] for deterministic actions [23].
The syntactic form of successor state axiom for a relational fluent *F* is

$$Poss(a, s) \rightarrow$$
$$[F(\vec{x}, \text{do}(a, s)) \leftrightarrow \gamma_F^+(\vec{x}, a, s) \vee$$
$$(F(\vec{x}, s) \wedge \neg \gamma_F^-(\vec{x}, a, s))],$$

where $\gamma_F^+(\vec{x}, a, s)$ and $\gamma_F^-(\vec{x}, a, s)$ indicate the conditions under which if the action *a* is executed in situation *s*, $F(\vec{x}, \text{do}(a, s))$ becomes true and false, respectively.
For example, the succession state axiom of fluent *assigned(p, d, s)*, meaning a patient *p* is assigned to a doctor *d* can be defined as follows:

$$Poss(a, s) \rightarrow$$
assigned $(p, d, \text{do}(a, s)) \leftrightarrow [(\exists t) a = \text{assign}(p, d, t) \vee$
$(\text{assigned}(p, d, s) \wedge \neg(\exists t) a = \text{revokeAssignment}(p, d, t) \wedge$
$\neg(\exists t) a = \text{leave}(p, t))]$

Here, $\gamma_F^+(\vec{x}, a, s)$ corresponds to the formula: $(\exists t) a = \text{assign}(p, d, t)$ and $\gamma_F^-(\vec{x}, a, s)$ is the formula: $(\exists t) a = \text{revokeAssignment}(p, d, t) \vee (\exists t) a = \text{leave}(p, t)$. The action *assign* makes the fluent *assigned* true, and the actions *revokeAssignment* and *leave* turn the fluent *assigned* to false.
It is assumed that no action can turn *F* to be both true and false in a situation, i.e.,
$\neg \exists s \exists a \gamma_F^+(\vec{x}, a, s) \wedge \gamma_F^-(\vec{x}, a, s)$.
For a functional fluent, the syntactic form of successor state axiom is

$$Poss(a, s) \rightarrow$$
$$[F(\vec{x}, \text{do}(a, s)) = y \leftrightarrow \gamma_F^+(\vec{x}, y, a, s) \vee$$
$$(y = F(\vec{x}, s) \wedge \neg(\exists y') \gamma_F^-(\vec{x}, y', a, s))],$$

where, $\gamma_F\left(\vec{x}, y, a, s\right)$ is any first-order formula with free variables among $\vec{x}$, y, a, t, and whose only term of sort of *situation* is s.

- Axioms describing the initial situation.
- In each application involving a particular action $A\left(\vec{x}, t\right)$, an axiom that gives the time of the action A: $time\left(A\left(\vec{x}, t\right)\right) = t$.

In the following, we denote Axioms $= \Sigma \cup A_{\mathrm{ss}} \cup A_{\mathrm{ap}} \cup A_{S_0}$, where

- Σ is the foundational axiomatic of the situation calculus.
- A_{ss} is a set of successor state axioms.
- A_{ap} is a set of action precondition axioms.
- A_{S_0} is a set of initial situation axioms. A_{S_0} is a set of sentences with the property that S_0 is the only term of sort situation mentioned by the fluents of a sentence of A_{S_0}. Thus, no fluent of a formula of A_{S_0} mentions a variable of sort situation or the function symbol *do*.

We denote Axioms $\vdash p$ the fact that the sentence p can be derived from the set of axioms *Axioms*. This kind of domain theories provides us with various reasoning capabilities, for instance planning [25]. Given a domain theory *Axioms* as above and a goal formula $G(s)$ with a single free-variable s, the planing task is to find a sequence of actions $\vec{a}$ such that

Axioms $\vdash s_0 \leq do(\vec{a}, s_0) \land \text{Executable}(do(\vec{a}, s_0)) \land G(do(\vec{a}, s_0))$,

where $do([a_1, \ldots, a_n], s)$ is an abbreviation for $do(a_n, do(a_{n-1}, \ldots, do(a_1, s) \ldots))$.

3   Security policy specification

The language we define to specify permissions and obligations in security policies is based on deontic logic of actions. We consider two modalities: permissions and obligations with deadline. They are called normative modalities in the following. Normative modalities are represented as dyadic conditional modalities. Permissions are specified using dyadic modality $P(\alpha|p)$, where α is an action of $\mathcal{A}$ and p is the condition of the permission. The condition is any formula built using fluents of $\mathcal{F}$ without situation. $P(\alpha|p)$ means that the action α is permitted when condition p holds. Obligations with deadline are specified using modality $O(\alpha < d|p)$ which intuitively means that when formula p starts to hold, there is an obligation to execute action α before the deadline condition d starts to hold. In the following, we assume that the deadline condition must be an atomic fluent predicate of $\mathcal{F}$. If the action α is executed before the deadline condition d starts to hold, then we shall say that the obligation is fulfilled. Else, we shall consider that the obligation is violated. We call *norm* a formula corresponding to a conditional permission or obligation with deadline. A security policy,

$\mathcal{P}$ is a finite set of norms. We shall now use the situation calculus to formally define the semantics of these different modalities.

4   Actual norm derivation and violation detection

The situation calculus is extended with fluents Perm(α) (there is an actual permission to do α) and Ob($\alpha < d$) (the obligation to do α before deadline d starts to be effective), where α is an action of $\mathcal{A}$ and d is a fluent of $\mathcal{F}$. We first extend the set of axioms previously defined with a permission definition axiom for every fluent predicate Perm(α), $\alpha \in \mathcal{A}$. For this purpose, let P_α be the set of conditional permissions having the form $P(\alpha|p)$. We denote $\psi_{P_\alpha} = p_1 \lor \ldots \lor p_n$, where each p_i for $i \in [1, \ldots, n]$ corresponds to the condition of a permission in P_α. If $P_\alpha = \emptyset$, then we assume that $\psi_{P_\alpha} = $ false. Using ψ_{P_α}, the successor state axiom for Perm(α, σ) is defined as follows:

$$\text{Poss}\,(a, \sigma) \rightarrow$$
$$\text{Perm}\,(\alpha, do\,(a, \sigma)) \leftrightarrow \left[\gamma_{\psi_{P_\alpha}}^{+}\,(a, \sigma) \lor \quad (1)\right.$$
$$\left.\left(\text{Perm}\,(\alpha, \sigma) \land \neg\gamma_{\psi_{P_\alpha}}^{-}\,(a, \sigma)\right)\right]$$

This axiom specifies that the permission to do an action becomes effective after the action that activates the context of the permission rule is executed. This permission remains effective until an action that turns the activation context to false is executed.

We can specify a predicate permitted which specifies that a given situation is secure with respect to access control requirements as follows:

Permitted(S_0) $\land$

$(\forall a \forall \sigma)\,[\text{Permitted}\,(do\,(a, \sigma)) \leftrightarrow (\text{Perm}\,(a, \sigma) \land \text{Permitted}\,(\sigma))]$

We can then specify a condition to prove that the system specification represented by a given set of *Axioms* is secure with respect to access control requirements as follows:

Axioms $\vdash (\forall\sigma)\,(\text{Executable}\,(\sigma) \rightarrow \text{Permitted}\,(\sigma))$

which corresponds to proving that predicate permitted is an integrity constraint in every executable situation. We call this integrity constraint the 'close policy requirement'. It is easy to show that a sufficient condition to prove the close policy requirement consists in strengthening the action precondition axiom of every action α with the guarded condition that this action must be permitted:

$$\forall\sigma, \text{poss}\,(\alpha, \sigma) \leftrightarrow (\phi\,(\sigma) \land \text{Perm}\,(\alpha, \sigma))$$

Using permitted situations, we introduce a notion of *legal plan*. Given a goal formula G, a legal plan consists of finding a permitted situation that satisfies G.

Let us now turn to the obligation definition axiom for every fluent predicate Ob($\alpha < d$), where $\alpha \in \mathcal{A}$ and $d \in \mathcal{F}$. Notice that since the sets $\mathcal{A}$ and $\mathcal{F}$ are finite, we have a finite set of successor state axioms to define for $\text{Ob}(\alpha < d)$. We define $O_{\alpha,d}$ to be the set of conditional obligations with deadline in P having the form $\text{Ob}(\alpha' < d'|p)$, such that $\alpha = \alpha'$ and d and d' are logically equivalent. We say that two fluent predicates d and d' are logically equivalent with respect to a set of *Axioms* if we can prove that $d \leftrightarrow d'$ is an integrity constraint of *Axioms*. We denote $\psi_{O_{\alpha,d}} = p_1 \vee \ldots \vee p_n$, where each p_i for $i \in [1,\ldots,n]$ corresponds to the condition of an obligation in $O_{\alpha,d}$. If $O_{\alpha,d} = \emptyset$, then we assume that $\psi_{O_{\alpha,d}} = \text{false}$. Using $\psi_{O_{\alpha,d}}$, the successor state axiom for $\text{Ob}(\alpha < d)$ is defined as follows:

$$\text{Poss}(a,\sigma) \rightarrow$$
$$\text{Ob}(\alpha < d, \text{do}(a,\sigma)) \leftrightarrow \Big[\gamma^+_{\psi_{O_{\alpha,d}}}(a,\sigma) \vee \tag{2}$$
$$\Big(\text{Ob}(\alpha < d, \sigma) \wedge \neg(a = \alpha) \wedge \neg\gamma^+_d(a,\sigma) \wedge \neg\gamma^-_{\psi_{O_{\alpha,d}}}(a,\sigma) \Big) \Big]$$

This axiom says that the obligation to do α before deadline d is activated when $\psi_{O_{\alpha,d}}$ starts to be true. This obligation is deactivated when it is fulfilled (i.e., action α is done) or it is violated (i.e., deadline d starts to be true) or condition $\psi_{O_{\alpha,d}}$ ends to be true (i.e., it is no longer relevant to do α).

We can characterize situations where the obligations are fulfilled by the following fluent:

$$\text{Poss}(a,\sigma) \rightarrow$$
$$\text{Fulfil}(\alpha < d, \text{do}(a,\sigma)) \leftrightarrow \big[(\text{Ob}(\alpha < d, \sigma) \wedge a = \alpha \wedge \neg\gamma^+_d(\alpha,\sigma)) \vee$$
$$\text{Fulfil}(\alpha < d, \sigma) \big] \tag{3}$$

Notice that if in a given situation σ, it simultaneously happens that the obligatory action is executed and the associated deadline is activated, then the decision is to consider that the obligation is violated and not fulfilled. This is called obligation with strict deadline. We can also define $O(\alpha \leq d|p)$ so that in the same situation, the obligation is fulfilled and not violated.

Finally, we define the succession state axiom of the fluent $\text{Violated}(\alpha < d, \sigma)$:

$$\text{Poss}(a,\sigma) \rightarrow$$
$$\text{Violated}(\alpha < d, \text{do}(a,\sigma)) \leftrightarrow \big[(\text{Ob}(\alpha < d, \sigma) \wedge \gamma^+_d(a,\sigma)) \vee$$
$$\text{Violated}(\alpha < d, \sigma) \big] \tag{4}$$

This axiom specifies that an obligation to do α is violated, when the associated deadline comes true when it was still active, and it was never executed. The axiom also specifies that in a given situation σ, if it simultaneously happens that the obligatory action is executed and the associated deadline is activated, then the decision is to consider that the obligation is violated.

Concerning system obligations, we consider them as a special case of obligations with deadline, written as follows: $O(\alpha)$. As there is no deadline associated with

these obligations, we assume that $\gamma^+_d(a,\sigma) = \gamma^-_d(a,\sigma) = \text{false}$. Thus, we can derive the succession state axiom characterizing the situations when system obligations are active using axiom 2.

$$\text{Poss}(a,\sigma) \rightarrow \Big(\text{Ob}(\alpha, \text{do}(a,\sigma)) \leftrightarrow \gamma^+_{\psi_{O_\alpha}}(a,\sigma) \Big) \tag{5}$$

This axiom says that the system obligation to do α is activated only in the situations when ψ_{O_α} starts to be true and they are deactivated immediately after. Thus, a system obligation should be fulfilled immediately after its activation. This can be derived using the axiom 3 as follows:

$$\text{Poss}(a,\sigma) \rightarrow$$
$$\text{Fulfil}(\alpha, \text{do}(a,\sigma)) \leftrightarrow [(\text{Ob}(\alpha,\sigma) \wedge a = \alpha) \vee \text{Fulfil}(\alpha,\sigma)]$$

When an obligation system is not executed immediately after its activation, a violation is detected using the following axiom:

$$\text{Poss}(a,\sigma) \rightarrow$$
$$\text{Violated}(\alpha, \text{do}(a,\sigma)) \leftrightarrow [(\text{Ob}(\alpha,\sigma) \wedge \neg(a = \alpha)) \vee \text{Violated}(\alpha,\sigma)]$$

5   Policy conflict detection

In this section, we define two kinds of conflict:

- conflict between obligation with deadline rules
- conflict between permission and obligation with deadline rules

The conflict between obligations is detected through the definition of the following situations:

- *situation locally enforceable* is defined in relation with a particular obligation and characterizes the fact that this obligation can be fulfilled by following the executable plan.
- *situation globally enforceable* characterizes the fact that all the active obligations can be enforced in an executable plan without violating the associated deadlines.

The conflict between permission and obligation with deadline rules is detected through the definition of the following situations:

- *situation legal locally enforceable* is defined in relation with a particular obligation and characterizes the fact that this obligation can be fulfilled by following an executable plan constituted of permitted actions (*legal plan*).
- *situation legal globally enforceable* characterizes the fact that all the active obligations can be enforced in an executable and legal plan without violating the associated deadlines.

5.1 Obligation conflicts

In a given situation, an active obligation is enforceable if it can be fulfilled following an executable plan.

$$\text{Enforceable}(\alpha < d, \sigma) \leftrightarrow [\text{Ob}(\alpha < d, \sigma) \wedge$$
$$(\exists \sigma', \sigma < \sigma') \left(\text{Fulfil}(\alpha < d, \sigma') \wedge \text{Executable}(\sigma')\right)]$$

It may happen that in one situation, every active obligation is enforceable, but it is still not possible to enforce all of them without violating the associated deadlines. If all the active obligations in a situation σ can be executed without violating at least one of them, we say that this situation is globally enforceable. To characterize this, we introduce the formula G-Enforceable(σ).

$$\text{G-Enforceable}(\sigma) \leftrightarrow (\exists \sigma', \sigma' > \sigma)$$
$$(\forall \alpha, d) \left(\text{Ob}(\alpha < d, \sigma) \rightarrow \left(\text{Fulfil}(\alpha < d, \sigma') \wedge \text{Executable}(\sigma')\right)\right)$$

Proving that a given situation σ is globally enforceable, amounts to proving the existence of an executable situation where all the active obligations in σ are fulfilled. If such a situation does not exist, we say that the policy is *feasibility conflictual* in σ. If the set of actions and the set of fluents are finite, we can prove that the existence of such a situation is decidable and can be solved in NEXPTIME complexity. This complexity of planning in the situation calculus is high but is similar to other planners, like Strips for example [26].

5.2 Conflict between permission and obligation rules

In traditional deontic logic like Standard Deontic Logic (SDL), obligation implying permission is an an axiom of the logic. However, if the obligation is associated with a deadline, then $\text{Ob}(\alpha < d, \sigma) \wedge \neg \text{Perm}(\alpha, \sigma)$ may be satisfiable in some situation σ. As we consider the close security requirement, then every executed action must be explicitly permitted. Thus, we define the legal local requirement as follows:

$$L\text{-Enforceable}(\alpha < d, \sigma) \leftrightarrow [\text{Ob}(\alpha < d, \sigma) \wedge$$
$$(\exists \sigma', \sigma < \sigma') \left(\text{Fulfil}(\alpha < d, \sigma') \wedge \text{Permitted}(\sigma')\right)]$$

This means that there is a legal path that allows filling the active obligation. If in addition the path is executable, then the obligation is strongly enforceable.

$$S\text{-Enforceable}(\alpha < d, \sigma) \leftrightarrow [\text{Ob}(\alpha < d, \sigma) \wedge$$
$$(\exists \sigma', \sigma < \sigma') \left(\text{Fulfil}(\alpha < d, \sigma') \wedge \text{Permitted}(\sigma') \wedge \text{Executable}(\sigma')\right)]$$

If all the active obligations in a situation σ can be executed in a permitted situation without violating at least one of them, we say that this situation is legal globally enforceable. The legally global requirement is defined as follows:

$$\text{LG-Enforceable}(\sigma) \leftrightarrow (\exists \sigma', \sigma < \sigma')$$
$$(\forall \alpha, \forall d) \left[\text{Ob}(\alpha < d, \sigma) \rightarrow \left(\text{Fulfil}(\alpha < d, \sigma') \wedge \text{Permitted}(\sigma')\right)\right]$$

The policy is considered legally conflictual in situation σ if it is not legally enforceable. If in addition the plan is executable, the situation is called strongly globally enforceable.

$$\text{SG-}Enforceable(s) \leftrightarrow (\exists s', s < s')$$
$$(\forall \alpha, \forall d) \left[\text{Ob}(\alpha < d, s) \rightarrow \left(\text{Fulfil}(\alpha < d, s') \wedge \text{Legal}(s') \wedge \text{Executable}(s')\right)\right]$$

In what follows, we assume the existence of a temporal reasoning component that allows us to infer, for example, that $T_1 = T_2$ when $T_1 \leq T_1$ and $T_2 \leq T_2$, and we are able to solve linear equations and inequalities over the reals using the Simplex algorithm [27]. Algorithm 1 detects the different types of conflict we have defined using recursive search as defined in Algorithm 2. Note that in Algorithm 2, we allow the execution of parallel actions; otherwise, we can use constraints to specify the actions which cannot be done in parallel. These constraints can be compiled into precondition axioms of these actions [22]. In this work and to simplify, we omit the use of constraints. Note that we suppose that if a situation we check is globally enforceable (respectively legally globally enforceable), then this situation must be executable (respectively permitted). Proving that a situation is executable (respectively permitted) can be done using regression [23], where testing is reduced to proving first-order theorem in the initial situation.

Algorithm 1 ConflictDetection(s, N, conflictType)

Require: s: the situation to check
  N: the maximal depth
  conflictType: the type of the searched conflict,
  "FC" for feasibility conflict,
      "LC" for legally conflict and
      "SC" for strong conflict
Ensure: No: if there is no conflict of type conflictType in the policy at situation s; otherwise, Yes.

  $\mathcal{O} = \{\alpha \in \mathcal{A}$ **such that** $\text{Ob}(\alpha < d, s)\}$ {set of active obligations in s}
  $s' \leftarrow$ recursiveSearch(s, N, $\mathcal{O}$, conflictType)
  if $\neg(s' = \text{NULL})$ **then**
    return No {there is no conflict of type conflictType in the policy at s and s' is the plan which leads to fulfill all the active obligations in s}
  else
    return Yes {there is a conflict of type conflictType in the policy at situation s}
  end if

Algorithm 2 recursiveSearch(s, N, $\mathcal{O}$, conflictType)

Require: s: the current situation

N: the current depth (initially the given maximum depth)

$\mathcal{O}$: set of active obligations in s

conflictType: the type of the searched conflict, "FC" for feasibility conflict,

"LC" for legally conflict and

"SC" for strong conflict

Ensure: Null: if the depth of the current path exceeds the given maximum depth or,

situation when all obligations in $\mathcal{O}$ are fulfilled if it exists otherwise,

the next situation to give to the next call for recursion

---

switch (conflictType)

case "FC":

$\mathcal{E} \leftarrow \{a \in \mathcal{A}, \text{Poss}(a,s) \land \text{Start}(s) \leq \text{Time}(a)\}$ {the set of actions that can lead from s to an eventual executable situation}

case "LC":

$\mathcal{E} \leftarrow \{a \in \mathcal{A}, \text{Perm}(a,s)\}$ {the set of actions that can lead from s to an eventual legal situation}

case "SC":

$\mathcal{E} \leftarrow \{a \in \mathcal{A}, \text{Poss}(a,s) \land \text{Start}(s) \leq \text{Time}(a) \land \text{Perm}(a,s)\}$ {the set of actions that can lead from s to an eventual legal and executable situation}

end switch

while true **do**

  if $N < 0$ **then**

    return NULL

  end if

  for all $a \in \mathcal{E}$ **do**

    $s' \leftarrow \text{do}(a,s)$

    $N \leftarrow N - 1$

    if $(\forall \alpha, d \in \mathcal{O})\text{Fulfil}(\alpha < d, s')$ **then**

      return s'

    end if

    $s'' \leftarrow \text{recursiveSearch}(s', N, \mathcal{O}, \text{conflictType})$

    if $\neg(s'' = \text{NULL}) \land (\forall \alpha, d \in \mathcal{O})\text{Fulfil}(\alpha < d, s''))$ **then**

      return s''

    end if

    $N \leftarrow N + 1$

  end for

  return NULL

end while

---

6 Formal specification of the case study's security policy

To illustrate our approach, let us consider a security policy containing the following rules:

- *Rule 1*: The doctor *must* complete the admission note of the patient assigned to him within 30 units of time following his admission to the hospital.
- *Rule 2*: The doctor *must* complete the medical observation of the patient assigned to him within 30 units of time following his admission to the hospital.
- *Rule 3*: End deadline for completing the admission note of a patient must occur after 30 units of time of his admission to the hospital.
- *Rule 4*: End deadline for completing the medical observation of a patient must occur after 40 units of time of his admission to the hospital.
- *Rule 5*: The doctor is permitted to start writing observation or admission note of an inpatient assigned to him when he is not writing another document.
- *Rule 6*: The doctor is permitted to complete observation or admission note at least 5 units of time after he began to write it.

Normally, we should specify a permission rule for each action in $\mathcal{A}$. But for simplicity, we quote just one permission rule regarding the action of writing documents.

To give the specification of the example policy, we should determine the set of fluents $\mathcal{F}$, the set of the actions $\mathcal{A}$, the succession state axioms of all fluents, and the preconditions axioms of all actions.

- Set $\mathcal{F}$ of fluents:

    - assigned(p, d, s). The patient p is assigned to a doctor d in situation s.
    - inpatient(p, t, s). The patient p is admitted to the hospital at time t in the situation s.
    - leaving(p, s). The patient p leaves the hospital in s.
    - deadline(*type*, p, t, s). The deadline to write document of type *type* concerning patient p created at time t is elapsed in s.
    - writingDoc(d, type, p, t, t', s). d is writing the document of type *type* concerning patient p created at time t and began to be written at t' in s.
    - writtenDoc(d, type, p, t, s). The document of type *type* concerning patient p and created at time t has been written in s by d.
    - doctor(d). d is a doctor.

- Set $\mathcal{A}$ of actions:

    - assign(p, d, t). The action to assign at time t the patient p to the doctor d.
    - revokeAssignment(p, d, t). The action to revoke at time t assignment of the patient p to the doctor d.

- patientAdmission(p, t). The action to admit at time t the patient p at the hospital.
- leave(p, t). The patient p leaves the hospital at time t.
- EndDeadline$(type, p, t, t')$: The action to warn at time t' that the accorded deadline for writing document of patient p expires.
- StartWrite$(d, type, p, t)$, EndWrite$(d, type, p, t)$: d starts (respectively ends) to write document of type corresponding to patient p at time t; type is one of the following elements: *Observation* or *AdmssionNote*.

- Fluent succession state axioms: Patient p will be assigned to doctor d when the action of assignment is executed, since then p remains assigned to d unless there is a revocation of assignment or the patient leaves the hospital.

$\text{Poss}(a, s) \rightarrow$

$$\text{assigned}(p, d, \text{do}(a, s)) \leftrightarrow \big[(\exists t) a = \text{assign}(p, d, t) \vee \quad (6)$$
$$(\text{assigned}(p, d, s) \wedge \neg(\exists t) a = \text{revokeAssignment}(p, d, t) \wedge$$
$$\neg(\exists t) a = \text{leave}(p, t))\big]$$

Patient p is hospitalized if he was admitted to the hospital and did not leave.

$\text{Poss}(a, s) \rightarrow$

$$\text{inpatient}(p, t, \text{do}(a, s)) \leftrightarrow \big[a = \text{patientAdmission}(p, t) \vee \quad (7)$$
$$(\text{inpatient}(p, t, s) \wedge \neg(\exists t') a = \text{leave}(p, t'))\big]$$

Action *EndDeadline* is executed to denote that the delay accorded to write documents is elapsed. When the deadline is considered expired, it remains expired forever.

$\text{Poss}(a, s) \rightarrow \quad (8)$

$$\text{deadline}(type, p, t, \text{do}(a, s)) \leftrightarrow$$
$$\big[(\exists t') a = \text{endDeadline}(type, p, t, t') \vee \text{deadline}(type, p, t, s)\big]$$

A document is in a writing process if its writing began before and is not completed yet.

$\text{Poss}(a, \sigma) \rightarrow \quad (9)$

$$\text{writingDoc}(d, type, p, t, t', \text{do}(a, s)) \leftrightarrow$$
$$\big[a = \text{startWrite}(d, type, p, t') \vee (\text{writingDoc}(d, type, p, t, t', s) \wedge$$
$$\neg(\exists t'') a = \text{endWrite}(d, type, p, t''))\big]$$

A document is considered written if the writing process is completed.

$\text{Poss}(a, \sigma) \rightarrow \quad (10)$

$$\text{writtenDoc}(d, type, p, t, \text{do}(a, s)) \leftrightarrow$$
$$\big[(\exists t') a = \text{endWrite}(d, type, p, t') \vee \text{writtenDoc}(d, type, p, t, s)\big]$$

- Action precondition axioms: In what follows, all action precondition axioms are written using equivalent conditions except *startWrite* action. This is because we consider that all these actions are always permitted (even if we did not mention the permission rules associated with them for simplicity). In contrast, precondition axiom of actions *startWrite* and *endWrite* will be rewritten later to take into account the permission rule associated with them. It is assumed that a patient can be assigned at any time to a doctor except if the patient is already assigned to him.

$$\text{Poss}(\text{assign}(p, d, t), \sigma) \leftrightarrow (\neg\text{assigned}(p, d, \sigma) \wedge \text{start}(\sigma) \leq t)$$

The assignment revocation of patients is necessarily applied to a patient who is already assigned to a doctor.

$$\text{Poss}(\text{revokeAssignment}(p, d, t), \sigma) \leftrightarrow (\text{assigned}(p, d, \sigma) \wedge \text{start}(\sigma) \leq t)$$

It is assumed that a patient assigned to a doctor can be admitted at any time to a hospital except if he is already hospitalized.

$$\text{Poss}(\text{patientAdmission}(p, t), \sigma) \leftrightarrow (\text{assigned}(p, d, \sigma) \wedge$$
$$\neg(\exists t') \text{inpatient}(p, t', \sigma) \wedge \text{start}(\sigma) \leq t)$$

Leaving the hospital concerns patients which are hospitalized.

$$\text{Poss}(\text{leave}(p, t), \sigma) \leftrightarrow ((\exists t') \text{inpatient}(p, t', \sigma) \wedge \text{start}(\sigma) \leq t)$$

Action *EndDeadline*$(type, p, t, t_{\text{ed}})$ is executed when the accorded deadline to write document of type *type* is elapsed since the moment t of a patient hospitalization; deadline is 30 units of time when *type* is admission note and 40 units of time when it is medical observation. It is assumed in addition that it is not possible to execute the end of deadline for the same document more than once.

$$\text{Poss}(\text{endDeadline}(type, p, t, t_{\text{ed}}), \sigma) \leftrightarrow$$
$$\big[\text{inpatient}(p, t', \sigma) \wedge ((t_{\text{ed}} = t' + 40 \wedge type = \text{observation}) \vee$$
$$(t_{\text{ed}} = t' + 30 \wedge type = \text{admissionNote})) \wedge \neg\text{deadline}(type, p, t, \sigma)\big]$$

It is assumed that the action to start writing a document is necessarily executed on a document that is not in a writing process.

$$\text{Poss}(\text{startWrite}(d, type, p, t, t_{\text{sw}}), \sigma) \rightarrow$$
$$\neg\text{writingDoc}(d, type, p, t, t', \sigma) \wedge \neg\text{writtenDoc}(d, type, p, t, \sigma) \wedge$$
$$\text{start}(\sigma) \leq t_{\text{sw}}$$

The writing end is applied to an ongoing writing document.

$$\text{Poss}(\text{endWrite}(d, type, p, t, t_{\text{ew}}), \sigma) \leftrightarrow$$
$$\big[(\exists t') \text{writingDoc}(d', type, p, t, t', \sigma) \wedge \text{start}(\sigma) \leq t_{\text{ew}}\big]$$

We can now give the specification of the aforementioned security rules.

Rule 1 : $O\left(\text{write}\left(d,\text{type},p,t,t'\right) < \text{deadline}(\text{type},p,t)\,\big|\,\text{doctor}(d)\wedge$
$\text{assigned}(p,d)\wedge\text{inpatient}(p,t)\wedge\text{type}=\text{admissionNote})$

Rule 2 : $O\left(\text{write}\left(d,\text{type},p,t,t'\right) < \text{deadline}(\text{type},p,t)\,\big|\,\text{doctor}(d)\wedge$
$\text{assigned}(p,d)\wedge\text{inpatient}(p,t)\wedge\text{type}=\text{observation})$

Rule 3 : $O\left(\text{endDeadline}\left(\text{admissionNotes},p,t,t'\right)\,\big|\,\text{inpatient}(p,t)\wedge$
$t' = t+30)$

Rule 4 : $O\left(\text{endDeadline}\left(\text{observation},p,t,t'\right)\,\big|\,\text{inpatient}(p,t)\wedge$
$t' = t+40)$

Rule 5 : $P\left(\text{startWrite}\left(d,\text{type},p,t,t_{\text{sw}}\right)\,\big|\,\text{doctor}(d)\wedge\text{assigned}(p,d)\wedge$
$\text{inpatient}(p,t,s)\wedge\text{type}=(\text{observation}\vee\text{admissionNote})\wedge$
$\neg\left(\exists\text{type}',p',t',t''\right)\text{writingDoc}\left(d,\text{type}',p',t',t''\right))$

Rule 6 : $P\left(\text{endtWrite}\left(d,\text{type},p,t,t_{\text{ew}}\right)\,\big|\,\text{writingDoc}(d,\text{type},p,t,t')\wedge$
$t_{\text{ew}}\geq t'+5)$

According to the specification of obligation rules, we can see that we have one set of conditional obligations with deadlines: $O_{\text{write}(d,\text{type},p,t,t_{\text{w}}),\text{deadline}(\text{type},p,t,s)}$. The corresponding formula $\psi_{O_{\text{write}(d,\text{type},p,t,t_{\text{w}}),\text{deadline}(\text{type},p,t,\sigma)}}$, after simplification, is as follows:

$$\psi_{O_{\text{write}(d,\text{type},p,t,t_{\text{w}}),\text{deadline}(\text{type},p,t,\sigma)}} \leftrightarrow$$
$$\text{doctor}(d)\wedge\text{assigned}(p,d,\sigma)\wedge\text{inpatient}(p,t,\sigma)\wedge$$
$$\text{type}=(\text{observation}\vee\text{admissionNote}))$$

According to axiom (2), to derive concrete obligations, we should calculate the following formulas:

$$\gamma^{+}_{\psi_{O_{\text{write}(d,\text{type},p,t,t_{\text{w}}),\text{deadline}(\text{type},p,t,\sigma)}}}(a,\sigma) \leftrightarrow$$
$$\text{assigned}(p,d,\sigma)\wedge a=\text{patientAdmission}(p,t)$$

$$\gamma^{-}_{\psi_{O_{\text{write}(d,\text{type},p,t,t_{\text{w}}),\text{deadline}(\text{type},p,t,\sigma)}}}(a,\sigma) \leftrightarrow$$
$$a=\text{revokeAssignment}(p,d,t')\vee a=\text{leave}(p,t')$$

The above formula is calculated using the succession state axiom of fluent *assigned* (6). Finally, the formula $\gamma^{+}_{\text{deadline}(\text{type},p,t)}(a,\sigma)$ is calculated using succession state axiom of fluent *deadline* (8).

$$\gamma^{+}_{\text{deadline}(\text{type},p,t)}(a,\sigma) \leftrightarrow a=\text{endDeadline}(\text{type},p,t,t')$$

Thus, the concrete obligations concerning rules 1 and 2 are as follows:

$\text{Poss}(a,\sigma) \rightarrow$
$\text{Ob}(\text{write}(d,\text{type},p,t,t_{\text{w}}),\text{do}(a,\sigma)) \leftrightarrow$
$\big[(\text{assigned}(p,d,\sigma)\wedge a=\text{patientAdmission}(p,t))\vee$
$(\text{Ob}(\text{write}(d,\text{type},p,t),\sigma)\wedge$
$\neg(\exists t')a=\text{endWrite}(d,\text{type},p,t,t')\wedge$
$\neg(\exists t')a=\text{endDeadline}(\text{type},p,t,t')\wedge$
$\neg(\exists t')a=\text{revokeAssignment}(p,d,t')\wedge\neg(\exists t')a=\text{leave}(p,t'))\big]$

Similarly, we can derive the situations where the system obligations are active.

$\text{Poss}(a,\sigma) \rightarrow$
$\text{Ob}\left(\text{endDeadline}(\text{type},p,t,t',\text{do}(a,\sigma)\right) \leftrightarrow$
$\big[(a=\text{patientAdmission}(p,t)\wedge$
$((\text{type}=\text{admissionNote}\wedge t'=t+30)\vee\text{type}=\text{observation}\wedge$
$t'=t+40))\vee$
$(\text{Ob}(\text{endDeadline}(\text{type},p,t,t'),\sigma)\wedge$
$\neg(\exists t')\,a=\text{endDeadline}\left(\text{type},p,t,t'\right)\wedge\neg(\exists t')\,a=\text{leave}\left(p,t'\right))\big]$

Using rule 5 and succession state axiom of fluent *assigned* (6), the actions and the conditions under which *startWrite* will be permitted are given by the following formula:

$$\gamma^{+}_{\psi_{P_{\text{startWrite}(d,\text{type},p,t,t_{\text{sw}})}}}(a,\sigma) \leftrightarrow$$
$$\big[\text{assigned}(p,d,\sigma)\wedge\text{type}=(\text{observation}\vee\text{admissionNote})\wedge$$
$$\neg\left(\exists\text{type}',p',t',t'_{\text{sw}}\right)\text{writingDoc}\left(d,\text{type}',p',t',t'_{\text{sw}},\sigma\right)\wedge$$
$$a=\text{patientAdmission}(p,t)\big]\vee$$
$$\big[\text{inpatient}(p,t,\sigma)\wedge(\exists\text{type}',p',t',t'_{\text{sw}})\text{writingDoc}\left(d,\text{type}',p',t',t'_{\text{sw}},\sigma\right)\wedge$$
$$a=\text{endWrite}\left(d,\text{type}',p',t',t_{\text{ew}}\right)\big]$$

On the other side, the actions and the conditions under which *startWrite* will be no longer permitted are given by the following formula:

$$\gamma^{-}_{\psi_{P_{\text{startWrite}(d,\text{type},p,t,t_{\text{sw}})}}}(a,\sigma) \leftrightarrow$$
$$(\exists t')\,a=\text{revokeAssignment}\left(p,d,t'\right)\vee(\exists t')\,a=\text{leave}\left(p,t'\right)\vee$$
$$(\exists\text{type}',p',t',t'')\,a=\text{startWrite}\left(d,\text{type}',p',t',t''\right)$$

Then, the active permission for startWrite is calculated using axiom (1).

$\text{Poss}(a,\sigma) \rightarrow$
$\text{Perm}\left(\text{startWrite}\left(d,\text{type},p,t,t_{\text{sw}}\right),\text{do}(a,\sigma)\right) \leftrightarrow$
$\big[\text{assigned}(p,d,\sigma)\wedge\text{type}=(\text{observation}\vee\textit{admissionNote})\wedge$ (11)
$\big[(\neg(\exists\text{type}',p',t',t'_{\text{sw}})\text{writingDoc}(d,\text{type}',p',t',t'_{\text{sw}},\sigma)\wedge$ (12)
$a=\text{patientAdmission}(p,t))\vee$ (13)
$(\text{inpatient}(p,t,\sigma)\wedge$ (14)
$(\exists\text{type}',p',t',t'_{\text{sw}})\text{writingDoc}\left(d,\text{type}',p',t',t'_{\text{sw}},\sigma\right)\wedge$ (15)
$a=\text{endWrite}(d,\text{type}',p',t',t_{\text{ew}}))\big]\vee$ (16)
$(\text{Perm}\left(\text{startWrite}\left(d,\text{type},p,t,t_{\text{sw}}\right),\sigma\right)\wedge$
$\neg(\exists t')\,a=\text{revokeAssignment}\left(p,d,t'\right)\wedge$
$\neg(\exists t')\,a=\text{leave}\left(p,t'\right)\wedge$
$\neg(\exists\text{type}',p',t',t'_{\text{sw}})\,a=\text{startWrite}\left(d,\text{type}',p',t',t'_{\text{sw}}\right))$

The lines 11, 12, and 13 of the axiom above express the fact that a doctor which is not writing a document is permitted to write the observation and the admission note of a patient assigned to him as soon as this patient is admitted in the hospital. The lines 11, 14, 15, and 16 express the fact that when a patient is hospitalized and his doctor is writing a document, the doctor will be permitted to write the observation and the admission note of this patient after he completes the writing document. Finally, the precondition axiom for starting writing documents is as follows:

$$\text{Poss}(\text{startWrite}(d, \text{type}, p, t, t_{sw}), \sigma) \leftrightarrow$$
$$\text{Perm}(\text{startWrite}(d, \text{type}, p, t, t_{sw}), \sigma) \wedge$$
$$\neg \text{writingDoc}(d, \text{type}, t, \sigma) \wedge \neg \text{writtenDoc}(d, \text{type}, p, t, \sigma)$$

Using rule 6 and the succession state axiom (10) of *writingDoc*, we can calculate the situation when the end for writing document is permitted.

$$\text{Poss}(a, \sigma) \rightarrow$$
$$\text{Perm}(\text{endWrite}(d, \text{type}, p, t, t_e), \text{do}(a, \sigma)) \leftrightarrow$$
$$a = \text{startWrite}(d, \text{type}, p, t, t_s) \wedge t_e \geq t_s + 5 \vee$$
$$\text{Perm}(\text{endWrite}(d, \text{type}, p, t, t_e), \sigma) \wedge$$
$$\neg a = \text{endWrite}(d, \text{type}, p, t, t'_e)$$

7 Implementation

We implement our model using the logic programming language Golog [8,13], based on the situation calculus. Regarding our need to solve linear equations and inequalities, we use the Common Logic Programming System ECLIPSE 3.5.2, which provides a built-in Simplex algorithm for solving linear equations and inequalities over the reals.

The point of departure for the implementation is to get the list of all active obligations in a given situation S. This is given using the predicate *activeObligations(ActiveObligationsList,S)*:

```
activeObligations
(ActiveObligationsList,S):-findall(Rule,ob(Rule,S),
                    ActiveObligationsList).
```

Given the list of active obligations, seeking the situation where all these obligations are fulfilled is made using the procedure *plan*.

```
proc(plan(N,L),
      ?(all(r,member(r,L) =>
      fulfil(r))):?(reportStats)#
      ?(N > 0):
      pi(a,?(primitiveAction(a)):a:
      ?(-badSituation):
      pi(n,?(n is N-1):plan(n,L)))).
```

Here, *primitiveAction* is a predicate characterizing all the actions of the domain. If $N = 0$, the execution of the procedure ends. If $N > 0$, a primitive action a is selected.

The Golog interpreter checks if the selected action a is possible and verifies that $\text{start}(s) \leq \text{time}(a)$, where s is the current situation. If so, a is executed and $\text{do}(a, s)$ becomes the new current executable situation.

We can change the following instruction of Golog:

```
do(E,S,do(E, S)) :- primitiveAction(E), poss(E,S),
                start(S,T1),time(E, T2),T1 <= T2.
```

and replace it with the following statement for searching a legal plan:

```
do(E,S,do(E, S)) :- primitiveAction(E),perm(E, S),
                start(S,T1),time(E,T2),T1 <= T2.
```

In our implementation, we make no change in the Golog interpreter, but every precondition axiom of an action includes the fact that this action is permitted using the fluent *perm*. Thus, we test whether a situation is strongly enforceable or not using the predicate *sEnforceable(N,S1)*.

```
sEnforceable(N,S1):- initializeCPU,
              activeObligations
              (ActiveObligationsList,S1),
              do(plan(N,
              ActiveObligationsList),S1,S),
              prettyPrintSituation(S).
```

Let us start by seeing how we can write some axioms of our example using Golog. The complete description of axioms is described in Additional file 1.

7.1 Examples of succession state axioms

```
ob(write(D,Type,P,T),
   do(A,S)):- (assigned(P,D,S),
            A=patientAdmission(P,T));
            (ob(write(D,observation,P,T),S),
            not A=endWrite(D,observation,P,T,T1),
            not A=endDeadline(observation,P,T,T2),
            not A=leave(P,T3),
            not A=revokeAssignation(P,D,T4)).
fulfil(write(D,Type,P,T),
      do(A,S)):- (ob(write(D,Type,P,T),S),
               (A=endWrite(D,Type,P,T,T2));
               fulfil(write(D,Type,P,T),S)).
```

7.2 Examples of action precondition axioms

```
poss(startWrite(D,observation,
      P,T,T1),S):- inpatient(P,T,S),
               assigned(P,D,S),
               not writingDoc(D,Type1,P1,T3,T4,S),
               not writtenDoc(D,observation,P,T,S).

poss(endWrite(D,Type,P,T,T1),S):- writingDoc
                       (D,Type,P,T,T2,S),
                       T1 $>= T2+5.
```

In addition to the succession state axioms and precondition axioms of actions, we suppose having the following axioms in the initial situation s_0.

```
start(s0, 0).
doctor(jean).
```

7.3 Description of bad situations

The badSituation test is used to remove partial plans which are known in advance to be unsuccessful. For example, a branch resulting from the execution of an action that disables an active obligation can be eliminated. A branch resulting from the execution of an action that activates the deadline corresponding to an active obligation may also be removed. We will see in the following how this can be done in the implementation of our example.

If a violation of an active obligation occurs after the execution of an action, it is no longer necessary to continue searching a solution from the resulting situation.

```
badSituation(do(A,S)):- A=endDeadline(Type,P,T,T1),
                        not fulfil(write
                        (D,Type,P,T),S),!.
badSituation(do(A,S)):- A=endDeadline(Type,P,T,T1),
                        poss(endDeadline(Type1,
                        P1,T2,T3),S),T3 $< T1,!.
badSituation(S):- ob(endDeadline(Type,P,T,T1),S),
                  start(S,T2), not (T1$>=T2),!.
```

If an active obligation is deactivated after the execution of an action, it is no longer necessary to continue searching a solution from the resulting situation.

```
badSituation(do(A,S)):- A=leave(P,T),!.
badSituation(do(A,S)):- A=revokeAssignation(P,D,T),!.
```

The construction of these bad situations can be done using the succession state axioms of fluent *Ob* and *Fulfil*. Thus, these optimizations can be generalized to any policy without losing the completeness of the planning search. In our example, the execution of actions *patientAdmission* and *assign* activates other obligations and have no impact on the fulfillment of obligations which are already active. Therefore, the path resulting from their execution can be eliminated in the solution search.

```
badSituation(do(A,S)):- A=assign(P,D,T),!.
badSituation(do(A,S)):- A=patientAdmission(P,T),!.
```

This optimization is closely related to our example because there is nothing that prevents to have actions in the policy that are necessary to fulfill obligations, but their execution leads to activate other obligations simultaneously.

We have performed tests that check the strongly enforceability of situations constructed as follows: the first situation checked by the first test, denoted $s1$ is the result of the assignment of a single patient $p1$ to the doctor jean at time 4 followed by his admission in the hospital at time 5.

```
test1:- sEnforceable(6,do(patientAdmission(p1,5),
        do(assign(p1,jean,4),s0))).
```

The next situation $s2$ is the assignment of another patient $p2$ to jean at time 6 from the situation $s1$ followed by the admission of $p2$ in the hospital at time 7.

```
test2:- sEnforceable(12,do(patientAdmission(p2,7),
        do(assign(p2,jean,6),
        do(patientAdmission(p1,5),
        do(assign(p1,jean,4),s0)))))).
```

We build 20 tests. Their complete description is in Additional file 2. The planning depth research is calculated as follows. In our application domain, there are seven actions, four of them are removed from the planning through the specification of *badSituation*. The remainder actions are *startWrite*, *endWrite*, and *endDeadline*. In the database, there is one doctor Jean and two types of documents, so for each patient, these actions are possible twice, one for each type of document. When one of these actions is executed, it is not possible to execute it again according to their precondition axioms. Thus, when all these actions are performed one after the other, it is no longer possible to perform other actions except those which are discarded from the planning search. Thereby, whenever a patient is added, the minimum depth ensuring the decidability of solution research is increased by six.

We conducted two series of tests depending on the deadlines associated with the obligations to write documents. The experiment was run on a machine equipped with an Intel 32 bit, 2.60 GHz, x4 processor, and 3.8 GB RAM, running ECLIPSE 3.5.2 on ubuntu Linux (v.13.04).

7.4 The first series of tests

The deadline for writing admission note is 30 units of time, and the observation is 40 units of time (see Additional file 3). In this series of tests, the maximum number of patients, who can be admitted in the hospital and assigned to *jean*, without causing conflict between the obligations is 4. Indeed, the policy is not conflictual in the first four situations. As example, the following legal plan generates a situation when all the active obligations in the situation $s1$ are fulfilled which means that $s1$ is strongly globally enforceable.

```
[eclipse 2]: test1.

  CPU time (sec): 0.00

[assign(p1,jean,4),patientAdmission(p1,5),
startWrite(jean, admissionNote,p1,5,_{3}74),
endWrite(jean,admissionNote,p1,5,_{1}095),
startWrite(jean,observation,p1,5,_{2}264),
endWrite(jean,observation,p1,5,_{3}112),
endDeadline(admissionNote,p1,5,35),
endDeadline(observation,p1,5,45)]
more? n.


Linear Store:

_{3}112 $>= 15+1*_{2}321+1*_{1}187+1*_{4}31
_{2}264 $>= 10+1*_{1}187+1*_{4}31
_{1}095 $>= 10+1*_{4}31
_{3}74 $>= 5
```

The above plan contains uninstantiated temporal variables. The value of these variables is just constrained by the inequalities in ECLIPSE's linear constraint store, although there may be cases when plans are fully specified like the following third test which proves that the policy remains consistent after the admission of three patients.

```
[eclipse 4]: test3.

  CPU time (sec): 0.03

[assign(p1,jean,4),patientAdmission(p1,5),
assign(p2,jean,6),patientAdmission(p2,7),
assign(p3,jean,8),patientAdmission(p3,9),
startWrite(jean,admissionNote,p3,9,9),
endWrite(jean,admissionNote,p3,9,14),
startWrite(jean,admissionNote,p2,7,14),
endWrite(jean,admissionNote,p2,7,19),
startWrite(jean,admissionNote,p1,5,19),
endWrite(jean,admissionNote,p1,5,24),
startWrite(jean,observation,p3,9,24),
endWrite(jean,observation,p3,9,29),
startWrite(jean,observation,p2,7,29),
endWrite(jean,observation,p2,7,34),
startWrite(jean,observation,p1,5,34),
endDeadline(admissionNote,p1,5,35),
endDeadline(admissionNote,p2,7,37),
endWrite(jean,observation,p1,5,39),
endDeadline(admissionNote,p3,9,39),
endDeadline(observation,p1,5,45),
endDeadline(observation,p2,7,47),
endDeadline(observation,p3,9,49)]
more? n.
```

Finally, the fifth test shows how the admission of a fifth patient produces a conflict.

```
[eclipse 6]: test5.

No (1460.33s cpu)
```

7.5 The second series of tests

The deadline for writing admission note is 1,000 units of time, and the observation is 1,100 units of time (see Additional file 4).

In this series of tests, we check 20 situations. Table 1 summarizes the results obtained and the execution time for each tested situation. Figure 1 shows how the execution time for finding a plan is increasing with the number of active obligations in these situations. On average, there are $2 \times nb$ actions, which can be executed from a given situation, where nb is a number of admitted patients. Moreover, the plan to achieve the desired goal is made up of $nb \times 6$ actions. Then, the number of worlds to explore is the order of $(2 \times nb)^{nb \times 6}$. This explains the increment in the time duration, each time a patient is admitted.

8 Related work

Most traditional security models are static and respond to access requests just by yes (accept) or no (deny). Recently, there are more and more works on security models that model obligations [3,28-31]. Formalization of obligations differs from one model to another. In XACML [32], obligations are all operations that must be met in conjunction with the application of the authorization decision. In [3,28,33], distinction is made between provisions and obligations. Provisions are actions or conditions that must be met before authorizing access. Obligations are actions that must be executed by users or system after the access is given. The ABC model (authorization, obligation, and condition) [34] was specifically designed to express security policies including usage control constraints. The expression of a constraint to be satisfied before the use of an object can be expressed as contextual authorization. However, constraints to meet during or after the use of an object relate to obligations that the user must follow. The NOMAD model [35] is based on a formalization in temporal and deontic logic to express contextual obligations which should be met before, during, or after the execution of an action. It is also possible to specify a deadline after which some obligation will be considered violated if the action was not performed. Authors in [36], define a core language to specify the access and usage control requirements and then give a formalism based on the logic of temporal actions (TLA) [37] to specify the behavior of the policy controller in charge of evaluating such policy. In this approach, a permission is associated with two conditions, the first must be true at the time of query evaluation,

Table 1 The summary of second series of tests

Tests	Patient number	Active obligation number	The minimum research depth	CPU time (s)	Strongly globally enforceable?
s1	1	4	6	0	Yes
s2	2	8	12	0.01	Yes
s3	3	12	18	0.03	Yes
s4	4	16	24	0.06	Yes
s5	5	20	30	0.1	Yes
s6	6	24	36	0.2	Yes
s7	7	28	42	0.36	Yes
s8	8	32	48	0.66	Yes
s9	9	36	54	1.1	Yes
s10	10	40	60	1.78	Yes
s11	11	44	66	2.78	Yes
s12	12	48	72	4.16	Yes
s13	13	52	78	6.03	Yes
s14	14	56	84	6.04	Yes
s15	15	60	90	8.60	Yes
s16	16	64	96	11.95	Yes
s17	17	68	102	16.43	Yes
s18	18	72	108	21.75	Yes
s19	19	76	114	28.89	Yes
s20	20	80	120	37.97	Yes

This table describes the most important parameters influencing the time of executions: the number of active obligations and the depth of the solution search.

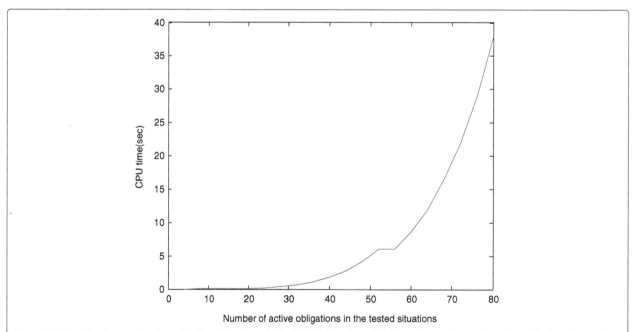

Figure 1 CPU utilization vs. Number of active obligations in the tested situations. This figure shows the cpu time elapsed before giving a first solution where all active obligations in the situations tested are fulfilled.

and the second must always be true as long as access is in progress. The authors also introduce a concept to reset a current access. Regarding obligations, they are associated with two conditions. Once the first condition is satisfied, the obligation is triggered, then the controller sends a notification to the user to perform the appropriate obligation, the second condition determines when the obligation should be considered violated. If the user does not satisfy the obligation before the second condition becomes true, a penalty is applied to him. The authors in [38] talk about what they called deontic conflicts. The types of conflict that the authors have classified in this category are those that occur between permission and prohibition and those which occurs between obligation and obligation waiver. As in the used formalism, the authors do not use prohibition and obligation waiver modalities, they do not deal with these conflicts in their work. But in this category, there is another kind of conflict which is the conflict between the obligations with deadlines and permissions. In our work, this conflict is detected when there is no plan consisting of permitted actions that lead to fulfilling an obligation requirement in its deadline. In other words, it is possible that in a given situation, a mandatory action is permitted and it can be fulfilled in its deadline, but it is not possible to execute because it is necessary to first execute other actions which are not permitted. Certainly, the authors define another type of conflict called temporal conflicts which occur when two deontic assignments at the same time initiate and terminate obligation. This is a particular case of what we detect in what we call the global conflict between the obligations with deadlines. Indeed, in a given situation, it may be possible to fulfill an active obligation in its deadline but given that there are other active obligations, at the same time it is not possible to fulfill them together without violating one of them. The conflict in the temporal constraints is actually a special case of a 'logical' conflict which we detect with the concept of executable plan.

9 Conclusions

In this paper, we use deontic modalities to specify close security policies including obligations with deadline. Then, we use the temporal sequential situations calculus to derive concrete permissions and obligations. Furthermore, we show how the situation calculus allows us to detect if there is a policy conflict in a given situation using the planning task. Moreover, we have illustrated our approach by using a case study from the health care community. Specifically, we are interested in obligations with deadlines concerning completion of the patients' medical records. We show how we can use our language to express the obligations of this example. In addition, we present the implementation that we did, using the logic programming language based on Golog.

On the other hand, obligations are generally associated with penalties when their violation occurs. The regulation of a hospital may specify the penalties triggered when medical records are not completed on due time. For example, if medical folders are not completed on time, the medical records department can establish for the president of the Executive Committee of the Medical Council of doctors the list of doctors and the number of folders that remain incomplete for each of them. While receiving this list, the director of professional services can inform by warning all doctors of the list that their privileges are automatically suspended until they complete their late folders. Our ongoing work along these lines consists, when we have a conflict, to specify whether the subject is accountable for this conflict. Furthermore, when we have several subjects, it is important to specify whether the violation of an obligation is not due to a violation of another subject obligation that has indirectly delayed fulfillment of the first obligation.

Our future work also includes conflict resolution. A conflicting situation means that there are subjects who cannot accomplish their active obligations one after another without violation. In such a situation, it will be interesting to know if there are active obligations of another subject in the same situation that could solve this conflict and then derive if this subject has enough free time to perform some active obligations of the first subject. This is one of the possible solutions to solve the conflict. We can also detect the rules responsible for the conflict and then update the policy with new deadlines for these rules.

Endnote
[a] The difficulty in logic of expressing the dynamics of a situation without explicitly specifying everything that is not affected by the actions.

Additional files

Additional file 1: conflictualSituation.pl. This is a prolog file which contains the description of the implementation of the studied example.

Additional file 2: test.pl. This is a prolog file which contains the description of the 20 performed tests. Each test represent a situation. Each situation is the result of an admission of another patient relative to the previous situation.

Additional file 3: deadlines_30_40.pl. This is a prolog file which initializes the deadline values for the first series of tests.

Additional file 4: deadlines_1000_1100.pl. This is a prolog file which initializes the deadline values for the second series of tests.

Competing interests
The authors declare that they have no competing interests.

Acknowledgements
This work is supported by the ITEA2 Predykot project (Grant agreement no.10035).

References

1. F Cuppens, N Cuppens-Boulahia, T Sans, Nomad: a security model with non atomic actions and deadlines, in *CSFW*, (2005), pp. 186–196

2. Y Elrakaiby, F Cuppens, N Cuppens-Boulahia, Formal enforcement and management of obligation policies. Data Knowl. Eng. **71**(1), 127–147 (2012)

3. M Hilty, A Pretschner, D Basin, C Schaefer, T Walter, A policy language for distributed usage control, in *Proceedings of the 12th European Conference on Research in Computer Security (ESORICS'07)* (Springer-Verlag Berlin, 2007), pp. 531–546

4. JD Moffett, MS Sloman, Policy conflict analysis in distributed system management. J. Organ. Comput. **4**(1), 1–22 (1994)

5. E Bertino, S Jajodia, P Samarati, Supporting multiple access control policies in database systems, in *Proceedings of the 1996 IEEE Symposium on Security and Privacy* (IEEE Computer Society Washington, D.C. 1996), p. 94

6. G Dinolt, L Benzinger, M Yatabe, Combining components and policies, in *Proceedings of the Computer Security Foundations Workshop VII* (Franconia, USA, 1994)

7. S Benferhat, R El Baida, F Cuppens, A stratification-based approach for handling conflicts in access control, in *SACMAT 2003, Proceedings of the 8th ACM Symposium on Access Control Models and Technologies, Como, Italy* (ACM New York, 2003), pp. 189–195. ISBN:1-58113-681-1

8. R Reiter, Sequential, temporal Golog, in *Principles of Knowledge Representation and Reasoning: Proceedings of the 6th International Conference (KR' 98)* (Morgan Kaufmann, San Francisco, 1998), pp. 547–556

9. S Hanks, D McDermott, ed. by ML Ginsberg, Default reasoning, nonmonotonic logics, and the frame problem, in *Readings in Nonmonotonic Reasoning* (Morgan Kaufmann, San Francisco, 1987), pp. 390–395

10. C Green, Application of theorem proving to problem solving, in *Proceedings of the 1st International Joint Conference on Artificial Intelligence (IJCAI'69)* (Morgan Kaufmann, San Francisco, 1969), pp. 219–239

11. RRO, Règlement 965. Gestion Hospitalière. Dossiers de renseigments personnels sur la santé (1990)

12. N Essaouini, F Cuppens, N Cuppens-Boulahia, AAE Kalam, *Proceedings of the eighth International Conference on Availability, Reliability and Security.* (IEEE Computer Society, Los Alamitos, 2013)

13. HJ Levesque, R Reiter, Y Lesperance, F Lin, RB Scherl, GOLOG: a logic programming language for dynamic do- mains. J. Logic Program. **31**(1–3), 59–83 (1997)

14. JI Balla, WE Jamieson, Improving the continuity of care between general practitioners and public hospitals. Med. J. Aust. **161**(11–12), 656–659 (1994)

15. P Bolton, A quality assurance activity to improve discharge communication with general practice. J. Qual. Clin. Pract. **21**, 69–70 (2001)

16. DC Adams, JB Bristol, KR Poskitt, Surgical discharge summaries: improving the record. Ann. R. Coll. Surg. Engl. **75**(2), 96–99 (1993)

17. PJ Embi, *Perceived Impact of Computerized Physician Documentation on Education and Clinical Practice in a Teaching Hospital.* (Oregon Health & Science University, Portland, 2002)

18. RJ Mageean, Study of "discharge communications" from hospital. Br. Med. J. **293**(6557), 1283–1284 (1986)

19. AN Raval, GE Marchioriz, JM Arnold, Improving the continuity of care following discharge of patients hospitalized with heart failure: is the discharge summary adequate? Can. J. Cardiol. **19**(4), 365–370 (2003)

20. J McCarthy, *Situations, Actions and Causal Laws*, Technical report, Stanford University, 1963. Reprinted in Semantic Information Processing. (M Minskys, ed.) (MIT Press, Cambridge, 1968), pp. 410–417

21. R Reiter, ed. by L Aiello, J Doyle, and S Shapiro, Natural actions, concurrency and continuous time in the situation calculus, in *Principles of Knowledge Representation and Reasoning: Proceedings of the Fifth International Conference* (Morgan Kaufmann, San Francisco, 1996), pp. 2–13

22. F Lin, R Reiter, State constraints revisited. J. Logic Comput. **4**, 655–678 (1994). Special issue on actions and processes

23. R Reiter, ed. by V Lifschitz, The frame problem in the situation calculus: a simple solution (sometimes) and a completeness result for goal regression, in *Artificial Intelligence and Mathematical Theory of Computation: Papers in Honor of John McCarthy* (Academic Press San Diego, 1991), pp. 359–380

24. R Reiter, Proving properties of states in the situation calculus. Artif. Intell. **64**(2), 337–351 (1993)

25. CC Green, ed. by B Meltzer, D Michie, Theorem proving by resolution as a basis for question-answering systems, in *Machine Intelligence, volume 4* (American Elsevier New York, 1969), pp. 183–205

26. R Fikes, NJ Nilsson, STRIPS: a new approach to the application of theorem proving to problem solving. Artif. Intell. **2**(3/4), 189–208 (1971)

27. TW Frühwirth, A Herold, V Küchenhoff, T Le Provost, P Lim, E Monfroy, M Wallace, ed. by G Comyn, NE Fuchs, and M Ratcliffe, Constraint logic programming - an informal introduction, in *Proceedings of the Second International Logic Programming Summer School on Logic Programming in Action (LPSS '92)* (Springer-Verlag London, pp. 3–35

28. C Bettini, S Jajodia, XS Wang, D Wijesekera, Obligation monitoring in policy management, in *3rd International Workshop on Policies for Distributed Systems and Networks (POLICY 2002), 5–7 June 2002* (IEEE Computer Society Monterey, 2002)

29. N Damianou, N Dulay, E Lupu, M Sloman, The ponder policy specification language. Proceedings of the International Workshop on Policies for Distributed Systems and Networks (POLICY '01), 18–38 (2001)

30. Q Ni, E Bertino, J Lobo, An obligation model bridging access control policies and privacy policies, in *Proceedings of the 13th ACM Symposium on Access Control Models and Technologies (SACMAT '08)* (ACM New York, 2008), pp. 133–142

31. R Craven, J Lobo, J Ma, A Russo, E Lupu, A Bandara, Expressive policy analysis with enhanced system dynamicity, in *Proceedings of the 4th International Symposium on Information, Computer, and Communications Security (ASIACCS '09)* (ACM New York, 2009), pp. 239–250

32. Oasis, Extensible access control markup language tc v2.0, normative xacml 2.0 documents. OASIS Standard. http://www.oasis-open.org/specs/index.php. Accessed 1 Feb 2005

33. M Hilty, D Basin, A Pretschner, ed. by S di Vimercati, P Syverson, and D Gollmann, On obligations, in *Computer Security-ESORICS 2005, Lecture Notes in Computer Science*, vol. 3679 (Springer Berlin, 2005), pp. 98–117

34. J Park, R Sandhu, The UCONABC usage control model. ACM Trans. Inf. Syst. Secur. **7**(1), 128–174 (2004)

35. F Cuppens, N Cuppens-Boulahia, T Sans, Nomad: a security model with non atomic actions and deadlines, in *18th IEEE Computer Security Foundations Workshop (CSFW)* (Aix en Provence, France, 2005)

36. T Sans, F Cuppens, N Cuppens-Boulahia, A framework to enforce access control, usage control and obligations. Ann. Telecomm. **62**(11–12), 1329–1352 (2007)

37. L Lamport, The temporal logic of actions. ACM Trans. Program. Lang. Syst. **16**(3), 872–923 (1994)

38. S Goedertier, J Vanthienen, ed. by J Eder, S Dustdar, Designing compliant business processes with obligations and permissions, in *Business Process Management Workshops, Lecture Notes in Computer Science*, vol. 4103 (Springer Berlin, 2006), pp. 5–14

19

Universal distortion function for steganography in an arbitrary domain

Vojtěch Holub[*], Jessica Fridrich and Tomáš Denemark

Abstract

Currently, the most successful approach to steganography in empirical objects, such as digital media, is to embed the payload while minimizing a suitably defined distortion function. The design of the distortion is essentially the only task left to the steganographer since efficient practical codes exist that embed near the payload-distortion bound. The practitioner's goal is to design the distortion to obtain a scheme with a high empirical statistical detectability. In this paper, we propose a universal distortion design called universal wavelet relative distortion (UNIWARD) that can be applied for embedding in an arbitrary domain. The embedding distortion is computed as a sum of relative changes of coefficients in a directional filter bank decomposition of the cover image. The directionality forces the embedding changes to such parts of the cover object that are difficult to model in multiple directions, such as textures or noisy regions, while avoiding smooth regions or clean edges. We demonstrate experimentally using rich models as well as targeted attacks that steganographic methods built using UNIWARD match or outperform the current state of the art in the spatial domain, JPEG domain, and side-informed JPEG domain.

1 Introduction

Designing steganographic algorithms for empirical cover sources [1] is very challenging due to the fundamental lack of accurate models. The most successful approach today avoids estimating (and preserving) the cover source distribution because this task is infeasible for complex and highly non-stationary sources, such as digital images. Instead, message embedding is formulated as source coding with a fidelity constraint [2] - the sender hides her message while minimizing an embedding distortion. Practical embedding algorithms that operate near the theoretical payload-distortion bound are available for a rather general class of distortion functions [3,4].

The key element of this general framework is the distortion, which needs to be designed in such a way that tests on real imagery indicate a high level of security[a]. In [5], a heuristically defined distortion function was parametrized and then optimized to obtain the smallest detectability in terms of a margin between classes within a selected feature space (cover model). However, unless the cover model is a complete statistical descriptor of the empirical source, such optimized schemes may, paradoxically, end up being more detectable if the warden designs the detector 'outside of the model' [6,7], which brings us back to the main and rather difficult problem - modeling the source.

In the JPEG domain, by far the most successful paradigm is to minimize the rounding distortion with respect to the raw, uncompressed image, if available [8-12]. In fact, this 'side-informed embedding' can be applied whenever the sender possesses a higher-quality 'precover'[b] that is quantized to obtain the cover[c]. Currently, the most secure embedding method for JPEG images that does not use any side information is the uniform embedding distortion (UED) [13] that substantially improved upon the nsF5 algorithm [14] - the previous state of the art. Note that most embedding algorithms for the JPEG format use only non-zero DCT coefficients, which makes them naturally content-adaptive.

In the spatial domain, embedding costs are typically required to be low in complex textures or 'noisy' areas and high in smooth regions. For example, HUGO [15] defines the distortion as a weighted norm between higher-order statistics of pixel differences in cover and stego images [16], with high weights assigned to well-populated bins

---

*Correspondence: vholub1@binghamton.edu
Department of Electrical and Computer Engineering, Binghamton University, Binghamton, NY 13902, USA

and low weights to sparsely populated bins that correspond to more complex content. An alternative model-free approach called wavelet obtained weights (WOW) [17] uses a bank of directional high-pass filters to obtain the so-called directional residuals, which assess the content around each pixel along multiple different directions. By measuring the impact of embedding on every directional residual and by suitably aggregating these impacts, WOW forces the distortion to be high where the content is predictable in *at least one* direction (smooth areas and clean edges) and low where the content is unpredictable in every direction (as in textures). The resulting algorithm is highly adaptive and has been shown to better resists steganalysis using rich models [18] than HUGO [17].

The distortion function proposed in this paper bears similarity to that of WOW but is simpler and suitable for embedding in an arbitrary domain. Since the distortion is in the form of a sum of *relative* changes between the stego and cover images represented in the wavelet domain, hence its name universal wavelet relative distortion (UNIWARD).

After introducing the basic notation and terminology in Section 2, we describe the distortion function in its most general form in Section 3 - one suitable for embedding in both the spatial and JPEG domains and the other for side-informed JPEG steganography. We also describe the additive approximation of UNIWARD that will be exclusively used in this paper. In Section 4, we introduce the common core of all experiments - the cover source, steganalysis features, the classifier used to build the detectors, and the empirical measure of security. A study of the best settings for UNIWARD, formed by the choice of the directional filter bank and a stabilizing constant, appears in Section 5. Section 6 contains the results of all experiments in the spatial, JPEG, and side-informed JPEG domains as well as the comparison with previous art. The security is measured empirically using classifiers trained with rich media models on a range of payloads and quality factors. The paper is concluded in Section 7.

This paper is an extended and adjusted version of an article presented at the First ACM Information Hiding and Multimedia Security Workshop in Montpellier in June 2013 [19].

2 Preliminaries

2.1 Notation
Capital and lowercase boldface symbols stand for matrices and vectors, respectively. The symbols $\mathbf{X} = (X_{ij})$, $\mathbf{Y} = (Y_{ij}) \in \mathcal{I}^{n_1 \times n_2}$ will always be used for a cover (and the corresponding stego) image with $n_1 \times n_2$ elements attaining values in a finite set $\mathcal{I}$. The image elements will be either 8-bit pixel values, in which case $\mathcal{I} = \{0, \ldots, 255\}$, or quantized JPEG DCT coefficients, $\mathcal{I} = \{-1,024, \ldots, 1,023\}$, arranged into an $n_1 \times n_2$ matrix by replacing each 8×8

pixel block with the corresponding block of quantized coefficients. For simplicity and without loss on generality, we will assume that n_1 and n_2 are multiples of 8.

For side-informed JPEG steganography, a precover (raw, uncompressed) image will be denoted as $\mathbf{P} = (P_{ij}) \in \mathcal{I}^{n_1 \times n_2}$. When compressing $\mathbf{P}$, first a blockwise DCT transform is executed for each 8×8 block of pixels from a fixed grid. Then, the DCT coefficients are divided by quantization steps and rounded to integers. Let $\mathbf{P}^{(b)}$ be the bth 8×8 block when ordering the blocks, e.g., in a row-by-row fashion ($b = 1, \ldots, n_1 \cdot n_2/64$). With a luminance quantization matrix $\mathbf{Q} = \{q_{kl}\}$, $1 \leq k, l \leq 8$, we denote $\mathbf{D}^{(b)} = \text{DCT}(\mathbf{P}^{(b)})./\mathbf{Q}$ the raw (non-rounded) values of DCT coefficients. Here, the operation './' is an elementwise division of matrices and DCT(.) is the DCT transform used in the JPEG compressor. Furthermore, we denote $\mathbf{X}^{(b)} = [\mathbf{D}^{(b)}]$ the quantized DCT coefficients rounded to integers. We use the symbols $\mathbf{D}$ and $\mathbf{X}$ to denote the arrays of all raw and quantized DCT coefficients when arranging all blocks $\mathbf{D}^{(b)}$ and $\mathbf{X}^{(b)}$ in the same manner as the 8×8 pixel blocks in the uncompressed image. We will use the symbol $J^{-1}(\mathbf{X})$ for the JPEG image represented using quantized DCT coefficients $\mathbf{X}$ when decompressed to the spatial domain[d].

For matrix $\mathbf{A}$, $\mathbf{A}^{\mathrm{T}}$ is its transpose, and $|\mathbf{A}| = (|a_{ij}|)$ is the matrix of absolute values. The indices i, j will be used solely to index pixels or DCT coefficients, while u, v will be exclusively used to index coefficients in a wavelet decomposition.

2.2 DCT transform
We would like to point out that the JPEG format allows several different implementations of the DCT transform, DCT(.). The specific choice of the transform implementation may especially impact the security of side-informed steganography. In this paper, we work with the DCT(.) implemented as 'dct2' in Matlab when feeding in pixels represented as 'double'. In particular, a block of 8×8 DCT coefficients is computed from a precover block $\mathbf{P}^{(b)}$ as

$$\text{DCT}(\mathbf{P}^{(b)})_{kl} = \sum_{i,j=0}^{7} \frac{w_k w_l}{4} \cos \frac{\pi k(2i+1)}{16}$$
$$\times \cos \frac{\pi l(2j+1)}{16} P_{ij}^{(b)}, \quad (1)$$

where $k, l \in \{0, \ldots, 7\}$ index the DCT mode and $w_0 = 1/\sqrt{2}$, $w_k = 1$ for $k > 0$.

To obtain an actual JPEG image from a two-dimensional array of quantized coefficients $\mathbf{X}$ (cover) or $\mathbf{Y}$ (stego), we first create an (arbitrary) JPEG image of the same dimensions $n_1 \times n_2$ using Matlab's 'imwrite' with the same quality factor, read its JPEG structure using Sallee's Matlab JPEG Toolbox (http://dde.binghamton.edu/download/jpeg_toolbox.zip) and then merely replace the array of quantized coefficients in this structure with $\mathbf{X}$ and $\mathbf{Y}$ to obtain the cover and stego images, respectively. This way, we guarantee that both images were created using the same JPEG compressor and that all that we will be detecting are the embedding changes rather than compressor artifacts.

3 Universal distortion function UNIWARD

In this section, we provide a general description of the proposed universal distortion function UNIWARD and explain how it can be used to embed in the JPEG and the side-informed JPEG domains. The distortion depends on the choice of a directional filter bank and one scalar parameter whose purpose is stabilizing the numerical computations. The distortion design is finished in Section 5, which investigates the effect of the filter bank and the stabilizing constant on empirical security.

Since rich models [18,20–22] currently used in steganalysis are capable of detecting changes along 'clean edges' that can be well fitted using locally polynomial models, whenever possible the embedding algorithm should embed into textured/noisy areas that are not easily modellable in any direction. We quantify this using outputs of a directional filter bank and construct the distortion function in this manner.

3.1 Directional filter bank

By a directional filter bank, we understand a set of three linear shift-invariant filters represented with their kernels $\mathcal{B} = \{\mathbf{K}^{(1)}, \mathbf{K}^{(2)}, \mathbf{K}^{(3)}\}$. They are used to evaluate the smoothness of a given image $\mathbf{X}$ along the horizontal, vertical, and diagonal directions by computing the so-called directional residuals $\mathbf{W}^{(k)} = \mathbf{K}^{(k)} \star \mathbf{X}$, where '$\star$' is a mirror-padded convolution so that $\mathbf{W}^{(k)}$ has again $n_1 \times n_2$ elements. The mirror padding prevents introducing embedding artifacts at the image boundary.

While it is possible to use arbitrary filter banks, we will exclusively use kernels built from one-dimensional low-pass (and high-pass) wavelet decomposition filters $\mathbf{h}$ (and $\mathbf{g}$):

$$\mathbf{K}^{(1)} = \mathbf{h} \cdot \mathbf{g}^{\mathrm{T}}, \ \mathbf{K}^{(2)} = \mathbf{g} \cdot \mathbf{h}^{\mathrm{T}}, \ \mathbf{K}^{(3)} = \mathbf{g} \cdot \mathbf{g}^{\mathrm{T}}. \tag{2}$$

In this case, the filters correspond, respectively, to two-dimensional LH, HL, and HH wavelet directional high-pass filters, and the residuals coincide with the first-level undecimated wavelet LH, HL, and HH directional decomposition of $\mathbf{X}$. We constrained ourselves to wavelet filter banks because wavelet representations are known to provide good decorrelation and energy compactification for images of natural scenes (see, e.g., Chapter 7 in [23]).

3.2 Distortion function (non-side-informed embedding)

We are now ready to describe the universal distortion function. We do so first for embedding that does not use any precover. Given a pair of cover and stego images, $\mathbf{X}$ and $\mathbf{Y}$, represented in the spatial (pixel) domain, we will denote with $W_{uv}^{(k)}(\mathbf{X})$ and $W_{uv}^{(k)}(\mathbf{Y})$, $k = 1, 2, 3$, $u \in \{1, \ldots, n_1\}$, $v \in \{1, \ldots, n_2\}$, their corresponding uvth wavelet coefficient in the kth subband of the first decomposition level. The UNIWARD distortion function is the sum of relative changes of all wavelet coefficients with respect to the cover image:

$$D(\mathbf{X}, \mathbf{Y}) \triangleq \sum_{k=1}^{3} \sum_{u=1}^{n_1} \sum_{v=1}^{n_2} \frac{|W_{uv}^{(k)}(\mathbf{X}) - W_{uv}^{(k)}(\mathbf{Y})|}{\sigma + |W_{uv}^{(k)}(\mathbf{X})|}, \tag{3}$$

where $\sigma > 0$ is a constant stabilizing the numerical calculations.

The ratio in (3) is smaller when a large cover wavelet coefficient is changed (where texture and edges appear). Embedding changes are discouraged in regions where $|W_{uv}^{(k)}(\mathbf{X})|$ is small for at least one k, which corresponds to a direction along which the content is modellable.

For JPEG images, the distortion between the two arrays of quantized DCT coefficients, $\mathbf{X}$ and $\mathbf{Y}$, is computed by first decompressing the JPEG files to the spatial domain, and evaluating the distortion between the decompressed images, $J^{-1}(\mathbf{X})$ and $J^{-1}(\mathbf{Y})$, in the same manner as in (3):

$$D(\mathbf{X}, \mathbf{Y}) \triangleq D\left(J^{-1}(\mathbf{X}), J^{-1}(\mathbf{Y})\right). \tag{4}$$

Note that the distortion (3) is non-additive because changing pixel X_{ij} will affect $s \times s$ wavelet coefficients, where $s \times s$ is the size of the 2D wavelet support. Also, changing a JPEG coefficient X_{ij} will affect a block of 8×8 pixels and therefore a block of $(8 + s - 1) \times (8 + s - 1)$ wavelet coefficients. It is thus apparent that when changing neighboring pixels (or DCT coefficients), the embedding changes 'interact,' hence the non-additivity of D.

3.3 Distortion function (JPEG side-informed embedding)

By side-informed embedding in JPEG domain, we understand the following general principle. Given the raw DCT coefficient D_{ij} obtained from the precover $\mathbf{P}$, the embedder has the choice of rounding D_{ij} up or down to modulate its parity (usually the least significant bit of the rounded value). We denote with $e_{ij} = |D_{ij} - X_{ij}|$, $e_{ij} \in [0, 0.5]$, the rounding error for the ijth coefficient when compressing the precover $\mathbf{P}$ to the cover image $\mathbf{X}$. Rounding 'to the other side' leads to an embedding change, $Y_{ij} = X_{ij} + \mathrm{sign}(D_{ij} - X_{ij})$, which corresponds to a 'rounding error' $1 - e_{ij}$. Thus, every embedding change increases the distortion *with respect to the precover* by the difference between both rounding errors: $|D_{ij} - Y_{ij}| - |D_{ij} - X_{ij}| = 1 - 2e_{ij}$.

For the side-informed embedding in JPEG domain, we therefore define the distortion as the difference:

$$D^{(SI)}(\mathbf{X}, \mathbf{Y}) \triangleq D\left(\mathbf{P}, J^{-1}(\mathbf{Y})\right) - D\left(\mathbf{P}, J^{-1}(\mathbf{X})\right)$$

$$= \sum_{k=1}^{3} \sum_{u=1}^{n_1} \sum_{v=1}^{n_2} \left[\frac{|W_{uv}^{(k)}(\mathbf{P}) - W_{uv}^{(k)}\left(J^{-1}(\mathbf{Y})\right)|}{\sigma + |W_{uv}^{(k)}(\mathbf{P})|} \right.$$
$$\left. - \frac{|W_{uv}^{(k)}(\mathbf{P}) - W_{uv}^{(k)}\left(J^{-1}(\mathbf{X})\right)|}{\sigma + |W_{uv}^{(k)}(\mathbf{P})|} \right]. \quad (5)$$

Note that the linearity of DCT and the wavelet transforms guarantee that $D^{(SI)}(\mathbf{X}, \mathbf{Y}) \geq 0$. This is because rounding a DCT coefficient (to obtain $\mathbf{X}$) corresponds to adding a certain pattern (that depends on the modified DCT mode) in the wavelet domain. Rounding to the other side (to obtain $\mathbf{Y}$) corresponds to subtracting the same pattern but with a *larger* amplitude. This is why $|W_{uv}^{(k)}(\mathbf{P}) - W_{uv}^{(k)}(J^{-1}(\mathbf{Y}))| - |W_{uv}^{(k)}(\mathbf{P}) - W_{uv}^{(k)}(J^{-1}(\mathbf{X}))| \geq 0$ for all k, u, v.

We note at this point that (5) bears some similarity to the distortion used in Normalized Perturbed Quantization (NPQ) [11,12], where the authors also proposed the distortion as a *relative* change of cover DCT coefficients. The main difference is that we compute the distortion using a directional filter bank, allowing thus directional sensitivity and potentially better content adaptability. Furthermore, we do not eliminate DCT coefficients that are zeros in the cover. Finally, and most importantly, in contrast to NPQ, our design naturally incorporates the effect of the quantization step because the wavelet coefficients are computed from the decompressed JPEG image.

3.3.1 Technical issues with zero embedding costs

When running experiments with *any* side-informed JPEG steganography in which the embedding cost is zero, when $e_{ij} = 1/2$, we discovered a technical problem that, to the best knowledge of the authors, has not been disclosed elsewhere. The problem is connected to the fact that when $e_{ij} = 1/2$ the cost of rounding D_{ij} 'down' instead of 'up' should not be zero because, after all, this does constitute an embedding change. This does not affect the security much when the number of such DCT coefficients is small. With an increasing number of coefficients with $e_{ij} = 1/2$ (we will call them 1/2-coefficients), however, $1 - 2e_{ij}$ is no longer a good measure of statistical detectability and one starts observing a rather pathological behavior - with payload approaching zero, the detection error does not saturate at 50% (random guessing) but rather at a lower value and only reaches 50% for payloads nearly equal to zero[e]. The strength with which this phenomenon manifests depends on how many 1/2-coefficients are in the image, which in turn depends on two factors - the implementation of the DCT used to compute the costs and the JPEG quality factor. When using the slow DCT (implemented using 'dct2' in Matlab), the number 1/2-coefficients is small and does not affect security at least for low-quality factors. However, in the fast-integer implementation of DCT (e.g., Matlab's imwrite), all D_{ij} are multiples of 1/8. Thus, with decreasing quantization step (increasing JPEG quality factor), the number of 1/2-coefficients increases.

To avoid dealing with this issue in this paper, we used the slow DCT implemented using Matlab's dct2 as explained in Section 2.2 to obtain the costs. Even with the slow DCT, however, 1/2-coefficients do cause problems when the quality factor is high. As one can easily verify from the formula for the DCT (1), when $k, l \in \{0, 4\}$, the value of D_{kl} is always a rational number because the cosines are either 1 or $\sqrt{2}/2$, which, together with the multiplicative weights $\mathbf{w}$, gives again a rational number. In particular, the DC coefficient (mode 00) is always a multiple of 1/4, the coefficients of modes 04 and 40 are multiples of 1/8, and the coefficients corresponding to mode 44 are multiples of 1/16. For all other combinations of $k, l \in \{0, \ldots, 7\}$, D_{ij} is an irrational number. In practice, *any* embedding whose costs are zero for 1/2-coefficients will thus strongly prefer these four DCT modes, causing a highly uneven distribution of embedding changes among the DCT coefficients. Because rich JPEG models [24] utilize statistics collected for each mode separately, they are capable of detecting this statistical peculiarity even at low payloads. This problem becomes more serious with increasing quality factor.

These above embedding artifacts can be largely suppressed by prohibiting embedding changes in *all* 1/2-coefficients in modes 00, 04, 40, and 44[f]. In Figure 1, where we show the comparison of various side-informed embedding methods for quality factor 95, we intentionally included the detection errors for all tested schemes where this measure was not enforced to prove the validity of the above arguments.

The solution of the problem with 1/2-coefficients, which is clearly not optimal, is related to the more fundamental problem, which is how exactly the side information in the form of an uncompressed image should be utilized for the design of steganographic distortion functions. The authors postpone a detailed study of this quite intriguing problem to a separate paper.

3.4 Additive approximation of UNIWARD

Any distortion function $D(\mathbf{X}, \mathbf{Y})$ can be used for embedding in its additive approximation [4] using D to compute the cost ρ_{ij} of changing each pixel/DCT coefficient X_{ij}. A significant advantage of using an additive approximation is the simplicity of the overall design. The embedding can be implemented in a straightforward manner by applying nowadays a standard tool in steganography - the Syndrome-Trellis Codes (STCs) [3]. All experiments in

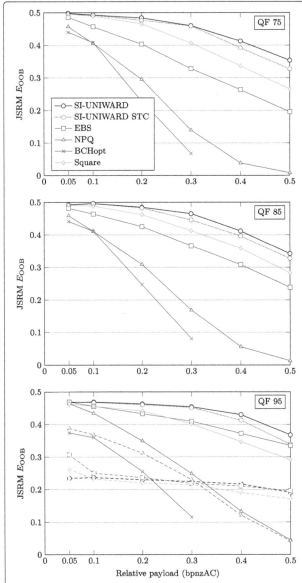

Figure 1 Comparison of various side-informed embedding methods. Detection error E_{OOB} for SI-UNIWARD and four other methods with the union of SRMQ1 and JRM and the ensemble classifier for JPEG quality factors 75, 85, and 95. The dashed lines in the graph for QF 95 correspond to the case when all the embedding methods use all coefficients, including the DCT modes 00, 04, 40, and 44 independently of the value of the rounding error e_{ij}.

The additive approximation to (3) and (5) will be denoted as $D_A(\mathbf{X}, \mathbf{Y})$ and $D_A^{(SI)}(\mathbf{X}, \mathbf{Y})$, respectively. For example,

$$D_A(\mathbf{X}, \mathbf{Y}) = \sum_{i=1}^{n_1} \sum_{j=1}^{n_2} \rho_{ij}(\mathbf{X}, Y_{ij})[X_{ij} \neq Y_{ij}], \qquad (7)$$

where $[S]$ is the Iverson bracket equal to 1 when the statement S is true and 0 when S is false.

Note that, due to the absolute values in $D(\mathbf{X}, \mathbf{Y})$ (3), $\rho_{ij}(\mathbf{X}, X_{ij} + 1) = \rho_{ij}(\mathbf{X}, X_{ij} - 1)$, which permits us to use a *ternary* embedding operation for the spatial and JPEG domains[h]. Practical embedding algorithms can be constructed using the ternary multi-layered version of STCs (Section 4 in [3]).

On the other hand, for the side-informed JPEG steganography, $D_A^{(SI)}(\mathbf{X}, \mathbf{Y})$ is inherently limited to a *binary* embedding operation because D_{ij} is either rounded up or down.

The embedding methods that use the additive approximation of UNIWARD for the spatial, JPEG, and side-informed JPEG domain will be called S-UNIWARD, J-UNIWARD, and SI-UNIWARD, respectively.

3.5 Relationship of UNIWARD to WOW

The distortion function of WOW bears some similarity to UNIWARD in the sense that the embedding costs are also computed from three directional residuals. The WOW embedding costs are, however, computed a different way that makes it rather difficult to use it for embedding in other domains, such as the JPEG domain[i].

To obtain a cost of changing pixel $X_{ij} \rightarrow Y_{ij}$, WOW first computes the embedding distortion in the wavelet domain weighted by the wavelet coefficients of the cover. This is implemented as a convolution $\xi_{ij}^{(k)} = |W_{uv}^{(k)}(\mathbf{X})| \star |W_{uv}^{(k)}(\mathbf{X}) - W_{uv}^{(k)}(\mathbf{X}_{\sim ij}Y_{ij})|$ (see Equation 2 in [17]). These so-called embedding suitabilities $\xi_{ij}^{(k)}$ are then aggregated over all three subbands using the reciprocal Hölder norm, $\rho_{ij}^{(WOW)} = \sum_{k=1}^{3} 1/\xi_{ij}^{(k)}$ to give WOW the proper content adaptivity in the spatial domain.

In principle, this approach could be used for embedding in the JPEG (or some other) domain in a similar way as in UNIWARD. However, notice that the suitabilities $\xi_{ij}^{(k)}$ increase with increasing JPEG quantization step (increasing spatial frequency), giving the high-frequency DCT coefficients smaller costs, $\rho_{ij}^{(WOW)}$, and thus a higher embedding probability than for the low-frequency coefficients. This creates both visible and statistically detectable artifacts. In contrast, the embedding costs in UNIWARD are higher for high-frequency DCT coefficients, desirably discouraging embedding changes in coefficients which are largely zeros.

this paper are carried out with additive approximations of UNIWARD.

The cost of changing X_{ij} to Y_{ij} and leaving all other cover elements unchanged is

$$\rho_{ij}(\mathbf{X}, Y_{ij}) \triangleq D(\mathbf{X}, \mathbf{X}_{\sim ij}Y_{ij}), \qquad (6)$$

where $\mathbf{X}_{\sim ij}Y_{ij}$ is the cover image $\mathbf{X}$ with only its ijth element changed: $X_{ij} \rightarrow Y_{ij}$[g]. Note that $\rho_{ij} = 0$ when $\mathbf{X} = \mathbf{Y}$.

4 Common core of all experiments

Before we move to the experimental part of this paper, which appears in Sections 5 and 6, we introduce the common core of all experiments: the cover source, steganalysis features, the classifier used to build the steganography detectors, and an empirical measure of security.

4.1 Cover source

All experiments are conducted on the BOSSbase database ver. 1.01 [25] containing 10,000 512×512 8-bit grayscale images coming from eight different cameras. This database is very convenient for our purposes because it contains uncompressed images that serve as precovers for side-informed JPEG embedding. Also, the images can be compressed to any desirable quality factor for the JPEG domain.

The steganographic security is evaluated empirically using binary classifiers trained on a given cover source and its stego version embedded with a fixed payload. Even though this setup is artificial and does not correspond to real-life applications, it allows assessment of security with respect to the payload size, which is the goal of academic investigations of this type[j].

4.2 Steganalysis features

Spatial domain steganography methods will be analyzed using the spatial rich model (SRM) [18] consisting of 39 symmetrized sub-models quantized with three different quantization factors with a total dimension of $34,671$[k]. JPEG domain methods (including the side-informed algorithms) will be steganalyzed using the union of a down-scaled version of the SRM with a single quantization step $q = 1$ (SRMQ1) with dimension $12,753$ and the JPEG rich model (JRM) [24] with dimension 22,510, giving the total feature dimension of 35,263.

4.3 Machine learning

All classifiers will be implemented using the ensemble [26] with Fisher linear discriminant as the base learner. The security is quantified using the ensemble's 'out-of-bag' (OOB) error E_{OOB}, which is an unbiased estimate of the minimal total testing error under equal priors, $P_E = \min_{P_{FA}} \frac{1}{2}(P_{FA} + P_{MD})$ [26]. The statistical detectability is usually displayed graphically by plotting E_{OOB} as a function of the relative payload. With the feature dimensionality and the database size, the statistical scatter of E_{OOB} over multiple ensemble runs with different seeds was typically so small that drawing error bars around the data points in the graphs would not show two visually discernible horizontal lines, which is why we omit this information in our graphs. As will be seen later, the differences in detectability between the proposed methods and prior art are so large that there should be no doubt about

the statistical significance of the improvement. The code for extractors of all rich models as well as the ensemble is available at http://dde.binghamton.edu/download.

5 Determining the parameters of UNIWARD

In this section, we study how the wavelet basis and the stabilizing constant σ in the distortion function UNIWARD affect the empirical security. We first focus on the parameter σ and then on the filter bank.

The original role of σ in UNIWARD [19] was to stabilize the numerical computations when evaluating the relative change of wavelet coefficients (3). As the following experiment shows, however, σ also strongly affects the content adaptivity of the embedding algorithm. In Figure 2, we show the embedding change probabilities for payload $\alpha = 0.4$ bpp (bits per pixel) for six values of the parameter σ. For this experiment, we selected the 8-tap Daubechies wavelet filter bank $\mathcal{B}$ whose 1D filters are shown in Figure 3[l]. Note that a small value of σ makes the embedding change probabilities undesirably sensitive to content. They exhibit unusual interleaved streaks of high and low values. This is clearly undesirable since the content (shown in the upper left corner of Figure 2) does not change as abruptly. On the other hand, a large σ makes the embedding change probabilities 'too smooth,' permitting thus UNIWARD to embed in regions with less complex content. Intuitively, we need to choose some middle ground for σ to avoid introducing a weakness into the embedding algorithm.

Because the SRM consists of statistics collected from the noise residuals of all pixels in the image, it 'does not see' the artifacts in the embedding probabilities - the interleaved bands of high and low values. Notice that the position of the bands is tied to the content and does not correspond to any fixed (content-independent) checkerboard pattern. Thus, we decided to introduce a new type of steganalysis features designed specifically to utilize the artifacts in the embedding probabilities to probe the security of this unusual selection channel for small values of σ.

5.1 Content-selective residuals

The idea behind the attack on the selection channel is to compute the statistics of noise residuals separately for pixels with a small embedding probability and then for pixels with a large embedding probability. The former will serve as a reference for the latter, giving strength to this attack. While it is true that the embedding probabilities estimated from the stego image will generally not exactly match those computed from the corresponding cover image[m], they will be close and 'good enough' for the attack to work.

We will use the first-order noise residuals (differences among neighboring pixels):

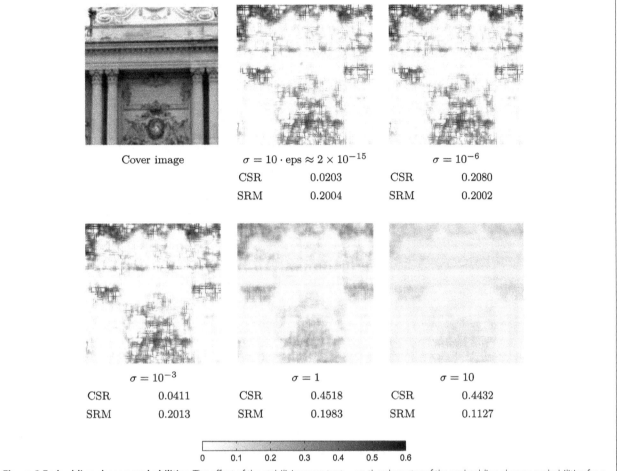

Figure 2 Embedding change probabilities. The effect of the stabilizing constant σ on the character of the embedding change probabilities for a 128×128 cover image shown in the upper left corner. The numerical values are the E_{OOB} obtained using the content-selective residual (CSR) and the SRM on BOSSbase 1.01 for relative payload $\alpha = 0.4$ bpp.

$$R_{ij} = X_{i,j} - X_{i,j+1}, \ i \in \{1, \ldots, n_1\}, \ j \in \{1, \ldots, n_2 - 1\}. \tag{8}$$

To curb the residuals' range and allow a compact statistical representation, R_{ij} will be truncated to the range $[-T, T]$, $R_{ij} \leftarrow \mathrm{trunc}_T(R_{ij})$, where T is a positive integer, and

$$\mathrm{trunc}_T(x) = \begin{cases} x & \text{when } -T \leq x \leq T \\ -T & \text{when } x < -T \\ T & \text{when } T < x. \end{cases} \tag{9}$$

Since this residual involves two adjacent pixels, we will divide all horizontally adjacent pixels in the image into four classes and compute the histogram for each class separately. Let $p_{ij}(\mathbf{X}, \overline{\alpha})$ denote the embedding change probability computed from image $\mathbf{X}$ when embedding payload of $\overline{\alpha}$ bpp. Given two thresholds $0 < t_s < t_L < 1$, we define the following four sets of residuals:

$$\mathcal{R}_{ss} = \{R_{ij} | p_{ij}(\mathbf{X}, \overline{\alpha}) < t_s \ \wedge \ p_{i,j+1}(\mathbf{X}, \overline{\alpha}) < t_s\} \tag{10}$$
$$\mathcal{R}_{sL} = \{R_{ij} | p_{ij}(\mathbf{X}, \overline{\alpha}) < t_s \ \wedge \ p_{i,j+1}(\mathbf{X}, \overline{\alpha}) > t_L\} \tag{11}$$
$$\mathcal{R}_{Ls} = \{R_{ij} | p_{ij}(\mathbf{X}, \overline{\alpha}) > t_L \ \wedge \ p_{i,j+1}(\mathbf{X}, \overline{\alpha}) < t_s\} \tag{12}$$
$$\mathcal{R}_{LL} = \{R_{ij} | p_{ij}(\mathbf{X}, \overline{\alpha}) > t_L \ \wedge \ p_{i,j+1}(\mathbf{X}, \overline{\alpha}) > t_L\}. \tag{13}$$

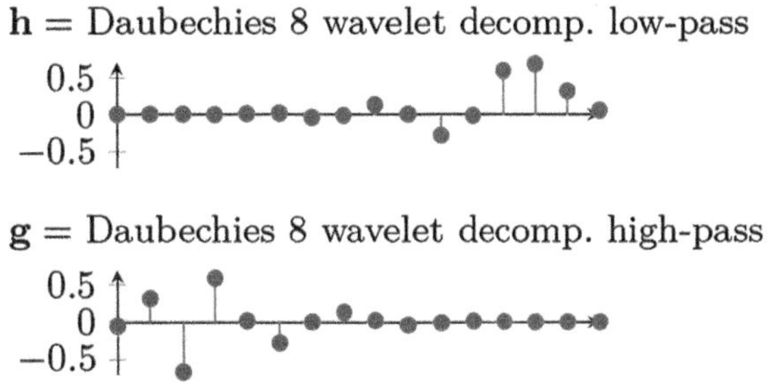

$\mathbf{h} =$ Daubechies 8 wavelet decomp. low-pass

$\mathbf{g} =$ Daubechies 8 wavelet decomp. high-pass

Figure 3 Daubechies wavelet filter bank. UNIWARD uses the Daubechies 8-tap wavelet directional filter bank built from one-dimensional low-pass and high-pass filters, **h** and **g**.

The so-called content-selective residual (CSR) features will be formed by the histograms of residuals in each set. Because the marginal distribution of each residual is symmetrical about zero, one can merge the histograms of residuals from $\mathcal{R}_{sL}$ and $\mathcal{R}_{Ls}$. The feature vector is thus the concatenation of $3 \times (2T + 1)$ histogram bins, $l = -T, \ldots, T$:

$$h_s(l) = \left| \{ R_{ij} | R_{ij} = l \ \wedge \ R_{ij} \in \mathcal{R}_{ss} \} \right| \tag{14}$$

$$h_L(l) = \left| \{ R_{ij} | R_{ij} = l \ \wedge \ R_{ij} \in \mathcal{R}_{LL} \} \right| \tag{15}$$

$$h_{sL}(l) = \left| \{ R_{ij} | R_{ij} = l \ \wedge \ R_{ij} \in \mathcal{R}_{sL} \cup \mathcal{R}_{Ls} \} \right|. \tag{16}$$

The set $\mathcal{R}_{ss}$ holds the residual values computed from pixels with a small embedding change probability, while the other sets hold residuals that are likely affected by embedding - their tails will become thicker.

All that remains is to specify the values of the parameters t_s, t_L, and $\overline{\alpha}$. Since the steganalyst will generally not know the payload embedded in the stego image[n], we need to choose a fixed value of $\overline{\alpha}$ that gives an overall good performance over a wide range of payloads. In our experiments, a medium value of $\overline{\alpha} = 0.4$ generally provided a good estimate of the interleaved bands in the embedding change probabilities. Finally, we conducted a grid search on images from BOSSbase to determine t_s and t_L. The found optimum was rather flat and located around $t_s = 0.05$, $t_L = 0.06$. The threshold T for $\text{trunc}_T(x)$ was kept fixed at $T = 10$.

For the value of σ as originally proposed in the workshop version of this paper [19], $\sigma = 10 \cdot \text{eps} \approx 2 \times 10^{-15}$ ('eps' defined as in Matlab), the detection error of the $3 \times (2 \times 10 + 1) = 63$-dimensional CSR feature vector turned out to be a reliable detection statistic. Figure 4 shows the detection error E_{OOB} as a function of the relative payload. This confirms our intuition that too small a value of σ introduces strong banding artifacts, the stego scheme becomes overly sensitive to content, and an approximate

knowledge on the faulty selection channel can be used to successfully attack S-UNIWARD.

As can be seen from Figure 2, the artifacts in the embedding change probabilities become gradually suppressed when increasing the value of the stabilizing constant σ. To determine the proper value of σ, we steganalyzed S-UNIWARD with both the CSR and SRM feature sets (and their union) on payload $\alpha = 0.4$ bpp as a function of σ (see Figure 5)[o]. The detection error using both the SRM and the CSR is basically constant until σ becomes close to 2^{-14} when a further increase of σ makes the CSR features ineffective for steganalysis. From $\sigma = 1$ the SRM starts detecting the embedding more accurately as the adaptivity of the scheme becomes lower. Also, at this value of σ, adding the CSR does not lower the detection error of the SRM. Based on this analysis, we decided to set the stabilizing constant of S-UNIWARD to $\sigma = 1$ and kept it at this value for the rest of the experiments in the spatial domain reported in this paper.

The attack based on content-selective residuals could be expanded to other residuals than pixel differences, and one could use higher-order statistics instead of histograms [27][p]. While the detection error for the original S-UNIWARD setting $\sigma = 10 \cdot \text{eps}$ can, indeed, be made smaller this way, expanding the CSR feature set has virtually no effect on the security of S-UNIWARD for $\sigma = 1$ and the optimality of this value.

We note that constructing a similar targeted attack against JPEG implementations of UNIWARD is likely not feasible because the distortion caused by a change in a DCT coefficient affects a block of 8×8 pixels and, consequently, 23×23 wavelet coefficients. The distortion 'averages out' and no banding artefacts show up in the embedding probability map. Steganalysis of J-UNIWARD with JSRM shown in Figure 6 indicates that the optimal σ

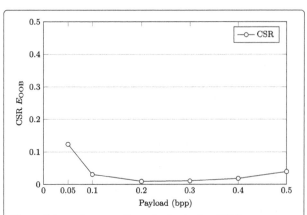

Figure 4 Detection error E_{OOB} obtained using CSR features as a function of relative payload for $\sigma = 10 \cdot$ **eps.**

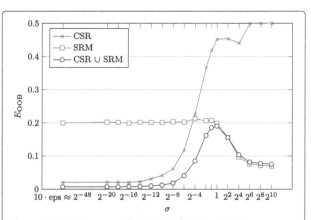

Figure 5 Detection error of S-UNIWARD. Payload 0.4 bpp implemented with various values of σ for the CSR and SRM features and their union.

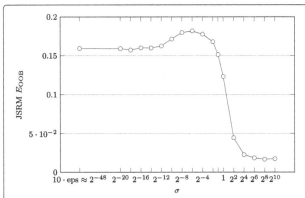

Figure 6 Steganalysis of J-UNIWARD with JSRM. Detection error E_{OOB} obtained using the merger of JRM and SRMQ1 (JSRM) features as a function σ for J-UNIWARD with payload $\alpha = 0.4$ bpnzAC and JPEG quality factor 75.

2^{-6} for J- and SI-UNIWARD. We report the results on a range of relative payloads 0.05, 0.1, 0.2, ..., 0.5 bpp, while JPEG domain (and side-informed JPEG) methods will be tested on the same payloads expressed in bits per non-zero cover AC DCT coefficient (bpnzAC).

6.1 Spatial domain

In the spatial domain, we compare the proposed method with HUGO [15], HUGO implemented using the Gibbs construction with bounding distortion (HUGO BD) [4], WOW [17], LSB matching (LSBM), and the edge-adaptive (EA) algorithm [28] With the exception of the EA algorithm, in which the costs and the embedding algorithm are inseparable, the results of all other algorithms are reported for embedding simulators that operate at the theoretical payload-distortion bound. The only algorithm that we implemented using STCs (with constraint height $h = 12$) to assess the coding loss is the proposed S-UNIWARD method.

For HUGO, we used the embedding simulator [25] with default settings $\gamma = 1$, $\sigma = 1$ and the switch --T with $T = 255$ to remove the weakness reported in [7]. HUGO BD starts with a distortion measure implemented as a weighted norm in the SPAM feature space, which is non-additive and not locally supported either. The bounding distortion is a method (see Section 7 in [4]) to give the distortion the form needed for the Gibbs construction to work - the local supportedness. HUGO BD was implemented using the Gibbs construction with two sweeps as described in the original publication with the same parameter settings as for HUGO. The non-adaptive LSBM was simulated at the ternary bound corresponding to uniform costs, $\rho_{ij} = 1$ for all i, j.

Figure 7 shows the E_{OOB} error for all stego methods as a function of the relative payload expressed in bits per pixel. While the security of the S-UNIWARD and WOW

for J-UNIWARD is 2^{-6}, which we selected for all experiments with J-UNIWARD and SI-UNIWARD in this paper.

5.2 Effect of the filter bank

As a final experiment of this section aimed at finding the best settings of UNIWARD, we studied the influence of the directional filter bank. We did so for a fixed payload $\alpha = 0.4$ bpp and two values of σ when steganalyzing using the CSR and SRM features. Table 1 shows the results for five different wavelet bases (http://wavelets.pybytes.com/wavelet/db8/) with varying parameters (support size s). The best results have been achieved with the 8-tap Daubechies wavelet, whose 1D low- and high-pass filters are displayed in Figure 3.

6 Experiments

In this section, we test the steganography using UNIWARD implemented with the 8-tap Daubechies directional filter bank and $\sigma = 1$ for S-UNIWARD and $\sigma =$

Table 1 Detection error E_{OOB} obtained using CSR and SRM features when using different filter banks in UNIWARD

	CSR		SRM	
	$\sigma = 10 \cdot eps$	$\sigma = 1$	$\sigma = 10 \cdot eps$	$\sigma = 1$
Haar	0.0649	0.3302	0.0339	0.0707
Daubechies 2	0.0278	0.4299	0.1313	0.1744
Daubechies 4	0.0106	0.4279	0.1763	0.1966
Daubechies 8	0.0203	0.4518	0.2001	0.1981
Daubechies 20	0.1934	0.4646	0.2046	0.1868
Symlet 8	0.0235	0.4410	0.1635	0.1919
Coiflet 1	0.0458	0.4426	0.0796	0.1444
Biorthogonal 44	0.0264	0.4388	0.0859	0.1683
Biorthogonal 68	0.0376	0.4459	0.1259	0.1820

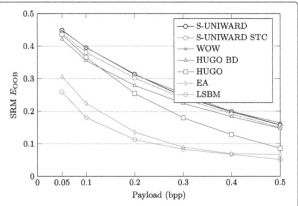

Figure 7 E_{OOB} error for all stego methods. Detection error E_{OOB} using SRM as a function of relative payload for S-UNIWARD and five other spatial domain steganographic schemes.

is practically the same due to the similarity of their distortion functions, the improvement over both versions of HUGO is quite apparent. HUGO BD performs better than HUGO especially for large payloads, where its detectability becomes comparable to that of S-UNIWARD. As expected, the non-adaptive LSBM performs poorly across all payloads, while EA appears only marginally better than LSBM.

In Figure 8, we contrast the probability of embedding changes for HUGO, WOW, and S-UNIWARD. The selected cover image has numerous horizontal and vertical edges and also some textured areas. Note that while HUGO embeds with high probability into the pillar edges as well as the horizontal lines above the pillars, S-UNIWARD directional costs force the changes solely into the textured areas. The placement of embedding changes for WOW and S-UNIWARD is quite similar, which is correspondingly reflected in their similar empirical security.

6.2 JPEG domain (non-side-informed)

For the JPEG domain without side information, we compare J-UNIWARD with nsF5 [14] and the recently proposed UED algorithm [13]. Since the costs used in UED are independent of the embedding change direction, we decided to include for comparison the UED implemented using *ternary* codes rather than binary, which indeed produced a more secure embedding algorithm[q]. All methods were again simulated at their corresponding payload-distortion bounds. The costs for nsF5 were uniform over all non-zero DCTs with zeros as the wet elements [29]. Figure 9 shows the results for JPEG quality factors 75, 85, and 95. As in the spatial domain, J-UNIWARD clearly outperformed both nsF5 and both versions of UED by a sizeable margin across all three quality factors. Furthermore, when using STCs with constraint height $h = 12$, the coding loss appears rather small.

6.3 JPEG domain (side-informed)

Working with the same three quality factors, we compare SI-UNIWARD with four other methods - the block entropy-weighted method of [10] (EBS), the NPQ [11], BCHopt [9], and the fourth method, which can be viewed as a modification (or simplification) of [9] or as [10] in which the normalization by block entropy has been removed. Following is a list of cost assignments for these four embedding methods; $\rho_{ij}^{(kl)}$ is the cost of changing DCT coefficient ij corresponding to DCT mode kl.

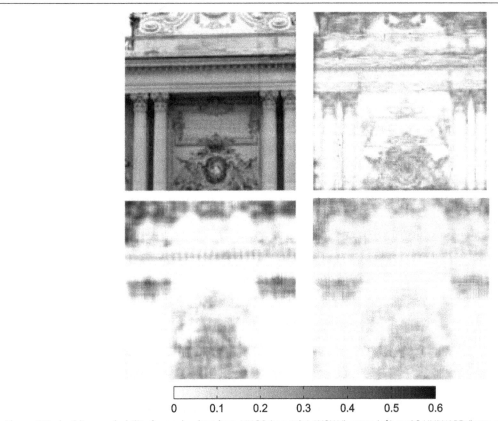

Figure 8 Embedding probability for payload 0.4 bpp. HUGO (top right), WOW (bottom left), and S-UNIWARD (bottom right) for a 128 × 128 grayscale cover image (top left).

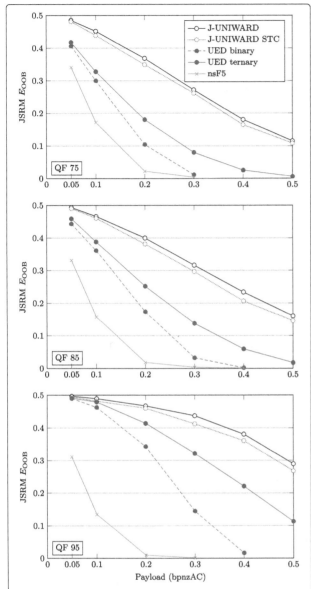

Figure 9 Results for JPEG quality factors 75, 85, and 95. Testing error E_{OOB} for J-UNIWARD, nsF5, and binary (ternary) UED on BOSSbase 1.01 with the union of SRMQ1 and JRM and ensemble classifier for quality factors 75, 85, and 95.

1. $\rho_{ij}^{(kl)} = \left(\dfrac{q_{kl}(0.5 - |e_{ij}|)}{H(\mathbf{X}^{(b)})} \right)^2$

2. $\rho_{ij}^{(kl)} = \dfrac{q_{kl}^{\lambda_1}(1 - 2|e_{ij}|)}{(\mu + |X_{ij}|)^{\lambda_2}}$

3. $\rho_{ij}^{(kl)}$ as defined in [9]

4. $\rho_{ij}^{(kl)} = \left(q_{kl}(1 - 2|e_{ij}|) \right)^2$

In method 1 (EBS), $H(\mathbf{X}^{(b)})$ is the block entropy defined as $H(\mathbf{X}^{(b)}) = -\sum_i h_i^{(b)} \log h_i^{(b)}$, where $h_i^{(b)}$ is the normalized histogram of all non-zero DCT coefficients in block $\mathbf{X}^{(b)}$. Per the experiments in [11], we set $\mu = 0$ as

NPQ embeds only in non-zero AC DCT coefficients, and $\lambda_1 = \lambda_2 = 1/2$ as this setting seemed to produce the most secure NPQ scheme for most payloads when tested with various feature sets. The cost ρ_{ij} for methods 1 to 4 is equal to zero when $e_{ij} = 1/2$. Methods 1 and 4 embed into all DCT coefficients, including the DC term and coefficients that would otherwise round to zero ($X_{ij} = 0$). We remind from Section 3.3.1 that methods 1, 2, and 4 avoid embedding into 1/2-coefficients from DCT modes 00, 04, 40, and 44. Since the cost assignment in method 3 (BCHopt) is inherently connected to its coding scheme, we kept this algorithm unchanged in our tests.

Figure 1 shows that SI-UNIWARD achieves the best security among the tested methods for all payloads and all JPEG quality factors. The coding loss is also quite negligible. Curiously, the weighting by block entropy in the EBS method paid off only for quality factor 95. For factors 85 and 75, the weighting actually increases the statistical detectability using our feature vector (*c.f.*, the 'Square' and 'EBS' curves). The dashed curves for quality factor 95 in Figure 1 are included to show the negative effect when 1/2-coefficients from DCT modes 00, 04, 40, and 44 are used for embedding (see the discussion in Section 3.3.1). In this case, the detection error levels off at approximately 25% to 30% for small-medium payloads because most embedding changes are executed at the above four DCT modes. Note that NPQ and BCHopt do not exhibit the pathological error saturation as strongly because they do not embed into the DC term (mode 00).

7 Conclusion

Perfect security seems unachievable for empirical cover sources, examples of which are digital images. Currently, the best the steganographer can do for such sources is to minimize the detectability when embedding a required payload. A standard way to approach this problem is to embed while minimizing a carefully crafted distortion function, which is tied to empirical statistical detectability. This converts the problem of secure steganography to one that has been largely resolved in terms of known bounds and general near-optimal practical coding constructions.

The contribution of this paper is a clean and universal design of the distortion function called UNIWARD, which is independent of the embedding domain. The distortion is always computed in the wavelet domain as a sum of relative changes of wavelet coefficients in the highest frequency undecimated subbands. The directionality of wavelet basis functions permits the sender to assess the neighborhood of each pixel for the presence of discontinuities in multiple directions (textures and 'noisy' regions) and thus avoid making embedding changes in those parts of the image that can be modeled along at least one direction (clean edges and smooth regions). This model-free heuristic approach has been implemented in the spatial, JPEG, and side-informed JPEG domains. In all three domains, the proposed steganographic schemes matched or outperformed current state-of-the-art steganographic methods. A quite significant improvement was especially obtained for the JPEG and side-informed JPEG domains. As demonstrated by experiments, the innovative concept to assess the costs of changing a JPEG coefficient in an alternative domain seems to be quite promising.

Although all proposed methods were implemented and tested with an additive approximation of UNIWARD, this distortion function is naturally defined in its non-additive version, meaning that changes made to neighboring pixels (DCT coefficients) interact in the sense that the total imposed distortion is not a sum of distortions of individual changes. This potentially allows UNIWARD to embed while taking into account the interaction among the changed image elements. We plan to explore this direction as part of our future effort.

Last but not the least, we have discovered a new phenomenon that hampers the performance of side-informed JPEG steganography that computes embedding costs based solely on the quantization error of DCT coefficients. When unquantized DCT coefficients that lie exactly in the middle of the quantization intervals are assigned zero costs, any embedding that minimizes distortion starts introducing embedding artifacts that are quite detectable using the JPEG rich model. While the makeshift solution proposed in this article is by no means optimal, it raises an important open question, which is how to best utilize the side information in the form of an uncompressed image when embedding data into the JPEG compressed form. The authors postpone detailed investigation of this phenomenon into their future effort.

Endnotes

[a]For a given empirical cover source, the statistical detectability is typically evaluated empirically using classifiers trained on cover and stego examples from the source.

[b]The concept of precover was used for the first time by Ker [30].

[c]Historically, the first side-informed embedding method was the embedding while dithering algorithm [31], in which a message was embedded to minimize the color quantization error when converting a true-color image to a palette image.

[d]The process J^{-1} involves rounding to integers and clipping to the dynamic range $\mathcal{I}$.

[e]This is because the embedding strongly prefers 1/2-coefficients.

[f]In practice, we assign very large costs to such coefficients.

[g]This notation was used in [4] and is also standard in the literature on Markov random fields [32].

[h]One might (seemingly rightfully) argue that the cost should depend on the polarity of the change. On the other hand, since the embedding changes with UNIWARD are restricted to textures, the equal costs are in fact plausible.

[i]This is one of the reasons why UNIWARD was conceived.

[j]Building a universal detector of steganography is not the goal of this paper.

[k]In Section 5, we will describe and work with another small feature set whose sole purpose will be to probe the security of the selection channel and to determine the proper value of the stabilizing constant σ.

[l]This filter bank was previously shown to provide the highest level of security for WOW [17] from among several tested filter banks. We thus selected the same bank here as a good initial candidate for the experiments.

[m]Also because the embedded payload α is unknown to the steganalyst.

[n]A study on building steganalyzers when the payload is not known appears in [33].

[o]When steganalyzing with the union of CSR and SRM using the ensemble classifier, we made sure that all 63 CSR features were included in each random feature subspace to avoid 'diluting' their strength in this type of classifier.

Also, the value of σ for extracting the embedding change probabilities $p_{ij}(\mathbf{X}; \overline{\alpha})$ was always fixed at $\sigma = 10 \cdot eps$ as the location of interleaved bands of high and low probabilities are more accurately estimated this way than with the value used in S-UNIWARD for the actual message embedding.

[p]Note for reviewers: A preprint of this article is available upon request.

[q]The authors of UED were apparently unaware of this possibility to further boost the security of their algorithm.

Competing interests
The authors declare that they have no competing interests.

Acknowledgements
The work on this paper was supported by the Air Force Office of Scientific Research under the research grant number FA9950-12-1-0124. The U.S. Government is authorized to reproduce and distribute reprints for governmental purposes notwithstanding any copyright notation thereon. The views and conclusions contained herein are those of the authors and should not be interpreted as necessarily representing the official policies, either expressed or implied of AFOSR or the U.S. Government. The authors would like to thank Tomáš Filler and Jan Kodovský for the useful discussions.

References
1.   R Böhme, *Advanced Statistical Steganalysis*. (Springer-Verlag, Berlin, 2010)
2.   CE Shannon, Coding theorems for a discrete source with a fidelity criterion. IRE Nat. Conv. Rec. **4**, 142–163 (1959)

3. T Filler, J Judas, J Fridrich, Minimizing additive distortion in steganography using syndrome-trellis codes. IEEE Trans. Inf. Forensics Secur. **6**(3), 920–935 (2011)

4. T Filler, J Fridrich, Gibbs construction in steganography. IEEE Trans. Inf. Forensics Secur. **5**(4), 705–720 (2010)

5. T Filler, J Fridrich, Design of adaptive steganographic schemes for digital images, in *Proceedings SPIE, Electronic Imaging, Media Watermarking, Security and Forensics III*, vol. 7880, ed. by A Alattar, ND Memon, EJ Delp, and J Dittmann (San Francisco, 2011), pp. 1–14

6. R Böhme, A Westfeld, Breaking Cauchy model-based JPEG steganography with first order statistics, in *Computer Security - ESORICS 2004. Proceedings 9th European Symposium on Research in Computer Security*, ed. by P Samarati, PYA Ryan, D Gollmann, R Molvapages, Sophia Antipolis, France. Lecture Notes in Computer Science, vol. 3193 (Springer, Berlin, 2004), pp. 125–140

7. J Kodovský, J Fridrich, V Holub, On dangers of overtraining steganography to incomplete cover model, in *Proceedings of the 13th ACM Multimedia & Security Workshop*, ed. by J Dittmann, S Craver, and C Heitzenrater (Niagara Falls, 2011), pp. 69–76

8. Y Kim, Z Duric, D Richards, Modified matrix encoding technique for minimal distortion steganography, in *8th International Workshop on Information Hiding*, ed. by JL Camenisch, CS Collberg, NF Johnson, P Sallee, Alexandria, 10–12 July 2006. Lecture Notes in Computer Science, vol. 4437 (Springer-Verlag, New York, 2006), pp. 314–327

9. V Sachnev, HJ Kim, R Zhang, Less detectable JPEG steganography method based on heuristic optimization and BCH syndrome coding, in *Proceedings of the 11th ACM Multimedia & Security Workshop*, ed. by J Dittmann, S Craver, and J Fridrich (Princeton, 2009), pp. 131–140

10. C Wang, J Ni, An efficient JPEG steganographic scheme based on the block–entropy of DCT coefficients, in *Proceedings of IEEE ICASSP* (Kyoto, 25–30 March 2012)

11. F Huang, J Huang, Y-Q Shi, New channel selection rule for JPEG steganography. IEEE Trans. Inf. Forensics Secur. **7**(4), 1181–1191 (2012)

12. F Huang, W Luo, J Huang, Y-Q Shi, Distortion function designing for JPEG steganography with uncompressed side-image, in *1st ACM Information Hiding and Multimedia Security Workshop* (Montpellier, 17–19 June 2013)

13. L Guo, J Ni, Y-Q Shi, An efficient JPEG steganographic scheme using uniform embedding, in *Fourth IEEE International Workshop on Information Forensics and Security* (Tenerife, 2–5 December 2012)

14. J Fridrich, T Pevný, J Kodovský, Statistically undetectable JPEG steganography: dead ends, challenges, and opportunities, in *Proceedings of the 9th ACM Multimedia & Security Workshop*, ed. by J Dittmann, J Fridrich (Dallas, 20–21 September 2007), pp. 3–14

15. T Pevný, T Filler, P Bas, Using high-dimensional image models to perform highly undetectable steganography, in *Information Hiding*, ed. by R Böhme, R Safavi-Naini. 12th International Conference, IH 2010, Calgary, 28–30 June 2010. Lecture Notes in Computer Science, vol. 6387 (Springer Heidelberg, 2010), pp. 161–177

16. T Pevný, P Bas, J Fridrich, Steganalysis by subtractive pixel adjacency matrix. IEEE Trans. Inf. Forensics Secur. **5**(2), 215–224 (2010)

17. V Holub, J Fridrich, Designing steganographic distortion using directional filters, in *Fourth IEEE International Workshop on Information Forensics and Security* (Tenerife, 2–5 December 2012)

18. J Fridrich, J Kodovský, Rich models for steganalysis of digital images. IEEE Trans. Inf. Forensics Secur. **7**(3), 868–882 (2011)

19. V Holub, J Fridrich, Digital image steganography using universal distortion, in *1st ACM Information Hiding and Multimedia Security Workshop* (Montpellier, 17–19 June 2013)

20. J Fridrich, J Kodovský, M Goljan, V Holub, Steganalysis of content-adaptive steganography in spatial domain, in *Information Hiding, 13th International Conference*, Lecture Notes in Computer Science, ed. by T Filler, T Pevný, A Ker, S Craver (Czech Republic Prague, May 18–20, 2011), pp. 102–117

21. G Gül, F Kurugollu, A new methodology in steganalysis: breaking highly undetactable steganograpy (HUGO), Information Hiding, *ed. by T Filler, T Pevný, A Ker, S Craver, 13th International Conference, IH 2011, Prague, 18–20 May 2011. Lecture Notes in Computer Science*, vol. 6958 (Springer, Heidelberg, 2011), pp. 71–84

22. Y-Q Shi, P Sutthiwan, L Chen, Textural features for steganalysis, in *Information Hiding*, ed. by M Kirchner, D Ghosal. 14th International Conference, IH 2012, Berkeley, 15–18 May 2012. Lecture Notes in Computer Science, vol. 7692 (Springer, Heidelberg, 2012), pp. 63–77

23. M Vetterli, J Kovacevic, *Wavelets and Subband Coding*. (Prentice Hall, Englewood Cliffs, 1995)

24. J Kodovský, J Fridrich, Steganalysis of JPEG images using rich models, in *Proceedings SPIE, Electronic Imaging, Media Watermarking, Security, and Forensics 2012*, vol. 8303, ed. by A Alattar, ND Memon, and EJ Delp (San Francisco, 23–26 2012 January), pp. 0A 1–13

25. T Filler, T Pevný, P Bas, BOSS (Break Our Steganography System). http://www.agents.cz/boss, accessed date 20/12/13

26. J Kodovský, J Fridrich, V Holub, Ensemble classifiers for steganalysis of digital media. IEEE Trans. Inf. Forensics Secur. **7**(2), 432–444 (2012)

27. T Denemark, J Fridrich, V Holub, in *Proceedings SPIE, Electronic Imaging, Media Watermarking, Security, and Forensics 2014*, vol. 9028, ed. by A Alattar, ND Memon, and CD Heitzenrater (San Francisco, 2–6 February 2014), p. TBD

28. W Luo, F Huang, J Huang, Edge adaptive image steganography based on LSB matching revisited. IEEE Trans. Inf. Forensics Secur. **5**(2), 201–214 (2010)

29. J Fridrich, M Goljan, D Soukal, P Lisoněk, Writing on wet paper, in *Proceedings SPIE, Electronic Imaging, Security, Steganography, and Watermarking of Multimedia Contents VII*, vol. 5681, ed. by EJ Delp, PW Wong (San Jose, 16–20 January 2005), pp. 328–340

30. AD Ker, A fusion of maximal likelihood and structural steganalysis, in *Information Hiding*, ed. by T Furon, F Cayre, G Doërr, P Bas. 9th International Workshop, IH 2007, Saint Malo, 11–13 June 2007. Lecture Notes in Computer Science, vol. 4567 (Springer-Verlag, Berlin), pp. 204–219

31. J Fridrich, R Du, Secure steganographic methods for palette images, in *Information Hiding*, ed. by A Pfitzmann, 3rd International Workshop, IH 1999, Dresden, 29 September–1 October 1999. Lecture Notes in Computer Science, vol. 1768 (Springer-Verlag, New York, 1999), pp. 47–60

32. G Winkler, *Image Analysis, Random Fields and Markov Chain Monte Carlo Methods: A Mathematical Introduction (Stochastic Modelling and Applied Probability)*, 2nd edition. (Springer, Berlin, 2003)

33. T Pevný, Detecting messages of unknown length, in *Proceedings SPIE, Electronic Imaging, Media Watermarking, Security and Forensics III*, vol. 7880, ed. by A Alattar, ND Memon, EJ Delp, and J Dittmann (San Francisco, January 23–26, 2011), pp. OT 1–12

Permissions

List of Contributors

Dominik Engel
University of Applied Sciences, Urstein Sued 1, 5412 Puch/Salzburg Austria
Dept. of Computer Sciences, University of Salzburg, Jakob Haringer Str. 2, 5020 Salzburg, Austria

Thomas Stütz
University of Applied Sciences, Urstein Sued 1, 5412 Puch/Salzburg Austria
Dept. of Computer Sciences, University of Salzburg, Jakob Haringer Str. 2, 5020 Salzburg, Austria

Andreas Uhl
Dept. of Computer Sciences, University of Salzburg, Jakob Haringer Str. 2, 5020 Salzburg, Austria

Donny J Ohan
Department of Computer Science, Sam Houston State University, Huntsville, TX 77340, USA

Narasimha Shashidhar
Department of Computer Science, Sam Houston State University, Huntsville, TX 77340, USA

Rimba Whidiana Ciptasari
Department of Informatics, Telkom University, Bandung 40257, Indonesia
Graduate School of Information Science and Electrical Engineering, Kyushu University, 744 Motooka, Nishi-ku, Fukuoka 819-0395, Japan

Kyung-Hyune Rhee
Department of IT Convergence and Application Engineering, Pukyong National University, 599-1, Daeyeon 3-Dong, Nam-Gu, Busan 608-737, Korea

Kouichi Sakurai
Graduate School of Information Science and Electrical Engineering, Kyushu University, 744 Motooka, Nishi-ku, Fukuoka 819-0395, Japan

Christian Richthammer
Department of Information Systems, University of Regensburg, Regensburg 93053, Germany

Michael Netter
Department of Information Systems, University of Regensburg, Regensburg 93053, Germany

Moritz Riesner
Department of Information Systems, University of Regensburg, Regensburg 93053, Germany

Johannes Sänger
Department of Information Systems, University of Regensburg, Regensburg 93053, Germany

Günther Pernul
Department of Information Systems, University of Regensburg, Regensburg 93053, Germany

Vaibhav Garg
Department of Computer Science, Drexel University, Philadelphia, PA 19104, USA

Thomas Koster
School of Informatics and Computing, Indiana University, Bloomington, IN 47408, USA

Linda Jean Camp
School of Informatics and Computing, Indiana University, Bloomington, IN 47408, USA

Saiful Islam
Department of Computer Science and Engineering, Indian Institute of Technology Kanpur, Kanpur 208016, India

Mangat R Modi
Department of Computer Science and Engineering, Indian Institute of Technology Kanpur, Kanpur 208016, India

Phalguni Gupta
Department of Computer Science and Engineering, Indian Institute of Technology Kanpur, Kanpur 208016, India

Roger Piqueras Jove
AT&T Security Research Center, New York, NY 10007, USA

Joshua Lackey
AT&T Security Research Center, New York, NY 10007, USA

Arvind Raghavan
Blue CloverDevices, San Bruno, CA 94066, USA

Zekeriya Erkin
Department of Intelligent Systems, Delft University of Technology, Delft, 2628 CD, The Netherlands

Thijs Veugen
Department of Intelligent Systems, Delft University of Technology, Delft, 2628 CD, The Netherlands
TNO, P.O. Box 5050, Delft, 2600 GB, The Netherlands

Tomas Toft
Computer Science Department, Aarhus University, IT-Parken, Åbogade 34, Aarhus N 8200, Denmark

Reginald L Lagendijk
Department of Intelligent Systems, Delft University of Technology, Delft, 2628 CD, The Netherlands

Yousra Chabchoub
ISEP, 21 rue d'assas, Paris 75006, France

Raja Chiky
ISEP, 21 rue d'assas, Paris 75006, France

Betul Dogan
ISEP, 21 rue d'assas, Paris 75006, France

Anh Thu Phan Ho
Institut-Telecom-LAGIS, Telecom-Lille, Rue Guglielmo Marconi, Villeneuve-d'Ascq 59650, France

Bao An Mai Hoang
LAGIS, Telecom-Lille, Rue Guglielmo Marconi, Villeneuve-d'Ascq 59650, France

Wadih Sawaya
Institut-Telecom-LAGIS, Telecom-Lille, Rue Guglielmo Marconi, Villeneuve-d'Ascq 59650, France

Patrick Bas
CNRS-LAGIS, Cite Scientifique, 59651, Villeneuve-d'Ascq 59650, France

Jake M Drew
Computer Science and Engineering Department, Southern Methodist University, 6425 Boaz Lane Dallas, TX 75205, USA

Tyler Moore
Computer Science and Engineering Department, Southern Methodist University, 6425 Boaz Lane Dallas, TX 75205, USA

Karl-Peter Fuchs
Department of Informatics, University of Hamburg, Vogt-Kölln-Str. 30, 22527 Hamburg, Germany

Dominik Herrmann
Department of Informatics, University of Hamburg, Vogt-Kölln-Str. 30, 22527 Hamburg, Germany

Andrea Micheloni
Department of Informatics, University of Hamburg, Vogt-Kölln-Str. 30, 22527 Hamburg, Germany

Hannes Federrath
Department of Informatics, University of Hamburg, Vogt-Kölln-Str. 30, 22527 Hamburg, Germany

Eirini Karapistoli
Interdepartmental Programme of Postgraduate Studies in Information Systems, University of Macedonia, Egnatias 156, Thessaloniki 54006, Greece

Anastasios A Economides
Interdepartmental Programme of Postgraduate Studies in Information Systems, University of Macedonia, Egnatias 156, Thessaloniki 54006, Greece

Xin Hu
Security Research Department, IBM T.J. Watson Research Center, 1101 Kitchawan Rd, Yorktown Heights, NY, USA

TingWang
Security Research Department, IBM T.J. Watson Research Center, 1101 Kitchawan Rd, Yorktown Heights, NY, USA

Marc Ph Stoecklin
IBM Zurich Research Lab, Saumerstrasse 4, 8803 Ruschlikon, Switzerland

Douglas L Schales
Security Research Department, IBM T.J. Watson Research Center, 1101 Kitchawan Rd, Yorktown Heights, NY, USA

Jiyong Jang
Security Research Department, IBM T.J. Watson Research Center, 1101 Kitchawan Rd, Yorktown Heights, NY, USA

Reiner Sailer
Security Research Department, IBM T.J. Watson Research Center, 1101 Kitchawan Rd, Yorktown Heights, NY, USA

Wadood Abdul
Laboratory SIC-XLIM, University of Poitiers, bat. SP2MI, av. Marie et Pierre Curie, 86960, Chasseneuil C'edex, France

Philippe Carré
Laboratory SIC-XLIM, University of Poitiers, bat. SP2MI, av. Marie et Pierre Curie, 86960, Chasseneuil C'edex, France

Philippe Gaborit
MLaboratory DMI-XLIM, University of Limoges, 123, av. A. Thomas, 87060, Limoges, France

José Marinho
Instituto Politécnico de Coimbra, ISEC, DEIS, Rua Pedro Nunes - Quinta da Nora, 3030-199 Coimbra, Portugal
DEI-UC - Department of Informatics Engineering, University of Coimbra, Pólo II - Pinhal de Marrocos, 3030-290 Coimbra, Portugal

Jorge Granjal
DEI-UC - Department of Informatics Engineering, University of Coimbra, Pólo II - Pinhal de Marrocos, 3030-290 Coimbra, Portugal
CISUC - Centre for Informatics and Systems of the University of Coimbra, Pólo II - Pinhal de Marrocos, 3030-290 Coimbra, Portugal

Edmundo Monteiro
DEI-UC - Department of Informatics Engineering, University of Coimbra, Pólo II - Pinhal de Marrocos, 3030-290 Coimbra, Portugal
CISUC - Centre for Informatics and Systems of the University of Coimbra, Pólo II - Pinhal de Marrocos, 3030-290 Coimbra, Portugal

Pratik Narang
BITS-Pilani, Hyderabad Campus, Hyderabad, Telangana 500078, India

Chittaranjan Hota
BITS-Pilani, Hyderabad Campus, Hyderabad, Telangana 500078, India

VN Venkatakrishnan
University of Illinois at Chicago, Chicago, IL 60607, USA.

Nada Essaouini
Télécom Bretagne, 2 rue Châtaigneraie, Cesson Sévigné Cedex 3, France
Cadi Ayyad University, ENSA, Boulevard Abdelkrim Al Khattabi, Marrakesh, Marrakesh 40000, Morocco

Frédéric Cuppens
Télécom Bretagne, 2 rue Châtaigneraie, Cesson Sévigné Cedex 3, France

Nora Cuppens-Boulahia
Télécom Bretagne, 2 rue Châtaigneraie, Cesson Sévigné Cedex 3, France

Anas Abou El Kalam
Cadi Ayyad University, ENSA, Boulevard Abdelkrim Al Khattabi, Marrakesh, Marrakesh 40000, Morocco

Vojtěch Holub
Department of Electrical and Computer Engineering, Binghamton University, Binghamton, NY 13902, USA

Jessica Fridrich
Department of Electrical and Computer Engineering, Binghamton University, Binghamton, NY 13902, USA

Tomáš Denemark
Department of Electrical and Computer Engineering, Binghamton University, Binghamton, NY 13902, USA

Printed in the USA
CPSIA information can be obtained
at www.ICGtesting.com
JSHW051429221024
72173JS00006B/1412